Great Ideas in History, Politics, and Philosophy

Great Ideas in History, Politics, and Philosophy

A Reader

J. Caleb Clanton
Richard C. Goode
Editors

BAYLOR UNIVERSITY PRESS

Cover and book design by Kasey McBeath
Cover art: Plato illustration by Shutterstock/Marusya Chaika; Frederick Douglass and Teresa of Avila illustrations by Andrew Tang
Typesetting by Scribe Inc.

Library of Congress Cataloging-in-Publication Data
Names: Clanton, J. Caleb, 1978- editor. | Goode, Richard C., 1960- editor.
Title: Great ideas in history, politics, and philosophy : a reader /
   J. Caleb Clanton, Richard C. Goode, editors.
Description: Waco, Texas : Baylor University Press, [2021] | Summary: "An
   anthology of major Western and Eastern literary, historical,
   philosophical, political, ethical, and religious texts"-- Provided by
   publisher.
Identifiers: LCCN 2021015490 (print) | LCCN 2021015491 (ebook) | ISBN
   9781481316187 (paperback) | ISBN 9781481316194 (epub) | ISBN
   9781481316606 (pdf)
Subjects: LCSH: Humanities. | Literature--Collections. | History--Sources.
   | Intellectual life--History.
Classification: LCC AC1 .G73 2021 (print) | LCC AC1 (ebook) | DDC
   001.3--dc23
LC record available at https://lccn.loc.gov/2021015490
LC ebook record available at https://lccn.loc.gov/2021015491

To our students, past and present.

Contents

Acknowledgments

Several people have been gracious with their time and energy in helping us put this volume together, and we owe them a word of thanks. For their input on the various selections contained herein, we gratefully acknowledge our faculty colleagues in the disciplines of history, political science, and philosophy at Lipscomb University. Our heartfelt thanks go to Howard Miller, Tim Johnson, Jerry Gaw, Neal Allison, Marc Schwerdt, Susan Haynes, and Lee Mayo. For helpful input on how to improve the manuscript, we thank Scot Danforth, Paul Contino, Chris Metress, Tracy Shilcutt, Paul Begin, Chris Collins, and Kraig Martin, as well as two anonymous reviewers. Thanks go also to Josh Strahan, Lauren White, and Leonard Allen for their advice and support in bringing this project to fruition.

A special word of thanks goes to David G. Holmes, dean of the College of Liberal Arts and Sciences at Lipscomb, for his insight on part of this project, as well as his support of our research in general. And our gratitude goes also to the provost of Lipscomb University, W. Craig Bledsoe, for supporting the general education initiative that initially gave birth to this project.

Lastly, we want to express our appreciation to all of the students with whom we have had, and continue to have, the good pleasure to discuss the great ideas only sampled in this volume. This book is dedicated to them with our respect and gratitude.

Preface: On Great Ideas

Suppose you had no more than about thirty minutes to gain some preliminary exposure to one or more of the greatest ideas that have shaped human experience, cultures, and civilizations throughout history. Where might you turn? The internet is an obvious choice, of course. But *even if* the whole world were at your fingertips, that fact alone wouldn't necessarily guide your next step. In fact, it might just leave you feeling overwhelmed or even paralyzed. Which great books or historical documents should you consider? And which excerpts should you turn to first? Remember: you have just thirty minutes to work with.

This anthology is meant to help. It offers a chronologically ordered array of reasonably short, seminal passages from some of the most significant (primarily nonfiction) texts in human history—texts that inform enduring questions related to the pursuit of wisdom and worldview, religious faith, historical and moral reflection, and civic and political life. The selections compiled here are drawn from several key historical contexts, including, among others, ancient Greece, China, India, and Rome; Judaism, early Christendom, and classical Islam; medieval Europe; the Renaissance and exploration period; the early modern period and Enlightenment; and early U.S. history. The goal is to help readers acquaint themselves with some of the towering perspectives, reflections, meditations, views, arguments, and documents in the disciplines of history, philosophy, religion, and political science/government. And since the point of reading great texts is to grapple with the ideas contained in them, this volume serves that end by giving readers easy entry points and, hence, streamlined access to some of the most crucial passages. Ultimately, our hope is to equip readers to join in on important conversations that are at once timeless and timely.

I.

The term "great ideas" is perhaps inevitably vague, in large part because there are a variety of ways in which something might be considered great. We sometimes mean to say that an idea is great in a normative or prescriptive sense—that xvi | Preface: On Great Ideas

is, we mean that it is great insofar as it is especially good, valuable, beautiful, or commendable in some way. In other cases, however, we have a more normatively benign sense of the term "great" in mind—that is, we mean that the idea is great simply insofar as it has been consequential in shaping human experience in some way.

Consider a parallel case. The popular news magazine *Time* has long published its annual "Person of the Year" issue in which an individual or group or even inanimate object is recognized for having made, for better or worse, a profound impact on humanity during the preceding year. Of course, sometimes those who are given this title deserve praise and admiration for their contributions. For example, in 2014, *Time* recognized as persons of the year "the Ebola Fighters"—the health-care professionals, missionaries, ambulance drivers, and other frontline workers who valiantly battled the Ebola outbreak in Africa during the months prior to publication. In other cases, however, *Time* has named morally atrocious figures as persons of the year—perhaps none more notorious or reviled than Adolf Hitler in 1938. This was hardly meant as an approval of Hitler, but rather simply as a biting acknowledgment of his heinous role in shaping the course of human events. To accuse *Time* of somehow sympathizing with Hitler or the Nazis is simply to misunderstand the sense in which *Time* was using the title "Person of the Year": no one can deny Hitler's horrible impact during the twentieth century, just as no one should praise it either.

A similar distinction holds with respect to the title "great ideas." Sometimes we might say that an idea is great precisely because it is exemplary or deserving of our affirmation—that it has helped get at an unplumbed truth in some penetrating way, or that it has lifted the human spirit, or that it has helped civilize us or brought us closer to God, or that it has somehow conduced to our improvement. In other words, some ideas are great because they are *praiseworthy*. But sometimes we might say that an idea is great simply insofar as it has been *consequential*—it matters just because it has made a profound impact or otherwise shaped human affairs, worldviews, and civilizations. The distinction between the different senses of the word "great" is an important one to keep in mind, because an idea might be great in the second sense, even though it is really quite reprehensible in the first.

There are of course additional senses in which we might reasonably peg something a "great idea." For example, we might say that an idea is great simply insofar as it is well-known or *recognizable*—despite whether it is praiseworthy or has been consequential. Alternatively, we might say that an idea is great not because the author or text is praiseworthy, consequential, or even recognizable, but strictly because it raises or gives poignant expression to perspectives, questions, or points of controversy central to human experience. In other words, some ideas are great just because they are *provocative* of the queries and considerations with which humans need to wrestle.

The key point here is just that the term "great ideas" admits of multiple meanings. Some ideas are great in *all* of the senses we have mentioned. Others are great only in one of the narrower senses. We stress this point because this anthology includes a range of what might reasonably count as great ideas—great *qua* praiseworthy, great *qua* consequential or influential, great *qua* recognizable, and/or great *qua* provocative. And we stress that point so as not to be misunderstood or misconstrued: we are not claiming or otherwise intimating that all of the various ideas canvassed in this volume are somehow great in the sense of being praiseworthy. We simply don't believe that. However, they are all great in at least one of the other reasonable senses of the term "great"—whether because they have been consequential, or readily recognizable, or simply because they provoke questions with which we cannot help but wrestle given the kind of creatures we are. And so it should go without saying that we are *not* somehow affirming, endorsing, or recommending all of the ideas touched on in this anthology. But we *are*, however, endorsing a critical engagement with them. In other words, while we are by no means suggesting that all of these ideas ought to be accepted or affirmed, we do think there is real value in critically engaging with them all.

And here's why: to engage with an idea is, first of all, to try to understand the idea, and to try to understand why it was first articulated, as well as why it is, or at least was, consequential or provocative. If we engage in this practice well enough, we can hope to get better at thinking clearly. After all, it can take some effort to grasp a difficult point made in an ancient text, for example. But we are made better by the intellectual muscle that this effort works in us. Additionally, when we try to understand an idea's impetus, influence, or provocation, we not only get a better handle on human psychologies and the cultural backdrops that can affect them, but we also become more charitable and empathetic toward others—both then and there, and here and now.

Still, we don't engage with ideas simply to understand and appreciate them. We engage with ideas in order to put them to the test and weigh them in the balance. Does this or that idea get at the truth? Does it illuminate something that really matters? Does it capture what is good and right? Does it make us better or abler in some way? Ultimately, we engage with ideas in order to challenge them—and to be challenged by them. At their best, these engagements move us incrementally toward the truth, and toward becoming the sorts of people we ought to become. Of course, some ideas are wrong or even vile, and so engaging with them might seem far less vital, or even dangerous. But in *critically* evaluating even those ideas—the ones we take to be false or otherwise hold in contempt—we can be made better. After all, those engagements can give us insight into what we should avoid *and why*. And if nothing else, those sorts of critical engagements can better reinforce the positions we already hold by helping us to see more clearly than before why they actually make sense.

2.

What we are discussing here—critically engaging and evaluating a range of ideas that have emerged throughout human history—falls squarely within the territory staked out by the academic disciplines of the humanities. And we think that the sort of inquiry undertaken by the humanities—what we might simply think of as *humanistic inquiry*—is important for reasons that all too often go underappreciated these days, perhaps because those reasons are so fundamental that they can fly below the radar screen, so to speak. In many ways, the humanities have fallen on hard times in higher education and, perhaps especially, in our K–12 schools. (After all, many K–12 curricula fail to even include *any* discussion of religion or philosophy, even if they include some cursory study of, say, literature, history, or civics.) This can seem strange because the value of studying the great ideas of human history can seem so patently obvious! What is true, and how can we know that? Is there a God? What is a *person*, and do we have souls? What is morally permissible and obligatory, and how can we arrive at that decision? How do we live rightly and well together? Who should wield power in society? How and toward what ends? What liberties should be protected, and why? What is the responsibility of the individual to the whole, and vice versa? How might we become more humane and less barbaric? What does it take to flourish and lead a meaningful life? What is justice, and why does it matter? Questions like these are clearly important!

Yet while this might seem obvious to some, we should remember that this is clearly less than obvious to others. And in a day and age when the humanistic disciplines are being criticized, downsized, or eliminated by the institutions that claim to be harbingers of higher education, and in a day and age when politicians angle for applause by taking potshots at the humanities, and in a day and age when students and their parents, as well as college administrators and even faculty, seem eager to vocalize their suspicions about the utility of studying the humanities, it is appropriate to make clear why humanistic inquiry still matters—just as it has always mattered.

Humanistic inquiry matters because it helps shape untutored human nature toward its fullest potential—to mature us as human beings and form us as persons. No one doubts that we need the know-how to take on this or that job role in life, or that we need to achieve some level of material success. But achieving a life of success isn't the same thing as achieving a life of significance and purpose, or a life of integrity, resilience, and virtue. So training for success isn't enough. We need to shape ourselves to be the sort of people who are faithful to the sorts of things that matter the most. So while some areas of inquiry might help us *train* for this or that role, humanistic inquiry can help *educate* us to become more fully human in the right sort of way.

Humanistic inquiry matters not only because it shapes us as humans, but also because it can actually help us to be better in our roles as scientists, health-care professionals, engineers, businessmen, lawyers, postal workers, mothers and fathers, spouses, and citizens. For one thing, studying the humanities equips us with the skills and competencies needed to pursue these vocations in their own right. But—what is more—studying the humanities helps us to pursue these vocations in the right way. Yes, we want our scientists to know *what* the world is like, and we want them to help us to see *how* we achieve this or that end. But we need this knowledge to be chastened by a serious consideration about *whether* we ought to pursue this or that end in the first place. We need our doctors to treat us as *persons* and not just as patients or—worse—lab experiments. We need engineers who not only know how to build a solid bridge but also where to put it and *why*. We need businesses that make money, but with *integrity* and responsibility. And so on. Humanistic inquiry can help us to become more humane in our various roles as humans.

Humanistic inquiry can also help us develop the concepts, categories, vocabulary, language, questions, concerns, worries, values, and personal and intellectual virtues that prepare a person for positions of leadership and service to others. It is all too crucial that our leaders have a reservoir of these sorts of resources ready at hand *before* they step on the job. Not only do old dogs rarely learn new tricks, but taking a time-out during a moment of crisis to study up on the tricks that are needed most is almost never an option. Crises aren't the right time to be saying "Wait, wait: What should I think in light of so much uncertainty?" or "How should I be when confronted with this sort of challenge?" Real leaders have already put in the hard work it takes to forge the right kinds of character traits and intellectual resources, precisely so that they are present when they are needed the most. We cannot wait for those in positions of leadership to learn certain things on the job; we need them to have already thought about certain questions. What insights have our forebears left us? What mistakes must we take care to avoid? What is wise and just in this sort of situation? How can we work together through crisis? The study of the humanities is crucial if we want the sort of leaders that we so badly need.

And, importantly, humanistic inquiry can help us also to reflect on what pulls us together—and what pulls us apart—as humans. Knowing this can help promote deliberation over mob rule, peace over war, cooperation over strife, and the common good over mere self-interest. Humanistic inquiry matters because it can help us to get better at seeking the truth about vast areas of human experience, particularly on questions that are not, and cannot be, settled under a microscope or in a public opinion survey. And that matters because, in times of great uncertainty and discord and polarization, we need to get better at distinguishing the real deal from the phony baloney.

Of course, that's not the only reason that getting at the truth matters. Ultimately, getting at the truth matters simply because *truth matters*—period.

3.

In the same way that we are not affirming or endorsing all of the ideas contained in this volume (but rather a critical engagement with them), we are also *not* suggesting or attempting to imply that this compilation is even remotely exhaustive of the great ideas that deserve to be engaged. We know that our critics might take a quick glance at the table of contents, for example, and complain that we have failed to include some rather important texts and ideas that really deserve inclusion. We freely concede this point. For one thing, we have not included selections drawn from sacred books such as the Bible or the Koran, and for the most part we have not included works of fiction and poetry, which means that we have not included great works by the likes of Euripides, Virgil, Ovid, Shakespeare, Milton, Cervantes, and many others. We did this mostly in order to focus on ideas and primary sources in history, politics, and philosophy. But even within the domain of the non-literature humanities, we have omitted lots of important texts and ideas.

Yet we are not signaling, nor do we actually think, that if a text is omitted from this volume that it somehow is *less* than great. The reality is that the practical constraints of space, together with our desire as editors to include a chronologically and conceptually diverse array of ideas meant that some very worthwhile authors and texts simply did not, because they could not, make the cut. The perfect anthology of great ideas would contain them all, of course. But, then again, such an anthology would be so long that it would likely scare away even the most ambitious readers. And in the end, we don't think it makes much sense to let perfection be the enemy of the good. Nonetheless, some of our critics will no doubt complain about the selections we have made—as well our omissions—and they will indict us on those grounds. Our reply is steady and simple: the ideas and texts compiled in this anthology are intended to be a place to begin, not necessarily a place to end. Our agenda is to start conversations, not shut them down.

We also recognize that a critic might complain that our table of contents is chock-full of those authors, texts, and ideas that we have judged to be the *most* important and in such a way that is perhaps invariably reflective of our own biases and prejudices—whether *we* are conscious of it or not. Perhaps. It is true, for example, that while we have tried to make this anthology inclusive of a wide range of authors and texts, our table of contents is nonetheless tilted, as it were, toward Western and Christian intellectual traditions. We do not mean thereby to imply that these traditions are somehow identical to *The* Universal Intellectual Tradition, in such a way that would neglect or dismiss or silence other important intellectual traditions. Nor do we mean to represent these traditions as necessarily triumphant over all others on every point of inquiry. Our aim is not to jury-rig the inquiry. However, we acknowledge that the contours of one's inquiries are informed, at least in part, by the inputs to that inquiry, and the inquiry shaped by this anthology is no exception. So we are also forced to acknowledge that the inquiry we are hoping to instigate is not complete; thus, we concede that it should be undertaken with a spirit of humility and an openness to additional ideas beyond the ones compiled here.

Still, we—all of us—always already find ourselves rooted in some sort of tradition that has, for better or for worse, done something to shape us and the various contexts in which we exist. Ideally, that tradition should be seen to include its critics, as well as the characters who are on the margins of it. In any case, that tradition is the place where we *begin*—not necessarily end—even if we dislike that tradition, critique it, move beyond it, or even reject it. After all, even critiquing an intellectual tradition requires some familiarity with it! And one rather legitimate worry these days is that Americans often don't know much about their own religious, philosophical, political, and cultural heritage. If that is correct, then there are real goods to be had in engaging with the intellectual traditions of the West and of Christendom that have shaped us. This is not a matter of simple nostalgia. For one thing, it is about self-knowledge and clearheaded thinking—the sort that might assist us in taking the plank out of our own eye, so to speak. When we are blind to those ideas and traditions that have shaped us, we run the risk of deliberating in ways that are hobbled with naïve arrogance, hypocrisy, misinformation, and prejudice. As one contemporary philosopher aptly puts it: "Once we accept the basic psycho-analytic insight that the partly forgotten past colours the significance of what we do today, then if we refuse to scrutinize the past, the risk is that we will lack a proper awareness of the true motivational structure of our present activities, decisions, and projects, and that the resulting distortion may have highly damaging consequences."[*] Ultimately, there is little way around the fact that Western and Christian histories have significantly imprinted the contexts in which we find ourselves. And the same goes for most of our readers. Knowing the language of those contexts allows for a greater, deeper, and richer interaction with them. If one wishes to restore, or reform, or even revolutionize the broken parts of this history, then knowing what has deformed and impaired it can help one heal or transform or abandon it. Moreover, to be literate and conversant in a diverse range of settings and populations requires not only self-knowledge but the development of an extensive lexicon. And the Western and Christian traditions are, if nothing else, a rich resource.

Nor do we mean to be sending any hidden messages to the reader in concluding the anthology with selections drawn from early U.S. history. This decision is not reflective of some sort of subtle wink and nod in the direction of American exceptionalism or triumphalism. Our decision to conclude with the early American tradition was motivated by the need (given limitations on space) to draw the line somewhere, and that line is as good a line as any, especially given that most of our readers can be reasonably expected to hail from the American context. And we stopped with the *early* American tradition insofar as we have restricted ourselves to making use of texts that are in the public domain.

We are aware of the sometimes acrimonious "canon wars" that academicians have waged with one another when lists of must-read texts are compiled or proposed, especially among curriculum committees. We are not even trying to settle the score on those debates here. Instead, our goal has been to contemplate a reasonably *inclusive*—dare we say "loose"?—canon of texts and ideas in history, politics, and philosophy, one that includes those who have critiqued and even rejected the traditions with which they have been associated. But we readily acknowledge the limits of our efforts, especially given the parameters within which we are working. So our defense, again, is to appeal to fallibility: We do not think, nor do we mean to suggest, that these texts and ideas are the only ones that warrant attention or that they deserve some special weighting in the grand scheme of things. But they nonetheless do warrant critical

---

* John Cottingham, "Why Should Analytic Philosophers Do History of Philosophy?" in *Analytic Philosophy and History of Philosophy*, ed. Tom Sorell and G. A. J. Rogers, 25–41 (Oxford: Clarendon Press, 2005), 37–38.

engagement in their own right. And, ultimately, this anthology is meant to invite readers to engage in a conversation of significance—a conversation about what it means to be human. Giving even more effort than we already have to introduce or defend the selections that follow this brief preface will serve only to delay and frustrate the inquiry that lies ahead, and the ideas contained within have for the most part survived quite well enough on their own without our, or anyone else's, commentary.

Readers will notice that some of the selections contained in this volume include peculiar locutions, unorthodox spellings, and strange capitalizations—even though these texts were originally written in English or have been translated into English. The explanation behind this is simply that, as editors, we chose to present these selections, as much as possible, in the same form as they appear in the published text from which they are drawn. Similarly, we have not changed pronouns for the sake of greater gender inclusivity; rather, we have left all pronouns as they appear in the published form from which they are drawn. Lastly, the reader will notice that we have tried to minimize the scholarly apparatus in this volume—footnotes, editorial comments, and the like. However, each selection is preceded with a very brief introduction, and we cite the published source from which the selection is taken in a footnote. Lastly, we have intentionally made every effort to limit ourselves to material that is now in the public domain, primarily in order to minimize the cost of producing this volume—ultimately, for the sake of greater educational access.

J. C. C.

R. C. G.

1

Homer

from *Iliad*

Very little is known about the life of Homer (ninth or eighth century BC), except that he is traditionally regarded as the blind author of the two greatest epic poems of Greek antiquity, namely the *Iliad* and its sequel, the *Odyssey*. The *Iliad* is set amidst the final year of the Trojan War, during which several Greek kingdoms have laid siege on Troy, with special focus on the dispute between King Agamemnon and the legendary warrior Achilles. The following excerpt is the opening passage of that poem.

———————————

Sing, O goddess, the anger of Achilles son of Peleus, that brought countless ills upon the Achaeans. Many a brave soul did it send hurrying down to Hades, and many a hero did it yield a prey to dogs and vultures, for so were the counsels of Jove fulfilled from the day on which the son of Atreus, king of men, and great Achilles, first fell out with one another.

And which of the gods was it that set them on to quarrel? It was the son of Jove and Leto; for he was angry with the king and sent a pestilence upon the host to plague the people, because the son of Atreus had dishonoured Chryses his priest. Now Chryses had come to the ships of the Achaeans to free his daughter, and had brought with him a great ransom: moreover he bore in his hand the sceptre of Apollo wreathed with a suppliant's wreath and he besought the Achaeans, but most of all the two sons of Atreus, who were their chiefs.

"Sons of Atreus," he cried, "and all other Achaeans, may the gods who dwell in Olympus grant you to sack the city of Priam, and to reach your homes in safety; but free my daughter, and accept a ransom for her, in reverence to Apollo, son of Jove."

SOURCE: Homer, *The Iliad of Homer*, trans. Samuel Butler (London: Longmans, Green, and Co., 1898), 1–9.

On this the rest of the Achaeans with one voice were for respecting the priest and taking the ransom that he offered; but not so Agamemnon, who spoke fiercely to him and sent him roughly away. "Old man," said he, "let me not find you tarrying about our ships, nor yet coming hereafter. Your sceptre of the god and your wreath shall profit you nothing. I will not free her. She shall grow old in my house at Argos far from her own home, busying herself with her loom and visiting my couch; so go, and do not provoke me or it shall be the worse for you."

The old man feared him and obeyed. Not a word he spoke, but went by the shore of the sounding sea and prayed apart to King Apollo whom lovely Leto had borne. "Hear me," he cried, "O god of the silver bow, that protectest Chryse and holy Cilla and rulest Tenedos with thy might, hear me oh thou of Sminthe. If I have ever decked your temple with garlands, or burned your thigh-bones in fat of bulls or goats, grant my prayer, and let your arrows avenge these my tears upon the Danaans."

Thus did he pray, and Apollo heard his prayer. He came down furious from the summits of Olympus, with his bow and his quiver upon his shoulder, and the arrows rattled on his back with the rage that trembled within him. He sat himself down away from the ships with a face as dark as night, and his silver bow rang death as he shot his arrow in the midst of them. First he smote their mules and their hounds, but presently he aimed his shafts at the people themselves, and all day long the pyres of the dead were burning.

For nine whole days he shot his arrows among the people, but upon the tenth day Achilles called them in assembly—moved thereto by Juno, who saw the Achaeans in their death-throes and had compassion upon them. Then, when they were got together, he rose and spoke among them.

"Son of Atreus," said he, "I deem that we should now turn roving home if we would escape destruction, for we are being cut down by war and pestilence at once. Let us ask some priest or prophet, or some reader of dreams (for dreams, too, are of Jove) who can tell us why Phoebus Apollo is so angry, and say whether it is for some vow that we have broken, or hecatomb that we have not offered, and whether he will accept the savour of lambs and goats without blemish, so as to take away the plague from us."

With these words he sat down, and Calchas son of Thestor, wisest of augurs, who knew things past present and to come, rose to speak. He it was who had guided the Achaeans with their fleet to Ilius, through the prophesyings with which Phoebus Apollo had inspired him. With all sincerity and goodwill he addressed them thus:—

"Achilles, loved of heaven, you bid me tell you about the anger of King Apollo, I will therefore do so; but consider first and swear that you will stand by me heartily in word and deed, for I know that I shall offend one who rules the Argives with might, to whom all the Achaeans are in subjection. A plain man cannot stand against the anger of a king, who if he swallow his displeasure now, will yet nurse revenge till he has wreaked it. Consider, therefore, whether or no you will protect me."

And Achilles answered, "Fear not, but speak as it is borne in upon you from heaven, for by Apollo, Calchas, to whom you pray, and whose oracles you reveal to us, not a Danaan at our ships shall lay his hand upon you, while I yet live to look upon the face of the earth—no, not though you name Agamemnon himself, who is by far the foremost of the Achaeans."

Thereon the seer spoke boldly. "The god," he said, "is angry neither about vow nor hecatomb, but for his priest's sake, whom Agamemnon has dishonoured, in that he would not free his daughter nor take a ransom for her; therefore has he sent these evils upon us, and will yet send others. He will not deliver the Danaans from this pestilence till Agamemnon has restored the girl without fee or ransom to her father, and has sent a holy hecatomb to Chryse. Thus we may perhaps appease him."

With these words he sat down, and Agamemnon rose in anger. His heart was black with rage, and his eyes flashed fire as he scowled on Calchas and said, "Seer of evil, you never yet prophesied smooth things concerning me, but have ever loved to foretell that which was evil. You have brought me neither comfort nor performance; and now you come seeing among Danaans, and saying that Apollo has plagued us because I would not take a ransom for this girl, the daughter of Chryses. I have set my heart on keeping her in my own house, for I love her better even than my own wife Clytemnestra, whose peer she is alike in form and feature, in understanding and accomplishments. Still I will give her up if I must, for I would have the people live, not die; but you must find me a prize instead, or I alone among the Argives shall be without one. This is not well; for you behold, all of you, that my prize is to go elsewhither."

And Achilles answered, "Most noble son of Atreus, covetous beyond all mankind, how shall the Achaeans find you another prize? We have no common store from which to take one. Those we took from the cities have been awarded; we cannot disallow the awards that have been made already. Give this girl, therefore, to the god, and if ever Jove grants us to sack the city of Troy we will requite you three and fourfold."

Then Agamemnon said, "Achilles, valiant though you be, you shall not thus outwit me. You shall not overreach and you shall not persuade me. Are you to keep your own prize, while I sit tamely under my loss and give up the girl at your bidding? Let the Achaeans find me a prize in fair exchange to my liking, or I will come and take your own, or that of Ajax or of Ulysses; and he to whomsoever I may come shall rue my coming. But of this we will take thought hereafter; for the present, let us draw a ship into the sea, and find a crew for her expressly; let us put a hecatomb on board, and let us send Chryseis also; further, let some chief man among us be in command, either Ajax, or Idomeneus, or yourself, son of Peleus, mighty warrior that you are, that we may offer sacrifice and appease the anger of the god."

Achilles scowled at him and answered, "You are steeped in insolence and lust of gain. With what heart can any of the Achaeans do your bidding, either on foray or in open fighting? I came not warring here for any ill the Trojans had done me. I have no quarrel with them. They have not raided my cattle nor my horses, nor cut down my harvests on the rich plains of Phthia; for between me and them there is a great space, both mountain and sounding sea. We have followed you, Sir Insolence! for your pleasure, not ours—to gain satisfaction from the Trojans for your shameless self and for Menelaus. You forget this, and threaten to rob me of the prize for which I have toiled, and which the sons of the Achaeans have given me. Never when the Achaeans sack any rich city of the Trojans do I receive so good a prize as you do, though it is my hands that do the better part of the fighting. When the sharing comes, your share is far the largest, and I, forsooth, must go back to my ships, take what I can get and be thankful, when my labour of fighting is done. Now, therefore, I shall go back to Phthia; it will be much better for me to return home with my ships, for I will not stay here dishonoured to gather gold and substance for you."

And Agamemnon answered, "Fly if you will, I shall make you no prayers to stay you. I have others here who will do me honour, and above all Jove, the lord of counsel. There is no king here so hateful to me as you are, for you are ever quarrelsome and ill affected. What though you be brave? Was it not heaven that made you so? Go home, then, with your ships and comrades to lord it over the Myrmidons. I care neither for you nor for your anger; and thus will I do: since Phoebus Apollo is taking Chryseis from me, I shall send her with my ship and my followers, but I shall come to your tent and take your own prize Briseis, that you may learn how much stronger I am than you are, and that another may fear to set himself up as equal or comparable with me."

The son of Peleus was furious, and his heart within his shaggy breast was divided whether to draw his sword, push the others aside, and kill the son of Atreus, or to restrain himself and check his anger. While he was thus in two minds, and was drawing his mighty sword from its scabbard, Minerva came down from heaven (for Juno had sent her in the love she bore to them both), and seized the son of Peleus by his yellow hair, visible to him alone, for of the others no man could see her. Achilles turned in amaze, and by the fire that flashed from her eyes at once knew that she was Minerva. "Why are you here," said he, "daughter of aegis-bearing Jove? To see the pride of Agamemnon, son of Atreus? Let me tell you—and it shall surely be—he shall pay for this insolence with his life."

And Minerva said, "I come from heaven, if you will hear me, to bid you stay your anger. Juno has sent me, who cares for both of you alike. Cease, then, this brawling, and do not draw your sword; rail at him if you will, and your railing will not be vain, for I tell you—and it shall surely be—that you shall hereafter receive gifts three times as splendid by reason of this present insult. Hold, therefore, and obey."

"Goddess," answered Achilles, "however angry a man may be, he must do as you two command him. This will be best, for the gods ever hear the prayers of him who has obeyed them."

He stayed his hand on the silver hilt of his sword, and thrust it back into the scabbard as Minerva bade him. Then she went back to Olympus among the other gods, and to the house of aegis-bearing Jove.

But the son of Peleus again began railing at the son of Atreus, for he was still in a rage. "Wine-bibber," he cried, "with the face of a dog and the heart of a hind, you never dare to go out with the host in fight, nor yet with our chosen men in ambuscade. You shun this as you do death itself. You had rather go round and rob his prizes from any man who contradicts you. You devour your people, for you are king over a feeble folk; otherwise, son of Atreus, henceforward you would insult no man. Therefore I say, and swear it with a great oath—nay, by this my sceptre which shalt sprout neither leaf nor shoot, nor bud anew from the day on which it left its parent stem upon the mountains—for the axe stripped it of leaf and bark, and now the sons of the Achaeans bear it as judges and guardians of the decrees of heaven—so surely and solemnly do I swear that hereafter they shall look fondly for Achilles and shall not find him. In the day of your distress, when your men fall dying by the murderous hand of Hector, you shall not know how to help them, and shall rend your heart with rage for the hour when you offered insult to the bravest of the Achaeans."

With this the son of Peleus dashed his gold-bestudded sceptre on the ground and took his seat, while the son of Atreus was beginning fiercely from his place upon the other side. Then uprose smooth-tongued Nestor, the facile speaker of the Pylians, and the words fell from his lips sweeter than honey. Two generations of men born and bred in Pylos had passed away under his rule, and he was now reigning over the third. With all sincerity and goodwill, therefore, he addressed them thus:—

"Of a truth," he said, "a great sorrow has befallen the Achaean land. Surely Priam with his sons would rejoice, and the Trojans be glad at heart if they could hear this quarrel between you two, who are so excellent in fight and counsel. I am older than either of you; therefore be guided by me. Moreover I have been the familiar friend of men even greater than you are, and they did not disregard my counsels. Never again can I behold such men as Pirithous and Dryas shepherd of his people, or as Caeneus, Exadius, godlike Polyphemus, and Theseus son of Aegeus, peer of the immortals. These were the mightiest men ever born upon this earth: mightiest were they, and when they fought the fiercest tribes of mountain savages they utterly overthrew them. I came from distant Pylos, and went about among them, for they would have me come, and I fought as it was in me to do. Not a man now living could withstand them, but they heard my words, and were persuaded by them. So be it also with yourselves, for this is the more excellent way. Therefore, Agamemnon, though you be strong, take not this girl away, for the sons of the Achaeans have already given her to Achilles; and you, Achilles, strive not further with the king, for no man who by the grace of Jove wields a sceptre has like honour with Agamemnon. You are strong, and have a goddess for your mother; but Agamemnon is stronger than you, for he has more people under him. Son of Atreus, check your anger, I implore you; end this quarrel with Achilles, who in the day of battle is a tower of strength to the Achaeans."

And Agamemnon answered, "Sir, all that you have said is true, but this fellow must needs become our lord and master: he must be lord of all, king of all, and captain of all, and this shall hardly be. Granted that the gods have made him a great warrior, have they also given him the right to speak with railing?"

Achilles interrupted him. "I should be a mean coward," he cried, "were I to give in to you in all things. Order other people about, not me, for I shall obey no longer. Furthermore I say—and lay my saying to your heart—I shall fight neither you nor any man about this girl, for those that take were those also that gave. But of all else that is at my ship you shall carry away nothing by force. Try, that others may see; if you do, my spear shall be reddened with your blood."

When they had quarrelled thus angrily, they rose, and broke up the assembly at the ships of the Achaeans. The son of Peleus went back to his tents and ships with the son of Menoetius and his company, while Agamemnon drew a vessel into the water and chose a crew of twenty oarsmen. He escorted Chryseis on board and sent moreover a hecatomb for the god. And Ulysses went as captain.

Hesiod

from *Theogony*

Along with Homer, Hesiod (ca. 750–650 BC) is among the earliest and most important poets to shape and memorialize ancient Greek culture and religion. A farmer native to Boeotia in central Greece, Hesiod is best known for his *Works and Days*, as well as his *Theogony*, from which the following is a brief excerpt. The *Theogony* is a key source of information about Greek mythology, in which Hesiod gives special attention to the putative origins of the world and the Greek gods.

Hail, children of Zeus! Grant lovely song and celebrate the holy race of the deathless gods who are for ever, those that were born of Earth and starry Heaven and gloomy Night and them that briny Sea did rear. Tell how at the first gods and earth came to be, and rivers, and the boundless sea with its raging swell, and the gleaming stars, and the wide heaven above, and the gods who were born of them, givers of good things, and how they divided their wealth, and how they shared their honours amongst them, and also how at the first they took many-folded Olympus. These things declare to me from the beginning, ye Muses who dwell in the house of Olympus, and tell me which of them first came to be.

Verily at the first Chaos came to be, but next wide-bosomed Earth, the ever-sure foundation of all the deathless ones who hold the peaks of snowy Olympus, and dim Tartarus in the depth of the wide-pathed Earth, and Eros (Love), fairest among the deathless gods, who unnerves the limbs and overcomes the mind and wise counsels of all gods and all men within them. From Chaos came forth Erebus and black Night; but of Night were born Aether and

SOURCE: Hesiod, *The Homeric Hymns and Homerica*, trans. Hugh G. Evelyn-White (New York: G. P. Putnam's Sons, 1920), 85, 87, 89.

Day, whom she conceived and bare from union in love with Erebus. And Earth first bare starry Heaven, equal to herself, to cover her on every side, and to be an ever-sure abiding-place for the blessed gods. And she brought forth long Hills, graceful haunts of the goddess-Nymphs who dwell amongst the glens of the hills. She bare also the fruitless deep with his raging swell, Pontus, without sweet union of love. But afterwards she lay with Heaven and bare deep-swirling Oceanus, Coeus and Crius and Hyperion and Iapetus, Theia and Rhea, Themis and Mnemosyne and gold-crowned Phoebe and lovely Tethys. After them was born Cronos the wily, youngest and most terrible of her children, and he hated his lusty sire.

3

Confucius

from *Analects*

The ancient Chinese educator, philosopher, and politician Confucius (551–479 BC) is widely regarded as perhaps the single most foundational thinker in East Asian civilizations, a status which in turn handily makes him one of the most influential thinkers throughout human history in general. The *Analects*, from which the following is an excerpt, is a posthumously compiled collection of aphoristic sayings traditionally attributed to Confucius. It emphasizes his views about the character traits of the superior person, and it highlights one of the most famous teachings of Confucianism, namely a principle of negative reciprocity: don't do unto others what you don't want done to yourself.

Book XV. Wei Ling Kung.

CHAPTER I. 1. The duke Ling of Wei asked Confucius about tactics. Confucius replied, "I have heard all about sacrificial vessels, but I have not learned military matters." On this, he took his departure the next day.

2. When he was in Ch'in, their provisions were exhausted, and his followers became so ill that they were unable to rise.

3. Tsze-loo, with evident dissatisfaction, said, "Has the superior man likewise to endure *in this way*?" The Master said, "The superior man may indeed have to endure want, but the mean man, when he is in want, gives way to unbridled license."

CHAPTER II. 1. The Master said, "Ts'ze, you think, I suppose, that I am one who learns many things and keeps them in memory?"

SOURCE: James Legge, ed. and trans., *The Chinese Classics*, vol. 1, *Confucian Analects, the Great Learning, and the Doctrine of the Mean* (Hongkong: At the Author's and London: Trübner & Co., 1861), 158–65.

2. Tsze-kung replied, "Yes,—but perhaps it is not so?"

3. "No," was the answer; "I *seek* a unity all-pervading."

CHAPTER III. The Master said, "Yew, those who know virtue are few."

CHAPTER IV. The Master said, "May not Shun be instanced as having governed efficiently without exertion? What did he do? He did nothing but gravely and reverently occupy his royal seat."

CHAPTER V. 1. Tsze-chang asked how a man should conduct himself, *so as to be everywhere appreciated.*

2. The Master said, "Let his words be sincere and truthful, and his actions honorable and careful;—such conduct may be practised among the rude tribes of the South or the North. If his words be not sincere and truthful and his actions not honorable and careful, will he, with such conduct, be appreciated, even in his neighborhood?

3. "When he is standing, let him see those two things, as it were, fronting him. When he is in a carriage, let him see them attached to the yoke. Then may he subsequently carry them into practice."

4. Tsze-chang wrote these counsels on the end of his sash.

CHAPTER VI. 1. The Master said, "Truly straightforward was the historiographer Yu. When good government prevailed in his State, he was like an arrow. When bad government prevailed, he was like an arrow.

2. "A superior man indeed is Keu Pih-yuh! When good government prevails in his state, he is to be found in office. When bad government prevails, he can roll his principles up, and keep them in his breast."

CHAPTER VII. The Master said, "When a man may be spoken with, not to speak to him is to err in reference to the man. When a man may not be spoken with, to speak to him is to err in reference to our words. The wise err neither in regard to their man nor to their words."

CHAPTER VIII. The Master said, "The determined scholar and the man of virtue will not seek to live at the expense of injuring their virtue. They will even sacrifice their lives to preserve their virtue complete."

CHAPTER IX. Tsze-kung asked about the practice of virtue. The Master said, "The mechanic, who wishes to do his work well, must first sharpen his tools. When you are living in any state, take service with the most worthy among its great officers, and make friends of the most virtuous among its scholars."

CHAPTER X. 1. Yen Yuen asked how the government of a country should be administered.

2. The Master said, "Follow the seasons of Hea.

3. "Ride in the state carriage of Yin.

4. "Wear the ceremonial cap of Chow.

5. "Let the music be the Shaou with its pantomimes.

6. "Banish the songs of Ch'ing, and keep far from specious talkers. The songs of Ch'ing are licentious; specious talkers are dangerous."

CHAPTER XI. The Master said, "If a man take no thought about what is distant, he will find sorrow near at hand."

CHAPTER XII. The Master said, "It is all over! I have not seen one who loves virtue as he loves beauty."

CHAPTER XIII. The Master said, "Was not Tsang Wăn like one who had stolen his situation? He knew the virtue and the talents of Hwuy of Lew-hea, and yet did not *procure that he should* stand with him *in court.*"

CHAPTER XIV. The Master said, "He who requires much from himself and little from others, will keep himself from *being the object of* resentment."

CHAPTER XV. The Master said, "When a man is not *in the habit of* saying—'What shall I think of this? What shall I think of this?' I can indeed do nothing with him!"

CHAPTER XVI. The Master said, "When a number of people are together, for a whole day, without their conversation turning on righteousness, and when they are fond of carrying out *the suggestions of* a small shrewdness;—theirs is indeed a hard case."

CHAPTER XVII. The Master said, "The superior man *in everything* considers righteousness to be essential. He performs it according to the rules of propriety. He brings it forth in humility. He completes it with sincerity. This is indeed a superior man."

CHAPTER XVIII. The Master said, "The superior man is distressed by his want of ability. He is not distressed by men's not knowing him."

CHAPTER XIX. The Master said, "The superior man dislikes the thought of his name not being mentioned after his death."

CHAPTER XX. The Master said, "What the superior man seeks, is in himself. What the mean man seeks, is in others."

CHAPTER XXI. The Master said, "The superior man is dignified, but does not wrangle. He is sociable, but not a partizan."

CHAPTER XXII. The Master said, "The superior man does not promote a man *simply* on account of his words, nor does he put aside *good* words because of the man."

CHAPTER XXIII. Tsze-kung asked, saying, "Is there one word which may serve as a rule of practice for all one's life?" The Master said, "Is not RECIPROCITY such a word? What you do not want done to yourself, do not do to others."

CHAPTER XXIV. 1. The Master said, "In my dealings with men, whose evil do I blame, whose goodness do I praise, beyond what is proper? If I do sometimes exceed in praise, there must be ground for it in my examination *of the individual.*

2. "This people supplied the ground why the three dynasties pursued the path of straightforwardness."

4

Lao-Tze

from *Tao Teh King*

The ancient Chinese philosopher Lao-Tze (ca. sixth century BC), otherwise known as Laozi or Lao-Tzu, is a foundational thinker in Taoism (or Daoism), and is even contemplated as a deity within religious versions of it. According to some accounts, he was a contemporary of Confucius, though this point is disputed among scholars. The work traditionally attributed to Lao-Tze, whose name simply means "Old Master," is commonly known as the *Tao Teh King* (sometimes *Tao-te ching* or *Daodejing*) and is an influential set of his teachings on the Way (Tao) and on virtue.

-----

13. 1. Favour and disgrace would seem equally to be feared; honour and great calamity, to be regarded as personal conditions (of the same kind).

2. What is meant by speaking thus of favour and disgrace? Disgrace is being in a low position (after the enjoyment of favour). The getting that (favour) leads to the apprehension (of losing it), and the losing it leads to the fear of (still greater calamity):—this is what is meant by saying that favour and disgrace would seem equally to be feared.

And what is meant by saying that honour and great calamity are to be (similarly) regarded as personal conditions? What makes me liable to great calamity is my having the body (which I call myself); if I had not the body, what great calamity could come to me?

3. Therefore he who would administer the kingdom, honouring it as he honours his own person, may be employed to govern it, and he who would administer it with the love which he bears to his own person may be entrusted with it.

SOURCE: James Legge, trans., *The Sacred Books of China: The Texts of Taoism* (Oxford: Clarendon Press, 1891), 56–62, 64–65.

14. 1. We look at it, and we do not see it, and we name it "the Equable." We listen to it, and we do not hear it, and we name it "the Inaudible." We try to grasp it, and do not get hold of it, and we name it "the Subtle." With these three qualities, it cannot be made the subject of description; and hence we blend them together and obtain The One.

2. Its upper part is not bright, and its lower part is not obscure. Ceaseless in its action, it yet cannot be named, and then it again returns and becomes nothing. This is called the Form of the Formless, and the Semblance of the Invisible; this is called the Fleeting and Indeterminable.

3. We meet it and do not see its Front; we follow it, and do not see its Back. When we can lay hold of the Tao of old to direct the things of the present day, and are able to know it as it was of old in the beginning, this is called (unwinding) the clue of Tao.

15. 1. The skilful masters (of the Tao) in old times, with a subtle and exquisite penetration, comprehended its mysteries, and were deep (also) so as to elude men's knowledge. As they were thus beyond men's knowledge, I will make an effort to describe of what sort they appeared to be.

2. Shrinking looked they like those who wade through a stream in winter; irresolute like those who are afraid of all around them; grave like a guest (in awe of his host); evanescent like ice that is melting away; unpretentious like wood that has not been fashioned into anything; vacant like a valley, and dull like muddy water.

3. Who can (make) the muddy water (clear)? Let it be still, and it will gradually become clear. Who can secure the condition of rest? Let movement go on, and the condition of rest will gradually arise.

4. They who preserve this method of the Tao do not wish to be full (of themselves). It is through their not being full of themselves that they can afford to seem worn and not appear new and complete.

16. 1. The (state of) vacancy should be brought to the utmost degree, and that of stillness guarded with unwearying vigour. All things alike go through their processes of activity, and (then) we see them return (to their original state). When things (in the vegetable world) have displayed their luxuriant growth, we see each of them return to its root. This returning to their root is what we call the state of stillness; and that stillness may be called a reporting that they have fulfilled their appointed end.

2. The report of that fulfilment is the regular, unchanging rule. To know that unchanging rule is to be intelligent; not to know it leads to wild movements and evil issues. The knowledge of that unchanging rule produces a (grand) capacity and forbearance, and that capacity and forbearance lead to a community (of

feeling with all things). From this community of feeling comes a kingliness of character; and he who is king-like goes on to be heaven-like. In that likeness to heaven he possesses the Tao. Possessed of the Tao, he endures long; and to the end of his bodily life, is exempt from all danger of decay.

17. 1. In the highest antiquity, (the people) did not know that there were (their rulers). In the next age they loved them and praised them. In the next they feared them; in the next they despised them. Thus it was that when faith (in the Tao) was deficient (in the rulers) a want of faith in them ensued (in the people).

2. How irresolute did those (earliest rulers) appear, showing (by their reticence) the importance which they set upon their words! Their work was done and their undertakings were successful, while the people all said, "We are as we are, of ourselves!"

18. 1. When the Great Tao (Way or Method) ceased to be observed, benevolence and righteousness came into vogue. (Then) appeared wisdom and shrewdness, and there ensued great hypocrisy.

2. When harmony no longer prevailed throughout the six kinships, filial sons found their manifestation; when the states and clans fell into disorder, loyal ministers appeared.

19. 1. If we could renounce our sageness and discard our wisdom, it would be better for the people a hundredfold. If we could renounce our benevolence and discard our righteousness, the people would again become filial and kindly. If we could renounce our artful contrivances and discard our (scheming for) gain, there would be no thieves nor robbers.

2. Those three methods (of government)
Thought olden ways in elegance did fail
And made these names their want of worth to veil;
But simple views, and courses plain and true
Would selfish ends and many lusts eschew . . .

[. . . .]

21. The grandest forms of active force
From Tao come, their only source.
Who can of Tao the nature tell?
Our sight it flies, our touch as well.
Eluding sight, eluding touch,
The forms of things all in it crouch;
Eluding touch, eluding sight,
There are their semblances, all right.
Profound it is, dark and obscure;

Things' essences all there endure.
Those essences the truth enfold
Of what, when seen, shall then be told.
Now it is so; 'twas so of old.
Its name—what passes not away;
So, in their beautiful array,
Things form and never know decay.

How know I that it is so with all the beauties of existing things? By this (nature of the Tao).

5

Sun Tzŭ

from *On the Art of War*

Not much is known with any certainty about the life of Sun Tzŭ (trad. 544–496 BC). In fact, his historicity is even disputed among scholars. However, he is presumed to be the Chinese general, military strategist, and Taoist thinker who penned *On the Art of War*, from which the following is an excerpt. *On the Art of War* is perhaps the oldest known military treatise in existence. And while it deals explicitly with a variety of details relevant to war-making and ruling, it has also been influential beyond military science in other areas of human endeavor that involve strategic thinking.

I. Laying Plans

1. Sun Tzŭ said: The art of war is of vital importance to the State.

2. It is a matter of life and death, a road either to safety or to ruin. Hence it is a subject of inquiry which can on no account be neglected.

3. The art of war, then, is governed by five constant factors, to be taken into account in one's deliberations, when seeking to determine the conditions obtaining in the field.

4. These are: (1) The Moral Law; (2) Heaven; (3) Earth; (4) The Commander; (5) Method and discipline.

5, 6. *The Moral Law* causes the people to be in complete accord with their ruler, so that they will follow him regardless of their lives, undismayed by any danger.

7. *Heaven* signifies night and day, cold and heat, times and seasons.

SOURCE: Sun Tzŭ, *On the Art of War: The Oldest Military Treatise in the World*, trans. Lionel Giles (London: Luzac & Co., 1910), 1–8, 17–25.

8. *Earth* comprises distances, great and small; danger and security; open ground and narrow passes; the chances of life and death.

9. *The Commander* stands for the virtues of wisdom, sincerity, benevolence, courage and strictness.

10. By *Method and discipline* are to be understood the marshalling of the army in its proper subdivisions, the gradations of rank among the officers, the maintenance of roads by which supplies may reach the army, and the control of military expenditure.

11. These five heads should be familiar to every general: he who knows them will be victorious; he who knows them not will fail.

12. Therefore, in your deliberations, when seeking to determine the military conditions, let them be made the basis of a comparison, in this wise:—

13. (1) Which of the two sovereigns is imbued with the Moral law?

(2) Which of the two generals has most ability?

(3) With whom lie the advantages derived from Heaven and Earth?

(4) On which side is discipline most rigorously enforced?

(5) Which army is stronger?

(6) On which side are officers and men more highly trained?

(7) In which army is there the greater constancy both in reward and punishment?

14. By means of these seven considerations I can forecast victory or defeat.

15. The general that hearkens to my counsel and acts upon it, will conquer:—let such a one be retained in command! The general that hearkens not to my counsel nor acts upon it, will suffer defeat:—let such a one be dismissed!

16. While heeding the profit of my counsel, avail yourself also of any helpful circumstances over and beyond the ordinary rules.

17. According as circumstances are favorable, one should modify one's plans.

18. All warfare is based on deception.

19. Hence, when able to attack, we must seem unable; when using our forces, we must seem inactive; when we are near, we must make the enemy believe we are far away; when far away, we must make him believe we are near.

20. Hold out baits to entice the enemy. Feign disorder, and crush him.

21. If he is secure at all points, be prepared for him. If he is in superior strength, evade him.

22. If your opponent is of choleric temper, seek to irritate him. Pretend to be weak, that he may grow arrogant.

23. If he is taking his ease, give him no rest. If his forces are united, separate them.

24. Attack him where he is unprepared, appear where you are not expected.

25. These military devices, leading to victory, must not be divulged beforehand.

26. Now the general who wins a battle makes many calculations in his temple ere the battle is fought. The general who loses a battle makes but few calculations beforehand. Thus do many calculations lead to victory, and few calculations to defeat: how much more no calculation at all! It is by attention to this point that I can foresee who is likely to win or lose.

[. . . .]

III. Attack by Stratagem

1. Sun Tzŭ said: In the practical art of war, the best thing of all is to take the enemy's country whole and intact; to shatter and destroy it is not so good. So, too, it is better to recapture an army entire than to destroy it, to capture a regiment, a detachment or a company entire than to destroy them.

2. Hence to fight and conquer in all your battles is not supreme excellence; supreme excellence consists in breaking the enemy's resistance without fighting.

3. Thus the highest form of generalship is to baulk the enemy's plans; the next best is to prevent the junction of the enemy's forces; the next in order is to attack the enemy's army in the field; and the worst policy of all is to besiege walled cities.

4. The rule is, not to besiege walled cities if it can possibly be avoided. The preparation of mantlets, movable shelters, and various implements of war, will take up three whole months; and the piling up of mounds over against the walls will take three months more.

5. The general, unable to control his irritation, will launch his men to the assault like swarming ants, with the result that one-third of his men are slain, while the town still remains untaken. Such are the disastrous effects of a siege.

6. Therefore the skillful leader subdues the enemy's troops without any fighting; he captures their cities without laying siege to them; he overthrows their kingdom without lengthy operations in the field.

7. With his forces intact he will dispute the mastery of the Empire, and thus, without losing a man, his triumph will be complete. This is the method of attacking by stratagem.

8. It is the rule in war, if our forces are ten to the enemy's one, to surround him; if five to one, to attack him; if twice as numerous, to divide our army into two.

9. If equally matched, we can offer battle; if slightly inferior in numbers, we can avoid the enemy; if quite unequal in every way, we can flee from him.

10. Hence, though an obstinate fight may be made by a small force, in the end it must be captured by the larger force.

11. Now the general is the bulwark of the State; if the bulwark is complete at all points; the State will be strong; if the bulwark is defective, the State will be weak.

12. There are three ways in which a ruler can bring misfortune upon his army:—

13. (1) By commanding the army to advance or to retreat, being ignorant of the fact that it cannot obey. This is called hobbling the army.

14. (2) By attempting to govern an army in the same way as he administers a kingdom, being ignorant of the conditions which obtain in an army. This causes restlessness in the soldier's minds.

15. (3) By employing the officers of his army without discrimination, through ignorance of the military principle of adaptation to circumstances. This shakes the confidence of the soldiers.

16. But when the army is restless and distrustful, trouble is sure to come from the other feudal princes. This is simply bringing anarchy into the army, and flinging victory away.

17. Thus we may know that there are five essentials for victory:

(1) He will win who knows when to fight and when not to fight.
(2) He will win who knows how to handle both superior and inferior forces.
(3) He will win whose army is animated by the same spirit throughout all its ranks.
(4) He will win who, prepared himself, waits to take the enemy unprepared.
(5) He will win who has military capacity and is not interfered with by the sovereign.

Victory lies in the knowledge of these five points.

18. Hence the saying: If you know the enemy and know yourself, you need not fear the result of a hundred battles. If you know yourself but not the enemy, for every victory gained you will also suffer a defeat. If you know neither the enemy nor yourself, you will succumb in every battle.

Doctrines of Gautama Buddha

The Four Noble Truths and Eightfold Path

Born into a family of privilege near today's India-Nepal border, Gautama (ca. 560–480 BC) encountered a sick and elderly man one day. From that moment on, the question of suffering hounded him. He left his wife, family, and life of ease to practice ascetic solitude in hope of discerning the causes of, and relief from, suffering. He achieved through meditation an enlightened understanding (*bodhi*) of the Four Noble Truths of suffering, and the Eightfold Path for the cessation of it, which is described in the following excerpt. For decades, he shared his enlightenment with others, forming monastic communities to practice the Buddhist philosophy, and thereby launching one of the world's great religions. As Buddhism spread across the Asian continent, it acclimated to new cultural contexts. Chuang Tzǔ's Taoism, for example, resonated with Chinese environs.

Chapter XXVIII: Doctrines of Gautama Buddha

It is not possible, within the limits of a single chapter, to give our readers anything like a complete summary of the doctrines of Buddha's creed, and our attempt will rather be to present the substance of the great lessons and ideas which Gautama preached and inculcated among his countrymen.

Buddhism is, in its essence, a system of self-culture and self-restraint. Doctrines and beliefs are of secondary importance, for the effort to end human suffering by living a holy life, free from passions and desires, was the cardinal idea with which Gautama was impressed on the day on which he was "enlightened" under the Bo-tree in Bodh Gaya, and it was the central idea which he preached to the last day of his life.

SOURCE: Romesh Chunder Dutt, *History of India*, ed. A. V. Williams Jackson, vol. 1, *From the Earliest Times to the Sixth Century B.C.* (London: The Grolier Society, 1906), 304–7.

When he went from Bodh Gaya to Benares, and first preached his religion to his five former disciples, he explained to them the Fourfold Wisdom and the Eightfold Path, which form the essence of Buddhism.

"This, Bhikkhus, is the Noble Truth of Suffering. Birth is suffering, decay is suffering, illness is suffering, death is suffering. Presence of objects we hate is suffering, not to obtain what we desire is suffering. Briefly, the fivefold clinging to existence (the five elements) is suffering.

"This, Bhikkhus, is the Noble Truth of the Cause of Suffering. Thirst, that leads to rebirth accompanied by pleasure and lust, finding its delight here and there, thirst for pleasure, thirst for existence, thirst for prosperity.

"This, O Bhikkhus, is the Noble Truth of the Cessation of Suffering. It ceases with the complete cessation of thirst—a cessation which consists in the absence of every passion, with the abandoning of this thirst, with the doing away with it, with the deliverance from it, with the destruction of desire.

"This, O Bhikkhus, is the Noble Truth of the Path which leads to the cessation of suffering—the holy Eightfold Path of Right Belief, Right Aspiration, Right Speech, Right Conduct, Right Means of Livelihood, Right Exertion, Right Mindfulness, and Right Meditation."

The substance of this teaching is that life is suffering, the thirst for life and its pleasures is the cause of suffering, the extinction of that thirst is the cessation of suffering, and that such extinction can be brought about only by a holy life. It is impossible to convey in a few words all that is implied by the eight maxims into which a holy life is thus analyzed, but to Buddhists, trained in the traditions of their religion, these aphorisms speak volumes. Correct views and beliefs must be learnt and entertained; high aims and aspirations must always remain before the mind's eye; truthfulness and gentleness must characterize every word; uprightness and absolute integrity must mark the conduct. A livelihood must be sought and adhered to which does no harm to living things; there must be a lifelong perseverance in doing good, in acts of kindness, gentleness, and beneficence; the mind and intellect must be active and watchful; calm and tranquil meditation must fill the life with peace. A more beautiful picture of life was never conceived by poet or visionary; and a more perfect system of self-culture was never proclaimed by philosopher or saint.

The idea of self-culture was no doubt developed during the long course of meditation and good works in which Gautama passed his life. On the eve of his death he called together his brethren and recapitulated the entire system of self-culture under seven heads, and these are known as the Seven Jewels of the Buddhist Law.

"Which, then, O brethren, are the truths which, when I had perceived, I made known to you; which, when you have mastered, it behoves you to practise, meditate upon, and spread abroad, in order that pure religion may last long and be perpetuated, in order that it may continue to be for the good and the happiness of the great multitudes, out of pity for the world, to the good and the gain and the weal of gods and men. They are these: the four earnest meditations, the fourfold great struggle against sin, the four roads to saintship, the five moral powers, the five organs of spiritual sense, the seven kinds of wisdom, and the noble Eightfold Path."

7

Herodotus

from *The History*

Heralded as the "father of history" by none other than Cicero, Herodotus (ca. 484–425 BC) authored a lengthy narrative of the Greco-Persian wars (499–479 BC). In *The History*, he sought to "preserve from decay the remembrance of what men have done," especially the Greek victories over the Persians. Although Herodotus was sometimes slighted for the hyperbole in his narration, archaeological evidence has upheld several of the major points in his writing. Even in his own time, his descriptions of Asia Minor, Egypt, and Persia were exceptionally popular in ancient Athens, and they continue to provide a vital window into ancient cultures.

––––––––––––

80. And now when five days were gone, and the hubbub had settled down, the conspirators met together to consult about the situation of affairs. At this meeting speeches were made, to which many of the Greeks give no credence, but they were made nevertheless. Otanes recommended that the management of public affairs should be entrusted to the whole nation. "To me," he said, "it seems advisable that we should no longer have a single man to rule over us—the rule of one is neither good nor pleasant. Ye cannot have forgotten to what lengths Cambyses went in his haughty tyranny; and the haughtiness of the Magi ye yourselves have experienced. How indeed is it possible that monarchy should be a well-adjusted thing, when it allows a man to do as he likes without being answerable? Such licence is enough to stir strange and unwonted thoughts in the heart of the worthiest of men. Give a person this power, and straight-way his manifold good things puff him up with pride, while envy is so natural to human kind that it cannot but arise in him. But pride and envy

SOURCE: Herodotus, *The History of Herodotus*, trans. George Rawlinson, vol. 2 of *The Historians of Greece* (New York: The Tandy-Thomas Company, 1909), 122–26.

together include all wickedness—both of them leading on to deeds of savage violence. True it is that kings, possessing as they do all that heart can desire, ought to be void of envy; but the contrary is seen in their conduct towards the citizens. They are jealous of the most virtuous among their subjects, and wish their death; while they take delight in the meanest and basest, being ever ready to listen to the tales of slanderers. A king, besides, is beyond all other men inconsistent with himself. Pay him court in moderation, and he is angry because you do not show him more profound respect—show him profound respect, and he is offended again, because (as he says) you fawn on him. But the worst of all is, that he sets aside the laws of the land, puts men to death without trial, and subjects women to violence. The rule of the many, on the other hand, has, in the first place, the fairest of names, to wit, *isonomy*; and further, it is free from all those outrages which a king is wont to commit. There, places are given by lot, the magistrate is answerable for what he does, and measures rest with the commonalty. I vote, therefore, that we do away with monarchy, and raise the people to power. For the people are all in all."

81. Such were the sentiments of Otanes. Megabyzus spoke next, and advised the setting up of an oligarchy: "In all that Otanes has said to persuade you to put down monarchy," he observed, "I fully concur; but his recommendation that we should call the people to power seems to me not the best advice. For there is nothing so void of understanding, nothing so full of wantonness as the unwieldy rabble. It were folly not to be borne, for men, while seeking to escape the wantonness of a tyrant, to give themselves up to the wantonness of a rude unbridled mob. The tyrant, in all his doings, at least knows what he is about, but a mob is altogether devoid of knowledge; for how should there be any knowledge in a rabble, untaught, and with no natural sense of what is right and fit? It rushes wildly into state affairs with all the fury of a stream swollen in the winter, and confuses everything. Let the enemies of the Persians be ruled by democracies; but let us choose out from the citizens a certain number of the worthiest, and put the government into their hands. For thus both we ourselves shall be among the governors, and power being entrusted to the best men, it is likely that the best counsels will prevail in the state."

82. This was the advice which Megabyzus gave, and after him Darius came forward, and spoke as follows: "All that Megabyzus said against democracy was well said, I think; but about oligarchy he did not speak advisedly; for take these three forms of government—democracy, oligarchy, and monarchy—and let them each be at their best, I maintain that monarchy far surpasses the other two. What government can possibly be better than that of the very best men in the whole state? The counsels of such a man are like himself, and so he

governs the mass of the people to their heart's content; while at the same time his measures against evil-doers are kept more secret than in other states. Contrariwise, in oligarchies, where men vie with each other in the service of the commonwealth, fierce enmities are apt to arise between man and man, each wishing to be leader, and to carry his own measures; whence violent quarrels come, which lead to open strife, often ending in bloodshed. Then monarchy is sure to follow; and this too shows how far that rule surpasses all others. Again, in a democracy, it is impossible but that there will be malpractices: these malpractices, however, do not lead to enmities, but to close friendships, which are formed among those engaged in them, who must hold well together to carry on their villainies. And so things go on until a man stands forth as champion of the commonalty, and puts down the evil-doers. Straightway the author of so great a service is admired by all, and from being admired soon comes to be appointed king; so that here too it is plain that monarchy is the best government. Lastly, to sum up all in a word, whence, I ask, was it that we got the freedom which we enjoy?—did democracy give it us, or oligarchy, or a monarch? As a single man recovered our freedom for us, my sentence is that we keep to the rule of one. Even apart from this, we ought not to change the laws of our forefathers when they work fairly; for to do so is not well."

83. Such were the three opinions brought forward at this meeting: the four other Persians voted in favour of the last. Otanes, who wished to give his countrymen a democracy, when he found the decision against him, arose a second time, and spoke thus before the assembly: "Brother conspirators, it is plain that the king who is to be chosen will be one of ourselves, whether we make the choice by casting lots for the prize, or by letting the people decide which of us they will have to rule over them, or in any other way. Now, as I have neither a mind to rule nor to be ruled, I shall not enter the lists with you in this matter. I withdraw, however, on one condition—none of you shall claim to exercise rule over me or my seed forever." The six agreed to these terms, and Otanes withdrew and stood aloof from the contest. And still to this day the family of Otanes continues to be the only free family in Persia; those who belong to it submit to the rule of the king only so far as they themselves choose; they are bound, however, to observe the laws of the land like the other Persians.

8

Thucydides

from *History of the Peloponnesian War*

Author of the monumental *History of the Peloponnesian War*, Thucydides (ca. 460–400 BC) profoundly shaped the arts of historiography. He was attentive to chronological detail and to a close reading of the facts in the fight between Athens and Sparta. Instead of invoking the intervention of the gods in the outcome of the wars, Thucydides ascribes more of the responsibility to good and wise leaders. Like his fellow Greek historian Herodotus, Thucydides used historical narration to raise vital and enduring political and moral questions. Some have conjectured that President Abraham Lincoln may have drawn upon this Funeral Oration of Pericles in drafting his own Gettysburg Address.

The bones of the slain are brought to a tabernacle erected for the purpose three days before, and all are at liberty to deck out the remains of their friends at their own discretion. But when the grand procession is made, the cypress coffins are drawn on carriages, one for every tribe, in each of which are separately contained the bones of all who belonged to that tribe. One sumptuous bier is carried along empty for those that are lost, whose bodies could not be found among the slain. All who are willing, both citizens and strangers, attend the solemnity; and the women who were related to the deceased, stand near the sepulchre groaning and lamenting. They deposit the remains in the public sepulchre, which stands in the finest suburb of the city;—for it hath been the constant custom here to bury all who fell in war, except those at Marathon, whose extraordinary valour they judged proper to honour with a sepulchre on the field of battle. As soon as they are interred, someone selected for the office by the public voice, and ever a person in great esteem for

SOURCE: Thucydides, *History of the Peloponnesian War*, trans. William Smith (London: Jones & Co., 1831), 64–68.

his understanding, and of high dignity among them, pronounces over them the decent panegyric—and this done they depart. Through all the war, as the occasion recurred, this method was constantly observed. But over these, the first victims of it, Pericles the son of Xantippus was appointed to speak. So, when the proper time was come, walking from the sepulchre, and mounting a lofty pulpit erected for the purpose, from whence he might be heard more distinctly by the company, he thus began:

"Many of those who have spoken before me on these occasions, have commended the author of that law which we are now obeying, for having instituted an oration to the honour of those who sacrifice their lives in fighting for their country. For my part, I think it sufficient for men who have approved their virtue in action, by action to be honoured for it—by such as you see the public gratitude now performing about this funeral; and that the virtues of many ought not to be endangered by the management of any one person, when their credit must precariously depend on his oration, which may be good and may be bad. Difficult indeed it is, judiciously to handle a subject, where even probable truth will hardly gain assent. The hearer, enlightened by a long acquaintance, and warm in his affection, may quickly pronounce everything unfavourably expressed, in respect to what he wishes and what he knows,—whilst the stranger pronounceth all exaggerated, through envy of those deeds which he is conscious are above his own achievement. For the praises bestowed upon others are then only to be endured, when men imagine they can do those feats they hear to have been done: they envy what they cannot equal, and immediately pronounce it false. Yet, as this solemnity hath received its sanction from the authority of our ancestors, it is my duty also to obey the law, and to endeavour to procure, as far as I am able, the good will and approbation of all my audience.

"I shall therefore begin first with our forefathers, since both justice and decency require we should on this occasion bestow on them an honourable remembrance. In this our country they kept themselves always firmly settled, and through their valour handed it down free to every since-succeeding generation. Worthy indeed of praise are they, and yet more worthy are our immediate fathers: since, enlarging their own inheritance into the extensive empire which we now possess, they bequeathed that their work of toil to us their sons. Yet even these successes we ourselves here present, we who are yet in the strength and vigour of our days, have nobly improved, and have made such provisions for this our Athens, that now it is all-sufficient in itself to answer every exigence of war and of peace. I mean not here to recite those martial exploits by which these ends were accomplished, or the resolute defences we ourselves and our fathers have made against the formidable invasions of

Barbarians and Greeks—your own knowledge of these will excuse the long detail. But by what methods we have risen to this height of glory and power, by what polity and by what conduct we are thus aggrandized, I shall first endeavour to show; and then proceed to the praise of the deceased. These, in my opinion, can be no impertinent topics on this occasion; the discussion of them must be beneficial to this numerous company of Athenians and of strangers.

"We are happy in a form of government which cannot envy the laws of our neighbours;—for it hath served as a model to others, but is original at Athens. And this our form, as committed not to the few, but to the whole body of the people, is called a democracy. How different so ever in a private capacity, we all enjoy the same general equality our laws are fitted to preserve, and superior honours just as we excel. The public administration is not confined to a particular family, but is attainable only by merit. Poverty is not a hinderance, since whoever is able to serve his country, meets with no obstacle to preferment from his first obscurity. The offices of the state we go through without obstructions from one another; and live together in the mutual endearments of private life without suspicions; not angry with a neighbour for following the bent of his own humour, nor putting on that countenance of discontent, which pains though it cannot punish—so that in private life we converse without diffidence or damage, while we dare not on any account offend against the public, through the reverence we bear to the magistrates and the laws, chiefly to those enacted for redress of the injured, and to those unwritten, a breach of which is allowed disgrace. Our laws have further provided for the mind most frequent intermissions of care by the appointment of public recreations and sacrifices throughout the year, elegantly performed with a peculiar pomp, the daily delight of which is a charm that puts melancholy to flight. The grandeur of this our Athens causeth the produce of the whole earth to be imported here, by which we reap a familiar enjoyment, not more of the delicacies of our own growth than of those of other nations.

"In the affairs of war we excel those of our enemies, who adhere to methods opposite to our own. For we lay open Athens to general resort, nor ever drive any stranger from us whom either improvement or curiosity hath brought among us, lest any enemy should hurt us by seeing what is never concealed. We place not so great a confidence in the preparatives and artifices of war, as in the native warmth of our souls impelling us to action. In point of education, the youth of some people are inured by a course of laborious exercise, to support toil and exercise like men; but we, notwithstanding our easy and elegant way of life, face all the dangers of war as intrepidly as they. This may be proved by facts, since the Lacedaemonians never invade our territories barely with their own, but with the united strength of all their confederates. But, when we invade the dominions of our neighbours, for the most part we conquer without difficulty in an enemy's country those who fight in defence of their own habitations. The strength of our whole force no enemy yet hath ever experienced, because it is divided by our naval expeditions, or engaged in the different quarters of our service by land. But if anywhere they engage and defeat a small party of our forces, they boastingly give it out a total defeat; and if they are beat, they were certainly overpowered by our united strength. What though from a state of inactivity rather than laborious exercise, or with a natural rather than an acquired valour, we learn to encounter danger?—this good at least we receive from it, that we never droop under the apprehension of possible misfortunes, and when we hazard the danger, are found no less courageous than those who are continually inured to it. In these respects our whole community deserves justly to be admired, and in many we have yet to mention.

"In our manner of living we show an elegance tempered with frugality, and we cultivate philosophy without enervating the mind. We display our wealth in the season of beneficence, and not in the vanity of discourse. A confession of poverty is disgrace to no man, no effort to avoid it is disgrace indeed. There is visibly in the same persons an attention to their own private concerns and those of the public; and in others engaged in the labours of life, there is a competent skill in the affairs of government. For we are the only people who think him that does not meddle in state affairs—not indolent, but good for nothing. And yet we pass the soundest judgments, and are quick at catching the right apprehensions of things, not thinking that words are prejudicial to actions, but rather the not being duly prepared by previous debate, before we are obliged to proceed to execution. Herein consists our distinguishing excellence, that in the hour of action we show the greatest courage, and yet debate beforehand the expediency of our measures. The courage of others is the result of ignorance; deliberation makes them cowards. And those undoubtedly must be owned to have the greatest souls, who, most acutely sensible of the miseries of war and the sweets of peace, are not hence in the least deterred from facing danger.

"In acts of beneficence, further, we differ from the many. We preserve friends not by receiving but by conferring obligations. For he who does a kindness hath the advantage over him who by the law of gratitude becomes a debtor to his benefactor. The person obliged is compelled to act the more insipid part, conscious that a return of kindness is merely a payment and not an obligation. And we alone are splendidly beneficent to others, not so much from interested motives, as for the credit of pure liberality. I shall sum up what yet remains by only adding—that our Athens in general is the school of Greece; and that every single Athenian among us is excellently formed by his personal qualifications, for all the various scenes of active life, acting with a most graceful demeanour, and a most ready habit of despatch.

"That I have not on this occasion made use of a pomp of words, but the truth of facts, that height to which by such a conduct this state hath risen, is an undeniable proof. For we are now the only people of the world who are found by experience to be greater than in report—the only people who, repelling the attacks of an invading enemy, exempts their defeat from the blush of indignation, and to their tributaries yields no discontent, as if subject to men unworthy to command. That we deserve our power, we need no evidence to manifest. We have great and signal proofs of this, which entitle us to the admiration of the present and future ages. We want no Homer to be the herald of our praise; no poet to deck off a history with the charms of verse, where the opinion of exploits must suffer by a strict relation. Every sea has been opened by our fleets, and every land hath been penetrated by our armies, which have every where left behind them eternal monuments of our enmity and our friendship.

"In the just defence of such a state, these victims of their own valour, scorning the ruin threatened to it, have valiantly fought and bravely died. And every one of those who survive is ready, I am persuaded, to sacrifice life in such a cause. And for this reason have I enlarged so much on national points, to give the clearest proof that in the present war we have more at stake than men whose public advantages are not so valuable, and to illustrate, by actual evidence, how great a commendation is due to them who are now my subjects, and the greatest part of which they have already received. For the encomiums with which I have celebrated the state have been earned for it by the bravery of these, and of men like these. And such compliments might be thought too high and exaggerated, if passed on any Grecians but them alone. The fatal period to which these gallant souls are now reduced is the surest evidence of their merit—an evidence begun in their lives and completed in their deaths. For it is a debt of justice to pay superior honours to men who have devoted their lives in fighting for their country, though inferior to others in every virtue but that of valour. Their last service effaceth all former demerits—it extends to the public; their private demeanours reached only to a few. Yet not one of these was at all induced to shrink from danger, through fondness of those delights which the peaceful affluent life bestows—not one was the less lavish of his life, through that flattering hope attendant upon want, that poverty at length might be exchanged for affluence. One passion there was in their minds much stronger than these—the desire of vengeance on their enemies. Regarding this as the most honourable prize of dangers, they boldly rushed towards the mark, to glut revenge, and then to satisfy those secondary passions. The uncertain event they had already secured in hope; what their eyes showed plainly must be done, they trusted their own valour to accomplish, thinking it more glorious to defend themselves and die in the attempt, than to yield and live. From the reproach of cowardice indeed they fled, but presented their bodies to the shock of battle; when, insensible of fear, but triumphing in hope, in the doubtful charge they instantly dropped—and thus discharged the duty which brave men owe to their country.

"As for you, who now survive them—it is your business to pray for a better fate—but, to think it your duty also to preserve the same spirit and warmth of courage against your enemies; not judging of the expediency of this from a mere harangue—where any man, indulging a flow of words, may tell you what you yourselves know as well as he, how many advantages there are in fighting valiantly against your enemies—but rather, making the daily-increasing grandeur of this community the object of your thoughts, and growing quite enamoured of it. And when it really appears great to your apprehensions, think again, that this grandeur was acquired by brave and valiant men; by men who knew their duty, and in the moments of action were sensible of shame; who, whenever their attempts were unsuccessful, thought it dishonour their country should stand in need of any thing their valour could do for it, and so made it the most glorious present. Bestowing thus their lives on the public, they have every one received a praise that will never decay, a sepulchre that will always be most illustrious—not that in which their bones lie mouldering, but that in which their fame is preserved, to be on every occasion, when honour is the employ of either word or act, eternally remembered. This whole earth is the sepulchre of illustrious men: nor is it the inscriptions on the columns in their native soil alone that show their merit, but the memorial of them, better than all inscriptions, in every foreign nation, reposited more durably in universal remembrance than on their own tomb. From this very moment, emulating these noble patterns, placing your happiness in liberty, and liberty in valour, be prepared to encounter all the dangers of war. For, to be lavish of life is not so noble in those whom misfortunes have reduced to misery and despair, as in men who hazard the loss of a comfortable subsistence, and the enjoyment of all the blessings this world affords, by an unsuccessful enterprise. Adversity, after a series of ease and affluence, sinks deeper into the heart of a man of spirit, than the stroke of death insensibly received in the vigour of life and public hope.

"For this reason, the parents of those who are now gone, whoever of them may be attending here, I do not bewail—I shall rather comfort. It is well known to what unhappy accidents they were liable from the moment of their birth; and, that happiness belongs to men who have reached the most glorious period of life, as these now have who are to you the source of sorrow—these, whose life hath received its ample measure, happy in its continuance, and equally happy in its conclusion. I know it in truth a difficult task, to fix comfort in those breasts, which will have frequent remembrances in seeing the happiness of others, of what they once themselves enjoyed. And sorrow flows not from the absence of those good things we have never yet experienced, but from the loss of those to which we have been accustomed. They who are not yet by age exempted from issue, should be comforted in the hope of having more. The children yet to be born will be a private benefit to some, in causing them to forget such as no longer are, and will be a double benefit to their country, in preventing its desolation, and providing for its security. For those persons cannot in common justice be regarded as members of equal value to the public, who have no children to expose to danger for its safety.—But you, whose age is already far advanced, compute the greater share of happiness your longer time hath afforded for so much gain, persuaded in yourselves, the remainder will be but short, and enlighten that space by the glory gained by these. It is greatness of soul alone that never grows old: nor is it wealth that delights in the latter stage of life, as some give out, so much as honour.

"To you, the sons and brothers of the deceased, whatever number of you are here, a field of hardy contention is opened. For him who no longer is, everyone is ready to commend, so that to whatever height you push your deserts, you will scarce ever be thought to equal, but to be somewhat inferior to these. Envy will exert itself against a competitor while life remains: but when death stops the competition, affection will applaud without restraint.

"If after this it be expected from me to say any thing to you who are now reduced to a state of widowhood, about female virtue, I shall express it all in one short admonition;—It is your greatest glory not to be deficient in the virtue peculiar to your sex, and to give the men as little handle as possible to talk of your behaviour, whether well or ill.

"I have now discharged the province allotted me by the laws, and said what I thought most pertinent to this assembly. Our departed friends have by facts been already honoured. Their children from this day till they arrive at manhood shall be educated at the public expense of the state, which hath appointed so beneficial a meed for these and all future relics of the public contests. For wherever the greatest rewards are proposed for virtue, there the best of patriots are ever to be found. Now, let every one respectively indulge the decent grief for his departed friends, and then retire."

9

Plato

from *Apology*

The famous Athenian citizen Plato (ca. 429–347 BC) stands out among the most influential philosophers not only in the Western tradition, but in human history. A follower of Socrates, Plato founded what is sometimes heralded as the first university—namely, the Academy. His most famous student was none other than Aristotle. Most of Plato's works were written in dialogue form, and the character Socrates typically plays a lead role in the conversation presented. The following excerpt from Plato's *Apology* is a dramatic portrayal of Socrates' actual defense against the accusation that he had corrupted the youth in Athens. Ultimately, Socrates is convicted and sentenced to death.

Well, then, I will make my defence, and I will endeavor in the short time which is allowed to do away with this evil opinion of me which you have held for such a long time; and I hope I may succeed, if this be well for you and me, and that my words may find favor with you. But I know that to accomplish this is not easy—I quite see the nature of the task. Let the event be as God wills: in obedience to the law I make my defence.

I will begin at the beginning, and ask what the accusation is which has given rise to this slander of me, and which has encouraged Meletus to proceed against me. What do the slanderers say? They shall be my prosecutors, and I will sum up their words in an affidavit: "Socrates is an evil-doer, and a curious person, who searches into things under the earth and in heaven, and he makes the worse appear the better cause; and he teaches the aforesaid doctrines to others." That is the nature of the accusation, and that is what you have seen yourselves in the comedy of Aristophanes, who has introduced a man whom he

SOURCE: Plato, *Dialogues of Plato, Containing the Apology of Socrates, Crito, Phaedo, and Protagoras*, trans. Benjamin Jowett, rev. ed. (New York: Colonial Press, 1899), 12–31.

calls Socrates, going about and saying that he can walk in the air, and talking a deal of nonsense concerning matters of which I do not pretend to know either much or little—not that I mean to say anything disparaging of anyone who is a student of natural philosophy. I should be very sorry if Meletus could lay that to my charge. But the simple truth is, O Athenians, that I have nothing to do with these studies. Very many of those here present are witnesses to the truth of this, and to them I appeal. Speak then, you who have heard me, and tell your neighbors whether any of you have ever known me hold forth in few words or in many upon matters of this sort. . . . You hear their answer. And from what they say of this you will be able to judge of the truth of the rest.

As little foundation is there for the report that I am a teacher, and take money; that is no more true than the other. Although, if a man is able to teach, I honor him for being paid. There is Gorgias of Leontium, and Prodicus of Ceos, and Hippias of Elis, who go the round of the cities, and are able to persuade the young men to leave their own citizens, by whom they might be taught for nothing, and come to them, whom they not only pay, but are thankful if they may be allowed to pay them.

[. . . .]

I dare say that someone will ask the question, "Why is this, Socrates, and what is the origin of these accusations of you: for there must have been something strange which you have been doing? All this great fame and talk about you would never have arisen if you had been like other men: tell us, then, why this is, as we should be sorry to judge hastily of you." Now I regard this as a fair challenge, and I will endeavor to explain to you the origin of this name of "wise," and of this evil fame. Please to attend them. And although some of you may think I am joking, I declare that I will tell you the entire truth. Men of Athens, this reputation of mine has come of a certain sort of wisdom which I possess. If you ask me what kind of wisdom, I reply, such wisdom as is attainable by man, for to that extent I am inclined to believe that I am wise; whereas the persons of whom I was speaking have a superhuman wisdom, which I may fail to describe, because I have it not myself; and he who says that I have, speaks falsely, and is taking away my character. And here, O men of Athens, I must beg you not to interrupt me, even if I seem to say something extravagant. For the word which I will speak is not mine. I will refer you to a witness who is worthy of credit, and will tell you about my wisdom—whether I have any, and of what sort—and that witness shall be the god of Delphi. You must have known Chaerephon; he was early a friend of mine, and also a friend of yours, for he shared in the exile of the people, and returned with you. Well, Chaerephon, as you know, was very impetuous in all his doings, and he went to Delphi and boldly asked the oracle to tell him whether—as I was saying, I must beg you not to interrupt—he asked the oracle to tell him whether there was anyone wiser than I was, and the Pythian prophetess answered that there was no man wiser. Chaerephon is dead himself, but his brother, who is in court, will confirm the truth of this story.

Why do I mention this? Because I am going to explain to you why I have such an evil name. When I heard the answer, I said to myself, What can the god mean? and what is the interpretation of this riddle? for I know that I have no wisdom, small or great. What can he mean when he says that I am the wisest of men? And yet he is a god and cannot lie; that would be against his nature. After a long consideration, I at last thought of a method of trying the question. I reflected that if I could only find a man wiser than myself, then I might go to the god with a refutation in my hand. I should say to him, "Here is a man who is wiser than I am; but you said that I was the wisest." Accordingly I went to one who had the reputation of wisdom, and observed to him—his name I need not mention; he was a politician whom I selected for examination—and the result was as follows: When I began to talk with him, I could not help thinking that he was not really wise, although he was thought wise by many, and wiser still by himself; and I went and tried to explain to him that he thought himself wise, but was not really wise; and the consequence was that he hated me, and his enmity was shared by several who were present and heard me. So I left him, saying to myself, as I went away: Well, although I do not suppose that either of us knows anything really beautiful and good, I am better off than he is—for he knows nothing, and thinks that he knows. I neither know nor think that I know. In this latter particular, then, I seem to have slightly the advantage of him. Then I went to another, who had still higher philosophical pretensions, and my conclusion was exactly the same. I made another enemy of him, and of many others besides him.

After this I went to one man after another, being not unconscious of the enmity which I provoked, and I lamented and feared this: but necessity was laid upon me—the word of God, I thought, ought to be considered first. And I said to myself, Go I must to all who appear to know, and find out the meaning of the oracle. And I swear to you, Athenians, by the dog I swear!—for I must tell you the truth—the result of my mission was just this: I found that the men most in repute were all but the most foolish; and that some inferior men were really wiser and better.

[. . . .]

There is another thing:—young men of the richer classes, who have not much to do, come about me of their own accord; they like to hear the pretenders examined, and they often imitate me, and examine others themselves; there are plenty of persons, as they soon enough discover, who think that they know something, but really know little or nothing: and then those who are examined by them instead of being angry with themselves are angry with me: This confounded Socrates, they say; this villainous misleader of youth!—and then if somebody asks them, Why, what evil does he practise or teach? they do not know, and cannot tell; but in order that they may not appear to be at a loss, they repeat the ready-made charges which are used against all philosophers about teaching things up in the clouds and under the earth, and having no gods, and making the worse appear the better cause; for they do not like to confess that their pretence of knowledge has been detected—which is the truth: and as they are numerous and ambitious and energetic, and are all in battle array and have persuasive tongues, they have filled your ears with their loud and inveterate calumnies. And this is the reason why my three accusers, Meletus and Anytus and Lycon, have set upon me: Meletus, who has a quarrel with me on behalf of the poets; Anytus, on behalf of the craftsmen; Lycon, on behalf of the rhetoricians: and as I said at the beginning, I cannot expect to get rid of this mass of calumny all in a moment. And this, O men of Athens, is the truth and the whole truth; I have concealed nothing, I have dissembled nothing. And yet I know that this plainness of speech makes them hate me, and what is their hatred but a proof that I am speaking the truth?—this is the occasion and reason of their slander of me, as you will find out either in this or in any future inquiry.

I have said enough in my defence against the first class of my accusers; I turn to the second class, who are headed by Meletus, that good and patriotic man, as he calls himself. And now I will try to defend myself against them: these new accusers must also have their affidavit read. What do they say? Something of this sort: That Socrates is a doer of evil, and corrupter of the youth, and he does not believe in the gods of the state, and has other new divinities of his own. That is the sort of charge; and now let us examine the particular counts. He says that I am a doer of evil, who corrupt[s] the youth; but I say, O men of Athens, that Meletus is a doer of evil, and the evil is that he makes a joke of a serious matter, and is too ready at bringing other men to trial from a pretended zeal and interest about matters in which he really never had the smallest interest. And the truth of this I will endeavor to prove.

Come hither, Meletus, and let me ask a question of you. You think a great deal about the improvement of youth?

Yes, I do.

Tell the judges, then, who is their improver; for you must know, as you have taken the pains to discover their corrupter, and are citing and accusing me before them. Speak, then, and tell the judges who their improver is.

Observe, Meletus, that you are silent, and have nothing to say. But is not this rather disgraceful, and a very considerable proof of what I was saying, that you have no interest in the matter? Speak up, friend, and tell us who their improver is.

The laws.

But that, my good sir, is not my meaning. I want to know who the person is, who, in the first place, knows the laws.

The judges, Socrates, who are present in court.

What do you mean to say, Meletus, that they are able to instruct and improve youth?

Certainly they are.

What, all of them, or some only and not others?

All of them.

By the goddess Here, that is good news! There are plenty of improvers, then. And what do you say of the audience—do they improve them?

Yes, they do.

And the senators?

Yes, the senators improve them.

But perhaps the ecclesiasts corrupt them?—or do they too improve them?

They improve them.

Then every Athenian improves and elevates them; all with the exception of myself; and I alone am their corrupter? Is that what you affirm?

That is what I stoutly affirm.

I am very unfortunate if that is true. But suppose I ask you a question: Would you say that this also holds true in the case of horses? Does one man do them harm and all the world good? Is not the exact opposite of this true? One man is able to do them good, or at least not many; the trainer of horses, that is to say, does them good, and others who have to do with them rather injure them? Is not that true, Meletus, of horses, or any other animals? Yes, certainly. Whether you and Anytus say yes or no, that is no matter. Happy indeed would be the condition of youth if they had one corrupter only, and all the rest of the world were their improvers. And you, Meletus, have sufficiently shown that you never had a thought about the young: your carelessness is seen in your not caring about matters spoken of in this very indictment.

And now, Meletus, I must ask you another question: Which is better, to live among bad citizens, or among good ones? Answer, friend, I say; for that is a question which may be easily answered. Do not the good do their neighbors good, and the bad do them evil?

Certainly.

And is there anyone who would rather be injured than benefited by those who live with him? Answer, my good friend; the law requires you to answer—does anyone like to be injured?

Certainly not.

And when you accuse me of corrupting and deteriorating the youth, do you allege that I corrupt them intentionally or unintentionally?

Intentionally, I say.

But you have just admitted that the good do their neighbors good, and the evil do them evil. Now is that a truth which your superior wisdom has recognized thus early in life, and am I, at my age, in such darkness and ignorance as not to know that if a man with whom I have to live is corrupted by me, I am very likely to be harmed by him, and yet I corrupt him, and intentionally, too? that is what you are saying, and of that you will never persuade me or any other human being. But either I do not corrupt them, or I corrupt them unintentionally, so that on either view of the case you lie. If my offence is unintentional, the law has no cognizance of unintentional offences: you ought to have taken me privately, and warned and admonished me; for if I had been better advised, I should have left off doing what I only did unintentionally—no doubt I should; whereas you hated to converse with me or teach me, but you indicted me in this court, which is a place, not of instruction, but of punishment.

I have shown, Athenians, as I was saying, that Meletus has no care at all, great or small, about the matter. But still I should like to know, Meletus, in what I am affirmed to corrupt the young. I suppose you mean, as I infer from your indictment, that I teach them not to acknowledge the gods which the State acknowledges, but some other new divinities or spiritual agencies in their stead. These are the lessons which corrupt the youth, as you say.

Yes, that I say emphatically.

Then, by the gods, Meletus, of whom we are speaking, tell me and the court, in somewhat plainer terms, what you mean! for I do not as yet understand whether you affirm that I teach others to acknowledge some gods, and therefore do believe in gods and am not an entire atheist—this you do not lay to my charge; but only that they are not the same gods which the city recognizes—the charge is that they are different gods. Or, do you mean to say that I am an atheist simply, and a teacher of atheism?

I mean the latter—that you are a complete atheist.

That is an extraordinary statement, Meletus. Why do you say that? Do you mean that I do not believe in the godhead of the sun or moon, which is the common creed of all men?

I assure you, judges, that he does not believe in them; for he says that the sun is stone, and the moon earth.

Friend Meletus, you think that you are accusing Anaxagoras: and you have but a bad opinion of the judges, if you fancy them ignorant to such a degree as not to know that those doctrines are found in the books of Anaxagoras the Clazomenian, who is full of them. And these are the doctrines which the youth are said to learn of Socrates, when there are not unfrequently exhibitions of them at the theatre (price of admission one drachma at the most); and they might cheaply purchase them, and laugh at Socrates if he pretends to father such eccentricities. And so, Meletus, you really think that I do not believe in any god?

I swear by Zeus that you believe absolutely in none at all.

You are a liar, Meletus, not believed even by yourself. For I cannot help thinking, O men of Athens, that Meletus is reckless and impudent, and that he has written this indictment in a spirit of mere wantonness and youthful bravado. Has he not compounded a riddle, thinking to try me? He said to himself: I shall see whether this wise Socrates will discover my ingenious contradiction, or whether I shall be able to deceive him and the rest of them. For he certainly does appear to me to contradict himself in the indictment as much as if he said that Socrates is guilty of not believing in the gods, and yet of believing in them—but this surely is a piece of fun.

I should like you, O men of Athens, to join me in examining what I conceive to be his inconsistency; and do you, Meletus, answer. And I must remind you that you are not to interrupt me if I speak in my accustomed manner.

Did ever man, Meletus, believe in the existence of human things, and not of human beings? . . . I wish, men of Athens, that he would answer, and not be always trying to get up an interruption. Did ever any man believe in horsemanship, and not in horses? or in flute-playing, and not in flute-players? No, my friend; I will answer to you and to the court, as you refuse to answer for yourself. There is no man who ever did. But now please to answer the next question: Can a man believe in spiritual and divine agencies, and not in spirits or demigods?

He cannot.

I am glad that I have extracted that answer, by the assistance of the court; nevertheless you swear in the indictment that I teach and believe in divine or spiritual agencies (new or old, no matter for that); at any rate, I believe in spiritual agencies, as you say and swear in the affidavit; but if I believe in divine beings, I must believe in spirits or demigods; is not that true? Yes, that is true, for I may assume that your silence gives assent to that. Now what are spirits or demigods? are they not either gods or the sons of gods? Is that true?

Yes, that is true.

But this is just the ingenious riddle of which I was speaking: the demigods or spirits are gods, and you say first that I don't believe in gods, and then again that I do believe in gods; that is, if I believe in demigods. For if the demigods are the illegitimate sons of gods, whether by the Nymphs or by any other mothers, as is thought, that, as all men will allow, necessarily implies the existence of their parents. You might as well affirm the existence of mules, and deny that of horses and asses. Such nonsense, Meletus, could only have been intended by you as a trial of me. You have put this into the indictment because you had nothing real of which to accuse me. But no one who has a particle of understanding will ever be convinced by you that the same man can believe in divine and superhuman things, and yet not believe that there are gods and demigods and heroes.

I have said enough in answer to the charge of Meletus: any elaborate defence is unnecessary; but as I was saying before, I certainly have many enemies, and this is what will be my destruction if I am destroyed; of that I am certain; not Meletus, nor yet Anytus, but the envy and detraction of the world, which has been the death of many good men, and will probably be the death of many more; there is no danger of my being the last of them.

Someone will say: And are you not ashamed, Socrates, of a course of life which is likely to bring you to an untimely end? To him I may fairly answer: There you are mistaken: a man who is good for anything ought not to calculate the chance of living or dying; he ought only to consider whether in doing anything he is doing right or wrong—acting the part of a good man or of a bad.

[. . . .]

Men of Athens, do not interrupt, but hear me; there was an agreement between us that you should hear me out. And I think that what I am going to say will do you good: for I have something more to say, at which you may be inclined to cry out; but I beg that you will not do this. I would have you know that, if you kill such a one as I am, you will injure yourselves more than you will injure me. Meletus and Anytus will not injure me: they cannot; for it is not in the nature of things that a bad man should injure a better than himself. I do not deny that he may, perhaps, kill him, or drive him into exile, or deprive him of civil rights; and he may imagine, and others may imagine, that he is doing him a great injury: but in that I do not agree with him; for the evil of doing as Anytus is doing—of unjustly taking away another man's life—is greater far. And now, Athenians, I am not going to argue for my own sake, as you may think, but for yours, that you may not sin against the God, or lightly reject his boon by condemning me. For if you kill me you will not easily find another like me, who, if I may use such a ludicrous figure of speech, am a sort of gadfly, given to the State by the God; and the State is like a great and noble steed who is tardy in his motions owing to his very size, and requires to be stirred into life. I am that gadfly which God has given the State, and all day long and in all places am always fastening upon you, arousing and persuading and reproaching you. And as you will not easily find another like me, I would advise you to spare me. I dare say that you may feel irritated at being suddenly awakened when you are caught napping; and you may think that if you were to strike me dead, as Anytus advises, which you easily might, then you would sleep on for the remainder of your lives, unless God in his care of you gives you another gadfly. And that I am given to you by God is proved by this: that if I had been like other men, I should not have neglected all my own concerns, or patiently seen the neglect of them during all these years, and have been doing yours, coming to you individually, like a father or elder brother, exhorting you to regard virtue; this, I say, would not be like human nature. And had I gained anything, or if my exhortations had been paid, there would have been some sense in that: but now, as you will perceive, not even the impudence of my accusers dares to say that I have ever exacted or sought pay of anyone; they have no witness of that. And I have a witness of the truth of what I say; my poverty is a sufficient witness.

Someone may wonder why I go about in private, giving advice and busying myself with the concerns of others, but do not venture to come forward in public and advise the State. I will tell you the reason of this. You have often heard me speak of an oracle or sign which comes to me, and is the divinity which Meletus ridicules in the indictment. This sign I have had ever since I was a child. The sign is a voice which comes to me and always forbids me to do something which I am going to do, but never commands me to do anything, and this is what stands in the way of my being a politician. And rightly, as I think. For I am certain, O men of Athens, that if I had engaged in politics, I should have perished long ago and done no good either to you or to myself. And don't be offended at my telling you the truth: for the truth is that no man who goes to war with you or any other multitude, honestly struggling against the commission of unrighteousness and wrong in the state, will save his life; he who will really fight for the right, if he would live even for a little while, must have a private station and not a public one.

I can give you as proofs of this, not words only, but deeds, which you value more than words. Let me tell you a passage of my own life, which will prove to you that I should never have yielded to injustice from any fear of death, and that if I had not yielded I should have died at once. I will tell you a story—tasteless, perhaps, and commonplace, but nevertheless true. The only office of State which

I ever held, O men of Athens, was that of senator; the tribe Antiochis, which is my tribe, had the presidency at the trial of the generals who had not taken up the bodies of the slain after the battle of Arginusae; and you proposed to try them all together, which was illegal, as you all thought afterwards; but at the time I was the only one of the Prytanes who was opposed to the illegality, and I gave my vote against you; and when the orators threatened to impeach and arrest me, and have me taken away, and you called and shouted, I made up my mind that I would run the risk, having law and justice with me, rather than take part in your injustice because I feared imprisonment and death. This happened in the days of the democracy. But when the oligarchy of the Thirty was in power, they sent for me and four others into the rotunda, and bade us bring Leon the Salaminian from Salamis, as they wanted to execute him. This was a specimen of the sort of commands which they were always giving with the view of implicating as many as possible in their crimes; and then I showed, not in words only, but in deed, that, if I may be allowed to use such an expression, I cared not a straw for death, and that my only fear was the fear of doing an unrighteous or unholy thing. For the strong arm of that oppressive power did not frighten me into doing wrong; and when we came out of the rotunda the other four went to Salamis and fetched Leon, but I went quietly home. For which I might have lost my life, had not the power of the Thirty shortly afterwards come to an end. And to this many will witness.

Now do you really imagine that I could have survived all these years, if I had led a public life, supposing that like a good man I had always supported the right and had made justice, as I ought, the first thing? No, indeed, men of Athens, neither I nor any other. But I have been always the same in all my actions, public as well as private, and never have I yielded any base compliance to those who are slanderously termed my disciples, or to any other. For the truth is that I have no regular disciples: but if anyone likes to come and hear me while I am pursuing my mission, whether he be young or old, he may freely come. Nor do I converse with those who pay only, and not with those who do not pay; but anyone, whether he be rich or poor, may ask and answer me and listen to my words; and whether he turns out to be a bad man or a good one, that cannot be justly laid to my charge, as I never taught him anything. And if anyone says that he has ever learned or heard anything from me in private which all the world has not heard, I should like you to know that he is speaking an untruth.

But I shall be asked, Why do people delight in continually conversing with you? I have told you already, Athenians, the whole truth about this: they like to hear the cross-examination of the pretenders to wisdom; there is amusement in this. And this is a duty which the God has imposed upon me, as I am assured by oracles, visions, and in every sort of way in which the will of divine power was ever signified to anyone.

[. . . .]

But, setting aside the question of dishonor, there seems to be something wrong in petitioning a judge, and thus procuring an acquittal instead of informing and convincing him. For his duty is, not to make a present of justice, but to give judgment; and he has sworn that he will judge according to the laws, and not according to his own good pleasure; and neither he nor we should get into the habit of perjuring ourselves—there can be no piety in that. Do not then require me to do what I consider dishonorable and impious and wrong, especially now, when I am being tried for impiety on the indictment of Meletus. For if, O men of Athens, by force of persuasion and entreaty, I could overpower your oaths, then I should be teaching you to believe that there are no gods, and convict myself, in my own defence, of not believing in them. But that is not the case; for I do believe that there are gods, and in a far higher sense than that in which any of my accusers believe in them. And to you and to God I commit my cause, to be determined by you as is best for you and me.

[*Jury finds Socrates guilty.*]

There are many reasons why I am not grieved, O men of Athens, at the vote of condemnation. I expected this, and am only surprised that the votes are so nearly equal; for I had thought that the majority against me would have been far larger; but now, had thirty votes gone over to the other side, I should have been acquitted. And I may say that I have escaped Meletus. And I may say more; for without the assistance of Anytus and Lycon, he would not have had a fifth part of the votes, as the law requires, in which case he would have incurred a fine of a thousand drachmae, as is evident.

And so he proposes death as the penalty. And what shall I propose on my part, O men of Athens? Clearly that which is my due. And what is that which I ought to pay or to receive? What shall be done to the man who has never had the wit to be idle during his whole life; but has been careless of what the many care about—wealth and family interests, and military offices, and speaking in the assembly, and magistracies, and plots, and parties. Reflecting that I was really too honest a man to follow in this way and live, I did not go where I could do no good to you or to myself; but where I could do the greatest good privately to everyone of you, thither I went, and sought to persuade every man among you that he must look to himself, and seek virtue and wisdom before he looks to his private interests, and look to the state before he looks to the interests of the State; and that this should be the order which he observes in all his actions. What shall be done to such a one? Doubtless some good thing, O men of Athens, if he has his reward; and the good should be of a kind suitable to him. What would be a reward suitable to a poor man who is your benefactor, who desires leisure that he may instruct you? There can be no more fitting reward than maintenance in the Prytaneum, O men of Athens, a reward which he deserves far more than the citizen who has won the prize at Olympia in the horse or chariot race, whether the chariots were drawn by two horses or by many. For I am in want, and he has enough; and he only gives you the appearance of happiness, and I give you the reality. And if I am to estimate the penalty justly, I say that maintenance in the Prytaneum is the just return.

[*Jury sentences Socrates to death.*]

Plato

from *Euthyphro*

The following is an excerpt from Plato's *Euthyphro*, which is often thought to represent one of Plato's earlier works. In this dialogue, Socrates encounters Euthyphro at court. Socrates is standing trial for corrupting the youth, while Euthyphro is prosecuting his own father for murder, which is shocking news to Socrates. From there, the two engage in a feisty conversation about the nature of piety, which culminates in Socrates posing a famous and difficult dilemma for Euthyphro—a dilemma that has puzzled and influenced moral and religious thinkers for centuries.

[*At court, Socrates encounters Euthyphro, who is prosecuting his own father for murder.*]

Soc. And I, my dear friend, knowing this, am desirous of becoming your disciple. For I observe that no one appears to notice you—not even this Meletus; but his sharp eyes have found me out at once, and he has indicted me for impiety. And therefore, I adjure you to tell me the nature of piety and impiety, which you said that you knew so well, and of murder, and of other offences against the gods. What are they? Is not piety in every action always the same? and impiety, again—is it not always the opposite of piety, and also the same with itself, having, as impiety, one notion which includes whatever is impious?

Euth. To be sure, Socrates.

Soc. And what is piety, and what is impiety?

Euth. Piety is doing as I am doing; that is to say, prosecuting any one who is guilty of murder, sacrilege, or of any similar crime—whether he be your

SOURCE: Plato, *The Dialogues of Plato, Translated into English with Analyses and Introductions*, 5 vols., vol. 2, 3rd ed., revised and corrected throughout, trans. B. Jowett (New York: Oxford University Press, American Branch, 1892), 79–87.

father or mother, or whoever he may be—that makes no difference; and not to prosecute them is impiety. And please to consider, Socrates, what a notable proof I will give you of the truth of my words, a proof which I have already given to others:—of the principle, I mean, that the impious, whoever he may be, ought not to go unpunished. For do not men regard Zeus as the best and most righteous of the gods?—and yet they admit that he bound his father (Cronos) because he wickedly devoured his sons, and that he too had punished his own father (Uranus) for a similar reason, in a nameless manner. And yet when I proceed against my father, they are angry with me. So inconsistent are they in their way of talking when the gods are concerned, and when I am concerned.

Soc. May not this be the reason, Euthyphro, why I am charged with impiety—that I cannot away with these stories about the gods? and therefore I suppose that people think me wrong. But, as you who are well informed about them approve of them, I cannot do better than assent to your superior wisdom. What else can I say, confessing as I do, that I know nothing about them? Tell me, for the love of Zeus, whether you really believe that they are true.

Euth. Yes, Socrates; and things more wonderful still, of which the world is in ignorance.

Soc. And do you really believe that the gods fought with one another, and had dire quarrels, battles, and the like, as the poets say, and as you may see represented in the works of great artists? The temples are full of them; and notably the robe of Athene, which is carried up to the Acropolis at the great Panathenaea, is embroidered with them. Are all these tales of the gods true, Euthyphro?

Euth. Yes, Socrates; and, as I was saying, I can tell you, if you would like to hear them, many other things about the gods which would quite amaze you.

Soc. I dare say; and you shall tell me them at some other time when I have leisure. But just at present I would rather hear from you a more precise answer, which you have not as yet given, my friend, to the question, What is "piety"? When asked, you only replied, Doing as you do, charging your father with murder.

Euth. And what I said was true, Socrates.

Soc. No doubt, Euthyphro; but you would admit that there are many other pious acts?

Euth. There are.

Soc. Remember that I did not ask you to give me two or three examples of piety, but to explain the general idea which makes all pious things to be pious. Do you not recollect that there was one idea which made the impious impious, and the pious pious?

Euth. I remember.

Soc. Tell me what is the nature of this idea, and then I shall have a standard to which I may look, and by which I may measure actions, whether yours or those of any one else, and then I shall be able to say that such and such an action is pious, such another impious.

Euth. I will tell you, if you like.

Soc. I should very much like.

Euth. Piety, then, is that which is dear to the gods, and impiety is that which is not dear to them.

Soc. Very good, Euthyphro; you have now given me the sort of answer which I wanted. But whether what you say is true or not I cannot as yet tell, although I make no doubt that you will prove the truth of your words.

Euth. Of course.

Soc. Come, then, and let us examine what we are saying. That thing or person which is dear to the gods is pious, and that thing or person which is hateful to the gods is impious, these two being the extreme opposites of one another. Was not that said?

Euth. It was.

Soc. And well said?

Euth. Yes, Socrates, I thought so; it was certainly said.

Soc. And further, Euthyphro, the gods were admitted to have enmities and hatreds and differences?

Euth. Yes, that was also said.

Soc. And what sort of difference creates enmity and anger? Suppose for example that you and I, my good friend, differ about a number; do differences of this sort make us enemies and set us at variance with one another? Do we not go at once to arithmetic, and put an end to them by a sum?

Euth. True.

Soc. Or suppose that we differ about magnitudes, do we not quickly end the differences by measuring?

Euth. Very true.

Soc. And we end a controversy about heavy and light by resorting to a weighing machine?

Euth. To be sure.

Soc. But what differences are there which cannot be thus decided, and which therefore make us angry and set us at enmity with one another? I dare say the answer does not occur to you at the moment, and therefore I will suggest that these enmities arise when the matters of difference are the just and unjust, good and evil, honourable and dishonourable. Are not these the points about which men differ, and about which when we are unable satisfactorily to decide our differences, you and I and all of us quarrel, when we do quarrel?

Euth. Yes, Socrates, the nature of the differences about which we quarrel is such as you describe.

Soc. And the quarrels of the gods, noble Euthyphro, when they occur, are of a like nature?

Euth. Certainly they are.

Soc. They have differences of opinion, as you say, about good and evil, just and unjust, honourable and dishonourable: there would have been no quarrels among them, if there had been no such differences—would there now?

Euth. You are quite right.

Soc. Does not every man love that which he deems noble and just and good, and hate the opposite of them?

Euth. Very true.

Soc. But, as you say, people regard the same things, some as just and others as unjust,—about these they dispute; and so there arise wars and fightings among them.

Euth. Very true.

Soc. Then the same things are hated by the gods and loved by the gods, and are both hateful and dear to them?

Euth. True.

Soc. And upon this view the same things, Euthyphro, will be pious and also impious?

Euth. So I should suppose.

Soc. Then, my friend, I remark with surprise that you have not answered the question which I asked. For I certainly did not ask you to tell me what action is both pious and impious: but now it would seem that what is loved by the gods is also hated by them. And therefore, Euthyphro, in thus chastising your father you may very likely be doing what is agreeable to Zeus but disagreeable to Cronos or Uranus, and what is acceptable to Hephaestus but unacceptable to Herè, and there may be other gods who have similar differences of opinion.

Euth. But I believe, Socrates, that all the gods would be agreed as to the propriety of punishing a murderer: there would be no difference of opinion about that.

Soc. Well, but speaking of men, Euthyphro, did you ever hear any one arguing that a murderer or any sort of evil-doer ought to be let off?

Euth. I should rather say that these are the questions which they are always arguing, especially in courts of law: they commit all sorts of crimes, and there is nothing which they will not do or say in their own defence.

Soc. But do they admit their guilt, Euthyphro, and yet say that they ought not to be punished?

Euth. No; they do not.

Soc. Then there are some things which they do not venture to say and do: for they do not venture to argue that the guilty are to be unpunished, but they deny their guilt, do they not?

Euth. Yes.

Soc. Then they do not argue that the evil-doer should not be punished, but they argue about the fact of who the evil-doer is, and what he did and when?

Euth. True.

Soc. And the gods are in the same case, if as you assert they quarrel about just and unjust, and some of them say while others deny that injustice is done among them. For surely neither God nor man will ever venture to say that the doer of injustice is not to be punished?

Euth. That is true, Socrates, in the main.

Soc. But they join issue about the particulars—gods and men alike; and, if they dispute at all, they dispute about some act which is called in question, and which by some is affirmed to be just, by others to be unjust. Is not that true?

Euth. Quite true.

Soc. Well then, my dear friend Euthyphro, do tell me, for my better instruction and information, what proof have you that in the opinion of all the gods a servant who is guilty of murder, and is put in chains by the master of the dead man, and dies because he is put in chains before he who bound him can learn from the interpreters of the gods what he ought to do with him, dies unjustly; and that on behalf of such an one a son ought to proceed against his father and accuse him of murder. How would you show that all the gods absolutely agree in approving of his act? Prove to me that they do, and I will applaud your wisdom as long as I live.

Euth. It will be a difficult task; but I could make the matter very clear indeed to you.

Soc. I understand; you mean to say that I am not so quick of apprehension as the judges: for to them you will be sure to prove that the act is unjust, and hateful to the gods.

Euth. Yes indeed, Socrates; at least if they will listen to me.

Soc. But they will be sure to listen if they find that you are a good speaker. There was a notion that came into my mind while you were speaking; I said to myself: "Well, and what if Euthyphro does prove to me that all the gods regarded the death of the serf as unjust, how do I know anything more of the nature of piety and impiety? for granting that this action may be hateful to the gods, still piety and impiety are not adequately defined by these distinctions, for that which is hateful to the gods has been shown to be also pleasing and dear to them." And therefore, Euthyphro, I do not ask you to prove this; I will suppose, if you like, that all the gods condemn and abominate such an action. But I will amend the definition so far as to say that what all the gods hate is impious, and what they love pious or holy; and what some of them love and others hate is both or neither. Shall this be our definition of piety and impiety?

Euth. Why not, Socrates?

Soc. Why not! certainly, as far as I am concerned, Euthyphro, there is no reason why not. But whether this admission will greatly assist you in the task of instructing me as you promised, is a matter for you to consider.

Euth. Yes, I should say that what all the gods love is pious and holy, and the opposite which they all hate, impious.

Soc. Ought we to enquire into the truth of this, Euthyphro, or simply to accept the mere statement on our own authority and that of others? What do you say?

Euth. We should enquire; and I believe that the statement will stand the test of enquiry.

Soc. We shall know better, my good friend, in a little while. The point which I should first wish to understand is whether the pious or holy is beloved by the gods because it is holy, or holy because it is beloved of the gods.

Euth. I do not understand your meaning, Socrates.

Soc. I will endeavour to explain: we speak of carrying and we speak of being carried, of leading and being led, seeing and being seen. You know that in all such cases there is a difference, and you know also in what the difference lies?

Euth. I think that I understand.

Soc. And is not that which is beloved distinct from that which loves?

Euth. Certainly.

Soc. Well; and now tell me, is that which is carried in this state of carrying because it is carried, or for some other reason?

Euth. No; that is the reason.

Soc. And the same is true of what is led and of what is seen?

Euth. True.

Soc. And a thing is not seen because it is visible, but conversely, visible because it is seen; nor is a thing led because it is in the state of being led, or carried because it is in the state of being carried, but the converse of this. And now I think, Euthyphro, that my meaning will be intelligible; and my meaning is, that any state of action or passion implies previous action or passion. It does not become because it is becoming, but it is in a state of becoming because it becomes; neither does it suffer because it is in a state of suffering, but it is in a state of suffering because it suffers. Do you not agree?

Euth. Yes.

Soc. Is not that which is loved in some state either of becoming or suffering?

Euth. Yes.

Soc. And the same holds as in the previous instances; the state of being loved follows the act of being loved, and not the act the state.

Euth. Certainly.

Soc. And what do you say of piety, Euthyphro: is not piety, according to your definition, loved by all the gods?

Euth. Yes.

Soc. Because it is pious or holy, or for some other reason?

Euth. No, that is the reason.

Soc. It is loved because it is holy, not holy because it is loved?

Euth. Yes.

Soc. And that which is dear to the gods is loved by them, and is in a state to be loved of them because it is loved of them?

Euth. Certainly.

Soc. Then that which is dear to the gods, Euthyphro, is not holy, nor is that which is holy loved of God, as you affirm; but they are two different things.

Euth. How do you mean, Socrates?

Soc. I mean to say that the holy has been acknowledged by us to be loved of God because it is holy, not to be holy because it is loved.

Euth. Yes.

Soc. But that which is dear to the gods is dear to them because it is loved by them, not loved by them because it is dear to them.

Euth. True.

Soc. But, friend Euthyphro, if that which is holy is the same with that which is dear to God, and is loved because it is holy, then that which is dear to God would have been loved as being dear to God; but if that which is dear to God is dear to him because loved by him, then that which is holy would have been holy because loved by him. But now you see that the reverse is the case, and that they are quite different from one another. For one . . . is of a kind to be loved because it is loved, and the other . . . is loved because it is of a kind to be loved. Thus you appear to me, Euthyphro, when I ask you what is the essence of holiness, to offer an attribute only, and not the essence—the attribute of being loved by all the gods. But you still refuse to explain to me the nature of holiness. And therefore, if you please, I will ask you not to hide your treasure, but to tell me once more what holiness or piety really is, whether dear to the gods or not (for that is a matter about which we will not quarrel), and what is impiety?

Euth. I really do not know, Socrates, how to express what I mean. For somehow or other our arguments, on whatever ground we rest them, seem to turn round and walk away from us.

Soc. Your words, Euthyphro, are like the handiwork of my ancestor Daedalus; and if I were the sayer or propounder of them, you might say that my arguments walk away and will not remain fixed where they are placed because I am a descendant of his. But now, since these notions are your own, you must find some other gibe, for they certainly, as you yourself allow, show an inclination to be on the move.

Euth. Nay, Socrates, I shall still say that you are the Daedalus who sets arguments in motion; not I, certainly, but you make them move or go round, for they would never have stirred, as far as I am concerned.

Soc. Then I must be a greater than Daedalus: for whereas he only made his own inventions to move, I move those of other people as well. And the beauty of it is, that I would rather not. For I would give the wisdom of Daedalus, and the wealth of Tantalus, to be able to detain them and keep them fixed. But enough of this. As I perceive that you are lazy, I will myself endeavor to show you how you might instruct me in the nature of piety; and I hope that you will not grudge your labour.

11

Plato

from *Meno*

The following is a brief excerpt from Plato's *Meno*. In this particular dialogue, Socrates is engaged in an often heated exchange with Gorgias' student, Meno, about the fundamental nature of virtue and whether it can be taught—is it a matter of nature or nurture?—among other matters of great philosophical interest. Toward the end of the dialogue, Socrates attempts to ferret out the difference between knowledge and mere correct opinion or true belief. In so doing, he gives rudimentary articulation of the long-influential view that knowledge consists in justified, true belief.

––––––––––––

Soc. I am afraid, Meno, that you and I are not good for much, and that Gorgias has been as poor an educator of you as Prodicus has been of me. Certainly we shall have to look to ourselves, and try to find some one who will help in some way or other to improve us. This I say, because I observe that in the previous discussion none of us remarked that right and good action is possible to man under other guidance than that of knowledge . . . ;—and indeed if this be denied, there is no seeing how there can be any good men at all.

Men. How do you mean, Socrates?

Soc. I mean that good men are necessarily useful or profitable. Were we not right in admitting this? It must be so.

Men. Yes.

Soc. And in supposing that they will be useful only if they are true guides to us of action—there we were also right?

Men. Yes.

SOURCE: Plato, *The Dialogues of Plato, Translated into English with Analyses and Introductions*, 5 vols., vol. 2, 3rd ed., revised and corrected throughout, trans. B. Jowett (New York: Oxford University Press, American Branch, 1892), 59–61.

Soc. But when we said that a man cannot be a good guide unless he have knowledge . . . , in this we were wrong.

Men. What do you mean by the word "right"?

Soc. I will explain. If a man knew the way to Larisa, or anywhere else, and went to the place and led others thither, would he not be a right and good guide?

Men. Certainly.

Soc. And a person who had a right opinion about the way, but had never been and did not know, might be a good guide also, might he not?

Men. Certainly.

Soc. And while he has true opinion about that which the other knows, he will be just as good a guide if he thinks the truth, as he who knows the truth?

Men. Exactly.

Soc. Then true opinion is as good a guide to correct action as knowledge; and that was the point which we omitted in our speculation about the nature of virtue, when we said that knowledge only is the guide of right action; whereas there is also right opinion.

Men. True.

Soc. Then right opinion is not less useful than knowledge?

Men. The difference, Socrates, is only that he who has knowledge will always be right; but he who has right opinion will sometimes be right, and sometimes not.

Soc. What do you mean? Can he be wrong who has right opinion, so long as he has right opinion?

Men. I admit the cogency of your argument, and therefore, Socrates, I wonder that knowledge should be preferred to right opinion—or why they should ever differ.

Soc. And shall I explain this wonder to you?

Men. Do tell me.

Soc. You would not wonder if you had ever observed the images of Daedalus; but perhaps you have not got them in your country?

Men. What have they to do with the question?

Soc. Because they require to be fastened in order to keep them, and if they are not fastened they will play truant and run away.

Men. Well, what of that?

Soc. I mean to say that they are not very valuable possessions if they are at liberty, for they will walk off like runaway slaves; but when fastened, they are of great value, for they are really beautiful works of art. Now this is an illustration of the nature of true opinions: while they abide with us they are beautiful and fruitful, but they run away out of the human soul, and do not remain long, and therefore they are not of much value until they are fastened by the tie of the cause; and this fastening of them, friend Meno, is recollection, as you and I have agreed to call it. But when they are bound, in the first place, they have the nature of knowledge; and, in the second place, they are abiding. And this is why knowledge is more honourable and excellent than true opinion, because fastened by a chain.

Men. What you are saying, Socrates, seems to be very like the truth.

Soc. I too speak rather in ignorance; I only conjecture. And yet that knowledge differs from true opinion is no matter of conjecture with me. There are not many things which I profess to know, but this is most certainly one of them.

Men. Yes, Socrates; and you are quite right in saying so.

Soc. And am I not also right in saying that true opinion leading the way perfects action quite as well as knowledge?

Men. There again, Socrates, I think you are right.

Soc. Then right opinion is not a whit inferior to knowledge, or less useful in action; nor is the man who has right opinion inferior to him who has knowledge?

Men. True.

12

Plato

from *Republic*

The following passage is sometimes known simply as the "Allegory of the Cave," and it is a brief excerpt from Plato's best-known and most influential work, the *Republic*. In this dialogue, Socrates and his interlocutors (chiefly Glaucon and Adeimantus) are trying to figure out what the fundamental nature of justice is. In their efforts to gain insight, they try to imagine what a truly just and ideal city would look like. Socrates contends that a class of guardians would be needed to look out over the city in special ways. Accordingly, how those guardians are educated is of utmost importance, and so Socrates tries to contemplate what that educational process should be like.

And now, I [Socrates] said, let me show in a figure how far our nature is enlightened or unenlightened:—Behold! human beings living in an underground den, which has a mouth open towards the light and reaching all along the den; here they have been from their childhood, and have their legs and necks chained so that they cannot move, and can only see before them, being prevented by the chains from turning round their heads. Above and behind them a fire is blazing at a distance, and between the fire and the prisoners there is a raised way; and you will see, if you look, a low wall built along the way, like the screen which marionette players have in front of them, over which they show the puppets.

I see.

And do you see, I said, men passing along the wall carrying all sorts of vessels, and statues and figures of animals made of wood and stone and various materials, which appear over the wall? Some of them are talking, others silent.

SOURCE: Plato, *The Republic of Plato*, trans. B. Jowett, 3rd ed., revised and corrected throughout (Oxford: Clarendon Press, 1888), 214–20.

You have shown me a strange image, and they are strange prisoners.

Like ourselves, I replied; and they see only their own shadows, or the shadows of one another, which the fire throws on the opposite wall of the cave?

True, he said; how could they see anything but the shadows if they were never allowed to move their heads?

And of the objects which are being carried in like manner they would only see the shadows?

Yes, he said.

And if they were able to converse with one another, would they not suppose that they were naming what was actually before them?

Very true.

And suppose further that the prison had an echo which came from the other side, would they not be sure to fancy when one of the passers-by spoke that the voice which they heard came from the passing shadow?

No question, he replied.

To them, I said, the truth would be literally nothing but the shadows of the images.

That is certain.

And now look again, and see what will naturally follow if the prisoners are released and disabused of their error. At first, when any of them is liberated and compelled suddenly to stand up and turn his neck round and walk and look towards the light, he will suffer sharp pains; the glare will distress him, and he will be unable to see the realities of which in his former state he had seen the shadows; and then conceive some one saying to him, that what he saw before was an illusion, but that now, when he is approaching nearer to being and his eye is turned towards more real existence, he has a clearer vision,—what will be his reply? And you may further imagine that his instructor is pointing to the objects as they pass and requiring him to name them,—will he not be perplexed? Will he not fancy that the shadows which he formerly saw are truer than the objects which are now shown to him?

Far truer.

And if he is compelled to look straight at the light, will he not have a pain in his eyes which will make him turn away to take refuge in the objects of vision which he can see, and which he will conceive to be in reality clearer than the things which are now being shown to him?

True, he said.

And suppose once more, that he is reluctantly dragged up a steep and rugged ascent, and held fast until he is forced into the presence of the sun himself, is he not likely to be pained and irritated? When he approaches the light his eyes will be dazzled, and he will not be able to see anything at all of what are now called realities.

Not all in a moment, he said.

He will require to grow accustomed to the sight of the upper world. And first he will see the shadows best, next the reflections of men and other objects in the water, and then the objects themselves; then he will gaze upon the light of the moon and the stars and the spangled heaven; and he will see the sky and the stars by night better than the sun or the light of the sun by day?

Certainly.

Last of all he will be able to see the sun, and not mere reflections of him in the water, but he will see him in his own proper place, and not in another; and he will contemplate him as he is.

Certainly.

He will then proceed to argue that this is he who gives the season and the years, and is the guardian of all that is in the visible world, and in a certain way the cause of all things which he and his fellows have been accustomed to behold?

Clearly, he said, he would first see the sun and then reason about him.

And when he remembered his old habitation, and the wisdom of the den and his fellow-prisoners, do you not suppose that he would felicitate himself on the change, and pity them?

Certainly, he would.

And if they were in the habit of conferring honours among themselves on those who were quickest to observe the passing shadows and to remark which of them went before, and which followed after, and which were together; and who were therefore best able to draw conclusions as to the future, do you think that he would care for such honours and glories, or envy the possessors of them? Would he not say with Homer, "Better to be the poor servant of a poor master," and to endure anything, rather than think as they do and live after their manner?

Yes, he said, I think that he would rather suffer anything than entertain these false notions and live in this miserable manner.

Imagine once more, I said, such an one coming suddenly out of the sun to be replaced in his old situation; would he not be certain to have his eyes full of darkness?

To be sure, he said.

And if there were a contest, and he had to compete in measuring the shadows with the prisoners who had never moved out of the den, while his sight was still weak, and before his eyes had become steady (and the time which would be needed to acquire this new habit of sight might be very considerable), would he not be ridiculous? Men would say of him that up he went and down he came without his eyes; and that it was better not even to think of ascending; and if any one tried to loose another and lead him up to the light, let them only catch the offender, and they would put him to death.

No question, he said.

This entire allegory, I said, you may now append, dear Glaucon, to the previous argument; the prison-house is the world of sight, the light of the fire is the sun, and you will not misapprehend me if you interpret the journey upwards to be the ascent of the soul into the intellectual world according to my poor belief, which, at your desire, I have expressed—whether rightly or wrongly God knows. But, whether true or false, my opinion is that in the world of knowledge the idea of good appears last of all, and is seen only with an effort; and, when seen, is also inferred to be the universal author of all things beautiful and right, parent of light and of the lord of light in this visible world, and the immediate source of reason and truth in the intellectual; and that this is the power upon which he who would act rationally either in public or private life must have his eye fixed.

I agree, he said, as far as I am able to understand you.

Moreover, I said, you must not wonder that those who attain to this beatific vision are unwilling to descend to human affairs; for their souls are ever hastening into the upper world where they desire to dwell; which desire of theirs is very natural, if our allegory may be trusted.

Yes, very natural.

And is there anything surprising in one who passes from divine contemplations to the evil state of man, misbehaving himself in a ridiculous manner; if, while his eyes are blinking and before he has become accustomed to the surrounding darkness, he is compelled to fight in courts of law, or in other places, about the images or the shadows of images of justice, and is endeavouring to meet the conceptions of those who have never yet seen absolute justice?

Anything but surprising, he replied.

Any one who has common sense will remember that the bewilderments of the eyes are of two kinds, and arise from two causes, either from coming out of the light or from going into the light, which is true of the mind's eye, quite as much as of the bodily eye; and he who remembers this when he sees any one whose vision is perplexed and weak, will not be too ready to laugh; he will first ask whether that soul of man has come out of the brighter life, and is unable to see because unaccustomed to the dark, or having turned from darkness to the day is dazzled by excess of light. And he will count the one happy in his condition and state of being, and he will pity the other; or, if he have a mind to laugh at the soul which comes from below into the light, there will be more reason in this than in the laugh which greets him who returns from above out of the light into the den.

That, he said, is a very just distinction.

But then, if I am right, certain professors of education must be wrong when they say that they can put a knowledge into the soul which was not there before, like sight into blind eyes.

They undoubtedly say this, he replied.

Whereas, our argument shows that the power and capacity of learning exists in the soul already; and that just as the eye was unable to turn from darkness to light without the whole body, so too the instrument of knowledge can only by the movement of the whole soul be turned from the world of becoming into that of being, and learn by degrees to endure the sight of being, and of the brightest and best of being, or in other words, of the good.

Very true.

And must there not be some art which will effect conversion in the easiest and quickest manner; not implanting the faculty of sight, for that exists already, but has been turned in the wrong direction, and is looking away from the truth?

Yes, he said, such an art may be presumed.

And whereas the other so-called virtues of the soul seem to be akin to bodily qualities, for even when they are not originally innate they can be implanted later by habit and exercise, the virtue of wisdom more than anything else contains a divine element which always remains, and by this conversion is rendered useful and profitable; or, on the other hand, hurtful and useless. Did you never observe the narrow intelligence flashing from the keen eye of a clever rogue—how eager he is, how clearly his paltry soul sees the way to his end; he is the reverse of blind, but his keen eye-sight is forced into the service of evil, and he is mischievous in proportion to his cleverness?

Very true, he said.

But what if there had been a circumcision of such natures in the days of their youth; and they had been severed from those sensual pleasures, such as eating and drinking, which, like leaden weights, were attached to them at their birth, and which drag them down and turn the vision of their souls upon the things that are below—if, I say, they had been released from these impediments and turned in the opposite direction, the very same faculty in them would have seen the truth as keenly as they see what their eyes are turned to now.

Very likely.

Yes, I said; and there is another thing which is likely, or rather a necessary inference from what has preceded, that neither the uneducated and uninformed of the truth, nor yet those who never make an end of their education, will be able ministers of State; not the former, because they have no single aim of duty which is the rule of all their actions, private as well as public; nor the latter, because they will not act at all except upon compulsion, fancying that they are already dwelling apart in the islands of the blest.

Very true, he replied.

Then, I said, the business of us who are the founders of the State will be to compel the best minds to attain that knowledge which we have already shown to be the greatest of all—they must continue to ascend until they arrive at the good; but when they have ascended and seen enough we must not allow them to do as they do now.

What do you mean?

I mean that they remain in the upper world: but this must not be allowed; they must be made to descend again among the prisoners in the den, and partake of their labours and honours, whether they are worth having or not.

13

Aristotle

from *Nicomachean Ethics*

Along with his famous teacher Plato, Aristotle (384–322 BC) is the most important of the classical Greek philosophers, and he is handily among the most influential thinkers in human history as well. Founder of the school known as the Lyceum, Aristotle wrote profusely about an impressive array of topics ranging from botany, biology, and medicine, to logic, metaphysics, and ethics, to music, rhetoric, and theatre. His most famous pupil was none other than Alexander the Great. The following excerpts are taken from Aristotle's magnum opus in the area of moral philosophy, namely, his *Nicomachean Ethics*, which was presumably named in honor of his son, Nicomachus. In it, Aristotle tries to determine what the ultimate end of human existence is, as well as contemplate the virtues needed to achieve that end.

Book I: The End.

1. Every art and every kind of inquiry, and likewise every act and purpose, seems to aim at some good: and so it has been well said that the good is that at which everything aims.

But a difference is observable among these aims or ends. What is aimed at is sometimes the exercise of a faculty, sometimes a certain result beyond that exercise. And where there is an end beyond the act, there the result is better than the exercise of the faculty.

Now since there are many kinds of actions and many arts and sciences, it follows that there are many ends also; *e.g.* health is the end of medicine, ships of shipbuilding, victory of the art of war, and wealth of economy.

SOURCE: Aristotle, *The Nicomachean Ethics of Aristotle*, trans. F. H. Peters, 5th ed. (London: Kegan Paul, Trench, and Trübner & Co., Ltd., 1893), 1–52.

But when several of these are subordinated to some one art or science,— as the making of bridles and other trappings to the art of horsemanship, and this in turn, along with all else that the soldier does, to the art of war, and so on,—then the end of the master-art is always more desired than the ends of the subordinate arts, since these are pursued for its sake. And this is equally true whether the end in view be the mere exercise of a faculty or something beyond that, as in the above instances.

2. If then in what we do there be some end which we wish for on its own account, choosing all the others as means to this, but not every end without exception as a means to something else (for so we should go on *ad infinitum*, and desire would be left void and objectless),—this evidently will be the good or the best of all things. And surely from a practical point of view it much concerns us to know this good; for then, like archers shooting at a definite mark, we shall be more likely to attain what we want.

If this be so, we must try to indicate roughly what it is, and first of all to which of the arts or sciences it belongs.

It would seem to belong to the supreme art or science, that one which most of all deserves the name of master-art or master-science.

Now Politics seems to answer to this description. For it prescribes which of the sciences a state needs, and which each man shall study, and up to what point; and to it we see subordinated even the highest arts, such as economy, rhetoric, and the art of war.

Since then it makes use of the other practical sciences, and since it further ordains what men are to do and from what to refrain, its end must include the ends of the others, and must be the proper good of man.

For though this good is the same for the individual and the state, yet the good of the state seems a grander and more perfect thing both to attain and to secure; and glad as one would be to do this service for a single individual, to do it for a people and for a number of states is nobler and more divine.

This then is the aim of the present inquiry, which is a sort of political inquiry.

[. . . .]

5. Let us now take up the discussion at the point from which we digressed.

It seems that men not unreasonably take their notions of the good or happiness from the lives actually led, and that the masses who are the least refined suppose it to be pleasure, which is the reason why they aim at nothing higher than the life of enjoyment.

For the most conspicuous kinds of life are three: this life of enjoyment, the life of the statesman, and, thirdly, the contemplative life.

The mass of men show themselves utterly slavish in their preference for the life of brute beasts, but their views receive consideration because many of those in high places have the tastes of Sardanapalus.

Men of refinement with a practical turn prefer honour; for I suppose we may say that honour is the aim of the statesman's life.

But this seems too superficial to be the good we are seeking: for it appears to depend upon those who give rather than upon those who receive it; while we have a presentiment that the good is something that is peculiarly a man's own and can scarce be taken away from him.

Moreover, these men seem to pursue honour in order that they may be assured of their own excellence,—at least, they wish to be honoured by men of sense, and by those who know them, and on the ground of their virtue or excellence. It is plain, then, that in their view, at any rate, virtue or excellence is better than honour; and perhaps we should take this to be the end of the statesman's life, rather than honour.

But virtue or excellence also appears too incomplete to be what we want; for it seems that a man might have virtue and yet be asleep or be inactive all his life, and, moreover, might meet with the greatest disasters and misfortunes; and no one would maintain that such a man is happy, except for argument's sake. But we will not dwell on these matters now, for they are sufficiently discussed in the popular treatises.

The third kind of life is the life of contemplation: we will treat of it further on.

As for the money-making life, it is something quite contrary to nature; and wealth evidently is not the good of which we are in search, for it is merely useful as a means to something else. So we might rather take pleasure and virtue or excellence to be ends than wealth; for they are chosen on their own account. But it seems that not even they are the end, though much breath has been wasted in attempts to show that they are.

[. . . .]

7. . . . Let us return once more to the question, what this good can be of which we are in search.

It seems to be different in different kinds of action and in different arts,— one thing in medicine and another in war, and so on. What then is the good in each of these cases? Surely that for the sake of which all else is done. And that in medicine is health, in war is victory, in building is a house,—a different thing in each different case, but always, in whatever we do and in whatever we choose, the end. For it is always for the sake of the end that all else is done.

If then there be one end of all that man does, this end will be the realizable good,—or these ends, if there be more than one.

By this generalization our argument is brought to the same point as before. This point we must try to explain more clearly.

We see that there are many ends. But some of these are chosen only as means, as wealth, flutes, and the whole class of instruments. And so it is plain that not all ends are final.

But the best of all things must, we conceive, be something final.

If then there be only one final end, this will be what we are seeking,—or if there be more than one, then the most final of them.

Now that which is pursued as an end in itself is more final than that which is pursued as means to something else, and that which is never chosen as means than that which is chosen both as an end in itself and as means, and that is strictly final which is always chosen as an end in itself and never as means.

Happiness seems more than anything else to answer to this description: for we always choose it for itself, and never for the sake of something else; while honour and pleasure and reason, and all virtue or excellence, we choose partly indeed for themselves (for, apart from any result, we should choose each of them), but partly also for the sake of happiness, supposing that they will help to make us happy. But no one chooses happiness for the sake of these things, or as a means to anything else at all.

We seem to be led to the same conclusion when we start from the notion of self-sufficiency.

The final good is thought to be self-sufficing [or all-sufficing]. In applying this term we do not regard a man as an individual leading a solitary life, but we also take account of parents, children, wife, and, in short, friends and fellow-citizens generally, since man is naturally a social being. Some limit must indeed be set to this; for if you go on to parents and descendants and friends of friends, you will never come to a stop. But this we will consider further on: for the present we will take self-sufficing to mean what by itself makes life desirable and in want of nothing. And happiness is believed to answer to this description.

And further, happiness is believed to be the most desirable thing in the world, and that not merely as one among other good things: if it were merely one among other good things [so that other things could be added to it], it is plain that the addition of the least of other goods must make it more desirable; for the addition becomes a surplus of good, and of two goods the greater is always more desirable.

Thus it seems that happiness is something final and self-sufficing, and is the end of all that man does.

But perhaps the reader thinks that though no one will dispute the statement that happiness is the best thing in the world, yet a still more precise definition of it is needed.

This will best be gained, I think, by asking, What is the function of man? For as the goodness and the excellence of a piper or a sculptor, or the practiser of any art, and generally of those who have any function or business to do, lies in that function, so man's good would seem to lie in his function, if he has one.

But can we suppose that, while a carpenter and a cobbler has a function and a business of his own, man has no business and no function assigned him by nature? Nay, surely as his several members, eye and hand and foot, plainly have each his own function, so we must suppose that man also has some function over and above all these.

What then is it?

Life evidently he has in common even with the plants, but we want that which is peculiar to him. We must exclude, therefore, the life of mere nutrition and growth.

Next to this comes the life of sense; but this too he plainly shares with horses and cattle and all kinds of animals.

There remains then the life whereby he acts—the life of his rational nature, with its two sides or divisions, one rational as obeying reason, the other rational as having and exercising reason.

But as this expression is ambiguous, we must be understood to mean thereby the life that consists in the exercise of the faculties; for this seems to be more properly entitled to the name.

The function of man, then, is exercise of his vital faculties [or soul] on one side in obedience to reason, and on the other side with reason.

But what is called the function of a man of any profession and the function of a man who is good in that profession are generically the same, *e.g.* of a harper and of a good harper; and this holds in all cases without exception, only that in the case of the latter his superior excellence at his work is added; for we say a harper's function is to harp, and a good harper's to harp well.

(Man's function then being, as we say, a kind of life—that is to say, exercise of his faculties and action of various kinds with reason—the good man's function is to do this well and beautifully [or nobly]. But the function of anything is done well when it is done in accordance with the proper excellence of that thing.)

If this be so the result is that the good of man is exercise of his faculties in accordance with excellence or virtue, or, if there be more than one, in accordance with the best and most complete virtue.

But there must also be a full term of years for this exercise; for one swallow or one fine day does not make a spring, nor does one day or any small space of time make a blessed or happy man.

This, then, may be taken as a rough outline of the good; for this, I think, is the proper method,—first to sketch the outline, and then to fill in the details. But it would seem that, the outline once fairly drawn, any one can carry on the work and fit in the several items which time reveals to us or helps us to find. And this indeed is the way in which the arts and sciences have grown; for it requires no extraordinary genius to fill up the gaps.

[. . . .]

Book II: Moral Virtue.

1. Excellence, then, being of these two kinds, intellectual and moral, intellectual excellence owes its birth and growth mainly to instruction, and so requires time and experience, while moral excellence is the result of habit or custom. . . .

From this it is plain that none of the moral excellences or virtues is implanted in us by nature; for that which is by nature cannot be altered by training. For instance, a stone naturally tends to fall downwards, and you could not train it to rise upwards, though you tried to do so by throwing it up ten thousand times, nor could you train fire to move downwards, nor accustom anything which naturally behaves in one way to behave in any other way.

The virtues, then, come neither by nature nor against nature, but nature gives the capacity for acquiring them, and this is developed by training.

Again, where we do things by nature we get the power first, and put this power forth in act afterwards: as we plainly see in the case of the senses; for it is not by constantly seeing and hearing that we acquire those faculties, but, on the contrary, we had the power first and then used it, instead of acquiring the power by the use. But the virtues we acquire by doing the acts, as is the case with the arts too. We learn an art by doing that which we wish to do when we have learned it; we become builders by building, and harpers by harping. And so by doing just acts we become just, and by doing acts of temperance and courage we become temperate and courageous.

This is attested, too, by what occurs in states; for the legislators make their citizens good by training; i.e. this is the wish of all legislators, and those who do not succeed in this miss their aim, and it is this that distinguishes a good from a bad constitution.

Again, both the moral virtues and the corresponding vices result from and are formed by the same acts; and this is the case with the arts also. It is by harping that good harpers and bad harpers alike are produced: and so with builders and the rest; by building well they will become good builders, and bad builders by build-ing badly. Indeed, if it were not so, they would not want anybody to teach them, but would all be born either good or bad at their trades. And it is just the same with the virtues also. It is by our conduct in our intercourse with other men that we become just or unjust, and by acting in circumstances of danger, and training ourselves to feel fear or confidence, that we become courageous or cowardly. So, too, with our animal appetites and the passion of anger; for by behaving in this way or in that on the occasions with which these passions are concerned, some become temperate and gentle, and others profligate and ill-tempered. In a word, acts of any kind produce habits or characters of the same kind.

Hence we ought to make sure that our acts be of a certain kind; for the resulting character varies as they vary. It makes no small difference, therefore, whether a man be trained from his youth up in this way or in that, but a great difference, or rather all the difference.

2. But our present inquiry has not, like the rest, a merely speculative aim; we are not inquiring merely in order to know what excellence or virtue is, but in order to become good; for otherwise it would profit us nothing. We must ask therefore about these acts, and see of what kind they are to be; for, as we said, it is they that determine our habits or character.

First of all, then, that they must be in accordance with right reason is a common characteristic of them, which we shall here take for granted, reserv-ing for future discussion the question what this right reason is, and how it is related to the other excellences.

But let it be understood, before we go on, that all reasoning on matters of practice must be in outline merely, and not scientifically exact: for, as we said at starting, the kind of reasoning to be demanded varies with the subject in hand; and in practical matters and questions of expediency there are no invariable laws, any more than in questions of health.

And if our general conclusions are thus inexact, still more inexact is all reasoning about particular cases; for these fall under no system of scientifically established rules or traditional maxims, but the agent must always consider for himself what the special occasion requires, just as in medicine or navigation.

But though this is the case we must try to render what help we can.

First of all, then, we must observe that, in matters of this sort, to fall short and to exceed are alike fatal. This is plain (to illustrate what we cannot see by what we can see) in the case of strength and health. Too much and too little exercise alike destroy strength, and to take too much meat and drink, or to take too little, is equally ruinous to health, but the fitting amount pro-duces and increases and preserves them. Just so, then, is it with temperance also, and courage, and the other virtues. The man who shuns and fears everything and never makes a stand, becomes a coward; while the man who fears nothing at all, but will face anything, becomes foolhardy. So, too, the man who takes his fill of any kind of pleasure, and abstains from none, is a profligate, but the man who shuns all (like him whom we call a "boor") is devoid of sensibility. Thus temperance and courage are destroyed both by excess and defect, but preserved by moderation.

But habits or types of character are not only produced and preserved and destroyed by the same occasions and the same means, but they will also manifest themselves in the same circumstances. This is the case with palpable things like strength. Strength is produced by taking plenty of nourishment and doing plenty of hard work, and the strong man, in turn, has the greatest capacity for these. And the case is the same with the virtues: by abstaining from pleasure we become temperate, and when we have become temperate we are best able to abstain. And so with courage: by habituating ourselves to despise danger, and to face it, we become courageous; and when we have become courageous, we are best able to face danger.

3. The pleasure or pain that accompanies the acts must be taken as a test of the formed habit or character.

He who abstains from the pleasures of the body and rejoices in the abstinence is temperate, while he who is vexed at having to abstain is profligate; and again, he who faces danger with pleasure, or, at any rate, without pain, is courageous, but he to whom this is painful is a coward.

For moral virtue or excellence is closely concerned with pleasure and pain. It is pleasure that moves us to do what is base, and pain that moves us to refrain from what is noble. And therefore, as Plato says, man needs to be so trained from his youth up as to find pleasure and pain in the right objects. This is what sound education means.

[. . . .]

4. But here we may be asked what we mean by saying that men can become just and temperate only by doing what is just and temperate: surely, it may be said, if their acts are just and temperate, they themselves are already just and temperate, as they are grammarians and musicians if they do what is grammatical and musical.

We may answer, I think, firstly, that this is not quite the case even with the arts. A man may do something grammatical [or write something correctly] by chance, or at the prompting of another person: he will not be grammatical till he not only does something grammatical, but also does it grammatically [or like a grammatical person], *i.e.* in virtue of his own knowledge of grammar.

But, secondly, the virtues are not in this point analogous to the arts. The products of art have their excellence in themselves, and so it is enough if when produced they are of a certain quality; but in the case of the virtues, a man is not said to act justly or temperately [or like a just or temperate man] if what he does merely be of a certain sort—he must also be in a certain state of mind when he does it; *i.e.*, first of all, he must know what he is doing; secondly, he must choose it, and choose it for itself; and, thirdly, his act must be the expression of a formed and stable character. Now, of these conditions, only one, the knowledge, is necessary for the possession of any art; but for the possession of the virtues knowledge is of little or no avail, while the other conditions that result from repeatedly doing what is just and temperate are not a little important, but all-important.

The thing that is done, therefore, is called just or temperate when it is such as the just or temperate man would do; but the man who does it is not just or temperate, unless he also does it in the spirit of the just or the temperate man.

It is right, then, to say that by doing what is just a man becomes just, and temperate by doing what is temperate, while without doing thus he has no chance of ever becoming good.

But most men, instead of doing thus, fly to theories, and fancy that they are philosophizing and that this will make them good, like a sick man who listens attentively to what the doctor says and then disobeys all his orders. This sort of philosophizing will no more produce a healthy habit of mind than this sort of treatment will produce a healthy habit of body.

[. . . .]

6. We have thus found the genus to which virtue belongs; but we want to know, not only that it is a trained faculty, but also what species of trained faculty it is.

We may safely assert that the virtue or excellence of a thing causes that thing both to be itself in good condition and to perform its function well. The excellence of the eye, for instance, makes both the eye and its work good; for it is by the excellence of the eye that we see well. So the proper excellence of the horse makes a horse what he should be, and makes him good at running, and carrying his rider, and standing a charge.

If, then, this holds good in all cases, the proper excellence or virtue of man will be the habit or trained faculty that makes a man good and makes him perform his function well.

How this is to be done we have already said, but we may exhibit the same conclusion in another way, by inquiring what the nature of this virtue is.

Now, if we have any quantity, whether continuous or discrete, it is possible to take either a larger [or too large], or a smaller [or too small], or an equal [or fair] amount, and that either absolutely or relatively to our own needs.

By an equal or fair amount I understand a mean amount, or one that lies between excess and deficiency.

By the absolute mean, or mean relatively to the thing itself, I understand that which is equidistant from both extremes, and this is one and the same for all.

By the mean relatively to us I understand that which is neither too much nor too little for us; and this is not one and the same for all.

For instance, if ten be larger [or too large] and two be smaller [or too small], if we take six we take the mean relatively to the thing itself [or the arithmetical mean]; for it exceeds one extreme by the same amount by which it is exceeded by the other extreme: and this is the mean in arithmetical proportion.

But the mean relatively to us cannot be found in this way. If ten pounds of food is too much for a given man to eat, and two pounds too little, it does not follow that the trainer will order him six pounds: for that also may perhaps be too much for the man in question, or too little; too little for Milo, too much for the beginner. The same holds true in running and wrestling.

And so we may say generally that a master in any art avoids what is too much and what is too little, and seeks for the mean and chooses it—not the absolute but the relative mean.

If, then, every art or science perfects its work in this way, looking to the mean and bringing its work up to this standard (so that people are wont to say of a good work that nothing could be taken from it or added to it, implying that excellence is destroyed by excess or deficiency, but secured by observing the mean; and good artists, as we say, do in fact keep their eyes fixed on this in all that they do), and if virtue, like nature, is more exact and better than any art, it follows that virtue also must aim at the mean—virtue of course meaning moral virtue or excellence; for it has to do with passions and actions, and it is these that admit of excess and deficiency and the mean. For instance, it is possible to feel fear, confidence, desire, anger, pity, and generally to be affected pleasantly and painfully, either too much or too little, in either case wrongly; but to be thus affected at the right times, and on the right occasions, and towards the right persons, and with the right object, and in the right fashion, is the mean course and the best course, and these are characteristics of virtue. And in the same way our outward acts also admit of excess and deficiency, and the mean or due amount.

Virtue, then, has to deal with feelings or passions and with outward acts, in which excess is wrong and deficiency also is blamed, but the mean amount is praised and is right—both of which are characteristics of virtue.

Virtue, then, is a kind of moderation . . . inasmuch as it aims at the mean or moderate amount. . . .

Again, there are many ways of going wrong (for evil is infinite in nature, to use a Pythagorean figure, while good is finite), but only one way of going right; so that the one is easy and the other hard—easy to miss the mark and hard to hit. On this account also, then, excess and deficiency are characteristic of vice, hitting the mean is characteristic of virtue: "Goodness is simple, ill takes any shape."

Virtue, then, is a habit or trained faculty of choice, the characteristic of which lies in moderation or observance of the mean relatively to the persons concerned, as determined by reason, *i.e.* by the reason by which the prudent man would determine it. And it is a moderation, firstly, inasmuch as it comes in the middle or mean between two vices, one on the side of excess, the other on the side of defect; and, secondly, inasmuch as, while these vices fall short of or exceed the due measure in feeling and in action, it finds and chooses the mean, middling, or moderate amount.

Regarded in its essence, therefore, or according to the definition of its nature, virtue is a moderation or middle state, but viewed in its relation to what is best and right it is the extreme of perfection.

But it is not all actions nor all passions that admit of moderation; there are some whose very names imply badness, as malevolence, shamelessness, envy, and, among acts, adultery, theft, murder. These and all other like things are blamed as being bad in themselves, and not merely in their excess or deficiency. It is impossible therefore to go right in them; they are always wrong: rightness and wrongness in such things (*e.g.* in adultery) does not depend upon whether it is the right person and occasion and manner, but the mere doing of any one of them is wrong.

It would be equally absurd to look for moderation or excess or deficiency in unjust cowardly or profligate conduct; for then there would be moderation in excess or deficiency, and excess in excess, and deficiency in deficiency.

The fact is that just as there can be no excess or deficiency in temperance or courage because the mean or moderate amount is, in a sense, an extreme, so in these kinds of conduct also there can be no moderation or excess or deficiency, but the acts are wrong however they be done. For, to put it generally, there cannot be moderation in excess or deficiency, nor excess or deficiency in moderation.

7. But it is not enough to make these general statements [about virtue and vice]: we must go on and apply them to particulars [*i.e.* to the several virtues and vices]. For in reasoning about matters of conduct general statements are

too vague, and do not convey so much truth as particular propositions. It is with particulars that conduct is concerned: our statements, therefore, when applied to these particulars, should be found to hold good.

These particulars then [*i.e.* the several virtues and vices and the several acts and affections with which they deal], we will take from the following table.

Moderation in the feelings of fear and confidence is courage: of those that exceed, he that exceeds in fearlessness has no name (as often happens), but he that exceeds in confidence is foolhardy, while he that exceeds in fear, but is deficient in confidence, is cowardly.

Moderation in respect of certain pleasures and also (though to a less extent) certain pains is temperance, while excess is profligacy. But defectiveness in the matter of these pleasures is hardly ever found, and so this sort of people also have as yet received no name: let us put them down as "void of sensibility."

In the matter of giving and taking money, moderation is liberality, excess and deficiency are prodigality and illiberality. But both vices exceed and fall short in giving and taking in contrary ways: the prodigal exceeds in spending, but falls short in taking; while the illiberal man exceeds in taking, but falls short in spending. (For the present we are but giving an outline or summary, and aim at nothing more; we shall afterwards treat these points in greater detail.)

But, besides these, there are other dispositions in the matter of money: there is a moderation which is called magnificence (for the magnificent is not the same as the liberal man: the former deals with large sums, the latter with small), and an excess which is called bad taste or vulgarity, and a deficiency which is called meanness; and these vices differ from those which are opposed to liberality: how they differ will be explained later.

With respect to honour and disgrace, there is a moderation which is high-mindedness, an excess which may be called vanity, and a deficiency which is little-mindedness.

But just as we said that liberality is related to magnificence, differing only in that it deals with small sums, so here there is a virtue related to high-mindedness, and differing only in that it is concerned with small instead of great honours. A man may have a due desire for honour, and also more or less than a due desire: he that carries this desire to excess is called ambitious, he that has not enough of it is called unambitious, but he that has the due amount has no name. There are also no abstract names for the characters, except "ambition," corresponding to ambitious. And on this account those who occupy the extremes lay claim to the middle place. And in common parlance, too, the moderate man is sometimes called ambitious and sometimes unambitious, and sometimes the ambitious man is praised and sometimes the unambitious. Why this is we will explain afterwards; for the present we will follow out our plan and enumerate the other types of character.

In the matter of anger also we find excess and deficiency and moderation. The characters themselves hardly have recognized names, but as the moderate man is here called gentle, we will call his character gentleness; of those who go into extremes, we may take the term wrathful for him who exceeds, with wrathfulness for the vice, and wrathless for him who is deficient, with wrathlessness for his character.

Besides these, there are three kinds of moderation, bearing some resemblance to one another, and yet different. They all have to do with intercourse in speech and action, but they differ in that one has to do with the truthfulness of this intercourse, while the other two have to do with its pleasantness—one of the two with pleasantness in matters of amusement, the other with pleasantness in all the relations of life. We must therefore speak of these qualities also in order that we may the more plainly see how, in all cases, moderation is praiseworthy, while the extreme courses are neither right nor praiseworthy, but blamable.

In these cases also names are for the most part wanting, but we must try, here as elsewhere, to coin names ourselves, in order to make our argument clear and easy to follow.

In the matter of truth, then, let us call him who observes the mean a true [or truthful] person, and observance of the mean truth [or truthfulness]: pretence, when it exaggerates, may be called boasting, and the person a boaster; when it understates, let the names be irony and ironical.

With regard to pleasantness in amusement, he who observes the mean may be called witty, and his character wittiness; excess may be called buffoonery, and the man a buffoon; while boorish may stand for the person who is deficient, and boorishness for his character.

With regard to pleasantness in the other affairs of life, he who makes himself properly pleasant may be called friendly, and his moderation friendliness; he that exceeds may be called obsequious if he have no ulterior motive, but a flatterer if he has an eye to his own advantage; he that is deficient in this respect, and always makes himself disagreeable, may be called a quarrelsome or peevish fellow.

Moreover, in mere emotions and in our conduct with regard to them, there are ways of observing the mean; for instance, shame . . . is not a virtue, but yet the modest . . . man is praised. For in these matters also we speak of this man as observing the mean, of that man as going beyond it (as the shame-faced man whom the least thing makes shy), while he who is deficient in the feeling, or lacks it altogether, is called shameless; but the term modest . . . is applied to him who observes the mean.

Righteous indignation, again, hits the mean between envy and malevolence. These have to do with feelings of pleasure and pain at what happens to our neighbours. A man is called righteously indignant when he feels pain at the sight of undeserved prosperity, but your envious man goes beyond him and is pained by the sight of any one in prosperity, while the malevolent man is so far from being pained that he actually exults in the misfortunes of his neighbours.

But we shall have another opportunity of discussing these matters.

As for justice, the term is used in more senses than one; we will, therefore, after disposing of the above questions, distinguish these various senses, and show how each of these kinds of justice is a kind of moderation.

14

Aristotle

from *Politics*

In addition to his lasting deposits in other areas of human inquiry, Aristotle
also made important contributions to political thought. The following excerpt
is taken from his book known simply as the *Politics*. Here, Aristotle tries to
determine what, in general, is the best form of human government, and he
reflects on this topic in a way that connects up to the theory of virtue he developed in his *Nicomachean Ethics*.

IV.11. We have now to enquire what is the best constitution for most states,
and the best life for most men, neither assuming a standard of virtue which is
above ordinary persons, nor an education which is exceptionally favoured by
nature and circumstances, nor yet an ideal state which is an aspiration only, but
having regard to the life in which the majority are able to share, and to the form
of government which states in general can attain. As to those aristocracies, as
they are called, of which we were just now speaking, they either lie beyond the
possibilities of the greater number of states, or they approximate to the so-
called constitutional government, and therefore need no separate discussion.
And in fact the conclusion at which we arrive respecting all these forms rests
upon the same grounds. For if it has been truly said in the Ethics that the happy
life is the life according to unimpeded virtue, and that virtue is a mean, then
the life which is in a mean, and in a mean attainable by every one, must be the
best. And the same principles of virtue and vice are characteristic of cities and
of constitutions; for the constitution is in a figure the life of the city.

Now in all states there are three elements; one class is very rich, another
very poor, and a third in a mean. It is admitted that moderation and the mean

SOURCE: Aristotle, *The Politics of Aristotle*, trans. B. Jowett, 2 vols. (Oxford: Clarendon
Press, 1885), 1:126–43.

are best, and therefore it will clearly be best to possess the gifts of fortune in moderation; for in that condition of life men are most ready to listen to reason. But he who greatly excels in beauty, strength, birth or wealth, or on the other hand who is very poor, or very weak, or very much disgraced, finds it difficult to follow reason. Of these two the one sort grow into violent and great criminals, the others into rogues and petty rascals. And two sorts of offences correspond to them, the one committed from violence, the other from roguery. The petty rogues are disinclined to hold office, whether military or civil, and their aversion to these two duties is as great an injury to the state as their tendency to crime. Again, those who have too much of the goods of fortune, strength, wealth, friends, and the like, are neither willing nor able to submit to authority. The evil begins at home: for when they are boys, by reason of the luxury in which they are brought up, they never learn, even at school, the habit of obedience. On the other hand, the very poor, who are in the opposite extreme, are too degraded. So that the one class cannot obey, and can only rule despotically; the other knows not how to command and must be ruled like slaves. Thus arises a city, not of freemen, but of masters and slaves, the one despising, the other envying; and nothing can be more fatal to friendship and good fellowship in states than this: for good fellowship tends to friendship; when men are at enmity with one another, they would rather not even share the same path. But a city ought to be composed, as far as possible, of equals and similars; and these are generally the middle classes. Wherefore the city which is composed of middle-class citizens is necessarily best governed; they are, as we say, the natural elements of a state. And this is the class of citizens which is most secure in a state, for they do not, like the poor, covet their neighbours' goods; nor do others covet theirs, as the poor covet the goods of the rich; and as they neither plot against others, nor are themselves plotted against, they pass through life safely. Wisely then did Phocylides pray,—"Many things are best in the mean; I desire to be of a middle condition in my city."

Thus it is manifest that the best political community is formed by citizens of the middle class, and that those states are likely to be well-administered, in which the middle class is large, and larger if possible than both the other classes, or at any rate than either singly; for the addition of the middle class turns the scale, and prevents either of the extremes from being dominant. Great then is the good fortune of a state in which the citizens have a moderate and sufficient property; for where some possess much, and the others nothing, there may arise an extreme democracy, or a pure oligarchy; or a tyranny may grow out of either extreme,—either out of the most rampant democracy, or out of an oligarchy; but it is not so likely to arise out of a middle and nearly equal condition.

I will explain the reason of this hereafter, when I speak of the revolutions of the states. The mean condition of states is clearly best, for no other is free from faction; and where the middle class is large, there are least likely to be factions and dissensions. For a similar reason large states are less liable to faction than small ones, because in them the middle class is large; whereas in small states it is easy to divide all the citizens into two classes who are either rich or poor, and to leave nothing in the middle. And democracies are safer and more permanent than oligarchies, because they have a middle class which is more numerous and has a greater share in the government; for when there is no middle class, and the poor greatly exceed in number, troubles arise, and the state soon comes to an end. A proof of the superiority of the middle class is that the best legislators have been of a middle condition; for example, Solon, as his own verses testify; and Lycurgus, for he was not a king; and Charondas, and almost all legislators.

These considerations will help us to understand why most governments are either democratical or oligarchical. The reason is that the middle class is seldom numerous in them, and whichever party, whether the rich or the common people, transgresses the mean and predominates, draws the government to itself, and thus arises either oligarchy or democracy. There is another reason—the poor and the rich quarrel with one another, and whichever side gets the better, instead of establishing a just or popular government, regards political supremacy as the prize of victory, and the one party sets up a democracy and the other an oligarchy. Both the parties which had the supremacy in Hellas looked only to the interest of their own form of government, and established in states, the one, democracies, and the other, oligarchies; they thought of their own advantage, of the public not at all. For these reasons the middle form of government has rarely, if ever, existed, and among a very few only. One man alone of all who ever ruled in Hellas was induced to give this middle constitution to states. But it has now become a habit among the citizens of states, not even to care about equality; all men are seeking for dominion, or, if conquered, are willing to submit.

What then is the best form of government, and what makes it the best is evident; and of other states, since we say that there are many kinds of democracy and many of oligarchy, it is not difficult to see which has the first and which the second or any other place in the order of excellence, now that we have determined which is the best. For that which is nearest to the best must of necessity be better, and that which is furthest from it worse, if we are judging absolutely and not relatively to given conditions: I say "relatively to given conditions," since a particular government may be preferable for some, but another form may be better for others.

12. We have now to consider what and what kind of government is suitable to what and what kind of men. I may begin by assuming, as a general principle common to all governments, that the portion of the state which desires permanence ought to be stronger than that which desires the reverse. Now every city is composed of quality and quantity. By quality I mean freedom, wealth, education, good birth, and by quantity, superiority of numbers. Quality may exist in one of the classes which make up the state, and quantity in the other. For example, the meanly-born may be more in number than the well-born, or the poor than the rich, yet they may not so much exceed in quantity as they fall short in quality; and therefore there must be a comparison of quantity and quality. Where the number of the poor is more than proportioned to the wealth of the rich, there will naturally be a democracy, varying in form with the sort of people who compose it in each case. If, for example, the husbandmen exceed in number, the first form of democracy will then arise; if the artisans and labouring class, the last; and so with the intermediate forms. But where the rich and the notables exceed in quality more than they fall short in quantity, there oligarchy arises, similarly assuming various forms according to the kind of superiority possessed by the oligarchs.

The legislator should always include the middle class in his government; if he makes his laws oligarchical, to the middle class let him look; if he makes them democratical, he should equally by his laws try to attach this class to the state. There only can the government ever be stable where the middle class exceeds one or both of the others, and in that case there will be no fear that the rich will unite with the poor against the rulers. For neither of them will ever be willing to serve the other, and if they look for some form of government more suitable to both, they will find none better than this, for the rich and the poor will never consent to rule in turn, because they mistrust one another. The arbiter is always the one trusted, and he who is in the middle is an arbiter. The more perfect the admixture of the political elements, the more lasting will be the state. Many even of those who desire to form aristocratical governments make a mistake, not only in giving too much power to the rich, but in attempting to overreach the people. There comes a time when out of a false good there arises a true evil, since the encroachments of the rich are more destructive to the state than those of the people.

13. The devices by which oligarchies deceive the people are five in number; they relate to (1) the assembly; (2) the magistracies; (3) the courts of law; (4) the use of arms; (5) gymnastic exercises. (1) The assemblies are thrown open to all, but either the rich only are fined for non-attendance, or a much larger fine is inflicted upon them. (2) As to the magistracies, those who are

qualified by property cannot decline office upon oath, but the poor may. (3) In the law-courts the rich, and the rich only, are fined if they do not serve, the poor are let off with impunity, or, as in the laws of Charondas, a large fine is inflicted on the rich, and a smaller one on the poor. In some states all citizens who have registered themselves are allowed to attend the assembly and to try causes; but if after registration they do not attend in the assembly or at the courts, heavy fines are imposed upon them. The intention is that through fear of the fines they may avoid registering themselves, and then they cannot sit in the law-courts or in the assembly. (4) Concerning the possession of arms, and (5) gymnastic exercises, they legislate in a similar spirit. For the poor are not obliged to have arms, but the rich are fined for not having them; and in like manner no penalty is inflicted on the poor for non-attendance at the gymnasium, and consequently, having nothing to fear, they do not attend, whereas the rich are liable to a fine, and therefore they take care to attend.

These are the devices of oligarchical legislators, and in democracies they have counter devices. They pay the poor for attending the assemblies and the law-courts, and they inflict no penalty on the rich for non-attendance. It is obvious that he who would duly mix the two principles should combine the practice of both, and provide that the poor should be paid to attend, and the rich fined if they do not attend, for then all will take part; if there is no such combination, power will be in the hands of one party only. The government should be confined to those who carry arms. As to the property qualification, no absolute rule can be laid down, but we must see what is the highest qualification sufficiently comprehensive to secure that the number of those who have the rights of citizens exceeds the number of those excluded. Even if they have no share in office, the poor, provided only that they are not outraged or deprived of their property, will be quiet enough.

But to secure gentle treatment for the poor is not an easy thing, since a ruling class is not always humane. And in time of war the poor are apt to hesitate unless they are fed; when fed, they are willing enough to fight. In some states the government is vested, not only in those who are actually serving, but also in those who have served; among the Malians, for example, the governing body consisted of the latter, while the magistrates were chosen from those actually on service. And the earliest government which existed among the Hellenes, after the overthrow of the kingly power, grew up out of the warrior class, and was originally taken from the knights (for strength and superiority in war at that time depended on cavalry); indeed, without discipline, infantry are useless, and in ancient times there was no military knowledge or tactics, and therefore the strength of armies lay in their cavalry. But when cities increased and the heavy armed grew in strength, more had a share in the government; and this is the reason why the states, which we call constitutional governments, have been hitherto called democracies. Ancient constitutions, as might be expected, were oligarchical and royal; their population being small they had no considerable middle class; the people were weak in numbers and organization, and were therefore more contented to be governed.

I have explained why there are various forms of government, and why there are more than is generally supposed; for democracy, as well as other constitutions, has more than one form: also what their differences are, and whence they arise, and what is the best form of government, speaking generally, and to whom the various forms of government are best suited; all this has now been explained.

14. Having thus gained an appropriate basis of discussion we will proceed to speak of the points which follow next in order. We will consider the subject not only in general but with reference to particular states. All states have three elements, and the good law-giver has to regard what is expedient for each state. When they are well-ordered, the state is well-ordered, and as they differ from one another, constitutions differ. What is the element first (1) which deliberates about public affairs; secondly (2) which is concerned with the magistrates and determines what they should be, over whom they should exercise authority, and what should be the mode of electing them; and thirdly (3) which has judicial power?

The deliberative element has authority in matters of war and peace, in making and unmaking alliances; it passes laws, inflicts death, exile, confiscation, audits the accounts of magistrates. All these powers must be assigned either to all the citizens or to some of them, for example, to one or more magistracies; or different causes to different magistracies, or some of them to all, and others of them only to some. That all things should be decided by all is characteristic of democracy; this is the sort of equality which the people desire. But there are various ways in which all may share in the government; they may deliberate, not all in one body, but by turns, as in the constitution of Telecles the Milesian. There are other states in which the boards of magistrates meet and deliberate, but come into office by turns, and are elected out of the tribes and the very smallest divisions of the state, until every one has obtained office in his turn. The citizens, on the other hand, are assembled only for the purposes of legislation, and to consult about the constitution, and to hear the edicts of the magistrates. In another variety of democracy the citizens form one assembly, but meet only to elect magistrates, to pass laws, to advise about war and peace, and to make scrutinies. Other matters are referred severally to special magistrates, who are elected by vote or by lot out of all the citizens. Or again, the citizens meet about election to offices and about scrutinies, and deliberate concerning war or alliances, while other matters are administered by the magistrates, who, as far as is possible, are elected by vote. I am speaking of those magistracies in which special knowledge is required. A fourth form of democracy is when all the citizens meet to deliberate about everything, and the magistrates decide nothing, but only make the preliminary enquiries; and that is the way in which the last and worst form of democracy, corresponding, as we maintain, to the close family oligarchy and to tyranny, is at present administered. All these modes are democratical.

On the other hand, that some should deliberate about all is oligarchical. This again is a mode which, like the democratical, has many forms. When the deliberative class being elected out of those who have a moderate qualification are numerous and they respect and obey the law without altering it, and any one who has the required qualification shares in the government, then, just because of this moderation, the oligarchy inclines towards polity. But when only selected individuals and not the whole people share in the deliberations of the state, then, although, as in the former case, they observe the law, the government is a pure oligarchy. Or, again, when those who have the power of deliberation are self-elected, and son succeeds father, and they and not the laws are supreme—the government is of necessity oligarchical. Where, again, particular persons have authority in particular matters;—for example, when the whole people decide about peace and war and hold scrutinies, but the magistrates regulate everything else, and they are elected either by vote or by lot—there the form of government is an aristocracy or polity. And if some questions are decided by magistrates elected by vote, and others by magistrates elected by lot, either absolutely or out of select candidates, or elected both by vote and by lot—these practices are partly characteristic of an aristocratical government, and partly of a pure constitutional government.

These are the various forms of the deliberative body; they correspond to the various forms of government. And the government of each state is administered according to one or other of the principles which have been laid down. Now it is for the interest of democracy, according to the most prevalent notion of it (I am speaking of that extreme form of democracy, in which the people are supreme even over the laws), with a view to better deliberation to adopt the custom of oligarchies respecting courts of law. For in oligarchies the rich who are wanted to be judges are compelled to attend under pain of a fine, whereas in democracies the poor are paid to attend. And this practice of oligarchies should be adopted by democracies in their public assemblies, for they will advise better if they all deliberate together,—the people with the notables and the notables with the people. It is also a good plan that those who deliberate should be elected by vote or by lot in equal numbers out of the different classes; and that if the people greatly exceed in number those who have political training, pay should not be given to all, but only to as many as would balance the number of the notables, or that the number in excess should be eliminated by lot. But in oligarchies either certain persons should be chosen out of the mass, or a class of officers should be appointed such as exist in some states, who are termed probuli and guardians of the law; and the citizens should occupy themselves exclusively with matters on which these have previously deliberated; for so the people will have a share in the deliberations of the state, but will not be able to disturb the principles of the constitution. Again, in oligarchies either the people ought to accept the measures of the government, or not to pass anything contrary to them; or, if all are allowed to share in counsel, the decision should rest with the magistrates. The opposite of what is done in constitutional governments should be the rule in oligarchies; the veto of the majority should be final, their assent not final, but the proposal should be referred back to the magistrates. Whereas in constitutional governments they take the contrary course; the few have the negative not the affirmative power; the affirmation of everything rests with the multitude.

These, then, are our conclusions respecting the deliberative, that is, the supreme element in states.

15. Next we will proceed to consider the distribution of offices; this, too, being a part of politics concerning which many questions arise:—What shall their number be? Over what shall they preside, and what shall be their duration? Sometimes they last for six months, sometimes for less; sometimes they are annual, whilst in other cases offices are held for still longer periods. Shall they be for life or for a long term of years; or, if for a short term only, shall the same persons hold them over and over again, or once only? Also about the appointment to them,—from whom are they to be chosen, by whom, and how? We should first be in a position to say what are the possible varieties of them, and then we may proceed to determine which are suited to different forms of government. But what are to be included under the term 'offices'? That is a question not quite so easily answered. For a political community requires many officers; and not every one who is chosen by vote or by lot is to be regarded as a ruler. In the first place there are the priests, who must be distinguished from political officers; masters of choruses and heralds, even ambassadors, are elected by vote [but still they are not political officers]. Some duties of superintendence again are political, extending either to all the citizens in a single sphere

of action, like the office of the general who superintends them when they are in the field, or to a section of them only, like the inspectorships of women or of youth. Other offices are concerned with household management, like that of the corn measurers who exist in many states and are elected officers. There are also menial offices which the rich have executed by their slaves. Speaking generally, they are to be called offices to which the duties are assigned of deliberating about certain measures and of judging and commanding, especially the last; for to command is the especial duty of a magistrate. But the question is not of any importance in practice; no one has ever brought into court the meaning of the word, although such problems have a speculative interest.

What kinds of offices, and how many, are necessary to the existence of a state, and which, if not necessary, yet conduce to its well-being, are much more important considerations, affecting all states, but more especially small ones. For in great states it is possible, and indeed necessary, that every office should have a special function; where the citizens are numerous, many may hold office. And so it happens that vacancies occur in some offices only after long intervals, or the office is held once only; and certainly every work is better done which receives the sole, and not the divided attention of the worker. But in small states it is necessary to combine many offices in a few hands, since the small number of citizens does not admit of many holding office:—for who will there be to succeed them? And yet small states at times require the same offices and laws as large ones; the difference is that the one want them often, the others only after long intervals. Hence there is no reason why the care of many offices should not be imposed on the same person, for they will not interfere with each other. When the population is small, offices should be like the spits which also serve to hold a lamp. We must first ascertain how many magistrates are necessary in every state, and also how many are not exactly necessary, but are nevertheless useful, and then there will be no difficulty in judging what offices can be combined in one. We should also know when local tribunals are to have jurisdiction over many different matters, and when authority should be centralized: for example, should one person keep order in the market and another in some other place, or should the same person be responsible everywhere? Again, should offices be divided according to the subjects with which they deal, or according to the persons with whom they deal: I mean to say, should one person see to good order in general, or one look after the boys, another after the women, and so on? Further, under different constitutions, should the magistrates be the same or different? For example, in democracy, oligarchy, aristocracy, monarchy, should there be the same magistrates, although they are elected, not out of equal or similar classes of citizens, but differently under different constitutions—in aristocracies, for example, they are chosen from the educated, in oligarchies from the wealthy, and in democracies from the free,—or are there different offices proper to different constitutions, and may the same be suitable to some, but unsuitable to others? For in some states it may be convenient that the same office should have a more extensive, in other states a narrower sphere. Special offices are peculiar to certain forms of government:—for example [to oligarchies] that of probuli, which is not a democratic office, although a bule or council is. There must be some body of men whose duty is to prepare measures for the people in order that they may not be diverted from their business; when these are few in number, the state inclines to an oligarchy: or rather the probuli must always be few, and are therefore an oligarchical element. But when both institutions exist in a state, the probuli are a check on the council; for the counsellor is a democratic element, but the probuli are oligarchical. Even the power of the council disappears when democracy has taken that extreme form, in which the people themselves are always meeting and deliberating about everything. This is the case when the members of the assembly are wealthy or receive pay; for they have nothing to do and are always holding assemblies and deciding everything for themselves. A magistracy which controls the boys or the women, or any similar office, is suited to an aristocracy rather than to a democracy; for how can the magistrates prevent the wives of the poor from going out of doors? Neither is it an oligarchical office; for the wives of the oligarchs are too fine to be controlled.

Enough of these matters. I will now enquire into the appointment of offices. There are three questions to be answered, and the combinations of answers give all possible differences: first, who appoints? secondly, from whom? and thirdly, how? Each of these three may further differ in three ways: (1) All the citizens, or only some, appoint; (2) Either the magistrates are chosen out of all or out of some who are distinguished either by a property qualification, or by birth, or merit, or for some special reason, as at Megara only those were eligible who had returned from exile and fought together against the democracy; (3) They may be appointed either by vote or by lot. Again, these several modes may be combined, I mean that some officers may be elected by some, others by all, and some again out of some, and others out of all, and some by vote and others by lot. Each of these differences admits of four variations. (1) Either all may elect out of all by vote, or all out of all by lot; and either out of all collectively or by sections, as, for example, by tribes, and wards, and phratries, until all the citizens have been gone through; or the citizens may be in all cases eligible indiscriminately, and in some cases they may be elected by vote, and in some by lot. Again (2), if only some appoint, they may appoint out of all by vote, or out of all by lot; or out of some by vote, out of some by lot, and some offices may be appointed in one way and some in another, I mean if they are appointed by all they may be appointed partly by vote and partly by lot. Thus there will be twelve forms of appointment without including the two combinations in the mode of election. Of these varieties two are democratic forms, namely, when the choice is made by all the people out of all by vote or by lot, or by both, that is to say, some by lot and some by vote. The cases in which they do not all appoint at one time, but some appoint out of all or out of some by vote or by lot or by both, (I mean some by lot and some by vote,) or some out of all and others out of some both by lot and vote, are characteristic of a polity or constitutional government. That some should be appointed out of all by vote or by lot or by both, is oligarchical, and still more oligarchical when some are elected from all and some from some. That some should be elected out of all and some out of some, or again some by vote and others by lot, is characteristic of a constitutional government, which inclines to an aristocracy. That some should be chosen out of some, and some taken by lot out of some, is oligarchical though not equally oligarchical; oligarchical, too, is the appointment of some out of some in both ways, and of some out of all. But that all should elect by vote out of some is aristocratical.

These are the different ways of constituting magistrates, and in this manner officers correspond to different forms of government:—which are proper to which, or how they ought to be established, will be evident when we determine the nature of their powers. By powers I mean such power as a magistrate exercises over the revenue or in defence of the country; for there are various kinds of power: the power of the general, for example, is not the same with that which regulates contracts in the market.

16. Of the three parts of government, the judicial remains to be considered, and this we shall divide on the same principle. There are three points on which the varieties of law-courts depend:—The persons from whom they are appointed, the matters with which they are concerned, and the manner of their appointment. I mean, (1) are the judges taken from all, or from some only? (2) how many kinds of law-courts are there? (3) are the judges chosen by vote or by lot?

First, let me determine how many kinds of law-courts there are. They are eight in number: One is the court of audits or scrutinies; a second takes cognizance of [ordinary] offences against the state; a third is concerned with treason against the government; the fourth determines disputes respecting penalties, whether raised by magistrates or by private persons; the fifth decides the more important civil cases; the sixth tries cases of homicide, which are of various kinds, (1) premeditated, (2) unpremeditated, (3) cases in which the guilt is confessed but the justice is disputed; and there may be a fourth court (4) in which murderers who have fled from justice are tried after their return; such as the Court of Phreatto is said to be at Athens. But cases of this sort rarely happen at all even in large cities. The different kinds of homicide may be tried either by the same or by different courts. (7) There are courts for strangers:—of these there are two subdivisions, (1) for the settlement of their disputes with one another, (2) for the settlement of disputes between them and the citizens. And besides all these there must be (8) courts for small suits about sums of a drachma up to five drachmas, or a little more, which have to be determined, but they do not require many judges.

Nothing more need be said of these small suits, nor of the courts for homicide and for strangers:—I would rather speak of political cases, which, when mismanaged, create division and disturbances in states.

Now if all the citizens judge, in all the different cases which I have distinguished, they may be appointed by vote or by lot, or sometimes by lot and sometimes by vote. Or when a certain class of causes are tried, the judges who decide them may be appointed, some by vote, and some by lot. These then are the four modes of appointing judges from the whole people, and there will be likewise four modes, if they are elected from a part only; for they may be appointed from some by vote and judge in all causes; or they may be appointed from some by lot and judge in all causes; or they may be elected in some cases by vote, and in some cases taken by lot, or some courts, even when judging the same causes, may be composed of members some appointed by vote and some by lot. These then are the ways in which the aforesaid judges may be appointed.

Once more, the modes of appointment may be combined, I mean, that some may be chosen out of the whole people, others out of some, some out of both; for example, the same tribunal may be composed of some who were elected out of all, and of others who were elected out of some, either by vote or by lot or by both.

In how many forms law-courts can be established has now been considered. The first form, viz. that in which the judges are taken from all the citizens, and in which all causes are tried, is democratical; the second, which is composed of a few only who try all causes, oligarchical; the third, in which some courts are taken from all classes, and some from certain classes only, aristocratical and constitutional.

Chuang Tzŭ (Zhuangzi)

Nourishment of the Soul, from *Chuang Tzŭ*

From the storied history of Tao Buddhism, Chuang Tzŭ stands preeminent, influencing Chinese thought and culture almost beyond measure. Written in the fourth century BC, his short, simple, and iconoclastic teachings convey a way of being and living based less on mastery of protocols and norms, and more on an openness to the mysterious Tao that is beyond both words and silence. Thus, Chuang Tzŭ teaches of a way diverging from a virtue-driven striving, measured by outcomes. Instead, he counsels following the *wu wei*, a nondoing or nonaction. When one is in harmony with the Great Tao, therefore, both the action and the timing of the good action will come as one is open to the *wu wei*'s spontaneous and apophatic way.

Chapter III: Nourishment of the Soul.

Argument:—Life too short—Wisdom unattainable—Accommodation to circumstance—Liberty paramount—Death a release—The soul immortal.

My life has a limit, but my knowledge is without limit. To drive the limited in search of the limitless, is fatal; and the knowledge of those who do this is fatally lost.

In striving for others, avoid fame. In striving for self, avoid disgrace. Pursue a middle course. Thus you will keep a sound body, and a sound mind, fulfil your duties, and work out your allotted span.

Prince Hui's cook was cutting up a bullock. Every blow of his hand, every heave of his shoulders, every tread of his foot, every thrust of his knee, every *whshh* of rent flesh, every *chhk* of the chopper, was in perfect

SOURCE: *Chuang Tzŭ: Mystic, Moralist, and Social Reformer*, trans. Herbert A. Giles (London: Bernard Quaritch, 1889), 33–37.

harmony,—rhythmical like the dance of the Mulberry Grove, simultaneous like the chords of the Ching Shou.

[. . . .]

"Well done!" cried the Prince. "Yours is skill indeed."

"Sire," replied the cook; "I have always devoted myself to Tao. It is better than skill. When I first began to cut up bullocks, I saw before me simply *whole* bullocks. After three years' practice, I saw no more whole animals.

[Meaning that he saw them, so to speak, in sections.]

And now I work with my mind and not with my eye. When my senses bid me stop, but my mind urges me on, I fall back upon eternal principles. I follow such openings or cavities as there may be, according to the natural constitution of the animal. I do not attempt to cut through joints: still less through large bones.

[. . . .]

"A good cook changes his chopper once a year,—because he cuts. An ordinary cook, once a month,—because he hacks. But I have had this chopper nineteen years, and although I have cut up many thousand bullocks, its edge is as if fresh from the whetstone. For at the joints there are always interstices, and the edge of a chopper being without thickness, it remains only to insert that which is without thickness into such an interstice.

[. . . .]

By these means the interstice will be enlarged, and the blade will find plenty of room. It is thus that I have kept my chopper for nineteen years as though fresh from the whetstone.

"Nevertheless, when I come upon a hard part where the blade meets with a difficulty, I am all caution. I fix my eye on it. I stay my hand, and gently apply my blade, until with a *hwah* the part yields like earth crumbling to the ground. Then I take out my chopper, and stand up, and look around, and pause, until with an air of triumph I wipe my chopper and put it carefully away."

"Bravo!" cried the Prince. "From the words of this cook I have learnt how to take care of my life."

[. . . .]

When Hsien, of the Kung-wên family, beheld a certain official, he was horrified, and said, "Who is that man? How came he to lose a foot? Is this the work of God, or of man?

"Why, of course," continued Hsien, "it is the work of God, and not of man. When God brought this man into the world, he wanted him to be unlike other men. Men always have two feet. From this it is clear that God and not man made him as he is.

[. . . .]

"Now, wild fowl get a peck once in ten steps, a drink once in a hundred. Yet they do not want to be fed in a cage. For although they would thus be able to command food, they would not be free."

[. . . .]

When Lao Tzŭ died, Ch'in Shih went to mourn. He uttered three yells and departed.

A disciple asked him saying, "Were you not our Master's friend?"

"I was," replied Ch'in Shih.

"And if so, do you consider that a sufficient expression of grief at his loss?" added the disciple.

"I do," said Ch'in Shih. "I had believed him to be the man of all men, but now I know that he was not. When I went in to mourn, I found old persons weeping as if for their children, young ones wailing as if for their mothers. And for him to have gained the attachment of those people in this way, he too must have uttered words which should not have been spoken, and dropped tears which should not have been shed, thus violating eternal principles, increasing the sum of human emotion, and forgetting the source from which his own life was received. The ancients called such emotions the trammels of mortality. The Master came, because it was his time to be born; he went, because it was his time to die. For those who accept the phenomenon of birth and death in this sense, lamentation and sorrow have no place. The ancients spoke of death as of God cutting down a man suspended in the air. The fuel is consumed, but the fire may be transmitted, and we know not that it comes to an end."

[The soul, according to Chuang Tzŭ, if duly nourished and not allowed to wear itself out with the body in the pursuits of mortality, may become immortal and return beatified to the Great Unknown whence it came.]

16

Mencius

from *Kung–Sun Ch'ow*

The second-greatest Confucian after the master, Mencius (a westernized trans-
literation of "Mengzi") responded in the fourth century BC to the political and
social turmoil of China's Zhou dynasty. Where some looked to external political systems and civil structures to stabilize society, Mencius looked inward to a
sacred-social natural law. Humans are both individually and collectively good
and will flourish to the extent that they altruistically honor the bond connecting heaven, human nature, and culture. Thus, as seen in the following excerpt,
commonweal is made manifest in the natural compassion and concern for
each member of society, expressed in the four principles.

———————

VI. 1. Mencius said, "All men have a mind which cannot bear [to see the
sufferings of] others.

2. "The ancient kings had this commiserating mind, and they had likewise,
as a matter of course, a commiserating government. When with a commiserating mind there was practised a commiserating government, to bring all under
heaven to order was [as easy] as to make [a small thing] go round in the palm.

3. "The ground on which I say that all men have a mind which cannot bear
[to see the suffering of] others is this:—Even now-a-days, when men suddenly
see a child about to fall into a well, they will all experience a feeling of alarm and
distress. They will feel so not that they may thereon gain the favour of the child's
parents; nor that they may seek the praise of their neighbours and friends; nor
from a dislike to the reputation of [being unmoved by] such a thing.

4. "Looking at the matter from this case, [we may see that] to be without
this feeling of distress is not human, and that it is not human to be without the

SOURCE: James Legge, trans., *The Chinese Classics*, vol. 2, *The Life and Works of Mencius*
(London: Trübner & Co., 1875), 173–75.

feeling of shame and dislike, or to be without the feeling of modesty and complaisance, or to be without the feeling of approving and disapproving.

5. "That feeling of distress is the principle of benevolence; the feeling of shame and dislike is the principle of righteousness; the feeling of modesty and complaisance is the principle of propriety; and the feeling of approving and disapproving is the principle of knowledge.

6. "Men have these four principles just as they have their four limbs. When men, having these four principles, yet say of themselves that they cannot [manifest them], they play the thief with themselves; and he who says of his ruler that he cannot [manifest them], plays the thief with his ruler.

7. "Since we all have the four principles in ourselves, let us know to give them all their development and completion, and the issue will be like that of a fire which has begun to burn, or of a spring which has begun to find vent. Let them have their full development, and they will suffice to love and protect all [within] the four seas; let them be denied that development, and they will not suffice for a man to serve his parents with."

17

Epicurus

Letter to Menoeceus

Founder of the Athenian school known as the Garden, Epicurus (341–270 BC) was the chief architect of a prominent school of thought in the ancient Greek-speaking world for centuries, namely, Epicureanism. Epicureanism empha-sizes the importance of living a life of pleasure, eschewing the fear of death, and achieving a state of *ataraxia*—that is, a lack of mental perturbation. The following is a letter sent by Epicurus to Menoeceus, which offers a brief sum-mation of his vision for how we ought to live.

––––––––––––––

Let no one be slow to seek wisdom when he is young nor weary in the search thereof when he is grown old. For no age is too early or too late for the health of the soul. And to say that the season for philosophy has not yet come, or that it is passed and gone, is like saying that the season for happiness is not yet or that it is now no more. Therefore, both old and young ought to seek wisdom, that so a man as age comes over him may be young in good things, because of the grace of what has been, and while he is young may likewise be old, because he has no fear of the things which are to come. So we must exercise ourselves in the things which bring happiness, since, if that be present, we have every-thing, and, if that be absent, all our actions are directed toward attaining it.

Those things which without ceasing I have declared unto thee, those do and exercise thyself therein, holding them to be the elements of right life. First, believe that God is a being blessed and immortal, according to the notion of a God commonly held amongst men; and so believing, thou shalt not affirm of him aught that is contrary to immortality or that agrees not with blessed-ness, but shalt believe about him whatsoever may uphold both his blessedness

SOURCE: R. D. Hicks, *Stoic and Epicurean* (New York: Charles Scribner's Sons, 1910), 167–73.

and his immortality. For verily there are gods, and the knowledge of them is manifest; but they are not such as the multitude believe, seeing that men do not steadfastly maintain the notions they form respecting them. Not the man who denies the gods worshipped by the multitude, but he who affirms of the gods what the multitude believes about them, is truly impious. For the utterances of the multitude about the gods are not true preconceptions but false assumptions, according to which the greatest evils happen to the wicked and the greatest blessings happen to the good from the hand of the gods, seeing that they are always favourable to their own good qualities and take pleasure in men like unto themselves, but reject as alien whatever is not of their kind.

Accustom thyself to believe that death is nothing to us, for good and evil imply sentience and death is the privation of all sentience; therefore, a right understanding that death is nothing to us makes enjoyable the mortality of life, not by adding to life an illimitable time, but by taking away the yearning after immortality. For life has no terrors for him who has thoroughly apprehended that there are no terrors for him in ceasing to live. Foolish, therefore, is the man who says that he fears death, not because it will pain when it comes, but because it pains in the prospect. Whatsoever causes no annoyance when it is present causes only a groundless pain in the expectation. Death, therefore, the most awful of evils, is nothing to us, seeing that when we are, death is not come, and when death is come, we are not. It is nothing, then, either to the living or to the dead, for with the living it is not and the dead exist no longer. But in the world, at one time men shun death as the greatest of all evils, and at another time choose it as a respite from the evils in life. The wise man does not deprecate life nor does he fear the cessation of life. The thought of life is no offense to him nor is the cessation of life regarded as an evil. And even as men choose of good, not merely and simply the larger portion, but the more pleasant, so the wise seek to enjoy the time which is most pleasant and not merely that which is longest. And he who admonishes the young to live well and the old to make a good end, speaks foolishly, not merely because of the desirableness of life, but because the same exercise at once teaches to live well and to die well. Much worse is he who says that it were good not to be born, but when once one is born to pass with all speed through the gates of Hades. If he, in truth, believes this, why does he not depart from life? It were easy for him to do so if once he is firmly convinced. If he speaks only in mockery his words are foolishness, for those who hear believe him not.

We must remember that the future is neither wholly ours nor wholly not ours, so that neither must we count upon it as quite certain to come nor despair of it as quite certain not to come.

We must also reflect that of desires some are natural, some are groundless; and that of the natural some are necessary as well as natural, and some are natural only. And of the necessary desires, some are necessary as well as natural and some are natural only. And of the necessary desires, some are necessary if we are to be happy, some if the body is to be rid of uneasiness, some if we are even to live. He who has a clear and certain understanding of these things will direct every preference and aversion toward securing health of body and tranquillity of mind, seeing that this is the sum and end of a blessed life. For the end of all our actions is to be free from pain and fear, and when once we have attained this all the tempest of the soul is laid, seeing that the living creature has no need to go in search of something that is lacking nor to look for anything else by which the good of the soul and of the body will be fulfilled. When we are pained because of the absence of pleasure, then, and then only, do we feel the need of pleasure; but when we feel no pain, then we no longer stand in need of pleasure. Wherefore we call pleasure the alpha and omega of a blessed life. Pleasure is our first and kindred good. It is the starting-point of every choice and of every aversion, and to it we come back, inasmuch as we make feeling the rule by which to judge of every good thing.

And since pleasure is our first and native good, for that reason we do not choose every pleasure whatsoever, but ofttimes pass over many pleasures when a greater annoyance ensues from them. And ofttimes we consider pains superior to pleasures when submission to the pains for a long time brings us as its consequence a greater pleasure. While, therefore, all pleasure because it is naturally akin to us is good, not all pleasure is choiceworthy, just as all pain is an evil but all pain is not to be shunned. It is, however, by measuring one against another, and by looking at the conveniences and inconveniences, that all these matters must be judged. Sometimes we treat the good as an evil, and the evil, on the contrary, as a good. Again, we regard independence of outward things as a great good, not so as in all cases to use little, but so as to be contented with little if we have not much, being honestly persuaded that they have the sweetest enjoyment of luxury who stand least in need of it, and that whatever is natural is easily procured and only the vain and worthless hard to win. Plain fare is not more distasteful than a costly diet, when once the pain of want has been removed, while bread and water confer the highest possible pleasure when they are brought to hungry lips. To habituate one's self, therefore, to simple and inexpensive diet supplies all that is needful for health, and enables a man to meet the necessary requirements of life without shrinking, and it places us in a better condition when we approach at intervals a costly fare and renders us fearless of fortune.

When we say, then, that pleasure is the end and aim, we do not mean the pleasures of the prodigal or the pleasures of sensuality, as we are understood to do by some, through ignorance, prejudice, or wilful misinterpretation. By pleasure we mean the absence of pain in the body and trouble in the soul. It is not an unbroken succession of drinking feasts and of revelry, not sexual love, not the enjoyment of the fish and other delicacies of a luxurious table which produce a pleasant life; it is sober reasoning, searching out the grounds of every choice and avoidance, and banishing those beliefs through which the greatest tumults take possession of the soul. Of all this the beginning and the greatest good is prudence. Wherefore, prudence is a more precious thing even than philosophy; from it spring all the other virtues, for it teaches that we cannot lead a life of pleasure which is not also a life of prudence, honour, and justice; nor lead a life of prudence, honour, and justice which is not also a life of pleasure. For the virtues have grown into one with a pleasant life, and a pleasant life is inseparable from them.

Who, then, is superior, in thy judgment, to such a man? He holds a holy belief concerning the gods, and is altogether free from the fear of death. He has diligently considered the end fixed by nature, and understands how easily the limit of good things can be procured and attained; that as for evils either their duration or their poignancy is but slight. Destiny, which some introduce as sovereign over all things, he laughs to scorn, affirming rather that certain things happen of necessity, others by chance, others through our own agency. For he sees that necessity destroys responsibility and that chance or fortune is inconstant; whereas our own actions are free, and it is to them that praise and blame naturally attach. It were better, indeed, to accept the legends of the gods than to bow beneath that yoke of destiny which the natural philosophers have imposed. The one holds out some faint hope that we may escape by honouring the gods, while the necessity of the philosophers is deaf to all supplications. Nor does such an one make chance a god, as the world in general does (for in the acts of God nothing is irregular), nor yet regard it as a vacillating cause, for he believes that chance dispenses to men no good or evil which make life blessed though it furnishes means and occasions for great good and great evil. He believes that the misfortune of the wise is better than the prosperity of the fool. It is better, in short, that what is well judged in action should not owe its successful issue to the aid of chance.

Exercise thyself in these and kindred precepts day and night, both by thyself and with him who is like unto thee; then never, either in waking or in dream, wilt thou be disturbed but wilt live as a god amongst men. For by living in the midst of immortal blessings man loses all semblance of mortality.

from *Bhagavad-Gita*

Widely recognized as among the most important Hindu texts hailing from India, the *Bhagavad-Gita* (or the "Song of God") is routinely dated to the second century BC, though this dating is disputed, and some scholars have contended that it was likely composed between the fifth and the third centuries BC. This text makes up the sixth book of the world's longest known epic poem, *Mahabharata*, which has been traditionally attributed to a likely mythical author, the sage Vyasa. The *Bhagavad-Gita* has influenced a range of notable figures throughout history, including Henry David Thoreau and Ralph Waldo Emerson in the United States, along with Mohandas Gandhi during his nonviolent campaign for Indian independence from British rule during the twentieth century. The following excerpt is the second chapter of the *Gita*, wherein the young prince Arjuna is suddenly stricken with a moment of despondent hesitation before going into battle against his own kinsmen. Krishna, the avatar of the supreme god Vishnu, replies in a way that synthesizes various religious and philosophical ideas of the Hindu tradition.

Chapter II

Sanjaya:
Him [Arjuna], filled with such compassion and such grief,
With eyes tear-dimmed, despondent, in stern words
The Driver, Madhusudan, thus addressed:

Krishna:
How hath this weakness taken thee? Whence springs
The inglorious trouble, shameful to the brave,

SOURCE: *The Song Celestial, or Bhagavad-Gita (from the Mahabharata), Being a Discourse between Arjuna, Prince of India, and the Supreme Being under the Form of Krishna*, trans. Edwin Arnold, 3rd ed. (London: Trübner & Co., Ludgate Hill, 1886), 9–24.

Barring the path of virtue? Nay, Arjun!
Forbid thyself to feebleness! it mars
Thy warrior-name! cast off the coward-fit!
Wake! Be thyself! Arise, Scourge of thy Foes!

Arjuna:
How can I, in the battle, shoot with shafts
On Bhishma, or on Drona—O thou Chief!—
Both worshipful, both honourable men?

Better to live on beggar's bread
With those we love alive,
Than taste their blood in rich feasts spread,
And guiltily survive!
Ah! were it worse—who knows?—to be
Victor or vanquished here,
When those confront us angrily
Whose death leaves living drear?
In pity lost, by doubtings tossed,
My thoughts—distracted—turn
To Thee, the Guide I reverence most,
That I may counsel learn:
I know not what would heal the grief
Burned into soul and sense,
If I were earth's unchallenged chief—
A god—and these gone thence!

Sanjaya:
So spake Arjuna to the Lord of Hearts,
And sighing, "I will not fight!" held silence then.
To whom, with tender smile, (O Bharata!)
While the Prince wept despairing 'twixt those hosts,
Krishna made answer in divinest verse:

Krishna.
Thou grievest where no grief should be! thou speak'st
Words lacking wisdom! for the wise in heart
Mourn not for those that live, nor those that die.
Nor I, nor thou, nor any one of these,
Ever was not, nor ever will not be,
For ever and for ever afterwards.

All, that doth live, lives always! To man's frame
As there come infancy and youth and age,
So come there raisings-up and layings-down
Of other and of other life-abodes,
Which the wise know, and fear not. This that irks—
Thy sense-life, thrilling to the elements—
Bringing thee heat and cold, sorrows and joys,
'Tis brief and mutable! Bear with it, Prince!
As the wise bear. The soul which is not moved,
The soul that with a strong and constant calm
Takes sorrow and takes joy indifferently,
Lives in the life undying! That which is
Can never cease to be; that which is not
Will not exist. To see this truth of both
Is theirs who part essence from accident,
Substance from shadow. Indestructible,
Learn thou! the Life is, spreading life through all;
It cannot anywhere, by any means,
Be anywise diminished, stayed, or changed.
But for these fleeting frames which it informs
With spirit deathless, endless, infinite,
They perish. Let them perish, Prince! and fight!
He who shall say, "Lo! I have slain a man!"
He who shall think, "Lo! I am slain!" those both
Know naught! Life cannot slay. Life is not slain!
Never the spirit was born; the spirit shall cease to be never;
Never was time it was not; End and Beginning are dreams!
Birthless and deathless and changeless remaineth the spirit for
    ever;
Death hath not touched it at all, dead though the house of it
    seems!

Who knoweth it exhaustless, self-sustained,
Immortal, indestructible,—shall such
Say, "I have killed a man, or caused to kill?"

Nay, but as when one layeth
His worn-out robes away,
And taking new ones, sayeth,
"These will I wear to-day!"
So putteth by the spirit

Lightly its garb of flesh,
And passeth to inherit
A residence afresh.

I say to thee weapons reach not the Life;
Flame burns it not, waters cannot o'erwhelm,
Nor dry winds wither it. Impenetrable,
Unentered, unassailed, unharmed, untouched,
Immortal, all-arriving, stable, sure,
Invisible, ineffable, by word
And thought uncompassed, ever all itself,
Thus is the Soul declared! How wilt thou, then,—
Knowing it so,—grieve when thou shouldst not grieve?
How, if thou hearest that the man new-dead
Is, like the man new-born, still living man—
One same, existent Spirit—wilt thou weep?
The end of birth is death; the end of death
Is birth: this is ordained! and mournest thou,
Chief of the stalwart arm! for what befalls
Which could not otherwise befall? The birth
Of living things comes unperceived; the death
Comes unperceived; between them, beings perceive:
What is there sorrowful herein, dear Prince?

Wonderful, wistful, to contemplate!
Difficult, doubtful, to speak upon!
Strange and great for tongue to relate,
Mystical hearing for every one!
Nor wotteth man this, what a marvel it is,
When seeing, and saying, and hearing are done!

This Life within all living things, my Prince!
Hides beyond harm; scorn thou to suffer, then,
For that which cannot suffer. Do thy part!
Be mindful of thy name, and tremble not!
Nought better can betide a martial soul
Than lawful war; happy the warrior
To whom comes joy of battle—comes, as now,
Glorious and fair, unsought; opening for him
A gateway unto Heav'n. But, if thou shunn'st
This honourable field—a Kshattriya—

If, knowing thy duty and thy task, thou bidd'st
Duty and task go by—that shall be sin!
And those to come shall speak thee infamy
From age to age; but infamy is worse
For men of noble blood to bear than death!
The chiefs upon their battle-chariots
Will deem 'twas fear that drove thee from the fray.
Of those who held thee mighty-souled the scorn
Thou must abide, while all thine enemies
Will scatter bitter speech of thee, to mock
The valour which thou hadst; what fate could fall
More grievously than this? Either—being killed—
Thou wilt win Swarga's safety, or—alive
And victor—thou wilt reign an earthly king.
Therefore, arise, thou Son of Kunti! brace
Thine arm for conflict, nerve thy heart to meet—
As things alike to thee—pleasure or pain,
Profit or ruin, victory or defeat:
So minded, gird thee to the fight, for so
Thou shalt not sin!

Thus far I speak to thee
As from the "Sankhya"—unspiritually—
Hear now the deeper teaching of the Yog,
Which holding, understanding, thou shalt burst
Thy Karmabandh, the bondage of wrought deeds.
Here shall no end be hindered, no hope marred,
No loss be feared: faith—yea, a little faith—
Shall save thee from the anguish of thy dread.
Here, Glory of the Kurus! shines one rule—
One steadfast rule—while shifting souls have laws
Many and hard. Specious, but wrongful deem
The speech of those ill-taught ones who extol
The letter of their Vedas, saying, "This
Is all we have, or need;" being weak at heart
With wants, seekers of Heaven: which comes—they say—
As "fruit of good deeds done;" promising men
Much profit in new births for works of faith;
In various rites abounding; following whereon
Large merit shall accrue towards wealth and power;

Albeit, who wealth and power do most desire
Least fixity of soul have such, least hold
On heavenly meditation. Much these teach,
From Veds, concerning the "three qualities;"
But thou, be free of the "three qualities,"
Free of the "pairs of opposites," and free
From that sad righteousness which calculates;
Self-ruled, Arjuna! simple, satisfied!
Look! like as when a tank pours water forth
To suit all needs, so do these Brahmans draw
Text for all wants from tank of Holy Writ.
But thou, want not! ask not! Find full reward
Of doing right in right! Let right deeds be
Thy motive, not the fruit which comes from them.
And live in action! Labour! Make thine acts
Thy piety, casting all self aside,
Contemning gain and merit; equable
In good or evil: equability
Is Yog, is piety!

Yet, the right act
Is less, far less, than the right-thinking mind.
Seek refuge in thy soul; have there thy heaven!
Scorn them that follow virtue for her gifts!
The mind of pure devotion—even here—
Casts equally aside good deeds and bad,
Passing above them. Unto pure devotion
Devote thyself: with perfect meditation
Comes perfect act, and the right-hearted rise—
More certainly because they seek no gain—
Forth from the bands of body, step by step,
To highest seats of bliss. When thy firm soul
Hath shaken off those tangled oracles
Which ignorantly guide, then shall it soar
To high neglect of what's denied or said,
This way or that way, in doctrinal writ.
Troubled no longer by the priestly lore,
Safe shall it live, and sure; steadfastly bent
On meditation. This is Yog—and Peace!

Arjuna:
What is his mark who hath that steadfast heart,
Confirmed in holy meditation? How
Know we his speech, Kesava? Sits he, moves he
Like other men?

Krishna:
When one, O Pritha's Son!
Abandoning desires which shake the mind—
Finds in his soul full comfort for his soul,
He hath attained the Yog—that man is such!
In sorrows not dejected, and in joys
Not overjoyed; dwelling outside the stress
Of passion, fear, and anger; fixed in calms
Of lofty contemplation;—such an one
Is Muni, is the Sage, the true Recluse!
He who to none and nowhere overbound
By ties of flesh, takes evil things and good
Neither desponding nor exulting, such
Bears wisdom's plainest mark! He who shall draw
As the wise tortoise draws its four feet safe
Under its shield, his five frail senses back
Under the spirit's buckler from the world
Which else assails them, such an one, my Prince!
Hath wisdom's mark! Things that solicit sense
Hold off from the self-governed; nay, it comes,
The appetites of him who lives beyond
Depart,—aroused no more. Yet may it chance,
O Son of Kunti! that a governed mind
Shall some time feel the sense-storms sweep, and wrest
Strong self-control by the roots. Let him regain
His kingdom! let him conquer this, and sit
On Me intent. That man alone is wise
Who keeps the mastery of himself! If one
Ponders on objects of the sense, there springs
Attraction; from attraction grows desire,
Desire flames to fierce passion, passion breeds
Recklessness; then the memory—all betrayed—
Lets noble purpose go, and saps the mind,
Till purpose, mind, and man are all undone.
But, if one deals with objects of the sense

Not loving and not hating, making them
Serve his free soul, which rests serenely lord,
Lo! such a man comes to tranquillity;
And out of that tranquillity shall rise
The end and healing of his earthly pains,
Since the will governed sets the soul at peace.
The soul of the ungoverned is not his,
Nor hath he knowledge of himself; which lacked,
How grows serenity? and, wanting that,
Whence shall he hope for happiness?

The mind
That gives itself to follow shows of sense
Seeth its helm of wisdom rent away,
And, like a ship in waves of whirlwind, drives
To wreck and death. Only with him, great Prince!
Whose senses are not swayed by things of sense—
Only with him who holds his mastery,
Shows wisdom perfect. What is midnight-gloom
To unenlightened souls shines wakeful day
To his clear gaze; what seems as wakeful day
Is known for night, thick night of ignorance,
To his true-seeing eyes. Such is the Saint!

And like the ocean, day by day receiving
Floods from all lands, which never overflows
Its boundary-line not leaping, and not leaving,
Fed by the rivers, but unswelled by those;—

So is the perfect one! to his soul's ocean
The world of sense pours streams of witchery;
They leave him as they find, without commotion,
Taking their tribute, but remaining sea.

Yea! whoso, shaking off the yoke of flesh
Lives lord, not servant, of his lusts; set free
From pride, from passion, from the sin of "Self,"
Toucheth tranquillity! O Pritha's Son!
That is the state of Brahm! There rests no dread
When that last step is reached! Live where he will,
Die when he may, such passeth from all 'plaining,
To blest Nirvana, with the Gods, attaining.

19

Marcus Tullius Cicero

from *Treatise on the Laws*

Marcus Tullius Cicero (106–43 BC) was a Roman statesman, rhetorician, orator, lawyer, and scholar who is perhaps best known for his efforts in connection with staving off the eventual collapse of the Roman Republic during the emergence of the Roman Empire. He was ultimately assassinated and dismembered at Mark Antony's order for his part in supporting Octavian over Antony in his famous speeches to the Roman Senate. Cicero's philosophical work has influenced a wide range of thinkers, including the early Christian writer Augustine (who claimed that Cicero's work helped turn him toward philosophical learning and, hence, eventually to God), as well as the Protestant reformer John Calvin. Written sometime between 55 and 51 BC, Cicero's *Treatise on the Laws*, from which the following selection is an excerpt, is a dialogue between Marcus and Atticus about how humans can come to discover divine reason and justice through the proper use of natural reason, which in turn provides the basis for law.

Marcus.—I will not detain you long. Since you grant me the existence of God, and the superintendence of Providence, I maintain that he has been especially beneficent to man. This human animal—prescient, sagacious, complex, acute, full of memory, reason and counsel, which we call man,—is generated by the supreme God in a more transcendent condition than most of his fellow-creatures. For he is the only creature among the earthly races of animated beings endued with superior reason and thought, in which the rest are deficient. And what is there, I do not say in man alone, but in all heaven and

SOURCE: Marcus Tullius Cicero, *The Political Works of Marcus Tullius Cicero: Comprising His Treatise on the Commonwealth; and His Treatise on the Laws*, trans. Francis Barham, 2 vols, vol. 2, *The Treatise on the Laws* (London: Edmund Spettigue, 1842), 40–49.

earth, more divine than reason, which, when it becomes ripe and perfect, is justly termed wisdom?

There exists, therefore, since nothing is better than reason, and since this is the common property of God and man, a certain aboriginal rational intercourse between divine and human natures. This reason, which is common to both, therefore, can be none other than right reason; and since this *right reason* is what we call *Law*, God and men are said by Law to be consociated. Between whom, since there is a communion of law, there must be also a communication of Justice.

Law and Justice being thus the common rule of immortals and mortals, it follows that they are both the fellow-citizens of one city and commonwealth. And if they are obedient to the same rule, the same authority and denomination, they may with still closer propriety be termed fellow-citizens, since one celestial regency, one divine mind, one omnipotent Deity then regulates all their thoughts and actions.

This universe, therefore, forms one immeasurable Commonwealth and city, common alike to gods and mortals. And as in earthly states, certain particular laws, which we shall hereafter describe, govern the particular relationships of kindred tribes; so in the nature of things doth an universal law, far more magnificent and resplendent, regulate the affairs of that universal city where gods and men compose one vast association.

When we thus reason on universal nature, we are accustomed to reason after this method. We believe that in the long course of ages and the uninterrupted succession of celestial revolutions, the seed of the human race was sown on our planet, and being scattered over the earth, was animated by the divine gift of souls. Thus men retained from their terrestrial origin, their perishable and mortal bodies, while their immortal spirits were ingenerated by Deity. From which consideration we are bold to say that we possess a certain consanguinity and kindred fellowship with the celestials. And so far as we know, among all the varieties of animals, man alone retains the idea of the Divinity. And among men there is no nation so savage and ferocious as to deny the necessity of worshipping God, however ignorant it may be respecting the nature of his attributes. From whence we conclude that every man must recognize a Deity, who considers the origin of his nature and the progress of his life.

Now the law of virtue is the same in God and man, and cannot possibly be diverse. This virtue is nothing else than a nature perfect in itself, and developed in all its excellence. There exists therefore a similitude between God and man; nor can any knowledge be more appropriate and sterling than what relates to this divine similitude.

Nature, attentive to our wants, offers us her treasures with the most grace-ful profusion. And it is easy to perceive that the benefits which flow from her are true and veritable gifts, which Providence has provided on purpose for human enjoyment, and not the fortuitous productions of her exuberant fecun-dity. Her liberality appears, not only in the fruits and vegetables which gush from the bosom of the earth, but likewise in cattle and the beasts of the field. It is clear that some of these are intended for the advantage of mankind, a part for propagation, and a part for food. Innumerable arts have likewise been dis-covered by the teaching of nature; for her doth reason imitate, and skilfully discover all things necessary to the happiness of life.

With respect to man this same bountiful nature hath not merely allotted him a subtle and active spirit, but moreover favoured him with physical senses, like so many guardians and messengers. Thus has she improved our under-standing in relation to many obscure principles, and laid the foundation of practical knowledge; and in all respects moulded our corporeal faculties to the service of our intellectual genius. For while she has debased the forms of other animals, who live to eat rather than eat to live, she has bestowed on man an erect stature, and an open countenance, and thus prompted him to the con-templation of heaven, the ancient home of his kindred immortals. So exqui-sitely, too, hath she fashioned the features of the human face, as to make them symbolic of the most recondite thoughts and sentiments. As for our two elo-quent eyes . . . do they not speak forth every impulse and passion of our souls? And that which we call *expression*, in which we infinitely excel all the inferior animals, how marvellously it delineates all our speculations and feelings! Of this the Greeks well knew the meaning, though they had no word for it.

I will not enlarge on the wonderful faculties and qualities of the rest of the body, the modulation of the voice, and the power of oratory, which is perhaps the greatest instrument of our influence over human society. These matters do not belong to the occasion of our present discourse, and I think that Scipio has already sufficiently explained them in those books of mine which you have read.

As the Deity, therefore, was pleased to create man as the chief and president of all terrestrial creatures, so it is evident, without further argument, that hu-man nature has made the greatest advances by its intrinsic energy; that nature, which without any other instruction than her own, has developed the first rude principles of the understanding, and strengthened and perfected reason to all the appliances of science and art.

Atticus.—Good heavens, my Cicero! from what a tremendous distance are you deducing the principles of justice! However, I won't hurry too eagerly to what

I expect you to say on the Civil Law. But I will listen patiently, even if you spend the whole day in this kind of discourse, for assuredly these are grander topics which you introduce as a preamble than those to which they prepare the way.

Marcus.—You may well describe these topics as grand, which we are now briefly discussing. For of all the questions on which our philosophers argue, there is none which it is more important thoroughly to understand than this, *that man is born for justice, and that law and equity are not a mere establishment of opinion, but an institution of nature.* This truth will become still more apparent if we investigate the nature of human association and society.

There is no one thing more like to another, more homogeneous and analogous, than man is to man. And if the corruption of customs, and the variation of opinions, had not induced an imbecility of minds, and turned them aside from the course of nature, no one would more nearly resemble himself than all men would resemble all men. Therefore whatever definition we give of man, it must include the whole human race. And this is a good argument, that no portion of mankind can be heterogeneous or dissimilar from the rest; because, if this were the case, one definition could not include all men.

In fact, reason, which alone gives us so many advantages over beasts, by means of which we conjecture, argue, refute, discourse, and accomplish and conclude our designs, is assuredly common to all men; for the faculty of acquiring knowledge is similar in all human minds, though the knowledge itself may be endlessly diversified. By the same senses we all perceive the same objects, and that which strikes the sensibilities of the few, cannot be indifferent to those of the many. Those first rude elements of intelligence which, as I before observed, are the earliest developments of thought, are similarly exhibited by all men; and that faculty of speech which is the soul's interpreter, agrees in the ideas it conveys, though it may differ in the syllables that express them. And therefore there exists not a man in any nation, who, adopting his true nature for his true guide, may not improve in virtue.

Nor is this resemblance which all men bear to each other remarkable in those things only which accord to right reason. For it is scarcely less conspicuous in those corrupt practices by which right reason is most cruelly violated. For all men alike are captivated by voluptuousness, which is in reality no better than disgraceful vice, though it may seem to bear some natural relations to goodness; for by its delicious delicacy and luxury it insinuates error into the mind, and leads us to cultivate it as something salutary, forgetful of its poisonous qualities.

An error, scarcely less universal, induces us to shun death, as if it were annihilation; and to cling to life, because it keeps us in our present stage of existence, which is perhaps rather a misfortune than a desideratum. Thus, likewise, we erroneously consider pain as one of the greatest evils, not only on account of its present asperity, but also because it seems the precursor of mortality. Another common delusion obtains, which induces all mankind to associate renown with honesty, as if we are necessarily happy when we are renowned, and miserable when we happen to be inglorious.

In short, our minds are all similarly susceptible of inquietudes, joys, desires and fears; and if opinions are not the same in all men, it does not follow, for example, that the people of Egypt who deify dogs and cats, do not labour under superstition in the same way as other nations, though they may differ from them in the forms of its manifestation.

But in nothing is the uniformity of human nature more conspicuous than in its respect for virtue. What nation is there, in which kindness, benignity, gratitude, and mindfulness of benefits are not recommended? What nation in which arrogance, malice, cruelty, and unthankfulness, are not reprobated and detested! This uniformity of opinions, invincibly demonstrates that mankind was intended to compose one fraternal association. And to affect this, the faculty of reason must be improved till it instructs us in all the arts of well-living. If what I have said meets your approbation, I will proceed; or if any of my argument appears defective, I will endeavour to explain it.

Atticus.—We see nothing to object to, if I may reply for both of us.

Marcus.—It follows, then, in the line of our argument, *that nature made us just that we might participate our goods with each other, and supply each others' wants.* You observe in this discussion whenever I speak of nature, I mean *nature in its genuine purity,* and not in the corrupt state which is displayed by the depravity of evil custom, which is so great, that the natural and innate flame of virtue is often almost extinguished and stifled by the antagonist vices, which are accumulated around it.

But if our true nature would assert her rights, and teach men the noble lesson of the poet, who says, "I am a man, therefore no human interest can be indifferent to me,"—then would justice be administered equally by all and to all. For nature hath not merely given us reason, but right reason, and consequently that law, which is nothing else than right reason enjoining what is good, and forbidding what is evil.

Now if nature hath given us law, she hath also given us justice,—for as she has bestowed reason on all, she has equally bestowed the sense of justice on all. And therefore did Socrates deservedly execrate the man who first drew a distinction between the law of nature and the law of morals, for he justly conceived that this error is the source of most human vices.

It is to this essential union between the naturally honorable, and the politically expedient, that this sentence of Pythagoras refers:—"Love is universal: let its benefits be universal likewise." From whence it appears that when a wise man is attached to a good man by that friendship whose rights are so extensive, that phenomenon takes place which is altogether incredible to worldlings, and yet it is a necessary consequence, that he loves himself not more dearly than he loves his friend. For how can a difference of interests arise where all interests are similar? If there could be such a difference of interests, however minute, it would be no longer a true friendship, which vanishes immediately when, for the sake of our own benefit, we would sacrifice that of our friend.

20

Marcus Tullius Cicero

from *De Officiis*

The following is an excerpt from Cicero's *De Officiis* (or *On Moral Duties*) which was written during the final year of Cicero's life in the form of a letter to his son, Marcus. Among other things, this book deals with what is right and honorable and how that connects up to our most natural states.

----

5. You behold, indeed, my son Marcus, the very form and, as it were, the countenance of the right, which, were it seen by the eyes, as Plato says, would awaken the intensest love of wisdom. But whatever is right springs from one of four sources. It consists either in the perception and skilful treatment of the truth; or in maintaining good-fellowship with men, giving to every one his due, and keeping faith in contracts and promises; or in the greatness and strength of a lofty and unconquered mind; or in the order and measure that constitute moderation and temperance. Although these four are connected and intertwined with one another, yet duties of certain kinds proceed from each of them; as from the division first named, including wisdom and prudence, proceed the investigation and discovery of truth, as the peculiar office of that virtue. For in proportion as one sees clearly what is the inmost and essential truth with regard to any subject, and can demonstrate it with equal acuteness and promptness, he is wont to be regarded, and justly, as of transcendent discretion and wisdom. Therefore truth is submitted to this virtue as the material of which it treats, and with which it is conversant. The other three virtues have for their sphere the providing and preserving of those things on which the conduct of life depends, so that the fellowship and union

SOURCE: Marcus Tullius Cicero, *Cicero De Officiis*, in *Ethical Writings of Cicero: De Officiis; De Senectute; De Amicitia, and Scipio's Dream*, trans. Andrew P. Peabody (Boston: Little, Brown, and Co., 1887), 10–11, 33–35, 66–69.

of society may be maintained, and that superiority and greatness of mind may shine forth, not only in the increase of resources and the acquisition of objects of desire for one's self, and for those dependent on him, but much more in a position from which one can look down on these very things. But order, and consistency, and moderation, and similar qualities have their scope in affairs that demand not merely the movement of the mind, but some outward action; for it is by bringing to the concerns of daily life a certain method and order that we shall maintain honor and propriety.

[. . . .]

16. Still further, human society and fellowship will be best maintained, if where there is the most intimate relation, the greatest amount of kindness be bestowed. Here it may be well to trace back the social relations of men to their principles in nature. The first of these principles is that which is seen in the social union of the entire race of man. Its bond is reason as expressed in language, which by teaching, learning, imparting, discussing, deciding, conciliates mutual regard, and unites men by a certain natural fellowship; nor in any respect are we farther removed from the nature of beasts, in which, we often say, there is courage, as in the horse and the lion, but not justice, equity, goodness, inasmuch as they have neither reason nor language. Indeed, it is through this society, so broadly open to men with one another, to all with all, that common possession is to be maintained as to whatever nature has produced for the common use of men; so that while those things that are specially designated by the statutes and the civil law are held as thus decreed, according to these very laws other things may be regarded in the sense of the Greek proverb, "All things are common among friends." Indeed, all those things seem to be common among men, which are of the kind designated by Ennius in a single example, but comprehending many others:—

"Who kindly shows a wanderer his way,
Lights, as it were, a torch from his own torch,—
In kindling others' light, no less he shines."

This one instance suffices to illustrate the rule, that whatever one can give without suffering detriment should be given even to an entire stranger. Thus among common obligations we may reckon, to prohibit no one from drinking at a stream of running water; to permit any one who wishes to light fire from fire; to give faithful advice to one who is in doubt,—which things are useful to the receiver, and do no harm to the giver. But since the resources of individuals are small, while the multitude of those who need them is unbounded, this indiscriminate giving should have the limit suggested by Ennius, "No less he shines," so that we may have the means of generosity to those peculiarly our own.

[. . . .]

30. It is appropriate to every discussion of duty, always to bear in mind how far the nature of man excels that of cattle and other beasts. They feel nothing save sensual pleasure, and toward that they are borne by every instinct; but the mind of man is nourished by learning and reflection, is constantly thinking or doing something, and is led by the pleasure and profit derived from what is seen and heard. And even if one is unduly inclined to sensual pleasure, if he only be not on a level with brute beasts,—for there are some who are men, not in fact, but in name,—if he be ever so little above them, although captivated with the mere delight of the senses, he hides and dissembles the appetite for such pleasure from very shame. Hence it is inferred that bodily pleasure is unworthy of man's superior endowments, and ought to be despised and spurned; and if there be any one who sets some value on sensual gratification, he should carefully keep it within due limits. Thus food and the care of the body should be ordered with reference to health and strength, not to sensual pleasure. Indeed, if we will only bear in mind what excellence and dignity belong to human nature, we shall understand how base it is to give one's self up to luxury, and to live voluptuously and wantonly, and how honorable it is to live frugally, chastely, circumspectly, soberly.

But it is to be borne in mind that we are endowed by nature as it were with two characters, one of which is common to us with other men, inasmuch as we all partake of reason, and of the traits which raise us above the brutes, from which all that is right and becoming is derived, and from which we seek the method of ascertaining our duty; while the other is that which is assigned to each of us individually. For as in bodies there are great dissimilarities,— we see some excelling in speed for the race, others in strength for wrestling; also in personal appearance, some have dignity, others grace,—so in minds there are even greater diversities. Lucius Crassus and Lucius Philippus had a great deal of pleasantry; Caius Caesar, the son of Lucius, even more and more elaborate; while in their contemporaries, Marcus Scaurus and Marcus Drusus the younger, there was an unusual severity of manner; in Caius Laelius, much mirthfulness; in his friend Scipio, greater ambition, a more austere type of character. Among the Greeks, too, we have learned that Socrates was pleasant and facetious, and had a jocose way of talking, and meant more than he said . . . ; on the other hand, that Pythagoras and Pericles obtained the highest authority in their intercourse with men without any seasoning of mirthfulness. We are informed that, of the Carthaginians, Hannibal was crafty, and of our own commanders, that Quintus Maximus readily practised concealment, kept silence, dissembled, laid snares, anticipated the plans of his enemies. In these traits the Greeks assign the foremost place to Themistocles and Jason of Pherae, and accord pre-eminent praise to the cunning and crafty procedure of Solon, who, for his own safety, and that he might render additional service to the state, feigned insanity. There are others of very unlike character, simple and open, who think that nothing should be done covertly or insidiously, votaries of truth, enemies of fraud; others still, who will endure anything whatever, and will be subservient to any one whomsoever, till they attain what they desire, as we saw in the case of Sulla and of Marcus Crassus. Of this class of men we learn that Lysander, the Lacedaemonian, was unsurpassed in crafty plotting and in his power of endurance, while Callicratidas, who succeeded Lysander in the command of the fleet, was of the opposite character. Also in speech, we sometimes see a man of surpassing ability contrive to appear like one of the multitude, as we witnessed in Catulus, both father and son, and in Quintus Mucius Mancia. We have heard from those of an earlier generation that this was the habit of Publius Scipio Nasica, and, on the other hand, that his father, the man who avenged the nefarious enterprises of Tiberius Gracchus, had nothing genial in his address. We learn, too, that Xenocrates, indeed the sternest of philosophers, was on this very score eminent and renowned. There are other innumerable diversities of nature and of manners, which yet give no good ground for obloquy.

21

Livy

from *History of Rome* (Stories of Lucretia and Cincinnatus)

Like so many ancient historians, Livy (ca. 60 BC–17 AD) told history on the grand scale. His *History of Rome*, for example, comprised scores of volumes, and traversed several centuries—from Rome's founding to the age of Augustus Caesar. For Livy, however, history was less a comprehensive chronicle of facts, and more a morality play, shedding light on the power and intrigue of notable forebears. Concerned that Roman morality was in a state of decline, he invited readers to assess their own ethical views in light of that of their ancestors. As in the stories of Lucretia and Cincinnatus, which are included below, questions of personal virtue and social responsibility are front and center. Why does Lucretia respond as she does? What made Cincinnatus an iconic leader?

Book I, Chapter LVII

[Story of Lucretia]

The Rutuli, a nation eminently powerful in wealth, considering that country and that age, were in possession of Ardea; and that circumstance was the very cause of the war, because the Roman king, exhausted by the magnificence of the public works, was anxious both to be enriched himself, and also to soothe down the minds of his subjects, exasperated also with his government, independently of his other tyrannical conduct, because they were indignant they were so long kept by the king in the occupation of mechanics, and in servile labour. The experiment was made, if Ardea could be taken in the first assault; when that did not succeed, the enemy were begun to be distressed with a siege and circumvallations. In these quarters furloughs were, as is usual in

SOURCE: *A Literal Translation of the First Three Books of Prendeville's Livy* (Dublin: John Cumming, 1830), 75–77, 201–6.

a war rather tedious than vigorous, granted with sufficient liberality, more so, however, to the principal officers than to the soldiers. The youths of the royal family, especially, used to spend their leisure hours in feastings and convivial parties amongst themselves. It happened, as they were drinking with Sex. Tarquinius, where also Collatinus Tarquinius, the son of Egerius, was supping, that mention was made of their wives; each praised his own to a surprising degree; the dispute then growing warm, Collatinus says, "That there was no need of words—that it could indeed be easily ascertained how much his Lucretia excelled the rest. Why do we not, as we possess the vigour of youth, mount our horses, and inspect in person the disposition of our wives? That that must be the strongest proof to each which shall meet his eyes, when the husband's arrival is unexpected." They were heated with wine. "Come then," say they all. They fly off to Rome, with their horses at full speed. Whither when they arrived, as the first shades of night were overspreading the earth, they proceed forthwith to Collatia; where they find Lucretia, not like the king's daughters-in-law, whom they had seen wasting their time in banquetting and luxurious indulgence with those of their own class, but sitting in the middle of her house, at that late hour of night, attentive to her wool, amidst her maids, who were working by candle-light. The honour of this female competition was awarded to Lucretia. Her consort, on his arrival, and the Tarquins were courteously received—the successful husband politely invites the royal youths. There a criminal passion of violating Lucretia by force takes possession of Sex. Tarquin; her beauty, as well as approved chastity, incite him to the act. And for that time indeed they return to the camp, after this nocturnal frolic of youth.

Chapter LVIII

After the lapse of a few days, Sex. Tarquinius, unknown to Collatinus, came to Collatia with a single attendant; where being kindly received by those who were ignorant of his design, when he had been shewn in after supper to the strangers' apartment, being fired with passion, when every thing around seemed secure and all buried in sleep, he approached Lucretia with a drawn sword, as she lay asleep; and, having pressed the lady's bosom with his left hand, said, "Hush, Lucretia, I am Sextus Tarquinius; my sword is in my hand; you shall die if you utter a word." When the female, being affrighted out of her sleep, saw no succour nigh, and death immediately threatening her; then Tarquin declared his love, intreated, mingled threats with prayers, and worked upon her female feelings on every side; when he saw her inflexible, and not yielding even from the dread of death, he adds dishonour to fear—he declares he will place his murdered slave naked by her dead body, that she might be said to have been slain in base adultery. By which terror when his lust, as it were triumphant, had overcome her obstinate chastity, and Tarquin departed from thence, elated at having overpowered a female's honour, Lucretia, distressed at so heavy a misfortune, dispatches one and the same messenger to Rome to her father, and to Ardea to her husband, with directions to come each with one trusty friend; that such was the occasion of action and expedition, that an atrocious deed had happened. Sp. Lucretius came with P. Valerius, the son of Volesus—Collatinus, with L. Junius Brutus, with whom as he happened to be on his return to Rome, he was met by his wife's messenger. They find Lucretia sitting disconsolate in her chamber; on the arrival of her friends, a flood of tears burst forth; and on her husband inquiring, "Is all well?" "Far from it," she replies; "for what can be well with a woman, when she has lost her chastity? Collatinus, the traces of another man are in your bed. But my person alone is violated, my heart is pure—death shall be witness. But give me your right hands and faith, that the adulterer shall not go unpunished. Sextus Tarquinius is the man who, an enemy in the disguise of a guest, has last night in arms obtained hence by force a triumph fatal to me, and, if you be men, to himself." They all pledge their honour in succession. They console her sick at heart, by turning the culpability from her, who suffered by compulsion, to the perpetrator of the offence; that it is the mind that transgresses, not the body; and that guilt is wanting, where intention is wanting. "You," said she, "will look to what is due to him; but I, though I acquit myself of the offence, do not release myself from the punishment; nor shall any woman hereafter live with sullied chastity by the example of Lucretia." She plunges into her heart a knife, which she kept concealed under her garment; and falling forward on the wound, she dropped down lifeless. Her husband and father shriek out together.

[. . . .]

Book III, Chapter XXVI

[Story of Cincinnatus]

A vast number of the Sabines came almost to the walls of the city, committing destructive depredations; the fields were laid desolate, terror was struck into the city. Then the commons cordially took up arms; two great armies were enlisted, the tribunes protesting against it in vain. Nautius led one against the Sabines: having pitched his camp at Eretum, by means of small detachments, generally by nocturnal incursions, he caused such devastation in the Sabine country, that compared with that, the Roman territories seemed almost untouched by the war. Minucius had neither the same success, nor energy of mind in conducting business; for, though he had encamped not far from the enemy, without having received any very considerable loss, he timidly kept himself within his camp. Which when the enemy had perceived, their boldness, as is usual, increased from the other's fear, and attacking the camp by night, when open force had not succeeded, they draw lines of circumvallation round it on the next day; but, before these shut up the egress, by opposing a barrier all round, five horsemen, having made their way between the enemy's out-posts, conveyed intelligence to Rome that the consul and his army were besieged. Nothing could happen so unexpected, nor so unhoped-for. The consternation, therefore, was so great, the alarm so great, as if the enemy were besieging the city, not the camp. They call home the consul Nautius; in whom, as there appeared not sufficient protection, and as they agreed that a dictator should be appointed, who might restore their afflicted fortune, L. Quinctius Cincinnatus is named with universal approbation. This is a circumstance worthy of the attention of all, who despise every thing in comparison to riches, and who fancy there is no place for high honour, or merit, except where opulence affluently abounds. L. Quinctius, the sole hope of the empire of the Roman people, cultivated a farm of four acres, which is now called the "Quinctian meadows," beyond the Tiber, opposite the very place where the dock yards now are. There, leaning on a stake, while digging a ditch, or being in the act of ploughing, (certain it is, as is agreed on all sides, that he was employed in agricultural labour,) a salutation being mutually offered and returned, being requested "that, in the name of good luck to himself and the commonwealth, he would put on his gown, and hear the commands of the senate;" being surprised, and asking, "was all well?" he orders his wife, Racilia, to bring him his gown quickly from the cottage. Attired in which, when he came forward, after wiping off the dust and perspiration, the deputies congratulating him, salute him dictator; invite him to the city, and state to him what great terror pervaded the army. A vessel had been prepared for Quinctius by the government, and his three sons going out to meet him, receive him when landed on the other side, after them, his other relatives and friends; and then, the major part of the senate. Attended by this numerous train, and preceded by the lictors, he is conducted to his house, and a great concourse of the commons took place. But the latter by no means beheld Quinctius with so much satisfaction, deeming both the power itself excessive, and the man invested with that power too arbitrary. And on that night indeed, nothing more was done, than watch kept in the city.

Chapter XXVII

On the following day, the dictator, when he had come into the Forum before day-light, names as his master of horse L. Tarquitius, of a patrician family, but who, though on account of his poverty he had served as a foot-soldier, was accounted by far the first among the Roman youths. Attended by his master of the horse, he came into the public assembly; proclaims a suspension of civil business, orders the shops to be closed throughout the entire city, and forbids any person to attend to any private business. He next orders that as many as were of the military age should attend, under arms, in the Campus Martius, before sun-set, with dressed victuals for five days, and twelve stakes each; those whose age was too unfit for military service, he ordered to dress his victuals for the neighbouring soldier, whilst the latter was preparing his arms, and procuring stakes. Thus the young men run in all directions, to look for palisades. They took them from whatever place was most convenient to each; no one was prevented; and they all attended with alacrity, pursuant to the dictator's proclamation. After that, the dictator himself leads forward the legions, and the master of horse his cavalry, in a regularly formed body, being prepared not more for a march than a battle, if the occasion should so require it. In both divisions there were used those exhortations which the juncture itself demanded—"That they should quicken their pace; that there was need of expedition, that they might be able to reach the enemy in the night; that a Roman consul and his army were besieged; that they were now shut up for the third day; that it was unknown what a single night or day may bring about; that the issue of the most important affairs often turned on a moment of time." They also called out to each other, gratifying their leaders, "Standard-bearer, hasten; soldier, follow." At midnight they arrive at Algidum; and when they perceived that they were now close to the enemy, they plant their standards (i.e. halt).

Chapter XXVIII

The dictator then, having rode round, and examined, as far as his view could extend by night, what was the situation, and what the form of their camp, commanded the tribunes of the soldiers to order the baggage to be heaped together in one place, and the soldiers with their arms and stakes to return into their respective ranks; what he commanded was executed. He then draws his whole army in a long line round the enemy's camp, in the same order that had been observed in the march; and orders that, when the signal were given, they should all raise a shout, and that on the shout being raised, every man should dig a trench in front of himself, and fix his stakes. This order being issued, the signal immediately followed; the soldiers executed their orders: the shout resounds round the enemy; it then passes the enemy's camp, and reaches the camp of the consul; in the one place it produces consternation, in the other, immense joy. The Romans, congratulating each other, that it was the shout of their countrymen, and that relief was at hand, terrify the enemy in their turn from the out-posts and watch-stations. The consul declares, "That the attack should not be deferred; for that by that shout their arrival alone was not indicated, but also the commencement of the action by their friends; and that it was surprising, if the enemy's camp was not assaulted on the outer side:" he therefore orders his soldiers to take up arms and follow him. The engagement was begun by the consular legions during the night; they intimate to the dictator, by their shout, that the affair was at issue on that side also. The Æqui were now making preparations to prevent lines of circumvallation from being drawn round them; when, the engagement being begun by the enemy inside them, turning their attention from those engaged in the works to the combatants within, lest a sally might be made through the midst of their camp, they left the night at the dictator's disposal for the work; and the fight with the consul continued till daylight. At break of day, they were now surrounded by the dictator's works, and scarcely supported the fight against one army; then their rampart is assaulted by Quinctius's army, which had just returned to their arms, after the completion of their work: here a new attack was pressing upon them, and the former had in no degree slackened its fury. Then, being turned by the urgency of the double danger from resistance to prayers, they entreated, on one side, the dictator, on the other, the consul, not to make victory consist in their entire destruction, and to allow them to retire from the place with the loss of their arms. Being ordered by the consul to apply to the dictator, the latter, being highly incensed, added ignominy to defeat. He commands Gracchus Cloelius, their general, and the other principal persons, to be brought before him in chains, and the town of Corbio to be evacuated; "That he did not want the blood of the Æqui; that they were at liberty to depart; but, in order that an acknowledgment that their nation had been subdued and vanquished should at length be extorted, that they must pass under the yoke." The yoke is formed of three spears, two of them being fixed in the ground, and over these one being tied across: under this yoke the dictator sent the Æqui.

Chapter XXIX

Having gained possession of the enemy's camp, which abounded in every thing, for he had sent them away quite bare, he gave all the plunder to his own soldiers exclusively; rebuking the consular army and the consul himself, he says, "Soldiers, you shall have no share of the spoil taken from that enemy to whom you have almost become a prey yourselves: and you, L. Minucius, shall command these legions as lieutenant-general, until you begin to have a spirit worthy of a consul." Thus Minucius resigns the consulship, and, being so ordered, remains with the army. But at that time, so submissively obedient was the mind to more skilful command, that this army, more mindful of the benefit conferred than the disgrace inflicted, both voted a golden crown, a pound in weight, to the dictator, and, at his departure, hailed him as their patron. At Rome, the senate, being convened by Q. Fabius, præfect of the city, ordained, that Quinctius should enter the city in triumph, in the same line of march in which he was coming: the leaders of the enemy were led before his chariot; the military ensigns were borne before him; the army, laden with plunder, followed after. Banquets are said to have been laid out before the houses of all the citizens; and, partaking of the feast, they followed the chariot, with the triumphal hymn and customary jests, in the manner of revellers. On that day, the freedom of the state was, with the approbation of all, conferred on L. Mamilius, of Tusculum. The dictator would have resigned his office forthwith, had not the assembly for the trial of M. Volscius, the false witness, obliged him to continue: the dread of the dictator prevented the tribunes from opposing that assembly. Volscius, being found guilty, went into exile to Lanuvium. Quinctius, on the sixteenth day, abdicated the dictatorship, which he had received for six months. During those days the consul, Nautius, fought a successful battle with the Sabines, at Eretum. In addition to the devastation of their lands, this calamity also befel the Sabines. Fabius Quintus was sent to Algidum, as successor to Minucius. At the close of the year, the subject of the law was agitated by the tribunes; but as two armies were from home, the patricians succeeded in their request, that no measure should be brought before the people. The commons gained their point so far, as to create the same men tribunes for the fifth time. They report, that wolves were seen in the Capitol, and were put to flight by dogs; and that, on account of this prodigy, the Capitol was purified. These were the transactions in that year.

22

Josephus

from *The Jewish War*

Born Yosef ben Matityahu, Flavius Josephus (37–100 AD) led a varied life. As a member of Judaism's Pharisee sect, he was inclined to accommodate to Roman occupation, so long as the Romans provided religious freedom. However, as pressures leading to the First Jewish War (66–70 AD) mounted, he assumed command of a rebel Jewish garrison in Galilee, which ended in his capture by Roman General (and soon Emperor) Vespasian. After acquiring his freedom, Josephus cast his lot with Rome, changing his name to Flavius Josephus. His work *The Jewish War* is a unique text in that it is authored by a Jew, yet with sympathetic treatment of both the colonized and the colonizer. His other famous history, *Antiquities of the Jews*, covers Jewish history from creation to Titus' destruction of Jerusalem, and references Jesus of Nazareth and John the Baptist.

Vol. IV, Book VI

Chapter VIII
[On Titus' Destruction of Jerusalem]

5. . . . So the Romans being now become masters of the walls, they both placed their ensigns upon the towers, and made joyful acclamations for the victory they had gained, as having found the end of this war much lighter than its beginning: for when they had gotten upon the last wall, without any bloodshed, they could hardly believe what they found to be true; but seeing nobody to oppose them, they stood in doubt what such an unusual solitude could mean. But when they went in numbers into the lanes of the city, with their swords

SOURCE: Flavius Josephus, *The Works of Josephus, With a Life Written by Himself*, vol. 4, trans. William Whiston (New York: Oakley, Mason and Co., 1870), 289–94, 335–36, 339–42 [856/1145, 902/1145, 906/1145].

drawn, they slew those whom they overtook without mercy, and set fire to the houses whither the Jews were fled, and burnt every soul in them, and laid waste a great many of the rest; and when they were come to the houses to plunder them, they found in them entire families of dead men, and the upper rooms full of putrid corpses, that is, of such as died by the famine: they then stood in horror at this sight and went out without touching any thing. But although they had this commiseration, for such as were destroyed in that manner, yet had they not the same for those that were still alive, but they ran every one through whom they met with, and obstructed the very lanes with their dead bodies, and made the whole city run down with blood, to such a degree, indeed, that the fire of many of the houses was quenched with these men's blood. And truly so it happened, that though the slayers left off at the evening, yet did the fire greatly prevail in the night; and as all was burning, came that eighth day of the month Gorpieus [Elul,] upon Jerusalem, a city that had been liable to so many miseries during this siege, that, had it always enjoyed as much happiness from its first foundation, it would certainly have been the envy of the world. Nor did it, on any other account, so much deserve these sore misfortunes, as by producing such a generation of men as were the occasion of this its overthrow.

Chapter IX

1. Now, when Titus was come into this [upper] city, he admired not only some other places of strength in it, but particularly those strong towers which the tyrants, in their mad conduct, had relinquished: for when he saw their solid altitude, and the largeness of their several stones, and the exactness of their joints, as also how great was their breadth, and how extensive their length, he expressed himself after the manner following:—"We have certainly had God for our assistant in this war, and it was no other than God who ejected the Jews out of these fortifications; for what could the hands of men or any machines do towards overthrowing these towers?" At which time he had many such discourses to his friends: he also let such go free as had been bound by the tyrants, and were left in the prisons. To conclude, when he had entirely demolished the rest of the city, and overthrew its walls, he left these towers as a monument of his good fortune, which had proved his auxiliaries, and enabled him to take what otherwise could not have been taken by him.

2. And now, since his soldiers were already quite tired with killing men, and yet there appeared to be a vast multitude still remaining alive, Cæsar gave orders that they should kill none but those that were in arms and opposed them, but should take the rest alive. But, together with those whom they had orders to slay, they slew the aged and the infirm; but for those that were in their flourishing age, and who might be useful to them, they drove them together

into the temple and shut them up within the walls of the court of the women; over which Cæsar set one of his freedmen, as also Fronto, one of his own friends, which last was to determine every one's fate, according to his merits. So this Fronto slew all those that had been seditious and robbers, who were impeached one by another; but of the young men he chose out the tallest and most beautiful, and reserved them for the triumph: and as for the rest of the multitude, that were about seventeen years old, he put them into bonds and sent them to the Egyptian mines. Titus also sent a great number into the provinces, as a present to them, that they might be destroyed upon their theatres by the sword and by the wild beasts; but those that were under seventeen years of age were sold for slaves. Now, during the days wherein Fronto was distinguishing these men, there perished for want of food, eleven thousand; some of which did not taste any food, through the hatred their guards bore to them, and others would not take in any when it was given them. The multitude also was so very great, that they were in want even of corn for their sustenance.

3. Now, the number of those that were carried captive during this whole war, was collected to be ninety-seven thousand; as was the number of those that perished during the whole siege eleven hundred thousand, the greater part of whom were, indeed, of the same nation [with the citizens of Jerusalem,] but not belonging to the city itself; for they were come up from all the country to the feast of unleavened bread, and were on a sudden shut up by an army, which at the very first occasioned so great a straitness among them that there came a pestilential destruction upon them, and soon afterward such a famine, as destroyed them more suddenly. And that this city could contain so many people in it, is manifest by that number of them which was taken under Cestius, who being desirous of informing Nero of the flower of the city, who otherwise was disposed to contemn that nation, entreated the high-priests, if the thing were possible, to take the number of their whole multitude. So these high-priests, upon the coming of that feast which is called the *Passover*, when they slay their sacrifices from the ninth hour till the eleventh, but so that a company not less than ten belong to every sacrifice (for it is not lawful for them to feast singly by themselves;) and many of us are twenty in a company. Now, the number of sacrifices was two hundred fifty-six thousand and five hundred, which, upon the allowance of no more than ten that feast together, amounts to two millions seven hundred thousand and two hundred persons that were pure and holy; for as to those that have the leprosy, or the gonorrhœa, or women that have their monthly courses, or such as are otherwise polluted, it is not lawful for them to be partakers of this sacrifice; nor, indeed, for any foreigners neither, who come hither to worship.

4. Now this vast multitude is, indeed, collected out of remote places; but the entire nation was now shut up by fate, as in a prison, and the Roman army encompassed the city when it was crowded with inhabitants. Accordingly the multitude of those that therein perished exceeded all the destructions that either men or God ever brought upon the world: for to speak only of what was publicly known, the Romans slew some of them, some they carried captives, and others they made a search for under ground, and when they found where they were, they broke up the ground, and slew all they met with. There were also found slain there above two thousand persons, partly by their own hands, and partly by one another, but chiefly destroyed by the famine: but then the ill-savor of the dead bodies was most offensive to those that lighted upon them, insomuch that some were obliged to get away immediately, while others were so greedy of gain that they would go in among the dead bodies that lay on heaps, and tread upon them; for a great deal of treasure was found in these caverns and the hope of gain made every way of getting it to be esteemed lawful. Many also of those that had been put in prison by the tyrants were now brought out; for they did not leave off their barbarous cruelty at the very last: yet did God avenge himself upon them both, in a manner agreeable to justice. As for John, he wanted food, together with his brethren, in these caverns, and begged that the Romans would now give him their right hand for his security which he had often proudly rejected before; but for Simon, he struggled hard with the distress he was in, till he was forced to surrender himself, as we shall relate hereafter; so he was reserved for the triumph, and to be then slain; as was John condemned to perpetual imprisonment. And now the Romans set fire to the extreme parts of the city, and burnt them down, and entirely demolished its walls.

[. . . .]

Vol. IV, Book VII

Chapter VIII
[Eleazar's Speeches at Masada]

6. . . . "Since we long ago, my generous friends, resolved never to be servants to the Romans, nor to any other than to God himself, who alone is the true and just Lord of mankind, the time is now come that obliges us to make that resolution true in practice: and let us not at this time bring a reproach upon ourselves for self-contradiction, while we formerly would not undergo slavery, though it were then without danger, but must now, together with slavery, choose such punishments also as are intolerable: I mean this upon the supposition that the Romans once reduce us under their power while we are

alive. We were the very first that revolted from them, and we are the last that fight against them; and I cannot but esteem it as a favor that God hath granted us, that it is still in our power to die bravely and in a state of freedom, which hath not been the case of others who were conquered unexpectedly. It is very plain that we shall be taken within a day's time; but it is still an eligible thing to die after a glorious manner, together with our dearest friends. This is what our enemies themselves cannot by any means hinder, although they be very desirous to take us alive. Nor can we propose to ourselves any more to fight them and beat them. It had been proper, indeed, for us to have conjectured at the purpose of God much sooner, and at the very first, when we were so desirous of defending our liberty, and when we received such sore treatment from one another, and worse treatment from our enemies, and to have been sensible that the same God who had of old taken the Jewish nation into his favor, had now condemned them to destruction; for had he either continued favorable, or been but in a lesser degree displeased with us, he had not overlooked the destruction of so many men, or delivered his most holy city to be burnt and demolished by our enemies. To be sure we weakly hoped to have preserved ourselves, and ourselves alone, still in a state of freedom, as if we had been guilty of no sins ourselves against God, nor been partners with those of others; we also taught other men to preserve their liberty. Wherefore, consider how God hath convinced us that our hopes were in vain, by bringing such distress upon us in the desperate state we are now in, and which is beyond all our expectations; for the nature of this fortress, which was in itself unconquerable, hath not proved a means of our deliverance; and even while we have still great abundance of food, and a great quantity of arms, and other necessaries more than we want, we are openly deprived by God himself of all hope of deliverance; for that fire which was driven upon our enemies did not of its own accord, turn back upon the wall which we had built: this was the effect of God's anger against us for our manifold sins, which we have been guilty of in a most insolent and extravagant manner with regard to our own countrymen; the punishments of which let us not receive from the Romans, but from God himself, as executed by our own hands; for these will be more moderate than the other. Let our wives die before they are abused, and our children before they have tasted of slavery; and after we have slain them, let us bestow that glorious benefit upon one another mutually, and preserve ourselves in freedom, as an excellent funeral monument for us. But first let us destroy our money and the fortress by fire; for I am well assured that this would be a great grief to the Romans, that they shall not be able to seize upon our bodies and shall fail of our wealth also: and let us spare nothing but our provisions; for they will be a testimony when we are dead that we were not subdued for want of necessaries, but that, according to our original resolution, we have preferred death before slavery.

7. . . . . "The circumstances we are now in ought to be an inducement to us to bear such calamity courageously, since it is by the will of God and by necessity that we are to die; for it now appears that God hath made such a decree against the whole Jewish nation, that we are to be deprived of this life which [he knew] we would not make a due use of: for do not you ascribe the occasion of our present condition to yourselves, nor think the Romans are the true occasion that this war we have had with them is become so destructive to us all: these things have not come to pass by their power, but a more powerful cause hath intervened, and made us afford them an occasion of their appearing to be conquerors over us. What Roman weapons, I pray you, were those by which the Jews of Cæsarea were slain? On the contrary, when they were no way disposed to rebel, but were all the while keeping their seventh day festival and did not so much as lift up their hands against the citizens of Cæsarea, yet did those citizens run upon them in great crowds, and cut their throats and the throats of their wives and children, and this without any regard to the Romans themselves, who never took us for their enemies till we revolted from them. But some may be ready to say, that truly the people of Cæsarea had always a quarrel against those that lived among them, and that, when an opportunity offered itself, they only satisfied the old rancor they had against them. What then shall we say to those of Scythopolis, who ventured to wage war with us on account of the Greeks? Nor did they do it by way of revenge upon the Romans, when they acted in concert with our countrymen. Wherefore, you see how little our good-will and fidelity to them profited us, while they were slain, they and their whole families, after the most inhuman manner, which was all the requital that was made them for the assistance they had afforded the others: for that very same destruction which they had prevented from falling upon the others did they suffer themselves from them, as if they had been ready to be the actors against them. It would be too long for me to speak at this time of every destruction brought upon us: for you cannot but know that there was not any one Syrian city which did not slay their Jewish inhabitants, and were not more bitter enemies to us than were the Romans themselves: nay, even those of Damascus, when they were able to allege no tolerable pretence against us, filled their city with the most barbarous slaughters of our people, and cut the throats of eighteen thousand Jews, with their wives and children. And as to the multitude of those that were slain in Egypt, and that with torments also, we have been informed they were more than sixty thousand: those, indeed, being in a foreign country, and so naturally meeting with nothing to oppose

against their enemies, were killed in the manner forementioned. As for all those of us who have waged war against the Romans in our own country, had we not sufficient reason to have sure hopes of victory? for we had arms and walls, and fortresses so prepared as not to be easily taken, and courage not to be moved by any dangers in the cause of liberty, which encouraged us all to revolt from the Romans. But then these advantages sufficed us but for a short time, and only raised our hopes, while they really appeared to be the origin of our miseries; for all we had hath been taken from us, and all hath fallen under our enemies, as if these advantages were only to render their victory over us the more glorious, and were not disposed for the preservation of those by whom these preparations were made. And as for those that are already dead in the war, it is reasonable we should esteem them blessed, for they are dead in defending and not in betraying their liberty; but as to the multitude of those that are now under the Romans, who would not pity their condition? and who would not make haste to die, before he would suffer the same miseries with them? Some of them have been put upon the rack, and tortured with fire and whippings, and so died. Some have been half-devoured by wild beasts and yet have been reserved alive to be devoured by them a second time, in order to afford laughter and sport to our enemies; and such of those as are alive, still are to be looked on as the most miserable, who being so desirous of death could not come at it. And where is now that great city, the metropolis of the Jewish nation? which was fortified by so many walls round about, which had so many fortresses and large towers to defend it, which could hardly contain the instruments prepared for the war, and which had so many ten thousands of men to fight for it? Where is this city that was believed to have God himself inhabitant therein? It is now demolished to the very foundations, and hath nothing but that monument of it preserved, I mean the camp of those that hath destroyed it, which still dwells upon its ruins; some unfortunate old men also lie upon the ashes of the temple, and a few women are there preserved alive by the enemy for our bitter shame and reproach. Now, who is there that revolves these things in his mind, and yet is able to bear the sight of the sun, though he might live out of danger? Who is there so much his country's enemy, or so unmanly, and so desirous of living, as not to repent that he is still alive? and I cannot but wish that we had all died before we had seen that holy city demolished by the hands of our enemies or the foundations of our holy temple dug up after so profane a manner. But since we had a generous hope that deluded us, as if we might, perhaps, have been able to avenge ourselves on our enemies on that account, though it be now become vanity, and hath left us alone in this distress, let us make haste to die bravely. Let us pity ourselves, our children, and our wives, while it is in our own power to show pity to them; for we were born to die, as well as those were whom we have begotten, nor is it in the power of the most happy of our race to avoid it. But for abuses and slavery, and the sight of our wives led away after an ignominious manner, with their children, these are not such evils as are natural and necessary among men; although such as do not prefer death before those miseries, when it is in their power to so do, must undergo even them on account of their own cowardice. We revolted from the Romans with great pretensions to courage; and when at the very last, they invited us to preserve ourselves, we would not comply with them. Who will not, therefore, believe that they will certainly be in a rage at us, in case they can take us alive? Miserable will then be the young men who will be strong enough in their bodies to sustain many torments; miserable also will be those of elder years, who will not be able to bear those calamities which young men might sustain. One man will be obliged to hear the voice of his son imploring help of his father, when his hands are bound. But certainly our hands are still at liberty, and have a sword in them; let them, then, be subservient to us in our glorious design; let us die before we become slaves under our enemies, and let us go out of the world, together with our children and our wives, in a state of freedom. This it is that our laws command us to do; this it is that our wives and children crave at our hands; nay, God himself hath brought this necessity upon us; while the Romans desire the contrary, and are afraid lest any of us should die before we are taken. Let us, therefore, make haste, and, instead of affording them so much pleasure as they hope for in getting us under their power, let us leave them an example which shall at once cause their astonishment at our death, and their admiration of our hardiness therein."

23

Ignatius of Antioch

Epistle to the Magnesians

Renowned among the Apostolic Fathers (i.e., those who knew or were directly influenced by the Apostles), Ignatius (ca. 35–107 AD) was the second or third bishop of Antioch (Syria). In addition to his teachings on the nature of Jesus (i.e., both fully God and fully human), Ignatius was also a strong proponent of monepiscopacy—illustrating the church polity used by the generations just after the apostolic era. In the following selection, for example, Ignatius encouraged the honor due to those appointed to the bishopric. Arrested and sentenced to death for his faith, Ignatius wrote several letters to various churches as he was marched to Rome for his execution—including the following Epistle to the Magnesians.

Ignatius, who is also called Theophorus, to the [Church] blessed in the grace of God the Father, in Jesus Christ our Saviour, in whom I salute the Church which is at Magnesia, near the Maeander, and wish it abundance of happiness in God the Father, and in Jesus Christ.

Chap. I.—Reason of Writing the Epistle.

Having been informed of your godly love, so well-ordered, I rejoiced greatly, and determined to commune with you in the faith of Jesus Christ. For as one who has been thought worthy of the most honourable of all names; in those bonds which I bear about, I commend the Churches, in which I pray for a union both of the flesh and spirit of Jesus Christ, the constant source of our

SOURCE: *The Ante-Nicene Fathers: Translations of the Writings of the Fathers down to A.D. 325*, vol. 1, *The Apostolic Fathers, with Justin Martyr and Irenaeus*, ed. Alexander Roberts and James Donaldson, revised and chronologically arranged with brief prefaces and occasional notes by A. Cleveland Coxe (New York: Charles Scribner's Sons, 1903), 59–65 [shorter version].

life, and of faith and love, to which nothing is to be preferred, but especially of Jesus and the Father, in whom, if we endure all the assaults of the prince of this world, and escape them, we shall enjoy God.

Chap. II.—I Rejoice in Your Messengers.

Since, then, I have had the privilege of seeing you, through Damas your most worthy bishop, and through your worthy presbyters Bassus and Apollonius, and through my fellow servant the deacon Sotio, whose friendship may I ever enjoy, inasmuch as he is subject to the bishop as to the grace of God, and to the presbytery as to the law of Jesus Christ, [I now write to you].

Chap. III.—Honour Your Youthful Bishop.

Now it becomes you also not to treat your bishop too familiarly on account of his youth, but to yield him all reverence, having respect to the power of God the Father, as I have known even holy presbyters do, not judging rashly, from the manifest youthful appearance [of their bishop], but as being themselves prudent in God, submitting to him, or rather not to him, but to the Father of Jesus Christ, the bishop of us all. It is therefore fitting that you should, after no hypocritical fashion, obey [your bishop], in honour of Him who has willed us [so to do], since he that does not so deceives not [by such conduct] the bishop that is visible, but seeks to mock Him that is invisible. And all such conduct has reference not to man, but to God, who knows all secrets.

Chap. IV.—Some Wickedly Act Independently of the Bishop.

It is fitting, then, not only to be called Christians, but to be so in reality: as some indeed give one the title of bishop, but do all things without him. Now such persons seem to me to be not possessed of a good conscience, seeing they are not stedfastly gathered together according to the commandment.

Chap. V.—Death Is the Fate of All Such.

Seeing, then, all things have an end, these two things are simultaneously set before us—death and life; and every one shall go unto his own place. For as there are two kinds of coins, the one of God, the other of the world, and each of these has its special character stamped upon it, [so is it also here]. The unbelieving are of this world; but the believing have, in love, the character of God the Father by Jesus Christ, by whom, if we are not in readiness to die into His passion, His life is not in us.

Chap. VI.—Preserve Harmony.

Since therefore I have, in the persons before mentioned, beheld the whole multitude of you in faith and love, I exhort you to study to do all things with a divine harmony, while your bishop presides in the place of God, and your presbyters in the place of the assembly of the apostles, along with your deacon, who are most dear to me, and are entrusted with the ministry of Jesus Christ, who was with the Father before the beginning of time, and in the end was revealed. Do ye all then, imitating the same divine conduct, pay respect to one another, and let no one look upon his neighbour after the flesh, but do ye continually love each other in Jesus Christ. Let nothing exist among you that may divide you; but be ye united with your bishop, and those that preside over you, as a type and evidence of your immortality.

Chap. VII.—Do Nothing without the Bishop and Presbyters.

As therefore the Lord did nothing without the Father, being united to Him, neither by Himself nor by the apostles, so neither do ye anything without the bishop and presbyters. Neither endeavour that anything appear reasonable and proper to yourselves apart; but being come together into the same place, let there be one prayer, one supplication, one mind, one hope, in love and in joy undefiled. There is one Jesus Christ, than whom nothing is more excellent. Do ye therefore all run together as into one temple of God, as to one altar, as to one Jesus Christ, who came forth from one Father, and is with and has gone to one.

Chap. VIII.—Caution against False Doctrines.

Be not deceived with strange doctrines, nor with old fables, which are unprofitable. For if we still live according to the Jewish law, we acknowledge that we have not received grace. For the divinest prophets lived according to Christ Jesus. On this account also they were persecuted, being inspired by His grace to fully convince the unbelieving that there is one God, who has manifested Himself by Jesus Christ His Son, who is His eternal Word, not proceeding forth from silence, and who in all things pleased Him that sent Him.

Chap. IX.—Let Us Live with Christ.

If, therefore, those who were brought up in the ancient order of things have come to the possession of a new hope, no longer observing the Sabbath, but living in the observance of the Lord's Day, on which also our life has sprung up again by Him and by His death—whom some deny, by which mystery we have obtained faith, and therefore endure, that we may be found the disciples of Jesus Christ, our only Master—how shall we be able to live apart from Him, whose disciples the prophets themselves in the Spirit did wait for Him as their Teacher? And therefore He whom they rightly waited for, being come, raised them from the dead.

Chap. X.—Beware of Judaizing.

Let us not, therefore, be insensible to His kindness. For were He to reward us according to our works, we should cease to be. Therefore, having become His disciples, let us learn to live according to the principles of Christianity. For whosoever is called by any other name besides this, is not of God. Lay aside, therefore, the evil, the old, the sour leaven, and be ye changed into the new leaven, which is Jesus Christ. Be ye salted in Him, lest anyone among you should be corrupted, since by your savour ye shall be convicted. It is absurd to profess Christ Jesus, and to Judaize. For Christianity did not embrace Judaism, but Judaism Christianity, that so every tongue which believeth might be gathered together to God.

Chap. XI.—I Write These Things to Warn You.

These things [I address to you], my beloved, not that I know any of you to be in such a state, but, as less than any of you, I desire to guard you beforehand, that ye fall not upon the hooks of vain doctrine, but that ye attain to full assurance in regard to the birth, and passion, and resurrection which took place in the time of the government of Pontius Pilate, being truly and certainly accomplished by Jesus Christ, who is our hope, from which may no one of you ever be turned aside.

Chap. XII.—Ye Are Superior to Me.

May I enjoy you in all respects, if indeed I be worthy! For though I am bound, I am not worthy to be compared to any of you that are at liberty. I know that ye are not puffed up, for ye have Jesus Christ in yourselves. And all the more when I commend you, I know that ye cherish modesty of spirit; as it is written, "The righteous man is his own accuser."

Chap. XIII.—Be Established in Faith and Unity.

Study, therefore, to be established in the doctrines of the Lord and the apostles, that so all things, whatsoever ye do, may prosper both in the flesh and spirit; in faith and love; in the Son, and in the Father, and in the Spirit; in the beginning and in the end; with your most admirable bishop, and the well-compacted spiritual crown of your presbytery, and the deacons who are according to God. Be ye subject to the bishop, and to one another, as Jesus Christ to the Father, according to the flesh, and the apostles to Christ, and to the Father, and to the Spirit; that so there may be a union both fleshly and spiritual.

Chap. XIV.—Your Prayers Requested.

Knowing as I do that ye are full of God, I have but briefly exhorted you. Be mindful of me in your prayers, that I may attain to God; and of the Church which is in Syria, whence I am not worthy to derive my name: for I stand in need of your united prayer in God, and your love, that the Church which is in Syria may be deemed worthy of being refreshed by your Church.

Chap. XV.—Salutations.

The Ephesians from Smyrna (whence I also write to you), who are here for the glory of God, as ye also are, who have in all things refreshed me, salute you, along with Polycarp, the bishop of the Smyrnaeans. The rest of the Churches, in honour of Jesus Christ, also salute you. Fare ye well in the harmony of God, ye who have obtained the inseparable Spirit, who is Jesus Christ.

24

Plutarch

from *Lives*

Although he is often described as a historian, Plutarch (ca. 45–120 AD) understood his work as biography, raising questions about virtue. He often paired Greek and Roman figures, providing a synopsis of their lives in order to invite ethical comparisons of their characters and pivotal decisions, as seen in the following excerpt. Although his reputation was more enduring in the Greek East than in the Latin West, his work was rediscovered during the Renaissance period and continued to be influential through the eighteenth century. Several notable figures of America's Revolutionary era, for example, found inspiration and guidance in his work.

The Comparison of Demosthenes and Cicero

These are the most memorable circumstances recorded in history of Demosthenes and Cicero which have come to our knowledge. But omitting an exact comparison of their respective faculties in speaking, yet thus much seems fit to be said; that Demosthenes, to make himself a master in rhetoric, applied all the faculties he had, natural or acquired, wholly that way; that he far surpassed in force and strength of eloquence all his contemporaries in political and judicial speaking, in grandeur and majesty all the panegyrical orators, and in accuracy and science all the logicians and rhetoricians of his day; that Cicero was highly educated, and by his diligent study became a most accomplished general scholar in all these branches, having left behind him numerous philosophical treatises of his own on Academic principles; as, indeed, even in his written speeches, both political and judicial, we see him continually trying

SOURCE: Plutarch, *Plutarch's Lives: The "Dryden Plutarch," Revised by Arthur Hugh Clough*, vol. 3 (New York: E. P. Dutton & Co., 1912), 223–27.

to show his learning by the way. And one may discover the different temper of each of them in their speeches. For Demosthenes's oratory was without all embellishment and jesting, wholly composed for real effect and seriousness; not smelling of the lamp, as Pytheas scoffingly said, but of the temperance, thoughtfulness, austerity, and grave earnestness of his temper. Whereas Cicero's love of mockery often ran him into scurrility; and in his love of laughing away serious arguments in judicial cases by jests and facetious remarks, with a view to the advantage of his clients, he paid too little regard to what was decent: saying, for example, in his defence of Cælius, that he had done no absurd thing in such plenty and affluence to indulge himself in pleasures, it being a kind of madness not to enjoy the things we possess, especially since the most eminent philosophers have asserted pleasures to be the chiefest good. So also we are told that when Cicero, being consul, undertook the defence of Murena against Cato's prosecution, by way of bantering Cato, he made a long series of jokes upon the absurd *paradoxes*, as they are called, of the Stoic set; so that a loud laughter passing from the crowd to the judges, Cato, with a quiet smile, said to those that sat next him, "My friends, what an amusing consul we have."

And, indeed, Cicero was by natural temper very much disposed to mirth and pleasantry, and always appeared with a smiling and serene countenance. But Demosthenes had constant care and thoughtfulness in his look, and a serious anxiety, which he seldom, if ever laid aside; and, therefore, was accounted by his enemies, as he himself confessed, morose and ill-mannered.

Also, it is very evident, out of their several writings, that Demosthenes never touched upon his own praises but decently and without offence when there was need of it, and for some weightier end; but, upon other occasions modestly and sparingly. But Cicero's immeasurable boasting of himself in his orations argues him guilty of an uncontrollable appetite for distinction, his cry being evermore that arms should give place to the gown, and the soldier's laurel to the tongue. And at last we find him extolling not only his deeds and actions, but his orations also, as well those that were only spoken, as those that were published; as if he were engaged in a boyish trial of skill, who should speak best, with the rhetoricians, Isocrates and Anaximenes, not as one who could claim the task to guide and instruct the Roman nation, the—

"Soldier full-armed, terrific to the foe."

It is necessary, indeed, for a political leader to be an able speaker; but it is an ignoble thing for any man to admire and relish the glory of his own eloquence. And, in this matter, Demosthenes had a more than ordinary gravity and magnificence of mind, accounting his talent in speaking nothing more than a mere accomplishment and matter of practice, the success of which must depend greatly on the good-will and candour of his hearers, and regarding those who pride themselves on such accounts to be men of a low and petty disposition.

The power of persuading and governing the people did, indeed, equally belong to both, so that those who had armies and camps at command stood in need of their assistance; as Charas, Diopithes, and Leosthenes of Demosthenes's, Pompey and young Cæsar of Cicero's, as the latter himself admits in his Memoirs addressed to Agrippa and Mæcenas. But what are thought and commonly said most to demonstrate and try the tempers of men, namely, authority and place, by moving every passion, and discovering every frailty, these are things which Demosthenes never received; nor was he ever in a position to give such proof of himself, having never obtained any eminent office, nor led any of those armies into the field against Philip which he raised by his eloquence. Cicero, on the other hand, was sent quæstor into Sicily, and proconsul into Cilicia and Cappadocia, at a time when avarice was at the height, and the commanders and governors who were employed abroad, as though they thought it a mean thing to steal, set themselves to seize by open force; so that it seemed no heinous matter to take bribes, but he that did it most moderately was in good esteem. And yet he, at this time, gave the most abundant proofs alike of his contempt of riches and of his humanity and good-nature. And at Rome, when he was created consul in name, but indeed received sovereign and dictatorial authority against Catiline and his conspirators, he attested the truth of Plato's prediction, that then the miseries of states would be at an end, when by a happy fortune, supreme power, wisdom, and justice should be united in one.

It is said, to the reproach of Demosthenes, that his eloquence was mercenary; that he privately made orations for Phormion and Apollodorus, though adversaries in the same cause; that he was charged with moneys received from the king of Persia, and condemned for bribes from Harpalus. And should we grant that all those (and they are not few) who have made these statements against him have spoken what is untrue, yet that Demosthenes was not the character to look without desire on the presents offered him out of respect and gratitude by royal persons, and that one who lent money on maritime usury was likely to be thus indifferent, is what we cannot assert. But that Cicero refused, from the Sicilians when he was quæstor, from the king of Cappadocia when he was proconsul, and from his friends at Rome when he was in exile, many presents, though urged to receive them, has been said already.

Moreover, Demosthenes's banishment was infamous, upon conviction for bribery; Cicero's very honourable, for ridding his country of a set of villains. Therefore, when Demosthenes fled his country, no man regarded it; for

Cicero's sake the senate changed their habit, and put on mourning, and would not be persuaded to make any act before Cicero's return was decreed. Cicero, however, passed his exile idly in Macedonia. But the very exile of Demosthenes made up a great part of the services he did for his country; for he went through the cities of Greece, and everywhere, as we have said joined in the conflict on behalf of the Grecians, driving out the Macedonian ambassadors, and approving himself a much better citizen than Themistocles and Alcibiades did in the like fortune. And, after his return, he again devoted himself to the same public service, and continued firm to his opposition to Antipater and the Macedonians. Whereas Lælius reproached Cicero in the senate for sitting silent when Cæsar, a beardless youth, asked leave to come forward contrary to the law, as a candidate for the consulship; and Brutus, in his epistles, charges him with nursing and rearing a greater and more heavy tyranny than that they had removed.

Finally, Cicero's death excites our pity; for an old man to be miserably carried up and down by his servants, flying and hiding himself from that death which was, in the course of nature, so near at hand; and yet at last to be murdered. Demosthenes, though he seemed at first a little to supplicate, yet, by his preparing and keeping the poison by him, demands our admiration; and still more admirable was his using it. When the temple of the god no longer afforded him a sanctuary, he took refuge, as it were, at a mightier altar, freeing himself from arms and soldiers, and laughing to scorn the cruelty of Antipater.

25

Epictetus

from *Enchiridion*

Epictetus (ca. 50–135 AD) was a Greek Stoic philosopher who spent a portion of his life as a slave until he was freed in Rome, where he taught for a while until he eventually fled to Nicopolis. Although Epictetus was by no means the founder of Stoicism—it was founded centuries earlier by Zeno of Citium (344–262 BC)—he is nonetheless an important representative of this school of thought. This is in part because only small fragments and testimonia from Stoicism's earliest architects remain, whereas we do have complete works from Epictetus, along with those of Seneca (ca. 1–65 AD) and Marcus Aurelius (121–180 AD). Stoicism holds that the good life consists in aligning one's internal states of mind with the way things are in the mind-external world. The following are aphorisms from Epictetus' *Enchiridion*, which is a relatively short handbook or manual on how to live the Stoic way.

––––––––––

I. There are things which are within our power, and there are things which are beyond our power. Within our power are opinion, aim, desire, aversion, and, in one word, whatever affairs are our own. Beyond our power are body, property, reputation, office, and, in one word, whatever are not properly our own affairs.

Now the things within our power are by nature free, unrestricted, unhindered; but those beyond our power are weak, dependent, restricted, alien. Remember then, that, if you attribute freedom to things by nature dependent, and take what belongs to others for your own; you will be hindered, you will lament, you will be disturbed, you will find fault both with Gods and men. But

SOURCE: Epictetus, *Enchiridion*, in *The Works of Epictetus, Consisting of His Discourses, in Four Books, the Enchiridion, and Fragments*, trans. based on that of Elizabeth Carter by Thomas Wentworth Higginson (Boston: Little, Brown, and Co., 1865), 375–85.

if you take for your own only that which is your own, and view what belongs to others just as it really is, then no one will ever compel you, no one will restrict you, you will find fault with no one, you will accuse no one, you will do nothing against your will; no one will hurt you, you will not have an enemy, nor will you suffer any harm.

Aiming therefore at such great things, remember that you must not allow yourself any inclination, however slight, towards the attainment of the others; but that you must entirely quit some of them, and for the present postpone the rest. But if you would have these, and possess power and wealth likewise, you may miss the latter in seeking the former; and you will certainly fail of that, by which alone happiness and freedom are procured.

Seek at once, therefore, to be able to say to every unpleasing semblance, "You are but a semblance and by no means the real thing." And then examine it by those rules which you have; and first and chiefly, by this: whether it concerns the things which are within our own power, or those which are not; and if it concerns anything beyond our power, be prepared to say that it is nothing to you.

II. Remember that desire demands the attainment of that of which you are desirous; and aversion demands the avoidance of that to which you are averse; that he who fails of the object of his desires, is disappointed; and he who incurs the object of his aversion, is wretched. If, then, you shun only those undesirable things which you can control, you will never incur anything which you shun. But if you shun sickness, or death, or poverty, you will run the risk of wretchedness. Remove aversion, then, from all things that are not within our power, and transfer it to things undesirable, which are within our power. But for the present altogether restrain desire; for if you desire any of the things not within our own power, you must necessarily be disappointed; and you are not yet secure of those which are within our power, and so are legitimate objects of desire. Where it is practically necessary for you to pursue or avoid anything, do even this with discretion, and gentleness, and moderation.

III. With regard to whatever objects either delight the mind, or contribute to use, or are tenderly beloved, remind yourself of what nature they are, beginning with the merest trifles: if you have a favorite cup, that it is a cup of which you are fond; for thus, if it is broken, you can bear it: if you embrace your child, or your wife, that you embrace a mortal; and thus, if either of them dies, you can bear it.

IV. When you set about any action, remind yourself of what nature the action is. If you are going to bathe, represent to yourself the incidents usual in the bath; some persons pouring out, others pushing in, others scolding, others pilfering. And thus you will more safely go about this action, if you say to yourself, "I will now go to bathe, and keep my own will in harmony with nature." And so with regard to every other action. For thus, if any impediment arises in bathing, you will be able to say, "It was not only to bathe that I desired, but to keep my will in harmony with nature; and I shall not keep it thus, if I am out of humor at things that happen."

V. Men are disturbed not by things, but by the views which they take of things. Thus death is nothing terrible, else it would have appeared so to Socrates. But the terror consists in our notion of death, that it is terrible. When, therefore, we are hindered, or disturbed, or grieved, let us never impute it to others, but to ourselves; that is, to our own views. It is the action of an uninstructed person to reproach others for his own misfortunes; of one entering upon instruction, to reproach himself; and of one perfectly instructed, to reproach neither others nor himself.

VI. Be not elated at any excellence not your own. If a horse should be elated, and say, "I am handsome," it might be endurable. But when you are elated, and say, "I have a handsome horse," know that you are elated only on the merit of the horse. What, then, is your own? The use of the phenomena of existence. So that when you are in harmony with nature in this respect, you will be elated with some reason; for you will be elated at some good of your own.

VII. As in a voyage, when the ship is at anchor, if you go on shore to get water, you may amuse yourself with picking up a shell-fish or a truffle in your way; but your thoughts ought to be bent towards the ship, and perpetually attentive, lest the captain should call; and then you must leave all these things, that you may not have to be carried on board the vessel, bound like a sheep. Thus likewise in life, if, instead of a truffle or shell-fish, such a thing as a wife or a child be granted you, there is no objection; but if the captain calls, run to the ship, leave all these things, and never look behind. But if you are old, never go far from the ship, lest you should be missing when called for.

VIII. Demand not that events should happen as you wish; but wish them to happen as they do happen, and you will go on well.

IX. Sickness is an impediment to the body, but not to the will, unless itself pleases. Lameness is an impediment to the leg, but not to the will; and say this to yourself with regard to everything that happens. For you will find it to be an impediment to something else, but not truly to yourself.

X. Upon every accident, remember to turn towards yourself and inquire what faculty you have for its use. If you encounter a handsome person, you will find continence the faculty needed; if pain, then fortitude; if reviling, then patience. And when thus habituated, the phenomena of existence will not overwhelm you.

XI. Never say of anything, "I have lost it"; but, "I have restored it." Has your child died? It is restored. Has your wife died? She is restored. Has your estate been taken away? That likewise is restored. "But it was a bad man who took it." What is it to you, by whose hands He who gave it hath demanded it again? While He permits you to possess it, hold it as something not your own; as do travellers at an inn.

XII. If you would improve, lay aside such reasonings as these: "If I neglect my affairs, I shall not have a maintenance; if I do not punish my servant, he will be good for nothing." For it were better to die of hunger, exempt from grief and fear, than to live in affluence with perturbation; and it is better that your servant should be bad than you unhappy.

Begin therefore with little things. Is a little oil spilt or a little wine stolen? Say to yourself, "This is the price paid for peace and tranquillity; and nothing is to be had for nothing." And when you call your servant, consider that it is possible he may not come at your call; or, if he does, that he may not do what you wish. But it is not at all desirable for him, and very undesirable for you, that it should be in his power to cause you any disturbance.

XIII. If you would improve, be content to be thought foolish and dull with regard to externals. Do not desire to be thought to know anything; and though you should appear to others to be somebody, distrust yourself. For be assured, it is not easy at once to keep your will in harmony with nature, and to secure externals; but while you are absorbed in the one, you must of necessity neglect the other.

XIV. If you wish your children, and your wife, and your friends, to live forever, you are foolish; for you wish things to be in your power which are not so; and what belongs to others, to be your own. So likewise, if you wish your servant to be without fault, you are foolish; for you wish vice not to be vice, but something else. But if you wish not to be disappointed in your desires, that is in your own power. Exercise, therefore, what is in your power. A man's master is he who is able to confer or remove whatever that man seeks or shuns. Whoever then would be free, let him wish nothing, let him decline nothing, which depends on others; else he must necessarily be a slave.

XV. Remember that you must behave as at a banquet. Is anything brought round to you? Put out your hand, and take a moderate share. Does it pass by you? Do not stop it. Is it not yet come? Do not yearn in desire towards it, but wait till it reaches you. So with regard to children, wife, office, riches; and you will some time or other be worthy to feast with the Gods. And if you do not so much as take the things which are set before you, but are able even to forego them, then you will not only be worthy to feast with the Gods, but to rule with them also. For, by thus doing, Diogenes and Heraclitus, and others like them, deservedly became divine, and were so recognized.

XVI. When you see any one weeping for grief, either that his son has gone abroad, or that he has suffered in his affairs; take care not to be overcome by the apparent evil. But discriminate, and be ready to say, "What hurts this man is not this occurrence itself, for another man might not be hurt by it;—but the view he chooses to take of it." As far as conversation goes, however, do not disdain to accommodate yourself to him, and if need be, to groan with him. Take heed, however, not to groan inwardly too.

XVII. Remember that you are an actor in a drama of such sort as the author chooses. If short, then in a short one; if long, then in a long one. If it be his pleasure that you should act a poor man, see that you act it well; or a cripple, or a ruler, or a private citizen. For this is your business, to act well the given part; but to choose it, belongs to another.

XVIII. When a raven happens to croak unluckily, be not overcome by appearances, but discriminate, and say, "Nothing is portended to *me*; but either to my paltry body, or property, or reputation, or children, or wife. But to *me* all portents are lucky, if I will. For whatsoever happens, it belongs to me to derive advantage therefrom."

XIX. You can be unconquerable, if you enter into no combat, in which it is not in your own power to conquer. When, therefore, you see any one eminent in honors or power, or in high esteem on any other account, take heed not to be bewildered by appearances and to pronounce him happy; for if the essence of good consists in things within our own power, there will be no room for envy or emulation. But, for your part, do not desire to be a general, or a senator, or a consul, but to be free; and the only way to this is, a disregard of things which lie not within our own power.

XX. Remember that it is not he who gives abuse or blows who affronts; but the view we take of these things as insulting. When, therefore, any one provokes you, be assured that it is your own opinion which provokes you. Try, therefore, in the first place, not to be bewildered by appearances. For if you once gain time and respite, you will more easily command yourself.

XXI. Let death and exile, and all other things which appear terrible, be daily before your eyes, but death chiefly; and you will never entertain any abject thought, nor too eagerly covet anything.

XXII. If you have an earnest desire towards philosophy, prepare yourself from the very first to have the multitude laugh and sneer, and say, "He is returned to us a philosopher all at once"; and "Whence this supercilious look?" Now for your part, do not have a supercilious look indeed; but keep steadily to those things which appear best to you, as one appointed by God to this particular station. For remember that, if you are persistent, those very persons who at first ridiculed, will afterwards admire you. But if you are conquered by them, you will incur a double ridicule.

XXIII. If you ever happen to turn your attention to externals, for the pleasure of any one, be assured that you have ruined your scheme of life. Be contented, then, in everything, with being a philosopher; and, if you wish to seem so likewise to any one, appear so to yourself, and it will suffice you.

XXIV. Let not such considerations as these distress you: "I shall live in discredit, and be nobody anywhere." For if discredit be an evil, you can no more be involved in evil through another, than in baseness. Is it any business of yours, then, to get power, or to be admitted to an entertainment? By no means. How then, after all, is this discredit? And how is it true that you will be nobody anywhere; when you ought to be somebody in those things only which are within your own power, in which you may be of the greatest consequence? "But my friends will be unassisted." What do you mean by unassisted? They will not have money from you; nor will you make them Roman citizens. Who told you, then, that these are among the things within our own power; and not rather the affairs of others? And who can give to another the things which he himself has not? "Well, but get them, then, that we too may have a share." If I can get them with the preservation of my own honor, and fidelity, and self-respect, show me the way, and I will get them; but if you require me to lose my own proper good, that you may gain what is no good, consider how unreasonable and foolish you are. Besides, which would you rather have, a sum of money, or a faithful and honorable friend? Rather assist me, then, to gain this character, than require me to do those things by which I may lose it. Well, but my country, say you, as far as depends upon me, will be unassisted. Here again, what assistance is this you mean? It will not have porticos nor baths of your providing? And what signifies that? Why, neither does a smith provide it with shoes, nor a shoemaker with arms. It is enough if every one fully performs his own proper business. And were you to supply it with another faithful and honorable citizen, would not he be of use to it? Yes. Therefore neither are you yourself useless to it. "What place then," say you, "shall I hold in the state?" Whatever you can hold with the preservation of your fidelity and honor. But if, by desiring to be useful to that, you lose these, how can you serve your country, when you have become faithless and shameless?

XXV. Is any one preferred before you at an entertainment, or in courtesies, or in confidential intercourse? If these things are good, you ought to rejoice that he has them; and if they are evil, do not be grieved that you have them not. And remember that you cannot be permitted to rival others in externals, without using the same means to obtain them. For how can he, who will not haunt the door of any man, will not attend him, will not praise him, have an equal share with him who does these things? You are unjust, then, and unreasonable, if you are unwilling to pay the price for which these things are sold, and would have them for nothing. For how much are lettuces sold? An obolus, for instance. If another, then, paying an obolus takes the lettuces, and you, not paying it, go without them, do not imagine that he has gained any advantage over you. For as he has the lettuces, so you have the obolus which you did not give. So, in the present case, you have not been invited to such a person's entertainment; because you have not paid him the price for which a supper is sold. It is sold for praise; it is sold for attendance. Give him, then, the value, if it be for your advantage. But if you would at the same time not pay the one, and yet receive the other, you are unreasonable and foolish. Have you nothing, then, in place of the supper? Yes, indeed you have; not to praise him whom you do not like to praise; not to bear the insolence of his lackeys.

from *Didache*

chapters 1–5

Although referenced in early Christian writings, the *Didache* (or *The Teaching of the Twelve Apostles*) was lost until the late nineteenth century. Of unknown authorship, its style and content fit material associated with the Apostolic Fathers (i.e., those who knew or were directly influenced by the apostles), thereby dating it to the early second century. Perhaps designed for catechumens, the text provides insight into postapostolic thought and practice. The first part discusses Christian ethics. The text's second part explains practices of worship (e.g., baptism and Eucharist), while a third section provides guidelines for distinguishing true from false teachers. The following excerpt is the text's first part.

I. There are two paths, one of life and one of death, and the difference is great between the two paths.

Now the path of life is this—first, thou shalt love the God who made thee, thy neighbour as thyself, and all things that thou wouldest not should be done unto thee, do not thou unto another. And the doctrine of these maxims is as follows. Bless them that curse you, and pray for your enemies. Fast on behalf of those that persecute you; for what thank is there if ye love them that love you? do not even the Gentiles do the same? But do ye love them that hate you, and ye will not have an enemy. Abstain from fleshly and worldly lusts. If any one give thee a blow on thy right cheek, turn unto him the other also, and thou shalt be perfect; if any one compel thee to go a mile, go with him two; if a man take away thy cloak, give him thy coat also; if a man take from thee what is thine, ask not for it again, for neither art thou able to do so. Give to every one

SOURCE: *The Didache, or Teaching of the Twelve Apostles, Restored to Its Original State from Various Sources*, trans. Charles H. Hoole (London: David Nutt, 1894), 75–79.

that asketh of thee, and ask not again, for the Father wishes that from his own gifts there should be given to all. Blessed is he who giveth according to the commandment, for he is free from guilt; but woe unto him that receiveth. For if a man receive being in need, he shall be free from guilt; but he who receiveth when not in need, shall pay a penalty as to why he received and for what purpose; and when he is in tribulation he shall be examined concerning the things that he has done, and shall not depart thence until he has paid the last farthing. For of a truth it has been said on these matters, Let thy almsgiving abide in thy hands until thou knowest to whom thou hast given.

II. But the second commandment of the teaching is this. Thou shalt not kill; thou shalt not commit adultery; thou shalt not corrupt youth; thou shalt not commit fornication; thou shalt not steal; thou shalt not use soothsaying; thou shalt not practice sorcery; thou shalt not kill a child by abortion, neither shalt thou slay it when born; thou shalt not covet the goods of thy neighbour; thou shalt not commit perjury; thou shalt not bear false witness; thou shalt not speak evil; thou shalt not bear malice; thou shalt not be double-minded or double-tongued, for to be double-tongued is the snare of death. Thy speech shall not be false or empty, but concerned with action. Thou shalt not be covetous, or rapacious, or hypocritical, or malicious, or proud; thou shalt not take up an evil design against thy neighbour; thou shalt not hate any man, but some thou shalt confute, concerning some thou shalt pray, and some thou shalt love beyond thine own soul.

III. My child, fly from everything that is evil, and from everything that is like to it. Be not wrathful, for wrath leadeth unto slaughter; be not jealous, or contentious, or quarrelsome, for from all these things slaughter ensues. My child, be not lustful, for lust leadeth unto fornication; be not a filthy talker; be not a lifter up of the eye, for from all these things come adulteries. My child, be not an observer of omens, since it leadeth to idolatry, nor a user of spells, nor an astrologer, nor a travelling purifier, nor wish to see these things, for from all these things idolatry ariseth. My child, be not a liar, for lying leadeth unto theft; be not covetous or conceited, for from all these things thefts arise. My child, be not a murmurer, since it leadeth unto blasphemy; be not self-willed or evil-minded, for from all these things blasphemies are produced; but be thou meek, for the meek shall inherit the earth; be thou long-suffering, and compassionate, and harmless, and peaceable, and good, and fearing alway the words that thou hast heard. Thou shalt not exalt thyself, neither shalt thou put boldness into thy soul. Thy soul shall not be joined unto the lofty, but thou shalt walk with the just and humble. Accept the things that happen to thee as good, knowing that without God nothing happens.

IV. My child, thou shalt remember both night and day him that speaketh unto thee the word of God; thou shalt honour him as thou dost the Lord, for where the teaching of the Lord is given, there is the Lord; thou shalt seek out day by day the favour of the saints, that thou mayest rest in their words; thou shalt not desire schism, but shalt set at peace them that contend; thou shalt judge righteously; thou shalt not accept the person of any one to convict him of transgression; thou shalt not doubt whether a thing shall be or not. Be not a stretcher out of thy hand to receive, and a drawer of it back in giving. If thou hast, give by means of thy hands a redemption for thy sins. Thou shalt not doubt to give, neither shalt thou murmur when giving; for thou shouldest know who is the fair recompenser of the reward. Thou shalt not turn away from him that is in need, but shalt share with thy brother in all things, and shalt not say that things are thine own; for if ye are partners in what is immortal, how much more in what is mortal? Thou shalt not remove thine heart from thy son or from thy daughter, but from their youth shalt teach them the fear of God. Thou shalt not command with bitterness thy servant or thy handmaid, who hope in the same God as thyself, lest they fear not in consequence the God who is over both; for he cometh not to call with respect of persons, but those whom the Spirit hath prepared. And do ye servants submit yourselves to your masters with reverence and fear, as being the type of God. Thou shalt hate all hypocrisy and everything that is not pleasing to God; thou shalt not abandon the commandments of the Lord, but shalt guard that which thou hast received, neither adding thereto nor taking therefrom; thou shalt confess thy transgressions in the church, and shalt not come unto prayer with an evil conscience. This is the path of life.

V. But the path of death is this. First of all, it is evil and full of cursing; there are found murders, adulteries, lusts, fornication, thefts, idolatries, soothsaying, sorceries, robberies, false witnessings, hypocrisies, double-mindedness, craft, pride, malice, self-will, covetousness, filthy talking, jealousy, audacity, arrogance; there are they who persecute the good—lovers of a lie, not knowing the reward of righteousness, not cleaving to the good nor to righteous judgment, watching not for the good but for the bad, from whom meekness and patience are afar off, loving things that are vain, following after recompense, having no compassion on the needy, nor labouring for him that is in trouble, not knowing him that made them, murderers of children, corrupters of the image of God, who turn away from him that is in need, who oppress him that is in trouble, unjust judges of the poor, erring in all things. From all these, children, may ye be delivered.

Justin Martyr

from *Second Apology*

One of the foremost Christian apologists of the second century, Justin (ca. 100–165) studied classical philosophy before converting to Christianity. Even after his conversion, he continued wearing his philosopher's robe, laboring to reconcile faith and reason. Having embraced Christianity less as competing with Greek ideas, he saw the new movement more as a completion or fulfillment of the reason promoted by the Greeks. His *Second Apology*, from which the following is an excerpt, is an address to the Roman Senate, in which he contends that Christian faith was ultimately the most rational way of thinking. Ultimately, the Roman Prefect had Justin arrested and beheaded. Killed for advocating "true philosophy," Christian history has granted him the martyr's "crown."

Chap. VIII.—All Have Been Hated in Whom the Word Has Dwelt.

And those of the Stoic school—since, so far as their moral teaching went, they were admirable, as were also the poets in some particulars, on account of the seed of reason [the Logos] implanted in every race of men—were, we know, hated and put to death,—Heraclitus for instance, and, among those of our own time, Musonius and others. For, as we intimated, the devils have always effected, that all those who anyhow live a reasonable and earnest life, and shun vice, be hated. And it is nothing wonderful; if the devils are proved to cause those to be much worse hated who live not according to a part only of the word diffused [among men] but by the knowledge and contemplation

SOURCE: Justin Martyr, *Second Apology*, in *The Ante-Nicene Fathers: Translations of the Writings of the Fathers down to A.D. 325*, vol. 1, *The Apostolic Fathers with Justin Martyr and Irenaeus*, ed. Alexander Roberts and James Donaldson, revised and chronologically arranged with brief prefaces and occasional notes by A. Cleveland Coxe (New York: Charles Scribner's Sons, 1903), 191–93.

of the whole Word, which is Christ. And they, having been shut up in eternal fire, shall suffer their just punishment and penalty. For if they are even now overthrown by men through the name of Jesus Christ, this is an intimation of the punishment in eternal fire which is to be inflicted on themselves and those who serve them. For thus did both all the prophets foretell, and our own teacher Jesus teach.

Chap. IX.—Eternal Punishment Not a Mere Threat.

And that no one may say what is said by those who are deemed philosophers, that our assertions that the wicked are punished in eternal fire are big words and bugbears, and that we wish men to live virtuously through fear, and not because such a life is good and pleasant; I will briefly reply to this, that if this be not so, God does not exist; or, if He exists, He cares not for men, and neither virtue nor vice is anything, and, as we said before, lawgivers unjustly punish those who transgress good commandments. But since these are not unjust, and their Father teaches them by the word to do the same things as Himself, they who agree with them are not unjust. And if one object that the laws of men are diverse, and say that with some, one thing is considered good, another evil, while with others what seemed bad to the former is esteemed good, and what seemed good is esteemed bad, let him listen to what we say to this. We know that the wicked angels appointed laws conformable to their own wickedness, in which the men who are like them delight; and the right Reason, when He came, proved that not all opinions nor all doctrines are good, but that some are evil, while others are good. Wherefore, I will declare the same and similar things to such men as these, and, if need be, they shall be spoken of more at large. But at present I return to the subject.

Chap. X.—Christ Compared with Socrates.

Our doctrines, then, appear to be greater than all human teaching; because Christ, who appeared for our sakes, became the whole rational being, both body, and reason, and soul. For whatever either lawgivers or philosophers uttered well, they elaborated by finding and contemplating some part of the Word. But since they did not know the whole of the Word, which is Christ, they often contradicted themselves. And those who by human birth were more ancient than Christ, when they attempted to consider and prove things by reason, were brought before the tribunals as impious persons and busybodies. And Socrates, who was more zealous in this direction than all of them, was accused of the very same crimes as ourselves. For they said that he was introducing new divinities, and did not consider those to be gods whom the state recognised. But he cast out from the state both Homer and the rest of the poets, and taught men to reject the wicked demons and those who did the things which the poets related; and he exhorted them to become acquainted with the God who was to them unknown, by means of the investigation of reason, saying, "That it is neither easy to find the Father and Maker of all, nor, having found Him, is it safe to declare Him to all." But these things our Christ did through His own power. For no one trusted in Socrates so as to die for this doctrine, but in Christ, who was partially known even by Socrates (for He was and is the Word who is in every man, and who foretold the things that were to come to pass both through the prophets and in His own person when He was made of like passions, and taught these things), not only philosophers and scholars believed, but also artisans and people entirely uneducated, despising both glory, and fear, and death; since He is a power of the ineffable Father, not the mere instrument of human reason.

Chap. XI.—How Christians View Death.

But neither should we be put to death, nor would wicked men and devils be more powerful than we, were not death a debt due by every man that is born. Wherefore we give thanks when we pay this debt. And we judge it right and opportune to tell here, for the sake of Crescens and those who rave as he does, what is related by Xenophon. Hercules, says Xenophon, coming to a place where three ways met, found Virtue and Vice, who appeared to him in the form of women: Vice, in a luxurious dress, and with a seductive expression rendered blooming by such ornaments, and her eyes of a quickly melting tenderness, said to Hercules that if he would follow her, she would always enable him to pass his life in pleasure and adorned with the most graceful ornaments, such as were then upon her own person; and Virtue, who was of squalid look and dress, said, But if you obey me, you shall adorn yourself not with ornament nor beauty that passes away and perishes, but with everlasting and precious graces. And we are persuaded that every one who flees those things that seem to be good, and follows hard after what are reckoned difficult and strange, enters into blessedness. For Vice, when by imitation of what is incorruptible (for what is really incorruptible she neither has nor can produce) she has thrown around her own actions, as a disguise, the properties of virtue, and qualities which are really excellent, leads captive earthly-minded men, attaching to Virtue her own evil properties. But those who understood the excellences which belong to that which is real, are also uncorrupt in virtue. And this every sensible person ought to think both of Christians and of the athletes, and of those who did what the poets relate of the so-called gods, concluding as much from our contempt of death, even when it could be escaped.

Chap. XII.—Christians Proved Innocent by Their Contempt of Death.

For I myself, too, when I was delighting in the doctrines of Plato, and heard the Christians slandered, and saw them fearless of death, and of all other things which are counted fearful, perceived that it was impossible that they could be living in wickedness and pleasure. For what sensual or intemperate man, or who that counts it good to feast on human flesh, could welcome death that he might be deprived of his enjoyments, and would not rather continue always the present life, and attempt to escape the observation of the rulers; and much less would he denounce himself when the consequence would be death? This also the wicked demons have now caused to be done by evil men. For having put some to death on account of the accusations falsely brought against us, they also dragged to the torture our domestics, either children or weak women, and by dreadful torments forced them to admit those fabulous actions which they themselves openly perpetrate; about which we are the less concerned, because none of these actions are really ours, and we have the unbegotten and ineffable God as witness both of our thoughts and deeds. For why did we not even publicly profess that these were the things which we esteemed good, and prove that these are the divine philosophy, saying that the mysteries of Saturn are performed when we slay a man, and that when we drink our fill of blood, as it is said we do, we are doing what you do before that idol you honour, and on which you sprinkle the blood not only of irrational animals, but also of men, making a libation of the blood of the slain by the hand of the most illustrious and noble man among you? And imitating Jupiter and the other gods in sodomy and shameless intercourse with woman, might we not bring as our apology the writings of Epicurus and the poets? But because we persuade men to avoid such instruction, and all who practise them and imitate such examples, as now in this discourse we have striven to persuade you, we are assailed in every kind of way. But we are not concerned, since we know that God is a just observer of all. But would that even now some one would mount a lofty rostrum, and shout with a loud voice, "Be ashamed, be ashamed, ye who charge the guiltless with those deeds which yourselves openly commit, and ascribe things which apply to yourselves and to your gods to those who have not even the slightest sympathy with them. Be ye converted; become wise."

Chap. XIII.—How the Word Has Been in All Men.

For I myself, when I discovered the wicked disguise which the evil spirits had thrown around the divine doctrines of the Christians, to turn aside others from joining them, laughed both at those who framed these falsehoods, and at the disguise itself, and at popular opinion; and I confess that I both boast and with all my strength strive to be found a Christian; not because the teachings of Plato are different from those of Christ, but because they are not in all respects similar, as neither are those of the others, Stoics, and poets, and historians. For each man spoke well in proportion to the share he had of the spermatic word, seeing what was related to it. But they who contradict themselves on the more important points appear not to have possessed the heavenly wisdom, and the knowledge which cannot be spoken against. Whatever things were rightly said among all men, are the property of us Christians. For next to God, we worship and love the Word who is from the unbegotten and ineffable God, since also He became man for our sakes, that becoming a partaker of our sufferings, He might also bring us healing. For all the writers were able to see realities darkly through the sowing of the implanted word that was in them. For the seed and imitation impacted according to capacity is one thing, and quite another is the thing itself, of which there is the participation and imitation according to the grace which is from Him.

Chap. XIV.—Justin Prays That This Appeal Be Published.

And we therefore pray you to publish this little book, appending what you think right, that our opinions may be known to others, and that these persons may have a fair chance of being freed from erroneous notions and ignorance of good, who by their own fault are become subject to punishment; that so these things may be published to men, because it is in the nature of man to know good and evil; and by their condemning us, whom they do not understand, for actions which they say are wicked, and by delighting in the gods who did such things, and even now require similar actions from men, and by inflicting on us death or bonds or some other such punishment, as if we were guilty of these things, they condemn themselves, so that there is no need of other judges.

Chap. XV.—Conclusion.

And I despised the wicked and deceitful doctrine of Simon of my own nation. And if you give this book your authority, we will expose him before all, that, if possible, they may be converted. For this end alone did we compose this treatise. And our doctrines are not shameful, according to a sober judgment, but are indeed more lofty than all human philosophy: and if not so, they are at least unlike the doctrines of the Sotadists, and Philænidians, and Dancers, and Epicureans, and such other teachings of the poets, which all are allowed to acquaint themselves with, both as acted and as written. And henceforth we shall be silent, having done as much as we could, and having added the prayer that all men everywhere may be counted worthy of the truth. And would that you also, in a manner becoming piety and philosophy, would for your own sakes judge justly!

28

Marcus Aurelius

from *Meditations*

Marcus Aurelius Antoninus (121–180) was adopted by Emperor Pius Antoninus as a boy and eventually became the Roman Emperor from 161 until 180—a period marked by war, insurrections, and disease. Influenced by the Stoic philosopher Epictetus, Marcus would eventually become one of the most important proponents of Stoicism in his own right. His most famous written work is his *Meditations*, which reads like a series of practical reflections written to himself on how to apply Stoic principles to life.

———————————

VIII.

This reflection also tends to the removal of the desire of empty fame, that it is no longer in thy power to have lived the whole of thy life, or at least thy life from thy youth upwards, like a philosopher; but both to many others and to thyself it is plain that thou art far from philosophy. Thou hast fallen into disorder then, so that it is no longer easy for thee to get the reputation of a philosopher; and thy plan of life also opposes it. If then thou hast truly seen where the matter lies, throw away the thought, How thou shalt seem [to others], and be content if thou shalt live the rest of thy life in such wise as thy nature wills. Observe then what it wills, and let nothing else distract thee; for thou hast had experience of many wanderings without having found happiness anywhere,— not in syllogisms, nor in wealth, nor in reputation, nor in enjoyment, nor anywhere. Where is it then? In doing what man's nature requires. How then shall a man do this? If he has principles from which come his affects and his acts. What principles? Those which relate to good and bad: the belief that there is

SOURCE: Marcus Aurelius Antoninus, *The Thoughts of the Emperor Marcus Aurelius Antoninus*, trans. George Long (Boston: Little, Brown, and Co., 1889), 194–212.

nothing good for man which does not make him just, temperate, manly, free; and that there is nothing bad which does not do the contrary to what has been mentioned.

2. On the occasion of every act ask thyself, How is this with respect to me? Shall I repent of it? A little time and I am dead, and all is gone. What more do I seek, if what I am now doing is the work of an intelligent living being, and a social being, and one who is under the same law with God?

3. Alexander and Caius and Pompeius, what are they in comparison with Diogenes and Heraclitus and Socrates? For they were acquainted with things, and their causes [forms], and their matter, and the ruling principles of these men were the same [or conformable to their pursuits]. But as to the others, how many things had they to care for, and to how many things were they slaves!

4. [Consider] that men will do the same things nevertheless, even though thou shouldst burst.

5. This is the chief thing: Be not perturbed, for all things are according to the nature of the universal; and in a little time thou wilt be nobody and nowhere, like Hadrianus and Augustus. In the next place, having fixed thy eyes steadily on thy business look at it, and at the same time remembering that it is thy duty to be a good man, and what man's nature demands, do that without turning aside; and speak as it seems to thee most just, only let it be with a good disposition and with modesty and without hypocrisy.

6. The nature of the universal has this work to do,—to remove to that place the things which are in this, to change them, to take them away hence, and to carry them there. All things are change, yet we need not fear anything new. All things are familiar [to us]; but the distribution of them still remains the same.

7. Every nature is contented with itself when it goes on its way well; and a rational nature goes on its way well when in its thoughts it assents to nothing false or uncertain, and when it directs its movements to social acts only, and when it confines its desires and aversions to the things which are in its power, and when it is satisfied with everything that is assigned to it by the common nature. For of this common nature every particular nature is a part, as the nature of the leaf is a part of the nature of the plant; except that in the plant the nature of the leaf is part of a nature which has not perception or reason, and is subject to be impeded; but the nature of man is part of a nature which is not subject to impediments, and is intelligent and just, since it gives to everything in equal portions and according to its worth, times, substance, cause [form], activity, and incident. But examine, not to discover that any one thing compared with any other single thing is equal in all respects, but by taking all the

parts together of one thing and comparing them with all the parts together of another.

8. Thou hast not leisure [or ability] to read. But thou hast leisure [or ability] to check arrogance: thou hast leisure to be superior to pleasure and pain: thou hast leisure to be superior to love of fame, and not to be vexed at stupid and ungrateful people, nay even to care for them.

9. Let no man any longer hear thee finding fault with the court life or with thy own. . . .

10. Repentance is a kind of self-reproof for having neglected something useful; but that which is good must be something useful, and the perfect good man should look after it. But no such man would ever repent of having refused any sensual pleasure. Pleasure then is neither good nor useful.

11. This thing, what is it in itself, in its own constitution? What is its substance and material? And what its causal nature [or form]? And what is it doing in the world? And how long does it subsist?

12. When thou risest from sleep with reluctance, remember that it is according to thy constitution and according to human nature to perform social acts, but sleeping is common also to irrational animals. But that which is according to each individual's nature is also more peculiarly its own, and more suitable to its nature, and indeed also more agreeable. . . .

13. Constantly, and, if it be possible, on the occasion of every impression on the soul, apply to it the principles of Physic, of Ethic, and of Dialectic.

14. Whatever man thou meetest with, immediately say to thyself: What opinions has this man about good and bad? For if with respect to pleasure and pain and the causes of each, and with respect to fame and ignominy, death and life, he has such and such opinions, it will seem nothing wonderful or strange to me if he does such and such things; and I shall bear in mind that he is compelled to do so.

15. Remember that as it is a shame to be surprised if the fig-tree produces figs, so it is to be surprised if the world produces such and such things of which it is productive; and for the physician and the helmsman it is a shame to be surprised if a man has a fever, or if the wind is unfavorable.

16. Remember that to change thy opinion and to follow him who corrects thy error is as consistent with freedom as it is to persist in thy error. For it is thy own, the activity which is exerted according to thy own movement and judgment, and indeed according to thy own understanding too.

17. If a thing is in thy own power, why dost thou do it? but if it is in the power of another, whom dost thou blame,—the atoms [chance] or the gods? Both are foolish. Thou must blame nobody. For if thou canst, correct [that which is

the cause]; but if thou canst not do this, correct at least the thing itself; but if thou canst not do even this, of what use is it to thee to find fault? for nothing should be done without a purpose.

18. That which has died falls not out of the universe. If it stays here, it also changes here, and is dissolved into its proper parts, which are elements of the universe and of thyself. And these too change, and they murmur not.

19. Everything exists for some end,—a horse, a vine. Why dost thou wonder? Even the sun will say, I am for some purpose, and the rest of the gods will say the same. For what purpose then art thou,—to enjoy pleasure? See if common sense allows this.

20. Nature has had regard in everything no less to the end than to the beginning and the continuance, just like the man who throws up a ball. What good is it then for the ball to be thrown up, or harm for it to come down, or even to have fallen? and what good is it to the bubble while it holds together, or what harm when it is burst? The same may be said of a light also.

21. Turn it [the body] inside out, and see what kind of thing it is; and when it has grown old, what kind of thing it becomes, and when it is diseased.

Short lived are both the praiser and the praised, and the rememberer and the remembered: and all this in a nook of this part of the world; and not even here do all agree, no, not any one with himself: and the whole earth too is a point.

22. Attend to the matter which is before thee, whether it is an opinion or an act or a word.

Thou sufferest this justly: for thou choosest rather to become good tomorrow than to be good to-day.

23. Am I doing anything? I do it with reference to the good of mankind. Does anything happen to me? I receive it and refer it to the gods, and the source of all things, from which all that happens is derived.

24. Such as bathing appears to thee,—oil, sweat, dirt, filthy water, all things disgusting,—so is every part of life and everything.

25. Lucilla saw Verus die, and then Lucilla died. Secunda saw Maximus die, and then Secunda died. Epitynchanus saw Diotimus die, and then Epitynchanus died. Antoninus saw Faustina die, and then Antoninus died. Such is everything. Celer saw Hadrianus die, and then Celer died. And those sharp-witted men, either seers or men inflated with pride, where are they,—for instance the sharp-witted men, Charax and Demetrius the Platonist, and Eudaemon, and any one else like them? All ephemeral, dead long ago. Some indeed have not been remembered even for a short time, and others have become the heroes of fables, and again others have disappeared even from fables. Remember this

then, that this little compound, thyself, must either be dissolved, or thy poor breath must be extinguished, or be removed and placed elsewhere.

26. It is satisfaction to a man to do the proper works of a man. Now it is a proper work of a man to be benevolent to his own kind, to despise the movements of the senses, to form a just judgment of plausible appearances, and to take a survey of the nature of the universe and of the things which happen in it.

27. There are three relations [between thee and other things]: the one to the body which surrounds thee; the second to the divine cause from which all things come to all; and the third to those who live with thee.

28. Pain is either an evil to the body—then let the body say what it thinks of it—or to the soul; but it is in the power of the soul to maintain its own serenity and tranquillity, and not to think that pain is an evil. For every judgment and movement and desire and aversion is within, and no evil ascends so high.

29. Wipe out thy imaginations by often saying to thyself: Now it is in my power to let no badness be in this soul, nor desire, nor any perturbation at all; but looking at all things I see what is their nature, and I use each according to its value.—Remember this power which thou hast from nature.

30. Speak both in the senate and to every man, whoever he may be, appropriately, not with any affectation: use plain discourse.

31. Augustus' court, wife, daughter, descendants, ancestors, sister, Agrippa, kinsmen, intimates, friends; Areius, Maecenas, physicians, and sacrificing priests,—the whole court is dead. Then turn to the rest, not considering the death of a single man [but of a whole race], as of the Pompeii; and that which is inscribed on the tombs,—The last of his race. Then consider what trouble those before them have had that they might leave a successor; and then, that of necessity some one must be the last. Again, here consider the death of a whole race.

32. It is thy duty to order thy life well in every single act; and if every act does its duty as far as is possible, be content; and no one is able to hinder thee so that each act shall not do its duty.—But something external will stand in the way.—Nothing will stand in the way of thy acting justly and soberly and considerately.—But perhaps some other active power will be hindered.—Well, but by acquiescing in the hindrance and by being content to transfer thy efforts to that which is allowed, another opportunity of action is immediately put before thee in place of that which was hindered, and one which will adapt itself to this ordering of which we are speaking.

33. Receive [wealth or prosperity] without arrogance; and be ready to let it go.

34. If thou didst ever see a hand cut off, or a foot, or a head, lying anywhere apart from the rest of the body, such does a man make himself, as far as he can, who is not content with what happens, and separates himself from others, or

does anything unsocial. Suppose that thou hast detached thyself from the natural unity,—for thou wast made by nature a part, but now thou hast cut thyself off,—yet here there is this beautiful provision, that it is in thy power again to unite thyself. God has allowed this to no other part, after it has been separated and cut asunder, to come together again. But consider the kindness by which he has distinguished man, for he has put it in his power not to be separated at all from the universal; and when he has been separated, he has allowed him to return and to be united and to resume his place as a part.

35. As the nature of the universal has given to every rational being all the other powers that it has, so we have received from it this power also. For as the universal nature converts and fixes in its predestined place everything which stands in the way and opposes it, and makes such things a part of itself, so also the rational animal is able to make every hindrance its own material, and to use it for such purposes as it may have designed.

36. Do not disturb thyself by thinking of the whole of thy life. Let not thy thoughts at once embrace all the various troubles which thou mayest expect to befall thee: but on every occasion ask thyself, What is there in this which is intolerable and past bearing? for thou wilt be ashamed to confess. In the next place remember that neither the future nor the past pains thee, but only the present. But this is reduced to a very little, if thou only circumscribest it, and chidest thy mind if it is unable to hold out against even this.

37. Does Panthea or Pergamus now sit by the tomb of Verus? Does Chaurias or Diotimus sit by the tomb of Hadrianus? That would be ridiculous. Well, suppose they did sit there, would the dead be conscious of it? and if the dead were conscious, would they be pleased? and if they were pleased, would that make them immortal? Was it not in the order of destiny that these persons too should first become old women and old men and then die? What then would those do after these were dead? All this is foul smell and blood in a bag.

38. If thou canst see sharp, look and judge wisely, says the philosopher.

39. In the constitution of the rational animal I see no virtue which is opposed to justice; but I see a virtue which is opposed to love of pleasure, and that is temperance.

40. If thou takest away thy opinion about that which appears to give thee pain, thou thyself standest in perfect security.—Who is this self?—The reason.—But I am not reason.—Be it so. Let then the reason itself not trouble itself. But if any other part of thee suffers, let it have its own opinion about itself. . . .

41. Hindrance to the perceptions of sense is an evil to the animal nature. Hindrance to the movements [desires] is equally an evil to the animal

nature. And something else also is equally an impediment and an evil to the constitution of plants. So then that which is a hindrance to the intelligence is an evil to the intelligent nature. Apply all these things then to thyself. Does pain or sensuous pleasure affect thee? The senses will look to that. Has any obstacle opposed thee in thy efforts towards an object? If indeed thou wast making this effort absolutely [unconditionally, or without any reservation], certainly this obstacle is an evil to thee considered as a rational animal. But if thou takest [into consideration] the usual course of things, thou hast not yet been injured nor even impeded. The things however which are proper to the understanding no other man is used to impede, for neither fire, nor iron, nor tyrant, nor abuse, touches it in any way. When it has been made a sphere, it continues a sphere. . . .

42. It is not fit that I should give myself pain, for I have never intentionally given pain even to another.

43. Different things delight different people; but it is my delight to keep the ruling faculty sound without turning away either from any man or from any of the things which happen to men, but looking at and receiving all with welcome eyes and using everything according to its value.

44. See that thou secure this present time to thyself: for those who rather pursue posthumous fame do not consider that the men of after time will be exactly such as these whom they cannot bear now; and both are mortal. And what is it in any way to thee if these men of after time utter this or that sound, or have this or that opinion about thee?

45. Take me and cast me where thou wilt; for there I shall keep my divine part tranquil, that is, content, if it can feel and act comformably to its proper constitution. Is this [change of place] sufficient reason why my soul should be unhappy and worse than it was, depressed, expanded, shrinking, affrighted? and what wilt thou find which is sufficient reason for this?

46. Nothing can happen to any man which is not a human accident, nor to an ox which is not according to the nature of an ox, nor to a vine which is not according to the nature of a vine, nor to a stone which is not proper to a stone. If then there happens to each thing both what is usual and natural, why shouldst thou complain? For the common nature brings nothing which may not be borne by thee.

47. If thou art pained by any external thing, it is not this thing that disturbs thee, but thy own judgment about it. And it is in thy power to wipe out this judgment now. But if anything in thy own disposition gives thee pain, who hinders thee from correcting thy opinion? And even if thou art pained because thou art not doing some particular thing which seems to thee to be right, why

dost thou not rather act than complain?—But some insuperable obstacle is in the way?—Do not be grieved then, for the cause of its not being done depends not on thee.—But it is not worth while to live, if this cannot be done.—Take thy departure then from life contentedly, just as he dies who is in full activity, and well pleased too with the things which are obstacles.

48. Remember that the ruling faculty is invincible, when self-collected it is satisfied with itself, if it does nothing which it does not choose to do, even if it resist from mere obstinacy. What then will it be when it forms a judgment about anything aided by reason and deliberately? Therefore the mind which is free from passions is a citadel, for man has nothing more secure to which he can fly for refuge and for the future be inexpugnable. He then who has not seen this is an ignorant man; but he who has seen it and does not fly to this refuge is unhappy.

49. Say nothing more to thyself than what the first appearances report. Suppose that it has been reported to thee that a certain person speaks ill of thee. This has been reported; but that thou hast been injured, that has not been reported. I see that my child is sick. I do see; but that he is in danger, I do not see. Thus then always abide by the first appearances, and add nothing thyself from within, and then nothing happens to thee. Or rather add something like a man who knows everything that happens in the world.

50. A cucumber is bitter—Throw it away.—There are briers in the road—Turn aside from them.—This is enough. Do not add, And why were such things made in the world? For thou wilt be ridiculed by a man who is acquainted with nature, as thou wouldst be ridiculed by a carpenter and shoemaker if thou didst find fault because thou seest in their workshop shavings and cuttings from the things which they make. And yet they have places into which they can throw these shavings and cuttings, and the universal nature has no external space; but the wondrous part of her art is that though she has circumscribed herself, everything within her which appears to decay and to grow old and to be useless she changes into herself, and again makes other new things from these very same, so that she requires neither substance from without nor wants a place into which she may cast that which decays. She is content then with her own space, and her own matter, and her own art.

51. Neither in thy actions be sluggish nor in thy conversation without method, nor wandering in thy thoughts, nor let there be in thy soul inward contention nor external effusion, nor in life be so busy as to have no leisure.

Suppose that men kill thee, cut thee in pieces, curse thee. What then can these things do to prevent thy mind from remaining pure, wise, sober, just? For instance, if a man should stand by a limpid pure spring, and curse it, the spring never ceases sending up potable water; and if he should cast clay into it or filth, it will speedily disperse them and wash them out, and will not be at all polluted. How then shalt thou possess a perpetual fountain [and not a mere well]? By forming thyself hourly to freedom conjoined with contentment, simplicity, and modesty.

52. He who does not know what the world is, does not know where he is. And he who does not know for what purpose the world exists, does not know who he is, nor what the world is. But he who has failed in any one of these things could not even say for what purpose he exists himself. What then dost thou think of him who [avoids or] seeks the praise of those who applaud, of men who know not either where they are or who they are?

53. Dost thou wish to be praised by a man who curses himself thrice every hour? wouldst thou wish to please a man who does not please himself? Does a man please himself who repents of nearly everything that he does?

54. No longer let thy breathing only act in concert with the air which surrounds thee, but let thy intelligence also now be in harmony with the intelligence which embraces all things. For the intelligent power is no less diffused in all parts and pervades all things for him who is willing to draw it to him than the aerial power for him who is able to respire it.

55. Generally, wickedness does no harm at all to the universe; and particularly the wickedness [of one man] does no harm to another. It is only harmful to him who has it in his power to be released from it as soon as he shall choose.

56. To my own free will the free will of my neighbor is just as indifferent as his poor breath and flesh. For though we are made especially for the sake of one another, still the ruling power of each of us has its own office, for otherwise my neighbor's wickedness would be my harm, which God has not willed, in order that my unhappiness may not depend on another.

57. The sun appears to be poured down, and in all directions indeed it is diffused, yet it is not effused. For this diffusion is extension: Accordingly its rays are called Extensions . . . because they are extended. . . . But one may judge what kind of a thing a ray is, if he looks at the sun's light passing through a narrow opening into a darkened room, for it is extended in a right line, and as it were is divided when it meets with any solid body which stands in the way and intercepts the air beyond; but there the light remains fixed and does not glide or fall off. Such then ought to be the outpouring and diffusion of the understanding, and it should in no way be an effusion, but an extension, and it should make no violent or impetuous collision with the obstacles which are in its way; nor yet fall down, but be fixed, and enlighten that which receives it. For a body will deprive itself of the illumination, if it does not admit it.

58. He who fears death either fears the loss of sensation or a different kind of sensation. But if thou shalt have no sensation, neither wilt thou feel any harm; and if thou shalt acquire another kind of sensation, thou wilt be a different kind of living being and thou wilt not cease to live.

59. Men exist for the sake of one another. Teach them then, or bear with them.

60. In one way an arrow moves, in another way the mind. The mind indeed, both when it exercises caution and when it is employed about inquiry, moves straight onward not the less, and to its object.

61. Enter into every man's ruling faculty; and also let every other man enter into thine.

Irenaeus

from Against Heresies

Born in Asia Minor, but ministering in southern Gaul (France), Irenaeus (ca. 130–200) is one of the foremost ante-Nicene Christian theologians. His most notable work, *Against Heresies* (ca. 180), provided an extended response to such unorthodox beliefs as Gnosticism, Docetism, and Ebionism. The following excerpt from Book IV is one of the texts used to argue that the doctrine of transubstantiation is of ancient origin, and not a medieval contrivance. The excerpt from Book V highlights Irenaeus' concern to root out heretical perspectives.

Book IV

Chap. XVIII.—Concerning Sacrifices and Oblations, and Those Who Truly Offer Them.

4. Inasmuch, then, as the Church offers with single-mindedness, her gift is justly reckoned a pure sacrifice with God. As Paul also says to the Philippians, "I am full, having received from Epaphroditus the things that were sent from you, the odour of a sweet smell, a sacrifice acceptable, pleasing to God." For it behoves us to make an oblation to God, and in all things to be found grateful to God our Maker, in a pure mind, and in faith without hypocrisy, in well-grounded hope, in fervent love, offering the first-fruits of His own created things. And the Church alone offers this pure oblation to the Creator, offering to Him, with giving of thanks, [the things taken] from His creation. But the

SOURCE: Irenaeus, *Against Heresies*, in *The Ante-Nicene Fathers: Translations of the Writings of the Fathers down to A.D. 325*, vol. 1, *The Apostolic Fathers with Justin Martyr and Irenaeus*, ed. Alexander Roberts and James Donaldson, revised and chronologically arranged with brief prefaces and occasional notes by A. Cleveland Coxe (New York: Charles Scribner's Sons, 1903), 485–86, 526–27.

Jews do not offer thus: for their hands are full of blood; for they have not received the Word, through whom it is offered to God. Nor, again, do any of the conventicles (*synagogae*) of the heretics [offer this]. For some, by maintaining that the Father is different from the Creator, do, when they offer to Him what belongs to this creation of ours, set Him forth as being covetous of another's property, and desirous of what is not His own. Those, again, who maintain that the things around us originated from apostasy, ignorance, and passion, do, while offering unto Him the fruits of ignorance, passion, and apostasy, sin against their Father, rather subjecting Him to insult than giving Him thanks. But how can they be consistent with themselves, [when they say] that the bread over which thanks have been given is the body of their Lord, and the cup His blood, if they do not call Himself the Son of the Creator of the world, that is, His Word, through whom the wood fructifies, and the fountains gush forth, and the earth gives "first the blade, then the ear, then the full corn in the ear."

5. Then, again, how can they say that the flesh, which is nourished with the body of the Lord and with His blood, goes to corruption, and does not partake of life? Let them, therefore, either alter their opinion, or cease from offering the things just mentioned. But our opinion is in accordance with the Eucharist, and the Eucharist in turn establishes our opinion. For we offer to Him His own, announcing consistently the fellowship and union of the flesh and Spirit. For as the bread, which is produced from the earth, when it receives the invocation of God, is no longer common bread, but the Eucharist, consisting of two realities, earthly and heavenly; so also our bodies, when they receive the Eucharist, are no longer corruptible, having the hope of the resurrection to eternity.

6. Now we make offering to Him, not as though He stood in need of it, but rendering thanks for His gift, and thus sanctifying what has been created. For even as God does not need our possessions, so do we need to offer something to God; as Solomon says: "He that hath pity upon the poor, lendeth unto the Lord." For God, who stands in need of nothing, takes our good works to Himself for this purpose, that He may grant us a recompense of His own good things, as our Lord says: "Come, ye blessed of My Father, receive the kingdom prepared for you. For I was an hungered, and ye gave Me to eat: I was thirsty, and ye gave Me drink: I was a stranger, and ye took Me in: naked, and ye clothed Me; sick, and ye visited Me; in prison, and ye came to Me." As, therefore, He does not stand in need of these [services], yet does desire that we should render them for our own benefit, lest we be unfruitful; so did the Word give to the people that very precept as to the making of oblations, although He stood in no need of them, that they might learn to serve God: thus is it,

therefore, also His will that we, too, should offer a gift at the altar, frequently and without intermission. The altar, then, is in heaven (for towards that place are our prayers and oblations directed); the temple likewise [is there], as John says in the Apocalypse, "And the temple of God was opened:" the tabernacle also: "For, behold," He says, "the tabernacle of God, in which He will dwell with men."

[. . . .]

Book V

Chap. I.—Christ Alone Is Able to Teach Divine Things, and to Redeem Us: He, the Same, Took Flesh of the Virgin Mary, Not Merely in Appearance, but Actually, by the Operation of the Holy Spirit, in Order to Renovate Us. Strictures on the Conceits of Valentinus and Ebion.

1. For in no other way could we have learned the things of God, unless our Master, existing as the Word, had become man. For no other being had the power of revealing to us the things of the Father, except His own proper Word. For what other person "knew the mind of the Lord," or who else "has become His counsellor?" Again, we could have learned in no other way than by seeing our Teacher, and hearing His voice with our own ears, that, having become imitators of His works as well as doers of His words, we may have communion with Him, receiving increase from the perfect One, and from Him who is prior to all creation. We—who were but lately created by the only best and good Being, by Him also who has the gift of immortality, having been formed after His likeness (predestinated, according to the prescience of the Father, that we, who had as yet no existence, might come into being), and made the first-fruits of creation—have received, in the times known beforehand, [the blessings of salvation] according to the ministration of the Word, who is perfect in all things, as the mighty Word, and very man, who, redeeming us by His own blood in a manner consonant to reason, gave Himself as a redemption for those who had been led into captivity. And since the apostasy tyrannized over us unjustly, and, though we were by nature the property of the omnipotent God, alienated us contrary to nature, rendering us its own disciples, the Word of God, powerful in all things, and not defective with regard to His own justice, did righteously turn against that apostasy, and redeem from it His own property, not by violent means, as the [apostasy] had obtained dominion over us at the beginning, when it insatiably snatched away what was not its own, but by means of persuasion, as became a God of counsel, who does not use violent means to obtain what He desires; so that neither should justice be infringed upon, nor the ancient handiwork of God go to destruction. Since the Lord

thus has redeemed us through His own blood, giving His soul for our souls, and His flesh for our flesh, and has also poured out the Spirit of the Father for the union and communion of God and man, imparting indeed God to men by means of the Spirit, and, on the other hand, attaching man to God by His own incarnation, and bestowing upon us at His coming immortality durably and truly, by means of communion with God,—all the doctrines of the heretics fall to ruin.

2. Vain indeed are those who allege that He appeared in mere seeming. For these things were not done in appearance only, but in actual reality. But if He did appear as a man, when He was not a man, neither could the Holy Spirit have rested upon Him,—an occurrence which did actually take place—as the Spirit is invisible; nor, [in that case], was there any degree of truth in Him, for He was not that which He seemed to be. But I have already remarked that Abraham and the other prophets beheld Him after a prophetical manner, foretelling in vision what should come to pass. If, then, such a being has now appeared in outward semblance different from what he was in reality, there has been a certain prophetical vision made to men; and another advent of His must be looked forward to, in which He shall be such as He has now been seen in a prophetic manner. And I have proved already, that it is the same thing to say that He appeared merely to outward seeming, and [to affirm] that He received nothing from Mary. For He would not have been one truly possessing flesh and blood, by which He redeemed us, unless He had summed up in Himself the ancient formation of Adam. Vain therefore are the disciples of Valentinus who put forth this opinion, in order that they may exclude the flesh from salvation, and cast aside what God has fashioned.

3. Vain also are the Ebionites, who do not receive by faith into their soul the union of God and man, but who remain in the old leaven of [the natural] birth, and who do not choose to understand that the Holy Ghost came upon Mary, and the power of the Most High did overshadow her: wherefore also what was generated is a holy thing, and the Son of the Most High God the Father of all, who effected the incarnation of this being, and showed forth a new [kind of] generation; that as by the former generation we inherited death, so by this new generation we might inherit life. Therefore do these men reject the commixture of the heavenly wine, and wish it to be water of the world only, not receiving God so as to have union with Him, but they remain in that Adam who had been conquered and was expelled from Paradise: not considering that as, at the beginning of our formation in Adam, that breath of life which proceeded from God, having been united to what had been fashioned, animated the man, and manifested him as a being endowed with reason; so also, in [the times of] the

end, the Word of the Father and the Spirit of God, having become united with the ancient substance of Adam's formation, rendered man living and perfect, receptive of the perfect Father, in order that as in the natural [Adam] we all were dead, so in the spiritual we may all be made alive. For never at any time did Adam escape the *hands* of God, to whom the Father speaking, said, "Let Us make man in Our image, after Our likeness." And for this reason in the last times (*fine*), not by the will of the flesh, nor by the will of man, but by the good pleasure of the Father, His hands formed a living man, in order that Adam might be created [again] after the image and likeness of God.

30

Clement of Alexandria

from *Stromata*

Clement of Alexandria (150–215) was an important early Christian apologist who tried to justify the Christian faith to classically trained philosophers. In the second and third centuries, popular prejudice presumed that Christianity was for the uneducated. Clement set out to prove quite the opposite. In the following excerpt, Clement acknowledges the truth found in Greek philosophy, but only as far as it could go without the aid of divine revelation. Christian-informed philosophy contributes important elements, enabling it to move ever closer to the truth. In this piece, Clement uses the term "gnostic," a Greek word for knowledge. Gnosticism in that era could refer to a dualistic heresy in which the flesh was evil, while the spirit was good. Here, however, Clement repurposes the term "gnostic" to suggest a knowledge informed by Christian revelation.

Book VII

Chap. I.—The Gnostic a True Worshipper of God, and Unjustly Calumniated by Unbelievers as an Atheist.

It is now time to show the Greeks that the Gnostic alone is truly pious; so that the philosophers, learning of what description the true Christian is, may condemn their own stupidity in rashly and inconsiderately persecuting the [Christian] name, and without reason calling those impious who know the true God. And clearer arguments must be employed, I reckon, with the philosophers, so that they may be able, from the exercise they have already had

SOURCE: Clement of Alexandria, *Stromata*, in *The Ante-Nicene Fathers: Translations of the Writings of the Fathers down to A.D. 325*, vol. 2, *Fathers of the Second Century: Hermas, Tatian, Athenagoras, Theophilus, and Clement of Alexandria*, ed. Alexander Roberts and James Donaldson, revised and chronologically arranged with brief prefaces and occasional notes by A. Cleveland Coxe (New York: Charles Scribner's Sons, 1905), 523–28.

through their own training, to understand, although they have not yet shown themselves worthy to partake of the power of believing.

[. . . .]

It is, then, our purpose to prove that the Gnostic alone is holy and pious, and worships the true God in a manner worthy of Him; and that worship meet for God is followed by loving and being loved by God. He accordingly judges all excellence to be honourable according to its worth; and judges that among the objects perceived by our senses, we are to esteem rulers, and parents, and every one advanced in years; and among subjects of instruction, the most ancient philosophy and primeval prophecy; and among intellectual ideas, what is oldest in origin, the timeless and unoriginated First Principle, and Beginning of existences—the Son—from whom we are to learn the remoter Cause, the Father, of the universe, the most ancient and the most beneficent of all; not capable of expression by the voice, but to be reverenced with reverence, and silence, and holy wonder, and supremely venerated; declared by the Lord, as far as those who learned were capable of comprehending, and understood by those chosen by the Lord to acknowledge; "whose senses," says the apostle, "were exercised." . . .

Similarly, also, in the Church, the elders attend to the department which has improvement for its object; and the deacons to the ministerial. In both these ministries the angels serve God, in the management of earthly affairs; and the Gnostic himself ministers to God, and exhibits to men the scheme of improvement, in the way in which he has been appointed to discipline men for their amendment. For he is alone pious that serves God rightly and unblameably in human affairs. For as that treatment of plants is best through which their fruits are produced and gathered in, through knowledge and skill in husbandry, affording men the benefit accruing from them; so the piety of the Gnostic, taking to itself the fruits of the men who by his means have believed, when not a few attain to knowledge and are saved by it, achieves by his skill the best harvest. And as Godliness . . . is the habit which preserves what is becoming to God, the godly man is the only lover of God, and such will he be who knows what is becoming, both in respect of knowledge and of the life which must be lived by him, who is destined to be divine . . ., and is already being assimilated to God. So then he is in the first place a lover of God. For as he who honours his father is a lover of his father, so he who honours God is a lover of God.

Thus also it appears to me that there are three effects of gnostic power: the knowledge of things; second, the performance of whatever the Word suggests;

and the third, the capability of delivering, in a way suitable to God, the secrets veiled in the truth.

[. . . .]

Chap. II.—The Son the Ruler and Saviour of All.

. . . And that He whom we call Saviour and Lord is the Son of God, the prophetic Scriptures explicitly prove. So the Lord of all, of Greeks and of Barbarians, persuades those who are willing. For He does not compel him who (through choosing and fulfilling, from Him, what pertains to laying hold of it the hope) is able to receive salvation from Him.

It is He who also gave philosophy to the Greeks by means of the inferior angels. For by an ancient and divine order the angels are distributed among the nations. But the glory of those who believe is "the Lord's portion." For either the Lord does not care for all men; and this is the case either because He is unable (which is not to be thought, for it would be a proof of weakness), or because He is unwilling, which is not the attribute of a good being. And He who for our sakes assumed flesh capable of suffering, is far from being luxuriously indolent. Or He does care for all, which is befitting for Him who has become Lord of all. For He is Saviour; not [the Saviour] of some, and of others not. But in proportion to the adaptation possessed by each, He has dispensed His beneficence both to Greeks and Barbarians, even to those of them that were predestinated, and in due time called, the faithful and elect. Nor can He who called all equally, and assigned special honours to those who have believed in a specially excellent way, ever envy any. Nor can He who is the Lord of all, and serves above all the will of the good and almighty Father, ever be hindered by another. But neither does envy touch the Lord, who without beginning was impassible; nor are the things of men such as to be envied by the Lord. But it is another, he whom passion hath touched, who envies. And it cannot be said that it is from ignorance that the Lord is not willing to save humanity, because He knows not how each one is to be cared for. For ignorance applies not to the God who, before the foundation of the world, was the counsellor of the Father. For He was the Wisdom "in which" the Sovereign God "delighted." For the Son is the power of God, as being the Father's most ancient Word before the production of all things, and His Wisdom. He is then properly called the Teacher of the beings formed by Him. Nor does He ever abandon care for men, by being drawn aside from pleasure, who, having assumed flesh, which by nature is susceptible of suffering, trained it to the condition of impassibility.

[. . . .]

Now that which is lovable leads, to the contemplation of itself, each one who, from love of knowledge, applies himself entirely to contemplation.

Wherefore also the Lord, drawing the commandments, both the first which He gave, and the second, from one fountain, neither allowed those who were before the law to be without law, nor permitted those who were unacquainted with the principles of the Barbarian philosophy to be without restraint. For, having furnished the one with the commandments, and the other with philosophy, He shut up unbelief to the Advent. Whence every one who believes not is without excuse. For by a different process of advancement, both Greek and Barbarian, He leads to the perfection which is by faith.

And if any one of the Greeks, passing over the preliminary training of the Hellenic philosophy, proceeds directly to the true teaching, he distances others, though an unlettered man, by choosing the compendious process of salvation by faith to perfection.

Everything, then, which did not hinder a man's choice from being free, He made and rendered auxiliary to virtue, in order that there might be revealed somehow or other, even to those capable of seeing but dimly, the one only almighty, good God—from eternity to eternity saving by His Son.

And, on the other hand, He is in no respect whatever the cause of evil. For all things are arranged with a view to the salvation of the universe by the Lord of the universe, both generally and particularly. It is then the function of the righteousness of salvation to improve everything as far as practicable. For even minor matters are arranged with a view to the salvation of that which is better, and for an abode suitable for people's character. Now everything that is virtuous changes for the better; having as the proper cause of change the free choice of knowledge, which the soul has in its own power. But necessary corrections, through the goodness of the great overseeing Judge, both by the attendant angels, and by various acts of anticipative judgment, and by the perfect judgment, compel egregious sinners to repent.

[. . . .]

Chap. III.—The Gnostic Aims at the Nearest Likeness Possible to God and His Son.

. . . Now the Greek philosophy, as it were, purges the soul, and prepares it beforehand for the reception of faith, on which the Truth builds up the edifice of knowledge.

This is the true athlete—he who in the great stadium, the fair world, is crowned for the true victory over all the passions. For He who prescribes the contest is the Almighty God, and He who awards the prize is the only-begotten Son of God. Angels and gods are spectators; and the contest, embracing all the varied exercises, is "not against flesh and blood," but against the spiritual powers of inordinate passions that work through the flesh. He who obtains the mastery in these struggles, and overthrows the tempter, menacing, as it were, with certain contests, wins immortality. For the sentence of God in most righteous judgment is infallible. The spectators are summoned to the contest, and the athletes contend in the stadium; the one, who has obeyed the directions of the trainer, wins the day. For to all, all rewards proposed by God are equal; and He Himself is unimpeachable. And he who has power receives mercy, and he that has exercised will is mighty.

So also we have received mind, that we may know what we do. And the maxim "Know thyself" means here to know for what we are born. And we are born to obey the commandments, if we choose to be willing to be saved. Such is the Nemesis, through which there is no escaping from God. Man's duty, then, is obedience to God, who has proclaimed salvation manifold by the commandments. And confession is thanksgiving. For the beneficent first begins to do good. And he who on fitting considerations readily receives and keeps the commandments, is faithful . . .; and he who by love requites benefits as far as he is able, is already a friend. One recompense on the part of men is of paramount importance—the doing of what is pleasing to God. As being His own production, and a result akin to Himself, the Teacher and Saviour receives acts of assistance and of improvement on the part of men as a personal favour and honour; as also He regards the injuries inflicted on those who believe on Him as ingratitude and dishonour to Himself. For what other dishonour can touch God? Wherefore it is impossible to render a recompense at all equivalent to the boon received from the Lord.

31

Tertullian

from *Prescription against Heretics*

Born in Carthage in northern Africa, Tertullian (ca. 160–225) was a major influence on Western Christian theology. Trained as a lawyer, he converted to Christianity about 197, and was a principal apologist defending Christianity against Greco-Roman critique. Whereas some apologists worked to reconcile the tensions between philosophical and Christian thought, Tertullian dismissed pagan thought almost out of hand. In his view, truth was available through divine revelation and was handed down by apostolic succession, rather than being attained by human reason. This excerpt illustrates the dichotomy Tertullian found between "Athens" and "Jerusalem," the "church" and the "academy"—a significant and perennial question.

Chap. I.—Introductory. Heresies Must Exist, and Even Abound; They Are a Probation to Faith.

The character of the times in which we live is such as to call forth from us even this admonition, that we ought not to be astonished at the heresies (which abound) neither ought their existence to surprise us, for it was foretold that they should come to pass; nor the fact that they subvert the faith of some, for their final cause is, by affording a trial to faith, to give it also the opportunity of being "approved." Groundless, therefore, and inconsiderate is the offence of the many who are scandalized by the very fact that heresies prevail to such a degree. How great (might their offence have been) if they had not existed. When it has been determined that a thing must by all means be, it receives the

SOURCE: Tertullian, *Prescription against Heretics*, in *The Ante-Nicene Fathers: Translations of the Writings of the Fathers down to A.D. 325*, vol. 3, *Latin Christianity: Its Founder, Tertullian. I. Apologetic; II. Anti-Marcion; III. Ethical*, ed. Alexander Roberts and James Donaldson, revised and chronologically arranged with brief prefaces and occasional notes by A. Cleveland Coxe (New York: Charles Scribner's Sons, 1903), 243–46.

(final) cause for which it has its being. This secures the power through which it exists, in such a way that it is impossible for it not to have existence.

[....]

Chap. III.—Weak People Fall an Easy Prey to Heresy, Which Derives Strength from the General Frailty of Mankind. Eminent Men Have Fallen from Faith: Saul, David, Solomon. The Constancy of Christ.

It is usual, indeed, with persons of a weaker character, to be so built up (in confidence) by certain individuals who are caught by heresy, as to topple over into ruin themselves. How comes it to pass, (they ask), that this woman or that man, who were the most faithful, the most prudent, and the most approved in the church, have gone over to the other side? Who that asks such a question does not in fact reply to it himself, to the effect that men whom heresies have been able to pervert ought never to have been esteemed prudent, or faithful, or approved? This again is, I suppose, an extraordinary thing, that one who has been approved should afterwards fall back? Saul, who was good beyond all others, is afterwards subverted by envy. David, a good man "after the Lord's own heart," is guilty afterwards of murder and adultery. Solomon, endowed by the Lord with all grace and wisdom, is led into idolatry, by women. For to the Son of God alone was it reserved to persevere to the last without sin. But what if a bishop, if a deacon, if a widow, if a virgin, if a doctor, if even a martyr, have fallen from the rule (of faith), will heresies on that account appear to possess the truth? Do we prove the faith by the persons, or the persons by the faith? No one is wise, no one is faithful, no one excels in dignity, but the Christian; and no one is a Christian but he who perseveres even to the end. You, as a man, know any other man from the outside appearance. You think as you see. And you see as far only as you have eyes. But says (the Scripture), "the eyes of the Lord are lofty." "Man looketh at the outward appearance, but God looketh at the heart." "The Lord (beholdeth and) knoweth them that are His;" and "the plant which (my heavenly Father) hath not planted, He rooteth up;" and "the first shall," as He shows, "be last;" and He carries "His fan in His hand to purge His threshing-floor." Let the chaff of a fickle faith fly off as much as it will at every blast of temptation, all the purer will be that heap of corn which shall be laid up in the garner of the Lord. Did not certain of the disciples turn back from the Lord Himself, when offended? Yet the rest did not therefore think that they must turn away from following Him, but because they knew that He was the Word of Life, and had come from God, they continued in His company to the very last, after He had gently inquired of them whether they also would go away. It is a comparatively small thing, that certain men, like Phygellus, and

Hermogenes, and Philetus, and Hymenæus, deserted His apostle: the betrayer of Christ was himself one of the apostles. We are surprised at seeing His churches forsaken by some men, although the things which we suffer after the example of Christ Himself, show us to be Christians. "They went out from us," says (St. John,) "but they were not of us. If they had been of us, they would no doubt have continued with us."

[. . . .]

Chap. VI.—Heretics Are Self-Condemned. Heresy Is Self-Will, Whilst Faith Is Submission of Our Will to the Divine Authority. The Heresy of Apelles.

On this point, however, we dwell no longer, since it is the same Paul who, in his Epistle to the Galatians, counts "heresies" among "the sins of the flesh," who also intimates to Titus, that "a man who is a heretic" must be "rejected after the first admonition," on the ground that "he that is such is perverted, and committeth sin, as a self-condemned man." Indeed, in almost every epistle, when enjoining on us (the duty) of avoiding false doctrines, he sharply condemns heresies. Of these the practical effects are false doctrines, called in Greek *heresies*, a word used in the sense of that *choice* which a man makes when he either teaches them (to others) or takes up with them (for himself). For this reason it is that he calls the heretic *self-condemned*, because he has himself chosen that for which he is condemned. We, however, are not permitted to cherish any object after our own will, nor yet to make choice of that which another has introduced of his private fancy. In the Lord's apostles we possess our authority; for even they did not of themselves choose to introduce anything, but faithfully delivered to the nations (of mankind) the doctrine which they had received from Christ. If, therefore, even an angel from heaven should preach any other gospel (than theirs), he would be called accursed by us. The Holy Ghost had even then foreseen that there would be in a certain virgin (called) Philumene an angel of deceit, "transformed into an angel of light," by whose miracles and illusions Apelles was led (when) he introduced his new heresy.

Chap. VII.—Pagan Philosophy the Parent of Heresies. The Connection between Deflections from Christian Faith and the Old System of Pagan Philosophy.

These are "the doctrines" of men and "of demons" produced for itching ears of the spirit of this world's wisdom: this the Lord called "foolishness," and "chose the foolish things of the world" to confound even philosophy itself. For (philosophy) it is which is the material of the world's wisdom, the rash interpreter of the nature and the dispensation of God. Indeed heresies are themselves instigated by philosophy. From this source came the Æons, and I [know] not what infinite forms, and the trinity of man in the system of Valentinus, who was of Plato's school. From the same source came Marcion's better god, with all his tranquillity; he came of the Stoics. Then, again, the opinion that the soul dies is held by the Epicureans; while the denial of the restoration of the body is taken from the aggregate school of all the philosophers; also, when matter is made equal to God, then you have the teaching of Zeno; and when any doctrine is alleged touching a god of fire, then Heraclitus comes in. The same subject-matter is discussed over and over again by the heretics and the philosophers; the same arguments are involved. Whence comes evil? Why is it permitted? What is the origin of man? and in what way does he come? Besides the question which Valentinus has very lately proposed—Whence comes God? Which he settles with the answer: From *enthymesis* and *ectroma*. Unhappy Aristotle! who invented for these men dialectics, the art of building up and pulling down; an art so evasive in its propositions, so far-fetched in its conjectures, so harsh, in its arguments, so productive of contentions—embarrassing even to itself, retracting everything, and really treating of nothing! Whence spring those "fables and endless genealogies," and "unprofitable questions," and "words which spread like a cancer?" From all these, when the apostle would restrain us, he expressly names *philosophy* as that which he would have us be on our guard against. Writing to the Colossians, he says, "See that no one beguile you through philosophy and vain deceit, after the tradition of men, and contrary to the wisdom of the Holy Ghost." He had been at Athens, and had in his interviews (with its philosophers) become acquainted with that human wisdom which pretends to know the truth, while it only corrupts it, and is itself divided into its own manifold heresies, by the variety of its mutually repugnant sects. What indeed has Athens to do with Jerusalem? What concord is there between the Academy and the Church? what between heretics and Christians? Our instruction comes from "the porch of Solomon," who had himself taught that "the Lord should be sought in simplicity of heart." Away with all attempts to produce a mottled Christianity of Stoic, Platonic, and dialectic composition! We want no curious disputation after possessing Christ Jesus, no inquisition after enjoying the gospel! With our faith, we desire no further belief. For this is our palmary faith, that there is nothing which we ought to believe besides.

Apostles' Creed

Two Versions

By the end of the first century AD, as Christianity spread beyond its roots in the eastern Mediterranean region, the young movement struggled to maintain consistency and unity. Alternative emphases and interpretations—often denounced as heresies—emerged. Irenaeus (130–200) and Clement of Alexandria (150–215) began talking in terms of a "rule of faith," a standard to discern whether candidates for baptism knew, and could affirm, key tenets of Christianity. In the following excerpt, Tertullian (ca. 160–225) illustrates the language that would eventually evolve into what history knows now as the Apostles' Creed. A contemporary version follows the passage from Tertullian.

---

from Tertullian, *Against Praxeas*

Chap. II.—The Catholic Doctrine of the Trinity and Unity. Sometimes Called the Divine Economy, or Dispensation of the Personal Relations of the Godhead.

In the course of time, then, the Father forsooth was born, and the Father suffered—God Himself, the Lord Almighty, whom in their preaching they declare to be Jesus Christ. We, however, as we indeed always have done (and more especially since we have been better instructed by the Paraclete, who leads men indeed into all truth), believe that there is one only God, but under the following dispensation . . . as it is called, that this one only God has also a Son, His Word, who proceeded from Himself, by whom all things were made, and without

SOURCES: Tertullian's *Against Praxeas* reprinted from *The Ante-Nicene Fathers: Translations of the Writings of the Fathers down to A.D. 325*, vol. 3, *Latin Christianity: Its Founder, Tertullian. I. Apologetic; II. Anti-Marcion; III. Ethical*, ed. Alexander Roberts and James Donaldson, revised and chronologically arranged with brief prefaces and occasional notes by A. Cleveland Coxe (New York: Charles Scribner's Sons, 1903), 598. The contemporary version is taken from the 1979 Book of Common Prayer.

whom nothing was made. Him *we believe* to have been sent by the Father into the Virgin, and to have been born of her—being both Man and God, the Son of Man and the Son of God, and to have been called by the name of Jesus Christ; *we believe* Him to have suffered, died, and been buried, according to the Scriptures, and, after He had been raised again by the Father and taken back to heaven, to be sitting at the right hand of the Father, *and* that He will come to judge the quick and the dead; who sent also from heaven from the Father, according to His own promise, the Holy Ghost, the Paraclete, the sanctifier of the faith of those who believe in the Father, and in the Son, and in the Holy Ghost. That this rule of faith has come down to us from the beginning of the gospel, even before any of the older heretics, much more before Praxeas, *a pretender* of yesterday, will be apparent both from the lateness of date which marks all heresies, and also from the absolutely novel character of our new-fangled Praxeas. In this principle also we must henceforth find a presumption of equal force against all heresies whatsoever—that whatever is first is true, whereas that is spurious which is later in date. But keeping this prescriptive rule inviolate, still some opportunity must be given for reviewing (the statements of heretics), with a view to the instruction and protection of divers persons; were it only that it may not seem that each per-version *of the truth* is condemned without examination, and simply prejudged; especially in the case of this heresy, which supposes itself to possess the pure truth, in thinking that one cannot believe in One Only God in any other way than by saying that the Father, the Son, and the Holy Ghost are the very self-same Person. As if in this way also one were not All, in that All are of One, by unity (that is) of substance; while the mystery of the dispensation is still guard-ed, which distributes the Unity into a Trinity, placing in their order the three *Persons*—the Father, the Son, and the Holy Ghost: three, however, not in con-dition, but in degree; not in substance, but in form; not in power, but in aspect; yet of one substance, and of one condition, and of one power, inasmuch as He is one God, from whom these degrees and forms and aspects are reckoned, under the name of the Father, and of the Son, and of the Holy Ghost. How they are susceptible of number without division, will be shown as our treatise proceeds.

The following is a contemporary version of the Apostles' Creed from the 1979 Book of Common Prayer.

> I believe in God, the Father almighty,
> creator of heaven and earth.
>
> I believe in Jesus Christ, his only Son, our Lord.
> He was conceived by the power of the Holy Spirit
> and born of the Virgin Mary.

He suffered under Pontius Pilate,
was crucified, died, and was buried.

He descended to the dead.
On the third day he rose again.
He ascended into heaven,
and is seated at the right hand of the Father.
He will come again to judge the living and the dead.

I believe in the Holy Spirit,
the holy catholic Church,
the communion of saints,
the forgiveness of sins,
the resurrection of the body,
and the life everlasting.

Amen.

from *The Passion of Perpetua and Felicitas*

How Perpetua (ca. 181–203) came to the Christian faith is unknown, but it is known that she lived in Carthage in northern Africa, was married, and had a young child. During Emperor Severus' persecution of Christians, she and several other catechumens—including her slave, Felicitas—were taken into custody. Perpetua's father appealed to her sense of responsibility as a young mother. Nonetheless, under the sentence of death, she sought baptism and inclusion in the Christian community. Consequently, she, Felicitas, and several other Christians were martyred in the Carthage amphitheater, as retold in the following excerpt. From Christianity's earliest days, her story has long been a staple in martyrology.

Chap. VI.—Argument. From the Prison They Are Led Forth with Joy into the Ampitheatre, Especially Perpetua and Felicitas. All Refuse to Put on Profane Garments. They Are Scourged, They Are Thrown to the Wild Beasts. Saturus Twice Is Unhurt. Perpetua and Felicitas Are Thrown Down; They Are Called Back to the Sanavivarian Gate. Saturus Wounded by a Leopard, Exhorts the Soldier. They Kiss One Another, and Are Slain with the Sword.

1. The day of their victory shone forth, and they proceeded from the prison into the amphitheatre, as if to an assembly, joyous and of brilliant countenances; if perchance shrinking, it was with joy, and not with fear. Perpetua followed with placid look, and with step and gait as a matron of Christ, beloved of God;

SOURCE: *The Passion of the Holy Martyrs Perpetua and Felicitas*, in *The Ante-Nicene Fathers: Translations of the Writings of the Fathers down to A.D. 325*, vol. 3, *Latin Christianity: Its Founder, Tertullian. I. Apologetic; II. Anti-Marcion; III. Ethical*, ed. Alexander Roberts and James Donaldson, revised and chronologically arranged with brief prefaces and occasional notes by A. Cleveland Coxe (New York: Charles Scribner's Sons, 1903), 704–6.

casting down the luster of her eyes from the gaze of all. Moreover, Felicitas, rejoicing that she had safely brought forth, so that she might fight with the wild beasts; from the blood and from the midwife to the gladiator, to wash after childbirth with a second baptism. And when they were brought to the gate, and were constrained to put on the clothing—the men, that of the priests of Saturn, and the women, that of those who were consecrated to Ceres—that noble-minded woman resisted even to the end with constancy. For she said, "We have come thus far of our own accord, for this reason, that our liberty might not be restrained. For this reason we have yielded our minds, that we might not do any such thing as this: we have agreed on this with you." Injustice acknowledged the justice; the tribune yielded to their being brought as simply as they were. Perpetua sang psalms, already treading under foot the head of the Egyptian; Revocatus, and Saturninus, and Saturus uttered threatenings against the gazing people about this martyrdom. When they came within sight of Hilarianus, by gesture and nod, they began to say to Hilarianus, "Thou judgest us," say they, "but God will judge thee." At this the people, exasperated, demanded that they should be tormented with scourges as they passed along the rank of the *venatores*. And they indeed rejoiced that they should have incurred any one of their Lord's passions.

2. But He who had said, "Ask, and you shall receive," gave to them when they asked, that death which each one had wished for. For when at any time they had been discoursing among themselves about their wish in respect of their martyrdom, Saturninus indeed had professed that he wished that he might be thrown to all the beasts; doubtless that he might wear a more glorious crown. Therefore in the beginning of the exhibition he and Revocatus made trial of the leopard, and moreover upon the scaffold they were harassed by the bear. Saturus, however, held nothing in greater abomination than a bear; but he imagined that he would be put an end to with one bite of a leopard. Therefore, when a wild boar was supplied, it was the huntsman rather who had supplied that boar who was gored by that same beast, and died the day after the shows. Saturus only was drawn out; and when he had been bound on the floor near to a bear, the bear would not come forth from his den. And so Saturus for the second time is recalled unhurt.

3. Moreover, for the young women the devil prepared a very fierce cow, provided especially for that purpose contrary to custom, rivalling their sex also in that of the beasts. And so, stripped and clothed with nets, they were led forth. The populace shuddered as they saw one young woman of delicate frame, and another with breasts still dropping from her recent childbirth. So, being recalled, they are unbound. Perpetua is first led in. She was tossed, and

fell on her loins; and when she saw her tunic torn from her side, she drew it over her as a veil for her middle, rather mindful of her modesty than her suffering. Then she was called for again, and bound up her dishevelled hair; for it was not becoming for a martyr to suffer with dishevelled hair, lest she should appear to be mourning in her glory. So she rose up; and when she saw Felicitas crushed, she approached and gave her her hand, and lifted her up. And both of them stood together; and the brutality of the populace being appeased, they were recalled to the Sanavivarian gate. Then Perpetua was received by a certain one who was still a catechumen, Rusticus by name, who kept close to her; and she, as if aroused from sleep, so deeply had she been in the Spirit and in an ecstasy, began to look round her, and to say to the amazement of all, "I cannot tell when we are to be led out to that cow." And when she had heard what had already happened, she did not believe it until she had perceived certain signs of injury in her body and in her dress, and had recognised the catechumen. Afterwards causing that catechumen and the brother to approach, she addressed them, saying, "Stand fast in the faith, and love one another, all of you, and be not offended at my sufferings."

4. The same Saturus at the other entrance exhorted the soldier Pudens, saying, "Assuredly here I am, as I have promised and foretold, for up to this moment I have felt no beast. And now believe with your whole heart. Lo, I am going forth to that beast, and I shall be destroyed with one bite of the leopard." And immediately at the conclusion of the exhibition he was thrown to the leopard; and with one bite of his he was bathed with such a quantity of blood, that the people shouted out to him as he was returning, the testimony of his second baptism, "Saved and washed, saved and washed." Manifestly he was assuredly saved who had been glorified in such a spectacle. Then to the soldier Pudens he said, "Farewell, and be mindful of my faith; and let not these things disturb, but confirm you." And at the same time he asked for a little ring from his finger, and returned it to him bathed in his wound, leaving to him an inherited token and the memory of his blood. And then lifeless he is cast down with the rest, to be slaughtered in the usual place. And when the populace called for them into the midst, that as the sword penetrated into their body they might make their eyes partners in the murder, they rose up of their own accord, and transferred themselves whither the people wished; but they first kissed one another, that they might consummate their martyrdom with the kiss of peace. The rest indeed, immoveable and in silence, received the sword-thrust; much more Saturus, who also had first ascended the ladder, and first gave up his spirit, for he also was waiting for Perpetua. But Perpetua, that she might taste some pain, being pierced between the ribs, cried out loudly, and she herself placed

the wavering right hand of the youthful gladiator to her throat. Possibly such a woman could not have been slain unless she herself had willed it, because she was feared by the impure spirit.

O most brave and blessed martyrs! O truly called and chosen unto the glory of our Lord Jesus Christ! Whom whoever magnifies, and honours, and adores, assuredly ought to read these examples for the edification of the Church, not less than the ancient ones, so that new virtues also may testify that one and the same Holy Spirit is always operating even until now, and God the Father Omnipotent, and His Son Jesus Christ our Lord, whose is the glory and infinite power for ever and ever. Amen.

34

Origen

from *Against Celsus*

The formative moment of Origen's life (ca. 185–254) likely came when his father, Leonidas, was arrested and martyred in 202. Desiring martyrdom himself, Origen dedicated his life to expressions of self-sacrifice. On one level, he practiced severe asceticism. On another level, he trained his brilliant mind on teaching and defending the Christian message. For example, he led the important Catechetical School in Alexandria, Egypt, wrote voluminously, and engaged detractors and their critiques of Christianity. When the philosopher Celsus ridiculed Christian teachings and practices, Origen took up the challenge, writing *Against Celsus* in 248. The following excerpt includes Origen's defense of Christian nonviolence.

Chap. LXXIII.

In the next place, Celsus urges us "to help the king with all our might, and to labour with him in the maintenance of justice, to fight for him; and if he requires it, to fight under him, or lead an army along with him." To this our answer is, that we do, when occasion requires, give help to kings, and that, so to say, a divine help, "putting on the whole armour of God." And this we do in obedience to the injunction of the apostle, "I exhort, therefore, that first of all, supplications, prayers, intercessions, and giving of thanks, be made for all men; for kings, and for all that are in authority;" and the more any one excels in piety, the more effective help does he render to kings, even more than is

SOURCE: Origen, *Against Celsus*, in *The Ante-Nicene Fathers: Translations of the Writings of the Fathers down to A.D. 325*, vol. 4, *Tertullian, Part Fourth; Minucius Felix; Commodian; Origen, Parts First and Second*, ed. Alexander Roberts and James Donaldson, revised and chronologically arranged with brief prefaces and occasional notes by A. Cleveland Coxe (New York: Charles Scribner's Sons, 1905), 667–68.

given by soldiers, who go forth to fight and slay as many of the enemy as they can. And to those enemies of our faith who require us to bear arms for the commonwealth, and to slay men, we can reply: "Do not those who are priests at certain shrines, and those who attend on certain gods, as you account them, keep their hands free from blood, that they may with hands unstained and free from human blood offer the appointed sacrifices to your gods; and even when war is upon you, you never enlist the priests in the army. If that, then, is a laudable custom, how much more so, that while others are engaged in battle, these too should engage as the priests and ministers of God, keeping their hands pure, and wrestling in prayers to God on behalf of those who are fighting in a righteous cause, and for the king who reigns righteously, that whatever is opposed to those who act righteously may be destroyed!" And as we by our prayers vanquish all demons who stir up war, and lead to the violation of oaths, and disturb the peace, we in this way are much more helpful to the kings than those who go into the field to fight for them. And we do take our part in public affairs, when along with righteous prayers we join self-denying exercises and meditations, which teach us to despise pleasures, and not to be led away by them. And none fight better for the king than we do. We do not indeed fight under him, although he require it; but we fight on his behalf, forming a special army—an army of piety—by offering our prayers to God.

Chap. LXXIV.

And if Celsus would have us to lead armies in defence of our country, let him know that we do this too, and that not for the purpose of being seen by men, or of vainglory. For "in secret," and in our own hearts, there are prayers which ascend as from priests in behalf of our fellow-citizens. And Christians are benefactors of their country more than others. For they train up citizens, and inculcate piety to the Supreme Being; and they promote those whose lives in the smallest cities have been good and worthy, to a divine and heavenly city, to whom it may be said, "Thou hast been faithful in the smallest city, come into a great one," where "God standeth in the assembly of the gods, and judgeth the gods in the midst;" and He reckons thee among them, if thou no more "die as a man, or fall as one of the princes."

Chap. LXXV.

Celsus also urges us to "take office in the government of the country, if that is required for the maintenance of the laws and the support of religion." But we recognise in each state the existence of another national organization, founded by the Word of God, and we exhort those who are mighty in word

and of blameless life to rule over Churches. Those who are ambitious of ruling we reject; but we constrain those who, through excess of modesty, are not
easily induced to take a public charge in the Church of God. And those who
rule over us well are under the constraining influence of the great King, whom
we believe to be the Son of God, God the Word. And if those who govern in the
Church, and are called rulers of the divine nation—that is, the Church—rule
well, they rule in accordance with the divine commands, and never suffer
themselves to be led astray by worldly policy. And it is not for the purpose of
escaping public duties that Christians decline public offices, but that they may
reserve themselves for a diviner and more necessary service in the Church
of God—for the salvation of men. And this service is at once necessary and
right. They take charge of all—of those that are within, that they may day by
day lead better lives, and of those that are without, that they may come to
abound in holy words and in deeds of piety; and that, while thus worshipping
God truly, and training up as many as they can in the same way, they may be
filled with the word of God and the law of God, and thus be united with the
Supreme God through His Son the Word, Wisdom, Truth, and Righteousness,
who unites to God all who are resolved to conform their lives in all things to
the law of God.

35

Eusebius of Caesarea

from *Life of Constantine*

Often known as the father of church history, Eusebius of Caesarea (260–340) chronicled Christian history from the first to the fourth centuries. Illustrating how historical narration is frequently a political act, Eusebius' writing regularly portrayed Constantine (272–337) as a heroic, even providential, figure. In the following excerpt, Eusebius records Constantine's call and conversion to Christianity, and Constantine's subsequent adoption of Christian identity and symbolism for his armies. Eusebius' narrative asserts how an outmatched Constantine defeated Maxentius at the Milvian Bridge (312) to become Rome's Western Emperor. The next year, Constantine would promulgate the Edict of Milan, setting the stage for the creation of a powerful Christendom that would shape the course of Western history for centuries.

Chapter XXVI: *How he resolved to deliver Rome from Maxentius.*

While, therefore, he regarded the entire world as one immense body, and perceived that the head of it all, the royal city of the Roman empire, was bowed down by the weight of a tyrannous oppression; at first he had left the task of liberation to those who governed the other divisions of the empire, as being his superiors in point of age. But when none of these proved able to afford relief, and those who had attempted it had experienced a disastrous termination of their enterprise, he said that life was without enjoyment to him as long as he saw the imperial city thus afflicted, and prepared himself for the overthrowal of the tyranny.

SOURCE: Eusebius, *The Life of the Blessed Emperor Constantine*, in *A Select Library of Nicene and Post-Nicene Fathers of the Christian Church*, 2nd series, vol. 1, *Eusebius: Church History, Life of Constantine the Great, and Oration in Praise of Constantine*, translated into English with prolegomena and explanatory notes, under the editorial supervision of Philip Schaff and Henry Wace (New York, The Christian Literature Company, 1890), 489–94.

Chapter XXVII: *That after reflecting on the Downfall of those who had worshiped Idols, he made Choice of Christianity.*

Being convinced, however, that he needed some more powerful aid than his military forces could afford him, on account of the wicked and magical enchantments which were so diligently practiced by the tyrant, he sought Divine assistance, deeming the possession of arms and a numerous soldiery of secondary importance, but believing the cooperating power of Deity invincible and not to be shaken. He considered, therefore, on what God he might rely for protection and assistance. While engaged in this enquiry, the thought occurred to him, that, of the many emperors who had preceded him, those who had rested their hopes in a multitude of gods, and served them with sacrifices and offerings, had in the first place been deceived by flattering predictions, and oracles which promised them all prosperity, and at last had met with an unhappy end, while not one of their gods had stood by to warn them of the impending wrath of heaven; while one alone who had pursued an entirely opposite course, who had condemned their error, and honored the one Supreme God during his whole life, had found him to be the Saviour and Protector of his empire, and the Giver of every good thing. Reflecting on this, and well weighing the fact that they who had trusted in many gods had also fallen by manifold forms of death, without leaving behind them either family or offspring, stock, name, or memorial among men: while the God of his father had given to him, on the other hand, manifestations of his power and very many tokens: and considering farther that those who had already taken arms against the tyrant, and had marched to the battlefield under the protection of a multitude of gods, had met with a dishonorable end (for one of them had shamefully retreated from the contest without a blow, and the other, being slain in the midst of his own troops, became, as it were, the mere sport of death); reviewing, I say, all these considerations, he judged it to be folly indeed to join in the idle worship of those who were no gods, and, after such convincing evidence, to err from the truth; and therefore felt it incumbent on him to honor his father's God alone.

Chapter XXVIII: *How, while he was praying, God sent him a Vision of a Cross of Light in the Heavens at Mid-day, with an Inscription admonishing him to conquer by that.*

Accordingly he called on him with earnest prayer and supplications that he would reveal to him who he was, and stretch forth his right hand to help him in his present difficulties. And while he was thus praying with fervent entreaty, a most marvelous sign appeared to him from heaven, the account of which it might have been hard to believe had it been related by any other person. But since the victorious emperor himself long afterwards declared it to the writer of this history, when he was honored with his acquaintance and society, and confirmed his statement by an oath, who could hesitate to accredit the relation, especially since the testimony of after-time has established its truth? He said that about noon, when the day was already beginning to decline, he saw with his own eyes the trophy of a cross of light in the heavens, above the sun, and bearing the inscription, CONQUER BY THIS. At this sight he himself was struck with amazement, and his whole army also, which followed him on this expedition, and witnessed the miracle.

Chapter XXIX: *How the Christ of God appeared to him in his Sleep, and commanded him to use in his Wars a Standard made in the Form of the Cross.*

He said, moreover, that he doubted within himself what the import of this apparition could be. And while he continued to ponder and reason on its meaning, night suddenly came on; then in his sleep the Christ of God appeared to him with the same sign which he had seen in the heavens, and commanded him to make a likeness of that sign which he had seen in the heavens, and to use it as a safeguard in all engagements with his enemies.

Chapter XXX: *The Making of the Standard of the Cross.*

At dawn of day he arose, and communicated the marvel to his friends: and then, calling together the workers in gold and precious stones, he sat in the midst of them, and described to them the figure of the sign he had seen, bidding them represent it in gold and precious stones. And this representation I myself have had an opportunity of seeing.

Chapter XXXI: *A Description of the Standard of the Cross, which the Romans now call the Labarum.*

Now it was made in the following manner. A long spear, overlaid with gold, formed the figure of the cross by means of a transverse bar laid over it. On the top of the whole was fixed a wreath of gold and precious stones; and within this, the symbol of the Saviour's name, two letters indicating the name of Christ by means of its initial characters, the letter P being intersected by X in its centre: and these letters the emperor was in the habit of wearing on his helmet at a later period. From the cross-bar of the spear was suspended a cloth, a royal piece, covered with a profuse embroidery of most brilliant precious stones; and which, being also richly interlaced with gold, presented an indescribable degree of beauty to the beholder. This banner was of a square form, and the upright staff, whose lower section was of great length, bore a golden half-length portrait of the pious emperor and his children on its upper part, beneath the trophy of the cross, and immediately above the embroidered banner.

The emperor constantly made use of this sign of salvation as a safeguard against every adverse and hostile power, and commanded that others similar to it should be carried at the head of all his armies.

Chapter XXXII: *How Constantine received Instruction, and read the Sacred Scriptures.*

These things were done shortly afterwards. But at the time above specified, being struck with amazement at the extraordinary vision, and resolving to worship no other God save Him who had appeared to him, he sent for those who were acquainted with the mysteries of His doctrines, and enquired who that God was, and what was intended by the sign of the vision he had seen.

They affirmed that He was God, the only begotten Son of the one and only God: that the sign which had appeared was the symbol of immortality, and the trophy of that victory over death which He had gained in time past when sojourning on earth. They taught him also the causes of His advent, and explained to him the true account of His incarnation. Thus he was instructed in these matters, and was impressed with wonder at the divine manifestation which had been presented to his sight. Comparing, therefore, the heavenly vision with the interpretation given, he found his judgment confirmed; and, in the persuasion that the knowledge of these things had been imparted to him by Divine teaching, he determined thenceforth to devote himself to the reading of the Inspired writings.

Moreover, he made the priests of God his counselors, and deemed it incumbent on him to honor the God who had appeared to him with all devotion. And after this, being fortified by well-grounded hopes in Him, he hastened to quench the threatening fire of tyranny.

[. . . .]

Chapter XXXVII: *Defeat of Maxentius's Armies in Italy.*

Constantine, however, filled with compassion on account of all these miseries, began to arm himself with all warlike preparation against the tyranny. Assuming therefore the Supreme God as his patron, and invoking His Christ to be his preserver and aid, and setting the victorious trophy, the salutary symbol, in front of his soldiers and bodyguard, he marched with his whole forces, trying to obtain again for the Romans the freedom they had inherited from their ancestors.

And whereas, Maxentius, trusting more in his magic arts than in the affection of his subjects, dared not even advance outside the city gates, but had guarded every place and district and city subject to his tyranny, with large bodies of soldiers, the emperor, confiding in the help of God, advanced against the first and second and third divisions of the tyrant's forces, defeated them all with ease at the first assault, and made his way into the very interior of Italy.

Chapter XXXVIII: *Death of Maxentius on the Bridge of the Tiber.*

And already he was approaching very near Rome itself, when, to save him from the necessity of fighting with all the Romans for the tyrant's sake, God himself drew the tyrant, as it were by secret cords, a long way outside the gates. And now those miracles recorded in Holy Writ, which God of old wrought against the ungodly (discredited by most as fables, yet believed by the faithful), did he in every deed confirm to all alike, believers and unbelievers, who were eye-witnesses of the wonders. For as once in the days of Moses and the Hebrew nation, who were worshipers of God, "Pharaoh's chariots and his host has he cast into the sea and his chosen chariot-captains are drowned in the Red Sea,"— so at this time Maxentius, and the soldiers and guards with him, "went down into the depths like stone," when, in his flight before the divinely-aided forces of Constantine, he essayed to cross the river which lay in his way, over which, making a strong bridge of boats, he had framed an engine of destruction, really against himself, but in the hope of ensnaring thereby him who was beloved by God. For his God stood by the one to protect him, while the other, godless, proved to be the miserable contriver of these secret devices to his own ruin. So that one might well say, "He hath made a pit, and dug it, and is fallen into the ditch which he made. His mischief shall return upon his own head, and his violence shall come down upon his own pate." Thus, in the present instance, under divine direction, the machine erected on the bridge, with the ambuscade concealed therein, giving way unexpectedly before the appointed time, the bridge began to sink, and the boats with the men in them went bodily to the bottom. And first the wretch himself, then his armed attendants and guards, even as the sacred oracles had before described, "sank as lead in the mighty waters." So that they who thus obtained victory from God might well, if not in the same words, yet in fact in the same spirit as the people of his great servant Moses, sing and speak as they did concerning the impious tyrant of old: "Let us sing unto the Lord, for he hath been glorified exceedingly: the horse and his rider hath he thrown into the sea. He is become my helper and my shield unto salvation." And again, "Who is like unto thee, O Lord, among the gods? Who is like thee, glorious in holiness, marvelous in praises, doing wonders?"

Chapter XXXIX: *Constantine's Entry into Rome.*

Having then at this time sung these and suchlike praises to God, the Ruler of all and the Author of victory, after the example of his great servant Moses, Constantine entered the imperial city in triumph. And here the whole body of the senate, and others of rank and distinction in the city, freed as it were from the restraint of a prison, along with the whole Roman populace, their countenances expressive of the gladness of their hearts, received him with acclamations and abounding joy; men, women, and children, with countless multitudes of servants, greeting him as deliverer, preserver, and benefactor, with incessant shouts. But he, being possessed of inward piety toward God, was neither rendered arrogant by these plaudits, nor uplifted by the praises he heard: but, being sensible that he had received help from God, he immediately rendered a thanksgiving to him as the Author of his victory.

Chapter XL: *Of the Statue of Constantine holding a Cross, and its Inscription.*

Moreover, by loud proclamation and monumental inscriptions he made known to all men the salutary symbol, setting up this great trophy of victory over his enemies in the midst of the imperial city, and expressly causing it to be engraven in indelible characters, that the salutary symbol was the safeguard of the Roman government and of the entire empire. Accordingly, he immediately ordered a lofty spear in the figure of a cross to be placed beneath the hand of a statue representing himself, in the most frequented part of Rome, and the following inscription to be engraved on it in the Latin language: BY VIRTUE OF THIS SALUTARY SIGN, WHICH IS THE TRUE TEST OF VALOR, I HAVE PRESERVED AND LIBERATED YOUR CITY FROM THE YOKE OF TYRANNY. I HAVE ALSO SET AT LIBERTY THE ROMAN SENATE AND PEOPLE, AND RESTORED THEM TO THEIR AN-CIENT DISTINCTION AND SPLENDOR.

Chapter XLI: *Rejoicings throughout the Provinces; and Constantine's Acts of Grace.*

Thus the pious emperor, glorying in the confession of the victorious cross, proclaimed the Son of God to the Romans with great boldness of testimony. And the inhabitants of the city, one and all, senate and people, reviving, as it were, from the pressure of a bitter and tyrannical domination, seemed to enjoy purer rays of light, and to be born again into a fresh and new life. All the nations, too, as far as the limit of the western ocean, being set free from the calamities which had heretofore beset them, and gladdened by joyous festivals, ceased not to praise him as the victorious, the pious, the common benefactor: all, indeed, with one voice and one mouth, declared that Constantine had appeared by the grace of God as a general blessing to mankind. The imperial edict also was everywhere published, whereby those who had been wrongfully deprived of their estates were permitted again to enjoy their own, while those who had unjustly suffered exile were recalled to their homes. Moreover, he freed from imprisonment, and from every kind of danger and fear, those who, by reason of the tyrant's cruelty, had been subject to these sufferings.

Chapter XLII: *The Honors conferred upon Bishops, and the Building of Churches.*

The emperor also personally inviting the society of God's ministers, distinguished them with the highest possible respect and honor, showing them favor in deed and word as persons consecrated to the service of his God. Accordingly, they were admitted to his table, though mean in their attire and outward appearance; yet not so in his estimation, since he thought he saw not the man as seen by the vulgar eye, but the God in him. He made them also his companions in travel, believing that He whose servants they were would thus help him. Besides this, he gave from his own private resources costly benefactions to the churches of God, both enlarging and heightening the sacred edifices, and embellishing the august sanctuaries of the church with abundant offerings.

36

Edict of Milan

From its founding Christianity had been an outlawed faith, subject to episodic and regional persecutions by Roman imperial authorities. The Edict of Milan (313), issued jointly by Emperor Licinius in the East and Emperor Constantine in the West, altered the course of history by recognizing Christianity as an accepted faith of the Empire. This pronouncement opened the way for Christianity to become the predominant faith of the Empire by the end of the fourth century. It also made possible an increased role of the state in the life and work of the church.

When I, Constantine Augustus, as well as I, Licinius Augustus, had fortunately met near Mediolanum (Milan), and were considering everything that pertained to the public welfare and security, we thought that, among other things which we saw would be for the good of many, those regulations pertaining to the reverence of the Divinity ought certainly to be made first, so that we might grant to the Christians and others full authority to observe that religion which each preferred; whence any Divinity whatsoever in the seat of the heavens may be propitious and kindly disposed to us and all who are placed under our rule. And thus by this wholesome counsel and most upright provision we thought to arrange that no one whatsoever should be denied the opportunity to give his heart to the observance of the Christian religion, of that religion which he should think best for himself, so that the Supreme Deity, to whose worship we freely yield our hearts, may show in all things His usual favor and benevolence. Therefore, your Worship should know that it has pleased us to remove all conditions whatsoever, which were in the rescripts formerly given to you officially, concerning the Christians and now any one of these who wishes to observe Christian religion may do so freely and openly,

SOURCE: *Translations and Reprints from the Original Sources of European History*, vol. 4 (Philadelphia: Department of History of the University of Pennsylvania, 1897), 29–30.

without molestation. We thought it fit to commend these things most fully to your care that you may know that we have given to those Christians free and unrestricted opportunity of religious worship. When you see that this has been granted to them by us, your Worship will know that we have also conceded to other religions the right of open and free observance of their worship for the sake of the peace of our times, that each one may have the free opportunity to worship as he pleases; this regulation is made we that we may not seem to detract from any dignity or any religion. Moreover, in the case of the Christians especially we esteemed it best to order that if it happens anyone heretofore has bought from our treasury from anyone whatsoever, those places where they were previously accustomed to assemble, concerning which a certain decree had been made and a letter sent to you officially, the same shall be restored to the Christians without payment or any claim of recompense and without any kind of fraud or deception. Those, moreover, who have obtained the same by gift, are likewise to return them at once to the Christians. Besides, both those who have purchased and those who have secured them by gift, are to appeal to the vicar if they seek any recompense from our bounty, that they may be cared for through our clemency. All this property ought to be delivered at once to the community of the Christians through your intercession, and without delay. And since these Christians are known to have possessed not only those places in which they were accustomed to assemble, but also other property, namely the churches, belonging to them as a corporation and not as individuals, all these things which we have included under the above law, you will order to be restored, without any hesitation or controversy at all, to these Christians, that is to say to the corporations and their conventicles:—providing, of course, that the above arrangements be followed so that those who return the same without payment, as we have said, may hope for an indemnity from our bounty. In all these circumstances you ought to tender your most efficacious intervention to the community of the Christians, that our command may be carried into effect as quickly as possible, whereby, moreover, through our clemency, public order may be secured. Let this be done so that, as we have said above, Divine favor towards us, which, under the most important circumstances we have already experienced, may, for all time, preserve and prosper our successes together with the good of the state. Moreover, in order that the statement of this decree of our good will may come to the notice of all, this rescript, published by your decree, shall be announced everywhere and brought to the knowledge of all, so that the decree of this, our benevolence, cannot be concealed.

37

Nicene Creed

Three Versions

About a decade after becoming Emperor, Constantine (272–337) convened a Christian church council at Nicaea to clarify orthodox doctrine on the person of Christ. Arius, a presbyter from Alexandria, Egypt, had been teaching that Christ is not coeternal with God the Father (i.e., "There was a time when He [Christ] was not"). This matter revealed important fault lines within the Christian communion. The Council of Nicaea (325), the first of Christianity's ecumenical councils, denounced Arianism, affirming Christ as coeternal and of the same substance with the Father. To teach and test adherence to this belief, the council drafted its Nicene Creed as a summary statement of orthodoxy. Having evolved, it is still in widespread liturgical use today.

(*Found in the Acts of the Ecumenical Councils of Ephesus and Chalcedon, in the Epistle of Eusebius of Cæsarea to his own Church, in the Epistle of St. Athanasius* Ad Jovianum Imp., *in the* Ecclesiastical Histories *of Theodoret and Socrates, and elsewhere . . .*)

The Synod at Nice set forth this Creed.

The Ecthesis of the Synod at Nice.

We believe in one God, the Father Almighty, maker of all things visible and invisible; and in one Lord Jesus Christ, the Son of God, the only-begotten of his Father, of the substance of the Father, God of God, Light of Light, very God of very God, begotten . . ., not made, being of one substance (. . .,

SOURCES: *A Select Library of Nicene and Post-Nicene Fathers of the Christian Church*, 2nd series, translated into English with prolegomena and explanatory notes, under the editorial supervision of Philip Schaff and Henry Wace, vol. 14, *The Seven Ecumenical Councils*, ed. Henry R. Percival (New York: The Christian Literature Company, 1900), 3. The contemporary version of the Nicene Creed is taken from the 1979 Book of Common Prayer.

consubstantialem) with the Father. By whom all things were made, both which be in heaven and in earth. Who for us men and for our salvation came down [from heaven] and was incarnate and was made man. He suffered and the third day he rose again, and ascended into heaven. And he shall come again to judge both the quick and the dead. And [we believe] in the Holy Ghost. And whosoever shall say that there was a time when the Son of God was not . . ., or that before he was begotten he was not, or that he was made of things that were not, or that he is of a different substance or essence [from the Father] or that he is a creature, or subject to change or conversion—all that so say, the Catholic and Apostolic Church anathematizes them.

[The following is the] Creed of Eusebius of Cæsarea, which he presented to the council, and which some suppose to have suggested the creed finally adopted. (*Found in his Epistle to his diocese; vide: St. Athanasius and Theodoret.*)

We believe in one only God, Father Almighty, Creator of things visible and invisible; and in the Lord Jesus Christ, for he is the Word of God, God of God, Light of Light, life of life, his only Son, the first-born of all creatures, begotten of the Father before all time, by whom also everything was created, who became flesh for our redemption, who lived and suffered amongst men, rose again the third day, returned to the Father, and will come again one day in his glory to judge the quick and the dead. We believe also in the Holy Ghost. We believe that each of these three is and subsists; the Father truly as Father, the Son truly as Son, the Holy Ghost truly as Holy Ghost; as our Lord also said, when he sent his disciples to preach: Go and teach all nations, and baptize them in the name of the Father, and of the Son, and of the Holy Ghost.

The following is a contemporary version of the Nicene Creed from the 1979 Book of Common Prayer.

> We believe in one God,
>> the Father, the Almighty,
>> maker of heaven and earth,
>> of all that is, seen and unseen.
> We believe in one Lord, Jesus Christ,
>> the only Son of God,
>> eternally begotten of the Father,
>> God from God, Light from Light,
>> true God from true God,
>> begotten, not made,
>> of one Being with the Father.

Through him all things were made.
For us and for our salvation
    he came down from heaven:
by the power of the Holy Spirit
    he became incarnate from the Virgin Mary,
    and was made man.
For our sake he was crucified under Pontius Pilate;
    he suffered death and was buried.
    On the third day he rose again
        in accordance with the Scriptures;
    he ascended into heaven
        and is seated at the right hand of the Father.
He will come again in glory to judge the living and the dead,
    and his kingdom will have no end.
We believe in the Holy Spirit, the Lord, the giver of life,
    who proceeds from the Father and the Son.
    With the Father and the Son he is worshiped and glorified.
    He has spoken through the Prophets.
    We believe in one holy catholic and apostolic Church.
    We acknowledge one baptism for the forgiveness of sins.
    We look for the resurrection of the dead,
        and the life of the world to come. Amen.

Athanasius of Alexandria

from *Life of Antony*

A founding figure in Christianity's "desert tradition," Antony (ca. 251–356) led a life of anchoritic monasticism that represented an alternative to Christianity's increasing acculturation to the Roman culture of the fourth century. As word spread of his life in the Egyptian desert, between the Nile and the Red Sea, his story inspired others to replicate his practices. Athanasius of Alexandria's biography of Antony (written shortly after the latter's death) then helped monasticism spread well beyond the Egyptian desert. The advent of this countercultural witness assumed the celebrated legacy of the early Christian martyrs.

---

3. As he [Antony] went into the church, hearing the Lord say in the Gospel "be not anxious for the morrow," he could stay no longer, but went out and gave those things also to the poor. Having committed his sister to known and faithful virgins, and put her into a convent to be brought up, he henceforth devoted himself outside his house to discipline, taking heed to himself and training himself with patience. For there were not yet so many monasteries in Egypt, and no monk at all knew of the distant desert; but all who wished to give heed to themselves practised the discipline in solitude near their own village. Now there was then in the next village an old man who had lived the life of a hermit from his youth up. Antony, after he had seen this man, imitated him in piety. And at first he began to abide in places outside the village: then if he heard of a good man anywhere, like the prudent bee, he went forth and sought him, nor turned back to his own place until he had seen him; and he returned, having got from

SOURCE: Athanasius of Alexandria, *Life of Antony*, in *A Select Library of Nicene and Post-Nicene Fathers of the Christian Church*, 2nd series, translated into English with prolegomena and explanatory notes, under the editorial supervision of Philip Schaff and Henry Wace, vol. 4, *St. Athanasius: Select Works and Letters*, ed. Archibald Robertson (New York: The Christian Literature Company, 1892), 196, 198, 200, 210–11.

the good man as it were supplies for his journey in the way of virtue. So dwelling there at first, he confirmed his purpose not to return to the abode of his fathers nor to the remembrance of his kinsfolk; but to keep all his desire and energy for perfecting his discipline. He worked, however, with his hands, having heard, "he who is idle let him not eat," and part he spent on bread and part he gave to the needy. And he was constant in prayer, knowing that a man ought to pray in secret unceasingly. For he had given such heed to what was read that none of the things that were written fell from him to the ground, but he remembered all, and afterwards his memory served him for books.

4. Thus conducting himself, Antony was beloved by all. He subjected himself in sincerity to the good men whom he visited, and learned thoroughly where each surpassed him in zeal and discipline. He observed the graciousness of one; the unceasing prayer of another; he took knowledge of another's freedom from anger and another's loving-kindness; he gave heed to one as he watched, to another as he studied; one he admired for his endurance, another for his fasting and sleeping on the ground; the meekness of one and the long-suffering of another he watched with care, while he took note of the piety towards Christ and the mutual love which animated all. Thus filled, he returned to his own place of discipline, and henceforth would strive to unite the qualities of each, and was eager to show in himself the virtues of all. With others of the same age he had no rivalry; save this only, that he should not be second to them in higher things. And this he did so as to hurt the feelings of nobody, but made them rejoice over him. So all they of that village and the good men in whose intimacy he was, when they saw that he was a man of this sort, used to call him God-beloved. And some welcomed him as a son, others as a brother.

[. . . .]

8. Thus tightening his hold upon himself, Antony departed to the tombs, which happened to be at a distance from the village; and having bid one of his acquaintances to bring him bread at intervals of many days, he entered one of the tombs, and the other having shut the door on him, he remained within alone. And when the enemy could not endure it, but was even fearful that in a short time Antony would fill the desert with the discipline, coming one night with a multitude of demons, he so cut him with stripes that he lay on the ground speechless from the excessive pain. For he affirmed that the torture had been so excessive that no blows inflicted by man could ever have caused him such torment. But by the Providence of God—for the Lord never overlooks them that hope in Him—the next day his acquaintance came bringing him the loaves. And having opened the door and seeing him lying on the ground as though dead, he lifted him up and carried him to the church in

the village, and laid him upon the ground. And many of his kinsfolk and the villagers sat around Antony as round a corpse. But about midnight he came to himself and arose, and when he saw them all asleep and his comrade alone watching, he motioned with his head for him to approach, and asked him to carry him again to the tombs without waking anybody.

[. . . .]

14. And so for nearly twenty years he continued training himself in solitude, never going forth, and but seldom seen by any. After this, when many were eager and wishful to imitate his discipline, and his acquaintances came and began to cast down and wrench off the door by force, Antony, as from a shrine, came forth initiated in the mysteries and filled with the Spirit of God. Then for the first time he was seen outside the fort by those who came to see him. And they, when they saw him, wondered at the sight, for he had the same habit of body as before, and was neither fat, like a man without exercise, nor lean from fasting and striving with the demons, but he was just the same as they had known him before his retirement. And again his soul was free from blemish, for it was neither contracted as if by grief, nor relaxed by pleasure, nor possessed by laughter or dejection, for he was not troubled when he beheld the crowd, nor overjoyed at being saluted by so many. But he was altogether even as being guided by reason, and abiding in a natural state. Through him the Lord healed the bodily ailments of many present, and cleansed others from evil spirits. And He gave grace to Antony in speaking, so that he consoled many that were sorrowful, and set those at variance at one, exhorting all to prefer the love of Christ before all that is in the world. And while he exhorted and advised them to remember the good things to come, and the loving-kindness of God towards us, "Who spared not His own Son, but delivered Him up for us all," he persuaded many to embrace the solitary life. And thus it happened in the end that cells arose even in the mountains, and the desert was colonised by monks, who came forth from their own people, and enrolled themselves for the citizenship in the heavens.

[. . . .]

55. So after certain days he went in again to the mountain. And henceforth many resorted to him, and others who were suffering ventured to go in. To all the monks therefore who came to him, he continually gave this precept: "Believe on the Lord and love Him; keep yourselves from filthy thoughts and fleshly pleasures, and as it is written in the Proverbs, be not deceived "by the fulness of the belly." Pray continually; avoid vainglory; sing psalms before sleep and on awaking; hold in your heart the commandments of Scripture; be mindful of the works of the saints that your souls being put in remembrance of the commandments may be brought into harmony with the zeal of the saints."

And especially he counselled them to meditate continually on the apostle's word, "Let not the sun go down upon your wrath." And he considered this was spoken of all commandments in common, and that not on wrath alone, but not on any other sin of ours, ought the sun to go down. For it was good and needful that neither the sun should condemn us for an evil by day nor the moon for a sin by night, or even for an evil thought. That this state may be preserved in us it is good to hear the apostle and keep his words, for he says, "Try your own selves and prove your own selves." Daily, therefore, let each one take from himself the tale of his actions both by day and night; and if he have sinned, let him cease from it; while if he have not, let him not be boastful. But let him abide in that which is good, without being negligent, nor condemning his neighbours, nor justifying himself, "until the Lord come who searcheth out hidden things" as saith the blessed apostle Paul. For often unawares we do things that we know not of; but the Lord seeth all things. Wherefore committing the judgment to Him, let us have sympathy one with another. Let us bear each other's burdens: but let us examine our own selves and hasten to fill up that in which we are lacking. And as a safeguard against sin let the following be observed. Let us each one note and write down our actions and the impulses of our soul as though we were going to relate them to each other. And be assured that if we should be utterly ashamed to have them known, we shall abstain from sin and harbour no base thoughts in our mind. For who wishes to be seen while sinning? or who will not rather lie after the commission of a sin, through the wish to escape notice? As then while we are looking at one another, we would not commit carnal sin, so if we record our thoughts as though about to tell them to one another, we shall the more easily keep ourselves free from vile thoughts through shame lest they should be known. Wherefore let that which is written be to us in place of the eyes of our fellow hermits, that blushing as much to write as if we had been caught, we may never think of what is unseemly. Thus fashioning ourselves we shall be able to keep the body in subjection, to please the Lord, and to trample on the devices of the enemy.

56. This was the advice he gave to those who came to him. And with those who suffered he sympathised and prayed. And oft-times the Lord heard him on behalf of many: yet he boasted not because he was heard, nor did he murmur if he were not. But always he gave the Lord thanks and besought the sufferer to be patient, and to know that healing belonged neither to him nor to man at all, but only to the Lord, who doeth good when and to whom He will. The sufferers therefore used to receive the words of the old man as though they were a cure, learning not to be downhearted but rather to be long-suffering. And those who were healed were taught not to give thanks to Antony but to God alone.

Basil of Caesarea

from *Homily VI on Luke 12*

Cappadocia, a region in today's Turkey, produced several important Christian theologians, of whom Basil of Caesarea (330–379) was among the most influential. His work in clarifying how Christ was simultaneously fully God and fully human became a standard explanation at the First Council of Constantinople (381)—only two years after Basil's death. In addition to key points of theology, Basil also had keen pastoral concerns. He contributed, for example, to the creation of Christian-based health-care service in Cappadocia, and was attentive to social inequities and disparities in wealth. In this homily, Basil draws upon the teachings in the Gospels, counseling Christians to calculate wealth by means other than the commonplace standards of society.

Homily VI., on Luke xii. 18, is on selfish wealth and greed.

Beware, says the preacher, lest the fate of the fool of the text be thine. "These things are written that we may shun their imitation. Imitate the earth, O man. Bear fruit, as she does, lest thou prove inferior to that which is without life. She produces her fruits, not that she may enjoy them, but for thy service. Thou dost gather for thyself whatever fruit of good works thou hast strewn, because the grace of good works returns to the giver. Thou hast given to the poor, and the gift becomes thine own, and comes back with increase. Just as grain that

SOURCE: Basil of Caesarea, *Homily VI on Luke 12*, in *A Select Library of Nicene and Post-Nicene Fathers of the Christian Church*, 2nd series, vol. 8, *St. Basil: Letters and Select Works*, translated into English with prolegomena and explanatory notes, under the editorial supervision of Philip Schaff and Henry Wace (New York: The Christian Literature Company, 1895), lvi–lvii. Treatise of De Spiritu Sancto, The Nine Homilies of the Hexaemeron, and the Letters of Saint Basil the Great, Archbishop of Caesarea translated with notes by The Rev. Blomfield Jackson.

has fallen on the earth becomes a gain to the sower, so the loaf thrown to the hungry man renders abundant fruit thereafter. Be the end of thy husbandry the beginning of the heavenly sowing. 'Sow,' it is written, 'to yourselves in righteousness.' Why then art thou distressed? Why dost thou harass thyself in thy efforts to shut up thy riches in clay and bricks? 'A good name is rather to be chosen than great riches.' If thou admire riches because of the honour that comes from them, bethink thee how very much more it tends to thine honour that thou shouldst be called the father of innumerable children than that thou shouldst possess innumerable staters in a purse. Thy wealth thou wilt leave behind thee here, even though thou like it not. The honour won by thy good deeds thou shalt convey with thee to the Master. Then all people standing round about thee in the presence of the universal Judge shall hail thee as feeder and benefactor, and give thee all the names that tell of loving kindness. Dost thou not see theatre-goers flinging away their wealth on boxers and buffoons and beast-fighters, fellows whom it is disgusting even to see, for the sake of the honour of a moment, and the cheers and clapping of the crowd? And art thou a niggard in thy expenses, when thou art destined to attain glory so great? God will welcome thee, angels will laud thee, mankind from the very beginning will call thee blessed. For thy stewardship of these corruptible things thy reward shall be glory everlasting, a crown of righteousness, the heavenly kingdom. Thou thinkest nothing of all this. Thy heart is so fixed on the present that thou despisest what is waited for in hope. Come then; dispose of thy wealth in various directions. Be generous and liberal in thy expenditure on the poor. Let it be said of thee, 'He hath dispersed, he hath given to the poor; his righteousness endureth for ever.' Do not press heavily on necessity and sell for great prices. Do not wait for a famine before thou openest thy barns. 'He that withholdeth corn, the people shall curse him.' Watch not for a time of want for gold's sake—for public scarcity to promote thy private profit. Drive not a huckster's bargains out of the troubles of mankind. Make not God's wrathful visitation an opportunity for abundance. Wound not the sores of men smitten by the scourge. Thou keepest thine eye on thy gold, and wilt not look at thy brother. Thou knowest the marks on the money, and canst distinguish good from bad. Thou canst not tell who is thy brother in the day of distress."

The conclusion is "'Ah!'—it is said—'words are all very fine: gold is finer.' I make the same impression as I do when I am preaching to libertines against their unchastity. Their mistress is blamed, and the mere mention of her serves but to enkindle their passions. How can I bring before your eyes the poor man's sufferings that thou mayest know out of what deep groanings thou art accumulating thy treasures, and of what high value will seem to thee in the day of judgment the famous words, 'Come, ye blessed of my Father, inherit the kingdom prepared for you from the foundation of the world: for I was an hungred and ye gave me meat: I was thirsty and ye gave me drink: . . . I was naked and ye clothed me.' What shuddering, what sweat, what darkness will be shed round thee, as thou hearest the words of condemnation!—'Depart from me, ye cursed, into outer darkness prepared for the devil and his angels: for I was an hungred and ye gave me no meat: I was thirsty and ye gave me no drink: . . . I was naked and ye clothed me not.' I have told thee what I have thought profitable. To thee now it is clear and plain what are the good things promised for thee if thou obey. If thou disobey, for thee the threat is written. I pray that thou mayest change to a better mind and thus escape its peril. In this way thy own wealth will be thy redemption. Thus thou mayest advance to the heavenly blessings prepared for thee by the grave of Him who hath called us all into His own kingdom, to Whom be glory and might for ever and ever. Amen."

40

Sulpicius Severus

from *Life of St. Martin*

Among those converted by Martin of Tours (316–397) was Sulpicius Severus, who returned the favor by writing the hagiographic *Life of St. Martin* (ca. 397). In his youth, Martin seemed to have an attraction to Christianity, to which he converted around 356. Drafted into the Roman military, Martin was unable to reconcile his military duties with his Christian faith. Thus, he announced that he could no longer serve in Rome's Legions. From that point forward, he would be a "soldier of Christ." In 371, Martin was consecrated Bishop of Tours (France) where he profoundly influenced the course of Western monasticism. He was among the first non-martyrs to be canonized as a Christian saint.

Chapter I. *Reasons for writing the Life of St. Martin.*

Most men being vainly devoted to the pursuit of worldly glory, have, as they imagined, acquired a memorial of their own names from this source; viz. devoting their pens to the embellishment of the lives of famous men. This course, although it did not secure for them a lasting reputation, still has undoubtedly brought them some fulfilment of the hope they cherished. It has done so, both by preserving their own memory, though to no purpose, and because, through their having presented to the world the examples of great men, no small emulation has been excited in the bosoms of their readers. Yet, notwithstanding these things, their labors have in no degree borne upon the

SOURCE: Sulpitius [Sulpicius] Severus, *The Life of St. Martin*, trans. Alexander Roberts, in *A Select Library of Nicene and Post-Nicene Fathers of the Christian Church*, 2nd series, vol. 11, *Sulpitius Severus. Vincent of Lerins. John Cassian*, translated into English with prolegomena and explanatory notes, under the editorial supervision of Philip Schaff and Henry Wace (New York: The Christian Literature Company, 1894), 3–6. Works of Sulpitius Severus translated, with preface, and notes, by Rev. Alexander Roberts.

blessed and never-ending life to which we look forward. For what has a glory, destined to perish with the world, profited those men themselves who have written on mere secular matters? Or what benefit has posterity derived from reading of Hector as a warrior, or Socrates as an expounder of philosophy? There can be no profit in such things, since it is not only folly to imitate the persons referred to, but absolute madness not to assail them with the utmost severity. For, in truth, those persons who estimate human life only by present actions, have consigned their hopes to fables, and their souls to the tomb. In fact, they gave themselves up to be perpetuated simply in the memory of mortals, whereas it is the duty of man rather to seek after eternal life than an eternal memorial and that, not by writing, or fighting, or philosophizing, but by living a pious, holy, and religious life. This erroneous conduct of mankind, being enshrined in literature, has prevailed to such an extent that it has found many who have been emulous either of the vain philosophy or the foolish excellence which has been celebrated. For this reason, I think I will accomplish something well worth the necessary pains, if I write the life of a most holy man, which shall serve in future as an example to others; by which, indeed, the readers shall be roused to the pursuit of true knowledge, and heavenly warfare, and divine virtue. In so doing, we have regard also to our own advantage, so that we may look for, not a vain remembrance among men, but an eternal reward from God. For, although we ourselves have not lived in such a manner that we can serve for an example to others, nevertheless, we have made it our endeavor that he should not remain unknown who was a man worthy of imitation. I shall therefore set about writing the life of St. Martin, and shall narrate both what he did previous to his episcopate, and what he performed as a bishop. At the same time, I cannot hope to set forth all that he was or did. Those excellences of which he alone was conscious are completely unknown, because, as he did not seek for honor from men, he desired, as much as he could accomplish it, that his virtues should be concealed. And even of those which had become known to us, we have omitted a great number, because we have judged it enough if only the more striking and eminent should be recorded. At the same time, I had in the interests of readers to see to it that, no undue amount of instances being set before them should make them weary of the subject. But I implore those who are to read what follows to give full faith to the things narrated, and to believe that I have written nothing of which I had not certain knowledge and evidence. I should, in fact, have preferred to be silent rather than to narrate things which are false.

Chapter II. *Military Service of St. Martin.*

Martin, then, was born at Sabaria in Pannonia, but was brought up at Tici-num, which is situated in Italy. His parents were, according to the judgment of the world, of no mean rank, but were heathens. His father was at first simply a soldier, but afterwards a military tribune. He himself in his youth following military pursuits was enrolled in the imperial guard, first under king Con-stantine, and then under Julian Cæsar. This, however, was not done of his own free will, for, almost from his earliest years, the holy infancy of the illustrious boy aspired rather to the service of God. For, when he was of the age of ten years, he betook himself, against the wish of his parents, to the Church, and begged that he might become a catechumen. Soon afterwards, becoming in a wonderful manner completely devoted to the service of God, when he was twelve years old, he desired to enter on the life of a hermit; and he would have followed up that desire with the necessary vows, had not his as yet too youthful age prevented. His mind, however, being always engaged on matters pertaining to the monasteries or the Church, already meditated in his boyish years what he afterwards, as a professed servant of Christ, fulfilled. But when an edict was issued by the ruling powers in the state, that the sons of veterans should be enrolled for military service, and he, on the information furnished by his father, (who looked with an evil eye on his blessed actions) having been seized and put in chains, when he was fifteen years old, was compelled to take the military oath, then showed himself content with only one servant as his at-tendant. And even to him, changing places as it were, he often acted as though, while really master, he had been inferior; to such a degree that, for the most part, he drew off his [servant's] boots and cleaned them with his own hand; while they took their meals together, the real master, however, generally acting the part of servant. During nearly three years before his baptism, he was en-gaged in the profession of arms, but he kept completely free from those vices in which that class of men become too frequently involved. He showed exceeding kindness towards his fellow-soldiers, and held them in wonderful affection; while his patience and humility surpassed what seemed possible to human nature. There is no need to praise the self-denial which he displayed: it was so great that, even at that date, he was regarded not so much as being a soldier as a monk. By all these qualities he had so endeared himself to the whole body of his comrades, that they esteemed him while they marvelously loved him. Although not yet made a new creature in Christ, he, by his good works, acted the part of a candidate for baptism. This he did, for instance, by aiding those who were in trouble, by furnishing assistance to the wretched, by supporting the needy, by clothing the naked, while he reserved nothing for himself from his military pay except what was necessary for his daily sustenance. Even then, far from being a senseless hearer of the Gospel, he so far complied with its precepts as to take no thought about the morrow.

Chapter III. *Christ appears to St. Martin.*

Accordingly, at a certain period, when he had nothing except his arms and his simple military dress, in the middle of winter, a winter which had shown itself more severe than ordinary, so that the extreme cold was proving fatal to many, he happened to meet at the gate of the city of Amiens a poor man destitute of clothing. He was entreating those that passed by to have compassion upon him, but all passed the wretched man without notice, when Martin, that man full of God, recognized that a being to whom others showed no pity, was, in that respect, left to him. Yet, what should he do? He had nothing except the cloak in which he was clad, for he had already parted with the rest of his garments for similar purposes. Taking, therefore, his sword with which he was girt, he divided his cloak into two equal parts, and gave one part to the poor man, while he again clothed himself with the remainder. Upon this, some of the by-standers laughed, because he was now an unsightly object, and stood out as but partly dressed. Many, however, who were of sounder understanding, groaned deeply because they themselves had done nothing similar. They especially felt this, because, being possessed of more than Martin, they could have clothed the poor man without reducing themselves to nakedness. In the following night, when Martin had resigned himself to sleep, he had a vision of Christ arrayed in that part of his cloak with which he had clothed the poor man. He contemplated the Lord with the greatest attention, and was told to own as his, the robe which he had given. Ere long, he heard Jesus saying with a clear voice to the multitude of angels standing round—"Martin, who is still but a catechumen, clothed me with this robe." The Lord, truly mindful of his own words (who had said when on earth—"Inasmuch as you have done these things to one of the least of these, you have done them unto me"), declared that he himself had been clothed in that poor man; and to confirm the testimony he bore to so good a deed, he condescended to show him himself in that very dress which the poor man had received. After this vision the sainted man was not puffed up with human glory, but, acknowledging the goodness of God in what had been done, and being now of the age of twenty years, he hastened to receive baptism. He did not, however, all at once, retire from military service, yielding to the entreaties of his tribune, whom he admitted to be his familiar tent-companion. For the tribune promised that, after the period of his office had expired, he too would retire from the world. Martin, kept back by the expectation of this event, continued, although but in name, to act the part of a soldier, for nearly two years after he had received baptism.

Chapter IV. *Martin retires from Military Service.*

In the meantime, as the barbarians were rushing within the two divisions of Gaul, Julian Cæsar, bringing an army together at the city of the Vaugiones, began to distribute a donative to the soldiers. As was the custom in such a case, they were called forward, one by one, until it came to the turn of Martin. Then, indeed, judging it a suitable opportunity for seeking his discharge—for he did not think it would be proper for him, if he were not to continue in the service, to receive a donative—he said to Cæsar, "Hitherto I have served *you* as a soldier: allow me now to become a soldier to God: let the man who is to serve thee receive thy donative: I am the soldier of Christ: it is not lawful for me to fight." Then truly the tyrant stormed on hearing such words, declaring that, from fear of the battle, which was to take place on the morrow, and not from any religious feeling, Martin withdrew from the service. But Martin, full of courage, yea all the more resolute from the danger that had been set before him, exclaims, "If this conduct of mine is ascribed to cowardice, and not to faith, I will take my stand unarmed before the line of battle tomorrow, and in the name of the Lord Jesus, protected by the sign of the cross, and not by shield or helmet, I will safely penetrate the ranks of the enemy." He is ordered, therefore, to be thrust back into prison, determined on proving his words true by exposing himself unarmed to the barbarians. But, on the following day, the enemy sent ambassadors to treat about peace and surrendered both themselves and all their possessions. In these circumstances who can doubt that this victory was due to the saintly man? It was granted him that he should not be sent unarmed to the fight. And although the good Lord could have preserved his own soldier, even amid the swords and darts of the enemy, yet that his blessed eyes might not be pained by witnessing the death of others, he removed all necessity for fighting. For Christ did not require to secure any other victory in behalf of his own soldier, than that, the enemy being subdued without bloodshed, no one should suffer death.

Augustine of Hippo

from *Confessions*

Augustine (354–430) was born in Tagaste in northern Africa and eventually became the Bishop of Hippo from 396–430. A prolific writer, he is easily one of the most influential of all the early Christian fathers and theologians. He is formally recognized today as a saint and as a Doctor of the Church by the Roman Catholic Church. St. Augustine's best-known works include the *City of God*, as well as his *Confessions*, from which the following is an excerpt. In this famous passage, Augustine is confessing to God about a particularly poignant example of moral perversity from his early years.

II.IV.9. Theft is punished by Thy law, O Lord, and by the law written in men's hearts, which iniquity itself cannot blot out. For what thief will suffer a thief? Even a rich thief will not suffer him who is driven to it by want. Yet had I a desire to commit robbery, and did so, compelled neither by hunger, nor poverty, but through a distaste for well-doing, and a lustiness of iniquity. For I pilfered that of which I had already sufficient, and much better. Nor did I desire to enjoy what I pilfered, but the theft and sin itself. There was a pear-tree close to our vineyard, heavily laden with fruit, which was tempting neither for its colour nor its flavour. To shake and rob this some of us wanton young fellows went, late one night (having, according to our disgraceful habit, prolonged our games in the streets until then), and carried away great loads, not to eat ourselves, but to fling to the very swine, having only eaten some of them; and to do this pleased us all the more because it was not permitted. Behold my heart, O my God; behold my heart, which Thou hadst pity upon when in the bottomless pit. Behold, now, let my heart tell Thee what it was seeking there, that I should be gratuitously wanton, having no

SOURCE: Augustine, *The Thirteen Books of the Confessions of St. Aur. Augustin*, trans. J. G. Pilkington in *A Select Library of the Nicene and Post-Nicene Fathers of the Christian Church*, ed. Philip Schaff, vol. 1, *The Confessions and Letters of St. Augustin, with a Sketch of His Life and Work* (Buffalo: The Christian Literature Company, 1886), 57–59.

inducement to evil but the evil itself. It was foul, and I loved it. I loved to perish. I loved my own error—not that for which I erred, but the error itself. Base soul, falling from Thy firmament to utter destruction—not seeking aught through the shame but the shame itself!

Chap. V.—He commits theft with his companions, not urged on by poverty, but from a certain distaste of well-doing.

10. There is a desirableness in all beautiful bodies, and in gold, and silver, and all things; and in bodily contact sympathy is powerful, and each other sense hath his proper adaptation of body. Worldly honour hath also its glory, and the power of command, and of overcoming; whence proceeds also the desire for revenge. And yet to acquire all these, we must not depart from Thee, O Lord, nor deviate from Thy law. The life which we live here hath also its peculiar attractiveness, through a certain measure of comeliness of its own, and harmony with all things here below. The friendships of men also are endeared by a sweet bond, in the oneness of many souls. On account of all these, and such as these, is sin committed; while through an inordinate preference for these goods of a lower kind, the better and higher are neglected,—even Thou, our Lord God, Thy truth, and Thy law. For these meaner things have their delights, but not like unto my God, who hath created all things; for in Him doth the righteous delight, and He is the sweetness of the upright in heart.

11. When, therefore, we inquire why a crime was committed, we do not believe it, unless it appear that there might have been the wish to obtain some of those which we designated meaner things, or else a fear of losing them. For truly they are beautiful and comely, although in comparison with those higher and celestial goods they be abject and contemptible. A man hath murdered another; what was his motive? He desired his wife or his estate; or would steal to support himself; or he was afraid of losing something of the kind by him; or, being injured, he was burning to be revenged. Would he commit murder without a motive, taking delight simply in the act of murder? Who would credit it? For as for that savage and brutal man, of whom it is declared that he was gratuitously wicked and cruel, there is yet a motive assigned. "Lest through idleness," he says, "hand or heart should grow inactive." And to what purpose? Why, even that, having once got possession of the city through that practice of wickedness, he might attain unto honours, empire, and wealth, and be exempt from the fear of the laws, and his difficult circumstances from the needs of his family, and the consciousness of his own wickedness. So it seems that even Catiline himself loved not his own villanies, but something else, which gave him the motive for committing them.

Chap. VI.—Why he delighted in that theft, when all things which under the appearance of good invite to vice are true and perfect in God alone.

12. What was it, then, that I, miserable one, so doted on in thee, thou theft of mine, thou deed of darkness, in that sixteenth year of my age? Beautiful thou wert not, since thou wert theft. But art thou anything, that so I may argue the case with thee? Those pears that we stole were fair to the sight, because they were Thy creation, Thou fairest of all, Creator of all, Thou good God—God, the highest good, and my true good. Those pears truly were pleasant to the sight; but it was not for them that my miserable soul lusted, for I had abundance of better, but those I plucked simply that I might steal. For, having plucked them, I threw them away, my sole gratification in them being my own sin, which I was pleased to enjoy. For if any of these pears entered my mouth, the sweetener of it was my sin in eating it. And now, O Lord my God, I ask what it was in that theft of mine that caused me such delight; and behold it hath no beauty in it—not such, I mean, as exists in justice and wisdom; nor such as is in the mind, memory, senses, and animal life of man; nor yet such as is the glory and beauty of the stars in their courses; or the earth, or the sea, teeming with incipient life, to replace, as it is born, that which decayeth; nor, indeed, that false and shadowy beauty which pertaineth to deceptive vices.

13. For thus doth pride imitate high estate, whereas Thou alone art God, high above all. And what does ambition seek but honours and renown, whereas Thou alone art to be honoured above all, and renowned for evermore? The cruelty of the powerful wishes to be feared; but who is to be feared but God only, out of whose power what can be forced away or withdrawn—when, or where, or whither, or by whom? The enticements of the wanton would fain be deemed love; and yet is naught more enticing than Thy charity, nor is aught loved more healthfully than that, Thy truth, bright and beautiful above all. Curiosity affects a desire for knowledge, whereas it is Thou who supremely knowest all things. Yea, ignorance and foolishness themselves are concealed under the names of ingenuousness and harmlessness, because nothing can be found more ingenuous than Thou; and what is more harmless, since it is a sinner's own works by which he is harmed? And sloth seems to long for rest; but what sure rest is there besides the Lord? Luxury would fain be called plenty and abundance; but Thou art the fulness and unfailing plenteousness of unfading joys. Prodigality presents a shadow of liberality; but Thou art the most lavish giver of all good. Covetousness desires to possess much; and Thou art the Possessor of all things. Envy contends for excellence; but what so excellent as Thou? Anger seeks revenge; who avenges more justly than Thou? Fear starts at unwonted and sudden chances which threaten things beloved, and is wary for their security; but what can happen that is unwonted or sudden to Thee? or who can deprive Thee of what Thou lovest? or where is there unshaken security

save with Thee? Grief languishes for things lost in which desire had delighted itself, even because it would have nothing taken from it, as nothing can be from Thee.

14. Thus doth the soul commit fornication when she turns away from Thee, and seeks without Thee what she cannot find pure and untainted until she returns to Thee. Thus all pervertedly imitate Thee who separate themselves far from Thee and raise themselves up against Thee. But even by thus imitating Thee they acknowledge Thee to be the Creator of all nature, and so that there is no place whither they can altogether retire from Thee. What, then, was it that I loved in that theft? And wherein did I, even corruptedly and pervertedly, imitate my Lord? Did I wish, if only by artifice, to act contrary to Thy law, because by power I could not, so that, being a captive, I might imitate an imperfect liberty by doing with impunity things which I was not allowed to do, in obscured likeness of Thy omnipotency? Behold this servant of Thine, fleeing from his Lord, and following a shadow! O rottenness! O monstrosity of life and profundity of death! Could I like that which was unlawful only because it was unlawful?

Chap. VII.—He gives thanks to God for the remission of his sins, and reminds everyone that the supreme God may have preserved us from greater sins.

15. "What shall I render unto the Lord," that whilst my memory recalls these things my soul is not appalled at them? I will love Thee, O Lord, and thank Thee, and confess unto Thy name, because Thou hast put away from me these so wicked and nefarious acts of mine. To Thy grace I attribute it, and to Thy mercy, that Thou hast melted away my sin as it were ice. To Thy grace also I attribute whatsoever of evil I have not committed; for what might I not have committed, loving as I did the sin for the sin's sake? Yea, all I confess to have been pardoned me, both those which I committed by my own perverseness, and those which, by Thy guidance, I committed not. Where is he who, reflecting upon his own infirmity, dares to ascribe his chastity and innocency to his own strength, so that he should love Thee the less, as if he had been in less need of Thy mercy, whereby Thou dost forgive the transgressions of those that turn to Thee? For whosoever, called by Thee, obeyed Thy voice, and shunned those things which he reads me recalling and confessing of myself, let him not despise me, who, being sick, was healed by that same Physician by whose aid it was that he was not sick, or rather was less sick. And for this let him love Thee as much, yea, all the more, since by whom he sees me to have been restored from so great a feebleness of sin, by Him he sees himself from a like feebleness to have been preserved.

Chap. VIII.—In his theft he loved the company of his fellow-sinners.

16. "What fruit had I then," wretched one, in those things which, when I remember them, cause me shame—above all in that theft, which I loved only for

the theft's sake? And as the theft itself was nothing, all the more wretched was I who loved it. Yet by myself alone I would not have done it—I recall what my heart was—alone I could not have done it. I loved, then, in it the companionship of my accomplices with whom I did it. I did not, therefore, love the theft alone—yea, rather, it was that alone that I loved, for the companionship was nothing. What is the fact? Who is it that can teach me, but He who illuminateth mine heart and searcheth out the dark corners thereof? What is it that hath come into my mind to inquire about, to discuss, and to reflect upon? For had I at that time loved the pears I stole, and wished to enjoy them, I might have done so alone, if I could have been satisfied with the mere commission of the theft by which my pleasure was secured; nor needed I have provoked that itching of my own passions, by the encouragement of accomplices. But as my enjoyment was not in those pears, it was in the crime itself, which the company of my fellow-sinners produced.

Chap. IX.—It was a pleasure to him also to laugh when seriously deceiving others.

17. By what feelings, then, was I animated? For it was in truth too shameful; and woe was me who had it. But still what was it? "Who can understand his errors?" We laughed, because our hearts were tickled at the thought of deceiving those who little imagined what we were doing, and would have vehemently disapproved of it. Yet, again, why did I so rejoice in this, that I did it not alone? Is it that no one readily laughs alone? No one does so readily; but yet sometimes, when men are alone by themselves, nobody being by, a fit of laughter overcomes them when anything very droll presents itself to their senses or mind. Yet alone I would not have done it—alone I could not at all have done it. Behold, my God, the lively recollection of my soul is laid bare before Thee—alone I had not committed that theft, wherein what I stole pleased me not, but rather the act of stealing; nor to have done it alone would I have liked so well, neither would I have done it. O Friendship too unfriendly! thou mysterious seducer of the soul, thou greediness to do mischief out of mirth and wantonness, thou craving for others' loss, without desire for my own profit or revenge; but when they say, "Let us go, let us do it," we are ashamed not to be shameless.

Chap. X.—With God there is true rest and life unchanging.

18. Who can unravel that twisted and tangled knottiness? It is foul. I hate to reflect on it. I hate to look on it. But thee do I long for, O righteousness and innocency, fair and comely to all virtuous eyes, and of a satisfaction that never palls! With thee is perfect rest, and life unchanging. He who enters into thee enters into the joy of his Lord, and shall have no fear, and shall do excellently in the most Excellent. I sank away from Thee, O my God, and I wandered too far from Thee, my stay, in my youth, and became to myself an unfruitful land.

42

Boethius

from *Consolation of Philosophy*

Anicius Manilus Severinus Boethius (ca. 475–526) was an aristocratic Roman statesman, governmental official, and thinker who wrote about a variety of topics ranging from logic, mathematics, and music to various issues in Christian theology. He is often thought to represent an important link from the ancient world to the medieval period in Western philosophy. His most famous work is his *Consolation of Philosophy*, which was presumably written while he was imprisoned for treason, a crime which he denied and for which he was ultimately executed. That text, from which the following is a brief excerpt, is an imaginary dialogue between the captive Boethius and the personification of philosophy.

Book II.

I. Thereafter for awhile she remained silent; and when she had restored my flagging attention by a moderate pause in her discourse, she thus began: 'If I have thoroughly ascertained the character and causes of thy sickness, thou art pining with regretful longing for thy former fortune. It is the change, as thou deemest, of this fortune that hath so wrought upon thy mind. Well do I understand that Siren's manifold wiles, the fatal charm of the friendship she pretends for her victims, so long as she is scheming to entrap them—how she unexpectedly abandons them and leaves them overwhelmed with insupportable grief. Bethink thee of her nature, character, and deserts, and thou wilt soon acknowledge that in her thou hast neither possessed, nor hast thou lost, aught of any worth. Methinks I need not spend much pains in bringing this to

SOURCE: Boethius, *The Consolation of Philosophy of Boethius*, trans. H. R. James (London: Elliot Stock, 1897), 43–51.

thy mind, since, even when she was still with thee, even while she was caress-
ing thee, thou usedst to assail her in manly terms, to rebuke her, with maxims
drawn from my holy treasure-house. But all sudden changes of circumstances
bring inevitably a certain commotion of spirit. Thus it hath come to pass that
thou also for awhile hast been parted from thy mind's tranquillity. But it is time
for thee to take and drain a draught, soft and pleasant to the taste, which, as it
penetrates within, may prepare the way for stronger potions. Wherefore I call
to my aid the sweet persuasiveness of Rhetoric, who then only walketh in the
right way when she forsakes not my instructions, and Music, my handmaid, I
bid to join with her singing, now in lighter, now in graver strain.

'What is it, then, poor mortal, that hath cast thee into lamentation and
mourning? Some strange, unwonted sight, methinks, have thine eyes seen.
Thou deemest Fortune to have changed towards thee; thou mistakest. Such
ever were her ways, ever such her nature. Rather in her very mutability hath
she preserved towards thee her true constancy. Such was she when she load-
ed thee with caresses, when she deluded thee with the allurements of a false
happiness. Thou hast found out how changeful is the face of the blind goddess.
She who still veils herself from others hath fully discovered to thee her whole
character. If thou likest her, take her as she is, and do not complain. If thou
abhorrest her perfidy, turn from her in disdain, renounce her, for baneful are
her delusions. The very thing which is now the cause of thy great grief ought
to have brought thee tranquillity. Thou hast been forsaken by one of whom
no one can be sure that she will not forsake him. Or dost thou indeed set
value on a happiness that is certain to depart? Again I ask, Is Fortune's presence dear to thee if she cannot be trusted to stay, and though she will bring
sorrow when she is gone? Why, if she cannot be kept at pleasure, and if her
flight overwhelms with calamity, what is this fleeting visitant but a token of
coming trouble? Truly it is not enough to look only at what lies before the
eyes; wisdom gauges the issues of things, and this same mutability, with its two
aspects, makes the threats of Fortune void of terror, and her caresses little to
be desired. Finally, thou oughtest to bear with whatever takes place within the
boundaries of Fortune's demesne, when thou hast placed thy head beneath
her yoke. But if thou wishest to impose a law of staying and departing on her
whom thou hast of thine own accord chosen for thy mistress, art thou not acting wrongfully, art thou not embittering by impatience a lot which thou canst
not alter? Didst thou commit thy sails to the winds, thou wouldst voyage not
whither thy intention was to go, but whither the winds drave thee; didst thou
entrust thy seed to the fields, thou wouldst set off the fruitful years against the
barren. Thou hast resigned thyself to the sway of Fortune; thou must submit

to thy mistress's caprices. What! art thou verily striving to stay the swing of the revolving wheel? Oh, stupidest of mortals, if it takes to standing still, it ceases to be the wheel of Fortune.'

Song I: Fortune's Malice.

Mad Fortune sweeps along in wanton pride,
Uncertain as Euripus' surging tide;
Now tramples mighty kings beneath her feet;
Now sets the conquered in the victor's seat.
She heedeth not the wail of hapless woe,
But mocks the griefs that from her mischief flow.
Such is her sport; so proveth she her power;
And great the marvel, when in one brief hour
She shows her darling lifted high in bliss,
Then headlong plunged in misery's abyss.

II. 'Now I would fain also reason with thee a little in Fortune's own words. Do thou observe whether her contentions be just. "Man," she might say, "why dost thou pursue me with thy daily complainings? What wrong have I done thee? What goods of thine have I taken from thee? Choose [as] thou wilt a judge, and let us dispute before him concerning the rightful ownership of wealth and rank. If thou succeedest in showing that any one of these things is the true property of mortal man, I freely grant those things to be thine which thou claimest. When nature brought thee forth out of thy mother's womb, I took thee, naked and destitute as thou wast, I cherished thee with my substance, and, in the partiality of my favour for thee, I brought thee up somewhat too indulgently, and this it is which now makes thee rebellious against me. I surrounded thee with a royal abundance of all those things that are in my power. Now it is my pleasure to draw back my hand. Thou hast reason to thank me for the use of what was not thine own; thou hast no right to complain, as if thou hadst lost what was wholly thine. Why, then, dost bemoan thyself? I have done thee no violence. Wealth, honour, and all such things are placed under my control. My handmaidens know their mistress; with me they come, and at my going they depart. I might boldly affirm that if those things the loss of which thou lamentest had been thine, thou couldst never have lost them. Am I alone to be forbidden to do what I will with my own? Unrebuked, the skies now reveal the brightness of day, now shroud the daylight in the darkness of night; the year may now engarland the face of the earth with flowers and fruits, now disfigure it with storms and cold. The sea is permitted to invite with smooth and tranquil surface to-day, to-morrow to roughen with wave and storm. Shall man's insatiate greed bind *me* to a constancy foreign to my character? This is my art, this the game I never cease to play. I turn the wheel that spins. I delight to see the high come down and the low ascend. Mount up, if thou wilt, but only on condition that thou wilt not think it a hardship to come down when the rules of my game require it. Wert thou ignorant of my character? Didst not know how Crœsus, King of the Lydians, erstwhile the dreaded rival of Cyrus, was afterwards pitiably consigned to the flame of the pyre, and only saved by a shower sent from heaven? Has it 'scaped thee how Paullus paid a meed of pious tears to the misfortunes of King Perseus, his prisoner? What else do tragedies make such woeful outcry over save the overthrow of kingdoms by the indiscriminate strokes of Fortune? Didst thou not learn in thy childhood how there stand at the threshold of Zeus 'two jars,' 'the one full of blessings, the other of calamities'? How if thou hast drawn over-liberally from the good jar? What if not even now have I departed wholly from thee? What if this very mutability of mine is a just ground for hoping better things? But listen now, and cease to let thy heart consume away with fretfulness, nor expect to live on thine own terms in a realm that is common to all.'

43

Benedict of Nursia

from *The Rule of St. Benedict*

With the western section of the Roman Empire in marked decline, Benedict of Nursia (ca. 480–550) drafted his Rule (*regula*) to stabilize monastic communities. His was by no means history's first Rule. The Rule of Augustine and the Rule of the Master preceded his. It was, however, the *Rule of St. Benedict* (530) that served as the principle foundation of cenobitic western monasticism for the next 1,500 years. Designed for his community at Monte Cassino, about eighty miles southeast of Rome, Benedict provided guidance for a life focused on an intimate relationship with God. The Rule also provided directions for the Abbot's shepherding of the community, the love and humility required of all community members, the ordered life of daily prayer and work, and the proper conservation of community resources.

Preface

Hearken, O Son, to the precepts of thy Master, and bend to Him the ear of thy heart: receive also with pleasure, and faithfully comply with the admonitions of a loving Father, that by pursuing the toilsome path of obedience, thou mayest return to Him, from whom thou hast departed, by following the broad and easy way of disobedience. To thee, therefore, I now direct my words, whosoever thou art, who, renouncing entirely thy own will, takest up the most powerful and brilliant armour of obedience, to fight under the standard of the Lord Jesus Christ, thy true King. First of all, then, when commencing any good work, let us beseech Him, with most fervent and persevering prayer, to perfect it; so that we may never have the misfortune to grieve Him by our evil doings, after having

SOURCE: Benedict, *The Holy Rule of St. Benedict*, trans. a Priest of Mount Melleray (London: Thomas Richardson and Son, 1865), 5–10, 22–26.

vouchsafed to reckon us among the number of His children. For we ought to be, at all times, obedient to Him, by the due employment of the talents He has entrusted to us, lest, if we provoke Him by our misdeeds, He should, one day, become in our regard, not only an angry Father, but even a dread Lord, and not alone deprive us of our inheritance, but consign us, moreover, as most wicked servants, to never-ending punishment, for refusing to follow Him to glory.

Wherefore, let us at length arise, awakened by that announcement of Scripture: "*It is now the hour for us to rise from sleep;*" and, having opened our eyes to the Divine light, let us hear with astonishment the admonitions addressed to us by the Voice of God, whilst day by day it crieth out saying, "*Today if you shall hear His Voice, harden not your hearts;*" and again, "*He that hath an ear, let him hear what the Spirit saith to the Churches.*" And what doth he say? "*Come, children, hearken to me; I will teach you the fear of the Lord.*" "*Walk whilst you have the light, that the darkness overtake you not.*"

And the Lord seeking out a labourer for His vineyard, among the multitude, to whom He addresses the foregoing admonitions, saith again: "*Who is the man that desireth life, who loveth to see good days?*" Shouldst thou hearing this make answer, and say, I am he, God saith to thee, If thou wilt have true and everlasting life "*Keep thy tongue from evil, and thy lips from speaking guile. Turn away from evil, and do good; seek after peace, and pursue it:*" and when you shall have done these things, Mine eyes shall be upon you; and Mine ears open to your prayers; and before you call upon Me, I will say, "*Lo! here I am.*" What can be sweeter to us, beloved brethren, than this invitation of the Lord? Behold! the Lord, in His loving-kindness, points out to us the way of life. Having, therefore, our loins girt about with faith, and the observance of good works, let us, with the Gospel as our guide, go forward in His paths; that we may deserve to see, in His kingdom, Him who hath called us. In which kingdom if we desire to dwell, we should be persuaded, that we can never attain to it, except by the practice of good works. But, that we may be fully convinced of this all-important truth, let us, with the prophet, interrogate the Lord Himself, saying to Him, "*Lord, who shall dwell in Thy Tabernacle; or who shall rest in Thy holy hill?*" After this interrogation, brethren, let us hear the Lord making answer, and showing us the way to His Tabernacle: "*He that walketh without blemish, and worketh justice; he that speaketh truth in his heart; who hath not used deceit in his tongue; nor hath done evil to his neighbour.*" He who repelling with scorn the wicked tempter, hath brought him to nought together with his temptations; he that hath taken hold of his evil suggestions while yet in their birth, and dashed them against the Rock, which is Christ. They who fear the Lord, do not pride themselves in their fidelity to the rules of a perfect life; but referring whatever of good they perceive in themselves solely to God, as to its principle and Author, they magnify Him working in them; saying with the prophet, "*Not to us, O Lord, not to us, but to Thy Name give glory.*" Thus it was, that Paul, the Apostle, did not glory in his preaching, as he himself testifies, saying, "*By the grace of God I am what I am;*" and again, "*He that glorieth, let him glory in the Lord.*" To this effect our Lord also saith in the Gospel, "*Every one therefore that heareth these My words, and doth them, shall be likened to a wise man, that built his house upon a rock; and the rain fell, and the floods came, and the winds blew, and they beat upon that house; and it fell not; for it was founded on a rock.*" In fine, the Lord daily awaits our compliance with these, His holy admonitions; so that, if He prolongs the term of our mortal life, it is, that we may ultimately amend our evil ways, according to that of the Apostle: "*Knowest thou not that the benignity of God leadeth thee to penance?*" for the merciful Lord saith, "*Is it My will, that a sinner should die; and not, that he should be converted from his ways, and live?*"

Having, then, brethren, asked the Lord, who is it that shall dwell in His tabernacle, we have heard what He has enjoined on those, who aspire to that happiness; with which injunctions, if we faithfully comply, we shall one day inherit the kingdom of heaven.

Let us, therefore, prepare ourselves to fight, heart and hand, beneath the standard of holy obedience to His precepts; and, to this end, let us beseech Him to strengthen our weakness by the assistance of His grace. If, moreover, we desire to escape the pains of hell, and to attain to life everlasting, let us, whilst there is yet time, and we abide in this mortal body, and thus have it in our power to do all that is commanded us, let us, I say, do speedily and with all fervour, what will be conducive to our eternal welfare.

We shall, therefore, proceed to establish a school where souls may be formed to the service of God; in doing so, we hope we shall ordain nothing too rigid; but though we should be somewhat severe, in some particulars, (which is but reasonable) in order to the reformation of vice, and the maintenance of charity, be not so frightened thereat, as to fly straightway from the path of salvation. This path is, indeed, narrow in the beginning; but when thou shalt have advanced therein, and grown strong in Faith; thy heart shall be enlarged; and thou shalt run in the way of God's commandments, with that unspeakable delight, which charity imparts to the soul. Thus, persevering in the monastery until death, as the obedient disciples and faithful followers of our Divine Master, we shall become partakers in the sufferings of Christ; and thereby deserve to be co-heirs with Him of His heavenly kingdom.

[. . . .]

Chapter IV: The Instruments of Good Works

1. To love the Lord thy God with thy whole heart, and with thy whole soul, and with thy whole strength.
2. To love thy neighbour as thyself.
3. Not to kill.
4. Not to commit adultery.
5. Not to steal.
6. Not to covet.
7. Not to bear false witness.
8. To honour all men.
9. Not to do to another what one will not have done to oneself.
10. To renounce oneself, in order to follow Christ.
11. To chastise the body.
12. Not to place one's happiness in the delights of the world.
13. To love fasting.
14. To refresh the poor.
15. To clothe the naked.
16. To visit the sick.
17. To bury the dead.
18. To relieve the oppressed.
19. To comfort those who are in sorrow.
20. To be estranged from the ways of the world.
21. To prefer nothing to the love of Christ.
22. Not to yield to anger.
23. Not to meditate revenge.
24. Not to harbour deceit in the heart.
25. To have unfeigned peace with all men.
26. Not to depart from charity.
27. Not to swear lest one should incur the guilt of perjury.
28. To speak the truth with candour.
29. Not to return evil for evil.
30. To injure no man, but to bear patiently an injury inflicted.
31. To love one's enemies.
32. Not to speak ill of those by whom one is reviled; but rather to bless them.
33. To suffer persecution for justice's sake.
34. Not to be proud.
35. Not to be given to wine.
36. Not to be greedy at meals.

37. Not to love sleep.
38. Not to be sluggish.
39. Not to be a murmurer.
40. Not to be a detractor.
41. To put one's hope in God.
42. Whatever of good one sees in oneself, to refer it to God and not to oneself.
43. To be persuaded, that whatever evil one does, comes from oneself, and to attribute it to oneself.
44. To fear the day of judgment.
45. To dread the torments of hell.
46. To long for eternal life with most ardent desire.
47. To keep death daily before one's eyes.
48. To watch continually over all one's actions.
49. To be convinced, that wherever we are, God beholds us.
50. To dash, instantly, against the rock, which is Christ, whatever evil thoughts the enemy suggests.
51. To manifest them to one's spiritual father.
52. To refrain from all sinful discourse.
53. Not to love much speaking.
54. Not to speak frivolous words, or such as are calculated to provoke laughter.
55. Not to love much or loud laughter.
56. To listen willingly to pious reading.
57. To pray often.
58. To confess to God the sins of one's past life; and to bewail them daily with sighs and tears.
59. To mortify the desires of the flesh; and to hate one's own will.
60. To obey the commands of the Abbot in all things, though he should himself, (which God forbid,) act in opposition to them; remembering that precept of our Lord: "*All things therefore whatsoever they shall say to you, observe and do; but according to their works do ye not.*"
61. Not to wish to be called holy before one is really so; but to be so in reality, that one may deserve the title.
62. To keep the commandments of God at all times.
63. To love chastity.
64. To hate no man.
65. Not to entertain feelings of envy or jealousy.
66. Not to love contention.

67. To shun haughtiness.
68. To respect our seniors.
69. To love one's juniors.
70. To pray for one's enemies, for the love of Christ.
71. To be reconciled to those with whom one is at variance, before the setting of the sun.
72. And never to despair of God's mercy.

These are the instruments of the spiritual calling, which, if we continually use, both day and night, and deliver up to our Divine Master, on the day of judgment, He shall give us that reward, which He Himself hath promised; and of which the Apostle says, "*That eye hath not seen, nor ear heard, neither hath it entered into the heart of man, what things God hath prepared for them that love Him.*"

The place or workshop where we are to apply ourselves to the assiduous exercise of that spiritual and Divine calling is no other than the enclosure of the Monastery, from which we are never to depart.

44

John of Damascus

from *Exposition of the Orthodox Faith*

In the eighth and ninth centuries, Eastern Orthodoxy debated whether images and pictures were appropriate in public and private Christian worship—a dispute known as the "Iconoclastic Controversy." In 730, Byzantine Emperor Leo III called for the destruction of such imagery, believing the representations to be a form of idolatry. John of Damascus (ca. 675–749), one of Eastern Orthodoxy's foremost theologians, provided a defense for the use of icons. He explained in one of his works, for example: "I do not worship matter, I worship the God of matter, who became matter for my sake, and deigned to inhabit matter, who worked out my salvation through matter. I venerate it, though not as God." Although untold ancient works were destroyed during the controversy, the use of icons was ultimately affirmed as an accepted practice for Eastern churches—well after John of Damascus' life.

Chapter XVI: *Concerning Images.*

But since some find fault with us for worshipping and honouring the image of our Saviour and that of our Lady, and those, too, of the rest of the saints and servants of Christ, let them remember that in the beginning God created man after His own image. On what grounds, then, do we shew reverence to each other unless because we are made after God's image? For as Basil, that much-versed expounder of divine things, says, the honour given to the image passes over to the prototype. Now a prototype is that which is imaged, from

SOURCE: John of Damascus, *Exposition of the Orthodox Faith*, trans. S. D. F. Salmond, in *A Select Library of Nicene and Post-Nicene Fathers of the Christian Church*, 2nd series, translated into English with prolegomena and explanatory notes, under the editorial supervision of Philip Schaff and Henry Wace, vol. 9, *St. Hilary of Poitiers. John of Damascus* (New York: Charles Scribner's Sons, 1899), 88 [467/493]

that which the derivative is obtained. Why was it that the Mosaic people honoured on all hands the tabernacle which bore an image and type of heavenly things, or rather of the whole creation? God indeed said to Moses, "*Look that thou make them after their pattern which was shewed thee in the mount.*" The Cherubim, too, which o'ershadow the mercy seat, are they not the work of men's hands? What, further, is the celebrated temple at Jerusalem? Is it not hand-made and fashioned by the skill of men?

Moreover the divine Scripture blames those who worship graven images, but also those who sacrifice to demons. The Greeks sacrificed and the Jews also sacrificed: but the Greeks to demons and the Jews to God. And the sacrifice of the Greeks was rejected and condemned, but the sacrifice of the just was very acceptable to God. For Noah sacrificed, and "*God smelled a sweet savour*," receiving the fragrance of the right choice and good-will towards Him. And so the graven images of the Greeks, since they were images of deities, were rejected and forbidden.

But besides this who can make an imitation of the invisible, incorporeal, uncircumscribed, formless God? Therefore to give form to the Deity is the height of folly and impiety. And hence it is that in the Old Testament the use of images was not uncommon. But after God in His bowels of pity became in truth man for our salvation, not as He was seen by Abraham in the semblance of a man, nor as He was seen by the prophets, but in being truly man, and after He lived upon the earth and dwelt among men, worked miracles, suffered, was crucified, rose again and was taken back to Heaven, since all these things actually took place and were seen by men, they were written for the remembrance and instruction of us who were not alive at that time in order that though we saw not, we may still, hearing and believing, obtain the blessing of the Lord. But seeing that not every one has a knowledge of letters nor time for reading, the Fathers gave their sanction to depicting these events on images as being acts of great heroism, in order that they should form a concise memorial of them. Often, doubtless, when we have not the Lord's passion in mind and see the image of Christ's crucifixion, His saving passion is brought back to remembrance, and we fall down and worship not the material but that which is imaged: just as we do not worship the material of which the Gospels are made, nor the material of the Cross, but that which these typify. For wherein does the cross, that typifies the Lord, differ from a cross that does not do so? It is just the same also in the case of the Mother of the Lord. For the honour which we give to her is referred to Him Who was made of her incarnate. And similarly also the brave acts of holy men stir us up to be brave and to emulate and imitate their valor and to glorify God. For as we said, the honour that is given to the best of fellow-servants is a proof of good-will towards our common Lady, and the honour rendered to the image passes over to the prototype. But this is an unwritten tradition, just as is also the worshipping towards the East and the worship of the Cross, and very many other similar things.

[. . . .]

Moreover that the Apostles handed down much that was unwritten, Paul, the Apostle of the Gentiles, tells us in these words: *"Therefore, brethren, stand fast and hold the traditions which ye have been taught of us, whether by word or by epistle."* And to the Corinthians he writes, *"Now I praise you, brethren, that ye remember me in all things, and keep the traditions as I have delivered them to you."*

45

The Venerable Bede

from *Ecclesiastical History of England* (Caedmon's Story)

An English Benedictine monk who lived in the Kingdom of Northumbria during the early middle ages, St. Bede, also known as the Venerable Bede (672/673–735), was a prolific scholar and teacher who wrote on a variety of topics ranging from nature to poetry and grammar to history and biography to his influential biblical commentaries. He is sometimes regarded as the father of English history, thanks in part to his best-known work, *The Ecclesiastical History of England*, which is a key source of information about the conversion of the Anglo-Saxon peoples to Christianity. That text, from which the following is an excerpt, is the first work to date events in time according to the birth of Christ. Bede was declared a Doctor of the Church by Pope Leo XIII in 1899.

There was in the monastery of this abbess a certain brother, marked in a special manner by the grace of God, for he was wont to make songs of piety and religion, so that whatever was expounded to him out of Scripture, he turned ere long into verse expressive of much sweetness and penitence, in English, which was his native language. By his songs the minds of many were often fired with contempt of the world, and desire of the heavenly life. Others of the English nation after him attempted to compose religious poems, but none could equal him, for he did not learn the art of poetry from men, neither was he taught by man, but by God's grace he received the free gift of song, for which reason he never could compose any trivial or vain poem, but only those which concern religion it behoved his religious tongue to utter. For having lived in the secular habit till he was well advanced in years, he had never learned anything of versifying; and for this reason sometimes at a banquet,

SOURCE: The Venerable Bede, *Bede's Ecclesiastical History of England*, trans. A. M. Sellar (London: George Bell and Sons, 1907), 277–81.

when it was agreed to make merry by singing in turn, if he saw the harp come towards him, he would rise up from table and go out and return home.

Once having done so and gone out of the house where the banquet was, to the stable, where he had to take care of the cattle that night, he there composed himself to rest at the proper time. Thereupon one stood by him in his sleep, and saluting him, and calling him by his name, said, "Cædmon, sing me something." But he answered, "I cannot sing, and for this cause I left the banquet and retired hither, because I could not sing." Then he who talked to him replied, "Nevertheless thou must needs sing to me." "What must I sing?" he asked. "Sing the beginning of creation," said the other. Having received this answer he straightway began to sing verses to the praise of God the Creator, which he had never heard, the purport whereof was after this manner: "Now must we praise the Maker of the heavenly kingdom, the power of the Creator and His counsel, the deeds of the Father of glory. How He, being the eternal God, became the Author of all wondrous works, Who being the Almighty Guardian of the human race, first created heaven for the sons of men to be the covering of their dwelling place, and next the earth." This is the sense but not the order of the words as he sang them in his sleep; for verses, though never so well composed, cannot be literally translated out of one language into another without loss of their beauty and loftiness. Awaking from his sleep, he remembered all that he had sung in his dream, and soon added more after the same manner, in words which worthily expressed the praise of God.

In the morning he came to the reeve who was over him, and having told him of the gift he had received, was conducted to the abbess, and bidden, in the presence of many learned men, to tell his dream, and repeat the verses, that they might all examine and give their judgement upon the nature and origin of the gift whereof he spoke. And they all judged that heavenly grace had been granted to him by the Lord. They expounded to him a passage of sacred history or doctrine, enjoining upon him, if he could, to put it into verse. Having undertaken this task, he went away, and returning the next morning, gave them the passage he had been bidden to translate, rendered in most excellent verse. Whereupon the abbess, joyfully recognizing the grace of God in the man, instructed him to quit the secular habit, and take upon him monastic vows; and having received him into the monastery, she and all her people admitted him to the company of the brethren, and ordered that he should be taught the whole course of sacred history. So he, giving ear to all that he could learn, and bearing it in mind, and as it were ruminating, like a clean animal, turned it into most harmonious verse; and sweetly singing it, made his masters in their turn his hearers. He sang the creation of the world, the origin of man, and all the history of Genesis, the departure of the children of Israel out of Egypt, their entrance into the promised land, and many other histories from Holy Scripture; the Incarnation, Passion, Resurrection of our Lord, and His Ascension into heaven; the coming of the Holy Ghost, and the teaching of the Apostles; likewise he made many songs concerning the terror of future judgement, the horror of the pains of hell, and the joys of heaven; besides many more about the blessings and the judgements of God, by all of which he endeavoured to draw men away from the love of sin, and to excite in them devotion to well-doing and perseverance therein. For he was a very religious man, humbly submissive to the discipline of monastic rule, but inflamed with fervent zeal against those who chose to do otherwise; for which reason he made a fair ending of his life.

For when the hour of his departure drew near, it was preceded by a bodily infirmity under which he laboured for the space of fourteen days, yet it was of so mild a nature that he could talk and go about the whole time. In his neighbourhood was the house to which those that were sick, and like to die, were wont to be carried. He desired the person that ministered to him, as the evening came on of the night in which he was to depart this life, to make ready a place there for him to take his rest. The man, wondering why he should desire it, because there was as yet no sign of his approaching death, nevertheless did his bidding. When they had lain down there, and had been conversing happily and pleasantly for some time with those that were in the house before, and it was now past midnight, he asked them, whether they had the Eucharist within? They answered, "What need of the Eucharist? for you are not yet appointed to die, since you talk so merrily with us, as if you were in good health." "Nevertheless," said he, "bring me the Eucharist." Having received It into his hand, he asked, whether they were all in charity with him, and had no complaint against him, nor any quarrel or grudge. They answered, that they were all in perfect charity with him, and free from all anger; and in their turn they asked him to be of the same mind towards them. He answered at once, "I am in charity, my children, with all the servants of God." Then strengthening himself with the heavenly Viaticum, he prepared for the entrance into another life, and asked how near the time was when the brothers should be awakened to sing the nightly praises of the Lord? They answered, "It is not far off." Then he said, "It is well, let us await that hour;" and signing himself with the sign of the Holy Cross, he laid his head on the pillow, and falling into a slumber for a little while, so ended his life in silence.

Thus it came to pass, that as he had served the Lord with a simple and pure mind, and quiet devotion, so he now departed to behold His Presence, leaving the world by a quiet death; and that tongue, which had uttered so many wholesome words in praise of the Creator, spake its last words also in His praise, while he signed himself with the Cross, and commended his spirit into His hands; and by what has been here said, he seems to have had foreknowledge of his death.

Li Po

The Sun

Li Po (700–761), also known as Li Bai or Li Bo or Li Pai, was a celebrated Chinese poet and traveler from the Sichuan Province during the Tang dynasty. His hundreds of poems helped contribute to what has been regarded by some as the golden age of Chinese poetry. They have been influential across the globe for centuries.

O Sun that rose in the eastern corner of Earth,
Looking as though you came from under the ground,
When you crossed the sky and entered the deep sea,
Where did you stable your six dragon-steeds?
Now and of old your journeys have never ceased:
    Strong were that man's limbs
Who could run beside you on your travels to and fro.

The grass does not refuse
To flourish in the spring wind;
The leaves are not angry
At falling through the autumn sky.
Who with whip or spur
Can urge the feet of Time?
The things of the world flourish and decay,
Each at its own hour.

SOURCE: Li Po, "The Sun," in Arthur Waley, *The Poet Li Po, A.D. 701–762: A Paper Read before the China Society at the School of Oriental Studies on November 21, 1918* (London: East and West, Ltd., 1919), 16–17.

Hsi-ho, Hsi-ho,
Is it true that once you loitered in the West
While Lu Yang raised his spear, to hold
The progress of your light;
Then plunged and sank in the turmoil of the sea?
Rebels against Heaven, slanderers of Fate;
Many defy the Way.
But *I* will put | the Whole Lump | of Life in my bag,
And merge my being in the Primal Element.

47

Eginhard

from *Life of Charlemagne*

Eginhard (ca. 775–840), also known as Einhard or Einhart, was the student of Alcuin, who was himself the student of one of the Venerable Bede's own pupils. Eginhard was the close personal associate of Charlemagne, as well as his son and successor, Louis the Pious. The following is an excerpt from his most important work, *Life of Charlemagne*, which is often regarded as being among the earliest biographies of a European monarch and among the most important literary works of the early Middle Ages.

XVII. This King, who showed himself so great in extending his empire and subduing foreign nations, and was constantly occupied with plans to that end, undertook also very many works calculated to adorn and benefit his kingdom, and brought several of them to completion. Among these, the most deserving of mention are the basilica of the Holy Mother of God at Aix-la-Chapelle, built in the most admirable manner, and a bridge over the Rhine at Mayence, half a mile long, the breadth of the river at this point. This bridge was destroyed by fire the year before Charles died, but, owing to his death so soon after, could not be repaired, although he had intended to rebuild it in stone. He began two palaces of beautiful workmanship—one near his manor called Ingelheim, not far from Mayence; the other at Nimeguen, on the Waal, the stream that washes the south side of the island of the Batavians. But, above all, sacred edifices were the object of his care throughout his whole kingdom; and whenever he found them falling to ruin from age, he commanded the priests and fathers who had charge of them to repair them, and made sure by commissioners that his instructions were obeyed. He also fitted out a fleet for the war with the

SOURCE: Eginhard, *Life of Charlemagne*, trans. Samuel Epes Turner (New York: American Book Company, 1880), 45–67.

Northmen; the vessels required for this purpose were built on the rivers that flow from Gaul and Germany into the Northern Ocean. Moreover, since the Northmen continually overran and laid waste the Gallic and German coasts, he caused watch and ward to be kept in all the harbours, and at the mouths of rivers large enough to admit the entrance of vessels, to prevent the enemy from disembarking; and in the South, in Narbonensis and Septimania, and along the whole coast of Italy as far as Rome, he took the same precautions against the Moors, who had recently begun their piratical practices. Hence, Italy suffered no great harm in his time at the hands of the Moors, nor Gaul and Germany from the Northmen, save that the Moors got possession of the Etruscan town of Civita Vecchia by treachery, and sacked it, and the Northmen harried some of the islands in Frisia off the German coast.

XVIII. Thus did Charles defend and increase as well as beautify his kingdom, as is well known; and here let me express my admiration of his great qualities and his extraordinary constancy alike in good and evil fortune. I will now forthwith proceed to give the details of his private and family life.

After his father's death, while sharing the kingdom with his brother, he bore his unfriendliness and jealousy most patiently, and, to the wonder of all, could not be provoked to be angry with him. Later he married a daughter of Desiderius, King of the Lombards, at the instance of his mother; but he repudiated her at the end of a year for some reason unknown, and married Hildegard, a woman of high birth, of Suabian origin. He had three sons by her—Charles, Pepin, and Lewis—and as many daughters—Hruodrud, Bertha, and Gisela. He had three other daughters besides these—Theoderada, Hiltrud, and Ruodhaid—two by his third wife, Fastrada, a woman of East Frankish (that is to say, of German) origin, and the third by a concubine, whose name for the moment escapes me. At the death of Fastrada, he married Liutgard, an Alemannic woman, who bore him no children. After her death he had three concubines—Gersuinda, a Saxon, by whom he had Adaltrud; Regina, who was the mother of Drogo and Hugh; and Ethelind, by whom he had Theodoric. Charles's mother, Berthrada, passed her old age with him in great honour; he entertained the greatest veneration for her; and there was never any disagreement between them except when he divorced the daughter of King Desiderius, whom he had married to please her. She died soon after Hildegard, after living to see three grandsons and as many granddaughters in her son's house, and he buried her with great pomp in the Basilica of St. Denis, where his father lay. He had an only sister, Gisela, who had consecrated herself to a religious life from girlhood, and he cherished as much affection for her as for his mother. She also died a few years before him in the nunnery where she had passed her life.

XIX. The plan that he adopted for his children's education was, first of all, to have both boys and girls instructed in the liberal arts, to which he also turned his own attention. As soon as their years admitted, in accordance with the custom of the Franks, the boys had to learn horsemanship, and to practice war and the chase, and the girls to familiarize themselves with cloth-making, and to handle distaff and spindle, that they might not grow indolent through idleness, and he fostered in them every virtuous sentiment. He only lost three of all his children before his death, two sons and one daughter, Charles, who was the eldest, Pepin, whom he had made King of Italy, and Hruodrud, his oldest daughter, whom he had betrothed to Constantine, Emperor of the Greeks. Pepin left one son, named Bernard, and five daughters, Adelaide, Atula, Guntrada, Berthaid, and Theoderada. The King gave a striking proof of his fatherly affection at the time of Pepin's death: he appointed the grandson to succeed Pepin, and had the granddaughters brought up with his own daughters. When his sons and his daughter died, he was not so calm as might have been expected from his remarkably strong mind, for his affections were no less strong, and moved him to tears. Again, when he was told of the death of Hadrian, the Roman Pontiff, whom he had loved most of all his friends, he wept as much as if he had lost a brother, or a very dear son. He was by nature most ready to contract friendships, and not only made friends easily, but clung to them persistently, and cherished most fondly those with whom he had formed such ties. He was so careful of the training of his sons and daughters that he never took his meals without them when he was at home, and never made a journey without them; his sons would ride at his side, and his daughters follow him, while a number of his body-guard, detailed for their protection, brought up the rear. Strange to say, although they were very handsome women, and he loved them very dearly, he was never willing to marry any of them to a man of their own nation or to a foreigner, but kept them all at home until his death, saying that he could not dispense with their society. Hence, though otherwise happy, he experienced the malignity of fortune as far as they were concerned; yet he concealed his knowledge of the rumours current in regard to them, and of the suspicions entertained of their honour.

XX. By one of his concubines he had a son, handsome in face, but hunchbacked, named Pepin, whom I omitted to mention in the list of his children. When Charles was at war with the Huns, and was wintering in Bavaria, this Pepin shammed sickness, and plotted against his father in company with some of the leading Franks, who seduced him with vain promises of the royal authority. When his deceit was discovered, and the conspirators were punished, his head was shaved, and he was suffered, in accordance with his wishes, to devote himself to a religious life in the monastery of Prüm. A formidable conspiracy against Charles had previously been set on foot in Germany, but all the traitors were banished, some of them without mutilation, others after their eyes had been put out. Three of them only lost their lives; they drew their swords and re-sisted arrest, and, after killing several men, were cut down, because they could not be otherwise overpowered. It is supposed that the cruelty of Queen Fastra-da was the primary cause of these plots, and they were both due to Charles's apparent acquiescence in his wife's cruel conduct, and deviation from the usual kindness and gentleness of his disposition. All the rest of his life he was regard-ed by everyone with the utmost love and affection, so much so that not the least accusation of unjust rigour was ever made against him.

XXI. He liked foreigners, and was at great pains to take them under his protection. There were often so many of them, both in the palace and the king-dom, that they might reasonably have been considered a nuisance; but he, with his broad humanity, was very little disturbed by such annoyances, because he felt himself compensated for these great inconveniences by the praises of his generosity and the reward of high renown.

XXII. Charles was large and strong, and of lofty stature, though not dispro-portionately tall (his height is well known to have been seven times the length of his foot); the upper part of his head was round, his eyes very large and an-imated, nose a little long, hair fair, and face laughing and merry. Thus his ap-pearance was always stately and dignified, whether he was standing or sitting; although his neck was thick and somewhat short, and his belly rather promi-nent; but the symmetry of the rest of his body concealed these defects. His gait was firm, his whole carriage manly, and his voice clear, but not so strong as his size led one to expect. His health was excellent except during the four years preceding his death, when he was subject to frequent fevers; at the last he even limped a little with one foot. Even in those years he consulted rather his own inclination, than the advice of physicians, who were almost hateful to him, because they wanted him to give up roasts, to which he was accustomed, and to eat boiled meat instead. In accordance with the national custom, he took frequent exercise on horseback and in the chase, accomplishments in which scarcely any people in the world can equal the Franks. He enjoyed the exhala-tions from natural warm springs, and often practiced swimming, in which he was such an adept that none could surpass him; and hence it was that he built his palace at Aix-la-Chapelle, and lived there constantly during his latter years until his death. He used not only to invite his sons to his bath, but his nobles and friends, and now and then a troop of his retinue or body-guard, so that a hundred or more persons sometimes bathed with him.

XXIII. He used to wear the national, that is to say, the Frank, dress—next his skin a linen shirt and linen breeches, and above these a tunic fringed with silk; while hose fastened by bands covered his lower limbs, and shoes his feet, and he protected his shoulders and chest in winter by a close-fitting coat of otter or marten skins. Over all he flung a blue cloak, and he always had a sword girt about him usually one with a gold or silver hilt and belt; he sometimes carried a jeweled sword, but only on great feast-days or at the reception of ambassadors from foreign nations. He despised foreign costumes however handsome, and never allowed himself to be robed in them except twice in Rome, when he donned the Roman tunic, chlamys, and shoes; the first time at the request of Pope Hadrian, the second to gratify Leo, Hadrian's successor. On great feast-days he made use of embroidered clothes, and shoes bedecked with precious stones; his cloak was fastened by a golden buckle, and he appeared crowned with a diadem of gold and gems: but on other days his dress varied little from the common dress of the people.

Charles was temperate in eating, and particularly so in drinking, for he abominated drunkenness in anybody, much more in himself and those of his household; but he could not easily abstain from food, and often complained that fasts injured his health. He very rarely gave entertainments, only on great feast-days, and then to large numbers of people. His meals ordinarily consisted of four courses, not counting the roast, which his huntsmen used to bring in on the spit; he was more fond of this than of any other dish. While at table, he listened to reading or music. The subjects of the readings were the stories and deeds of olden time: he was fond, too, of St. Augustine's books, and especially of the one entitled "The City of God." He was so moderate in the use of wine and all sorts of drink that he rarely allowed himself more than three cups in the course of a meal. In summer, after the midday meal, he would eat some fruit, drain a single cup, put off his clothes and shoes, just as he did for the night, and rest for two or three hours. He was in the habit of awaking and rising from bed four or five times during the night. While he was dressing and putting on his shoes, he not only gave audience to his friends, but if the Count of the Palace told him of any suit in which his judgment was necessary, he had the parties brought before him forthwith, took cognizance of the case, and gave his decision, just as if he were sitting on the judgment-seat. This was not the only business that he transacted at this time, but he performed any duty of the day whatever, whether he had to attend to the matter himself, or to give commands concerning it to his officers.

XXV. Charles had the gift of ready and fluent speech, and could express whatever he had to say with the utmost clearness. He was not satisfied with command of his native language merely, but gave attention to the study of foreign ones, and in particular was such a master of Latin that he could speak it as well as his native tongue; but he could understand Greek better than he could speak it. He was eloquent, indeed, that he might have passed for a teacher of eloquence. He most zealously cultivated the liberal arts, held those who taught them in great esteem, and conferred great honours upon them. He took lessons in grammar of the deacon Peter of Pisa, at that time an aged man. Another deacon, Albin of Britain, surnamed Alcuin, a man of Saxon extraction, who was the greatest scholar of the day, was his teacher in other branches of learning. The King spent much time and labour with him studying rhetoric, dialectics, and especially astronomy; he learned to reckon, and used to investigate the motions of the heavenly bodies most curiously, with an intelligent scrutiny. He also tried to write, and used to keep tablets and blanks in bed under his pillow, that at leisure hours he might accustom his hand to form the letters; however, as he did not begin his efforts in due season, but late in life, they met with ill success.

XXVI. He cherished with the greatest fervour and devotion the principles of the Christian religion, which had been instilled into him from infancy. Hence it was that he built the beautiful basilica at Aix-la-Chapelle, which he adorned with gold and silver and lamps, and with rails and doors of solid brass. He had the columns and marbles for this structure brought from Rome and Ravenna, for he could not find such as were suitable elsewhere. He was a constant worshipper at this church as long as his health permitted, going morning and evening, even after nightfall, besides attending mass; and he took care that all the services there conducted should be administered with the utmost possible propriety, very often warning the sextons not to let any improper or unclean thing be brought into, the building, or remain in it. He provided it with a great number of sacred vessels of gold and silver, and with such a quantity of clerical robes that not even the doorkeepers, who fill the humblest office in the church, were obliged to wear their every-day clothes when in the exercise of their duties. He was at great pains to improve the church reading and psalmody, for he was well skilled in both, although he neither read in public nor sang, except in a low tone and with others.

XXVII. He was very forward in succouring the poor, and in that gratuitous generosity which the Greeks call alms, so much so that he not only made a point of giving in his own country and his own kingdom, but when he discovered that there were Christians living in poverty in Syria, Egypt, and Africa, at Jerusalem, Alexandria, and Carthage, he had compassion on their wants, and used to send money over the seas to them. The reason that he zealously strove to make friends with the kings beyond seas was that he might get help and relief to the Christians living under their rule. He cherished the Church of St. Peter the Apostle at Rome above all over holy and sacred places, and heaped its treasury with a vast wealth of gold, silver, and precious stones. He sent great and countless gifts to the popes; and throughout his whole reign the wish that he had nearest at heart was to re-establish the ancient authority of the city of Rome under his care and by his influence, and to defend and protect the Church of St. Peter, and to beautify and enrich it out of his own store above all other churches. Although he held it in such veneration, he only repaired to Rome to pay his vows and make his supplications four times during the whole forty-seven years that he reigned.

XXVIII. When he made his last journey thither, he had also other ends in view. The Romans had inflicted many injuries upon the Pontiff Leo, tearing out his eyes and cutting out his tongue, so that he had been compelled to call upon the King for help. Charles accordingly went to Rome, to set in order the affairs of the Church, which were in great confusion, and passed the whole winter there. It was then that he received the titles of Emperor and Augustus, to which he at first had such an aversion that he declared that he would not have set foot in the Church the day that they were conferred, although it was a great feast-day, if he could have foreseen the design of the Pope. He bore very patiently with the jealousy which the Roman emperors showed upon his assuming these titles, for they took this step very ill; and by dint of frequent embassies and letters, in which he addressed them as brothers, he made their haughtiness yield to his magnanimity, a quality in which he was unquestionably much their superior.

XXIX. It was after he had received the imperial name that, finding the laws of his people very defective (the Franks have two sets of laws, very different in many particulars), he determined to add what was wanting, to reconcile the discrepancies, and to correct what was vicious and wrongly cited in them. However, he went no further in this matter than to supplement the laws by a few capitularies, and those imperfect ones; but he caused the unwritten laws of all the tribes that came under his rule to be compiled and reduced to writing. He also had the old rude songs that celebrate the deeds and wars of the ancient kings written out for transmission to posterity. He began a grammar of his native language. He gave the months names in his own tongue, in place of the Latin and barbarous names by which they were formerly known among the Franks. He likewise designated the winds by twelve appropriate names; there were hardly more than four distinctive ones in use before.

48

Ibn Sina (Avicenna)

from *Avicenna's Offering to the Prince: A Compendium on the Soul*

Ibn Sina (ca. 980–1037), also commonly known as Avicenna, was among the most important Islamic minds of the premodern world. A Persian physician, scientist, poet, theologian, and philosopher, he is famous for his monumental medical work, *The Canon of Medicine*, which was widely used as a standard medical textbook for centuries, making it one of the most significant works in the history of medicine. He is noteworthy also for his important philosophical case for the existence of the soul. The following is an excerpt from his compendium on the soul in which he contends that mental essence (soul) is distinct from body.

Section Tenth

To Establish that there is a Mental Essence, Distinct from Bodies, which stands towards Human Souls in the stead of Light toward Sight, and in the stead of a Source or Fountain; and To Establish that Souls, if they leave the Bodies, unite therewith.

As to the mental essence, we find it in infants devoid of every mental form. Then, later on in life, we find in it self-evident axiomatic mentally-grasped notions, without effort of learning and without reflection. So that the arising of them within it will not fail of being either through sense and experience, or else through divine outpouring reaching to it. But it is not licit to hold that the arising of such primary mental form will be through experience, seeing that

SOURCE: Abû-'Aly al-Husayn Ibn 'Abdallah Ibn Sînâ, *Avicenna's Offering to the Prince: A Compendium on the Soul*, trans. Edward Abbott van Dyck with grateful acknowledgement of the substantial help obtained from Dr. S. Landauer's Concise German Translation, and from James Middleton MacDonald's Literal English Translation (Verona, Italy: n.p., 1906), 89–94.

experience does not afford and supply a necessary and inevitable judgment, since experience does not go so far as to believe or disbelieve definitively the existence of something different to the judgment drawn from what it has perceived. Indeed experience, although it shows us that every animal we perceive moves on chewing the lower jaw, yet it does not supply us with a convincing judgment that such is the case with every animal; for were this true, it would not be licit for the crocodile to exist which moves his upper jaw on chewing. Therefore not every judgment we have arrived at, as to things, through our sensuous perception, is applicable to and holds good of all that we have perceived or have not perceived of such things, but it may so be that what we have not perceived differ from what we have perceived. Whereas our conception that a whole is greater than a part is not [formed] because we have sensuously felt every part and every whole that are so related, seeing that even such an experience will not garanty to us that there will be no whole and no part differently related.

Likewise the dictum concerning the impossibility of two opposites (contrasts) coming together in one and the same thing, and that things which are equal to one and the same thing are equal to one another. And likewise the dictum concerning our holding proofs to be true if they be valid, for the belief in and conviction of their validity does not become valid by and through learning and effort of study; else this would draw out ad infinitum [inasmuch as each proof rests upon given presuppositions, whose validity would in its turn have to be proved]. Nor is this gained from sense, for the reason that we have mentioned. Consequently both the latter as well as the former [certainty] are gained from a godly outflow reaching unto the rational soul, and the rational soul reaching unto it; so that this mental form arises therein. Also, as to this outflow, unless it have in its own self such a generic (universal) mental form, it would not be able to engrave it within the rational soul. Hence such form is in the outflow's own self. And whatsoever Self has in it a mental form is an essence, other than a body, and not within a body, and standing of itself. Therefore this outflow unto which the soul reaches is a mental essence, not a body, not in a body, standing of itself, and one which stands towards the rational soul in the stead of light to sight; yet however with this difference, namely that light supplies unto sight the power of perceiving only, and not the perceived form, whereas this essence supplies, exclusively by and through its sole and single self, unto the rational power, the power of perceiving, and brings about therein the perceived forms also, as we have set forth above.

Now, if the rational soul's conceiving rational forms be a source of completion and perfection for it, and be effected and brought about on reaching unto this essence, and if worldly earthly labors, such as its thought, its sorrows and joy, its longings, hamper the power and withold it from reaching thereunto, so that it will not reach thereunto save only through abandoning these powers and getting rid of them, there being nothing to stop it from continued Reaching save the living body,—then consequently if it quit the body it will not cease to be reaching unto its Perfector and attached to Him.

Again, what reaches unto its Perfector and attaches itself to Him is safe against corruption, all the more so if even during disconnection from Him it has not undergone corruption. Wherefore the soul after death shall ever remain and continue unwavering [and undying] and attached to this noble essence, which is called generic universal mind, and in the language of the lawgivers the Divine Knowledge.

As to the other powers, such as the animal and the vegetable: Whereas every one of them performs its proper peculiar action only by and through the live body, and in no other way, consequently they will never quit live bodies, but will die with their death, seeing that every thing which is, and yet has no action, is idle and useless. Yet nevertheless the rational soul does gain, by its connection with them, from them their choicest and purest lye and wash, and leaves for death the husks. And were it not so, the rational soul would not use them in consciousness. Wherefore the rational soul shall surely depart (migrate, travel) taking along the kernels of the other powers after death ensues.

We have thus made a clear statement concerning souls, and got at which souls are [ever]lasting, and which of them will not be fitted out and armed with [ever]lastingness. It still remains for us, in connection with this research, to show how a soul exists within live bodies, and the aim and end for which it is found within the same, and what measure will be bestowed upon it, in the hereafter, of eternal delight and perpetual punishment, and of [temporary] punishment that ceases after a duration of time that shall ensue upon the decease of the live body; and to treat of the notion that is designated by the lawgivers as intercession (mediation), and of the quality (attribute) of the four angels and the throne-bearers. Were it not however that the custom prevails to isolate such research from the research whose path we have been treading, out of high esteem and reverence for it, and to make the latter research precede in order of treatment the former, to the end of levelling the road and paving it solidly, I should (would) have followed up these [ten] sections with a full and complete treatment of the subject dealt with in them. Notwithstanding all this, were it not for fear of wearying by prolixity, I would have disregarded the demands of custom herein. Thus then whatever it may please the Prince—God prolong his highness—to command as to treating singly of such notions, I shall put forth, in humble compliance and obedience, my utmost effort, God Almighty willing; and may wisdom never cease to revive through him after fainting, to flourish after withering, so that its sway may be renewed through his sway, and through his days its days may come back again, and that through his prestige the prestige of its devotees be exalted, and the seekers after its favor abound, so God almighty will.

49

Anselm of Canterbury and Gaunilon

from *Proslogium* (on the Ontological Argument)

St. Anselm of Canterbury (1033–1109) was a Benedictine monk and philosopher-theologian who served as Archbishop of Canterbury from 1093 until his death. He is perhaps the single most important Western thinker of the eleventh century, as well as one of the most significant Christian thinkers of all time, in part because of his contributions pertaining to perfect being theology, atonement theory, and the free will/predestination debate, among others. Formally recognized as one of only thirty-six Doctors of the Church by the Roman Catholic Church, Anselm is known as the Magnificent Doctor. He is perhaps most famous today for his formulation of the ontological argument for God's existence in his book *Proslogium*. The following is an excerpt from that particular text, along with a critical response to it from Anselm's contemporary and fellow Benedictine, Gaunilon (or Gaunilo).

Chapter II.

Truly there is a God, although the fool hath said in his heart, There is no God.

And so, Lord, do thou, who dost give understanding to faith, give me, so far as thou knowest it to be profitable, to understand that thou art as we believe; and that thou art that which we believe. And, indeed, we believe that thou art a being than which nothing greater can be conceived. Or is there no such nature, since the fool hath said in his heart, there is no God? (Psalms xiv. 1). But, at any rate, this very fool, when he hears of this being of which I speak—a being

SOURCE: St. Anselm, *Proslogium; Monologium; an Appendix in Behalf of the Fool by Gaunilon; and Cur Deus Homo*, trans. Sidney Norton Deane (Chicago: Open Court Publishing Company, 1903), 7–10, 150–51, 158–59.

than which nothing greater can be conceived—understands what he hears, and what he understands is in his understanding; although he does not understand it to exist.

For, it is one thing for an object to be in the understanding, and another to understand that the object exists. When a painter first conceives of what he will afterwards perform, he has it in his understanding, but he does not yet understand it to be, because he has not yet performed it. But after he has made the painting, he both has it in his understanding, and he understands that it exists, because he has made it.

Hence, even the fool is convinced that something exists in the understanding, at least, than which nothing greater can be conceived. For, when he hears of this, he understands it. And whatever is understood, exists in the understanding. And assuredly that, than which nothing greater can be conceived, cannot exist in the understanding alone. For, suppose it exists in the understanding alone: then it can be conceived to exist in reality; which is greater.

Therefore, if that, than which nothing greater can be conceived, exists in the understanding alone, the very being, than which nothing greater can be conceived, is one, than which a greater can be conceived. But obviously this is impossible. Hence, there is no doubt that there exists a being, than which nothing greater can be conceived, and it exists both in the understanding and in reality.

Chapter III.

God cannot be conceived not to exist.—God is that, than which nothing greater can be conceived.—That which can be conceived not to exist is not God.

And it assuredly exists so truly, that it cannot be conceived not to exist. For, it is possible to conceive of a being which cannot be conceived not to exist; and this is greater than one which can be conceived not to exist. Hence, if that, than which nothing greater can be conceived, can be conceived not to exist, it is not that, than which nothing greater can be conceived. But this is an irreconcilable contradiction. There is, then, so truly a being than which nothing greater can be conceived to exist, that it cannot even be conceived not to exist; and this being thou art, O Lord, our God.

So truly, therefore, dost thou exist, O Lord, my God, that thou canst not be conceived not to exist; and rightly. For, if a mind could conceive of a being better than thee, the creature would rise above the Creator; and this is most absurd. And, indeed, whatever else there is, except thee alone, can be conceived not to exist. To thee alone, therefore, it belongs to exist more truly than all other beings, and hence in a higher degree than all others. For, whatever else exists does not exist so truly, and hence in a less degree it belongs to it to exist. Why, then, has the fool said in his heart, there is no God (Psalms xiv. 1), since it is so evident, to a rational mind, that thou dost exist in the highest degree of all? Why, except that he is dull and a fool?

Chapter IV.

How the fool has said in his heart what cannot be conceived.—A thing may be conceived in two ways: (1) when the word signifying it is conceived; (2) when the thing itself is understood. As far as the word goes, God can be conceived not to exist; in reality he cannot.

But how has the fool said in his heart what he could not conceive; or how is it that he could not conceive what he said in his heart? since it is the same to say in the heart, and to conceive. But, if really, nay, since really, he both conceived, because he said in his heart; and did not say in his heart, because he could not conceive; there is more than one way in which a thing is said in the heart or conceived. For, in one sense, an object is conceived, when the word signifying it is conceived; and in another, when the very entity, which the object is, is understood.

In the former sense, then, God can be conceived not to exist; but in the latter, not at all. For no one who understands what fire and water are can conceive fire to be water, in accordance with the nature of the facts themselves, although this is possible according to the words. So, then, no one who understands what God is can conceive that God does not exist; although he says these words in his heart, either without any or with some foreign, signification. For, God is that than which a greater cannot be conceived. And he who thoroughly understands this, assuredly understands that this being so truly exists, that not even in concept can it be non-existent. Therefore, he who understands that God so exists, cannot conceive that he does not exist.

I thank thee, gracious Lord, I thank thee; because what I formerly believed by thy bounty, I now so understand by thine illumination, that if I were unwilling to believe that thou dost exist, I should not be able not to understand this to be true.

[. . . .]

[Gaunilon's Answer in Behalf of the Fool]

. . . How, then, is the veritable existence of that being proved to me from the assumption, by hypothesis, that it is greater than all other beings? For I should still deny this, or doubt your demonstration of it, to this extent, that I should not admit that this being is in my understanding and concept even in the way in which many objects whose real existence is uncertain and doubtful, are in my understanding and concept. For it should be proved first that this being itself really exists somewhere; and then, from the fact that it is greater than all, we shall not hesitate to infer that it also subsists in itself.

6. For example: it is said that somewhere in the ocean is an island, which, because of the difficulty, or rather the impossibility, of discovering what does not exist, is called the lost island. And they say that this island has an inestimable wealth of all manner of riches and delicacies in greater abundance than is told of the Islands of the Blest; and that having no owner or inhabitant, it is more excellent than all other countries, which are inhabited by mankind, in the abundance with which it is stored.

Now if some one should tell me that there is such an island, I should easily understand his words, in which there is no difficulty. But suppose that he went on to say, as if by a logical inference: "You can no longer doubt that this island which is more excellent than all lands exists somewhere, since you have no doubt that it is in your understanding. And since it is more excellent not to be in the understanding alone, but to exist both in the understanding and in reality, for this reason it must exist. For if it does not exist, any land which really exists will be more excellent than it; and so the island already understood by you to be more excellent will not be more excellent."

If a man should try to prove to me by such reasoning that this island truly exists, and that its existence should no longer be doubted, either I should believe that he was jesting, or I know not which I ought to regard as the greater fool: myself, supposing that I should allow this proof; or him, if he should suppose that he had established with any certainty the existence of this island. For he ought to show first that the hypothetical excellence of this island exists as a real and indubitable fact, and in no wise as any unreal object, or one whose existence is uncertain, in my understanding.

[. . . .]

[Anselm's Apologetic Reply to Gaunilon]

. . . But, you say, it is as if one should suppose an island in the ocean, which surpasses all lands in its fertility, and which, because of the difficulty, or rather the impossibility, of discovering what does not exist, is called a lost island; and should say that there can be no doubt that this island truly exists in reality, for this reason, that one who hears it described easily understands what he hears.

Now I promise confidently that if any man shall devise anything existing either in reality or in concept alone (except that than which a greater cannot be conceived) to which he can adapt the sequence of my reasoning, I will discover that thing, and will give him his lost island, not to be lost again.

But it now appears that this being than which a greater is inconceivable cannot be conceived not to be, because it exists on so assured a ground of truth; for otherwise it would not exist at all.

Hence, if any one says that he conceives this being not to exist, I say that at the time when he conceives of this either he conceives of a being than which a greater is inconceivable, or he does not conceive at all. If he does not conceive, he does not conceive of the non-existence of that of which he does not conceive. But if he does conceive, he certainly conceives of a being which cannot be even conceived not to exist. For if it could be conceived not to exist, it could be conceived to have a beginning and an end. But this is impossible.

He, then, who conceives of this being conceives of a being which cannot be even conceived not to exist; but he who conceives of this being does not conceive that it does not exist; else he conceives what is inconceivable. The non-existence, then, of that than which a greater cannot be conceived is inconceivable.

50

Al Ghazzali

from *Confessions of Al Ghazzali*

The Persian philosopher, theologian, and mystic Abu Hamid Muhammad ibn Muhammad At-tusi Al Ghazzali, also known simply as Al Ghazzali (ca. 1058–1111), was one of the most influential minds of classical Islam and is best known for his work *The Incoherence of the Philosophers*, in which he rejects the application of Greek philosophy, meaning Aristotelian logic, to religious interpretation, thus rebuking previous Muslim philosophers, such as Ibn Sina (Avicenna), who had worked to integrate faith and reason. Al Ghazzali's autobiographical *Confessions*, from which the following selection is taken, describes a crisis of faith he experienced beginning in 1095, which was resolved when he adopted Sufism, a mystical practice in Islam that seeks to develop a spiritual, rather than rational, understanding of divine truth.

Ghazzali's Search for Truth:

"In the name of the most merciful God."

Quoth the Imām Ghazzali:

Glory be to God, Whose praise should precede every writing and every speech! May the blessings of God rest on Muhammed His Prophet and His Apostle, on his family and companions, by whose guidance error is escaped!

You have asked me, O brother in the faith, to expound the aim and the mysteries of religious sciences, the boundaries and depths of theological doctrines. You wish to know my experiences while disentangling truth lost in the medley of sects and divergencies of thought, and how I have dared to climb from the low levels of traditional belief to the topmost summit of assurance. You desire

SOURCE: Al Ghazzali, *The Confessions of Al Ghazzali*, trans. Claud Field (London: John Murray, 1909), 11–21, 41–50.

to learn what I have borrowed, first of all from scholastic theology; and secondly from the method of the Ta'limites, who, in seeking truth, rest upon the authority of a leader; and why, thirdly, I have been led to reject philosophic systems; and finally, what I have accepted of the doctrine of the Sufis, and the sum total of truth which I have gathered in studying every variety of opinion. You ask me why, after resigning at Bagdad a teaching post which attracted a number of hearers, I have, long afterwards, accepted a similar one at Nishapur. Convinced as I am of the sincerity which prompts your inquiries, I proceed to answer them, invoking the help and protection of God.

Know then, my brothers (may God direct you in the right way), that the diversity in beliefs and religions, and the variety of doctrines and sects which divide men, are like a deep ocean strewn with shipwrecks, from which very few escape safe and sound. Each sect, it is true, believes itself in possession of the truth and of salvation, "each party," as the Koran saith, "rejoices in its own creed"; but as the chief of the apostles, whose word is always truthful, has told us, "My people will be divided into more than seventy sects, of whom only one will be saved." This prediction, like all others of the Prophet, must be fulfilled.

From the period of adolescence, that is to say, previous to reaching my twentieth year to the present time when I have passed my fiftieth, I have ventured into this vast ocean; I have fearlessly sounded its depths, and, like a resolute diver, I have penetrated its darkness and dared its dangers and abysses. I have interrogated the beliefs of each sect and scrutinised the mysteries of each doctrine, in order to disentangle truth from error and orthodoxy from heresy. I have never met one who maintained the hidden meaning of the Koran without investigating the nature of his belief, nor a partisan of its exterior sense without inquiring into the results of his doctrine. There is no philosopher whose system I have not fathomed, nor theologian the intricacies of whose doctrine I have not followed out.

Sufism has no secrets into which I have not penetrated; the devout adorer of Deity has revealed to me the aim of his austerities; the atheist has not been able to conceal from me the real reason of his unbelief. The thirst for knowledge was innate in me from an early age; it was like a second nature implanted by God, without any will on my part. No sooner had I emerged from boyhood than I had already broken the fetters of tradition and freed myself from hereditary beliefs.

Having noticed how easily the children of Christians become Christians, and the children of Moslems embrace Islam, and remembering also the traditional saying ascribed to the Prophet, "Every child has in him the germ of Islam, then his parents make him Jew, Christian, or Zoroastrian," I was moved by a keen desire to learn what was this innate disposition in the child, the nature of the accidental beliefs imposed on him by the authority of his parents and his masters, and finally the unreasoned convictions which he derives from their instructions.

Struck with the contradictions which I encountered in endeavouring to disentangle the truth and falsehood of these opinions, I was led to make the following reflection: "The search after truth being the aim which I propose to myself, I ought in the first place to ascertain what are the bases of certitude." In the next place I recognised that certitude is the clear and complete knowledge of things, such knowledge as leaves no room for doubt nor possibility of error and conjecture, so that there remains no room in the mind for error to find an entrance. In such a case it is necessary that the mind, fortified against all possibility of going astray, should embrace such a strong conviction that, if, for example, any one possessing the power of changing a stone into gold, or a stick into a serpent, should seek to shake the bases of this certitude, it would remain firm and immovable. Suppose, for instance, a man should come and say to me, who am firmly convinced that ten is more than three, "No; on the contrary, three is more than ten, and, to prove it, I change this rod into a serpent," and supposing that he actually did so, I should remain none the less convinced of the falsity of his assertion, and although his miracle might arouse my astonishment, it would not instil any doubt into my belief.

I then understood that all forms of knowledge which do not unite these conditions (imperviousness to doubt, etc.) do not deserve any confidence, because they are not beyond the reach of doubt, and what is not impregnable to doubt cannot constitute certitude.

The Subterfuges of the Sophists

I then examined what knowledge I possessed, and discovered that in none of it, with the exception of sense-perceptions and necessary principles, did I enjoy that degree of certitude which I have just described. I then sadly reflected as follows: "We cannot hope to find truth except in matters which carry their evidence in themselves—that is to say, in sense-perceptions and necessary principles; we must therefore establish these on a firm basis. Is my absolute confidence in sense-perceptions and on the infallibility of necessary principles analogous to the confidence which I formerly possessed in matters believed on the authority of others? Is it only analogous to the reliance most people place on their organs of vision, or is it rigorously true without admixture of illusion or doubt?"

I then set myself earnestly to examine the notions we derive from the evidence of the senses and from sight in order to see if they could be called in question. The result of a careful examination was that my confidence in them was shaken. Our sight for instance, perhaps the best practised of all our senses, observes a shadow, and finding it apparently stationary pronounces it devoid of movement. Observation and experience, however, show subsequently that a shadow moves not suddenly, it is true, but gradually and imperceptibly, so that it is never really motionless.

Again, the eye sees a star and believes it as large as a piece of gold, but mathematical calculations prove, on the contrary, that it is larger than the earth. These notions, and all others which the senses declare true, are subsequently contradicted and convicted of falsity in an irrefragable manner by the verdict of reason.

Then I reflected in myself: "Since I cannot trust to the evidence of my senses, I must rely only on intellectual notions based on fundamental principles, such as the following axioms: 'Ten is more than three. Affirmation and negation cannot coexist together. A thing cannot both be created and also existent from eternity, living and annihilated simultaneously, at once necessary and impossible.'" To this the notions I derived from my senses made the following objections: "Who can guarantee you that you can trust to the evidence of reason more than to that of the senses? You believed in our testimony till it was contradicted by the verdict of reason, otherwise you would have continued to believe it to this day. Well, perhaps, there is above reason another judge who, if he appeared, would convict reason of falsehood, just as reason has confuted us. And if such a third arbiter is not yet apparent, it does not follow that he does not exist."

To this argument I remained some time without reply; a reflection drawn from the phenomena of sleep deepened my doubt. "Do you not see," I reflected, "that while asleep you assume your dreams to be indisputably real? Once awake, you recognise them for what they are—baseless chimeras. Who can assure you, then, of the reliability of notions which, when awake, you derive from the senses and from reason? In relation to your present state they may be real; but it is possible also that you may enter upon another state of being which will bear the same relation to your present state as this does to your condition when asleep. In that new sphere you will recognise that the conclusions of reason are only chimeras."

This possible condition is, perhaps, that which the Sufis call "ecstasy" ("hāl"), that is to say, according to them, a state in which, absorbed in themselves and in the suspension of sense-perceptions, they have visions beyond the reach of intellect. Perhaps also Death is that state, according to that saying of the Prince of prophets: "Men are asleep; when they die, they wake." Our present life in relation to the future is perhaps only a dream, and man, once dead, will see things in direct opposition to those now before his eyes; he will then understand that word of the Koran, "To-day we have removed the veil from thine eyes and thy sight is keen."

Such thoughts as these threatened to shake my reason, and I sought to find an escape from them. But how? In order to disentangle the knot of this difficulty, a proof was necessary. Now a proof must be based on primary assumptions, and it was precisely these of which I was in doubt. This unhappy state lasted about two months, during which I was, not, it is true, explicitly or by profession, but morally and essentially a thoroughgoing sceptic.

God at last deigned to heal me of this mental malady; my mind recovered sanity and equilibrium, the primary assumptions of reason recovered with me all their stringency and force. I owed my deliverance, not to a concatenation of proofs and arguments, but to the light which God caused to penetrate into my heart—the light which illuminates the threshold of all knowledge. To suppose that certitude can be only based upon formal arguments is to limit the boundless mercy of God. Some one asked the Prophet the explanation of this passage in the Divine Book: "God opens to Islam the heart of him whom He chooses to direct." "That is spoken," replied the Prophet, "of the light which God sheds in the heart." "And how can man recognise that light?" he was asked. "By his detachment from this world of illusion and by a secret drawing towards the eternal world," the Prophet replied.

On another occasion he said: "God has created His creatures in darkness, and then has shed upon them His light." It is by the help of this light that the search for truth must be carried on. As by His mercy this light descends from time to time among men, we must ceaselessly be on the watch for it. This is also corroborated by another saying of the Apostle: "God sends upon you, at certain times, breathings of His grace; be prepared for them."

My object in this account is to make others understand with what earnestness we should search for truth, since it leads to results we never dreamt of. Primary assumptions have not got to be sought for, since they are always present to our minds; if we engage in such a search, we only find them persistently elude our grasp. But those who push their investigation beyond ordinary limits are safe from the suspicion of negligence in pursuing what is within their reach.

The Different Kinds of Seekers after Truth

When God in the abundance of His mercy had healed me of this malady, I ascertained that those who are engaged in the search for truth may be divided into three groups.

I. Scholastic theologians, who profess to follow theory and speculation.

II. The Philosophers, who profess to rely upon formal logic.

III. The Sufis, who call themselves the elect of God and possessors of intuition and knowledge of the truth by means of ecstasy.

"The truth," I said to myself, "must be found among these three classes of men who devote themselves to the search for it. If it escapes them, one must give up all hope of attaining it. Having once surrendered blind belief, it is impossible to return to it, for the essence of such belief is to be unconscious of itself. As soon as this unconsciousness ceases it is shattered like a glass whose fragments cannot be again reunited except by being cast again into the furnace and refashioned." Determined to follow these paths and to search out these systems to the bottom, I proceeded with my investigations in the following order: Scholastic theology; philosophical systems; and, finally Sufism.

[. . . .]

Sufism

When I had finished my examination of these doctrines I applied myself to the study of Sufism. I saw that in order to understand it thoroughly one must combine theory with practice. The aim which the Sufis set before them is as follows: To free the soul from the tyrannical yoke of the passions, to deliver it from its wrong inclinations and evil instincts, in order that in the purified heart there should only remain room for God and for the invocation of His holy name.

As it was more easy to learn their doctrine than to practise it, I studied first of all those of their books which contain it: *The Nourishment of Hearts*, by Abu Talib of Mecca, the works of Hareth el Muhasibi, and the fragments which still remain of Junaid, Shibli, Abu Yezid Bustami and other leaders (whose souls may God sanctify). I acquired a thorough knowledge of their researches, and I learned all that was possible to learn of their methods by study and oral teaching. It became clear to me that the last stage could not be reached by mere instruction, but only by transport, ecstasy, and the transformation of the moral being.

To define health and satiety, to penetrate their causes and conditions, is quite another thing from being well and satisfied. To define drunkenness, to know that it is caused by vapours which rise from the stomach and cloud the seat of intelligence, is quite a different thing to being drunk. The drunken man has no idea of the nature of drunkenness, just because he is drunk and not in a condition to understand anything, while the doctor, not being under the influence of drunkenness, knows its character and laws. Or if the doctor fall ill, he has a theoretical knowledge of the health of which he is deprived.

In the same way there is a considerable difference between knowing renouncement, comprehending its conditions and causes, and practising renouncement and detachment from the things of this world. I saw that Sufism consists in experiences rather than in definitions, and that what I was lacking belonged to the domain, not of instruction, but of ecstasy and initiation.

The researches to which I had devoted myself, the path which I had traversed in studying religious and speculative branches of knowledge, had given me a firm faith in three things—God, Inspiration, and the Last Judgment. These three fundamental articles of belief were confirmed in me, not merely by definite arguments, but by a chain of causes, circumstances, and proofs which it is impossible to recount. I saw that one can only hope for salvation by devotion and the conquest of one's passions, a procedure which presupposes renouncement and detachment from this world of falsehood in order to turn towards eternity and meditation on God. Finally, I saw that the only condition of success was to sacrifice honours and riches and to sever the ties and attachments of worldly life.

Coming seriously to consider my state, I found myself bound down on all sides by these trammels. Examining my actions, the most fair-seeming of which were my lecturing and professorial occupations, I found to my surprise that I was engrossed in several studies of little value, and profitless as regards my salvation. I probed the motives of my teaching and found that, in place of being sincerely consecrated to God, it was only actuated by a vain desire of honour and reputation. I perceived that I was on the edge of an abyss, and that without an immediate conversion I should be doomed to eternal fire. In these reflections I spent a long time. Still a prey to uncertainty, one day I decided to leave Bagdad and to give up everything; the next day I gave up my resolution. I advanced one step and immediately relapsed. In the morning I was sincerely resolved only to occupy myself with the future life; in the evening a crowd of carnal thoughts assailed and dispersed my resolutions. On the one side the world kept me bound to my post in the chains of covetousness, on the other side the voice of religion cried to me, "Up! Up! thy life is nearing its end, and thou hast a long journey to make. All thy pretended knowledge is nought but falsehood and fantasy. If thou dost not think now of thy salvation, when wilt thou think of it? If thou dost not break thy chains to-day, when wilt thou break them?" Then my resolve was strengthened, I wished to give up all and flee; but the Tempter, returning to the attack, said, "You are suffering from a transitory feeling; don't give way to it, for it will soon pass. If you obey it, if you give up this fine position, this honourable post exempt from trouble and rivalry, this seat of authority safe from attack, you will regret it later on without being able to recover it."

Thus I remained, torn asunder by the opposite forces of earthly passions and religious aspirations, for about six months from the month Rajab of the year A.D. 1096. At the close of them my will yielded and I gave myself up to destiny. God caused an impediment to chain my tongue and prevented me from lecturing. Vainly I desired, in the interest of my pupils, to go on with my teaching, but my mouth became dumb. The silence to which I was condemned cast me into a violent despair; my stomach became weak; I lost all appetite; I could neither swallow a morsel of bread nor drink a drop of water.

The enfeeblement of my physical powers was such that the doctors, despairing of saving me, said, "The mischief is in the heart, and has communicated itself to the whole organism; there is no hope unless the cause of his grievous sadness be arrested."

Finally, conscious of my weakness and the prostration of my soul, I took refuge in God as a man at the end of himself and without resources. "He who hears the wretched when they cry" (*Koran*, xxvii. 63) deigned to hear me; He made easy to me the sacrifice of honours, wealth, and family. I gave out publicly that I intended to make the pilgrimage to Mecca, while I secretly resolved to go to Syria, not wishing that the Caliph (may God magnify him) or my friends should know my intention of settling in that country. I made all kinds of clever excuses for leaving Bagdad with the fixed intention of not returning thither. The Imāms of Irak criticised me with one accord. Not one of them could admit that this sacrifice had a religious motive, because they considered my position as the highest attainable in the religious community. "Behold how far their knowledge goes!" (*Koran*, liii. 31). All kinds of explanations of my conduct were forthcoming. Those who were outside the limits of Irak attributed it to the fear with which the Government inspired me. Those who were on the spot and saw how the authorities wished to detain me, their displeasure at my resolution and my refusal of their request, said to themselves, "It is a calamity which one can only impute to a fate which has befallen the Faithful and Learning!"

At last I left Bagdad, giving up all my fortune. Only, as lands and property in Irak can afford an endowment for pious purposes, I obtained a legal authorisation to preserve as much as was necessary for my support and that of my children; for there is surely nothing more lawful in the world than that a learned man should provide sufficient to support his family. I then betook myself to Syria, where I remained for two years, which I devoted to retirement, meditation, and devout exercises. I only thought of self-improvement and discipline and of purification of the heart by prayer in going through the forms of devotion which the Sufis had taught me. I used to live a solitary life in the Mosque of Damascus, and was in the habit of spending my days on the minaret after closing the door behind me.

From thence I proceeded to Jerusalem, and every day secluded myself in the Sanctuary of the Rock. After that I felt a desire to accomplish the Pilgrimage, and to receive a full effusion of grace by visiting Mecca, Medina, and the Tomb of the Prophet. After visiting the shrine of the Friend of God (Abraham), I went to the Hedjāz. Finally, the longings of my heart and the prayers of my children brought me back to my country, although I was so firmly resolved at first never to revisit it. At any rate I meant, if I did return, to live there solitary and in religious meditation; but events, family cares, and vicissitudes of life changed my resolutions and troubled my meditative calm. However irregular the intervals which I could give to devotional ecstasy, my confidence in it did not diminish; and the more I was diverted by hindrances, the more steadfastly I returned to it.

Ten years passed in this manner. During my successive periods of meditation there were revealed to me things impossible to recount. All that I shall say for the edification of the reader is this: I learnt from a sure source that the Sufis are the true pioneers on the path of God; that there is nothing more beautiful than their life, nor more praiseworthy than their rule of conduct, nor purer than their morality. The intelligence of thinkers, the wisdom of philosophers, the knowledge of the most learned doctors of the law would in vain combine their efforts in order to modify or improve their doctrine and morals; it would be impossible. With the Sufis, repose and movement, exterior or interior, are illumined with the light which proceeds from the Central Radiance of Inspiration. And what other light could shine on the face of the earth? In a word, what can one criticise in them? To purge the heart of all that does not belong to God is the first step in their cathartic method. The drawing up of the heart by prayer is the keystone of it, as the cry "Allahu Akbar" (God is great) is the keystone of prayer, and the last stage is the being lost in God. I say the last stage, with reference to what may be reached by an effort of will; but, to tell the truth, it is only the first stage in the life of contemplation, the vestibule by which the initiated enter.

From the time that they set out on this path, revelations commence for them. They come to see in the waking state angels and souls of prophets; they hear their voices and wise counsels. By means of this contemplation of heavenly forms and images they rise by degrees to heights which human language cannot reach, which one cannot even indicate without falling into great and inevitable errors. The degree of proximity to Deity which they attain is regarded by some as intermixture of being (*haloul*), by others as identification (*ittihād*), by others as intimate union (*wasl*). But all these expressions are wrong, as we have explained in our work entitled *The Chief Aim*. Those who have reached that stage should confine themselves to repeating the verse—

> What I experience I shall not try to say;
> Call me happy, but ask me no more.

In short, he who does not arrive at the intuition of these truths by means of ecstasy, knows only the *name* of inspiration. The miracles wrought by the saints are, in fact, merely the earliest forms of prophetic manifestation. Such was the state of the Apostle of God when, before receiving his commission, he retired to Mount Hira to give himself up to such intensity of prayer and meditation that the Arabs said: "Muhammed is become enamoured of God."

This state, then, can be revealed to the initiated in ecstasy, and to him who is incapable of ecstasy, by obedience and attention, on condition that he frequents the society of Sufis till he arrives, so to speak, at an imitative initiation. Such is the faith which one can obtain by remaining among them, and intercourse with them is never painful.

But even when we are deprived of the advantage of their society, we can comprehend the possibility of this state (revelation by means of ecstasy) by a chain of manifest proofs. We have explained this in the treatise entitled *Marvels of the Heart*, which forms part of our work, *The Revival of the Religious Sciences*. The certitude derived from proofs is called "knowledge"; passing into the state we describe is called "transport"; believing the experience of others and oral transmission is "faith." Such are the three degrees of knowledge, as it is written, "The Lord will raise to different ranks those among you who have believed and those who have received knowledge from Him" (*Koran*, lviii. 12).

But behind those who believe comes a crowd of ignorant people who deny the reality of Sufism, hear discourses on it with incredulous irony, and treat as charlatans those who profess it. To this ignorant crowd the verse applies: "There are those among them who come to listen to thee, and when they leave thee, ask of those who have received knowledge, 'What has he just said?' These are they whose hearts God has sealed up with blindness and who only follow their passions."

Among the number of convictions which I owe to the practice of the Sufi rule is the knowledge of the true nature of inspiration. This knowledge is of such great importance that I proceed to expound it in detail.

51

Pope Urban II

from Fulcher of Chartres' *Speech of Urban II*
at the Council of Clermont

The following excerpt contains Pope Urban II's summons in 1095, which initiated the first in a series of Christian crusades. The Seljuk Turk threat to the Byzantine Empire and Eastern Orthodoxy prompted Urban's call, with military crusaders promised high—even eternal—rewards. With crusades occurring episodically for over two hundred years, waves of armed Europeans headed eastward to reclaim the Holy Lands from Muslims. In retrospect, the litany of humanitarian abuses against Muslims, Jews, and occasionally other Christians appears indefensible, leaving a troubling mark on Western Christianity's record.

"Most beloved brethren: Urged by necessity, I, Urban, by the permission of God chief bishop and prelate over the whole world, have come into these parts as an ambassador with a divine admonition to you, the servants of God. I hoped to find you as faithful and as zealous in the service of God as I had supposed you to be. But if there is in you any deformity or crookedness contrary to God's law, with divine help I will do my best to remove it. For God has put you as stewards over his family to minister to it. Happy indeed will you be if he finds you faithful in your stewardship. You are called shepherds; see that you do not act as hirelings. But be true shepherds, with your crooks always in your hands. Do not go to sleep, but guard on all sides the flock committed to you. For if through your carelessness or negligence a wolf carries away one

SOURCE: Fulcher of Chartres, "The Speech of Urban II at the Council of Clermont, 1095," in *A Source Book for Mediæval History: Selected Documents Illustrating the History of Europe in the Middle Age*, ed. Oliver J. Thatcher and Edgar Holmes McNeal (New York: Charles Scribner's Sons, 1905), 514–17.

of your sheep, you will surely lose the reward laid up for you with God. And after you have been bitterly scourged with remorse for your faults, you will be fiercely overwhelmed in hell, the abode of death. For according to the gospel you are the salt of the earth [Matt. 5:13]. But if you fall short in your duty, how, it may be asked, can it be salted? O how great the need of salting! It is indeed necessary for you to correct with the salt of wisdom this foolish people which is so devoted to the pleasures of this world, lest the Lord, when He may wish to speak to them, find them putrefied by their sins unsalted and stinking. For if He shall find worms, that is, sins, in them, because you have been negligent in your duty, He will command them as worthless to be thrown into the abyss of unclean things. And because you cannot restore to Him His great loss, He will surely condemn you and drive you from His loving presence. But the man who applies this salt should be prudent, provident, modest, learned, peaceable, watchful, pious, just, equitable, and pure. For how can the ignorant teach others? How can the licentious make others modest? And how can the impure make others pure? If anyone hates peace, how can he make others peaceable? Or if anyone has soiled his hands with baseness, how can he cleanse the impurities of another? We read also that if the blind lead the blind, both will fall into the ditch [Matt. 15:14]. But first correct yourselves, in order that, free from blame, you may be able to correct those who are subject to you. If you wish to be the friends of God, gladly do the things which you know will please Him. You must especially let all matters that pertain to the church be controlled by the law of the church. And be careful that simony does not take root among you, lest both those who buy and those who sell [church offices] be beaten with the scourges of the Lord through narrow streets and driven into the place of destruction and confusion. Keep the church and the clergy in all its grades entirely free from the secular power. See that the tithes that belong to God are faithfully paid from all the produce of the land; let them not be sold or withheld. If anyone seizes a bishop let him be treated as an outlaw. If anyone seizes or robs monks, or clergymen, or nuns, or their servants, or pilgrims, or merchants, let him be anathema [that is, cursed]. Let robbers and incendiaries and all their accomplices be expelled from the church and anthematized. If a man who does not give a part of his goods as alms is punished with the damnation of hell, how should he be punished who robs another of his goods? For thus it happened to the rich man in the gospel [Luke 16:19]; he was not punished because he had stolen the goods of another, but because he had not used well the things which were his.

"You have seen for a long time the great disorder in the world caused by these crimes. It is so bad in some of your provinces, I am told, and you are so weak in the administration of justice, that one can hardly go along the road by day or night without being attacked by robbers; and whether at home or abroad one is in danger of being despoiled either by force or fraud. Therefore it is necessary to reenact the truce, as it is commonly called, which was proclaimed a long time ago by our holy fathers. I exhort and demand that you, each, try hard to have the truce kept in your diocese. And if anyone shall be led by his cupidity or arrogance to break this truce, by the authority of God and with the sanction of this council he shall be anathematized."

After these and various other matters had been attended to, all who were present, clergy and people, gave thanks to God and agreed to the pope's proposition. They all faithfully promised to keep the decrees. Then the pope said that in another part of the world Christianity was suffering from a state of affairs that was worse than the one just mentioned. He continued:

"Although, O sons of God, you have promised more firmly than ever to keep the peace among yourselves and to preserve the rights of the church, there remains still an important work for you to do. Freshly quickened by the divine correction, you must apply the strength of your righteousness to another matter which concerns you as well as God. For your brethren who live in the east are in urgent need of your help, and you must hasten to give them the aid which has often been promised them. For, as the most of you have heard, the Turks and Arabs have attacked them and have conquered the territory of Romania [the Greek empire] as far west as the shore of the Mediterranean and the Hellespont, which is called the Arm of St. George. They have occupied more and more of the lands of those Christians, and have overcome them in seven battles. They have killed and captured many, and have destroyed the churches and devastated the empire. If you permit them to continue thus for awhile with impunity, the faithful of God will be much more widely attacked by them. On this account I, or rather the Lord, beseech you as Christ's heralds to publish this everywhere and to persuade all people of whatever rank, foot-soldiers and knights, poor and rich, to carry aid promptly to those Christians and to destroy that vile race from the lands of our friends. I say this to those who are present, it is meant also for those who are absent. Moreover, Christ commands it.

"All who die by the way, whether by land or by sea, or in battle against the pagans, shall have immediate remission of sins. This I grant them through the power of God with which I am invested. O what a disgrace if such a despised and base race, which worships demons, should conquer a people which has the faith of omnipotent God and is made glorious with the name of Christ! With what reproaches will the Lord overwhelm us if you do not aid those who, with us, profess the Christian religion! Let those who have been accustomed unjustly to wage private warfare against the faithful now go against the infidels and end with victory this war which should have been begun long ago. Let those who, for a long time, have been robbers, now become knights. Let those who have been fighting against their brothers and relatives now fight in a proper way against the barbarians. Let those who have been serving as mercenaries for small pay now obtain the eternal reward. Let those who have been wearing themselves out in both body and soul now work for a double honor. Behold! on this side will be the sorrowful and poor, on that, the rich; on this side, the enemies of the Lord, on that, his friends. Let those who go not put off the journey, but rent their lands and collect money for their expenses; and as soon as winter is over and spring comes, let them eagerly set out on the way with God as their guide."

52

Ibn Tufail

from *Hayy ibn Yaqdhan*

Abu Bakr Muhammad ibn Abd al-Malik ibn Muhammad ibn Tufail al-Qaisi al-Andalusi, also known as Abu Jaafar Ebn Tophail, or simply Ibn Tufail (1109/1110–1185/1186), was an important Arab Andalusian Muslim physician, philosopher, and theologian. The following is an excerpt from his most famous work, *Hayy ibn Yaqdhan*, which is a philosophical novel wherein a boy grows up among wild animals on a (humanly) unoccupied island for nearly fifty years, eventually educating himself through careful observation and experimentation to the point at which he comes to have divine knowledge. The story plots out a key position in the various medieval debates about the relationship between faith and reason.

———————

11. Thus he went on, Living only upon what he Suck'd till he was Two Years Old, and then he began to step a little and Breed his Teeth. He always followed the *Roe*, and she shew'd all the tenderness to him imaginable; and us'd to carry him to places where Fruit Trees grew, and fed him with the Ripest and Sweetest Fruits which fell from the Trees; and for Nuts or such like, she us'd to break the Shell with her Teeth, and give him the Kernel; still Suckling him, as often as he pleas'd, and when he was thirsty she shew'd him the way to the water. If the Sun shin'd too hot and scorch'd him, she shaded him; if he was cold she cherish'd him and kept him warm; and when Night came she brought him home to his old Place, and covered him partly with her own Body, and partly with some Feathers which were left in the Ark, which had been put in with him when he was first expos'd. Now, when they went out in the Morning, and

SOURCE: Ibn Tufail, *The Improvement of Human Reason, Exhibited in the Life of Hai Ebn Yokdhan: Written in Arabick above 500 Years ago, by Abu Jaafar Ebn Tophail*, trans. Simon Ockley (London: Edm. Powell in Blackfriars, and J. Morphew near Stationers-hall, 1708), 37–53.

when they came home again at Night, there always went with them an Herd of Deer, which lay in the same place where they did; so that the Boy being always amongst them learn'd their voice by degrees, and imitated it so exactly that there was scarce any sensible difference; nay, when he heard the voice of any Bird or Beast, he'd come very near it, being of a most excellent Apprehension. But of all the voices which he imitated, he made most use of the Deers, which he was Master of, and could express himself as they do, either when they want help, call their Mates, when they would have them come nearer, or go farther off. (For you must know that the Brute Beasts have different Sounds to express these different things.) Thus he contracted such an Acquaintance with the Wild Beasts, that they were not afraid of him, nor he of them.

12. By this time he began to have the Ideas of a great many things fix'd in his mind, so as to have a desire to some, and an aversion to others, even when they were absent. In the mean while he consider'd all the several sorts of Animals, and saw that they were all clothed either with Hair, Wool, or several sorts of Feathers: he consider'd their great Swiftness and Strength, and that they were all arm'd with Weapons defensive, as Horns, Teeth, Hoofs, Spurs, Nails, and the like. But that he himself was Naked and Defenceless, Slow and Weak, in respect of them. For whenever there happened any Controversy about gathering of such ripe Fruits as fell from the Trees; he always came off by the worst, for they could both keep their own, and take away his, and he could neither beat them off, nor run away from them.

13. He observ'd besides that his Fellow-Fawns, tho' their Fore-heads were smooth at first, yet afterwards had Horns bud out, and tho' they were feeble at first, yet afterwards grew very Vigorous and Swift. All these things he perceived in them, which were not in himself; and when he had consider'd the Matter, he could not imagine what should be the reason of this Difference; then he consider'd such Animals as had any Defect or Natural Imperfection, but amongst them all he could find none like himself. He took Notice that the Passages of the Excrements were cover'd in all other Creatures besides himself: that by which they voided their grosser Excrements, with a Tail; and that which serv'd for the voiding of their Urine, with Hair or some such like thing. Besides, he observ'd that their Privy parts, were more concealed than his own were.

14. All these things were matter of great Grief to him, and when he had perplex'd himself very much with the thoughts of them, and was now near seven Years Old, he despair'd utterly of having those things grow upon him, the want of which made him so uneasy. He therefore resolv'd to help himself, and thereupon gets him some Broad Leaves of Trees, of which he made two

Coverings, one to wear behind, the other before; and made a Girdle of Palm-Trees and Rushes Twisted together, to Hang his coverings upon, and Ty'd it about his waste, and so wore it. But alas it would not last long, for the Leaves wither'd and dropt away; so that he was forc'd to get more, which he doubled and put together as well as he could, Plaiting the Leaves one upon another, which made it a little more durable, but not much. Then having broke a Bough from a Tree and fitted the Ends of it to his Mind, he stript off the Twigs and made it smooth; with this he began to attack the Wild Beasts, assaulting the weaker, and defending himself against the stronger. By this means he began a little to know his own Strength, and perceiv'd that his Hands were better than their Feet; because by the help of them, he had provided wherewithal to cover his Nakedness, and also gotten him a Defensive Weapon, so that now he had no need of a Tail, nor of those Natural Weapons which he had so wish'd for at first.

15. He was now above Seven Years Old, and because the repairing of his Covering of Leaves so often, was very troublesome to him, he had a design of taking the Tail of some Dead Beast, and wearing it himself; but when he perceiv'd that all Beasts did constantly avoid those which were Dead of the same kind, it made him doubt whether it might be safe or not; at last, by chance he found a Dead Eagle, and observing that none of the Beasts shew'd any aversion to that Carcass, he concluded that this would suit his purpose: and in the first place, he cuts off the Wings, and the Tail whole, and spreads the Feathers open; then he drew off the Skin, and divided it into two equal parts, one of which he wore upon his Back, with the other he covered his Navel and Secrets: the Tail he wore behind, and the Wings were plac'd upon each Arm. This Dress of his answer'd several Ends; for in the first place it cover'd his Nakedness, and help'd to keep him warm, and then it made him so frightful to the Beasts, that none of them car'd to meddle with him, or come near him; only the *Roe* his Nurse, which never left him, nor he, her; and when she grew Old and Feeble, he us'd to lead her where there was the best Food, and pluck the best Fruits for her, and give her them to eat.

16. Notwithstanding this she grew lean and weak, and continu'd a while in a languishing Condition, till at last she Dyed, and then all her Motions and Actions ceas'd. When the Boy perceiv'd her in this Condition, he was ready to dye for Grief. He call'd her with the same voice which she us'd to answer to, and made what Noise he could, but there was no Motion, no Alteration. Then he began to peep into her Eyes and Ears, but could perceive no visible defect in either; in like manner he examin'd all the parts of her Body, and found nothing amiss, but every thing as it should be. He had a vehement desire to find,

if possible, that part [where] the defect was, that he might remove it, and she return to her former State, of Life and Vigour. But he was altogether at a loss, how to compass his design, nor could he possibly bring it about.

17. That which put him upon this search, was what he observ'd in himself. He took Notice that when he shut his Eyes, or held any thing before them, he could see nothing at all, till that Obstacle was removed; and so when he put his Fingers into his Ears, that he could not hear, till he took 'em out again; and when he closed his Nostrils together, he smelt nothing till they were open'd; from whence he concluded, that all his Senses and Actions were liable to Obstacles and Impediments, upon the removal of which, the same Operations return'd to their former course. Therefore, when he had examined every External Part of her, and found no visible defect, and yet at the same time perceiv'd an Universal Cessation of Motion in the whole Body, not peculiar to one Member, but common to them all, he began to imagine that the hurt was in some part, which was most remote from the sight, and hidden in the inward part of the Body; and that this Part was of such nature and use, that without its help, none of the other External Parts could exercise their proper Functions; and that if this Part suffer any hurt, the damage was Universal, and a Cessation of the whole ensu'd.

18. This made him very desirous to find that part if possible, that he might remove the defect from it, that so it might be as it us'd to be, and the whole Body might enjoy the Benefit of it, and the same course of Actions follow as before. He had before observ'd, in the Bodies of Wild Beasts and other Animals, that all their Members were solid, and that there were only three Cavities, *viz.* The Skull, the Breast, and the Belly; he imagined therefore that this Part which he wanted, must needs be in one of these Cavities, and above all, he had a strong persuasion that it was in the middlemost of them. He verily believ'd, that all the Members stood in need of this part, and that from thence it must necessarily follow, that the Seat of it must be in the Centre. And when he reflected upon his own Body, he felt such a part in his Breast, of which he had this notion, *viz.* That it was impossible for him to subsist without it, so much as the twinkling of an eye, tho' he could at the same time conceive a possibility of subsisting without his other parts, *viz.* his Hands, Feet, Ears, Nose, Eyes, or even his Head. And upon this account, whenever he fought with any Wild Beast, he always took particular care to guard his Breast; because of the Apprehension which he had of that Part, which was contain'd in it.

19. Having, by this way of reasoning, assur'd himself that the disaffected Part lay in the Breast; he was resolv'd to make a search, in order to find it out; that whatsoever the Impediment was, he might remove it if possible; but then

again, he was afraid on the other side, lest his Undertaking should be worse than the Disease, and prove prejudicial. He began to consider next, whether or no he had ever remembred any Beasts, or other Animals, which he had seen in that condition, recover again, and return to the same State which they were in before: but he could call to Mind no such Instance; from whence he concluded, that if she was let alone there would be no hopes at all, but if he should be so fortunate as to find that Part, and find the Impediment, there might be some hope. Upon this he resolv'd to open her Breast and make enquiry; in order to which he provides himself with sharp Flints, and Splinters of dry Cane almost like Knives, with which he made an incision between the Ribs, and cutting through the Flesh, came to the *Diaphragma*; which he finding very Tough and not easily broken, assur'd himself, that such a Covering must needs belong to that part which he lookt for, and that if he could once get through that, he should find it. He met with some difficulty in his Work, because his Instruments were none of the best, for he had none but such as were made either of Flint or Cane.

20. However, he sharpned 'em again and renewed his Attempt with all the Skill he was Master of. At last he broke through, and the first part he met with was the Lungs, which he at first sight mistook, for that part which he search'd for, and turn'd 'em about this way and that way, to see if he could find in them the cause of the Disease. He first happen'd upon that Lobe which lay next the side [which he had open'd] and when he perceiv'd that it did lean sideways, he was satisfy'd that it was not the part he look'd for, because he was fully perswaded, that that must needs be in the midst of the Body, as well in regard of Latitude as Longitude. He proceeded in his search, till at last he found the Heart, which when he saw closed with a very strong Cover, and fastned with strong Ligaments, and covered by the Lungs on that side which he had open'd; he began to say to himself. "If this part be so on the other side as it is on this which I have open'd, then 'tis certainly in the midst, and without doubt the same I look for; especially considering the Conveniency of the Situation, the Comliness and Regularity of its Figure, the Firmness and Solidity of the Flesh, and besides, its being guarded with such a Membrane as I have not observ'd in any part." Upon this he searches the other side, and finding the same Membrane on the inside of the Ribs, and the Lungs in the same posture, which he had observ'd on that side which he had open'd first, he concluded the Heart to be the part which he look'd for.

21. Therefore he first Attacks the *Pericardium*, which, after a long tryal and a great deal of pains, he made shift to tear; and when he had laid the Heart bare, and perceiv'd that it was solid on every side, he began to examin it, to see

if he could find any hurt in it; but finding none, he squeez'd it with his Hands, and perceiv'd that it was hollow. He began [then] to think that what he look'd for, might possibly be contain'd in that Cavity. When he came to open it, he found in it two Cavities, one on the right side, the other on the left. That on the right side was full of clotted Blood, that on the left quite empty. "Then (says he,) without all doubt, one of those two Cavites must needs be the Receptacle of what I look for; as for that on this side there's nothing in it but congealed Blood, which was not so, be sure, till the whole Body was in that condition in which it now is" (for he had observ'd that all Blood congeals when it flows from the Body, and that this Blood did not differ in the least from any other,) "and therefore what I look for, cannot by any means, be such a matter as this; for that which I mean, is something which is peculiar to this place, which I find I could not subsist without, so much as the Twinkling of an Eye. And this is that which I look'd for at first. For as for this Blood, how often have I lost a great deal of it in my Skirmishes with the Wild Beasts, and yet it never did me any considerable harm, nor rendred me incapable of performing any Action of Life, and therefore what I look for is not in this Cavity. Now as for the Cavity on the left side, I find 'tis altogether empty, and I have no reason in the World to think that it was made in vain, because I find every part appointed for such and such particular Functions. How then can this Ventricle of the Heart, which I see is of so excellent a Frame, serve for no use at all? I cannot think but that the same thing which I am in search of, once dwelt here, but has now deserted his Habitation and left it empty, and that the Absence of that thing, has occasion'd this Privation of Sense and Cessation of Motion, which happen'd to the Body." Now when he perceiv'd that the Being which had inhabited there before, had left its House before it fell to Ruine, and forsaken it when as yet it continu'd whole and entire, he concluded that it was highly probable that it would never return to it any more, after its being so cut and mangled.

22. Upon this the whole Body seem'd to him a very inconsiderable thing, and worth nothing in respect of that Being, he believed once inhabited, and now had left it. Therefore he applied himself wholly to the consideration of that Being. *What it was?* and *how it subsisted? what joyn'd it to the Body? Whether it went, and by what passage, when it left the Body? What was the Cause of its Departure, whether it were forc'd to leave its Mansion, or left the Body of its own accord? and in case it went away Voluntarily, what it was that rendred the Body so disagreeable to it, as to make it forsake it?* And whilst his Mind was perplext with such variety of Thoughts, he laid aside all concern for the Carcass, and threw it away; for now he perceiv'd that his Mother, which had Nurs'd him so Tenderly and had Suckled him, was *that something* which was departed: and

from it proceeded all those Actions by which she shew'd her Care of him, and Affection to him, and not from this unactive Body; but that the Body was to it only as an Instrument or Tool, like his Cudgel which he had made for himself, with which he used to Fight with the Wild Beasts. So that now, all his regard to the Body was remov'd, and transferr'd to that by which the Body is governed, and by whose Power it moves. Nor had he any other desire but to make enquiry after that.

23. In the mean time the Carcass of the *Roe* began to putrifie, and emit Noisome Vapours, which still increas'd his aversion to it, so that he did not care to see it. 'Twas not long after that he chanc'd to see two Ravens engag'd so furiously; that one of them struck down the other Stark Dead; and when he had done, he began to scrape with his Claws till he had digg'd a Pit, in which he Buried the Carcass of his Adversary. Our Philosopher observing this, said to himself. *How well has this Raven done in Burying the Body of his Companion, tho' he did ill in Killing him? How much greater reason was there for me to have been forward in performing this Office to my Mother?* Upon this he makes a Grave, and lays his Mother into it, and Buries her. He proceeded in his Enquiry concerning what that should be by which the Body was govern'd, but could not Apprehend what it was; when he look'd upon the rest of the Roes, and perceiv'd that they were of the same form and figure with his Mother, he believ'd that there was in every one of them something which govern'd and actuated them, like that which had actuated and govern'd his Mother formerly: and for the sake of that likeness he us'd to keep in their Company, and shew affection towards them. He continued a while in this condition, Contemplating the various kinds of Animals and Plants, and walking about the Coast of his Island, to see if he could find any thing like himself; (as he observ'd that every Individual Animal, and Plant, had a great many more like it.) But all his search was in vain. And when he perceiv'd that his Island was encompass'd by the Sea, he thought that there was no other Land in the World but only that Island.

[24.] It happen'd that by Collision a Fire was kindled among a parcel of Reeds or Canes; which scar'd him at first, as being a Sight which he was altogether a Stranger to; so that he stood at a distance a good while, strangely surpriz'd, at last he came nearer and nearer by degrees, still observing the Brightness of its Light and marvellous Efficacy in consuming every thing it touch'd, and changing it into its own Nature; till at last, his Admiration of it, and that innate Boldness and Fortitude, which God had implanted in his Nature prompted him on, that he ventur'd to come near it, and stretch'd out his Hand to take some of it. But when it burnt his Fingers and he found there was no dealing with it that way, he endeavour'd to take a stick, which the Fire had not as yet wholly seiz'd upon; so taking hold on that part which was untouch'd he easily gain'd his purpose, and carried it Home to his Lodging (for he had contriv'd for himself a convenient place) there he kept this Fire and added Fuel to it, admir'd it wonderfully, and tended it night and day; at night especially, because its Light and Heat supply'd the absence of the Sun; so that he was extreamly delighted with it, and reckon'd it the most excellent of all those things which he had about him. And when he observ'd that it always mov'd upwards, he perswaded himself that, it was one of those Celestial Substances which he saw shining in the Firmament, and he was continually trying of its power, by throwing things into it, which he perceiv'd it operated upon and consum'd, sometimes sooner, sometimes slower, according as the Bodies which he put into it were more or less combustible.

25. Amongst other things which he put in to try its strength, he once flung in some Fish which had been thrown ashore by the Water, and as soon as e're he smelt the Steam, it rais'd his Appetite, so that he had a Mind to Taste of them; which he did, and found 'em very agreeable and from that time he began to use himself to the Eating of Flesh, and applied himself to Fishing and Hunting till he understood those sports very well: upon this account he admir'd his Fire more and more, because it help'd him to several sorts of Provision which he was altogether unacquainted with before.

53

Moses Maimonides

from *Guide for the Perplexed*

Maimonides (1135–1204), born Moses Ben Maimon and sometimes known as "The RaMBaM," was a celebrated physician and Jewish rabbi. He stands out as the single most important Jewish intellectual of the medieval period, and he produced a variety of significant and influential medical, philosophical, and theological works, including, most notably, his fourteen-volume compilation of Jewish law and philosophy known as the *Mishneh Torah*, as well as his work *The Guide for the Perplexed*, from which the following is an excerpt. Here, Maimonides discusses our knowledge of God's existence in relation to God's incorporeality.

Chapter XLVI

We have already stated . . . that there is a great difference between bringing to view the existence of a thing and demonstrating its true essence. We can lead others to notice the existence of an object by pointing to its accidents, actions, or even most remote relations to other objects: e.g., if you wish to describe the king of a country to one of his subjects who does not know him, you can give a description and an account of his existence in many ways. You will either say to him, the tall man with a fair complexion and grey hair is the king, thus describing him by his accidents; or you will say, the king is the person round whom are seen a great multitude of men on horse and on foot, and soldiers with drawn swords, over whose head banners are waving, and before whom trumpets are sounded; or it is the person living in the palace in a particular region of a certain country; or it is the person who ordered the building of that wall, or the construction of that bridge; or by some other

SOURCE: Moses Maimonides, *The Guide for the Perplexed*, trans. M. Friedländer, 4th ed. rev. (New York: E. P. Dutton & Co., 1904), 59–63.

similar acts and things relating to him. His existence can be demonstrated in a still more indirect way, e.g., if you are asked whether this land has a king, you will undoubtedly answer in the affirmative. "What proof have you?" "The fact that this banker here, a weak and little person, stands before this large mass of gold pieces, and that poor man, tall and strong, who stands before him asking in vain for alms of the weight of a carob-grain, is rebuked and is compelled to go away by the mere force of words; for had he not feared the king, he would, without hesitation, have killed the banker, or pushed him away and taken as much of the money as he could." Consequently, this is a proof that this country has a ruler and his existence is proved by the well-regulated affairs of the country, on account of which the king is respected and the punishments decreed by him are feared. In this whole example nothing is mentioned that indicated his characteristics, and his essential properties, by virtue of which he is king. The same is the case with the information concerning the Creator given to the ordinary classes of men in all prophetical books and in the Law. For it was found necessary to teach all of them that God exists, and that He is in every respect the most perfect Being, that is to say, He exists not only in the sense in which the earth and the heavens exist, but He exists and possesses life, wisdom, power, activity, and all other properties which our belief in His existence must include. . . . That God exists was therefore shown to ordinary men by means of similes taken from physical bodies; that He is living, by a simile taken from motion, because ordinary men consider only the body as fully, truly, and undoubtedly existing; that which is connected with a body but is itself not a body, although believed to exist, has a lower degree of existence on account of its dependence on the body for existence. That, however, which is neither itself a body, nor a force within a body, is not existent according to man's first notions, and is above all excluded from the range of imagination. In the same manner motion is considered by the ordinary man as identical with life; what cannot move voluntarily from place to place has no life, although motion is not part of the definition of life, but an accident connected with it. The perception by the senses, especially by hearing and seeing, is best known to us; we have no idea or notion of any other mode of communication between the soul of one person and that of another than by means of speaking, i.e., by the sound produced by lips, tongue, and the other organs of speech. When, therefore, we are to be informed that God has a *knowledge* of things, and that communication is made by Him to the Prophets who convey it to us, they represent Him to us as seeing and hearing, i.e., as perceiving and knowing those things which can be seen and heard. They represent Him to us as speaking, i.e., that communications from Him reach the Prophets; that is to be understood by the term "prophecy," as will be fully explained. God is described as working, because we do not know any other mode of producing a thing except by direct touch. He is said to have a soul in the sense that He is living, because all living beings are generally supposed to have a soul; although the term soul is, as has been shown, a homonym.

Again, since we perform all these actions only by means of corporeal organs, we figuratively ascribe to God the organs of locomotion, as feet, and their soles; organs of hearing, seeing, and smelling, as ear, eye, and nose; organs and substance of speech, as mouth, tongue, and sound; organs for the performance of work, as hand, its fingers, its palm, and the arm. In short, these organs of the body are figuratively ascribed to God, who is above all imperfection, to express that He performs certain acts; and these acts are figuratively ascribed to Him to express that He possesses certain perfections different from those acts themselves. E.g., we say that He has eyes, ears, hands, a mouth, a tongue, to express that He sees, hears, acts, and speaks; but seeing and hearing are attributed to Him to indicate simply that He perceives. You thus find in Hebrew instances in which the perception of the one sense is named instead of the other; thus, "See the word of the Lord" (Jer. ii. 31), in the same meaning as "Hear the word of the Lord," for the sense of the phrase is, "Perceive what He says"; similarly the phrase, "See the smell of my son" (Gen. xxvii. 27) has the same meaning as "Smell the smell of my son," for it relates to the perception of the smell. In the same way are used the words, "And all the people saw the thunders and the lightnings" (Exod. xx. 15), although the passage also contains the description of a prophetical vision, as is well known and understood among our people. Action and speech are likewise figuratively applied to God, to express that a certain influence has emanated from Him, as will be explained (chap. lxv and chap. lxvi.). The physical organs which are attributed to God in the writings of the Prophets are either organs of locomotion, indicating life; organs of sensation, indicating perception; organs of touch, indicating action; or organs of speech, indicating the divine inspiration of the Prophets, as will be explained.

The object of all these indications is to establish in our minds the notion of the existence of a living being, the Maker of everything, who also possesses a knowledge of the things which He has made. We shall explain, when we come to speak of the inadmissibility of Divine attributes, that all these various attributes convey but one notion, viz., that of the essence of God. The sole object of this chapter is to explain in what sense physical organs are ascribed to the Most Perfect Being, namely, that they are mere indications of the actions generally performed by means of these organs. Such actions being perfections respecting ourselves, are predicated of God, because we wish to express that He is most perfect in every respect, as we remarked above in explaining the Rabbinical phrase, "The language of the Torah is like the language of man." Instances of organs of locomotion being applied to the Creator occur as follows:—"My footstool" (Isa. lxvi. 1); "the place of the soles of my feet" (Ezek. xliii. 7). For examples of organs of touch applied to God, comp. "the hand of the Lord" (Exod. ix. 3); "with the finger of God" (*ib.* xxxi. 18); "the work of thy fingers" (Ps. viii. 4), "And thou hast laid thine hand upon me" (*ib.* cxxxix. 5); "The arm of the Lord" (Isa. liii. 1); "Thy right hand, O Lord" (Exod. xv. 6). In instances like the following, organs of speech are attributed to God: "The mouth of the Lord has spoken" (Isa. i. 20); "And He would open His lips against thee" (Job xi. 5); "The voice of the Lord is powerful" (Ps. xxix. 4); "And his tongue as a devouring fire" (Isa. xxx. 27). Organs of sensation are attributed to God in instances like the following: "His eyes behold, His eyelids try" (Ps. xi. 4); "The eyes of the Lord which run to and fro" (Zech. iv. 10); "Bow down thine ear unto me, and hear" (2 Kings xix. 16); "You have kindled a fire in my nostril" (Jer. xvii. 5). Of the inner parts of the human body only the heart is figuratively applied to God, because "heart" is a homonym, and denotes also "intellect"; it is besides the source of animal life. In phrases like "my bowels are troubled for him" (Jer. xxxi. 20); "The sounding of thy bowels" (Isa. lxiii. 15), the term "bowels" is used in the sense of "heart"; for the term "bowels" is used both in a general and in a specific meaning; it denotes specifically "bowels," but more generally it can be used as the name of any inner organ, including "heart." The correctness of this argument can be proved by the phrase "And thy law is within my bowels" (Ps. xl. 9), which is identical with "And thy law is within my heart." For that reason the prophet employed in this verse the phrase "my bowels are troubled" (and "the sounding of thy bowels"); the verb *hamah* is in fact used more frequently in connection with "heart," than with any other organ; comp. "My heart maketh a noise (*homeh*) in me" (Jer. iv. 19). Similarly, the shoulder is never used as a figure in reference to God, because it is known as a mere instrument of transport, and also comes into close contact with the thing which it carries. With far greater reason the organs of nutrition are never attributed to God; they are at once recognized as signs of imperfection. In fact all organs, both the external and the internal, are employed in the various actions of the soul; some, as e.g., all inner organs, are the means of preserving the individual for a certain time; others, as the organs of generation, are the means of preserving the species; others are the means of improving the condition of man and bringing his actions to perfection, as the hands, the feet, and the eyes, all of which tend to render motion, action, and perception more perfect. Animate beings require motion in order to be able to approach that which is conducive to their welfare, and to move away from the opposite; they require the senses in order to be able to discern what is injurious to them and what is beneficial. In addition, man requires various kinds of handiwork, to prepare his food, clothing, and dwelling; and he is compelled by his physical constitution to perform such work, namely, to prepare what is good for him. Some kinds of work also occur among certain animals, as far as such work is required by those animals. I do not believe that any man can doubt the correctness of the assertion that the Creator is not in need of anything for the continuance of His existence, or for the improvement of His condition. Therefore, God has no organs, or, what is the same, He is not corporeal; His actions are accomplished by His Essence, not by any organ, and as undoubtedly physical forces are connected with the organs, He does not possess any such forces, that is to say, He has, besides His Essence, nothing that could be the cause of His action, His knowledge, or His will, for attributes are nothing but forces under a different name. It is not my intention to discuss the question in this chapter. Our Sages laid down a general principle, by which the literal sense of the physical attributes of God mentioned by the prophets is rejected; a principle which evidently shows that our Sages were far from the belief in the corporeality of God, and that they did not think any person capable of misunderstanding it, or entertaining any doubt about it. For that reason they employ in the Talmud and the Midrashim phrases similar to those contained in the prophecies, without any circumlocution; they knew that there could not be any doubt about their metaphorical character, or any danger whatever of their being misunderstood; and that all such expressions would be understood as figurative [language], employed to communicate to the intellect the notion of His existence. Now, it was well known that in figurative language God is compared to a king who commands, cautions, punishes, and rewards, his subjects, and whose servants and attendants publish his orders, so that they might be acted upon, and they also execute whatever he wishes. Thus the Sages adopted that figure, used it frequently, and introduced such speech, consent and refusal of a king, and other usual acts of kings, as became necessary by that figure. In all these instances they were sure that no doubt or confusion would arise from it. The general principle alluded to above is contained in the following saying of our Sages, mentioned in Bereshith Rabba (c. xxvii.), "Great was the power of the Prophets; they compared the creature to its Creator; comp. 'And over the resemblance of the throne was a resemblance like the appearance of man'" (Ezek. i. 26). They have thus plainly stated that all those images which the Prophets perceived, i.e. in prophetic visions, are images created by God. This is perfectly correct; for every image in our imagination has been created. How pregnant is the expression, "Great is their boldness!" They indicated by it, that they themselves found it very remarkable; for whenever they perceived a word or act difficult to explain, or apparently objectionable, they used that phrase; e.g., a certain Rabbi has performed the act (of "ḥali ah") with a slipper, alone and by night. Another Rabbi, thereupon exclaimed "How great is his boldness to have followed the opinion of the minority." The Chaldee phrase *rab gubreh* in the original of the latter quotation, and the Hebrew *gadol koḥo* in that of the former quotation, have the same meaning, viz., Great is the power of (or the boldness of). Hence, in the preceding quotation, the sense is, How remarkable is the language which the Prophets were obliged to use when they speak of God the Creator in terms signifying properties of beings created by Him. This deserves attention. Our Sages have thus stated in distinct and plain terms that they are far from believing in the corporeality of God; and in the figures and forms seen in a prophetical vision, though belonging to created beings, the Prophets, to use the words of our Sages, "compared the creature to its Creator." If, however, after these explanations, any one wishes out of malice to cavil at them, and to find fault with them, though their method is neither comprehended nor understood by him, the Sages o.b.m. will sustain no injury by it.

54

Moses Maimonides

Thirteen Principles of the Faith

The following articles of the Jewish creed were originally formulated by Moses Maimonides in his commentary on the Mishnah. Liturgical expressions of those articles were eventually memorialized as the thirteen principles of the faith in the Jewish prayer book, from which the following is an excerpt. These thirteen principles are widely recognized as conveying the central accepted affirmations of Judaism.

---

1. I believe with perfect faith that the Creator, blessed be his name, is the Author and Guide of everything that has been created, and that he alone has made, does make, and will make all things.
2. I believe with perfect faith that the Creator, blessed be his name, is a Unity, and that there is no unity in any manner like unto his, and that he alone is our God, who was, is, and will be.
3. I believe with perfect faith that the Creator, blessed be his name, is not a body, and that he is free from all the accidents of matter, and that he has not any form whatsoever.
4. I believe with perfect faith that the Creator, blessed be his name, is the first and the last.
5. I believe with perfect faith that to the Creator, blessed by his name, and to him alone, it is right to pray, and that it is not right to pray to any being besides him.
6. I believe with perfect faith that all the words of the prophets are true.

SOURCE: *The Authorised Daily Prayer Book of the United Hebrew Congregations of the British Empire*, trans. S. Singer, 9th ed. (London: Eyre and Spottiswoode, 1912), 89–90.

7. I believe with perfect faith that the prophecy of Moses our teacher, peace be unto him, was true, and that he was the chief of the prophets, both of those that preceded and of those that followed him.

8. I believe with perfect faith that the whole Law, now in our possession, is the same that was given to Moses our teacher, peace be unto him.

9. I believe with perfect faith that this Law will not be changed, and that there will never be any other law from the Creator, blessed be his name.

10. I believe with perfect faith that the Creator, blessed be his name, knows every deed of the children of men, and all their thoughts, as it is said, It is he that fashioneth the hearts of them all, that giveth heed to all their deeds.

11. I believe with perfect faith that the Creator, blessed be his name, rewards those that keep his commandments, and punishes those that transgress them.

12. I believe with perfect faith in the coming of the Messiah, and, though he tarry, I will wait daily for his coming.

13. I believe with perfect faith that there will be a resurrection of the dead at the time when it shall please the Creator, blessed be his name, and exalted be the remembrance of him for ever and ever.

For thy salvation I hope, O Lord! I hope, O Lord, for thy salvation! O Lord, for thy salvation I hope!

55

Andreas Capellanus

from *The Art of Courtly Love* ("The Rules of Love")

Very little is known about Andreas Capellanus (ca. late twelfth century), except that he was the author of what is commonly known as *The Art of Courtly Love* and that he may have been a court chaplain, perhaps for the French Countess, Marie de Champagne (1145–1198). This work is historically significant for its documentary portrayal of romantic love during the medieval period. The following is the author's summation of the rules of love.

———————

    I. Marriage is not a just excuse for not loving.
    II. He who is not jealous cannot love.
    III. No one can be bound by a double love.
    IV. Love always increases or diminishes.
    V. What the lover takes from his beloved against her will has no relish.
    VI. A man can love only when he has reached full manhood.
    VII. A dead lover must be mourned by the survivor for two years.
    VIII. No one should be deprived of love without abundant reason.
    IX. No one can love unless he is compelled to do so by the persuasion of love.
    X. Love is always wont to shun the abode of avarice.
    XI. It is unseemly to love those whom one would be ashamed to marry.
    XII. A true lover does not wish to enjoy the love of another than his beloved.
    XIII. Love seldom lasts after it is divulged.
    XIV. Love easily won becomes contemptible; love won with difficulty is held dear.

SOURCE: Thomas Frederick Crane, *Italian Social Customs of the Sixteenth Century and Their Influence on the Literatures of Europe* (New Haven: Yale University Press, 1920), 35–36.

XV. Every lover is wont to turn pale at the sight of his beloved.

XVI. A lover's heart trembles at the sudden sight of his beloved.

XVII. A new love drives away the old.

XVIII. Probity alone makes one worthy of love.

XIX. If love diminishes it soon ends and rarely revives.

XX. A lover is always timid.

XXI. A lover's affection is always increased by true jealousy.

XXII. A lover's zeal and affection are increased by suspicion of the beloved.

XXIII. He eats and sleeps less whom the thought of love distresses.

XXIV. Every act of the lover is bounded by the thought of the beloved.

XXV. A true lover believes nothing good but what he thinks will please the beloved.

XXVI. Love can refuse nothing to love.

XXVII. A lover cannot tire of the favors of his beloved.

XXVIII. A slight presumption forces the lover to suspect his beloved.

XXIX. He is not wont to love who is tormented by lewdness.

XXX. A true lover dwells in the uninterrupted contemplation of the beloved.

XXXI. Nothing forbids a woman to be loved by two men, and a man by two women.

Ibn al-Athir

from *Account of the Outbreak of the Tartars into the Lands of Islam*

The name "Tartar" (or Tatar) refers to a Turkic-speaking people of north-eastern Mongolia. In the early thirteenth century, Turkic nomads joined with Genghis Khan's force, which famously moved across Asia and into eastern Europe. The term "Tartar" then became a generic reference to this invading force. In the following excerpt, the Islamic historian Ibn al-Athir (1160–1233) provides an Arab Muslim perspective on the attack. Primarily focusing on the assault from the East, he includes also the onslaught from the Crusading West. If his perspective is representative, Muslims clearly felt caught between oppressor armies. About twenty-five years after Ibn al-Athir's death, Baghdad fell to the Mongolian force led by Hulagu Khan, which significantly altered the history and politics of Arab civilization.

For some years I continued averse from mentioning this event, deeming it so horrible that I shrank from recording it and ever withdrawing one foot as I advanced the other. To whom, indeed, can it be easy to write the announcement of the death-blow of Islam and the Muslims, or who is he on whom the remembrance thereof can weigh lightly? O would that my mother had not born me or that I had died and become a forgotten thing ere this befell! Yet, withal a number of my friends urged me to set it down in writing, and I hesitated long, but at last came to the conclusion that to omit this matter [from my history] could serve no useful purpose.

I say, therefore, that this thing involves the description of the greatest catastrophe and the most dire calamity (of the like of which days and nights are

SOURCE: Ibn al-Athir, *Account of the Outbreak of the Tartars into the Lands of Islam*, in Edward G. Browne, *A Literary History of Persia: From Firdawsi to Sa'di* (London: T. Fisher Unwin, 1906), 427–31.

innocent) which befell all men generally, and the Muslims in particular; so that, should one say that the world, since God Almighty created Adam until now, has not been afflicted with the like thereof, he would but speak the truth. For indeed history does not contain anything which approaches or comes near unto it. For of the most grievous calamities recorded was what Nebuchadnezzar inflicted on the children of Israel by his slaughter of them and his destruction of Jerusalem; and what was Jerusalem in comparison to the countries which these accursed miscreants destroyed, each city of which was double the size of Jerusalem? Or what were the children of Israel compared to those whom these slew? For verily those whom they massacred in a single city exceeded all the children of Israel. Nay, it is unlikely that mankind will see the like of this calamity, until the world comes to an end and perishes, except the final outbreak of Gog and Magog. For even Antichrist will spare such as follow him, though he destroy those who oppose him, but these [Tartars] spared none, slaying women and men and children, ripping open pregnant women and killing unborn babes. Verily to God do we belong, and unto Him do we return, and there is no strength and no power save in God, the High, the Almighty, in face of this catastrophe, whereof the sparks flew far and wide, and the hurt was universal; and which passed over the lands like clouds driven by the wind. For these were a people who emerged from the confines of China, and attacked the cities of Turkistán, like Káshghar and Balásághún, and thence advanced on the cities of Transoxiana, such as Samarqand, Bukhárá and the like, taking possession of them, and treating their inhabitants in such wise as we shall mention; and of them one division then passed on into Khurásán, until they had made an end of taking possession, and destroying, and slaying, and plundering, and thence passing on to Ray, Hamadán and the Highlands, and the cities contained therein, even to the limits of Iráq, whence they marched on the towns of Ádharbayján and Arrániyya, destroying them and slaying most of their inhabitants, of whom none escaped save a small remnant; and all this in less than a year; this is a thing whereof the like has not been heard. And when they had finished with Ádharbayján and Arrániyya, they passed on to Darband-i-Shirwán, and occupied its cities, none of which escaped save the fortress wherein was their King; wherefore they passed by it to the countries of the Lán and the Lakiz and the various nationalities which dwell in that region, and plundered, slew, and destroyed them to the full. And thence they made their way to the lands of Qipcháq, who are the most numerous of the Turks, and slew all such as withstood them, while the survivors fled to the fords and mountain-tops, and abandoned their country, which these Tartars overran. All this they did in the briefest space of time, remaining only for so long as their march required and no more.

Another division, distinct from that mentioned above, marched on Ghazna and its dependencies, and those parts of India, Sistán and Kirmán which border thereon, and wrought therein deeds like unto the other, nay, yet more grievous. Now this is a thing the like of which ear has not heard; for Alexander, concerning whom historians agree that he conquered the world, did not do so with such swiftness, but only in the space of about ten years; neither did he slay, but was satisfied that men should be subject to him. But these Tartars conquered most of the habitable globe, and the best, the most flourishing and most populous part thereof, and that whereof the inhabitants were the most advanced in character and conduct, in about a year; nor did any country escape their devastations which did not fearfully expect them and dread their arrival.

Moreover they need no commissariat, nor the conveyance of supplies, for they have with them sheep, cows, horses, and the like quadrupeds, the flesh of which they eat, [needing] naught else. As for their beasts which they ride, these dig into the earth with their hoofs and eat the roots of plants, knowing naught of barley. And so, when they alight anywhere, they have need of nothing from without. As for their religion, they worship the sun when it rises, and regard nothing as unlawful, for they eat all beasts, even dogs, pigs, and the like; nor do they recognise the marriage-tie, for several men are in marital relations with one woman, and if a child is born, it knows not who is its father.

Therefore Islám and the Muslims have been afflicted during this period with calamities wherewith no people hath been visited. These Tartars (may God confound them!) came from the East, and wrought deeds which horrify all who hear of them, and which you shall, please God, see set forth in full detail in their proper connection. And of these [calamities] was the invasion of Syria by the Franks (may God curse them!) out of the West, and their attack on Egypt, and occupation of the port of Damietta therein, so that Egypt and Syria were like to be conquered by them, but for the grace of God and the help which He vouchsafed us against them, as we have mentioned under the year 614 (A.D. 1217–18). Of these [calamities], moreover, was that the sword was drawn between those [of the Muslims] who escaped from these two foes, and strife was rampant [amongst them], as we have also mentioned: and verily unto God do we belong and unto Him do we return! We ask God to vouchsafe victory to Islám and the Muslims, for there is none other to aid, help, or defend the True Faith. But if God intends evil to any people, naught can avert it, nor have they any ruler save Him. As for these Tartars, their achievements were only rendered possible by the absence of any effective obstacle; and the cause of this absence was that Muhammad Khwárazmsháh had overrun the [Muslim] lands, slaying and destroying their Kings, so that he remained alone ruling over all these countries; wherefore, when he was defeated by the Tartars, none was left in the lands to check those or protect these, that so God might accomplish a thing which was to be done.

It is now time for us to describe how they first burst forth into the [Muslim] lands.

[. . . .]

Stories have been related to me, . . ., which the hearer can scarcely credit, as to the terror of them [*i.e.*, the Mongols], which God Almighty cast into men's hearts; so that it is said that a single one of them would enter a village or a quarter wherein were many people, and would continue to slay them one after another, none daring to stretch forth his hand against this horseman. And I have heard that one of them took a man captive, but had not with him any weapon wherewith to kill him; and he said to his prisoner, "Lay your head on the ground and do not move;" and he did so, and the Tartar went and fetched his sword and slew him therewith. Another man related to me as follows:—"I was going," said he, "with seventeen others along a road, and there met us a Tartar horseman, and bade us bind one another's arms. My companions began to do as he bade them, but I said to them, 'He is but one man; wherefore, then, should we not kill him and flee?' They replied, 'We are afraid.' I said, 'This man intends to kill you immediately; let us therefore rather kill him, that perhaps God may deliver us.' But I swear by God that not one of them dared to do this, so I took a knife and slew him, and we fled and escaped." And such occurrences were many.

57

Magna Carta, 1215

Originally drafted by the Archbishop of Canterbury, the Magna Carta represents something of a truce agreement between an unpopular English crown and the rebellious and powerful barons who had grown tired of its ways. Signed by King John on June 15, 1215, the charter guaranteed in exchange for peace a schedule of legal rights, perhaps the most famous of which is that free men may not be denied justice or a fair trial. Although this attempt at a peace treaty soon failed—England quickly descended into civil war and the charter was declared null and void by Pope Innocent III—the Magna Carta remains an iconic document of lasting historical significance, in part because of how it inspired the idea of constitutional restrictions on governmental authority, which proved particularly influential for the founders of the United States of America.

John, by the grace of God, king of England, lord of Ireland, duke of Normandy and Aquitaine, and count of Anjou, to the archbishops, bishops, abbots, earls, barons, justiciars, foresters, sheriffs, stewards, servants, and to all his bailiffs and liege subjects, greeting. Know that, having regard to God and for the salvation of our souls, and those of all our ancestors and heirs, and unto the honour of God and the advancement of holy Church, and for the reform of our realm, [we have granted as underwritten] by advice of our venerable fathers, Stephen, archbishop of Canterbury, primate of all England and cardinal of the holy Roman Church, Henry archbishop of Dublin, William of London, Peter of Winchester, Jocelyn of Bath and Glastonbury, Hugh of Lincoln, Walter of Worcester, William of Coventry, Benedict of Rochester, bishops; of master Pandulf, subdeacon and member of the household of our lord the Pope, of brother Aymeric (master of the Knights of the Temple in England), and of the

SOURCE: William Sharp McKechnie, *Magna Carta: A Commentary on the Great Charter of King John, with an Historical Introduction*, 2nd ed., revised and in part rewritten (Glasgow: James Maclehose and Sons, 1914), 186–480.

illustrious men William Marshal, earl of Pembroke, William, earl of Salisbury, William, earl Warenne, William, earl of Arundel, Alan of Galloway (constable of Scotland), Waren Fitz Gerald, Peter Fitz Herbert, Hubert de Burgh (seneschal of Poitou), Hugh de Neville, Matthew Fitz Herbert, Thomas Basset, Alan Basset, Philip d'Aubigny, Robert of Roppesley, John Marshal, John Fitz Hugh, and others, our liegemen.

[1] In the first place we have granted to God, and by this our present charter confirmed for us and our heirs for ever that the English church shall be free, and shall have her rights entire, and her liberties inviolate; and we will that it be thus observed; which is apparent from this that the freedom of elections, which is reckoned most important and very essential to the English church, we, of our pure and unconstrained will, did grant, and did by our charter confirm and did obtain the ratification of the same from our lord, Pope Innocent III., before the quarrel arose between us and our barons: and this we will observe, and our will is that it be observed in good faith by our heirs for ever. We have also granted to all freemen of our kingdom, for us and our heirs forever, all the underwritten liberties, to be had and held by them and their heirs, of us and our heirs forever.

[2] If any of our earls or barons, or others holding of us in chief by military service shall have died, and at the time of his death his heir shall be full of age and owe "relief" he shall have his inheritance on payment of the ancient relief, namely the heir or heirs of an earl, £100 for a whole earl's barony; the heir or heirs of a baron, £100 for a whole barony; the heir or heirs of a knight, 100s. at most for a whole knight's fee; and whoever owes less let him give less, according to the ancient custom of fiefs.

[3] If, however, the heir of any one of the aforesaid has been under age and in wardship, let him have his inheritance without relief and without fine when he comes of age.

[4] The guardian of the land of an heir who is thus under age, shall take from the land of the heir nothing but reasonable produce, reasonable customs, and reasonable services, and that without destruction or waste of men or goods; and if we have committed the wardship of the lands of any such minor to the sheriff, or to any other who is responsible to us for its issues, and he has made destruction or waste of what he holds in wardship, we will take of him amends, and the land shall be committed to two lawful and discreet men of that fee, who shall be responsible for the issues to us or to him to whom we shall assign them; and if we have given or sold the wardship of any such land to anyone and he has therein made destruction or waste, he shall lose that wardship, and it shall be transferred to two lawful and discreet men of that fief, who shall be responsible to us in like manner as aforesaid.

[5] The guardian, moreover, so long as he has the wardship of the land, shall keep up the houses, parks, fishponds, stanks, mills, and other things pertaining to the land, out of the issues of the same land; and he shall restore to the heir, when he has come to full age, all his land, stocked with ploughs and "waynage," according as the season of husbandry shall require, and the issues of the land can reasonably bear.

[6] Heirs shall be married without disparagement, yet so that before the marriage takes place the nearest in blood to that heir shall have notice.

[7] A widow, after the death of her husband, shall forthwith and without difficulty have her marriage portion and inheritance; nor shall she give anything for her dower, or for her marriage portion, or for the inheritance which her husband and she held on the day of the death of that husband; and she may remain in the house of her husband for forty days after his death, within which time her dower shall be assigned to her.

[8] No widow shall be compelled to marry, so long as she prefers to live without a husband; provided always that she gives security not to marry without our consent, if she holds of us, or without the consent of the lord of whom she holds, if she holds of another.

[9] Neither we nor our bailiffs shall seize any land or rent for any debt, so long as the chattels of the debtor are sufficient to repay the debt; nor shall the sureties of the debtor be distrained so long as the principal debtor is able to satisfy the debt; and if the principal debtor shall fail to pay the debt, having nothing wherewith to pay it, then the sureties shall answer for the debt; and let them have the lands and rents of the debtor, if they desire them, until they are indemnified for the debt which they have paid for him, unless the principal debtor can show proof that he is discharged thereof as against the said sureties.

[10] If one who has borrowed from the Jews any sum, great or small, die before that loan be repaid, the debt shall not bear interest while the heir is under age, of whomsoever he may hold; and if the debt fall into our hands, we will not take anything except the principal sum contained in the bond.

[11] And if anyone die indebted to the Jews, his wife shall have her dower and pay nothing of that debt; and if any children of the deceased are left under age, necessaries shall be provided for them in keeping with the holding of the deceased; and out of the residue the debt shall be paid, reserving, however, service due to feudal lords; in like manner let it be done touching debts due to others than Jews.

[12] No scutage nor aid shall be imposed on our kingdom, unless by common counsel of our kingdom, except for ransoming our person, for making our eldest son a knight, and for once marrying our eldest daughter; and for

these there shall not be levied more than a reasonable aid. In like manner it shall be done concerning aids from the city of London.

[13] And the city of London shall have all its ancient liberties and free customs, as well by land as by water; furthermore, we decree and grant that all other cities, boroughs, towns, and ports shall have all their liberties and free customs.

[14] And for obtaining the common counsel of the kingdom anent the assessing of an aid (except in the three cases aforesaid) or of a scutage, we will cause to be summoned the archbishops, bishops, abbots, earls, and greater barons, severally by our letters; and we will moreover cause to be summoned generally, through our sheriffs and bailiffs, all others who hold of us in chief, for a fixed date, namely, after the expiry of at least forty days, and at a fixed place; and in all letters of such summons we will specify the reason of the summons. And when the summons has thus been made, the business shall proceed on the day appointed, according to the counsel of such as are present, although not all who were summoned have come.

[15] We will not for the future grant to any one licence to take an aid from his own free tenants, except to ransom his body, to make his eldest son a knight, and once to marry his eldest daughter; and on each of these occasions there shall be levied only a reasonable aid.

[16] No one shall be distrained for performance of greater service for a knight's fee, or for any other free tenement, than is due therefrom.

[17] Common pleas shall not follow our court, but shall be held in some fixed place.

[18] Inquests of *novel disseisin*, of *mort d'ancestor*, and of *darrein presentment*, shall not be held elsewhere than in their own country-courts, and that in manner following,—We, or, if we should be out of the realm, our chief justiciar, will send two justiciars through every county four times a year, who shall, along with four knights of the county chosen by the county, hold the said assizes in the county court, on the day and in the place of meeting of that court.

[19] And if any of the said assizes cannot be taken on the day of the county court, let there remain of the knights and freeholders, who were present at the county court on that day, as many as may be required for the efficient making of judgments, according as the business be more or less.

[20] A freeman shall not be amerced for a slight offence, except in accordance with the degree of the offence; and for a grave offence he shall be amerced in accordance with the gravity of the offence, yet saving always his "contenement"; and a merchant in the same way, saving his "merchandise"; and a villein shall be amerced in the same way, saving his "wainage"—if they

have fallen into our mercy: and none of the aforesaid amercements shall be imposed except by the oath of honest men of the neighbourhood.

[21] Earls and barons shall not be amerced except through their peers, and only in accordance with the degree of the offence.

[22] A clerk shall not be amerced in respect of his lay holding except after the manner of the others aforesaid; further, he shall not be amerced in accordance with the extent of his ecclesiastical benefice.

[23] No village or individual shall be compelled to make bridges at river banks, except those who from of old were legally bound to do so.

[24] No sheriff, constable, coroners, or others of our bailiffs, shall hold pleas of our Crown.

[25] All counties, hundreds, wapentakes, and trithings (except our demesne manors) shall remain at the old rents, and without any additional payment.

[26] If any one holding of us a lay fief shall die, and our sheriff or bailiff shall exhibit our letters patent of summons for a debt which the deceased owed to us, it shall be lawful for our sheriff or bailiff to attach and catalogue chattels of the deceased, found upon the lay fief, to the value of that debt, at the sight of law-worthy men, provided always that nothing whatever be thence removed until the debt which is evident shall be fully paid to us; and the residue shall be left to the executors to fulfil the will of the deceased; and if there be nothing due from him to us, all the chattels shall go to the deceased, saving to his wife and children their reasonable shares.

[27] If any freeman shall die intestate, his chattels shall be distributed by the hands of his nearest kinsfolk and friends, under supervision of the church, saving to every one the debts which the deceased owed to him.

[28] No constable or other bailiff of ours shall take corn or other provisions from any one without immediately tendering money therefor, unless he can have postponement thereof by permission of the seller.

[29] No constable shall compel any knight to give money in lieu of castle-guard, when he is willing to perform it in his own person, or (if he himself cannot do it from any reasonable cause) then by another responsible man. Further, if we have led or sent him upon military service, he shall be relieved from guard in proportion to the time during which he has been on service because of us.

[30] No sheriff or bailiff of ours, or other person, shall take the horses or carts of any freeman for transport duty, against the will of the said freeman.

[31] Neither we nor our bailiffs shall take, for our castles or for any other work of ours, wood which is not ours, against the will of the owner of that wood.

[32] We will not retain beyond one year and one day, the lands of those who have been convicted of felony, and the lands shall thereafter be handed over to the lords of the fiefs.

[33] All kydells for the future shall be removed altogether from Thames and Medway, and throughout all England, except upon the sea shore.

[34] The writ which is called *praecipe* shall not for the future be issued to anyone, regarding any tenement whereby a freeman may lose his court.

[35] Let there be one measure of wine throughout our whole realm; and one measure of ale; and one measure of corn, to wit, "the London quarter"; and one width of cloth (whether dyed, or russet, or "halberget"), to wit, two ells within the selvedges; of weights also let it be as of measures.

[36] Nothing in future shall be given or taken for a writ of inquisition of life or limbs, but freely it shall be granted, and never denied.

[37] If anyone holds of us by fee-farm, by socage, or by burgage, and holds also land of another lord by knight's service, we will not (by reason of that fee-farm, socage, or burgage,) have the wardship of the heir, or of such land of his as is of the fief of that other; nor shall we have wardship of that fee-farm, socage, or burgage, unless such fee-farm owes knight's service. We will not by reason of any small serjeanty which anyone may hold of us by the service of rendering to us knives, arrows, or the like, have wardship of his heir or of the land which he holds of another lord by knight's service.

[38] No bailiff for the future shall, upon his own unsupported complaint, put anyone to his "law," without credible witnesses brought for this purpose.

[39] No freeman shall be taken or [and] imprisoned or disseised or exiled or in any way destroyed, nor will we go upon him nor send upon him, except by the lawful judgment of his peers or [and] by the law of the land.

[40] To no one will we sell, to no one will we refuse or delay, right or justice.

[41] All merchants shall have safe and secure exit from England, and entry to England, with the right to tarry there and to move about as well by land as by water, for buying and selling by the ancient and right customs, quit from all evil tolls, except (in time of war) such merchants as are of the land at war with us. And if such are found in our land at the beginning of the war, they shall be detained, without injury to their bodies or goods, until information be received by us, or by our chief justiciar, how the merchants of our land found in the land at war with us are treated; and if our men are safe there, the others shall be safe in our land.

[42] It shall be lawful in future for any one (excepting always those imprisoned or outlawed in accordance with the law of the kingdom, and natives of any country at war with us, and merchants, who shall be treated as

is above provided) to leave our kingdom and to return, safe and secure by land and water, except for a short period in time of war, on grounds of public policy—reserving always the allegiance due to us.

[43] If anyone holding of some escheat (such as the honour of Wallingford, Nottingham, Boulogne, Lancaster, or of other escheats which are in our hands and are baronies) shall die, his heir shall give no other relief, and perform no other service to us than he would have done to the baron, if that barony had been in the baron's hand; and we shall hold it in the same manner in which the baron held it.

[44] Men who dwell without the forest need not henceforth come before our justiciars of the forest upon a general summons, except those who are impleaded, or who have become sureties for any person or persons attached for forest offences.

[45] We will appoint as justices, constables, sheriffs, or bailiffs only such as know the law of the realm and mean to observe it well.

[46] All barons who have founded abbeys, concerning which they hold charters from the kings of England, or of which they have long-continued possession, shall have the wardship of them, when vacant, as they ought to have.

[47] All forests that have been made such in our time shall forthwith be disafforested; and a similar course shall be followed with regard to river-banks that have been placed "in defence" by us in our time.

[48] All evil customs connected with forests and warrens, foresters and warreners, sheriffs and their officers, river-banks and their wardens, shall immediately be inquired into in each county by twelve sworn knights of the same county chosen by the honest men of the same county, and shall, within forty days of the said inquest, be utterly abolished, so as never to be restored, provided always that we previously have intimation thereof, or our justiciar, if we should not be in England.

[49] We will immediately restore all hostages and charters delivered to us by Englishmen, as sureties of the peace or of faithful service

[50] We will entirely remove from their bailiwicks, the relations of Gerard of Athée (so that in future they shall have no bailiwick in England); namely, Engelard of Cigogné, Peter, Guy, and Andrew of Chanceaux, Guy of Cigogné, Geoffrey of Martigny with his brothers, Philip Mark with his brothers and his nephew Geoffrey, and the whole brood of the same.

[51] As soon as peace is restored, we will banish from the kingdom all foreign-born knights, cross-bowmen, serjeants, and mercenary soldiers, who have come with horses and arms to the kingdom's hurt.

[52] If any one has been dispossessed or removed by us, without the legal judgment of his peers, from his lands, castles, franchises, or from his right, we will immediately restore them to him; and if a dispute arise over this, then let it be decided by the five-and-twenty barons of whom mention is made below in the clause for securing the peace. Moreover, for all those possessions, from which any one has, without the lawful judgment of his peers, been disseised or removed, by our father, King Henry, or by our brother, King Richard, and which we retain in our hand (or which are possessed by others, to whom we are bound to warrant them) we shall have respite until the usual term of crusaders; excepting those things about which a plea has been raised, or an inquest made by our order, before our taking of the cross; but as soon as we return from our expedition (or if perchance we desist from the expedition) we will immediately grant full justice therein.

[53] We shall have, moreover, the same respite and in the same manner in rendering justice concerning the disafforestation or retention of those forests which Henry our father and Richard our brother afforested, and concerning the wardship of lands which are of the fief of another (namely, such wardships as we have hitherto had by reason of a fief which anyone held of us by knight's service), and concerning abbeys founded on other fiefs than our own, in which the lord of the fee claims to have right; and when we have returned, or if we desist from our expedition, we will immediately grant full justice to all who complain of such things.

[54] No one shall be arrested or imprisoned upon the appeal of a woman, for the death of any other than her husband.

[55] All fines made with us unjustly and against the law of the land, and all amercements imposed unjustly and against the law of the land, shall be entirely remitted, or else it shall be done concerning them according to the decision of the five-and-twenty barons of whom mention is made below in the clause for securing the peace, or according to the judgment of the majority of the same, along with the aforesaid Stephen, archbishop of Canterbury, if he can be present, and such others as he may wish to bring with him for this purpose, and if he cannot be present the business shall nevertheless proceed without him, provided always that if any one or more of the aforesaid five-and-twenty barons are in a similar suit, they shall be removed as far as concerns this particular judgment, others being substituted in their places after having been selected by the rest of the same five-and-twenty for this purpose only, and after having been sworn.

[56] If we have disseised or removed Welshmen from lands or liberties, or other things, without the legal judgment of their peers in England or in

Wales, they shall be immediately restored to them; and if a dispute arise over this, then let it be decided in the marches by the judgment of their peers; for tenements in England according to the law of England, for tenements in Wales according to the law of Wales, and for tenements in the marches according to the law of the marches. Welshmen shall do the same to us and ours.

[57] Further, for all those possessions from which any Welshman has, without the lawful judgment of his peers, been disseised or removed by King Henry our father, or King Richard our brother, and which we retain in our hand (or which are possessed by others, to whom we are bound to warrant them) we shall have respite until the usual term of crusaders; excepting those things about which a plea has been raised or an inquest made by our order before we took the cross; but as soon as we return, (or if perchance we desist from our expedition), we will immediately grant full justice in accordance with the laws of the Welsh and in relation to the foresaid regions.

[58] We will immediately give up the son of Llywelyn and all the hostages of Wales, and the charters delivered to us as security for the peace.

[59] We will do towards Alexander, King of Scots, concerning the return of his sisters and his hostages, and concerning his franchises, and his right, in the same manner as we shall do towards our other barons of England, unless it ought to be otherwise according to the charters which we hold from William his father, formerly King of Scots; and this shall be according to the judgment of his peers in our court.

[60] Moreover, all these aforesaid customs and liberties, the observance of which we have granted in our kingdom as far as pertains to us towards our men, shall be observed by all of our kingdom, as well clergy as laymen, as far as pertains to them towards their men.

[61] Since, moreover, for God and the amendment of our kingdom and for the better allaying of the quarrel that has arisen between us and our barons, we have granted all these concessions, desirous that they should enjoy them in complete and firm endurance for ever, we give and grant to them the underwritten security, namely, that the barons choose five-and-twenty barons of the kingdom, whomsoever they will, who shall be bound with all their might, to observe and hold, and cause to be observed, the peace and liberties we have granted and confirmed to them by this our present Charter, so that if we, or our justiciar, or our bailiffs or any one of our officers, shall in anything be at fault toward anyone, or shall have broken any one of the articles of the peace or of this security, and the offence be notified to four barons of the foresaid five-and-twenty, the said four barons shall repair to us (or our justiciar, if we are out of the realm) and, laying the transgression before us, petition to have

that transgression redressed without delay. And if we shall not have corrected the transgression (or, in the event of our being out of the realm, if our justiciar shall not have corrected it) within forty days, reckoning from the time it has been intimated to us (or to our justiciar, if we should be out of the realm), the four barons aforesaid shall refer that matter to the rest of the five-and-twenty barons, and those five-and-twenty barons shall, together with the community of the whole land, distrain and distress us in all possible ways, namely, by seizing our castles, lands, possessions, and in any other way they can, until redress has been obtained as they deem fit, saving harmless our own person, and the persons of our queen and children; and when redress has been obtained, they shall resume their old relations towards us. And let whoever in the country desires it, swear to obey the orders of the said five-and-twenty barons for the execution of all the aforesaid matters, and along with them, to molest us to the utmost of his power; and we publicly and freely grant leave to every one who wishes to swear, and we shall never forbid anyone to swear. All those, moreover, in the land who of themselves and of their own accord are unwilling to swear to the twenty-five to help them in constraining and molesting us, we shall by our command compel the same to swear to the effect foresaid. And if any one of the five-and-twenty barons shall have died or departed from the land, or be incapacitated in any other manner which would prevent the foresaid provisions being carried out, those of the said twenty-five barons who are left shall choose another in his place according to their own judgment, and he shall be sworn in the same way as the others. Further, in all matters, the execution of which is intrusted to these twenty-five barons, if perchance these twenty-five are present and disagree about anything, or if some of them, after being summoned, are unwilling or unable to be present, that which the majority of those present ordain or command shall be held as fixed and established, exactly as if the whole twenty-five had concurred in this; and the said twenty-five shall swear that they will faithfully observe all that is aforesaid, and cause it to be observed with all their might. And we shall procure nothing from anyone, directly or indirectly, whereby any part of these concessions and liberties might be revoked or diminished; and if any such thing has been procured, let it be void and null, and we shall never use it personally or by another.

[62] And all the ill-will, hatreds, and bitterness that have arisen between us and our men, clergy and lay, from the date of the quarrel, we have completely remitted and pardoned to everyone. Moreover, all trespasses occasioned by the said quarrel, from Easter in the sixteenth year of our reign till the restoration of peace, we have fully remitted to all, both clergy and laymen, and completely forgiven, as far as pertains to us. And, on this head, we have caused to be made

for them letters testimonial patent of the lord Stephen, archbishop of Canterbury, of the lord Henry, archbishop of Dublin, of the bishops aforesaid, and of Master Pandulf as touching this security and the concessions aforesaid.

[63] Wherefore it is our will, and we firmly enjoin, that the English Church be free, and that the men in our kingdom have and hold all the aforesaid liberties, rights, and concessions, well and peaceably, freely and quietly, fully and wholly, for themselves and their heirs, of us and our heirs, in all respects and in all places for ever, as is aforesaid. An oath, moreover, has been taken, as well on our part as on the part of the barons, that all these conditions aforesaid shall be kept in good faith and without evil intent. Given under our hand—the above-named and many others being witnesses—in the meadow which is called Runnymede, between Windsor and Staines, on the fifteenth day of June, in the seventeenth year of our reign.

58

Thomas Aquinas

from *Summa Theologica* ("The Five Ways")

Thomas Aquinas (1224/5–1274) was a medieval Italian Dominican monk and philosopher-theologian whose influence within the Christian intellectual tradition, particularly within Roman Catholicism, is nearly unparalleled. Honored as the Angelic Doctor and as the Common Doctor, he is formally recognized as a saint by the Church. His most important work, *Summa Theologica*, is a massive systematic treatise on nearly every topic pertinent to God, humanity, and the world. The following is an excerpt from the first part of Aquinas' *Summa* in which he offers five related ways of arguing for the existence of God. In characteristic fashion, the passage opens with a brief consideration of the opposing viewpoint to which Aquinas replies with his own arguments.

Third Article: Whether God Exists?

We proceed thus to the Third Article:—

Objection 1. It seems that God does not exist; because if one of two contraries be infinite, the other would be altogether destroyed. But the word 'God' means that He is infinite goodness. If, therefore, God existed, there would be no evil discoverable; but there is evil in the world. Therefore God does not exist.

Obj. 2. Further, it is superfluous to suppose that what can be accounted for by a few principles has been produced by many. But it seems that everything we see in the world can be accounted for by other principles, supposing God did not exist. For all natural things can be reduced to one principle, which

SOURCE: Thomas Aquinas, *The "Summa Theologica" of St. Thomas Aquinas*, vol. 1, *Part I, QQ. I.–XXVI.*, trans. the Fathers of the English Dominican Province, 2nd and rev. ed. (London: Burns Oates & Washbourne Ltd., 1920), 24–27.

302 | Thomas Aquinas

is nature; and all voluntary things can be reduced to one principle, which is human reason, or will. Therefore there is no need to suppose God's existence.

On the contrary, It is said in the person of God: *I am Who am* (Exod. iii. 14).

I answer that, The existence of God can be proved in five ways.

The first and more manifest way is the argument from motion. It is certain, and evident to our senses, that in the world some things are in motion. Now whatever is in motion is put in motion by another, for nothing can be in motion except it is in potentiality to that towards which it is in motion; whereas a thing moves inasmuch as it is in act. For motion is nothing else than the reduction of something from potentiality to actuality. But nothing can be reduced from potentiality to actuality, except by something in a state of actuality. Thus that which is actually hot, as fire, makes wood, which is potentially hot, to be actually hot, and thereby moves and changes it. Now it is not possible that the same thing should be at once in actuality and potentiality in the same respect, but only in different respects. For what is actually hot cannot simultaneously be potentially hot; but it is simultaneously potentially cold. It is therefore impossible that in the same respect and in the same way a thing should be both mover and moved, *i.e.*, that it should move itself. Therefore, whatever is in motion must be put in motion by another. If that by which it is put in motion be itself put in motion, then this also must needs be put in motion by another, and that by another again. But this cannot go on to infinity, because then there would be no first mover, and, consequently, no other mover; seeing that subsequent movers move only inasmuch as they are put in motion by the first mover; as the staff moves only because it is put in motion by the hand. Therefore it is necessary to arrive at a first mover, put in motion by no other; and this everyone understands to be God.

The second way is from the nature of the efficient cause. In the world of sense we find there is an order of efficient causes. There is no case known (neither is it, indeed, possible) in which a thing is found to be the efficient cause of itself; for so it would be prior to itself, which is impossible. Now in efficient causes it is not possible to go on to infinity, because in all efficient causes following in order, the first is the cause of the intermediate cause, and the intermediate is the cause of the ultimate cause, whether the intermediate cause be several, or one only. Now to take away the cause is to take away the effect. Therefore, if there be no first cause among efficient causes, there will be no ultimate, nor any intermediate cause. But if in efficient causes it is possible to go on to infinity, there will be no first efficient cause, neither will there be an ultimate effect, nor any intermediate efficient causes; all of which is plainly false. Therefore it is necessary to admit a first efficient cause, to which everyone gives the name of God.

The third way is taken from possibility and necessity, and runs thus. We find in nature things that are possible to be and not to be, since they are found to be generated, and to corrupt, and consequently, they are possible to be and not to be. But it is impossible for these always to exist, for that which is possible not to be at some time is not. Therefore, if everything is possible not to be, then at one time there could have been nothing in existence. Now if this were true, even now there would be nothing in existence, because that which does not exist only begins to exist by something already existing. Therefore, if at one time nothing was in existence, it would have been impossible for anything to have begun to exist; and thus even now nothing would be in existence—which is absurd. Therefore, not all beings are merely possible, but there must exist something the existence of which is necessary. But every necessary thing either has its necessity caused by another, or not. Now it is impossible to go on to infinity in necessary things which have their necessity caused by another, as has been already proved in regard to efficient causes. Therefore we cannot but postulate the existence of some being having of itself its own necessity, and not receiving it from another, but rather causing in others their necessity. This all men speak of as God.

The fourth way is taken from the gradation to be found in things. Among beings there are some more and some less good, true, noble, and the like. But 'more' and 'less' are predicated of different things, according as they resemble in their different ways something which is the maximum, as a thing is said to be hotter according as it more nearly resembles that which is hottest; so that there is something which is truest, something best, something noblest, and, consequently, something which is uttermost being; for those things that are greatest in truth are greatest in being, as it is written in *Metaph*. ii. Now the maximum in any genus is the cause of all in that genus; as fire, which is the maximum of heat, is the cause of all hot things. Therefore there must also be something which is to all beings the cause of their being, goodness, and every other perfection; and this we call God.

The fifth way is taken from the governance of the world. We see that things which lack intelligence, such as natural bodies, act for an end, and this is evident from their acting always, or nearly always, in the same way, so as to obtain the best result. Hence it is plain that not fortuitously, but designedly, do they achieve their end. Now whatever lacks intelligence cannot move towards an end, unless it be directed by some being endowed with knowledge and intelligence; as the arrow is shot to its mark by the archer. Therefore some intelligent being exists by whom all natural things are directed to their end; and this being we call God.

Reply Obj. 1. As Augustine says (*Enchir.* xi.): *Since God is the highest good, He would not allow any evil to exist in His works, unless His omnipotence and goodness were such as to bring good even out of evil.* This is part of the infinite goodness of God, that He should allow evil to exist, and out of it produce good.

Reply Obj. 2. Since nature works for a determinate end under the direction of a higher agent, whatever is done by nature must needs be traced back to God, as to its first cause. So also whatever is done voluntarily must also be traced back to some higher cause other than human reason or will, since these can change and fail; for all things that are changeable and capable of defect must be traced back to an immovable and self-necessary first principle, as was shown in the body of the *Article*.

59

Thomas Aquinas

from *Summa Theologica* (from the Treatise on the Law)

The following are selected excerpts from Aquinas' influential treatise on the law, which is taken from his much larger masterwork, the *Summa Theologica*. This treatise is widely recognized to be one of the most important sources of the natural law tradition. Here, Aquinas explains the fundamental nature of law, the end toward which it is directed, and the relationship between the natural law and God. Aquinas begins each point with a question to which he offers a response.

Question XC. Of Laws.

Article I.—*Is law a function of reason?*

R. A law is a rule and measure of acts, whereby one is induced to act or is restrained from action. Now the rule and measure of human acts is reason: it being the part of reason to direct to the end, which is the first principle of conduct. Hence a law must be some function of reason.

Article II.—*Is law always directed to the general good?*

R. As reason is the principle of human acts, so in reason itself there is something which acts as a principle or mainspring in regard of all the rest; and upon this something law must mainly and chiefly bear. Now in matters of conduct, which are the domain of practical reason, the prime mainspring is the last end in view; and that is happiness. Hence law must especially regard the order that is to be followed in the attainment of happiness.

Again, seeing that every part is referred to the whole as the imperfect to the perfect, and one man is a part of a perfect community, it needs must

SOURCE: Thomas Aquinas, *Aquinas Ethicus: Or, the Moral Teaching of St. Thomas, A Translation of the Principal Portions of the Second Part of the "Summa Theologica,"* vol. 1, trans. Joseph Rickaby (London: Burns and Oates, 1892), 264–71, 281–85.

be that law peculiarly regards the order that is to be followed in view of the general happiness.

Since the name of *law* denotes something bearing upon the general good; every other precept prescribing a particular work lacks the character of law, except inasmuch as it is referred to the general good of the community.

Article III.—*Has the reason of any and every man the power of making laws?*

R. Law properly regards first and foremost the order that is to be taken towards the general good. Now to order anything towards the general good belongs either to the whole people, or to some one who is the vicegerent of the whole people. And therefore the framing of a law either belongs to the whole people or belongs to a public personage who has care of the whole people: because in all other things also the ordering of means to the end belongs to him to whom the end belongs as his special concern.

§ 1. To the text, "These are a law to themselves," it is to be said that a law is in a person, not only as in one regulating, but also by participation as in one regulated. In this latter way every man is a law to himself, inasmuch as he participates in the direction given by one who regulates him. Hence it is added in the same text: "Who show the work of the law written in their hearts."

§ 2. A private person cannot induce another to virtue efficaciously: for he can only admonish; but if his admonition is not received, he has no coercive power, which the law must have, if it is to induce people to virtue efficaciously. This coercive power is held by the multitude, or by a public personage, to whom it belongs to inflict penalties; and therefore it is for the holder of this power alone to make laws.

§ 3. As the individual is part of the household, so the household is part of the State; and the State is a perfect community. And therefore, as the good of one individual is not the last end, but is directed to the general good, so also the good of one single household is directed to the good of one single State, which is a perfect community. Hence he who governs a family, may make regulations or standing orders, not however such as to have the character of law.

Article IV.—*Is promulgation of the essence of law?*

R. A law is imposed on others by way of a rule and measure. Now a rule and measure is imposed by its application to the subjects ruled and measured. Hence, for a law to have the binding force which is proper to a law, it must be applied to the men who are to be regulated by it. Such application is made by the law being brought under their notice by promulgation. Hence promulgation is necessary for the law to have force.

And thus from the four preceding articles may be gathered the definition of a *law*, which is nothing else than *an ordinance of reason for the general good, emanating from him who has the care of the community, and promulgated.*

Question XCI. Of the Variety of Laws.

Article I.—*Is there any Eternal Law?*

R. A law is nothing else than the dictate of practical reason in the sovereign who governs a perfect community. Now it is manifest, supposing that the world is ruled by Divine Providence, that the whole community of the universe is governed by Divine Reason. And therefore the plan of government of things, as it is in God the Sovereign of the universe, bears the character of a law. And because the Divine Reason conceives nothing according to time, but has an eternal concept, therefore it is that this manner of law must be called eternal.

§ 1. To the objection that there was no subject from eternity on whom a law could be imposed, it is to be said that the things that are not in themselves exist with God, as being known and pre-ordained by Him, according to the text: "Who calleth those things that are not, as those that are."

Article II.—*Is there in us any natural law?*

R. Law being a rule and measure, may be in a thing in two ways: in one way as in one ruling and measuring, in another way as in one that is ruled and measured. Hence since all things subject to Divine Providence are ruled and measured by the Eternal Law, it is manifest that they all participate to some extent in the Eternal Law, inasmuch by the stamp of that law upon them they have their inclinations to their several acts and ends. But among the rest the rational creature is subject to Divine Providence in a more excellent way, being itself a partaker in Providence, providing for itself and others. Hence there is in it a participation of the Eternal Law, whereby it has a natural inclination to a due act and end: such participation in the Eternal Law in the rational creature is called the *natural law*. Hence when the Psalmist had said: "Offer up the sacrifice of justice," as if in answer to some inquiry what the works of justice are, he adds: "Many say, Who showeth us good things?" Answering this question, he says: "The light of Thy countenance, O Lord, is signed upon us," signifying that the light of natural reason, whereby we discern what is good and what evil, which is the effect of the natural law, is nothing else than an impression of the divine light upon us. Hence it is clear that the natural law is nothing else than a participation of the Eternal Law in the rational creature.

§ 3. Even irrational animals share in the Eternal Law in their own way, as also does the rational creature. But because the rational creature shares in it intellectually and rationally, therefore the participation of the Eternal Law in the rational creature is properly called a *law*; for law is a function of reason: but in the irrational creature it is not shared rationally; hence it cannot be called a *law* except by a similitude.

Article IV.— *Was it necessary that there should be any divine law?*

R. Besides the natural law and human law it was necessary for the guidance of human life to have a divine law. And this for four reasons: First, because it is by law that man is guided to the performance of proper acts in view of his last end. And if indeed man were ordained to an end that did not exceed the measure of the natural faculties of man, there would be no need of man's having any guidance on the part of reason beyond that of the natural law, and human law which is derived from it. But because man is ordained to an end of eternal blessedness, which exceeds the measure of the natural human faculties, therefore it was necessary that, over and above natural law and human law, he should be further guided to his end by a law given from God. Secondly, because of the uncertainty of human judgment, especially on contingent and particular matters, whence it is that different men come to form different judgments on human acts; whence also different and contrary laws arise. In order then that man might know without a doubt what to do and what to avoid, it was necessary for him to be guided in his acts by a law given from God, which can be relied upon for certain not to err. Thirdly, because man can make a law only upon matters of which he can be a judge. Now the judgment of man cannot pass upon interior acts, which are hidden, but only upon exterior movements which appear: and yet for the perfection of virtue rectitude in both sorts of acts is necessary. And therefore human law could not sufficiently restrain and direct interior acts: but to this end it was necessary for a divine law to supervene. Fourthly, because human law cannot punish or prevent all evil doings; for in the wish to take away all evils many good things would be taken away, and the profit of the public good would be impeded, which is necessary for the preservation of society. In order then that no evil might go unforbidden and unpunished, the supervening of the divine law was necessary, whereby all sins are prohibited. And these four causes are touched upon in the Psalm, where it is said: "The law of the Lord is unspotted," allowing no turpitude of sin: "converting souls," because it directs not only exterior but also interior acts: "the testimony of the Lord is faithful," for the certain knowledge of truth and right: "giving wisdom to little ones," in that it directs man to an end supernatural and divine.

§ 1. By the natural law the Eternal Law is sufficiently shared in according to the measure of the capacity of human nature. But to his supernatural last end man needs to be directed in some higher way. And therefore there is given by God an additional law, which is a higher participation of the Eternal Law.

[. . . .]

Question XCIV: Of the Natural Law.

Article II.—*Does the natural law contain several precepts or one only?*

R. A certain order is found in the things that fall under human apprehension. What first falls under apprehension is *being*, the idea of which is included in all things whatsoever any one apprehends. And therefore the first principle requiring no proof is this, that *there is no affirming and denying of the same thing at the same time*; a principle which is founded on the notion of *being* and *not-being*; and upon this principle all the rest are founded. As *being* is the first thing that falls under apprehension absolutely, so *good* is the first thing that falls under the apprehension of the practical reason. For every agent acts for an end, which end has a character of goodness. And therefore the first principle of practical reason is one founded on the nature of good, good being that which all things seek after. This then is the first precept of law, that *good is to be done and gone after, and evil is to be avoided*. All the other precepts of the natural law are founded upon this: so that all those things belong to the precepts of the law of nature as things to be done, or avoided, which practical reason naturally apprehends and recognizes as human goods [or evils]. But because good has the character of an end of action, and evil the contrary character, hence all those things to which man has a natural inclination are apprehended by reason as good, and consequently as things to be gone after, and followed out in act; and their contraries are apprehended as evils to be avoided. According then to the order of natural inclinations is the order of the precepts of the law of nature. First of all there is in man an inclination to that natural good which he shares along with all *substances*, inasmuch as every substance seeks the preservation of its own being, according to its nature. In virtue of this inclination there belongs to the natural law the taking of those means whereby the life of man is preserved, and things contrary thereto are kept off. Secondly, there is in man an inclination to things more specially belonging to him, in virtue of the nature which he shares with other *animals*. In this respect those things are said to be of the natural law, which nature has taught to all animals, as the intercourse of the sexes, the education of offspring, and the like. In a third way there is in man an inclination to good according to the *rational* nature which is proper to him; as man has a natural inclination to know the truth about God, and to live in society. In this respect there belong to the natural law such natural inclinations as to avoid ignorance, to shun offending other men, and the like.

Article III.—*Are all acts of virtue prescribed by the law of nature?*

R. To the law of nature belongs everything to which man is inclined according to his nature. Now every being is naturally inclined to an activity befitting itself according to its form. Hence as the proper *form* of man is his rational soul, there is a natural inclination in every man to act according to reason; that is, to act according to virtue. Hence from this point of view all acts of virtue are according to nature: for every one's own reason naturally dictates to him to act virtuously.

But if we speak of virtuous acts in detail, not all virtuous acts are prescribed by natural law: for many things are virtuously done, to which nature at first does not incline, but rational inquiry has found them conducive to human happiness.

Article V.—*Can the law of nature be changed?*

R. A change in the natural law may be understood in two ways. One way is the way of addition; and in that way there is nothing to hinder the natural law being changed: for many enactments useful to human life have been added over and above the natural law, as well by the divine law as by human laws. Another conceivable way in which the natural law might be changed is the way of subtraction, that something should cease to be of the natural law that was of it before. Understanding change in this sense, the natural law is absolutely immutable in its first principles: but as to secondary precepts, which are certain detailed conclusions closely related to the first principles, the natural law is not so changed as that its dictate is not right in most cases steadily to abide by: it may, however, be changed in some particular case, and in rare instances, through some special causes impeding the observance of these secondary precepts, as has been said above.

§ 3. There are two ways in which a thing may be said to be *of natural law*, in one way because nature inclines thereto, as to the axiom that wrong must not be done to another: in another way because nature does not induce the contrary—as we might say that for man to be naked is of natural law, because nature has not given him clothes, but art has invented that addition. Hence Isidore's saying: "A common possession of all things and one liberty is of natural law:" because slavery and the separation of properties were not induced by nature, but by the reason of men for the utility of human life; and so also in this the law of nature has not been changed except by addition.

Article VI.—*Can the natural law be abolished from the heart of man?*

R. Belonging to the natural law are, first, certain most general precepts, which are known to all: secondly, secondary precepts of a more special nature, being conclusions following upon primary principles. As to those general precepts, the natural law can in no way be blotted out from the human heart in the abstract: still it is blotted out in its application to a particular question of practice, inasmuch as reason is hindered from applying the abstract principle to a particular case by concupiscence or some other passion. But as to the other, the secondary precepts, the natural law may be blotted out of the hearts of men by evil persuasions, or by vicious customs and corrupt habits, as among some men the note of sin was not attached to robbery, or even to unnatural vice, as the Apostle says.

60

Pope Boniface VIII

Unam Sanctam (November 18, 1302)

Rising to the papacy in 1294, Pope Boniface VIII (1234–1303) sought to continue Gregory VII's and Innocent III's expansion of the Vatican's political power. Confrontations with France's Philip IV, however, stalled Boniface's plans. In the papal bull *Unam Sanctam* (1302), Boniface issued the medieval period's greatest claim for the papacy's temporal authority. Simply stated: eternal salvation was contingent upon political obedience to the Pope. Boniface, however, was unable to turn his rhetoric into the reality of political submission. Philip IV had Boniface captured, and although he was released in short order, Boniface died. Within a few years, Philip had the papacy relocated to Avignon, France, and obligated to French oversight.

We are compelled, our faith urging us, to believe and to hold—and we do firmly believe and simply confess—that there is one holy catholic and apostolic church, outside of which there is neither salvation nor remission of sins; her Spouse proclaiming it in the canticles: "My dove, my undefiled is but one, she is the choice one of her that bare her;" which represents one mystic body, of which body the head is Christ; but of Christ, God. In this church there is one Lord, one faith and one baptism. There was one ark of Noah, indeed, at the time of the flood, symbolizing one church; and this being finished in one cubit had, namely, one Noah as helmsman and commander. And, with the exception of this ark, all things existing upon the earth were, as we read, destroyed. This church, moreover, we venerate as the only one, the Lord saying through His prophet: "Deliver my soul from the sword, my darling from the power

SOURCE: Pope Boniface VIII, "The Bull 'Unam Sanctam,'" in *Select Historical Documents of the Middle Ages*, ed. and trans. Ernest F. Henderson (London: George Bell and Sons, 1905), 435–37.

of the dog." He prayed at the same time for His soul—that is, for Himself the Head—and for His body,—which body, namely, he called the one and only church on account of the unity of the faith promised, of the sacraments, and of the love of the church. She is that seamless garment of the Lord which was not cut but which fell by lot. Therefore of this one and only church there is one body and one head—not two heads as if it were a monster:—Christ, namely, and the vicar of Christ, St. Peter, and the successor of Peter. For the Lord Himself said to Peter, Feed my sheep. My sheep, He said, using a general term, and not designating these or those particular sheep; from which it is plain that He committed to Him all His sheep. If, then, the Greeks or others say that they were not committed to the care of Peter and his successors, they necessarily confess that they are not of the sheep of Christ; for the Lord says, in John, that there is one fold, one shepherd and one only. We are told by the word of the gospel that in this His fold there are two swords,—a spiritual, namely, and a temporal. For when the apostles said "Behold here are two swords"—when, namely, the apostles were speaking in the church—the Lord did not reply that this was too much, but enough. Surely he who denies that the temporal sword is in the power of Peter wrongly interprets the word of the Lord when He says: "Put up thy sword in its scabbard." Both swords, the spiritual and the material, therefore, are in the power of the church; the one, indeed, to be wielded for the church, the other by the church; the one by the hand of the priest, the other by the hand of kings and knights, but at the will and sufferance of the priest. One sword, moreover, ought to be under the other, and the temporal authority to be subjected to the spiritual. For when the apostle says "there is no power but of God, and the powers that are of God are ordained," they would not be ordained unless sword were under sword and the lesser one, as it were, were led by the other to great deeds. For according to St. Dionysius the law of divinity is to lead the lowest through the intermediate to the highest things. Not therefore, according to the law of the universe, are all things reduced to order equally and immediately; but the lowest through the intermediate, the intermediate through the higher. But that the spiritual exceeds any earthly power in dignity and nobility we ought the more openly to confess the more spiritual things excel temporal ones. This also is made plain to our eyes from the giving of tithes, and the benediction and the sanctification; from the acceptation of this same power, from the control over those same things. For, the truth bearing witness, the spiritual power has to establish the earthly power, and to judge it if it be not good. Thus concerning the church and the ecclesiastical power is verified the prophecy of Jeremiah: "See, I have this day set thee over the nations and over the kingdoms," and the other things which follow. Therefore if the earthly power err it shall be judged by the spiritual power; but if the lesser spiritual power err, by the greater. But if the greatest, it can be judged by God alone, not by man, the apostle bearing witness. A spiritual man judges all things, but he himself is judged by no one. This authority, moreover, even though it is given to man and exercised through man, is not human but rather divine, being given by divine lips to Peter and founded on a rock for him and his successors through Christ himself whom he has confessed; the Lord himself saying to Peter: "Whatsoever thou shalt bind," etc. Whoever, therefore, resists this power thus ordained by God, resists the ordination of God, unless he makes believe, like the Manichean, that there are two beginnings. This we consider false and heretical, since by the testimony of Moses, not "in the beginnings," but "in the beginning" God created the Heavens and the earth. Indeed we declare, announce and define, that it is altogether necessary to salvation for every human creature to be subject to the Roman pontiff.

The Lateran, Nov. 14, in our 8th year. As a perpetual memorial of this matter.

61

Dante Alighieri

from *Divine Comedy (Inferno)*

Together with Petrarch and Giovanni Boccaccio, the poet Dante Alighieri (1265–1321) is heralded as one of the founders of Italian literature. Heavily involved in politics during his youth, Dante was expelled from his home in Florence in 1301, when his faction, the White Guelphs, was defeated by its rivals. He spent the rest of his life in exile, during which he composed what is widely regarded as one of the most important works of the Middle Ages, *Divine Comedy*. Written in *terza rima*—a system of three-line stanzas with an interlocking rhyming scheme—this epic poem describes an allegorical journey through the afterlife guided by the Roman poet Virgil, and it is divided into three parts, namely, hell, purgatory, and heaven. Its ultimate theme is divine justice: after death, God punishes the wicked and rewards the virtuous in ways that are commensurate with their earthly behavior. The following is Canto IV from the first part of that poem, *Inferno*, in which Dante imagines the first and least terrible of nine circles of hell, which is populated by virtuous persons who had not accepted Christ.

Canto IV

Broke the deep lethargy within my head
    A heavy thunder, so that I upstarted,
    Like to a person who by force is wakened;
And round about I moved my rested eyes,
    Uprisen erect, and steadfastly I gazed,
    To recognize the place wherein I was.

SOURCE: Dante Alighieri, *The Divine Comedy*, vol. 1, trans. Henry Wadsworth Longfellow (London: George Routledge and Sons, 1867), 20–26.

True is it, that upon the verge I found me
    Of the abysmal valley dolorous,
    That gathers thunder of infinite ululations.
Obscure, profound it was, and nebulous,
    So that by fixing on its depths my sight
    Nothing whatever I discerned therein.
"Let us descend now into the blind world,"
    Began the Poet, pallid utterly;
    "I will be first, and thou shalt second be."
And I, who of his color was aware,
    Said: "How shall I come, if thou art afraid,
    Who 'rt wont to be a comfort to my fears?"
And he to me: "The anguish of the people
    Who are below here in my face depicts
    That pity which for terror thou hast taken.
Let us go on, for the long way impels us."
    Thus he went in, and thus he made me enter
    The foremost circle that surrounds the abyss.
There, in so far as I had power to hear,
    Were lamentations none, but only sighs,
    That tremulous made the everlasting air.
And this arose from sorrow without torment,
    Which the crowds had, that many were and great,
    Of infants and of women and of men.
To me the Master good: "Thou dost not ask
    What spirits these, which thou beholdest, are?
    Now will I have thee know, ere thou go farther,
That they sinned not; and if they merit had,
    'Tis not enough, because they had not baptism,
    Which is the portal of the Faith thou holdest;
And if they were before Christianity,
    In the right manner they adored not God;
    And among such as these am I myself.
For such defects, and not for other guilt,
    Lost are we, and are only so far punished,
    That without hope we live on in desire."
Great grief seized on my heart when this I heard,
    Because some people of much worthiness
    I knew, who in that Limbo were suspended.

"Tell me, my Master, tell me, thou my Lord,"
    Began I, with desire of being certain
    Of that Faith which o'ercometh every error,
"Came any one by his own merit hence,
    Or by another's, who was blessed thereafter?"
    And he, who understood my covert speech,
Replied: "I was a novice in this state,
    When I saw hither come a Mighty One,
    With sign of victory incoronate.
Hence he drew forth the shade of the First Parent,
    And that of his son Abel, and of Noah,
    Of Moses the lawgiver, and the obedient
Abraham, patriarch, and David, king,
    Israel with his father and his children,
    And Rachel, for whose sake he did so much,
And others many, and he made them blessed;
    And thou must know, that earlier than these
    Never were any human spirits saved."
We ceased not to advance because he spake,
    But still were passing onward through the forest,
    The forest, say I, of thick-crowded ghosts.
Not very far as yet our way had gone
    This side the summit, when I saw a fire
    That overcame a hemisphere of darkness.
We were a little distant from it still,
    But not so far that I in part discerned not
    That honorable people held that place.
"O thou who honorest every art and science,
    Who may these be, which such great honor have,
    That from the fashion of the rest it parts them?"
And he to me: "The honorable name,
    That sounds of them above there in thy life,
    Wins grace in Heaven, that so advances them."
In the mean time a voice was heard by me:
    "All honor be to the pre-eminent Poet;
    His shade returns again, that was departed."
After the voice had ceased and quiet was,
    Four mighty shades I saw approaching us;
    Semblance had they nor sorrowful nor glad.

To say to me began my gracious Master:
    "Him with that falchion in his hand behold,
    Who comes before the three, even as their lord.
That one is Homer, Poet sovereign;
    He who comes next is Horace, the satirist;
    The third is Ovid, and the last is Lucan.
Because to each of these with me applies
    The name that solitary voice proclaimed,
    They do me honor, and in that do well."
Thus I beheld assemble the fair school
    Of that lord of the song pre-eminent,
    Who o'er the others like an eagle soars.
When they together had discoursed somewhat,
    They turned to me with signs of salutation,
    And on beholding this, my Master smiled;
And more of honor still, much more, they did me,
    In that they made me one of their own band;
    So that the sixth was I, 'mid so much wit.
Thus we went on as far as to the light,
    Things saying 'tis becoming to keep silent,
    As was the saying of them where I was.
We came unto a noble castle's foot,
    Seven times encompassëd with lofty walls,
    Defended round by a fair rivulet;
This we passed over even as firm ground;
    Through portals seven I entered with these Sages;
    We came into a meadow of fresh verdure.
People were there with solemn eyes and slow,
    Of great authority in their countenance;
    They spake but seldom, and with gentle voices.
Thus we withdrew ourselves upon one side
    Into an opening luminous and lofty,
    So that they all of them were visible.
There opposite, upon the green enamel,
    Were pointed out to me the mighty spirits,
    Whom to have seen I feel myself exalted.
I saw Electra with companions many,
    'Mongst whom I knew both Hector and Æneas,
    Cæsar in armor with gerfalcon eyes;

I saw Camilla and Penthesilea
  On the other side, and saw the King Latinus,
  Who with Lavinia his daughter sat;
I saw that Brutus who drove Tarquin forth,
  Lucretia, Julia, Marcia, and Cornelia,
  And saw alone, apart, the Saladin.
When I had lifted up my brows a little,
  The Master I beheld of those who know,
  Sit with his philosophic family.
All gaze upon him, and all do him honor.
  There I beheld both Socrates and Plato,
  Who nearer him before the others stand;
Democritus, who puts the world on chance,
  Diogenes, Anaxagoras, and Thales,
  Zeno, Empedocles, and Heraclitus;
Of qualities I saw the good collector,
  Hight Dioscorides; and Orpheus saw I,
  Tully and Livy, and moral Seneca,
Euclid, geometrician, and Ptolemy,
  Galen, Hippocrates, and Avicenna,
  Averroes, who the great Comment made.
I cannot all of them portray in full,
  Because so drives me onward the long theme,
  That many times the word comes short of fact.
The sixfold company in two divides;
  Another way my sapient Guide conducts me
  Forth from the quiet to the air that trembles;
And to a place I come where nothing shines.

62

Ibn Batuta

from *Travels* (in Africa)

In 1325, the young religious scholar Ibn Batuta (1304–1369) set out from his home in northern Morocco on pilgrimage to Mecca. By the time he returned home, some twenty-four years later, he had traversed nearly seventy thousand miles, having visited Egypt, India, China, and the Swahili Coast of East Africa—all of it on ship, foot, camel, or horse. It was not enough to satisfy his wanderlust, though. So in late 1351, he took a caravan to Mali, a sub-Saharan African kingdom. When he returned three years later, he recorded his observations and adventures in *Rihla* (or *Travels*), which is among the most historically important travel journals of the premodern world. Part of its significance is in capturing a moment of discovery with all the attending excitement, risks, and challenges; part of its significance is in how its descriptions convey the sometimes unconscious biases and prejudices of the author in cross-cultural encounters.

We remained at Oualata fifty days. It is an exceedingly hot place, with a few small palm trees in it, under the shade of which they grow melons. The water of the place is found in pits, having been absorbed by the sand. Mutton is in great plenty. Their clothing is all brought from Egypt. The greater part of the inhabitants are merchants. Their women are exceedingly beautiful, and more respectable than the men. The character of these merchants is strange enough, for they are quite impervious to jealousy. No one is named after his father, but after his maternal uncle; and one's sister's son always inherits property in preference to one's own son: a custom I witnessed nowhere else, except among the infidel Hindus of Malabar. But these are Muslims, who retain their

SOURCE: Ibn Batuta, *The Travels of Ibn Batūta*, trans. Samuel Lee (London: Oriental Translation Committee, 1829), 234–41. Translation revised by H. D. Miller and used here with permission.

prayers by memory, study theology, and learn the Qur'an by rote. As to their women, they are not shy with regard to the men, nor do they veil themselves from them, although they constantly accompany them at prayers. Anyone who wishes to marry one of them may do so; but he must not take her with him out of the country; and, even if the woman should wish to go, her family will not allow her. It is a custom among them, that a man may have a mistress, of women strangers to him, who may come and associate with him, even in the presence of her own husband and of his wife. In like manner, a man will enter his own house, and see the friend of his wife with her alone, and talking with her, without the least emotion or attempt to disturb them: he will only come in and sit down on one side, till the man goes. Upon a certain day I went in to the Judge of Oualata, who was an eminent man, at that time my host, and with whom I had formed a friendship. I saw with him a handsome young woman, and wished to leave him: for I knew his wife, and that this was a different person. The woman smiled at me, but did not blush. He said: "This is my female friend; she is no stranger." I remonstrated with him, and said: "This is a strange woman; you are an eminent *qadi*, and Judge of the Muslims: how, then, can you be alone with her?" He said: "This is our custom; nor is there any suspicion from our being in society together." He did not, however, benefit by my advice, nor did I visit him after this.

I then proceeded from Oualata to Mali, the distance of which is a journey of four and twenty days, if one hastens. The roads are safe, so I hired a guide and proceeded with three of my companions. These roads abound with trees, which are high, and so large that a caravan may shade itself under one of them. As I passed by one of these trees, I saw a weaver weaving cloth within a cleft of its trunk. Some of these will grow so rotten inside, that the trunk will become like a well and be filled with the rain-water, and from this the people will drink. Sometimes the bees will be in these in such numbers that they will be filled with honey, which travelers take for their use. . . . Gourds grow so large in Sudan, that they will cut one into halves, and out of these make two large dishes. The greatest part of their vessels, moreover, are made of the gourd. After ten days from our leaving Oualata we came to the village Zaghari which is large, and inhabited by black merchants. Among these lives a number of white people, of the Ibadi sect of heretics.

We then left this place and came to the great river, which is the Nile. Upon it is the town of Karsakhu, from which the Nile descends to Kabara, then to Zagha, the inhabitants of which were the first in these parts to embrace Islam. They are religious, and fond of learning. From this place the Nile descends to Timbuktu, then to Gogo, of both which we shall give some account. It then proceeds to the town of Muli, which is the extreme district of Mali. It then goes on to Yuwi, the greatest district of Sudan, and the king of which is the most potent. No white person can enter here; for, if he attempts to do so, they will kill him before he reaches it. The Nile then descends from this place to the countries of Nubia, the inhabitants of which are Christians; then to Dongola, which is the largest district they possess; the king of which is named Ibn Kanz Oddin, who became a Muslim in the times of El Malik El Nasir. The Nile then descends to the cataracts, which terminate the regions of Sudan, dividing them from Upper Egypt.

From Karsakhu, I went to the river Sansara, which is about ten miles from Mali. I then went to the city of Mali, the residence of the King. I there inquired for the residence of the white people, and lodged with them; they treated me very honourably. The Muslim Judge of the blacks, who was a celebrated Haji, made me his guest, and sent me a present and a cow. I was sick two months in Mali. But God restored me.

It happened that Mansa Sulayman, the Sultan of Mali, a most avaricious and worthless man, made a feast by way of kindness. I was present at the entertainment with some of our theologians. When the assembly broke up, I saluted him, having been brought to his knowledge by the theologians. When I had left the place he sent me a meal, which he forwarded to the house of the Judge. Upon this occasion the Judge came walking hastily to me, and said: "Up, for the Sultan has sent you a present." I hastened, expecting that a dress of honour, some horses, and other valuables, had been sent; but, behold! they were only three crusts of bread, with a piece of fried fish, and a dish of sour milk. I smiled at their simplicity, and the great value they set on such trifles as these. I stayed here, after this meal, two months; but received nothing from him, although I had often met him in their friendly meetings. I one day, however, rose up in his presence, and said: "I have travelled the world over, and have seen its kings; and now, I have been four months in thy territories, but no present, or even provision from thee, has yet reached me. Now, what shall I say of thee, when I shall be interrogated on the subject hereafter?" Upon this, he gave me a house for my accommodation, with suitable provisions. After this, the theologians visited me in the month of Ramadan, and, out of their whole number, they gave me three and thirty *mithqals* of gold. Of all people, the blacks prostrate themselves most in presence of their king: for when any one of them is called upon to appear before him, he will immediately put off his usual clothing, and put on a worn-out dress, with a dirty cap; he will then enter the presence like a beggar, with his clothes lifted up to the middle of his legs; he will then beat the ground with both his elbows, and remain in the attitude of a person performing a prostration. When the Sultan addresses one of them, the person addressed will take up the garment off his back, and throw dust upon his head; and, as long as the Sultan speaks, everyone present will remain with his turban taken off. One of the best things in these parts is, the regard they pay to justice, for they hate injustice more than other people. The safety, too, is very great; so that a traveler may proceed alone among them, without the least fear of a thief or robber. Another of their good properties is, that when a merchant happens to die among them, they will make no effort to get possession of his property: but will allow the lawful successors to it to take it. Another is their constant custom of attending prayers with the congregation; for, unless one makes haste, he will find no place left to say his prayers in. Another is, their insisting on the Qur'an's being committed to memory: for if a man finds his son defective in this, he will confine him till he is quite perfect, nor will he allow him his liberty until he is so. As to their bad practices, they will allow their little daughters, as well as their male and female slaves, to go about quite naked. In the same manner will the women enter into the presence of the King, which his own daughters will also do. Nor do the free women ever clothe themselves till after marriage. The majority of them will eat carrion, dogs and donkeys.

I travelled, in the next place, from Mali, the Sultan having given me a hundred *mithqals* of gold, which place I left in the month Muharram, in the year fifty-four (A. D. February, 1353), and came to a wide tributary which branches out of the Nile, and upon the banks of which there were very large beasts. I wondered at them, and thought they were elephants from the great numbers there are in those parts: but when I saw them enter the water I enquired about them, and was told, that they were hippopotamuses, which go out to graze, and then return to the water. They are larger than the land horses, and have manes and tails: their heads are like those of horses, and their legs like those of elephants. I was told by some credible black pilgrims, that the infidels of some parts of Sudan will eat men; but that they will eat none but blacks, because, say they, the white are injurious on account of their not being ripe; and, that when their Sultan happens to send his ambassadors to one of the kings of the heathens, and intends to honour them with a feast, he also sends to them a black slave, whom they kill and eat, and then return their thanks for the honour and favour done them.

63

Petrarch

The Ascent of Mount Ventoux

Franscesco Petrarcha (1304–1374), known most commonly as simply Petrarch, was an Italian traveler, poet, classicist, and scholar who is widely recognized as having played a significant role in the advent of the Italian Renaissance and humanism. Along with Dante Alighieri and Giovanni Boccaccio, Petrarch is known for his lasting influence on the development of the modern Italian language. The following is a renowned letter that chronicles his climb up Mount Ventoux, which has been regarded as an exemplification of the spirit of a new, modern era.

To Dionisio da Borgo San Sepolcro.

To-day I made the ascent of the highest mountain in this region, which is not improperly called Ventosum. My only motive was the wish to see what so great an elevation had to offer. I have had the expedition in mind for many years; for, as you know, I have lived in this region from infancy, having been cast here by that fate which determines the affairs of men. Consequently the mountain, which is visible from a great distance, was ever before my eyes, and I conceived the plan of some time doing what I have at last accomplished to-day. The idea took hold upon me with especial force when, in re-reading Livy's *History of Rome*, yesterday, I happened upon the place where Philip of Macedon, the same who waged war against the Romans, ascended Mount Hæmus in Thessaly, from whose summit he was able, it is said, to see two seas, the Adriatic and the Euxine. Whether this be true or false I have not been able

SOURCE: Petrarch, "The Ascent of Mount Ventoux," in *Petrarch, the First Modern Scholar and Man of Letters: A Selection from His Correspondence with Boccaccio and Other Friends, Designed to Illustrate the Beginning of the Renaissance*, trans. James Harvey Robinson with Henry Winchester Rolfe (New York: G. P. Putnam's Sons, 1898), 307–20.

to determine, for the mountain is too far away, and writers disagree. Pomponius Mela, the cosmographer—not to mention others who have spoken of this occurrence—admits its truth without hesitation; Titus Livius, on the other hand, considers it false. I, assuredly, should not have left the question long in doubt, had that mountain been as easy to explore as this one. Let us leave this matter [to] one side, however, and return to my mountain here,—it seems to me that a young man in private life may well be excused for attempting what an aged king could undertake without arousing criticism.

When I came to look about for a companion I found, strangely enough, that hardly one among my friends seemed suitable, so rarely do we meet with just the right combination of personal tastes and characteristics, even among those who are dearest to us. This one was too apathetic, that one over-anxious; this one too slow, that one too hasty; one was too sad, another over-cheerful; one more simple, another more sagacious, than I desired. I feared this one's taciturnity and that one's loquacity. The heavy deliberation of some repelled me as much as the lean incapacity of others. I rejected those who were likely to irritate me by a cold want of interest, as well as those who might weary me by their excessive enthusiasm. Such defects, however grave, could be borne with at home, for charity suffereth all things, and friendship accepts any burden; but it is quite otherwise on a journey, where every weakness becomes much more serious. So, as I was bent upon pleasure and anxious that my enjoyment should be unalloyed, I looked about me with unusual care, balanced against one another the various characteristics of my friends, and without committing any breach of friendship I silently condemned every trait which might prove disagreeable on the way. And—would you believe it?—I finally turned homeward for aid, and proposed the ascent to my only brother, who is younger than I, and with whom you are well acquainted. He was delighted and gratified beyond measure by the thought of holding the place of a friend as well as of a brother.

At the time fixed we left the house, and by evening reached Malaucène, which lies at the foot of the mountain, to the north. Having rested there a day, we finally made the ascent this morning, with no companions except two servants; and a most difficult task it was. The mountain is a very steep and almost inaccessible mass of stony soil. But, as the poet has well said, "Remorseless toil conquers all." It was a long day, the air fine. We enjoyed the advantages of vigour of mind and strength and agility of body, and everything else essential to those engaged in such an undertaking, and so had no other difficulties to face than those of the region itself. We found an old shepherd in one of the mountain dales, who tried, at great length, to dissuade us from the ascent, saying that some fifty years before he had, in the same ardour of youth, reached the summit, but had gotten for his pains nothing except fatigue and regret, and clothes and body torn by the rocks and briars. No one, so far as he or his companions knew, had ever tried the ascent before or after him. But his counsels increased rather than diminished our desire to proceed, since youth is suspicious of warnings. So the old man, finding that his efforts were in vain, went a little way with us, and pointed out a rough path among the rocks, uttering many admonitions, which he continued to send after us even after we had left him behind. Surrendering to him all such garments or other possessions as might prove burdensome to us, we made ready for the ascent, and started off at a good pace. But, as usually happens, fatigue quickly followed upon our excessive exertion, and we soon came to a halt at the top of a certain cliff. Upon starting on again we went more slowly, and I especially advanced along the rocky way with a more deliberate step. While my brother chose a direct path straight up the ridge, I weakly took an easier one which really descended. When I was called back, and the right road was shown me, I replied that I hoped to find a better way round on the other side, and that I did not mind going farther if the path were only less steep. This was just an excuse for my laziness; and when the others had already reached a considerable height I was still wandering in the valleys. I had failed to find an easier path, and had only increased the distance and difficulty of the ascent. At last I became disgusted with the intricate way I had chosen, and resolved to ascend without more ado. When I reached my brother, who, while waiting for me, had had ample opportunity for rest, I was tired and irritated. We walked along together for a time, but hardly had we passed the first spur when I forgot about the circuitous route which I had just tried, and took a lower one again. Once more I followed an easy, roundabout path through winding valleys, only to find myself soon in my old difficulty. I was simply trying to avoid the exertion of the ascent; but no human ingenuity can alter the nature of things, or cause anything to reach a height by going down. Suffice it to say that, much to my vexation and my brother's amusement, I made this same mistake three times or more during a few hours.

After being frequently misled in this way, I finally sat down in a valley and transferred my winged thoughts from things corporeal to the immaterial, addressing myself as follows:—"What thou hast repeatedly experienced to-day in the ascent of this mountain, happens to thee, as to many, in the journey toward the blessed life. But this is not so readily perceived by men, since the motions of the body are obvious and external while those of the soul are invisible and hidden. Yes, the life which we call blessed is to be sought for on a high eminence, and strait is the way that leads to it. Many, also, are the hills that lie between, and we must ascend, by a glorious stairway, from strength to strength. At the top is at once the end of our struggles and the goal for which we are bound. All wish to reach this goal, but, as Ovid says, 'To wish is little; we must long with the utmost eagerness to gain our end.' Thou certainly dost ardently desire, as well as simply wish, unless thou deceivest thyself in this matter, as in so many others. What, then, doth hold thee back? Nothing, assuredly, except that thou wouldst take a path which seems, at first thought, more easy, leading through low and worldly pleasures. But nevertheless in the end, after long wanderings, thou must perforce either climb the steeper path, under the burden of tasks foolishly deferred, to its blessed culmination, or lie down in the valley of thy sins, and (I shudder to think of it!), if the shadow of death overtake thee, spend an eternal night amid constant torments." These thoughts stimulated both body and mind in a wonderful degree for facing the difficulties which yet remained. Oh, that I might traverse in spirit that other road for which I long day and night, even as to-day I overcame material obstacles by my bodily exertions! And I know not why it should not be far easier, since the swift immortal soul can reach its goal in the twinkling of an eye, without passing through space, while my progress to-day was necessarily slow, dependent as I was upon a failing body weighed down by heavy members.

One peak of the mountain, the highest of all, the country people call "Sonny," why, I do not know, unless by antiphrasis, as I have sometimes suspected in other instances; for the peak in question would seem to be the father of all the surrounding ones. On its top is a little level place, and here we could at last rest our tired bodies.

Now, my father, since you have followed the thoughts that spurred me on in my ascent, listen to the rest of the story, and devote one hour, I pray you, to reviewing the experiences of my entire day. At first, owing to the unaccustomed quality of the air and the effect of the great sweep of view spread out before me, I stood like one dazed. I beheld the clouds under our feet, and what I had read of Athos and Olympus seemed less incredible as I myself witnessed the same things from a mountain of less fame. I turned my eyes toward Italy, whither my heart most inclined. The Alps, rugged and snow-capped, seemed to rise close by, although they were really at a great distance; the very same Alps through which that fierce enemy of the Roman name once made his way, bursting the rocks, if we may believe the report, by the application of vinegar. I sighed, I must confess, for the skies of Italy, which I beheld rather with my mind than with my eyes. An inexpressible longing came over me to see once more my friend and my country. At the same time I reproached myself for this double weakness, springing, as it did, from a soul not yet steeled to manly resistance. And yet there were excuses for both of these cravings, and a number of distinguished writers might be summoned to support me.

Then a new idea took possession of me, and I shifted my thoughts to a consideration of time rather than place. "To-day it is ten years since, having completed thy youthful studies, thou didst leave Bologna. Eternal God! In the name of immutable wisdom, think what alterations in thy character this intervening period has beheld! I pass over a thousand instances. I am not yet in a safe harbour where I can calmly recall past storms. The time may come when I can review in due order all the experiences of the past, saying with St. Augustine, 'I desire to recall my foul actions and the carnal corruption of my soul, not because I love them, but that I may the more love thee, O my God.' Much that is doubtful and evil still clings to me, but what I once loved, that I love no longer. And yet what am I saying? I still love it, but with shame, but with heaviness of heart. Now, at last, I have confessed the truth. So it is. I love, but love what I would not love, what I would that I might hate. Though loath to do so, though constrained, though sad and sorrowing, still I do love, and I feel in my miserable self the truth of the well known words, 'I will hate if I can; if not, I will love against my will.' Three years have not yet passed since that perverse and wicked passion which had a firm grasp upon me and held undisputed sway in my heart began to discover a rebellious opponent, who was unwilling longer to yield obedience. These two adversaries have joined in close combat for the supremacy, and for a long time now a harassing and doubtful war has been waged in the field of my thoughts."

Thus I turned over the last ten years in my mind, and then, fixing my anxious gaze on the future, I asked myself, "If, perchance, thou shouldst prolong this uncertain life of thine for yet two lustres, and shouldst make an advance toward virtue proportionate to the distance to which thou hast departed from thine original infatuation during the past two years, since the new longing first encountered the old, couldst thou, on reaching thy fortieth year, face death, if not with complete assurance, at least with hopefulness, calmly dismissing from thy thoughts the residuum of life as it faded into old age?"

These and similar reflections occurred to me, my father. I rejoiced in my progress, mourned my weaknesses, and commiserated the universal instability of human conduct. I had well-nigh forgotten where I was and our object in coming; but at last I dismissed my anxieties, which were better suited to other surroundings, and resolved to look about me and see what we had come to see. The sinking sun and the lengthening shadows of the mountain were already warning us that the time was near at hand when we must go. As if suddenly wakened from sleep, I turned about and gazed toward the west. I was unable to discern the summits of the Pyrenees, which form the barrier between France and Spain; not because of any intervening obstacle that I know of but owing simply to the insufficiency of our mortal vision. But I could see with the utmost clearness, off to the right, the mountains of the region about Lyons, and to the left the bay of Marseilles and the waters that lash the shores of Aigues Mortes, altho' all these places were so distant that it would require a journey of several days to reach them. Under our very eyes flowed the Rhone.

While I was thus dividing my thoughts, now turning my attention to some terrestrial object that lay before me, now raising my soul, as I had done my body, to higher planes, it occurred to me to look into my copy of St. Augustine's *Confessions*, a gift that I owe to your love, and that I always have about me, in memory of both the author and the giver. I opened the compact little volume, small indeed in size, but of infinite charm, with the intention of reading whatever came to hand, for I could happen upon nothing that would be otherwise than edifying and devout. Now it chanced that the tenth book presented itself. My brother, waiting to hear something of St. Augustine's from my lips, stood attentively by. I call him, and God too, to witness that where I first fixed my eyes it was written: "And men go about to wonder at the heights of the mountains, and the mighty waves of the sea, and the wide sweep of rivers, and the circuit of the ocean, and the revolution of the stars, but themselves they consider not." I was abashed, and, asking my brother (who was anxious to hear more), not to annoy me, I closed the book, angry with myself that I should still be admiring earthly things who might long ago have learned from even the pagan philosophers that nothing is wonderful but the soul, which, when great itself, finds nothing great outside itself. Then, in truth, I was satisfied that I had seen enough of the mountain; I turned my inward eye upon myself, and from that time not a syllable fell from my lips until we reached the bottom again. Those words had given me occupation enough, for I could not believe that it was by a mere accident that I happened upon them. What I had there read I believed to be addressed to me and to no other, remembering that St. Augustine had once suspected the same thing in his own case, when, on opening the book of the Apostle, as he himself tells us, the first words that he saw there were, "Not in rioting and drunkenness, not in chambering and wantonness, not in strife and envying. But put ye on the Lord Jesus Christ, and make not provision for the flesh, to fulfil the lusts thereof."

The same thing happened earlier to St. Anthony, when he was listening to the Gospel where it is written, "If thou wilt be perfect, go and sell that thou hast, and give to the poor, and thou shalt have treasure in heaven: and come and follow me." Believing this scripture to have been read for his especial benefit, as his biographer Athanasius says, he guided himself by its aid to the Kingdom of Heaven. And as Anthony on hearing these words waited for nothing more, and as Augustine upon reading the Apostle's admonition sought no farther, so I concluded my reading in the few words which I have given. I thought in silence of the lack of good counsel in us mortals, who neglect what is noblest in ourselves, scatter our energies in all directions, and waste ourselves in a vain show, because we look about us for what is to be found only within. I wondered at the natural nobility of our soul, save when it debases itself of its own free will, and deserts its original estate, turning what God has given it for its honour into dishonour. How many times, think you, did I turn back that day, to glance at the summit of the mountain, which seemed scarcely a cubit high compared with the range of human contemplation,—when it is not immersed in the foul mire of earth? With every downward step I asked myself this: If we are ready to endure so much sweat and labour in order that we may bring our bodies a little nearer heaven, how can a soul struggling toward God, up the steeps of human pride and human destiny, fear any cross or prison or sting of fortune? How few, I thought, but are diverted from their path by the fear of difficulties or the love of ease! How happy the lot of those few, if any such there be! It is of them, assuredly, that the poet was thinking, when he wrote:

> Happy the man who is skilled to understand
> Nature's hid causes; who beneath his feet
> All terrors casts, and death's relentless doom,
> And the loud roar of greedy Acheron.

How earnestly should we strive, not to stand on mountain-tops, but to trample beneath us those appetites which spring from earthly impulses.

With no consciousness of the difficulties of the way, amidst these preoccupations which I have so frankly revealed, we came, long after dark, but with the full moon lending us its friendly light, to the little inn which we had left that morning before dawn. The time during which the servants have been occupied in preparing our supper, I have spent in a secluded part of the house, hurriedly jotting down these experiences on the spur of the moment, lest, in case my task were postponed, my mood should change on leaving the place, and so my interest in writing flag.

You will see, my dearest father, that I wish nothing to be concealed from you, for I am careful to describe to you not only my life in general but even my individual reflections. And I beseech you, in turn, to pray that these vague and wandering thoughts of mine may some time become firmly fixed, and, after having been vainly tossed about from one interest to another, may direct themselves at last toward the single, true, certain, and everlasting good.

MALAUCÈNE, APRIL 26.

64

Ibn Khaldun

from *Muqaddimah*

A native of Tunisia, Ibn Khaldun (1332–1406) was an important Arab Muslim historian. He is sometimes heralded as being among the progenitors of modern historiography, philosophy of history, ethnography, and even economic thought. He is considered noteworthy for being one of the earliest thinkers to articulate a secularized philosophy of history, which is on display in the following excerpt from his most famous work, *Muqaddimah*.

―――――――――

Know that the science of History is noble in its conception, abounding in instruction, and exalted in its aim. It acquaints us with the characteristics of the ancient peoples, the ways of life followed by the prophets, and the dynasties and government of kings, so that those who wish may draw valuable lessons for their guidance in religious and worldly affairs. The student of History, however, requires numerous sources of information and a great variety of knowledge; he must consider well and examine carefully in order to arrive at the truth and avoid errors and pitfalls. If he rely on bare tradition, without having thoroughly grasped the principles of common experience, the institutes of government, the nature of civilisation, and the circumstances of human society, and without judging what is past and invisible by the light of what is present before his eyes, then he will often be in danger of stumbling and slipping and losing the right road. Many errors committed by historians, commentators, and leading traditionists in their narrative of events have been caused by their reliance on mere tradition, which they have accepted without regard to its (intrinsic) worth, neglecting to refer it to its general principles, judge it by its analogies, and test it by the standard of wisdom,

SOURCE: Ibn Khaldun, excerpt from *Muqaddimah*, in Reynold A. Nicholson, *Translations of Eastern Poetry and Prose* (Cambridge: Cambridge University Press, 1922), 176–81.

knowledge of the natures of things, and exact historical criticism. Thus they have gone astray from the truth and wandered in the desert of imagination and error. Especially is this the case in computing sums of money and numbers of troops, when such matters occur in their narratives; for here falsehood and exaggeration are to be expected, and one must always refer to general principles and submit to the rules (of probability). For example, Mas'údí and many other historians relate that Moses—on whom be peace!—numbered the armies of the Israelites in the wilderness, after he had reviewed all the men capable of bearing arms who were twenty years old or above that age, and that they amounted to 600,000 or more. Now, in making this statement he forgot to consider whether Egypt and Syria are large enough to support armies of that size, for it is a fact attested by well-known custom and familiar experience that every kingdom keeps for its defence only such a force as it can maintain and furnish with rations and pay. Moreover, it would be impossible for armies so huge to march against each other or fight, because the territory is too limited in extent to allow of it, and because, when drawn up in ranks, they would cover a space twice or three times as far as the eye can reach, if not more. How should these two hosts engage in battle, or one of them gain the victory, when neither wing knows anything of what is happening on the other? The present time bears witness to the truth of my observations: water is not so like to water as the future to the past.

The Persian Empire was much greater than the kingdom of the Israelites, as appears from the conquest of the latter by Nebuchadnezzar, who attacked their country, made himself master of their dominions, and laid waste Jerusalem, the chief seat of their religion and power, although he was only the governor of a Persian province: it is said that he was the satrap of the western frontiers. The Persians ruled over the two 'Iráks, Khurásán, Transoxania, and the lands opening on the Caspian Sea—an empire far more extensive than that of the Israelites; yet their armies never equalled or even approached the number mentioned above. Their army at Ḳádisíya, the greatest they ever mustered, was 120,000 strong, and each of these was accompanied by a retainer. Saif, by whom this is related, adds that the whole force exceeded 200,000. According to 'Á'isha and Zuhrí, the troops under Rustam who were opposed to Sa'd at Ḳádisíya were only 60,000 strong, each man having a follower.

Again, if the Israelites had reached this total, vast would have been the extent of their kingdom and wide the range of their power. Provinces and kingdoms are small or great in proportion to the numbers of their soldiery and population, as we shall explain in the chapter concerning empires in the First Book. Now, it is well-known that the territories of the Israelites did not extend, in Syria, beyond al-Urdunn and Palestine, and in the Ḥijáz, beyond the districts of Yathrib (Medina) and Khaibar.

Furthermore, according to the trustworthy authorities, there were only four fathers (generations) between Moses and Israel. Moses was the son of 'Imrán the son of Yas-hur the son of Káhat or Káhit the son of Láwí or Láwá the son of Jacob or Isrá'ílu 'llah (Israel of God). This is his genealogy as given in the Pentateuch. The length of time separating them is recorded by Mas'údí, who says that when Israel entered Egypt and came to Joseph with his sons, the (twelve) Patriarchs and their children, seventy persons in all, they abode in Egypt under the dominion of the Pharaohs, the kings of the Copts, two hundred and twenty years until they went forth into the wilderness with Moses, on whom be peace. It is incredible that in the course of four generations their offspring should have multiplied so enormously.

That being so, the rule for distinguishing the true from the false in history is based on possibility or impossibility; that is to say, we must examine human society, by which I mean civilisation, and discriminate between the characteristics essential to it and inherent in its nature and those which are accidental and unimportant, recognising further those which cannot possibly belong to it. If we do that, we shall have a canon for separating historical fact and truth from error and falsehood by a method of proof that admits of no doubt; and then, if we hear an account of any of the things that happen in civilised society, we shall know how to distinguish what we judge to be worthy of acceptance from what we judge to be spurious, having in our hands an infallible criterion which enables historians to verify whatever they relate.

Such is the purpose of the First Book of the present work. And it would seem that this is an independent science. For it has a subject, namely, human civilisation and society; and problems, namely, to explain in succession the accidental features and essential characters of civilisation. This is the case with every science, the intellectual as well as those founded on authority.

The matter of the following discourse is novel, original, and instructive. I have discovered it by dint of deep thought and research. It appertains not to the science of oratory, which is only concerned with such language as will convince the multitude and be useful for winning them over to an opinion or persuading them to reject the same. Nor, again, does it form part of the science of civil government, *i.e.* the proper regulation of a household or city in accordance with moral and philosophical laws, in order that the people may be led to live in a way that tends to preserve and perpetuate the species. These two sciences may resemble it, but its subject differs from theirs. It appears to be a new invention; and indeed I have not met with a discourse upon it by anyone in the world. I do not know whether this is due to their neglect of the topic—and we need not think the worse of them for that—or whether, perhaps, they may have treated it exhaustively in books that have not come down to us. Amongst the races of mankind the sciences are many and the savants numerous, and the knowledge we have lost is greater in amount than all that has reached us. What has become of the sciences of the Persians, whose writings were destroyed by 'Umar (may God be well-pleased with him!) at the time of the conquest? Where are those of Chaldaea, Assyria, and Babylonia, with all that they produced and left behind them? Where are those of the Copts and of peoples yet more ancient? We have received the sciences of but one nation, the Greeks, and that only because Ma'mún took pains to have their books translated from the language in which they were composed. He was enabled to do this by finding plenty of translators and expending large sums on the work. Of the sciences of other peoples we know nothing.

[. . . .]

Now we shall set forth in this Book the various features of civilisation as they appear in human society: kingship, acquisition of wealth, the sciences, and the arts. We shall employ demonstrative methods to verify and elucidate the knowledge spread amongst all classes, to refute false opinions, and to remove uncertainties.

Man is distinguished from the other animals by attributes peculiar to himself. Amongst these are

(1) The sciences and arts produced by the faculty of reflection, which distinguishes men from the animals and exalts him above the rest of created beings.

(2) The need for an authority to restrain and a government to coerce him. Of the animals he is the only one that cannot exist without this. As for what is said concerning bees and locusts, even if they have something of the sort, they have it by instinct, not from reflection and consideration.

(3) The labour and industry which supply him with diverse ways and means of obtaining a livelihood, inasmuch as God has made nourishment necessary to him for the maintenance of his life and has directed him to seek it and search after it. *"He gave unto all things their nature: then He directed."*

(4) Civilisation, *i.e.* settling down and dwelling together in a city or in tents for the sake of social intercourse and for the satisfaction of their needs, because men are naturally disposed to help each other to subsist, as we shall explain presently. This civilisation is either nomadic (*badawí*) or residential (*ḥaḍarí*). The former is found in steppes and mountains, among the pastoral tribes of the desert and the inhabitants of remote sands; the latter in towns, villages, cities, and cultivated tracts, whither men resort for safety and in order

to be protected by walls. In all these circumstances it exhibits the phenomena characteristic of a social state. Accordingly, the matter of this Book must be comprised in six chapters.

I. Human society in general, its various divisions, and the part of the earth which it occupies.
II. Nomadic civilisation, with an account of the wild tribes and peoples.
III. Dynasties, the Caliphate, kingship, and the high offices of government.
IV. The settled civilisation of countries and cities.
V. Crafts, means of livelihood, and the various ways of making money.
VI. The sciences, and how they are acquired and learned.

65

Julian of Norwich

from *Revelations of Divine Love*

Although her actual name has been lost to history, most use the appellation Julian of Norwich (1342–ca. 1413) to refer to the author of *Revelations of Divine Love*. Over the course of two days in 1377, Julian purportedly experienced sixteen direct revelations, or shewings, giving her a mystical knowledge of God. Later she would become an anchorite, living in a room attached to St. Julian's church in Norwich, England—hence her name. In the following excerpt, Julian breaks with tradition and describes the Trinity in feminine terms.

The Fifty-eighth Chapter.

God, the blissful Trinity, which is everlasting Being, right as He is endless from without beginning, right so it was in His purpose endless, to make Mankind. Which fair nature first was prepared to His own Son, the Second Person; and when He would, by full accord of all the Trinity, He made us all at once. And in our making He knit us and united us to Himself, by which uniting we be kept as clean and as noble as we were made. By the virtue of that precious uniting we love our Maker and like Him, praise Him, and thank Him, and endlessly rejoice in Him. And this is the working which is wrought continually in each soul that shall be saved; which is the godly will aforesaid. And thus, in our making, God Almighty is our Natural Father. And God all wisdom is our natural Mother, with the love and the goodness of the Holy Ghost, which is all one God, one Lord. And in the knitting and in the union, He is our very true Spouse, and we His loved wife, and His fair maiden, with which wife He was never displeased, for He saith: "*I love thee, and thou lovest Me, and our love shall never part in two.*"

SOURCE: Julian of Norwich, *Revelations of Divine Love, Shewed to a Devout Anchoress, by Name, Mother Julian of Norwich* (London: Thomas Richardson and Sons, 1877), 218–26.

I beheld the working of all the Blessed Trinity, in which beholding I saw and understood these three properties: the property of the Fatherhood, the property of the Motherhood, and the property of the Lordship, in one God. In our Father Almighty we have our bliss and our keeping, and, in regard of our natural substance, which is in us, our making from without beginning. And in the Second Person, in wit and wisdom we have our keeping, and in regard of our sensuality our restoring and our saving; for He is our Mother, Brother, and Saviour. And in our good Lord the Holy Ghost we have our rewarding, and our yielding for our living and our travail, endlessly overpassing all that we desire in His marvellous courtesy, of high plenteous grace. For all our life is in three: in the first our being; and in the second we have our increasing; and in the third we have our fulfilling. The first is nature, the second is mercy, the third is grace. For the first, I saw and understood that the high might of the Trinity is our Father, and the deep wisdom of the Trinity is our Mother, and the great love of the Trinity is our Lord. And all these have we in nature, and in our substantial making. And furthermore I saw that the Second Person, which is our Mother substantially, the same dear worthy Person is now become our Mother sensual; for we be double of God's making: that is to say, substantial and sensual. Our substance is the higher part which we have in our Father God Almighty; and the Second Person of the Trinity is our Mother in nature in our substantial making, in whom we be grounded and rooted, and He is our Mother in Mercy, in our sensuality taking. And thus our Mother is to us divers manners working, in whom our parts be kept unseparated; for in our Mother Christ we profit and increase, and in mercy He reformeth us and restoreth. And by the virtue of His Passion, His death, and His uprising, He united us to our substance.

This worketh our Mother in mercy to all His children, which be to Him pliant and obedient. And grace worketh with mercy, and namely in two properties, as it was shewed. Which working belongeth to the Third Person, the Holy Ghost: He worketh rewarding and giving. Rewarding is a gift of trust, that the Lord doth to them that hath travailed. And giving is a courteous working which He doth freely of grace, fulfilling and overpassing all that is deserved of creatures. Thus in our Father God Almighty we have our being, and in our Mother of mercy Jesus Christ we have our reforming and our restoring, in whom our parts be united, and all made perfect man: and by yielding and giving in grace of the Holy Ghost we are fulfilled. And our substance is in our Father God Almighty; and our substance is in our Mother God All-Wisdom; and our substance is in our Lord God the Holy Ghost, all Goodness; for our Substance is whole in each Person of the Trinity, which is one God. And our sensuality is only in the Second Person Christ Jesus, in whom is the Father and the Holy Ghost. And in Him, and by Him, we be mightily taken out of hell, and out of the wretchedness in earth; and worshipfully brought up into heaven, and blissfully united to our substance, increased in riches and in nobleness by all the virtue of Christ, and by the grace and working of the Holy Ghost.

The Fifty-ninth Chapter.

And all this bliss we have by mercy and grace: which manner of bliss we might never have had and known, unless that property and goodness which is God had been contraried, whereby we have this bliss. For wickedness hath been suffered to rise contrary to that goodness, and the goodness of mercy and grace contraried against that wickedness, and turned all to goodness and worship, to all that shall be saved; for it is that property in God which doth good against evil. Thus Jesus Christ, that doth good against evil, is our very Mother. We have our being of Him, where the ground of Motherhood beginneth, with all the sweet keeping of love that endlessly followeth. As verily as God is our Father, as verily is God our Mother, and that shewed He in all, and namely in these sweet words where He saith: "*I it am;*" that is to say, "*I it am, the might and the goodness of the Fatherhood; I it am, the wisdom and the kindness of the Motherhood; I it am, the light and the grace that is all blessed love; I it am, the Trinity; I it am, the Unity; I it am the high sovereign goodness of all manner of thing; I it am that maketh thee to long; I it am, the endless fulfilling of all true desires.*" For where the soul is highest, noblest, and worshipfullest, yet it is lowest, meekest, and mildest.

And of this substantial ground we have all our virtues in our sensuality, by gift of nature, by helping, and speeding of mercy and grace, without which we may not profit. Our high Father Almighty God, which is being, He knoweth us, and loved us from before any time. Of which knowing, in His full marvellous deep charity, by the foreseeing endless counsel of all the Blessed Trinity, He would that the Second Person should become our Mother, our Brother, and our Saviour.

Whereof it followeth that as verily as God is our Father, as verily God is our Mother. Our Father willeth, our Mother worketh, our good Lord the Holy Ghost confirmeth. And therefore it belongeth to us to love our God, in whom we have our being, Him reverently thanking and praising for our making, mightily praying to our Mother of mercy and pity, and to our Lord the Holy Ghost, for help and grace. For in these three is all our life, nature, mercy, and grace; whereof we have mildness, patience, and pity, and hating of sin and wickedness: for it belongeth properly to virtues to hate sin and wickedness.

And thus is Jesus our very Mother in nature of our first making: and He is our very first mother in grace by taking of our nature made. All the fair working, and all the sweet kindly offices of dear worthy Motherhood be appropriated to the Second Person. For in Him we have this godly will, whole and safe without end, both in nature and in grace, of His own proper Goodness.

I understood three manner of beholdings of Motherhood in God. The first is, the ground of our natural making. The second is, taking of our nature, and there beginneth the Motherhood of grace. The third is, Motherhood in working: and therein is a forthspreading by the same grace, of length and breadth, and height and deepness without end, and all is one love.

66

Catherine of Siena

from *Dialogue of the Seraphic Virgin*

One of three women to be declared by the Vatican as Doctor of the Church, Catherine of Siena (1347–1380) is also central to the Italian identity. She was, for instance, influential in returning the papacy back to Rome, from its decades in Avignon, France. In the fourteenth century, she was best known for her public service toward the poor, sick, and imprisoned. Her enduring legacy, however, may be in her mystical approach to divine knowledge. The following excerpt illustrates her emphasis on faith, based less on a rational or intellectual knowledge, and more on a knowledge born out of direct experience and relationship with the divine.

Chapter I: A Treatise of Divine Providence

The soul, who is lifted by a very great and yearning desire for the honour of God and the salvation of souls, begins by exercising herself, for a certain space of time, in the ordinary virtues, remaining in the cell of self-knowledge, in order to know better the goodness of God towards her. This she does because knowledge must precede love, and only when she has attained love, can she strive to follow and to clothe herself with the truth. But, in no way, does the creature receive such a taste of the truth, or so brilliant a light therefrom, as by means of humble and continuous prayer, founded on knowledge of herself and of God; because prayer, exercising her in the above way, unites with God the soul that follows the footprints of Christ Crucified, and thus, by desire and affection, and union of love, makes her another Himself. Christ would seem to

SOURCE: Catherine of Siena, *The Dialogue of the Seraphic Virgin, Catherine of Siena: Dictated by Her, While in a State of Ecstasy, to Her Secretaries, and Completed in the Year of Our Lord 1370*, trans. Algar Thorold (London: Kegan Paul, Trench, Trübner & Co., 1896), 19–20.

have meant this, when He said: *To him who will love Me and will observe My commandment, will I manifest Myself; and he shall be one thing with Me and I with him.* In several places we find similar words, by which we can see that it is, indeed, through the effect of love, that the soul becomes another Himself. That this may be seen more clearly, I will mention what I remember having heard from a handmaid of God, namely, that, when she was lifted up in prayer, with great elevation of mind, God was not wont to conceal, from the eye of her intellect, the love which He had for His servants, but rather to manifest it; and, that among other things, He used to say: "Open the eye of your intellect, and gaze into Me, and you shall see the beauty of My rational creature. And look at those creatures who, among the beauties which I have given to the soul, creating her in My image and similitude, are clothed with the nuptial garment (that is the garment of love), adorned with many virtues, by which they are united with Me through love. And yet I tell you, if you should ask Me, who these are, I should reply" (said the sweet and amorous Word of God) "they are another Myself, inasmuch as they have lost and denied their own will, and are clothed with Mine, are united to Mine, are conformed to Mine." It is therefore true, indeed, that the soul unites herself with God by the affection of love.

So, that soul, wishing to know and follow the truth more manfully, and lifting her desires first for herself—for she considered that a soul could not be of use, whether in doctrine, example, or prayer, to her neighbour, if she did not first profit herself, that is, if she did not acquire virtue in herself—addressed four requests to the Supreme and Eternal Father. The first was for herself; the second for the reformation of the Holy Church; the third a general prayer for the whole world, and in particular for the peace of Christians who rebel, with much lewdness and persecution, against the Holy Church; in the fourth and last, she besought the Divine Providence to provide for things in general, and in particular, for a certain case with which she was concerned.

67

Thomas à Kempis

from *Imitation of Christ*

Thomas à Kempis (ca. 1380–1471) is best known for his *Imitation of Christ* (1420–1427), which endures as a classic in Western Christianity, able to cross sectarian divisions. The volume's thesis is that "We must imitate Christ's life and his ways if we are to be truly enlightened and set free from the darkness of our own hearts. Let it be the most important thing we do, then, to reflect on the life of Jesus Christ." Born in Germany, Thomas was influenced by the Brethren of the Common Life and their ascetic practices. He became an Augustinian monk, where he dedicated his life to writing, preaching, and spiritual direction.

Chapter LVI: *That we ought to Deny Ourselves, and to Imitate Christ by the Cross.*

1. My son, as much as you can go out of yourself, so much will you be able to enter into Me.

As the absence of all craving for outward things brings inward peace, so the setting aside of self inwardly unites you to God.

I wish you to learn perfect renunciation of yourself to My will, without opposition or complaint.

Follow Me; "I am the Way, the Truth, and the Life."

Without the Way, you cannot go; without the Truth, you cannot know; without the Life, you cannot live.

I am the Way, which you ought to follow; the Truth, which you ought to believe; the Life, which you ought to hope for.

I am the Way, unchangeable; the Truth, infallible; the Life, endless.

SOURCE: Thomas à Kempis, *Of the Imitation of Christ in Four Books*, trans. W. H. Hutchings (London: Rivingtons, 1881), 195–97, 203–5.

I am the straightest Way, the Sovereign Truth, the true Life, the blessed Life, the Life uncreated.

If you shall abide in My way, you shall know the truth, and the truth shall make you free, and you shall lay hold of eternal life.

2. If you wish to enter into life, keep the commandments.

If you wish to know the truth, believe Me.

If you wish to be perfect, sell all.

If you wish to be My disciple, deny yourself.

If you wish to obtain the blessed life, despise this present life.

If you wish to be exalted in Heaven, humble yourself in this world.

If you wish to reign with Me, bear the Cross with Me.

For only the servants of the Cross find the life of Blessedness and of true light.

3. O Lord Jesus, since Thy life was strict, and despised by the world, grant me grace to follow Thy steps, and share with Thee the contempt of the world.

For the servant is not greater than his Lord, nor the disciple above his master.

Let Thy servant be trained after Thy life, for in it is my safety and true holiness.

Whatever else I hear and read does not refresh me, nor give me full delight.

4. My son, since you know these things, and read them all, blessed shall you be if you do them.

"He that hath My commandments and keepeth them, he it is that loveth Me; and I will love him, and will manifest Myself unto him," and will make him sit together with Me in My Father's Kingdom.

Therefore, O Lord Jesus, as Thou hast said and promised, so may it happen unto me, and may I deserve it.

I have received, I have received from Thy hand the cross; I will bear it; I will bear it even unto death, as Thou hast laid it upon me.

Truly the life of a good Religious man is a cross, but it leads to Heaven.

We have begun; we may not go back, neither is it right to leave it.

5. Onward, brethren, onward let us go together! Jesus will be with us.

For the sake of Jesus we have taken up this cross; for the sake of Jesus let us continue to bear it.

He will be our Helper, Who is our Guide and Forerunner.

Behold our King marches before us, Who will fight for us.

Let us follow Him bravely, let no one shrink from fears; let us be prepared to die valiantly in battle, and let us not bring disgrace on our glory by turning back from the Cross.

[. . . .]

Chapter LIX: *That all Hope and Trust is to be Fixed in God Alone.*

1. O Lord, what is my hope which I have in this life, or what is my greatest comfort which I have from all visible things under heaven?

Is it not Thou Thyself, O Lord my God, whose mercies are without number?

When was it ever well with me without Thee? or when could it be ever ill with me, when Thou wert present?

I would rather be poor for Thee, than rich without Thee.

I would choose rather to be a pilgrim on earth with Thee, than to possess Heaven without Thee.

Where Thou art, there is Heaven; and where Thou art not, there is death and Hell.

Thou art my desire; and therefore I must sigh and cry after Thee, and call earnestly upon Thee.

In short, there is none whom I can fully trust in, to bring me the help which I need in my times of trial, but Thou alone, my God.

Thou art my hope, my confidence, and my comforter; and most faithful art Thou in all things.

2. All seek their own advantage: Thou aimest at my salvation and my advancement only, and turnest all things to my profit.

And if I am exposed by Thee to various temptations and trials, Thou orderest all things for my good, for Thou in a thousand ways art wont to prove Thy beloved servants.

In which trials Thou oughtest no less to be loved and praised, than if Thou didst fill me with heavenly consolations.

3. In Thee, therefore, O Lord my God, I place my whole trust and refuge; on Thee I cast all my tribulation and distress, for I find everything weak and unstable, which I behold out of Thee.

For neither do a number of friends profit us, nor can strong helpers assist, nor prudent advisers give useful counsel, nor books of learned men console, nor any precious substance redeem, nor any place, however secret, protect, unless Thou Thyself assist, help, strengthen, comfort, instruct, and guard us.

4. For all the things which seem calculated to bring peace and happiness, without Thee are nothing, and bring no true happiness at all.

Thou, therefore, art the end of all good, the highest life, the deepest wisdom that can be uttered; and to trust in Thee above all is the strongest comfort of all Thy servants.

To Thee do I look up; in Thee do I trust, my God, Father of mercies!

Bless and sanctify my soul with Heavenly blessing, that it may become Thy holy habitation, and the seat of Thy eternal glory; and let nothing be found where Thou deignest to dwell that may offend the eyes of Thy Majesty.

According to the multitude of Thy mercies and the greatness of Thy goodness look upon me: and hear the prayer of Thy poor servant—exiled far away in the region of the shadow of death.

Defend and preserve the soul of Thine unworthy servant amid the many risks of this corruptible life; and, by Thy grace accompanying me, direct me along the path of peace to the Country of never-failing joy and brightness.

Amen.

68

Joan of Arc

Letter to the King of England, March 22, 1429

Remembered as "The Maid of Orléans," Joan of Arc (1412–1431) was a religious mystic and military strategist. Born into an impoverished French family, her contributions at the siege of Orléans (1428–1429) helped repulse the English during a key phase of the Hundred Years War, thereby saving the city. It was during this siege that Joan sent a brash letter to England's monarch, correctly prophesying the impending defeat of his army. In 1430, however, English forces captured Joan as she protected her retreating forces. Now a pawn in a complex political game, she stood trial in 1431, indicted on blasphemy and seventy other charges. Upon conviction, she was, burned at the stake on May 30, 1431. Joan maintained that the voices she heard were sent by God, and that she was not deluded.

———————————

Jesu, Marie.

King of England; and you, Duke of Bedford, who call yourself Regent of the kingdom of France; you, William de la Pole, Earl of Suffolk; John, Lord Talbot; and you, Thomas, Lord Scales, who call yourselves lieutenants to the Duke of Bedford: Give satisfaction to the King of Heaven; give up to the maid who is sent hither by God, the King of Heaven, the keys of all the good towns in France which you have taken and broken into. She is come here by the order of God to reclaim the blood royal. She is quite ready to make peace, if you are willing to give her satisfaction, by giving and paying back to France what you have taken. And for you, archers, companions-in-arms, gentlemen and others, who are before the town of Orleans, return to your own countries, by God's

SOURCE: E. A. Ford, *Blessed Joan of Arc: Complete Story of Her Wonderful Life, Her Tragic Death, Her Rehabilitation, Her Beatification* (New York: Christian Press Association, 1910), 52–54.

order; and if this be not done, then hear the message of the Maid, who will shortly come upon you to your very great hurt.

King of England, I am a chieftain of war and, if this be not done, whereso-ever I find your followers in France I will make them leave, willingly or unwill-ingly; if they will not leave I will have them put to death.

I am sent here by God, the King of Heaven, to drive them all out of the whole of France. And if they will obey I will have mercy on them.

And do not think to yourselves that you will get possession of the realm of France from God, the King of Heaven, Son of the Blessed Mary; for King Charles will gain it, the true heir; and God, the King of Heaven, so wills it, and it is revealed to him, (the King) by the Maid, and he will enter Paris with a good company.

If you will not believe the message of God and of the Maid and act aright, in whatsoever place we find you, we will enter therein and make so great a disturbance that for a thousand years none in France will be so great.

And believe surely that the King of Heaven will send greater power to the Maid, to her and her good men-at-arms, than you can bring to the attack; and, when it comes to blows, we shall see who has the better right from the King of Heaven.

You, Duke of Burgundy, the Maid prays and enjoins you, that you do not come to grievous hurt. If you will give her satisfactory pledges, you may yet join with her, so that the French may do the fairest deed that has ever yet been done for Christendom.

And answer, if you wish to make peace in the City of Orleans; if this be not done you may shortly be reminded of it to your very great hurt.

Written this Tuesday in Holy Week, March 22, 1429.

69

Niccolò Machiavelli

from *The Prince*

Niccolò di Bernardo dei Machiavelli (1468–1527) was a Florentine politician and Renaissance thinker whose name is often associated with the kind of political dirty-handedness, deception, and manipulation he infamously endorsed as sometimes necessary for good statecraft. He is an important figure in political science, and he is best known for his political treatises, namely, *The Prince* and his *Discourses on the First Decade of Titus Livius*. The following excerpts are taken from *The Prince*, and they capture some of the reasons why he is associated with "Machiavellian" behavior.

Fourteenth Chapter: That Which Concerns a Prince on the Subject of the Art of War

A prince ought to have no other aim or thought, nor select anything else for his study, than war and its rules and discipline; for this is the sole art that belongs to him who rules, and it is of such force that it not only upholds those who are born princes, but it often enables men to rise from a private station to that rank. And, on the contrary, it is seen that when princes have thought more of ease than of arms they have lost their states. And the first cause of your losing it is to neglect this art; and what enables you to acquire a state is to be master of the art. Francesco Sforza, through being martial, from a private person became Duke of Milan; and the sons, through avoiding the hardships and troubles of arms, from dukes became private persons. For among other evils which being unarmed brings you, it causes you to be despised, and this is one of those ignominies against which a prince ought to guard himself, as

SOURCE: Nicolo Machiavelli, *The Prince*, trans. W. K. Marriot (New York: E. P. Dutton & Co., 1920), 115–18, 141–45.

is shown later on. Because there is nothing proportionate between the armed and the unarmed; and it is not reasonable that he who is armed should yield obedience willingly to him who is unarmed, or that the unarmed man should be secure among armed servants. Because, there being in the one disdain and in the other suspicion, it is not possible for them to work well together. And therefore a prince who does not understand the art of war, over and above the other misfortunes already mentioned, cannot be respected by his soldiers, nor can he rely on them. He ought never, therefore, to have out of his thoughts this subject of war, and in peace he should addict himself more to its exercise than in war; this he can do in two ways, the one by action, the other by study.

As regards action, he ought above all things to keep his men well organised and drilled, to follow incessantly the chase, by which he accustoms his body to hardships, and learns something of the nature of localities, and gets to find out how the mountains rise, how the valleys open out, how the plains lie, and to understand the nature of rivers and marshes, and in all this to take the greatest care. Which knowledge is useful in two ways. Firstly, he learns to know his country, and is better able to undertake its defence; afterwards, by means of the knowledge and observation of that locality, he understands with ease any other which it may be necessary for him to study hereafter; because the hills, valleys, and plains, and rivers and marshes that are, for instance, in Tuscany, have a certain resemblance to those of other countries, so that with a knowledge of the aspect of one country one can easily arrive at a knowledge of others. And the prince that lacks this skill lacks the essential which it is desirable that a captain should possess, for it teaches him to surprise his enemy, to select quarters, to lead armies, to array the battle, to besiege towns to advantage.

Philopoemen, Prince of the Achaeans, among other praises which writers have bestowed on him, is commended because in time of peace he never had anything in his mind but the rules of war; and when he was in the country with friends, he often stopped and reasoned with them: "If the enemy should be upon that hill, and we should find ourselves here with our army, with whom would be the advantage? How should one best advance to meet him, keeping the ranks? If we should wish to retreat, how ought we to set about it? If they should retreat, how ought we to pursue?" And he would set forth to them, as he went, all the chances that could befall an army; he would listen to their opinion and state his, confirming it with reasons, so that by these continual discussions there could never arise, in time of war, any unexpected circumstances that he could not deal with.

But to exercise the intellect the prince should read histories, and study there the actions of illustrious men, to see how they have borne themselves in war, to examine the causes of their victories and defeat, so as to avoid the latter and imitate the former; and above all do as an illustrious man did, who took as an exemplar one who had been praised and famous before him, and whose achievements and deeds he always kept in his mind, as it is said Alexander the Great imitated Achilles, Cæsar Alexander, Scipio Cyrus. And whoever reads the life of Cyrus, written by Xenophon, will recognise afterwards in the life of Scipio how that imitation was his glory, and how in chastity, affability, humanity, and liberality Scipio conformed to those things which have been written of Cyrus by Xenophon. A wise prince ought to observe some such rules, and never in peaceful times stand idle, but increase his resources with industry in such a way that they may be available to him in adversity, so that if fortune changes it may find him prepared to resist her blows.

[. . . .]

Eighteenth Chapter: Concerning the Way in Which Princes Should Keep Faith

Every one admits how praiseworthy it is in a prince to keep faith, and to live with integrity and not with craft. Nevertheless our experience has been that those princes who have done great things have held good faith of little account, and have known how to circumvent the intellect of men by craft, and in the end have overcome those who have relied on their word. You must know there are two ways of contesting, the one by the law, the other by force; the first method is proper to men, the second to beasts; but because the first is frequently not sufficient, it is necessary to have recourse to the second. Therefore it is necessary for a prince to understand how to avail himself of the beast and the man. This has been figuratively taught to princes by ancient writers, who describe how Achilles and many other princes of old were given to the Centaur Chiron to nurse, who brought them up in his discipline; which means solely that, as they had for a teacher one who was half beast and half man, so it is necessary for a prince to know how to make use of both natures, and that one without the other is not durable. A prince, therefore, being compelled knowingly to adopt the beast, ought to choose the fox and the lion; because the lion cannot defend himself against snares and the fox cannot defend himself against wolves. Therefore, it is necessary to be a fox to discover the snares and a lion to terrify the wolves. Those who rely simply on the lion do not understand what they are about. Therefore a wise lord cannot, nor ought he to, keep faith when such observance may be turned against him, and when the reasons that caused him to pledge it exist no longer. If men were entirely good this precept would not hold, but because they are bad, and will not keep faith with you, you too are not bound to observe it with them. Nor will there ever be wanting to a prince legitimate reasons to excuse this non-observance. Of this endless modern examples could be given, showing how many treaties and engagements have been made void and of no effect through the faithlessness of princes; and he who has known best how to employ the fox has succeeded best.

But it is necessary to know well how to disguise this characteristic, and to be a great pretender and dissembler; and men are so simple, and so subject to present necessities, that he who seeks to deceive will always find some one who will allow himself to be deceived. One recent example I cannot pass over in silence. Alexander the Sixth did nothing else but deceive men, nor ever thought of doing otherwise, and he always found victims; for there never was a man who had greater power in asserting, or who with greater oaths would affirm a thing, yet would observe it less; nevertheless his deceits always succeeded according to his wishes, because he well understood this side of mankind.

Therefore it is unnecessary for a prince to have all the good qualities I have enumerated, but it is very necessary to appear to have them. And I shall dare to say this also, that to have them and always to observe them is injurious, and that to appear to have them is useful; to appear merciful, faithful, humane, religious, upright, and to be so, but with a mind so framed that should you require not to be so, you may be able and know how to change to the opposite.

And you have to understand this, that a prince, especially a new one, cannot observe all those things for which men are esteemed, being often forced, in order to maintain the state, to act contrary to fidelity, friendship, humanity, and religion. Therefore it is necessary for him to have a mind ready to turn itself accordingly as the winds and variations of fortune force it, yet, as I have said above, not to diverge from the good if he can avoid doing so, but, if compelled, then to know how to set about it.

For this reason a prince ought to take care that he never lets anything slip from his lips that is not replete with the above-named five qualities, that he may appear to him who sees and hears him altogether merciful, faithful, humane, upright, and religious. There is nothing more necessary to appear to have than this last quality, inasmuch as men judge generally more by the eye than by the hand, because it belongs to everybody to see you, to few to come in touch with you. Every one sees what you appear to be, few really know what you are, and those few dare not oppose themselves to the opinion of the many, who have the majesty of the state to defend them; and in the actions of all men, and especially of princes, which it is not prudent to challenge, one judges by the result.

For that reason, let a prince have the credit of conquering and holding his state, the means will always be considered honest, and he will be praised by everybody; because the vulgar are always taken by what a thing seems to be and by what comes of it; and in the world there are only the vulgar, for the few find a place there only when the many have no ground to rest on.

One prince of the present time, whom it is not well to name, never preaches anything else but peace and good faith, and to both he is most hostile, and either, if he had kept it, would have deprived him of reputation and kingdom many a time.

70

Niccolò Machiavelli

from *Discourses on the First Decade of Titus Livius*

The following is an excerpt from Machiavelli's second-most important political treatise, namely, his *Discourses on the First Decade of Titus Livius*, which was written later in his life and published posthumously. It is partly a political history of ancient Rome, and was motivated by the instrumentalist idea that one can cull the past for its wisdom to achieve better political outcomes in the present.

Chapter LVIII.—That a People is wiser and more constant than a Prince.

That "*nothing is more fickle and inconstant than the multitude,*" is affirmed not by Titus Livius only, but by all other historians, in whose chronicles of human actions we often find the multitude condemning some citizen to death, and afterwards lamenting him and grieving greatly for his loss; as the Romans grieved and lamented for Manlius Capitolinus, whom they had themselves condemned to die. In relating which circumstance our author observes: "*In a short time the people, having no longer cause to fear him, began to deplore his death.*" And elsewhere, when speaking of what took place in Syracuse after the murder of Hieronymus, grandson of Hiero, he says, "*It is the nature of the multitude to be an abject slave, or a domineering master.*"

It may be that in attempting to defend a cause, which, as I have said, all writers are agreed to condemn, I take upon me a task so hard and difficult that I shall either have to relinquish it with shame or pursue it with opprobrium. Be that as it may, I neither do, nor ever shall judge it a fault, to support opinion

SOURCE: Niccolò Machiavelli, *Discourses on the First Decade of Titus Livius*, trans. Ninian Hill Thomson (London: Kegan Paul, Trench, & Co., 1883), 174–80.

by arguments, where it is not sought to impose them by violence or authority, I maintain, then, that this infirmity with which historians tax the multitude, may with equal reason be charged against every individual man, but most of all against princes, since all who are not controlled by the laws, will commit the very same faults as are committed by an uncontrolled multitude. Proof whereof were easy, since of all the many princes existing, or who have existed, few indeed are or have been either wise or good.

I speak of such princes as have had it in their power to break the reins by which they are controlled, among whom I do not reckon those kings who reigned in Egypt in the most remote antiquity when that country was governed in conformity with its laws; nor do I include those kings who reigned in Sparta, nor those who in our own times reign in France, which kingdom, more than any other whereof we have knowledge at the present day, is under the government of its laws. For kings who live, as these do, subject to constitutional restraint, are not to be counted when we have to consider each man's proper nature, and to see whether he resembles the multitude. For to draw a comparison with such princes as these, we must take the case of a multitude controlled as they are, and regulated by the laws, when we shall find it to possess the same virtues which we see in them, and neither conducting itself as an abject slave nor as a domineering master.

Such was the people of Rome, who, while the commonwealth continued uncorrupted, never either served abjectly nor domineered haughtily; but, on the contrary, by means of their magistrates and their ordinances, maintained their place, and when forced to put forth their strength against some powerful citizen, as in the case of Manlius, the decemvirs, and others who sought to oppress them, did so; but when it was necessary for the public welfare to yield obedience to the dictator or consuls, obeyed. And if the Roman people mourned the loss of the dead Manlius, it is no wonder; for they mourned his virtues, which had been of such a sort that their memory stirred the regret of all, and would have had power to produce the same feelings even in a prince; all writers being agreed that excellence is praised and admired even by its enemies. But if Manlius when he was so greatly mourned, could have risen once more from the dead, the Roman people would have pronounced the same sentence against him which they pronounced when they led him forth from the prison-house, and straightway condemned him to die. And in like manner we see that princes, accounted wise, have put men to death, and afterwards greatly lamented them, as Alexander mourned for Clitus and others of his friends, and Herod for Mariamne.

But what our historian says of the multitude, he says not of a multitude which like the people of Rome is controlled by the laws, but of an uncontrolled multitude like the Syracusans, who were guilty of all these crimes which infuriated and ungoverned men commit, and which were equally committed by Alexander and Herod in the cases mentioned. Wherefore the nature of a multitude is no more to be blamed than the nature of princes, since both equally err when they can do so without regard to consequences. Of which many instances, besides those already given, might be cited from the history of the Roman emperors, and of other princes and tyrants, in whose lives we find such inconstancy and fickleness, as we might look in vain for in a people.

I maintain, therefore, contrary to the common opinion which avers that a people when they have the management of affairs are changeable, fickle, and ungrateful, that these faults exist not in them otherwise than as they exist in individual princes; so that were any to accuse both princes and peoples, the charge might be true, but that to make exception in favour of princes is a mistake; for a people in command, if it be duly restrained, will have the same prudence and the same gratitude as a prince has, or even more, however wise he may be reckoned; and a prince on the other hand, if freed from the control of the laws, will be more ungrateful, fickle, and short-sighted than a people. And further, I say that any difference in their methods of acting results not from any difference in their nature, that being the same in both, or, if there be advantage on either side, the advantage resting with the people, but from their having more or less respect for the laws under which each lives. And whosoever attentively considers the history of the Roman people, may see that for four hundred years they never relaxed in their hatred of the regal name, and were constantly devoted to the glory and welfare of their country, and will find numberless proofs given by them of their consistency in both particulars. And should any allege against me the ingratitude they showed to Scipio, I reply by what has already been said at length on that head, where I proved that peoples are less ungrateful than princes. But as for prudence and stability of purpose, I affirm that a people is more prudent, more stable, and of better judgment than a prince. Nor is it without reason that the voice of the people has been likened to the voice of God; for we see that wide-spread beliefs fulfil themselves, and bring about marvellous results, so as to have the appearance of presaging by some occult quality either weal or woe. Again, as to the justice of their opinions on public affairs, we seldom find that after hearing two speakers of equal ability urging them in opposite directions, they do not adopt the sounder view, or are unable to decide on the truth of what they hear. And if, as I have said, a people errs in adopting courses which appear to it bold and advantageous, princes will likewise err when their passions are touched, as is far oftener the case with them than with a people.

We see, too, that in the choice of magistrates a people will choose far more honestly than a prince; so that while you shall never persuade a people that it is advantageous to confer dignities on the infamous and profligate, a prince may readily, and in a thousand ways, be drawn to do so. Again, it may be seen that a people, when once they have come to hold a thing in abhorrence, remain for many ages of the same mind; which we do not find happen with princes. For the truth of both of which assertions the Roman people are my sufficient witness, who, in the course of so many hundred years, and in so many elections of consuls and tribunes, never made four appointments of which they had reason to repent; and, as I have said, so detested the name of king, that no obligation they might be under to any citizen who affected that name, could shield him from the appointed penalty.

Further, we find that those cities wherein the government is in the hands of the people, in a very short space of time, make marvellous progress, far exceeding that made by cities which have been always ruled by princes; as Rome grew after the expulsion of her kings, and Athens after she freed herself from Pisistratus; and this we can ascribe to no other cause than that the rule of a people is better than the rule of a prince.

Nor would I have it thought that anything our historian may have affirmed in the passage cited, or elsewhere, controverts these my opinions. For if all the glories and all the defects both of peoples and of princes be carefully weighed, it will appear that both for goodness and for glory a people is to be preferred. And if princes surpass peoples in the work of legislation, in shaping civil institutions, in moulding statutes, and framing new ordinances, so far do the latter surpass the former in maintaining what has once been established, as to merit no less praise than they.

And to state the sum of the whole matter shortly, I say that popular governments have endured for long periods in the same way as the governments of princes, and that both have need to be regulated by the laws; because the prince who can do what he pleases is a madman, and the people which can do as it pleases is never wise. If, then, we assume the case of a prince bound, and of a people chained down by the laws, greater virtue will appear in the people than in the prince; while if we assume the case of each of them freed from all control, it will be seen that the people commits fewer errors than the prince, and less serious errors, and such as admit of readier cure. For a turbulent and unruly people may be spoken to by a good man, and readily brought back to good ways; but none can speak to a wicked prince, nor any remedy be found against him but by the sword. And from this we may infer which of the two suffers from the worse disease; for if the disease of the people may be healed by words, while that of the prince must be dealt with by the sword, there is none but will judge that evil to be the greater which demands the more violent remedy.

When a people is absolutely uncontrolled, it is not so much the follies which it commits or the evil which it actually does that excites alarm, as the mischief which may thence result, since in such disorders it becomes possible for a tyrant to spring up. But with a wicked prince the contrary is the case; for we dread present ill, and place our hopes in the future, persuading ourselves that the evil life of the prince may bring about our freedom. So that there is this distinction between the two, that with the one we fear what is, with the other what is likely to be. Again, the cruelties of a people are turned against him who it fears will encroach upon the common rights, but the cruelties of the prince against those who he fears may assert those rights.

The prejudice which is entertained against the people arises from this, that any man may speak ill of them openly and fearlessly, even when the government is in their hands; whereas princes are always spoken of with a thousand reserves and a constant eye to consequences.

But since the subject suggests it, it seems to me not out of place to consider what alliances we can most trust, whether those made with commonwealths or those made with princes.

71

Bartolomé de Las Casas

from *Tears of the Indians*

One of the few eyewitnesses to criticize early Spanish colonization of the Americas, Bartolomé de Las Casas (ca. 1474–1566) arrived in the Americas as a slaveholding *encomendero*. His conscience was stirred, however, by both the prophetic preaching of Fr. Antonio de Montesinos and Las Casas' own observation of conquistador atrocities. He eventually took vows as a Dominican friar and redirected his energies toward the defense of the Indigenous peoples, thereby leading to his unofficial title as the "Apostle to the Indians." To illustrate the magnitude of the devastation, Las Casas reported colonial abuses throughout the Indies. In the following excerpt, for instance, he depicts the atrocities in the Province of St. Martha. Englishmen, like J. Phillips, quickly translated and marketed Las Casas' books, stoking a righteous indignation against Spanish colonization. Condemning this so-called "Black Legend" of Spanish oppression, the English more often replicated than rectified Spanish approaches to colonizing the Americas.

If I had decreed to reckon up the impieties, slaughters, cruelties, violences, rapines, murders, and iniquities, and other crimes committed by the *Spaniards* against God, the King, and these innocent Nations, I should make [too] large a volume: yet I shall do my endevour, if God grant me life. For the present I will rehearse a part of those things which the Bishops of these Provinces wrote to the King our Soveraign Lord. There were letters dated the 25 of *May*, in the year, 1541. In which these words are written. "I tell your sacred Majesty,

SOURCE: Bartolomé de Las Casas, *The Tears of the Indians: Being an Historical and True Account of the Cruel Massacres and Slaughters of above Twenty Millions of Innocent People Committed by the Spaniards in the Islands of Hispaniola, Cuba, Jamaica, &c.*, trans. J. Phillips (London: Nathan Brook, 1656), 72–75.

that there is no remedy to ease this afflicted Nation, but to deliver it out of the power of these step-fathers, and to give it into the power of a loving husband, which may use it with more gentlenesse as befits it, and that as soon as may be; for if there be any delay, it must of necessity perish. And a little after he proceeds thus. By which it shall be apparent to your Majesty, how deservedly the Governors of these Provinces ought to be deprived of their dignity, that the Provinces may be eased; which if it be not suddenly done, these provinces will never be eased. This also your Majesty may further take notice of, that they are not men that live here but Devils, that there are no servants of God or the King to be found, but traytors both to the Law and King." Now certainly there is nothing more destructive to the peace of the Nation, and that hinders more the conversion of those that live there in peace, then the cruel and hard usage which the *Spaniards* afflict those innocent people with-all, which bred in them such a loathing of the *Spanish* name, that nothing is more odious and detestable. For the *Indians* call them *Yaes*, which in their language signifies Devils. And truly not without reason, for the actions of these people have been more like the actions of Devils, whereby it happens that the *Indians* se[e]ing such crimes committed by the *Spaniards* both of high and inferiour conditions, so void of pity and compassion, cannot chuse but think amisse both of God, the King, and . . . the Christians; and to labour to persuade them to the contrary, is a vain and fruitlesse labour, and whereby a greater advantage is given them to laugh at Christ and his Law. And as for the *Indians* that take armes to defend themselves they think it better to die once, then to fall into the hands of their enemies, and to be afflicted with many deaths. These things, most invincible *Cæsar*, I have learnt by experience. He addes further, Your Majesty hath in these Countreys more friends and servants then you are aware of; for there is no souldier of all those that serve in these parts, who does not publickly and openly professe, whether he rob, steal, kill or burn the subjects of your Majesty, for the obtaining of gold, but that he does it to do your Majesty service. Wherefore most invincible *Cæsar* it would be requisite, that you should signifie by the severe correction of some, how displeased you were with such services, whereby they shew themselves so disobedient and refractory to God himself. Which words are taken from the writings of the said Bishop of *St. Martha*, out of which it is manifest, what strange things have been committed, and are daily committed by them. They call the *Indians* Warlike, that continually flie to the Mountains to avoid the cruelty of the *Spaniards*, and they call those the *Indians* and Inhabitants of the Countrey, whom they have subjected to the hardship of a perpetual slavery by the terror of their massacres: by which they have been depopulated and wasted, as appears out of the letters of the foresaid

Bishop, who recites but a very few of those things that were committed. The *Indians* of these Regions us'd to break forth into these expressions, when they are forc'd naked through the craggie passages of the mountains, if at any time they chanced to faint with weariness (for then they are constantly beaten with canes, sometimes their teeth knockt out with the hilts of their swords, to make them rise and proceed on in their journeys without any rest) then were they wont I say to break forth into these expressions, Oh how envious art thou! I faint, kill me, and put an end to my daies: this they sigh forth, scarcly able to draw out their words, the certain signs of an inward anguish and deep distresse; but who can comprehend in words the hundredth part of these calamities and afflictions wherewith the *Spaniards* do torment the poor *Indians*; God of his mercy bring them to the knowledge of those who are able to remedy and prevent them for the future.

72

Francisco de Vitoria

from *De Indis et de Ivre Belli Reflectiones*

Shortly after Christopher Columbus' 1492 encounter with the Indigenous peoples of the Americas, legal and theological debates erupted in Europe over the rights of those peoples to their traditional lands. To the point: could Spanish colonizers rightly claim the land and enslave the peoples? Some scholars affirmed colonization and enslavement on the grounds that non-Christian peoples lacked the right to autonomy and land ownership. Moreover, on this view, Christian conquistadors could forcibly take the land according to just war principles. Francisco de Vitoria (ca. 1486–1546) offered a robust legal and theological rebuttal in defense of Indigenous rights. Drawing upon a range of Western and biblical sources, Vitoria here sets out the two sides, and then offers his claims for the American Indians' rights. He concludes his argument with a lengthy explanation of the just war theory, thereby updating an ancient doctrine for the modern era.

Fourth . . . I ask first whether the aborigines in question were true owners in both private and public law before the arrival of the Spaniards; that is, whether they were true owners of private property and possessions and also whether there were among them any who were the true princes and overlords of others. The answer might seem to be No, the reason being that slaves own no property, "for a slave can have nothing of his own" (*Inst.*, 2, 9, 3, and *Dig.*, 29, 2, 79), and so all his acquisitions belong to his master (*Inst.*, 1, 8, 1). But the aborigines in question are slaves. Therefore the matter is proved; for as Aristotle (*Politics*, bk. I) neatly and correctly says, "Some are by nature slaves,

SOURCE: Francisco de Vitoria, *De Indis et de Ivre Belli Reflectiones*, ed. Ernest Nys, trans. John Pawley Bate, in no. 7 of *The Classics of International Law*, ed. James Scott Brown (Washington, D.C.: Carnegie Institution of Washington, 1917), 120–23, 146–47, 187.

those, to wit, who are better fitted to serve than to rule." Now these are they who have not sufficient reason to govern even themselves, but only to do what they are bidden, and whose strength lies in their body rather than in their mind. But, of a surety, if there be any such, the aborigines in question are preëminently such, for they really seem little different from brute animals and are utterly incapable of governing, and it is unquestionably better for them to be ruled by others than to rule themselves. Aristotle says it is just and natural for such to be slaves. Therefore they and their like can not be owners. And it is immaterial that before the arrival of the Spaniards they had no other masters; for there is no inconsistency in a slave having no master, as the glossator on *Dig.*, 40, 12, 23, notes. Nay, the statement is expressly made in that passage of the *Digest* and it is the expressed case set out in *Dig.*, 45, 3, 36, pr., where it is said that a slave who has been abandoned by his master and not taken into possession by any one else can be taken into possession by any one. If, then, these were slaves they could be taken into possession by the Spaniards.

On the opposite side we have the fact that the people in question were in peaceable possession of their goods, both publicly and privately. Therefore, unless the contrary is shown, they must be treated as owners and not be disturbed in their possession unless cause be shown. . . .

Fifth. Now, some have maintained that grace is the title to dominion and consequently that sinners, at any rate those in mortal sin, have no dominion over anything. That was the error of the poor folk of Lyons, or Waldenses, and afterwards of John Wycliffe. One error of his, namely, that "no one is a civil owner, while he is in mortal sin," was condemned by the Council of Constance. . . . It is certain, however, that all dominion is by divine authority, for God himself is the creator of everything, and none but they to whom He has given dominion can have it. Now it is not agreeable to reason that He should give it to the disobedient and transgressors of his commandments, just as human princes do not give their property, such as towns and strongholds, to rebels, and if they have given it to them, they confiscate it. But we ought to judge about divine things through the medium of human things (*Romans*, ch. 1). Therefore God does not give dominion to the disobedient. And in token hereof God at times removes such from their exalted position, as in the cases of Saul (I *Sam.*, ch. 15 and 16), and of Nebuchadnezzar and Balthazar (*Daniel*, ch. 4 and 5). Again (*Genesis*, ch. 1), "Let us make man in our own image and likeness that he may have dominion over the fish of the sea," etc. It appears therefore that dominion is founded on the image of God. But the sinner displays no such image. Therefore he has no dominion. Further, such a one commits the crime of treason. Therefore he deserves to lose his dominion.

Likewise, St. Augustine says that the sinner is not worthy of the bread he eats. Also, the Lord had given our first parents dominion over paradise and then deprived them of it because of their sin (*Genesis*, ch. 1). . . .

Sixth. But against this doctrine I advance the proposition that mortal sin does not hinder civil dominion and true dominion. . . . If a sinner has not civil dominion (which is what they seem to be speaking of), he, therefore, has not natural dominion; but the consequent is untrue; therefore, etc. I prove the consequence; for natural dominion is a gift of God, just as civil dominion is, nay, more so, for civil dominion seems an institute of human law. Therefore, if for an offense against God a man loses civil dominion, he would for the same reason lose his natural dominion also. But the falsity of the consequent is demonstrated by the fact that the man in question does not lose dominion over his own acts and over his own limbs, for a sinner has a right to defend his own life.

[. . . .]

In the same way that God makes His sun to rise on the good and on the bad and sends His rain on the just and on the unjust, so also He has given temporal goods alike to good and to bad. Nor is this subject discussed, because it is in doubt, but in order that from one crime, to wit, from this insensate heresy, we may learn the character of all heretics.

[. . . .]

Christian princes cannot, even by the authorization of the Pope, restrain the Indians from sins against the law of nature or punish them because of those sins. My first proof is that the writers in question build on a false hypothesis, namely, that the Pope has jurisdiction over the Indian aborigines, as said above. My second proof is as follows: They mean to justify such coercion either universally for sins against the law of nature, such as theft, fornication, and adultery, or particularly for sins against nature, such as those which St. Thomas deals with (*Secunda Secundae*, qu. 154, arts. 11, 12), the phrase "sin against nature" being employed not only of what is contrary to the law of nature, but also of what is against the natural order and is called uncleanness in II *Corinthians*, ch. 12, according to the commentators, such as intercourse with boys and with animals or intercourse of woman with woman, whereon see *Romans*, ch. 1. Now, if they limit themselves to the second meaning, they are open to the argument that homicide is just as grave a sin, and even a graver sin, and, therefore, it is clear that, if it is lawful in the case of the sins of the kind named, therefore it is lawful also in the case of homicide. Similarly, blasphemy is a sin as grave and so the same is clear; therefore. If, however, they are to be understood in the first sense, that is, as speaking of all sin against the law of nature, the argument against them is that the coercion in question is not lawful for fornication; therefore not for the other sins which are contrary to the law of nature. The antecedent is clear from I *Corinthians*, ch. 5: "I wrote to you in an epistle not to company with fornicators," and besides "If any brother among you is called a fornicator or an idolater," etc.; and lower down: "For what have I to do to judge them also that are without?" Whereon St. Thomas says: "The prelates have received power over those only who have submitted themselves to the faith." Hence it clearly appears that St. Paul declares it not his business to pronounce judgment on unbelievers and fornicators and idolaters. So also it is not every sin against the law of nature that can be clearly shown to be such, at any rate to every one. Further, this is as much as to say that the aborigines may be warred into subjection because of their unbelief, for they are all idolaters. Further, the Pope can not make war on Christians on the ground of their being fornicators or thieves or, indeed, because they are sodomites; nor can he on that ground confiscate their land and give it to other princes; were that so, there would be daily changes of kingdoms, seeing that there are many sinners in every realm. And this is confirmed by the consideration that these sins are more heinous in Christians, who are aware that they are sins, than in barbarians, who have not that knowledge. Further, it would be a strange thing that the Pope, who can not make laws for unbelievers, can yet sit in judgment and visit punishment upon them.

A further and convincing proof is the following: The aborigines in question are either bound to submit to the punishment awarded to the sins in question or they are not. If they are not bound, then the Pope can not award such punishment. If they are bound, then they are bound to recognize the Pope as lord and lawgiver. Therefore, if they refuse such recognition, this in itself furnishes a ground for making war on them, which, however, the writers in question deny, as said above. And it would indeed be strange that the barbarians could with impunity deny the authority and jurisdiction of the Pope, and yet that they should be bound to submit to his award. Further, they who are not Christians can not be subjected to the judgment of the Pope, for the Pope has no other right to condemn or punish them than as vicar of Christ. But, the writers in question admit—both Innocent and Augustinus of Ancona, and the Archbishop and Sylvester, too—that they can not be punished because they do not receive Christ. Therefore not because they do not receive the judgment of the Pope, for the latter presupposes the former.

[. . . .]

All this can be summarized in a few canons or rules of warfare. First canon: Assuming that a prince has authority to make war, he should first of all not go seeking occasions and causes of war, but should, if possible, live in peace with all men, as St. Paul enjoins on us (*Romans*, ch. 12). Moreover, he should reflect that others are his neighbors, whom we are bound to love as ourselves, and that we all have one common Lord, before whose tribunal we shall have to render our account. For it is the extreme of savagery to seek for and rejoice in grounds for killing and destroying men whom God has created and for whom Christ died. But only under compulsion and reluctantly should he come to the necessity of war.

Second canon: When war for a just cause has broken out, it must not be waged so as to ruin the people against whom it is directed, but only so as to obtain one's rights and the defense of one's country and in order that from that war peace and security may in time result.

Third canon: When victory has been won and the war is over, the victory should be utilized with moderation and Christian humility, and the victor ought to deem that he is sitting as judge between two States, the one which has been wronged and the one which has done the wrong, so that it will be as judge and not as accuser that he will deliver the judgment whereby the injured state can obtain satisfaction, and this, so far as possible should involve the offending state in the least degree of calamity and misfortune, the offending individuals being chastised within lawful limits; and an especial reason for this is that in general among Christians all the fault is to be laid at the door of their princes, for subjects when fighting for their princes act in good faith and it is thoroughly unjust, in the words of the poet, that—

> *Quidquid delirant reges, plectantur Achivi*
> (For every folly their Kings commit the punishment should fall upon
>   the Greeks.)

73

Desiderius Erasmus

from *In Praise of Folly*

Desiderius Erasmus of Rotterdam (ca. 1466–1536) was a Dutch philologist, classicist, theologian, controversialist, and Christian humanist who played an influential role in the northern European Renaissance. He is well known for his translated Greek/Latin edition of the New Testament, but he is perhaps most famous for his scathing reflections on society and on the abuses and excesses within the Roman Catholic Church put forth in his work *In Praise of Folly*, from which the following is an excerpt. Some have assumed that Erasmus' critiques of the Church were at least part of what inspired Martin Luther's eventual Reformation, though it is clear that the two did not see eye to eye on many fronts, as evidenced by their disputes in personal correspondence, as well as in their published works. Erasmus never joined the Protestant movement.

And now for some reflections upon popes, cardinals, and bishops, who in pomp and splendour have almost equalled if not outgone secular princes. Now if any one consider that their upper crotchet of white linen is to signify their unspotted purity and innocence; that their forked mitres, with both divisions tied together by the same knot, are to denote the joint knowledge of the Old and New Testament; that their always wearing gloves, represents their keeping their hands clean and undefiled from lucre and covetousness; that the pastoral staff implies the care of a flock committed to their charge; that the cross carried before them expresses their victory over all carnal affections; he (I say) that considers this, and much more of the like nature, must needs conclude they are entrusted with a very weighty and difficult office. But alas, they

SOURCE: Erasmus, *In Praise of Folly, Illustrated with Many Curious Cuts, Designed, Drawn, and Etched by Hans Holbein, with Portrait, Life of Erasmus, and His Epistle Addressed to Sir Thomas More*, trans. White Kennett (London: Reeves & Turner, 1876), 154–64.

think it sufficient if they can but feed themselves; and as to their flock, either commend them to the care of Christ himself, or commit them to the guidance of some inferior vicars and curates; not so much as remembering what their name of bishop imports, to wit, labour, pains, and diligence, but by base simoniacal contracts, they are in a profane sense *Episcopi, i.e.,* overseers of their own gain and income.

So cardinals, in like manner, if they did but consider that the church supposes them to succeed in the room of the apostles; that therefore they must behave themselves as their predecessors, and so not be lords, but dispensers of spiritual gifts, of the disposal whereof they must one day render a strict account: or if they would but reflect a little on their habit, and thus reason with themselves, what means this white upper garment, but only an unspotted innocence? What signifies my inner purple, but only an ardent love and zeal to God? What imports my outermost pall, so wide and long that it covers the whole mule when I ride, nay, should be big enough to cover a camel, but only a diffusive charity, that should spread itself for a succour and protection to all, by teaching, exhorting, comforting, reproving, admonishing, composing of differences, courageously withstanding wicked princes, and sacrificing for the safety of our flock our life and blood, as well as our wealth and riches; though indeed riches ought not to be at all possessed by such as boast themselves successors to the apostles, who were poor, needy, and destitute: I say, if they did but lay these considerations to heart they would never be so ambitious of being created to this honour, they would willingly resign it when conferred upon them, or at least would be as industrious, watchful and laborious, as the primitive apostles were.

Now as to the popes of Rome, who pretend themselves Christ's vicars, if they would but imitate his exemplary life, in the being employed in an unintermitted course of preaching; in the being attended with poverty, nakedness, hunger, and a contempt of this world; if they did but consider the import of the word pope, which signifies a father; or if they did but practice their surname of most holy, what order or degrees of men would be in a worse condition? There would be then no such vigorous making of parties, and buying of votes, in the conclave upon a vacancy of that see: and those who by bribery, or other indirect courses, should get themselves elected, would never secure their sitting firm in the chair by pistol, poison, force, and violence. How much of their pleasure would be abated if they were but endowed with one dram of wisdom? Wisdom, did I say? Nay, with one grain of that salt which our Saviour bid them not lose the savour of. All their riches, all their honour, their jurisdictions, their Peter's patrimony, their offices, their dispensations, their licences, their indulgences, their long train and attendants (see in how short a compass I have abbreviated all their marketing of religion); in a word, all their perquisites would be forfeited and lost; and in their room would succeed watchings, fastings, tears, prayers, sermons, hard studies, repenting sighs, and a thousand such like severe penalties: nay, what's yet more deplorable, it would then follow, that all their clerks, amanuenses, notaries, advocates, proctors, secretaries, the offices of grooms, ostlers, serving-men, pimps (and somewhat else, which for modesty's sake I shall not mention); in short, all these troops of attendants, which depend on his holiness, would all lose their several employments. This indeed would be hard, but what yet remains would be more dreadful: the very Head of the Church, the spiritual prince, would then be brought from all his splendour to the poor equipage of a scrip and staff. But all this is upon the supposition only that they understood what circumstances they are placed in; whereas now, by a wholesome neglect of thinking, they live as well as heart can wish: whatever of toil and drudgery belongs to their office that they assign over to St. Peter, or St. Paul, who have time enough to mind it; but if there be any thing of pleasure and grandeur, that they assume to themselves, as being hereunto called: so that by my influence no sort of people live more to their own ease and content. They think to satisfy that Master they pretend to serve, our Lord and Saviour, with their great state and magnificence, with the ceremonies of instalments, with the titles of reverence and holiness, and with exercising their episcopal function only in blessing and cursing. The working of miracles is old and out-dated; to teach the people is too laborious; to interpret scripture is to invade the prerogative of the schoolmen; to pray is too idle; to shed tears is cowardly and unmanly; to fast is too mean and sordid; to be easy and familiar is beneath the grandeur of him, who, without being sued to and intreated, will scarce give princes the honour of kissing his toe; finally, to die for religion is too self-denying; and to be crucified as their Lord of Life, is base and ignominious. Their only weapons ought to be those of the Spirit; and of these indeed they are mighty liberal, as of their interdicts, their suspensions, their denunciations, their aggravations, their greater and lesser excommunications, and their roaring bulls, that fright whomever they are thundered against; and these most holy fathers never issue them out more frequently than against those, who, at the instigation of the devil, and not having the fear of God before their eyes, do feloniously and maliciously attempt to lessen and impair St. Peter's patrimony: and though that apostle tells our Saviour in the gospel, in the name of all the other disciples, we have left all, and followed you, yet they challenge as his inheritance, fields, towns, treasures, and large dominions; for the defending whereof, inflamed with a holy zeal, they fight with fire and sword, to the great loss and effusion of Christian blood, thinking they are apostolical maintainers of Christ's spouse, the church, when they have murdered all such as they call her enemies; though indeed the church has no enemies more bloody and tyrannical than such impious popes, who give dispensations for the not preaching of Christ; evacuate the main effect and design of our redemption by their pecuniary bribes and sales; adulterate the gospel by their forced interpretations, and undermining traditions; and lastly, by their lusts and wickedness grieve the Holy Spirit, and make their Saviour's wounds to bleed anew. Farther, when the Christian church has been all along first planted, then confirmed, and since established by the blood of her martyrs, as if Christ her head would be wanting in the same methods still of protecting her, they invert the order, and propagate their religion now by arms and violence, which was wont formerly to be done only with patience and sufferings. And though war be so brutish, as that it becomes beasts rather than men; so extravagant, that the poets feigned it an effect of the furies; so licentious, that it stops the course of all justice and honesty, so desperate, that it is best waged by ruffians and banditti, and so unchristian, that it is contrary to the express commands of the gospel; yet maugre all this, peace is too quiet, too inactive, and they must be engaged in the boisterousness of war. Among which undertaking popes, you shall have some so old that they can scarce creep, and yet they will put on a young, brisk resolution, will resolve to stick at no pains, to spare no cost, nor to waive any inconvenience, so they may involve laws, religion, peace, and all other concerns, whether sacred or civil, in unappeasable tumults and distractions. And yet some of their learned fawning courtiers will interpret this notorious madness for zeal, and piety, and fortitude, having found out the way how a man may draw his sword, and sheathe it in his brother's bowels, and yet not offend against the duty of the second table, whereby we are obliged to love our neighbours as ourselves. It is yet uncertain whether these Romish fathers have taken example from, or given precedent to, such other German bishops, who omitting their ecclesiastical habit, and other ceremonies, appear openly armed cap-a-pie, like so many champions and warriors, thinking no doubt that they come short of the duty of their function, if they die in any other place than the open field, fighting the battles of the Lord. The inferior clergy, deeming it unmannerly not to conform to their patrons and diocesans, devoutly tug and fight for their tithes with syllogisms and arguments, as fiercely as with swords, sticks, stones, or anything that came next to hand. When they read the rabbies, fathers, or other ancient writings, how quick-sighted are they in spying out any sentences, that they may frighten the people with, and make them believe that more than the tenth is due, passing by whatever they meet with in the same authors that minds them of the duty and difficulty of their own office. They never consider that their shaven crown is a token that they should pare off and cut away all the superfluous lusts of this world, and give themselves wholly to divine meditation; but instead of this, our bald-pated priests think they have done enough, if they do but mumble over such a fardel of prayers; which it is a wonder if God should hear or understand, when they whisper them so softly, and in so unknown a language, which they can scarce hear or understand themselves. This they have in common with other mechanics, that they are most subtle in the craft of getting money, and wonderfully skilled in their respective dues of tithes, offerings, perquisites, &c. Thus they are all content to reap the profit, but as to the burden, that they toss as a ball from one hand to another, and assign it over to any they can get or hire: for as secular princes have their judges and subordinate ministers to act in their name, and supply their stead; so ecclesiastical governors have their deputies, vicars, and curates, nay, many times turn over the whole care of religion to the laity. The laity, supposing they have nothing to do with the church (as if their baptismal vow did not initiate them members of it), make it over to the priests; of the priests again, those that are secular, thinking their title implies them to be a little too profane, assign this task over to the regulars, the regulars to the monks, the monks bandy it from one order to another, till it light upon the mendicants; they lay it upon the carthusians, which order alone keeps honesty and piety among them, but really keep them so close that no body ever yet could see them. Thus the Popes thrusting only their sickle into the harvest of profit, leave all the other toil of spiritual husbandry to the bishops, the bishops bestow it upon the pastors, the pastors on their curates, and the curates commit it to the mendicants, who return it again to such as well know how to make good advantage of the flock, by the benefit of their fleece.

74

Ignatius of Loyola

from *Spiritual Exercises*

A career military man, Ignatius of Loyola (1491–1556) was severely wounded in the 1521 Battle of Pamplona (Spain). During his prolonged convalescence, he read biographies of Christ and the saints, which prompted the redirection of his life. The next year he traveled to the monastery at Montserrat (near Barcelona) for a vigil before the Black Madonna. There, he would leave his sword and formally end his military career. Embarking on an extended retreat at Manresa, Loyola began composing his most famous work, *Spiritual Exercises*, and envisioning a new religious order within the Catholic Church. Organized along military lines, the Society of Jesus (the Jesuits) would have worldwide influence in missions and education. These eighteen rules capture something of the Jesuit charism.

TO HAVE THE TRUE SENTIMENT WHICH WE OUGHT TO HAVE
IN THE CHURCH MILITANT

Let the following Rules be observed.

First Rule. The first: All judgment laid aside, we ought to have our mind ready and prompt to obey, in all, the true Spouse of Christ our Lord, which is our holy Mother the Church Hierarchical.

Second Rule. The second: To praise confession to a Priest, and the reception of the most Holy Sacrament of the Altar once in the year, and much more each month, and much better from week to week, with the conditions required and due.

Third Rule. The third: To praise the hearing of Mass often, likewise hymns, psalms, and long prayers, in the church and out of it; likewise the hours set at the time fixed for each Divine Office and for all prayer and all Canonical Hours.

SOURCE: Ignatius of Loyola, *The Spiritual Exercises of St. Ignatius of Loyola*, trans. Fr. Elder Mullan, SJ (New York: P. J. Kenedy and Sons, 1914), 189–94.

Fourth Rule. The fourth: To praise much Religious Orders, virginity and continence, and not so much marriage as any of these.

Fifth Rule. The fifth: To praise vows of Religion, of obedience, of poverty, of chastity and of other perfections of supererogation. And it is to be noted that as the vow is about the things which approach to Evangelical perfection, a vow ought not to be made in the things which withdraw from it, such as to be a merchant, or to be married, etc.

Sixth Rule. To praise relics of the Saints, giving veneration to them and praying to the Saints; and to praise Stations, pilgrimages, Indulgences, pardons, Cruzadas, and candles lighted in the churches.

Seventh Rule. To praise Constitutions about fasts and abstinence, as of Lent, Ember Days, Vigils, Friday and Saturday; likewise penances, not only interior, but also exterior.

Eighth Rule. To praise the ornaments and the buildings of churches; likewise images, and to venerate them according to what they represent.

Ninth Rule. Finally, to praise all precepts of the Church, keeping the mind prompt to find reasons in their defence and in no manner against them.

Tenth Rule. We ought to be more prompt to find good and praise as well the Constitutions and recommendations as the ways of our Superiors. Because, although some are not or have not been such, to speak against them, whether preaching in public or discoursing before the common people, would rather give rise to fault-finding and scandal than profit; and so the people would be incensed against their Superiors, whether temporal or spiritual. So that, as it does harm to speak evil to the common people of Superiors in their absence, so it can make profit to speak of the evil ways to the persons themselves who can remedy them.

Eleventh Rule. To praise positive and scholastic learning. Because, as it is more proper to the Positive Doctors, as St. Jerome, St. Augustine and St. Gregory, etc., to move the heart to love and serve God our Lord in everything; so it is more proper to the Scholastics, as St. Thomas, St. Bonaventure, and to the Master of the Sentences, etc., to define or explain for our times the things necessary for eternal salvation; and to combat and explain better all errors and all fallacies. For the Scholastic Doctors, as they are more modern, not only help themselves with the true understanding of the Sacred Scripture and of the Positive and holy Doctors, but also, they being enlightened and clarified by the Divine virtue, help themselves by the Councils, Canons and Constitutions of our holy Mother the Church.

Twelfth Rule. We ought to be on our guard in making comparison of those of us who are alive to the blessed passed away, because error is committed not a little in this; that is to say, in saying, this one knows more than St. Augustine; he is another, or greater than, St. Francis; he is another St. Paul in goodness, holiness, etc.

Thirteenth Rule. To be right in everything, we ought always to hold that the white which I see, is black, if the Hierarchical Church so decides it, believing that between Christ our Lord, the Bridegroom, and the Church, His Bride, there is the same Spirit which governs and directs us for the salvation of our souls. Because by the same Spirit and our Lord Who gave the ten Commandments, our holy Mother the Church is directed and governed.

Fourteenth Rule. Although there is much truth in the assertion that no one can save himself without being predestined and without having faith and grace; we must be very cautious in the manner of speaking and communicating with others about all these things.

Fifteenth Rule. We ought not, by way of custom, to speak much of predestination; but if in some way and at some times one speaks, let him so speak that the common people may not come into any error, as sometimes happens, saying: Whether I have to be saved or condemned is already determined, and no other thing can now be, through my doing well or ill; and with this, growing lazy, they become negligent in the works which lead to the salvation and the spiritual profit of their souls.

Sixteenth Rule. In the same way, we must be on our guard that by talking much and with much insistence of faith, without any distinction and explanation, occasion be not given to the people to be lazy and slothful in works, whether before faith is formed in charity or after.

Seventeenth Rule. Likewise, we ought not to speak so much with insistence on grace that the poison of discarding liberty be engendered.

So that of faith and grace one can speak as much as is possible with the Divine help for the greater praise of His Divine Majesty, but not in such way, nor in such manners, especially in our so dangerous times, that works and free will receive any harm, or be held for nothing.

Eighteenth Rule. Although serving God our Lord much out of pure love is to be esteemed above all; we ought to praise much the fear of His Divine Majesty, because not only filial fear is a thing pious and most holy, but even servile fear—when the man reaches nothing else better or more useful—helps much to get out of mortal sin. And when he is out, he easily comes to filial fear, which is all acceptable and grateful to God our Lord, as being at one with the Divine Love.

75

Martin Luther

Ninety-Five Theses

Although the young Martin Luther (1483–1546) seemed destined for the practice of law, after a dramatic conversion experience in 1505, he became an ordained priest two years later. Having joined the faculty at the University of Wittenberg, and while teaching on the New Testament's Epistle to the Romans, Luther questioned how sinners might find right standing before God. Ultimately, he found the answer in the doctrine of justification by faith. Consequently, he began challenging such penitential systems as the indulgences. In October 1517, he drafted his famous ninety-five theses—points for dialogue and debate—centered on those prevailing systems. Those theses found surprising resonance with a wide audience. During a 1519 debate with Johann Eck, Luther publicly sided with executed heretic Jan Hus. Shortly thereafter, Pope Leo X excommunicated Luther in 1521. The Protestant Reformation is generally dated to Luther's actions.

Disputation of Doctor Martin Luther on the Power and Efficacy of Indulgences

October 31, 1517

Out of love for the truth and the desire to bring it to light, the following propositions will be discussed at Wittenberg, under the presidency of the Reverend Father Martin Luther, Master of Arts and of Sacred Theology, and Lecturer in Ordinary on the same at that place. Wherefore he requests that those who are unable to be present and debate orally with us, may do so by letter.

In the Name our Lord Jesus Christ. Amen.

SOURCE: Martin Luther, "A Disputation on the Power and Efficacy of Indulgences," trans. C. M. Jacobs, in *Works of Martin Luther*, vol. 1 (Philadelphia: A. J. Holman and General Council Publication Board, 1915), 29–38.

375

1. Our Lord and Master Jesus Christ, when He said *Poenitentiam agite* [repent or do penance], willed that the whole life of believers should be repentance.

2. This word cannot be understood to mean sacramental penance, i.e., confession and satisfaction, which is administered by the priests.

3. Yet it means not inward repentance only; nay, there is no inward repentance which does not outwardly work divers mortifications of the flesh.

4. The penalty [of sin], therefore, continues so long as hatred of self continues; for this is the true inward repentance, and continues until our entrance into the kingdom of heaven.

5. The pope does not intend to remit, and cannot remit any penalties other than those which he has imposed either by his own authority or by that of the Canons.

6. The pope cannot remit any guilt, except by declaring that it has been remitted by God and by assenting to God's remission; though, to be sure, he may grant remission in cases reserved to his judgment. If his right to grant remission in such cases were despised, the guilt would remain entirely unforgiven.

7. God remits guilt to no one whom He does not, at the same time, humble in all things and bring into subjection to His vicar, the priest.

8. The penitential canons are imposed only on the living, and, according to them, nothing should be imposed on the dying.

9. Therefore the Holy Spirit in the pope is kind to us, because in his decrees he always makes exception of the article of death and of necessity.

10. Ignorant and wicked are the doings of those priests who, in the case of the dying, reserve canonical penances for purgatory.

11. This changing of the canonical penalty to the penalty of purgatory is quite evidently one of the tares that were sown while the bishops slept.

12. In former times the canonical penalties were imposed not after, but before absolution, as tests of true contrition.

13. The dying are freed by death from all penalties; they are already dead to canonical rules, and have a right to be released from them.

14. The imperfect health [of soul], that is to say, the imperfect love, of the dying brings with it, of necessity, great fear; and the smaller the love, the greater is the fear.

15. This fear and horror is sufficient of itself alone (to say nothing of other things) to constitute the penalty of purgatory, since it is very near to the horror of despair.

16. Hell, purgatory, and heaven seem to differ as do despair, almost-despair, and the assurance of safety.

17. With souls in purgatory it seems necessary that horror should grow less and love increase.

18. It seems unproved, either by reason or Scripture, that they are outside the state of merit, that is to say, of increasing love.

19. Again, it seems unproved that they, or at least that all of them, are certain or assured of their own blessedness, though we may be quite certain of it.

20. Therefore by "full remission of all penalties" the pope means not actually "of all," but only of those imposed by himself.

21. Therefore those preachers of indulgences are in error, who say that by the pope's indulgences a man is freed from every penalty, and saved;

22. Whereas he remits to souls in purgatory no penalty which, according to the canons, they would have had to pay in this life.

23. If it is at all possible to grant to any one the remission of all penalties whatsoever, it is certain that this remission can be granted only to the most perfect, that is, to the very fewest.

24. It must needs be, therefore, that the greater part of the people are deceived by that indiscriminate and high-sounding promise of release from penalty.

25. The power which the pope has, in a general way, over purgatory, is just like the power which any bishop or curate has, in a special way, within his own diocese or parish.

26. The pope does well when he grants remission to souls [in purgatory], not by the power of the keys (which he does not possess), but by way of intercession.

27. They preach man who say that so soon as the penny jingles into the money-box, the soul flies out [of purgatory].

28. It is certain that when the penny jingles into the money-box, gain and avarice can be increased, but the result of the intercession of the Church is in the power of God alone.

29. Who knows whether all the souls in purgatory wish to be bought out of it, as in the legend of Sts. Severinus and Paschal.

30. No one is sure that his own contrition is sincere; much less that he has attained full remission.

31. Rare as is the man that is truly penitent, so rare is also the man who truly buys indulgences, i.e., such men are most rare.

32. They will be condemned eternally, together with their teachers, who believe themselves sure of their salvation because they have letters of pardon.

33. Men must be on their guard against those who say that the pope's pardons are that inestimable gift of God by which man is reconciled to Him;

34. For these "graces of pardon" concern only the penalties of sacramental satisfaction, and these are appointed by man.

35. They preach no Christian doctrine who teach that contrition is not necessary in those who intend to buy souls out of purgatory or to buy confessionalia.

36. Every truly repentant Christian has a right to full remission of penalty and guilt, even without letters of pardon.

37. Every true Christian, whether living or dead, has part in all the blessings of Christ and the Church; and this is granted him by God, even without letters of pardon.

38. Nevertheless, the remission and participation [in the blessings of the Church] which are granted by the pope are in no way to be despised, for they are, as I have said, the declaration of divine remission.

39. It is most difficult, even for the very keenest theologians, at one and the same time to commend to the people the abundance of pardons and [the need of] true contrition.

40. True contrition seeks and loves penalties, but liberal pardons only relax penalties and cause them to be hated, or at least, furnish an occasion [for hating them].

41. Apostolic pardons are to be preached with caution, lest the people may falsely think them preferable to other good works of love.

42. Christians are to be taught that the pope does not intend the buying of pardons to be compared in any way to works of mercy.

43. Christians are to be taught that he who gives to the poor or lends to the needy does a better work than buying pardons;

44. Because love grows by works of love, and man becomes better; but by pardons man does not grow better, only more free from penalty.

45. Christians are to be taught that he who sees a man in need, and passes him by, and gives [his money] for pardons, purchases not the indulgences of the pope, but the indignation of God.

46. Christians are to be taught that unless they have more than they need, they are bound to keep back what is necessary for their own families, and by no means to squander it on pardons.

47. Christians are to be taught that the buying of pardons is a matter of free will, and not of commandment.

48. Christians are to be taught that the pope, in granting pardons, needs, and therefore desires, their devout prayer for him more than the money they bring.

49. Christians are to be taught that the pope's pardons are useful, if they do not put their trust in them; but altogether harmful, if through them they lose their fear of God.

50. Christians are to be taught that if the pope knew the exactions of the pardon-preachers, he would rather that St. Peter's church should go to ashes, than that it should be built up with the skin, flesh and bones of his sheep.

51. Christians are to be taught that it would be the pope's wish, as it is his duty, to give of his own money to very many of those from whom certain hawkers of pardons cajole money, even though the church of St. Peter might have to be sold.

52. The assurance of salvation by letters of pardon is vain, even though the commissary, nay, even though the pope himself, were to stake his soul upon it.

53. They are enemies of Christ and of the pope, who bid the Word of God be altogether silent in some Churches, in order that pardons may be preached in others.

54. Injury is done the Word of God when, in the same sermon, an equal or a longer time is spent on pardons than on this Word.

55. It must be the intention of the pope that if pardons, which are a very small thing, are celebrated with one bell, with single processions and ceremonies, then the Gospel, which is the very greatest thing, should be preached with a hundred bells, a hundred processions, a hundred ceremonies.

56. The "treasures of the Church," out of which the pope grants indulgences, are not sufficiently named or known among the people of Christ.

57. That they are not temporal treasures is certainly evident, for many of the vendors do not pour out such treasures so easily, but only gather them.

58. Nor are they the merits of Christ and the Saints, for even without the pope, these always work grace for the inner man, and the cross, death, and hell for the outward man.

59. St. Lawrence said that the treasures of the Church were the Church's poor, but he spoke according to the usage of the word in his own time.

60. Without rashness we say that the keys of the Church, given by Christ's merit, are that treasure;

61. For it is clear that for the remission of penalties and of reserved cases, the power of the pope is of itself sufficient.

62. The true treasure of the Church is the Most Holy Gospel of the glory and the grace of God.

63. But this treasure is naturally most odious, for it makes the first to be last.

64. On the other hand, the treasure of indulgences is naturally most acceptable, for it makes the last to be first.

65. Therefore the treasures of the Gospel are nets with which they formerly were wont to fish for men of riches.

66. The treasures of the indulgences are nets with which they now fish for the riches of men.

67. The indulgences which the preachers cry as the "greatest graces" are known to be truly such, in so far as they promote gain.

68. Yet they are in truth the very smallest graces compared with the grace of God and the piety of the Cross.

69. Bishops and curates are bound to admit the commissaries of apostolic pardons, with all reverence.

70. But still more are they bound to strain all their eyes and attend with all their ears, lest these men preach their own dreams instead of the commission of the pope.

71. He who speaks against the truth of apostolic pardons, let him be anathema and accursed!

72. But he who guards against the lust and license of the pardon-preachers, let him be blessed!

73. The pope justly thunders against those who, by any art, contrive the injury of the traffic in pardons.

74. But much more does he intend to thunder against those who use the pretext of pardons to contrive the injury of holy love and truth.

75. To think the papal pardons so great that they could absolve a man even if he had committed an impossible sin and violated the Mother of God—this is madness.

76. We say, on the contrary, that the papal pardons are not able to remove the very least of venial sins, so far as its guilt is concerned.

77. It is said that even St. Peter, if he were now Pope, could not bestow greater graces; this is blasphemy against St. Peter and against the pope.

78. We say, on the contrary, that even the present pope, and any pope at all, has greater graces at his disposal; to wit, the Gospel, powers, gifts of healing, etc., as it is written in I. Corinthians xii.

79. To say that the cross, emblazoned with the papal arms, which is set up [by the preachers of indulgences], is of equal worth with the Cross of Christ, is blasphemy.

80. The bishops, curates and theologians who allow such talk to be spread among the people, will have an account to render.

81. This unbridled preaching of pardons makes it no easy matter, even for learned men, to rescue the reverence due to the pope from slander, or even from the shrewd questionings of the laity.

82. To wit:—"Why does not the pope empty purgatory, for the sake of holy love and of the dire need of the souls that are there, if he redeems an infinite number of souls for the sake of miserable money with which to build a Church? The former reasons would be most just; the latter is most trivial."

83. Again:—"Why are mortuary and anniversary masses for the dead continued, and why does he not return or permit the withdrawal of the endowments founded on their behalf, since it is wrong to pray for the redeemed?"

84. Again:—"What is this new piety of God and the pope, that for money they allow a man who is impious and their enemy to buy out of purgatory the pious soul of a friend of God, and do not rather, because of that pious and beloved soul's own need, free it for pure love's sake?"

85. Again:—"Why are the penitential canons long since in actual fact and through disuse abrogated and dead, now satisfied by the granting of indulgences, as though they were still alive and in force?"

86. Again:—"Why does not the pope, whose wealth is to-day greater than the riches of the richest, build just this one church of St. Peter with his own money, rather than with the money of poor believers?"

87. Again:—"What is it that the pope remits, and what participation does he grant to those who, by perfect contrition, have a right to full remission and participation?"

88. Again:—"What greater blessing could come to the Church than if the pope were to do a hundred times a day what he now does once, and bestow on every believer these remissions and participations?"

89. "Since the pope, by his pardons, seeks the salvation of souls rather than money, why does he suspend the indulgences and pardons granted heretofore, since these have equal efficacy?"

90. To repress these arguments and scruples of the laity by force alone, and not to resolve them by giving reasons, is to expose the Church and the pope to the ridicule of their enemies, and to make Christians unhappy.

91. If, therefore, pardons were preached according to the spirit and mind of the pope, all these doubts would be readily resolved; nay, they would not exist.

92. Away, then, with all those prophets who say to the people of Christ, "Peace, peace," and there is no peace!

93. Blessed be all those prophets who say to the people of Christ, "Cross, cross," and there is no cross!

94. Christians are to be exhorted that they be diligent in following Christ, their Head, through penalties, deaths, and hell;

95. And thus be confident of entering into heaven rather through many tribulations, than through the assurance of peace.

76

John Calvin

from *Institutes of the Christian Religion*

Together with Martin Luther, John Calvin (1509–1564) is perhaps the most prominent and widely influential thinker of the early Protestant Reformation. A French lawyer, apologist, theologian, and pastor, who wielded immense political power in the city of Geneva, where his congregation was located, he is famous for setting forth the basic systematic principles of Calvinist theology, which include his well-known positions on total depravity, divine sovereignty, and predestination. The following is an excerpt from Calvin's most important theological work, *Institutes of the Christian Religion*, in which he explains the basic framework of his religious epistemology.

Chapter I: The Knowledge of God and of Ourselves Mutually Connected.—Nature of the Connection.

1. Our wisdom, in so far as it ought to be deemed true and solid wisdom, consists almost entirely of two parts: the knowledge of God and of ourselves. But as these are connected together by many ties, it is not easy to determine which of the two precedes, and gives birth to the other. For, in the first place, no man can survey himself without forthwith turning his thoughts towards the God in whom he lives and moves; because it is perfectly obvious, that the endowments which we possess cannot possibly be from ourselves; nay, that our very being is nothing else than subsistence in God alone. In the second place, those blessings which unceasingly distil to us from heaven, are like streams conducting us to the fountain. Here, again, the infinitude of good which resides in God becomes more apparent from our poverty. In particular,

source: John Calvin, *Institutes of the Christian Religion*, trans. Henry Beveridge (Edinburgh: Calvin Translation Society, 1846), 37–68.

the miserable ruin into which the revolt of the first man has plunged us, compels us to turn our eyes upwards; not only that while hungry and famishing we may thence ask what we want, but being aroused by fear may learn humility. For as there exists in man something like a world of misery, and ever since we were stript of the divine attire our naked shame discloses an immense series of disgraceful properties, every man, being stung by the consciousness of his own unhappiness, in this way necessarily obtains at least some knowledge of God. Thus, our feeling of ignorance, vanity, want, weakness, in short, depravity and corruption, reminds us . . . that in the Lord, and none but He, dwell the true light of wisdom, solid virtue, exuberant goodness. We are accordingly urged by our own evil things to consider the good things of God; and, indeed, we cannot aspire to Him in earnest until we have begun to be displeased with ourselves. For what man is not disposed to rest in himself? Who, in fact, does not thus rest, so long as he is unknown to himself; that is, so long as he is contented with his own endowments, and unconscious or unmindful of his misery? Every person, therefore, on coming to the knowledge of himself, is not only urged to seek God, but is also led as by the hand to find him.

2. On the other hand, it is evident that man never attains to a true self-knowledge until he have previously contemplated the face of God, and come down after such contemplation to look into himself. For (such is our innate pride) we always seem to ourselves just, and upright, and wise, and holy, until we are convinced, by clear evidence, of our injustice, vileness, folly, and impurity. Convinced, however, we are not, if we look to ourselves only, and not to the Lord also—He being the only standard by the application of which this conviction can be produced. For, since we are all naturally prone to hypocrisy, any empty semblance of righteousness is quite enough to satisfy us instead of righteousness itself. And since nothing appears within us or around us that is not tainted with very great impurity, so long as we keep our mind within the confines of human pollution, anything which is in some small degree less defiled, delights us as if it were most pure: just as an eye, to which nothing but black had been previously presented, deems an object of a whitish, or even of a brownish hue, to be perfectly white.

[. . . .]

3. Hence that dread and amazement with which, as Scripture uniformly relates, holy men were struck and overwhelmed whenever they beheld the presence of God. When we see those who previously stood firm and secure so quaking with terror, that the fear of death takes hold of them, nay, they are, in a manner, swallowed up and annihilated, the inference to be drawn is, that men are never duly touched and impressed with a conviction of their

insignificance, until they have contrasted themselves with the majesty of God. Frequent examples of this consternation occur both in the Book of Judges and the Prophetical Writings; so much so, that it was a common expression among the people of God, "We shall die, for we have seen the Lord."

[. . . .]

But though the knowledge of God and the knowledge of ourselves are bound together by a mutual tie, due arrangement requires that we treat of the former in the first place, and then descend to the latter.

Chapter II: What It Is to Know God.—Tendency of This Knowledge.

1. By the knowledge of God, I understand that by which we not only conceive that there is some God, but also apprehend what it is for our interest, and conducive to his glory, what, in short, it is befitting to know concerning him. For, properly speaking, we cannot say that God is known where there is no religion or piety. I am not now referring to that species of knowledge by which men, in themselves lost and under curse, apprehend God as a Redeemer in Christ the Mediator. I speak only of that simple and primitive knowledge, to which the mere course of nature would have conducted us, had Adam stood upright. For although no man will now, in the present ruin of the human race, perceive God to be either a father, or the author of salvation, or propitious in any respect, until Christ interpose to make our peace; still it is one thing to perceive that God our Maker supports us by his power, rules us by his providence, fosters us by his goodness, and visits us with all kinds of blessings, and another thing to embrace the grace of reconciliation offered to us in Christ. Since, then, the Lord first appears, as well in the creation of the world as in the general doctrine of Scripture, simply as a Creator, and afterwards as a Redeemer in Christ,—a twofold knowledge of him hence arises: of these the former is now to be considered, the latter will afterwards follow in its order. But although our mind cannot conceive of God, without rendering some worship to him, it will not, however, be sufficient simply to hold that he is the only being whom all ought to worship and adore, unless we are also persuaded that he is the fountain of all goodness, and that we must seek everything in him, and in none but him. My meaning is: we must be persuaded not only that as he once formed the world, so he sustains it by his boundless power, governs it by his wisdom, preserves it by his goodness, in particular, rules the human race with justice and judgment, bears with them in mercy, shields them by his protection; but also that not a particle of light, or wisdom, or justice, or power, or rectitude, or genuine truth, will anywhere be found, which does not flow from

him, and of which he is not the cause; in this way we must learn to expect and ask all things from him, and thankfully ascribe to him whatever we receive. For this sense of the divine perfections is the proper master to teach us piety, out of which religion springs. By piety I mean that union of reverence and love to God which the knowledge of his benefits inspires. For, until men feel that they owe everything to God, that they are cherished by his paternal care, and that he is the author of all their blessings, so that nought is to be looked for away from him, they will never submit to him in voluntary obedience; nay, unless they place their entire happiness in him, they will never yield up their whole selves to him in truth and sincerity.

[2.] Those, therefore, who, in considering this question, propose to inquire what the essence of God is, only delude us with frigid speculations,—it being much more our interest to know what kind of being God is, and what things are agreeable to his nature. For, of what use is it to join Epicurus in acknowledging some God who has cast off the care of the world, and only delights himself in ease? What avails it, in short, to know a God with whom we have nothing to do? The effect of our knowledge rather ought to be, *first*, to teach us reverence and fear; and, *secondly*, to induce us, under its guidance and teaching, to ask every good thing from him, and, when it is received, ascribe it to him. For how can the idea of God enter your mind without instantly giving rise to the thought, that since you are his workmanship, you are bound, by the very law of creation, to submit to his authority?—that your life is due to him?—that whatever you do ought to have reference to him?

[. . . .]

Such is pure and genuine religion, namely, confidence in God coupled with serious fear—fear, which both includes in it willing reverence, and brings along with it such legitimate worship as is prescribed by the law. And it ought to be more carefully considered, that all men promiscuously do homage to God, but very few truly reverence him. On all hands there is abundance of ostentatious ceremonies, but sincerity of heart is rare.

Chapter III: The Knowledge of God Naturally Implanted in the Human Mind.

1. That there exists in the human mind, and indeed by natural instinct, some sense of Deity, we hold to be beyond dispute, since God himself, to prevent any man from pretending ignorance, has endued all men with some idea of his Godhead, the memory of which he constantly renews and occasionally enlarges, that all to a man, being aware that there is a God, and that he is their Maker, may be condemned by their own conscience when they neither

worship him nor consecrate their lives to his service. Certainly, if there is any quarter where it may be supposed that God is unknown, the most likely for such an instance to exist is among the dullest tribes farthest removed from civilisation. But, as a heathen tells us, there is no nation so barbarous, no race so brutish, as not to be imbued with the conviction that there is a God. Even those who, in other respects, seem to differ least from the lower animals, constantly retain some sense of religion; so thoroughly has this common conviction possessed the mind, so firmly is it stamped on the breasts of all men. Since, then, there never has been, from the very first, any quarter of the globe, any city, any household even, without religion, this amounts to a tacit confession, that a sense of Deity is inscribed on every heart. Nay, even idolatry is ample evidence of this fact. For we know how reluctant man is to lower himself, in order to set other creatures above him. Therefore, when he chooses to worship wood and stone rather than be thought to have no God, it is evident how very strong this impression of a Deity must be; since it is more difficult to obliterate it from the mind of man, than to break down the feelings of his nature,—these certainly being broken down, when, in opposition to his natural haughtiness, he spontaneously humbles himself before the meanest object as an act of reverence to God.

2. It is most absurd, therefore, to maintain, as some do, that religion was devised by the cunning and craft of a few individuals, as a means of keeping the body of the people in due subjection, while there was nothing which those very individuals, while teaching others to worship God, less believed than the existence of a God. I readily acknowledge, that designing men have introduced a vast number of fictions into religion, with the view of inspiring the populace with reverence or striking them with terror, and thereby rendering them more obsequious; but they never could have succeeded in this, had the minds of men not been previously imbued with that uniform belief in God, from which, as from its seed, the religious propensity springs. And it is altogether incredible that those who, in the matter of religion, cunningly imposed on their ruder neighbours, were altogether devoid of a knowledge of God. For though in old times there were some, and in the present day not a few are found who deny the being of a God, yet, whether they will or not, they occasionally feel the truth which they are desirous not to know. We do not read of any man who broke out into more unbridled and audacious contempt of the Deity than C. Caligula, and yet none showed greater dread when any indication of divine wrath was manifested. Thus, however unwilling, he shook with terror before the God whom he professedly studied to contemn. You may every day see the same thing happening to his modern imitators. The most audacious despiser

of God is most easily disturbed, trembling at the sound of a falling leaf. How so, unless in vindication of the divine majesty, which smites their consciences the more strongly the more they endeavour to flee from it. They all, indeed, look out for hiding-places, where they may conceal themselves from the presence of the Lord, and again efface it from their mind; but after all their efforts they remain caught within the net. Though the conviction may occasionally seem to vanish for a moment, it immediately returns, and rushes in with new impetuosity, so that any interval of relief from the gnawings of conscience is not unlike the slumber of the intoxicated or the insane, who have no quiet rest in sleep, but are continually haunted with dire horrific dreams. Even the wicked themselves, therefore, are an example of the fact that some idea of God always exists in every human mind.

3. All men of sound judgment will therefore hold, that a sense of Deity is indelibly engraven on the human heart. And that this belief is naturally engendered in all, and thoroughly fixed as it were in our very bones, is strikingly attested by the contumacy of the wicked, who, though they struggle furiously, are unable to extricate themselves from the fear of God. Though Diagoras, and others of like stamp, make themselves merry with whatever has been believed in all ages concerning religion, and Dionysius scoffs at the judgment of heaven, it is but a Sardonian grin; for the worm of conscience, keener than burning steel, is gnawing them within. I do not say with Cicero, that errors wear out by age, and that religion increases and grows better day by day. For the world . . . labours as much as it can to shake off all knowledge of God, and corrupts his worship in innumerable ways. I only say, that, when the stupid hardness of heart, which the wicked eagerly court as a means of despising God, becomes enfeebled, the sense of Deity, which of all things they wished most to be extinguished, is still in vigour, and now and then breaks forth. Whence we infer, that this is not a doctrine which is first learned at school, but one as to which every man is, from the womb, his own master; one which nature herself allows no individual to forget, though many, with all their might, strive to do so. Moreover, if all are born and live for the express purpose of learning to know God, and if the knowledge of God, in so far as it fails to produce this effect, is fleeting and vain, it is clear that all those who do not direct the whole thoughts and actions of their lives to this end fail to fulfil the law of their being. This did not escape the observation even of philosophers. For it is the very thing which Plato meant . . . when he taught, as he often does, that the chief good of the soul consists in resemblance to God; *i.e.*, when, by means of knowing him, she is wholly transformed into him. Thus Gryllus, also, in Plutarch . . . , reasons most skilfully, when he affirms that, if once religion is banished from the lives

of men, they not only in no respect excel, but are, in many respects, much more wretched than the brutes, since, being exposed to so many forms of evil, they continually drag on a troubled and restless existence: that the only thing, therefore, which makes them superior is the worship of God, through which alone they aspire to immortality.

Chapter IV: The Knowledge of God Stifled or Corrupted, Ignorantly or Maliciously.

1. But though experience testifies that a seed of religion is divinely sown in all, scarcely one in a hundred is found who cherishes it in his heart, and not one in whom it grows to maturity, so far is it from yielding fruit in its season. Moreover, while some lose themselves in superstitious observances, and others, of set purpose, wickedly revolt from God, the result is that, in regard to the true knowledge of him, all are so degenerate, that in no part of the world can genuine godliness be found. In saying that some fall away into superstition, I mean not to insinuate that their excessive absurdity frees them from guilt; for the blindness under which they labour is almost invariably accompanied with vain pride and stubbornness. Mingled vanity and pride appear in this, that when miserable men do seek after God, instead of ascending higher than themselves, as they ought to do, they measure him by their own carnal stupidity, and, neglecting solid inquiry, fly off to indulge their curiosity in vain speculation. Hence, they do not conceive of him in the character in which he is manifested, but imagine him to be whatever their own rashness has devised. This abyss standing open, they cannot move one footstep without rushing headlong to destruction. With such an idea of God, nothing which they may attempt to offer in the way of worship or obedience can have any value in his sight, because it is not him they worship, but, instead of him, the dream and figment of their own heart. This corrupt procedure is admirably described by Paul, when he says, that "thinking to be wise, they became fools" (Rom. i. 22). He had previously said that "they became vain in their imaginations," but lest any should suppose them blameless, he afterwards adds, that they were deservedly blinded, because, not contented with sober inquiry, because, arrogating to themselves more than they have any title to do, they of their own accord court darkness, nay, bewitch themselves with perverse, empty show. Hence it is that their folly, the result not only of vain curiosity, but of licentious desire and overweening confidence in the pursuit of forbidden knowledge, cannot be excused.

2. The expression of David (Psalm xiv. 1, liii. 1), "The fool hath said in his heart, There is no God," is primarily applied to those who, as will shortly

farther appear, stifle the light of nature, and intentionally [stupefy] themselves. We see many, after they have become hardened in a daring course of sin, madly banishing all remembrance of God, though spontaneously suggested to them from within, by natural sense. To show how detestable this madness is, the Psalmist introduces them as distinctly denying that there is a God, because, although they do not disown his essence, they rob him of his justice and providence, and represent him as sitting idly in heaven. Nothing being less accordant with the nature of God than to cast off the government of the world, leaving it to chance, and so to wink at the crimes of men that they may wanton with impunity in evil courses; it follows, that every man who indulges in security, after extinguishing all fear of divine judgment, virtually denies that there is a God. As a just punishment of the wicked, after they have closed their own eyes, God makes their hearts dull and heavy, and hence, seeing, they see not. David, indeed, is the best interpreter of his own meaning, when he says elsewhere, the wicked has "no fear of God before his eyes" (Psalm xxxvi. 1); and, again, "He hath said in his heart, God hath forgotten; he hideth his face; he will never see it." Thus, although they are forced to acknowledge that there is some God, they however, rob him of his glory by denying his power. For, as Paul declares, "If we believe not, he abideth faithful, he cannot deny himself" (2 Tim. ii. 13); so those who feign to themselves a dead and dumb idol, are truly said to deny God. It is, moreover, to be observed, that though they struggle with their own convictions, and would fain not only banish God from their minds, but from heaven also, [their] stupefaction is never so complete as to secure them from being occasionally dragged before the divine tribunal. Still, as no fear restrains them from rushing violently in the face of God, so long as they are hurried on by that blind impulse, it cannot be denied that their prevailing state of mind in regard to him is brutish oblivion.

3. In this way, the vain pretext which many employ to clothe their superstition is overthrown. They deem it enough that they have some kind of zeal for religion, how preposterous soever it may be, not observing that true religion must be conformable to the will of God as its unerring standard; that he can never deny himself, and is no spectre or phantom, to be metamorphosed at each individual's caprice. It is easy to see how superstition, with its false glosses, mocks God, while it tries to please him. Usually fastening merely on things on which he has declared he sets no value, it either contemptuously overlooks, or even undisguisedly rejects, the things which he expressly enjoins, or in which we are assured that he takes pleasure. Those, therefore, who set up a fictitious worship, merely worship and adore their own delirious fancies; indeed, they would never dare so to trifle with God, had they not

previously fashioned him after their own childish conceits. Hence that vague and wandering opinion of Deity is declared by an apostle to be ignorance of God: "Howbeit, then, when ye knew not God, ye did service unto them which by nature are no gods." And he elsewhere declares, that the Ephesians were "without God" (Eph. ii. 12) at the time when they wandered without any correct knowledge of him. It makes little difference, at least in this respect, whether you hold the existence of one God, or a plurality of gods, since, in both cases alike, by departing from the true God, you have nothing left but an execrable idol. It remains, therefore, to conclude with Lactantius (*Instit. Div.* lib. i. 2, 6), "No religion is genuine that is not in accordance with truth."

4. To this fault they add a second—viz. that when they do think of God it is against their will; never approaching him without being dragged into his presence, and when there, instead of the voluntary fear flowing from reverence of the divine majesty, feeling only that forced and servile fear which divine judgment extorts—judgment which, from the impossibility of escape, they are compelled to dread, but which, while they dread, they at the same time also hate. To impiety, and to it alone, the saying of Statius properly applies: "Fear first brought gods into the world" (*Theb.* lib. i.). Those whose inclinations are at variance with the justice of God, knowing that his tribunal has been erected for the punishment of transgression, earnestly wish that that tribunal were overthrown. Under the influence of this feeling they are actually warring against God, justice being one of his essential attributes. Perceiving that they are always within reach of his power, that resistance and evasion are alike impossible, they fear and tremble. Accordingly, to avoid the appearance of contemning a majesty by which all are overawed, they have recourse to some species of religious observance, never ceasing meanwhile to defile themselves with every kind of vice, and add crime to crime, until they have broken the holy law of the Lord in every one of its requirements, and set his whole righteousness at nought; . . .

[. . . .]

Chapter VI: The Need of Scripture, as a Guide and Teacher, in Coming to God as a Creator.

1. Therefore, though the effulgence which is presented to every eye, both in the heavens and on the earth, leaves the ingratitude of man without excuse, since God, in order to bring the whole human race under the same condemnation, holds forth to all, without exception, a mirror of his Deity in his works, another and better help must be given to guide us properly to God as a Creator. Not in vain, therefore, has he added the light of his Word in order that

he might make himself known unto salvation, and bestowed the privilege on those whom he was pleased to bring into nearer and more familiar relation to himself. For, seeing how the minds of men were carried to and fro, and found no certain resting-place, he chose the Jews for a peculiar people, and then hedged them in that they might not, like others, go astray. And not in vain does he, by the same means, retain us in his knowledge, since but for this, even those who, in comparison of others, seem to stand strong, would quickly fall away. For as the aged, or those whose sight is defective, when any book, however fair, is set before them, though they perceive that there is something written, are scarcely able to make out two consecutive words, but, when aided by glasses, begin to read distinctly, so Scripture, gathering together the impressions of Deity, which, till then, lay confused in their minds, dissipates the darkness, and shows us the true God clearly. God therefore bestows a gift of singular value, when, for the instruction of the Church, he employs not dumb teachers merely, but opens his own sacred mouth; when he not only proclaims that some God must be worshipped, but at the same time declares that He is the God to whom worship is due; when he not only teaches his elect to have respect to God, but manifests himself as the God to whom this respect should be paid.

The course which God followed towards his Church from the very first, was to supplement these common proofs by the addition of his Word, as a surer and more direct means of discovering himself. And there can be no doubt that it was by this help, Adam, Noah, Abraham, and the other patriarchs, attained to that familiar knowledge which, in a manner, distinguished them from unbelievers. I am not now speaking of the peculiar doctrines of faith by which they were elevated to the hope of eternal blessedness. It was necessary, in passing from death unto life, that they should know God, not only as a Creator, but as a Redeemer also; and both kinds of knowledge they certainly did obtain from the Word. In point of order, however, the knowledge first given was that which made them acquainted with the God by whom the world was made and is governed. To this first knowledge was afterwards added the more intimate knowledge which alone quickens dead souls, and by which God is known, not only as the Creator of the world, and the sole author and disposer of all events, but also as a Redeemer, in the person of the Mediator.

[. . . .]

3. For if we reflect how prone the human mind is to lapse into forgetfulness of God, how readily inclined to every kind of error, how bent every now and then on devising new and fictitious religions, it will be easy to understand how necessary it was to make such a depository of doctrine as would secure

it from either perishing by the neglect, vanishing away amid the errors, or being corrupted by the presumptuous audacity of men. It being thus manifest that God, foreseeing the inefficiency of his image imprinted on the fair form of the universe, has given the assistance of his Word to all whom he has ever been pleased to instruct effectually, we, too, must pursue this straight path, if we aspire in earnest to a genuine contemplation of God;—we must go, I say, to the Word, where the character of God, drawn from his works, is described accurately and to the life; these works being estimated, not by our depraved judgment, but by the standard of eternal truth. If, as I lately said, we turn aside from it, how great soever the speed with which we move, we shall never reach the goal, because we are off the course. We should consider that the brightness of the Divine countenance, which even an apostle declares to be inaccessible (1 Tim. vi. 16), is a kind of labyrinth,—a labyrinth to us inextricable, if the Word do not serve us as a thread to guide our path; and that it is better to limp in the way, than run with the greatest swiftness out of it. Hence the Psalmist, after repeatedly declaring (Psalm xciii. xcvi. xcvii. xcix. &c.) that superstition should be banished from the world in order that pure religion may flourish, introduces God as *reigning*; meaning by the term, not the power which he possesses and which he exerts in the government of universal nature, but the doctrine by which he maintains his due supremacy: because error never can be eradicated from the heart of man until the true knowledge of God has been implanted in it.

4. Accordingly, the same prophet, after mentioning that the heavens declare the glory of God, that the firmament showeth forth the works of his hands, that the regular succession of day and night proclaim his Majesty, proceeds to make mention of the Word:—"The law of the Lord," says he, "is perfect, converting the soul; the testimony of the Lord is sure, making wise the simple. The statutes of the Lord are right, rejoicing the heart; the commandment of the Lord is pure, enlightening the eyes" (Psalm xix. 1–9). For though the law has other uses besides . . ., the general meaning is, that it is the proper school for training the children of God; the invitation given to all nations, to behold him in the heavens and earth, proving of no avail. The same view is taken in the xxix. Psalm, where the Psalmist, after discoursing on the dreadful voice of God, which, in thunder, wind, rain, whirlwind, and tempest, shakes the earth, makes the mountains tremble, and breaks the cedars, concludes by saying, "that in his temple doth every one speak of his glory," unbelievers being deaf to all God's words when they echo in the air. In like manner another Psalm, after describing the raging billows of the sea, thus concludes, "Thy testimonies are very sure; holiness becometh thine house for ever" (Psalm xciii. 5). To the

same effect are the words of our Saviour to the Samaritan woman, when he told her that her nation and all other nations worshipped they knew not what; and that the Jews alone gave worship to the true God (John iv. 22). Since the human mind, through its weakness, was altogether unable to come to God if not aided and upheld by his sacred word, it necessarily followed that all mankind, the Jews excepted, inasmuch as they sought God without the Word, were labouring under vanity and error.

from *Schleitheim Confession of Faith*, 1527

The Reformation era of the sixteenth century took at least four expressions: the Protestant Reformation of Luther, Calvin, and others; the English Reformation; the Catholic Reformation illustrated by Ignatius of Loyola and the Council of Trent; and the Radical (or Anabaptist) Reformation. As a loose confederation of dissenters, the Anabaptists struggled to find clear focus and identity. The Schleitheim Confession, authored principally by Michael Sattler (1490–1527), helped to codify the Anabaptists' commitment to return to the "root," or *radix*, of the early Christian church—thus the origin of their name, "Radicals." The early Christian patterns that the Radicals sought to replicate are described in this Confession. Rejecting Anabaptist teaching, the Protestants and the Catholics found common cause in eradicating the Anabaptists. Despite severe persecution, Anabaptist tenets lived on in such groups as the Mennonites, Amish, Church of the Brethren, Baptists, and parts of the Stone-Campbell Movement.

Letter of the brotherly union of certain believing baptized children of God, who have assembled at Schleitheim, to the congregations of believing, baptized Christians:

Joy, peace, and mercy from our Father, through the union of the blood of Christ Jesus, together with the gifts of the Spirit (who is sent by the Father to all believers for strength and comfort and constancy in all distress unto the end, Amen) be with all who love God, and with the children of the light everywhere scattered abroad, wherever they are appointed by God our Father, wherever

SOURCE: Thomas Armitage, *A History of the Baptists: Traced by Their Vital Principles and Practices from the Time of Our Lord and Saviour Jesus Christ to the Year 1886* (New York: Bryan, Taylor, 1887), 949–52.

they are assembled with one accord in one God and Father of us all. Grace and peace in heart be with you all. Amen.

[. . . .]

But that ye may understand what these articles were, mark and understand. Scandal has been brought in among us by certain false brethren, so that some have turned from the faith, because they have presumed to use for themselves the freedom of the Spirit and of Christ. But such have erred from the truth and are given over (to their condemnation) to the wantonness and freedom of the flesh; and have thought faith and love may do and suffer all things, and nothing would injure or condemn them as long as they thus believed. Mark, ye members of God in Christ Jesus, faith in the Heavenly Father through Jesus Christ does not thus prove itself, does not work and deal in such way as these false brethren and sisters do and teach. Take heed to yourselves; be warned of such; for they serve not our Father, but their father, the devil. But ye are not so, for they who are of Christ have crucified the flesh, with all lusts and longings. You understand *me* well, and the brethren whom we mean. Separate yourselves from them, for they are turned away. Pray the Lord for their acknowledgment unto repentance and for our constancy to walk in the way we have entered, for the honor of God and his Christ. Amen.

The articles we have discussed, and in which we are one, are these: 1. Baptism. 2. Excommunication. 3. Breaking of bread. 4. Separation from abominations. 5. Shepherds in the congregation. 6. Sword. 7. Oath.

1. In the first place, mark this concerning baptism: Baptism should be given to all those who have learned repentance and change of life, and believe in truth that their sins have been taken away through Christ; and to all those who desire to walk in the resurrection of Jesus Christ, and to be buried with him in death, that with him they may rise; and to all those who with such intention themselves desire and request it of us. By this is excluded all infant baptism, the Pope's highest and first abomination. This has its foundation and witness in the Scriptures and in the usage of the Apostles—Matt. 28, Mark 16, Acts 2, 8, 16, 19. This we would with all simplicity, but firmly, hold and be assured of.

2. In the second place, we were united concerning excommunication, as follows: Excommunication should be pronounced on all those who have given themselves to the Lord, to walk in his commandments, and on all those who have been baptized into one body of Christ, and who call themselves brothers and sisters, and yet slip away and fall into sin and are overtaken unawares. They should be warned the second time privately, and the third time publicly rebuked before the whole congregation, or be excluded according to the command of Christ, Matt. 28. But this should take place, according to the order of

the Spirit of God, before the breaking of bread, that we may with one mind and with one love break and eat of one bread and drink of one cup.

3. Thirdly, we were one and agreed concerning breaking of bread, as follows: All who would break one bread for a memorial of the broken body of Christ, and all who would drink one draught as a memorial of the poured out blood of Christ, should beforehand be united to one body of Christ; that is, to the Church of God, of which the head is Christ, to wit, by baptism. For, as Paul shows, we cannot at the same time be partakers of the table of the Lord and of the table of the devil; we cannot at the same time partake and drink of the cup of the Lord and of the cup of the devil; that is, all who have communion with the dead works of darkness, they have no part with the light. All who follow the devil and the world have no part with those who are called from the world to God. All who lie in the wicked one have no part with the good. Hence, also, it should and must be, whoso has not the call of one God to one faith, to one baptism, to one spirit, to one body, common to all the children of God, he cannot be made one bread with them, as must be if we would in the truth break bread according to the command of Christ.

4. Fourthly, we were agreed concerning separation: This should be from the evil and wicked, whom the devil has planted in the world, to the end alone that we should not have association with them or run with them in the multitude of their abominations. And this because all who have not entered the obedience of faith, and who have not united themselves to God to do his will, are a great abomination before God, and naught can possibly grow or issue from them but abominable things. Now, in all creatures there is either goodness or evil; they either believe or are unbelieving; are darkness or light; of the world or out of the world; temples of God or of idols; Christ or Belial, and none may have part with the other. Now, the command of God is plain to us, in which he calls us to be ever separate from evil. Thus will he ever be our God, and we shall be his sons and daughters. Further, he warns us to go out from Babylon and carnal Egypt, that we be not partakers of their torment and sufferings, which the Lord will bring upon them.

From all this we should learn that everything that is not at one with our God and Christ is nothing else than abomination, which we should avoid and flee. By this is meant all Popish and anti-Popish work and worship, assembly, church-going, wine-houses, citizenship, and enjoyments of unbelief, and many other similar things which the world prizes, though they are done directly against the command of God, according to the measure of all unrighteousness, which is the world. From all this we should be separate and have no part with such, for they are clear abominations, which will make us abhorrent to our

Christ Jesus, who has delivered us from the service of the flesh and filled us for the service of God by the Spirit whom he has given to us. Therefore, there will also from us undoubtedly depart unchristian and devilish weapons—sword, armor, and the like—and all use of them for friend or against enemies, through power of the word of Christ, "Resist not evil."

5. Fifthly, we are united respecting the pastor in the congregation of God, thus: The pastor in the congregation should be one in entire accordance with the direction of Paul, who has a good report from those who are without the faith. His office should be to read, exhort, and teach; to warn, reprove, excommunicate in the congregation, and to lead in prayer for the bettering of all brethren and sisters; to take the bread, to break it, and in all things to care for the body of Christ, that it be edified and bettered, and that the mouth of the blasphemer be stopped. But he, when he is in want, must be supported by the congregation which elected him, so that he who serves the Gospel should also live from it, as the Lord has ordained.

But if a pastor should do anything worthy of reproof, nothing should be undertaken with him without two or three witnesses; and if they have sinned, they shall be reproved before all the people, that the others may fear.

But if the pastor is driven away, or is taken by the cross to the Lord, immediately another shall be chosen in his place, that the little flock of God be not destroyed.

6. Sixthly, we were united concerning the sword, thus: The sword is an ordinance of God outside of the perfection of Christ, which punishes and slays the wicked and protects and guards the good. In law the sword is ordained over the wicked for punishment and death, and the civil power is ordained to use it. But in the perfection of Christ, excommunication is pronounced only for warning and for exclusion of him who has sinned, without death of the flesh, only by warning and the command not to sin again. It is asked by many who do not know the will of Christ respecting us, whether a Christian may or should use the sword against the wicked in order to protect and guard the good, or for love?

The answer is unanimously revealed thus: Christ teaches and commands us that we should learn from him, for he is meek and lowly of heart, and so we will find rest for our souls. Now, Christ says to the heathen woman who was taken in adultery, not that they should stone her according to the law of his Father (yet he also said, "as the Father gave me commandment, even so I do"), but in mercy, and forgiveness, and warning to sin no more, and says, "Go and sin no more." So should we also closely follow according to the law of excommunication.

Secondly, It is asked concerning the sword, whether a Christian should pronounce judgment in worldly disputes and quarrels which unbelievers have with one another? The only answer is: Christ was not willing to decide or judge between brothers concerning inheritance, but refused to do it; so should we also do.

Thirdly, It is asked concerning the sword, Should one be a magistrate if he is elected thereto? To this the answer is: It was intended to make Christ a King, and he fled and did not regard the ordinance of his Father. Thus should we do and follow him, and we shall not walk in darkness. For he himself says, "Whosoever will come after me, let him deny himself and take up his cross and follow me." Also, he himself forbids the power of the sword and says, "The princes of the Gentiles exercise lordship," etc., "but it shall not be so among you." Further, Paul says, "for whom he did foreknow he also did predestinate to be conformed to the image of his son." Also, Peter says, "Christ has suffered (not ruled), leaving us an ensample that ye should follow his steps."

Lastly, it is remarked that it does not become a Christian to be a magistrate for these reasons: The rule of the magistrate is according to the flesh, that of the Christian according to the Spirit; their houses and dwelling remain in this world, the Christian's is in heaven; their citizenship is in this world, the Christian's citizenship is in heaven; the weapons of their contest and war are carnal and only against the flesh, but the weapons of the Christian are spiritual, against the fortresses of the devil; the worldly are armed with steel and iron, but the Christians are armed with the armor of God, with truth, righteousness, peace, faith, salvation, and with the word God. In short, as Christ our head was minded towards us, so should the members of the body of Christ through him be minded, that there be no schism in the body by which it be destroyed. For every kingdom divided against itself will be brought to destruction. Therefore, as Christ is, as it stands written of him, so must the members be, that his body be whole and one, to the edification of itself.

7. Seventhly, we were united concerning oaths, thus: The oath is an assurance among those who dispute or promise, and was spoken of in the law that it should take place with the name of God, only in truth and not in falsehood. Christ, who teaches the perfection of the law, forbids to his people all swearing, whether true or false, neither by heaven nor by earth, nor by Jerusalem, nor by our head, and that for the reason which he immediately after gives, "Because thou canst not make one hair white or black." Take heed, all swearing is therefore forbidden, because we are not able to make good that which is promised in the oath, since we cannot change the least thing upon us. Now, there are some who do not believe the simple command of God, but they speak and

ask thus: If God swore to Abraham by himself because he was God (when he promised him that he would do good to him and would be his God if he kept his commands), why should I not also swear if I promise a person something? Answer. Hear what the Scripture says: "God being willing more abundantly to shew unto the heirs of promise the immutability of his counsel, confirmed it with an oath, that by two immutable things, in which it was impossible for God to lie, we might have a strong consolation." Mark the meaning of this Scripture: God has power to do what he forbids to you, for to him all things are possible.

"God swore an oath to Abraham," says the Scripture, "in order that he might show his counsel to be immutable;" that is, no one can withstand or hinder his will, and therefore he can keep the oath. But, as was said by Christ above, "We have no power either to hold or to give," and therefore should not swear at all.

Further, some say God has not forbidden in the New Testament to swear, and he has commanded it in the Old; but it is only forbidden to swear by heaven, earth, Jerusalem, and by our head. Answer. Hear the Scriptures: "He that shall swear by heaven sweareth by the throne of God; and by him that sitteth thereon." Mark, swearing by heaven is forbidden, which is only the throne of God; how much more is it forbidden to swear by God himself! Ye fools and blind, which is the greater, the throne, or he who sits upon it?

Still, some say, If it is wrong to use God's name for the truth, yet the apostles, Peter and Paul, swore. Answer. Peter and Paul testify only that which God promised to Abraham by oath, and they themselves promised nothing, as the examples clearly show. But to testify and to swear are different things. When one swears he promises a thing in the future, as Christ was promised to Abraham, whom we received a long time afterwards. When one testifies he witnesses concerning that which is present, whether it be good or bad, as Simon spoke of Christ to Mary and testified, "Behold, this one is set for the fall and rising of many in Israel, and for a sign, which shall be spoken against." Similarly Christ has taught us when he says, "Let your communication be yea, yea, nay, nay; for whatsover is more than these cometh of the Evil One." He says, your speech or word shall be yea and nay, and his intention is clear.

Christ is simple yea and nay, and all who seek him simply will understand His word. Amen.

Dear brethren and sisters in the Lord, these are the articles which some brethren have understood wrongly and not in accordance with the true meaning, and thereby have confused many weak consciences, so that the name of God has been grossly blasphemed; for which cause it was necessary that we should be united in the Lord, which, God be praised, has taken place.

Now that ye have well understood the will of God, which has been manifested through us, it is necessary that ye from the heart and not wavering perform the known will of God. For ye well know what is the reward of that servant who sins wittingly.

All that ye have done unwittingly and that ye have confessed that ye have done wrong, that is forgiven you through believing prayer, which was made by us in the assembly for the sin and guilt of us all, through the gracious pardon of God and through the blood of Jesus Christ. Amen.

Mark all those who walk not according to the simplicity of divine truth, which is contained in this letter, as it was apprehended by us in the assembly, in order that each one among us be governed by the rule of discipline, and henceforth the entrance among us of false brethren and sisters be guarded against. Separate from you what is evil, so will the Lord be your God, and ye shall be his sons and daughters.

Dear brethren, be mindful how Paul exhorts Titus. He speaks thus: "The grace of God that bringeth salvation hath appeared to all men, teaching us that, denying ungodliness and worldly lusts, we should live soberly, righteously and godly in this present world, looking for that blessed hope and the glorious appearing of the great God and our Saviour Jesus Christ, who gave himself for us that he might redeem us from all iniquity and purify unto himself a peculiar people, zealous of good works." Think of this and practice it; so will the Lord of peace be with you.

The name of God be eternally praised and glorified. Amen.

The Lord give you his peace. Amen.

ACTA SCHLAITTEN AM RANDEN AUF MATTHIAE, *FEBRUARY 24TH, ANNO* MDXXVII.

from *Canons and Decrees of the Sacred and Ecumenical Council of Trent*

In the midst of the sixteenth century's era of religious reformations, Pope Paul III convened the Council of Trent (1546–1563) to reform the Catholic Church, and to attend to Protestant critiques. Tridentine reforms confirmed such matters as the authority of tradition along with Scripture, the Latin Vulgate as the standard version of Scripture, the role of human participation in God's saving grace, the seven sacraments, residency requirements for bishops in their respective sees, and the proper use of indulgences. The following excerpts illustrate Trent's teachings on justification, the sacraments and their proper oversight, and transubstantiation.

Sixth Session, Chapter VII: *What the Justification of the impious is, and what are the causes thereof.*

This disposition, or preparation, is followed by Justification itself, which is not remission of sins merely, but also the sanctification and renewal of the inward man, through the voluntary reception of the grace, and of the gifts, whereby man of unjust becomes just, and of an enemy a friend, that so he may be *an heir according to hope of life everlasting.*

Of this Justification the causes are these: the final cause indeed is the glory of God and of Jesus Christ, and life everlasting; while the efficient cause is a merciful God who *washes and sanctifies* gratuitously, *signing*, and anointing

SOURCE: *The Canons and Decrees of the Sacred and Œcumenical Council of Trent: Celebrated under the Sovereign Pontiffs Paul III., Julius III., and Pius IV.,* trans. J. Waterworth (London: C. Dolman, 1848), 34–36, 54–55, 76–77.

with the holy *Spirit of promise, who is the pledge of our inheritance*; but the meritorious cause is His most beloved only-begotten, our Lord Jesus Christ, who, when we were enemies, *for the exceeding charity wherewith he loved us*, merited Justification for us by His most holy Passion on the wood of the cross, and made satisfaction for us unto God the Father; the instrumental cause is the sacrament of baptism, which is the sacrament of faith, without which (faith) no man was ever justified; lastly, the alone formal cause is the justice of God, not that whereby He Himself is just, but that whereby He maketh us just, that, to wit, with which we being endowed by Him, *are renewed in the spirit of our mind*, and we are not only reputed, but are truly called, and are, just, receiving justice within us, each one according to his own measure, *which the Holy Ghost distributes to every one as He wills*, and according to each one's proper disposition and co-operation. For, although no one can be just, but he to whom the merits of the Passion of our Lord Jesus Christ are communicated, yet is this done in the said justification of the impious, when by the merit of that same most holy Passion, *the charity of God is poured forth*, by the Holy Spirit, *in the hearts* of those that are justified, and is inherent therein: whence, man, through Jesus Christ, in whom he is ingrafted, receives, in the said justification, together with the remission of sins, all these (gifts) infused at once, faith, hope, and charity. For faith, unless hope and charity be added thereto, neither unites man perfectly with Christ, nor makes him a living member of His body. For which reason it is most truly said, that *Faith without works is dead* and profitless; and, *In Christ Jesus neither circumcision, availeth anything, nor uncircumcision, but faith which worketh by charity*. This faith, Catechumens beg of the Church—agreeably to a tradition of the apostles—previously to the sacrament of Baptism; when they beg for the faith which bestows life everlasting, which, without hope and charity, faith cannot bestow: whence also do they immediately hear that word of Christ; *If thou wilt enter into life, keep the commandments*. Wherefore, when receiving true and Christian justice, they are bidden, immediately on being born again, to preserve it pure and spotless, as the *first robe* given them through Jesus Christ in lieu of that which Adam, by his disobedience, lost for himself and for us, that so they may bear it before the judgment-seat of our Lord Jesus Christ, and may have life everlasting.

[. . . .]

Seventh Session, On the Sacraments in General

Canon I.—If any one saith, that the sacraments of the New Law were not all instituted by Jesus Christ, our Lord; or, that they are more, or less, than seven, to wit, Baptism, Confirmation, the Eucharist, Penance, Extreme Unction,

Order, and Matrimony; or even that any one of these seven is not truly and properly a sacrament; let him be anathema.

[. . . .]

Canon IV.—If any one saith, that the sacraments of the New Law are not necessary unto salvation, but superfluous; and that, without them, or without the desire thereof, men obtain of God, through faith alone, the graces of justification;—though all (the sacraments) are not indeed necessary for every individual; let him be anathema.

[. . . .]

Canon VI.—If any one saith, that the sacraments of the New Law do not contain the grace which they signify; or, that they do not confer that grace on those who do not place an obstacle thereunto; as though they were merely outward signs of grace or justice received through faith, and certain marks of the Christian profession, whereby believers are distinguished amongst men from unbelievers; let him be anathema.

[. . . .]

Canon VIII.—If any one saith, that by the said sacraments of the New Law grace is not conferred through the act performed, but that faith alone in the divine promise suffices for the obtaining of grace; let him be anathema.

[. . . .]

Canon X.—If any one saith, that all Christians have power to administer the word, and all the sacraments; let him be anathema.

[. . . .]

Thirteenth Session, Chapter I: *On the real presence of our Lord Jesus Christ in the most holy sacrament of the Eucharist.*

In the first place, the holy Synod teaches, and openly and simply professes, that, in the august sacrament of the holy Eucharist, after the consecration of the bread and wine, our Lord Jesus Christ, true God and man, is truly, really, and substantially contained under the species of those sensible things. For neither are these things mutually repugnant,—that our Saviour Himself always sitteth at the right hand of the Father in heaven, according to the natural mode of existing, and that, nevertheless, He be, in many other places, sacramentally present to us in his own substance, by a manner of existing, which, though we can scarcely express it in words, yet can we, by the understanding illuminated by faith, conceive, and we ought most firmly to believe, to be possible unto God: for thus all our forefathers, as many as were in the true Church of Christ, who have treated of this most holy Sacrament, have most openly professed, that our Redeemer instituted this so admirable a sacrament at the last supper, when, after the blessing of the bread and wine, He testified, in express and clear words, that He gave them His own very Body, and His own Blood; words which,—recorded by the holy Evangelists, and afterwards repeated by Saint Paul, whereas they carry with them that proper and most manifest meaning in which they were understood by the Fathers,—it is indeed a crime the most unworthy that they should be wrested, by certain contentions and wicked men, to fictitious and imaginary tropes, whereby the verity of the flesh and blood of Christ is denied, contrary to the universal sense of the Church, which, as the *pillar and ground of truth*, has detested, as satanical, these inventions devised by impious men; she recognising, with a mind ever grateful and unforgetting, this most excellent benefit of Christ.

Chapter II: *On the reason of the Institution of this most holy sacrament.*

Wherefore, our Saviour, when about to depart out of this world to the Father, instituted this Sacrament, in which He poured forth as it were the riches of His divine love towards man, *making a remembrance of his wonderful works*; and He commanded us, in the participation thereof, to venerate His *memory*, and to *show forth his death until He come* to judge the world. And He would also that this sacrament should be received as the spiritual food of souls, whereby may be fed and strengthened those who live with His life who said, *He that eateth me, the same also shall live by me*; and as an antidote, whereby we may be freed from daily faults, and be preserved from mortal sins. He would, furthermore, have it be a pledge of our glory to come, and everlasting happiness, and thus be a symbol of that one body whereof He is the head, and to which He would fain have us as members be united by the closest bond of faith, hope, and charity, *that we might all speak the same things, and there might be no schisms amongst us.*

from *Thirty-Nine Articles of Religion (Church of England)*

As the Protestant Reformation emerged on the European continent, England's King Henry VIII initially remained allied with Rome. Soon, however, England also sought more autonomy from the Vatican. In 1534, Parliament issued the Act of Supremacy, which established England's monarch—not the Pope—as the head of the Church in England. Now independent, ecclesiastical leaders such as Archbishop Thomas Cranmer crafted the Ten Articles (1536), the Six Articles (1539), and the Forty-Two Articles (1553) to refine and define the doctrinal formula of the English Church. After the five-year return of the English Church to Rome during Queen Mary's reign (1553–1558), a new generation labored to establish the catholicity of the Church of England, vis-à-vis Protestantism and Catholicism, ultimately settling on the Thirty-Nine Articles in 1571. The genius of the Thirty-Nine Articles, excerpted below, may be in their brevity. They allow latitude for diverse viewpoints within the most fiercely contested issues of the Reformation era.

––––––––––

Article I: *Of Faith in the Holy Trinity.*

There is but one living and true God, everlasting, without body, parts or passions, of infinite power, wisdom, and goodness, the maker and preserver of all things both visible and invisible. And in unity of this Godhead there be three persons, of one substance, power, and eternity, the Father, the Son, and the Holy Ghost.

[. . . .]

SOURCE: Edgar C. S. Gibson, *The Thirty-Nine Articles of the Church of England: Explained with an Introduction*, 2nd ed. (London: Methuen, 1898), 90, 296, 357, 378, 388, 410, 415, 424, 459–60, 493, 511, 537, 573, 581, 585, 615, 620, 640, 676, 695, 716, 759–60, 783.

Article VIII: *Of the Three Creeds.*

The three Creeds, Nicene Creed, Athanasius' Creed, and that which is commonly called the Apostles' Creed, ought thoroughly to be received and believed: for they may be proved by most certain warrants of Holy Scripture.

Article IX: *Of Original or Birth Sin.*

Original sin standeth not in the following of Adam (as the Pelagians do vainly talk), but it is the fault and corruption of the nature of every man, that naturally is engendered of the offspring of Adam whereby man is very far gone from original righteousness, and is of his own nature inclined to evil, so that the flesh lusteth always contrary to the spirit, and therefore in every person born into this world, it deserveth God's wrath and damnation. And this infection of nature doth remain, yea in them that are regenerated, whereby the lust of the flesh . . . which some do expound the wisdom, some sensuality, some the affection, some the desire of the flesh, is not subject to the law of God. And although there is no condemnation for them that believe and are baptized: yet the apostle doth confess that concupiscence and lust hath of itself the nature of sin.

Article X: *Of Free will.*

The condition of man after the fall of Adam is such, that he cannot turn and prepare himself by his own natural strength and good works, to faith and calling upon God: Wherefore we have no power to do good works pleasant and acceptable to God, without the grace of God by Christ preventing us, that we may have a good will, and working with us, when we have that good will.

Article XI: *Of the Justification of Man.*

We are accounted righteous before God, only for the merit of our Lord and Saviour Jesus Christ, by faith, and not for our own works or deservings: Wherefore, that we are justified by faith only, is a most wholesome doctrine, and very full of comfort, as more largely is expressed in the Homily of Justification.

Article XII: *Of Good Works.*

Albeit that good works, which are the fruits of faith, and follow after justification, cannot put away our sins, and endure the severity of God's judgment: yet are they pleasing and acceptable to God in Christ, and do spring out necessarily of a true and lively faith, in so much that by them, a lively faith may be as evidently known, as a tree discerned by the fruit.

Article XIII: *Of Works before Justification.*

Works done before the grace of Christ, and the inspiration of His Spirit, are not pleasant to God, forasmuch as they spring not of faith in Jesu Christ, neither do they make men meet to receive grace, or (as the school authors say) deserve grace of congruity: yea, rather for that they are not done as God hath willed and commanded them to be done, we doubt not but they have the nature of sin.

Article XIV: *Of Works of Supererogation.*

Voluntary works besides, over and above God's commandments, which they call works of supererogation, cannot be taught without arrogancy and impiety. For by them men do declare that they do not only render unto God as much as they are bound to do, but that they do more for His sake than of bounden duty is required: whereas Christ saith plainly, When ye have done all that are commanded to you, say, We be unprofitable servants.

[. . . .]

Article XVII: *Of Predestination and Election.*

Predestination to life, is the everlasting purpose of God, whereby (before the foundations of the world were laid) He hath constantly decreed by His counsel secret to us, to deliver from curse and damnation those whom He hath chosen in Christ out of mankind, and to bring them by Christ to everlasting salvation, as vessels made to honour. Wherefore, they which be endued with so excellent a benefit of God, be called according to God's purpose by his Spirit working in due season: they through Grace obey the calling: they be justified freely: they be made sons of God by adoption: they be made like the image of his only-begotten Son Jesus Christ: they walk religiously in good works, and at length, by God's mercy, they attain to everlasting felicity.

As the godly consideration of predestination, and our election in Christ, is full of sweet, pleasant, and unspeakable comfort to godly persons, and such as feel in themselves the working of the Spirit of Christ, mortifying the works of the flesh, and their earthly members, and drawing up their mind to high and heavenly things, as well because it doth greatly establish and confirm their faith of eternal Salvation to be enjoyed through Christ as because it doth fervently kindle their love towards God: so, for curious and carnal persons, lacking the Spirit of Christ, to have continually before their eyes the sentence of God's predestination, is a most dangerous downfall, whereby the devil doth thrust them either into desperation, or into wretchlessness of most unclean living, no less perilous than desperation.

Furthermore, we must receive God's promises in such wise, as they be generally set forth to us in Holy Scripture: and, in our doings, that Will of God is to be followed, which we have expressly declared unto us in the Word of God.

[. . . .]

Article XIX: *Of the Church.*

The visible Church of Christ, is a congregation of faithful men, in the which the pure word of God is preached, and the sacraments be duly ministered, according to Christ's ordinance in all those things that of necessity are requisite to the same.

As the Church of Hierusalem, Alexandria, and Antioch have erred: so also the Church of Rome hath erred, not only in their living and manner of ceremonies, but also in matters of faith.

Article XX: *Of the Authority of the Church.*

The Church hath power to decree Rites or Ceremonies, and authority in controversies of faith: and yet it is not lawful for the Church to ordain anything that is contrary to God's word written, neither may it so expound one place of Scripture, that it be repugnant to another. Wherefore, although the Church be a witness and a keeper of holy Writ: yet, as it ought not to decree anything against the same, so besides the same, ought it not to enforce anything to be believed for necessity of salvation.

[. . . .]

Article XXII: *Of Purgatory.*

The Romish doctrine concerning Purgatory, Pardons, Worshipping, and Adoration, as well of Images, as of Reliques, and also invocation of Saints, is a fond thing, vainly invented, and grounded upon no warranty of Scripture, but rather repugnant to the word of God.

Article XXIII: *Of Ministering in the Congregation.*

It is not lawful for any man to take upon him the office of public preaching, or ministering the Sacraments in the congregation, before he be lawfully called and sent to execute the same. And those we ought to judge lawfully called and sent, which be chosen and called to this work by men who have public authority given unto them in the congregation, to call and send ministers into the Lord's vineyard.

Article XXIV: *Of Speaking in the Congregation, in such a tongue as the people understandeth.*

It is a thing plainly repugnant to the word of God, and the custom of the primitive Church, to have public prayer in the Church, or to minister the Sacraments in a tongue not understanded of the people.

Article XXV: *Of the Sacraments.*

Sacraments ordained of Christ, be not only badges or tokens of Christian men's profession: but rather they be certain sure witnesses and effectual signs of grace and God's goodwill towards us, by the which He doth work invisibly in us, and doth not only quicken, but also strengthen and confirm our faith in Him.

There are two Sacraments ordained of Christ our Lord in the Gospel, that is to say, Baptism, and the Supper of the Lord.

Those five, commonly called Sacraments, that is to say, Confirmation, Penance, Orders, Matrimony, and Extreme Unction, are not to be counted for Sacraments of the Gospel, being such as have grown partly of the corrupt following of the Apostles, partly are states of life allowed in the Scriptures: but yet have not like nature of Sacraments with Baptism and the Lord's Supper, for that they have not any visible sign or ceremony ordained of God.

The Sacraments were not ordained of Christ to be gazed upon, or to be carried about: but that we should duly use them. And in such only as worthily receive the same, they have a wholesome effect or operation: but they that receive them unworthily, purchase to themselves damnation, as S. Paul saith.

Article XXVI: *Of the Unworthiness of the ministers, which hinder[s] not the effect of the Sacraments.*

Although in the visible Church the evil be ever mingled with the good, and sometime the evil have chief authority in the ministration of the word and Sacraments: yet forasmuch as they do not the same in their own name but in Christ's, and do minister by His commission and authority, we may use their ministry, both in hearing the word of God, and in the receiving of the Sacraments. Neither is the effect of Christ's ordinance taken away by their wickedness, nor the grace of God's gifts diminished from such as by faith and rightly do receive the Sacraments ministered unto them, which be effectual, because of Christ's institution and promise, although they be ministered by evil men.

Nevertheless, it appertaineth to the discipline of the Church, that inquiry be made of evil ministers, and that they be accused by those that have knowledge of their offences; and finally, being found guilty by just judgment, be deposed.

Article XXVII: *Of Baptism.*

Baptism is not only a sign of profession, and mark of difference, whereby Christian men are discerned from other that be not christened: but is also a sign of regeneration or new birth, whereby as by an instrument, they that receive baptism rightly, are grafted into the Church; the promises of the forgiveness of sin, and of our adoption to be the sons of God, by the Holy Ghost, are visibly signed and sealed: faith is confirmed: and grace increased by virtue of prayer unto God.

The baptism of young children is in any wise to be retained in the Church, as most agreeable with the institution of Christ.

Article XXVIII: *Of the Lord's Supper.*

The Supper of the Lord is not only a sign of the love that Christians ought to have among themselves one to another; but rather it is a Sacrament of our redemption by Christ's death. Insomuch that to such as rightly, worthily, and with faith receive the same, the bread which we break is a partaking of the body of Christ: and likewise the cup of blessing is a partaking of the blood of Christ.

Transubstantiation (or the change of the substance of bread and wine) in the Supper of the Lord, cannot be proved by Holy Writ; but is repugnant to the plain words of Scripture, overthroweth the nature of a Sacrament, and hath given occasion to many superstitions.

The body of Christ is given, taken, and eaten in the Supper only after an heavenly and spiritual manner. And the mean whereby the body of Christ is received and eaten in the Supper, is faith.

The Sacrament of the Lord's Supper was not by Christ's ordinance reserved, carried about, lifted up, or worshipped.

[....]

Article XXX: *Of both kinds.*

The cup of the Lord is not to be denied to the lay people. For both the parts of the Lord's Sacrament, by Christ's ordinance and commandment, ought to be ministered to all Christian men alike.

[....]

Article XXXII: *Of the Marriage of Priests.*

Bishops, Priests, and Deacons are not commanded by God's law either to vow the estate of single life, or to abstain from marriage. Therefore it is lawful also for them, as for all other Christian men, to marry at their own discretion, as they shall judge the same to serve better to godliness.

[. . . .]

Article XXXIV: *Of the traditions of the Church.*

It is not necessary that traditions and ceremonies be in all places one, or utterly like, for at all times they have been diverse, and may be changed according to the diversity of countries, times, and men's manners, so that nothing be ordained against God's word. Whosoever through his private judgment, willingly and purposely doth openly break the traditions and ceremonies of the Church, which be not repugnant to the word of God, and be ordained and approved by common authority, ought to be rebuked openly (that other may fear to do the like), as he that offendeth against the common order of the Church, and hurteth the authority of the Magistrate, and woundeth the consciences of the weak brethren.

Every particular or national Church hath authority to ordain, change, and abolish ceremonies or rites of the Church ordained only by man's authority, so that all things be done to edifying.

[. . . .]

Article XXXVII: *Of the Civil Magistrates.*

The Queen's Majesty hath the chief power in this Realm of England, and other her dominions, unto whom the chief government of all estates of this Realm, whether they be Ecclesiastical or Civil, in all causes doth appertain, and is not, nor ought to be subject to any foreign jurisdiction.

Where we attribute to the Queen's Majesty the chief government, by which titles we understand the minds of some slanderous folks to be offended; we give not to our princes the ministering either of God's word, or of Sacraments, the which thing the Injunctions also lately set forth by Elizabeth our Queen, doth most plainly testify: But that only prerogative which we see to have been given always to all godly Princes in holy Scriptures by God Himself, that is, that they should rule all estates and degrees committed to their charge by God, whether they be Ecclesiastical or Temporal, and restrain with the civil sword the stubborn and evil-doers.

The bishop of Rome hath no jurisdiction in this Realm of England.

The laws of the Realm may punish Christian men with death, for heinous and grievous offences.

It is lawful for Christian men, at the commandment of the Magistrate, to wear weapons, and serve in the wars.

Article XXXVIII: *Of Christian Men's goods which are not common.*

The riches and goods of Christians are not common, as touching the right, title, and possession of the same, as certain Anabaptists do falsely boast. Notwithstanding every man ought of such things as he possesseth, liberally to give alms to the poor, according to his ability.

80

Teresa of Avila

from *Interior Castle*

A Spanish mystic and Carmelite reformer, Teresa of Avila's life (1515–1582) coincided with the sixteenth century's waves of religious reformations. Joining the Carmelite order in 1535, by 1562 she opened her first convent seeking to restore the order's early austerity. She went on to open several more. By about the age of forty, she received ecstatic visions, which infused her writing and work. *Interior Castle* (1577), an autobiographical work, has become a classic of Christian spirituality, in which she describes the mystical ascent of the soul to God by means of mental/contemplative prayer. Although the work, from which the following is an excerpt, was regarded as questionable in its time, Teresa ultimately became the first of three women to be declared Doctor of the Church by the Vatican.

The Seventh Mansions.

Chapter II

We will now speak of the divine and spiritual marriage, though such a sublime favour cannot be entirely possessed in this life, or perfectly accomplished, since if we once leave God we shall quite lose so great a good. The first time God bestows this favour His Majesty is pleased to discover himself to the soul by an imaginary vision of His Most Sacred Humanity, in order that she may fully understand it, and be not ignorant that she receives so immense a gift. To others He may appear in another form: to her of whom we speak our Lord showed himself immediately after she had communicated, in a figure of great splendour, beauty, and majesty, just as He was after His resurrection. He said

SOURCE: Teresa of Avila, *The Interior Castle; or, The Mansions*, trans. John Dalton (London: T. Jones, 1852), 178–84.

to her, "That now was the time she should consider His affairs as hers, and that he would take care of hers." Other words were uttered, more fit to be felt than spoken.

You may perhaps think that this was no novelty, because at other times our Lord represented himself to this soul in this same way. But this was so far different, that it left her quite out of herself, and quite astonished, both because this vision came with great force, and on account of the words which He spoke; and also because, in the interior of the soul, where He had represented himself, she had never heard any except in the preceding vision. You must understand, that there is an immense difference between this and the preceding mansions; and the difference is as great between the spiritual espousals and the spiritual marriage, as there is between those who are only affianced, and those who are really united in matrimony.

I have already mentioned, that though these comparisons be used (because none fitter can be found); yet it should be understood that here the body is no more remembered than if the soul were out of it, and much *less* in the spiritual marriage; for this secret union is effected in the interior centre of the soul, which must certainly be where God himself resides, and He (in my opinion) requires no door to enter at. In all that I have hitherto said, the effects seem to be brought about by means of the senses and faculties, and the representation of our Lord's humanity must certainly be of this nature. But that is far different which takes place here in the union of the spiritual marriage. Our Lord appears in this centre of the soul, not by an imaginary, but an intellectual vision, though it is more subtile than those I have mentioned before. Such did He appear to the Apostles, without entering in at the door, when He said to them "Pax vobis."

That which God here communicates to the soul in an instant is so great a secret, and so sublime a grace, and what she feels is such an excessive delight, that I know nothing to compare it to, except that our Lord is pleased at that moment to manifest to her the glory which is in heaven; and this He does in a more sublime way than by any vision or spiritual delight. More cannot be said (as far as can be understood) than that this soul becomes one with God; for as He himself is a spirit, His Majesty is pleased to discover the love He has for us, by making certain persons understand how it extends, in order that we may praise His greatness, because He has vouchsafed to unite himself to a creature in such a way, that as in the marriage state husband and wife can no more be separated, so He will never be separated from her.

The spiritual espousals is different, for this is often dissolved, and so also is union; for though "union" is the joining of two things into one, they may at last be divided, and may subsist apart. We generally see that this favour of our Lord quickly passes away, and the soul afterwards does not enjoy that company, that is, so as to know it. But in that other favour of our Lord this is not the case, for the soul always remains with her God in that centre.

Let us suppose "union" to be like two *tapers*, so exactly joined together, that the light of both makes but one; or that the wick, light, and wax, are all one and the same, but that, afterwards, one taper may be easily divided from the other, and then two distinct tapers will remain, and the wick will be distinct from the wax. But here (in the spiritual espousals) it is like water descending from heaven into a river or spring, where one is so mixed with the other, that it cannot be discovered which is the river-water, and which the rain-water. It is, also, like a small rivulet running into the sea, whose waters cannot be separated from each other; or as if there were two windows in a room, at which one great light entered; but which, though entering in divided, yet makes but one light within. This is, perhaps, that which St. Paul means, where he says: "He who adheres to God, is one with Him," alluding to this sublime marriage, which presupposes that God is united to the soul by union. He likewise says: "Mihi vivere Christus est, et mori lucrum" (To me to live is Christ, and to die is gain). I think the soul may say the same here; for here the butterfly dies—of which we have spoken, and this with very great joy—because now her life is Christ. This in time is best known by the effects, for it is clearly seen, by certain secret inspirations, that it is God who gives life to the soul; and these inspirations are often so very lively, that they cannot in any way be doubted, because the soul perceives them very well, though they cannot be expressed. But the feeling is so great, that sometimes it produces certain amorous words, which, it appears, one cannot help uttering; as for example: "O life of my life! my support which upholdest me!" together with other like expressions. From those divine breasts, wherewith it seems God continually supports the soul, streams of milk issue, which comfort all the people of the castle; for it seems our Lord wishes them to enjoy, in some manner, that abundance which the soul enjoys; and that, from this vast river, in which the little spring is swallowed up, there should, sometimes, flow a quantity of that water, in order to support those who are to serve these two spouses, in that which relates to the body. And just as if a person, who should be suddenly plunged in this water, without thinking of any such thing, could not help feeling himself wet; so, in the same manner, but with more certainty, are these operations I am speaking about discerned; because as a great quantity of water could not fall upon us, if there were no principle whence it descended; so here we clearly see, that there is one in our interior who sends forth these darts, and gives life to this life; and that there is a sun, from which proceeds that great light, which is conveyed to the powers from the interior of the soul.

She does not, as I have said, stir from this centre, nor does she lose her peace, for He Himself who gave it to the apostles, when they were assembled together, can give it to her also.

I have been thinking, that this salutation of our Lord contained more no doubt—than the mere words outwardly represented; the same may be said regarding our Lord telling the glorious Magdalen "to go in peace;" for as the words of our Lord are *deeds* in us, so these words must certainly produce such effects upon those souls who are already disposed, as to take from them all that is corporeal in the soul, and leave it a pure spirit, in order that it might be united with the Uncreated Spirit in this celestial union. It is very certain, that by disengaging ourselves from all creatures, and withdrawing ourselves from them for the love of God, the same Lord will fill us with Himself. When our Lord was once praying for His Apostles, He requested that they might be "one with the Father and with Him," as Christ our Lord was in the Father and the Father in Him. I know not what love can be greater than this: and here let us all not fail to enter into this union, since His Majesty has said, "I pray not for them only, but for all those who shall believe in me." He likewise said, "I am in them." How true, O my God! are these words, and how well does the soul in this prayer understand them! And we should all understand them, were it not through our own fault, since the words of Jesus Christ, our King and Lord, cannot fail. But as we do not prepare ourselves properly, and do not remove everything from us which might obstruct this light, hence we do not behold ourselves in this glass in which we look, and wherein our image is engraven.

But let us return to what we were saying. After our Lord has conducted the soul into His mansion, which is the centre of the soul, as they say—the empyreal heaven where God resides is not moved like the other part is; and so it seems, that when the soul enters there, those motions do not take place in the soul, which used to be in the faculties and imagination, so that they can hurt her or take away her peace.

I may seem to mean, that the soul by obtaining this favour becomes *secure* as regards her salvation, and does not afterwards relapse. But I do not say any such thing; and whenever I speak on this subject, and seem to mean that the soul is secure, my words must be understood thus, viz., as long as the Divine Majesty holds her in His hand, and she does not offend Him. I know for certain, that though she see herself in this state, and though it may continue some years, she does not, therefore, think herself secure; but rather she has greater fears than formerly, and is more careful to avoid any small offence against God, as I shall mention hereafter; she also has such ardent desires of serving Him, and such continual pain and confusion, to see how little she can do, and how much she is obliged to do, that it is no small cross, but rather a great mortification; for in doing penance, the greater it is, the more delight does the soul feel. Her true penance is, when God takes away her health and strength, so that she is unable to do any penance; and though I have in another place shown the great affliction this causes, yet here it is much greater; and all certainty must come from the root, into which she is grafted; just as a tree which grows near running water looks greener and bears fruit better. Why then should we be astonished at the desires which this soul has, since the true spirit of her has become one with that celestial water of which we spoke?

But to return to what I was saying. It is not intended that the faculties, senses, and passions should always enjoy this peace. The soul indeed does; but in the other mansions there are seasons of war, of troubles, and of pains, though in such a manner as not to take away her peace; and this happens very commonly.

It is so difficult to explain how the spirit is lodged in this centre of our soul, and even to believe it, that I fear, sisters, my inability to explain it may be some temptation to you not to believe what I say; for, to assert that there are crosses and troubles, and yet that the soul is at peace, is difficult to imagine. I wish to give you a few comparisons; and God grant they may prove such as may in some degree illustrate the subject. But should they not be to the purpose, yet I know that what I say is the truth. The king is in his palace, yet there may be many wars in his kingdom, and many offensive things done; still he does not on this account cease to be on his throne. And so it is here; though there be many tumults and many poisonous creatures in the other mansions, and the noise of them is heard, yet no such things enter into this mansion, or force the soul to remove from hence; and though they give her some pain, yet it is not in a way to disturb her and deprive her of her peace; for the passions are now subdued in such a way, that they are afraid to enter here, because they go away still more mortified. The whole body is in pain; but if the head be sound, no harm can be done to it. I smile at these comparisons, for they do not satisfy me; but I can find no better. Whatever you may think of them, I have spoken the truth.

from *Edict of Nantes*

Signed into law by French King Henry IV in 1598, the Edict of Nantes was one of Europe's first acts of religious tolerance. Extending religious rights and privileges to Huguenots (French Protestants), the pronouncement helped reduce the Wars of Religion, which had persisted since 1562. Specific freedoms provided in the Edict included the free exercise of religion (except in Paris), full civil rights for Protestants and Catholics, and state-funded support for both Catholic and Protestant ministers. The Edict was exceptionally controversial in its time, and less than a century later Louis XIV revoked it, reimposing restrictions on Protestants.

Henry, by the grace of God king of France and of Navarre, to all to whom these presents come, greeting:

Among the infinite benefits which it has pleased God to heap upon us, the most signal and precious is his granting us the strength and ability to withstand the fearful disorders and troubles which prevailed on our advent in this kingdom. The realm was so torn by innumerable factions and sects that the most legitimate of all the parties was fewest in numbers. God has given us strength to stand out against this storm; we have finally surmounted the waves and made our port of safety,—peace for our state. For which his be the glory all in all, and ours a free recognition of his grace in making use of our instrumentality in the good work. . . . We implore and await from the Divine Goodness the same protection and favor which he has ever granted to this kingdom from the beginning. . . .

We have, by this perpetual and irrevocable edict, established and proclaimed and do establish and proclaim:

SOURCE: Extracts from the Edict of Nantes, in *Readings in European History: A Collection of Extracts from the Sources Chosen with the Purpose of Illustrating the Progress of Culture in Western Europe since the German Invasions*, ed. James Harvey Robinson, 2 vols., vol. 2, *From the Opening of the Protestant Revolt to the Present Day* (Boston: Ginn, 1906), 183–85.

I. First, that the recollection of everything done by one party or the other between March, 1585, and our accession to the crown, and during all the preceding period of troubles, remain obliterated and forgotten, as if no such things had ever happened.

III. We ordain that the Catholic Apostolic and Roman religion shall be restored and reëstablished in all places and localities of this our kingdom and countries subject to our sway, where the exercise of the same has been interrupted, in order that it may be peaceably and freely exercised, without any trouble or hindrance: forbidding very expressly all persons, of whatsoever estate, quality, or condition, from troubling, molesting, or disturbing ecclesiastics in the celebration of divine service, in the enjoyment or collection of tithes, fruits, or revenues of their benefices, and all other rights and dues belonging to them; and that all those who during the troubles have taken possession of churches, houses, goods or revenues, belonging to the said ecclesiastics, shall surrender to them entire possession and peaceable enjoyment of such rights, liberties, and sureties as they had before they were deprived of them.

VI. And in order to leave no occasion for troubles or differences between our subjects, we have permitted, and herewith permit, those of the said religion called Reformed to live and abide in all the cities and places of this our kingdom and countries of our sway, without being annoyed, molested, or compelled to do anything in the matter of religion contrary to their consciences, ... upon condition that they comport themselves in other respects according to that which is contained in this our present edict.

VII. It is permitted to all lords, gentlemen, and other persons making profession of the said religion called Reformed, holding the right of high justice [or a certain feudal tenure], to exercise the said religion in their houses.

IX. We also permit those of the said religion to make and continue the exercise of the same in all villages and places of our dominion where it was established by them and publicly enjoyed several and divers times in the year 1597, up to the end of the month of August, notwithstanding all decrees and judgments to the contrary.

XIII. We very expressly forbid to all those of the said religion its exercise, either in respect to ministry, regulation, discipline, or the public instruction of children, or otherwise, in this our kingdom and lands of our dominion, otherwise than in the places permitted and granted by the present edict.

XIV. It is forbidden as well to perform any function of the said religion in our court or retinue, or in our lands and territories beyond the mountains, or in our city of Paris, or within five leagues of the said city.

XVIII. We also forbid all our subjects, of whatever quality and condition, from carrying off by force or persuasion, against the will of their parents, the children of the said religion, in order to cause them to be baptized or confirmed in the Catholic Apostolic and Roman Church; and the same is forbidden to those of the said religion called Reformed, upon penalty of being punished with especial severity.

XXI. Books concerning the said religion called Reformed may not be printed and publicly sold, except in cities and places where the public exercise of the said religion is permitted.

XXII. We ordain that there shall be no difference or distinction made in respect to the said religion, in receiving pupils to be instructed in universities, colleges, and schools; nor in receiving the sick and poor into hospitals, retreats, and public charities.

XXIII. Those of the said religion called Reformed shall be obliged to respect the laws of the Catholic Apostolic and Roman Church, recognized in this our kingdom, for the consummation of marriages contracted, or to be contracted, as regards the degrees of consanguinity and kinship.

82

Mayflower Compact

The charter under which the *Mayflower* sailed in 1620 approved a settlement in "Virginia," somewhere north of the Jamestown colony (1607). Due to storms, the ship landed instead at Cape Cod (today Massachusetts). With the season advancing toward winter, the decision was made to remain there. That meant, however, that the settlement was outside the charter's grant, thereby invalidating the original structure of the colony's governance. Moreover, contrary to popular lore, not all 102 passengers aboard the *Mayflower* were of the same mindset. Several were religious Separatists, i.e., those parting ways with the Church of England as an irredeemable communion. Others had less overtly religious motivations for sailing to North America. Given the circumstances and organizational questions, the eclectic group of Plymouth settlers crafted their own *Mayflower Compact*—the document to organize their life together in New England.

In ye name of God, Amen. We whose names are underwriten, the loyall subjects of our dread soveraigne Lord, King James, by ye grace of God, of Great Britaine, Franc, & Ireland king, defender of ye faith, &c., haveing undertaken, for ye glorie of God, and advancemente of ye Christian faith, and honour of our king & countrie, a voyage to plant ye first colonie in ye Northerne parts of Virginia, doe by these presents solemnly & mutualy in ye presence of God, and one of another, covenant & combine our selves togeather into a civill body politick, for our better ordering & preservation & furtherance of ye ends aforesaid; and by vertue hearof to enacte, constitute, and frame such just & equall lawes, ordinances, acts, constitutions, & offices, from time to time, as shall be thought most meete & convenient for ye generall good of ye Colonie, unto which we promise all due submission and

SOURCE: William Bradford, *History of Plymouth Plantation*, ed. Charles Deane (Boston: Massachusetts Historical Society, 1856), 89–90.

obedience. In witnes wherof we have hereunder subscribed our names at Cap-Codd ye 11. of November, in ye year of ye raigne of our soveraigne lord, King James, of England, France, & Ireland ye eighteenth, and of Scotland ye fiftie fourth. An°: Dom. 1620.

83

William Bradford

from *History of Plymouth Plantation*

Investors expected a financial return from the Plymouth Colony, which was founded in 1620 near the Cape Cod peninsula of Massachusetts. Initially, Pilgrims practiced an economic system known as the "common course and condition," which meant communal ownership of resources. Given the risks and hard work of living in Plymouth, colonists chaffed under such conditions. In 1623, economic structures were altered to allow for privatized landholding. Thus, colonists worked more for individual benefit than for investors. In the following excerpt, Gov. William Bradford describes the reenergizing benefit that this decision held for the colony.

All this whille no supply was heard of, neither knew they when they might expecte any. So they begane to thinke how they might raise as much corne as they could, and obtaine a beter crope then they had done, that they might not still thus languish in miserie. At length, after much debate of things, the Govr (with ye advise of ye cheefest amongst them) gave way that they should set corne every man for his owne perticuler, and in that regard trust to them selves; in all other things to goe on in ye generall way as before. And so assigned to every family a parcell of land, according to the proportion of their number for that end, only for present use (but made no devission for inheritance), and ranged all boys & youth under some familie. This had very good success; for it made all hands very industrious, so as much more corne was planted then other waise would have bene by any means ye Govr or any other could use, and saved him a great deall of trouble, and gave farr better contente. The women now wente willingly into ye feild, and tooke their litle-ons with them to set

SOURCE: William Bradford, *History of Plymouth Plantation*, ed. Charles Deane (Boston: Massachusetts Historical Society, 1856), 134–36.

corne, which before would aledg weaknes, and inabilitie; whom to have compelled would have bene thought great tiranie and oppression.

The experience that was had in this comone course and condition, tried
sundrie years, and that amongst godly and sober men, may well evince the
vanitie of that conceite of Platos & other ancients, applauded by some of later times;—that ye taking away of propertie, and bringing in comunitie into a
comone wealth, would make them happy and florishing; as if they were wiser
then God. For this comunitie (so farr as it was) was found to breed much
confusion & discontent, and retard much imploymet that would have been
to their benefite and comforte. For ye yong-men that were most able and fitte
for labour & service did repine that they should spend their time & streingth
to worke for other mens wives and children, with out any recompence. The
strong, or man of parts, had no more in devission of victails & cloaths, then he
that was weake and not able to doe a quarter ye other could; this was thought
injuestice. The aged and graver men to be ranked and equalised in labours, and
victails, cloaths, &c., with ye meaner & yonger sorte, thought it some indignite
& disrespect unto them. And for mens wives to be commanded to doe servise
for other men, as dresing their meate, washing their cloaths, &c., they deemd it
a kind of slaverie, neither could many husbands well brooke it. Upon ye poynte
all being to have alike, and all to doe alike, they thought them selves in ye like
condition, and one as good as another; and so, if it did not cut of those relations that God hath set amongest men, yet it did at least much diminish and
take of ye mutuall respects that should be preserved amongst them. And would
have bene worse if they had been men of another condition. Let none objecte
this is men's corruption, and nothing to ye course it selfe. I answer, seeing all
men have this corruption in them, God in his wisdome saw another course
fiter for them.

84

John Winthrop

from *A Model of Christian Charity*

On October 29, 1629, the Massachusetts Bay Colony elected John Winthrop (1588–1649) as their Governor. Thus, it fell to him to explicate the mission and vision of this Puritan "errand into the wilderness" of North America. On board his flagship, the *Arbella*, Winthrop delivered the "Model of Christian Charity" as something of a constitution for the colony. (This was contemplated as a political speech and not as a sermon, since political officials were not authorized to preach.) The goal of the enterprise, Winthrop asserted, was the creation of a providentially structured Bible Commonwealth, ordered on key Christian principles (e.g., personal sacrifice for the well-being of others and the greater good). If these New England–bound Puritans honored their divine calling, their demonstration plot in New England would prove to England, and to the world, that Christian love could serve as the political foundation for building strong and stable communities.

Christian Charitie.

A Modell hereof.

GOD ALMIGHTY in his most holy and wise providence, hath soe disposed of the condition of mankind, as in all times some must be rich, some poore, some high and eminent in power and dignitie; others mean and in submission.

The Reason hereof.

1 *Reas.* First to hold conformity with the rest of his world, being delighted to show forth the glory of his wisdom in the variety and difference of the creatures,

SOURCE: John Winthrop, "A Modell of Christian Charity," in *Collections of the Massachusetts Historical Society*, 3rd series, vol. 7 (Boston: Charles C. Little and James Brown, 1838), 33–38, 40–41, 44, 46–47.

and the glory of his power in ordering all these differences for the preservation and good of the whole; and the glory of his greatness, that as it is the glory of princes to have many officers, soe this great king will haue many stewards, counting himself more honoured in dispensing his gifts to man by man, than if he did it by his owne immediate hands.

2 *Reas.* Secondly that he might haue the more occasion to manifest the work of his Spirit: first upon the wicked in moderating and restraining them: soe that the riche and mighty should not eate upp the poore nor the poore and dispised rise upp against and shake off theire yoake. 2ly In the regenerate, in exerciseing his graces in them, as in the grate ones, theire love, mercy, gentleness, temperance &c., in the poore and inferior sorte, theire faithe, patience, obedience &c.

3 *Reas.* Thirdly, that every man might have need of others, and from hence they might be all knitt more nearly together in the Bonds of brotherly affection. From hence it appears plainly that noe man is made more honourable than another or more wealthy &c., out of any particular and singular respect to himselfe, but for the glory of his creator and the common good of the creature, man. Therefore God still reserves the propperty of these gifts to himself as Ezek. 16. 17. he there calls wealthe, *his gold and his silver*, and Prov. 3. 9. he claims theire service as his due, *honor the Lord with thy riches* &c.—All men being thus (by divine providence) ranked into two sorts, riche and poore; under the first are comprehended all such as are able to live comfortably by their own meanes duely improved; and all others are poore according to the former distribution. There are two rules whereby we are to walk one towards another: Justice and Mercy. These are always distinguished in their act and in their object, yet may they both concurre in the same subject in eache respect; as sometimes there may be an occasion of showing mercy to a rich man in some sudden danger or distresse, and alsoe doeing of meere justice to a poor man in regard of some perticular contract &c. There is likewise a double Lawe by which wee are regulated in our conversation towardes another; in both the former respects, the lawe of nature and the lawe of grace, or the morrall lawe or the lawe of the gospell, to omitt the rule of justice as not propperly belonging to this purpose otherwise than it may fall into consideration in some perticular cases. By the first of these lawes man as he was enabled soe withall is commanded to love his neighbour as himself. Upon this ground stands all the precepts of the morrall lawe, which concernes our dealings with men. To apply this to the works of mercy; this lawe requires two things. First that every man afford his help to another in every want or distresse. Secondly, that hee performe this out of the same affection which makes him carefull of his owne

goods, according to that of our Savior, (Math.) *Whatsoever ye would that men should do to you.* This was practised by Abraham and Lot in entertaining the angells and the old man of Gibea. The lawe of Grace or of the Gospell hath some difference from the former; as in these respects, First the lawe of nature was given to man in the estate of innocency; this of the Gospell in the estate of regeneracy. 2ly, the former propounds one man to another, as the same flesh and image of God; this as a brother in Christ allsoe, and in the communion of the same Spirit, and soe teacheth to put a difference between christians and others. *Doe good to all, especially to the household of faith*; upon this ground the Israelites were to putt a difference betweene the brethren of such as were strangers though not of the Canaanites.

3ly. The Lawe of nature would give no rules for dealing with enemies, for all are to be considered as friends in the state of innocency, but the Gospell commands loue to an enemy. Proofe. *If thine Enemy hunger, feed him; Love your Enemies, doe good to them that hate you.* Math. 5. 44.

This lawe of the Gospell propounds likewise a difference of seasons and occasions. There is a time when a christian must sell all and give to the poor, as they did in the Apostles times. There is a time allsoe when christians (though they give not all yet) must give beyond their abillity, as they of Macedonia, Cor. 2, 6. Likewise community of perills calls for extraordinary liberality, and soe doth community in some speciall service for the churche. Lastly, when there is no other means whereby our christian brother may be relieved in his distress, we must help him beyond our ability rather than tempt God in putting him upon help by miraculous or extraordinary meanes.

This duty of mercy is exercised in the kinds, Giueving, lending and forgiving.—

Quest. What rule shall a man observe in giueving in respect of the measure?

Ans. If the time and occasion be ordinary he is to giue out of his abundance. *Let him lay aside as God hath blessed him.* If the time and occasion be extraordinary, he must be ruled by them; taking this withall, that then a man cannot likely doe too much, especially if he may leave himselfe and his family under probable means of comfortable subsistence.

[. . . .]

Object. *The wise man's Eies are in his head*, saith Solomon, *and foreseeth the plague*; therefore he must forecast and lay upp against evill times when hee or his may stand in need of all he can gather.

Ans. This very Argument Solomon useth to persuade to liberallity, Eccle.: *Cast thy bread upon the waters*, and *for thou knowest not what evill may come upon the land.* Luke 26. *Make you friends of the riches of iniquity*; you will ask how this shall be? very well. For first he that giues to the poore, lends to the lord and he will repay him even in this life an hundredfold to him or his.—*The righteous is ever mercifull and lendeth and his seed enjoyeth the blessing*; and besides wee know what advantage it will be to us in the day of account when many such witnesses shall stand forth for us to witnesse the improvement of our tallent. And I would know of those whoe pleade soe much for laying up for time to come, whether they holde that to be Gospell, Math. 16. 19. *Lay not upp for yourselves Treasures upon Earth &c.* If they acknowledge it, what extent will they allowe it? if only to those primitive times, let them consider the reason whereopon our Saviour groundes it. The first is that they are subject to the moathe, the rust, the theife. Secondly, They will steale away the hearte; *where the treasure is there will ye heart be allsoe.* The reasons are of like force at all times. Therefore the exhortation must be generall and perpetuall, withallwayes in respect of the love and affection to riches and in regard of the things themselves when any speciall seruice for the churche or perticular Distresse of our brother doe call for the use of them; otherwise it is not only lawfull but necessary to lay upp as Joseph did to haue ready uppon such occasions, as the Lord (whose stewards wee are of them) shall call for them from us; Christ giues us an Instance of the first, when hee sent his disciples for the Ass, and bidds them answer the owner thus, the Lord hath need of him: soe when the Tabernacle was to be built, he sends to his people to call for their silver and gold, &c; and yeildes noe other reason but that it was for his worke. When Elisha comes to the widow of Sareptah and findes her preparing to make ready her pittance for herselfe and family, he bids her first provide for him, he challengeth first God's parte which she must first give before shee must serve her owne family. All these teache us that the Lord lookes that when hee is pleased to call for his right in any thing wee haue, our owne interest wee haue, must stand aside till his turne be served. For the other, wee need looke noe further then to that of John 1. *he whoe hath this world's goodes and seeth his brother to neede and shutts upp his compassion from him, how dwelleth the loue of God in him,* which comes punctually to this conclusion; if thy brother be in want and thou canst help him, thou needst not make doubt, what thou shouldst doe; if thou louest God thou must help him.

Quest. What rule must wee observe in lending?

Ans. Thou must observe whether thy brother hath present or probable or possible means of repaying thee, if there be none of those, thou must give him according to his necessity, rather then lend him as he requires; if he hath present means of repaying thee, thou art to look at him not as an act of mercy, but by way of Commerce, wherein thou arte to walk by the rule of justice; but if his means of repaying thee be only probable or possible, then is hee an object of thy mercy, thou must lend him, though there be danger of losing it, Deut. 15. 7. *If any of thy brethren be poore &c., thou shalt lend him sufficient.* That men might not shift off this duty by the apparent hazzard, he tells them that though the yeare of Jubile were at hand (when he must remitt it, if hee were not able to repay it before) yet he must lend him and that chearefully. *It may not greive thee to give him* (saith hee) and because some might object, why soe I should soone impoverishe myself and my family, he adds with all thy worke &c; for our Saviour, Math. 5. 42. *From him that would borrow of thee turne not away.*

Quest. What rule must we observe in forgiuing?

Ans. Whether thou didst lend by way of commerce or in mercy, if he hath nothing to pay thee, must forgive, (except in cause where thou hast a surety or a lawfull pleadge) Deut. 15. 2. Every seaventh yeare the Creditor was to quitt that which he lent to his brother if he were poore as appears ver. 8. *Save when there shall be no poore with thee.* In all these and like cases, Christ was a generall rule, Math. 7. 22. *Whatsoever ye would that men should doe to you, doe yee the same to them allsoe.*

[. . . .]

From hence we may frame these conclusions. 1. First of all, true Christians are of one body in Christ, 1 Cor. 12. 12. 13. 17. *Ye are the body of Christ and members of their parte.* All the partes of this body being thus vnited are made soe contiguous in a speciall relation as they must needes partake of each other's strength and infirmity; joy and sorrowe, weale and woe. 1 Cor. 12. 26. *If one member suffers, all suffer with it, if one be in honor, all rejoyce with it.* 2ly. The ligaments of this body which knitt together are loue. 3ly. Noe body can be perfect which wants its proper ligament. 5ly. This sensibleness and sympathy of each other's conditions will necessarily infuse into each parte a native desire and endeavour, to strengthen, defend, preserve and comfort the other. To insist a little on this conclusion being the product of all the former, the truthe hereof will appeare both by precept and patterne. 1 John 3. 10. *Yee ought to lay doune your lives for the brethren.* Gal. 6. 2. *beare ye one another's burthen's and soe fulfill the lawe of Christ.* For patterns wee haue that first of our Saviour whoe out of his good will in obedience to his father, becomeing a parte of this body and being knitt with it in the bond of loue, found such a natiue sensibleness of our infirmities and sorrowes as he willingly yielded himselfe to deathe to ease the infirmities of the rest of his body, and soe healed theire sorrowes. From the like sympathy of partes did the Apostles and many thousands of the Saintes lay doune theire lives for Christ. Againe the like wee may see in the members of this body among themselves. 1 Rom. 9. Paule could have been contented to have been separated from Christ, that the Jewes might not be cutt off from the body. It is very observable what hee professeth of his affectionate partaking with every member; *whoe is weake* (saith hee) *and I am not weake? whoe is offended and I burne not*; and againe, 2 Cor. 7. 13. *therefore wee are comforted because yee were comforted.* Of Epaphroditus he speaketh, Phil. 2. 30. *that he regarded not his owne life to do him service.* Soe Phebe and others are called *the servants of the churche.* Now it is apparent that they served not for wages, or by constrainte, but out of loue. The like we shall finde in the histories of the churche, in all ages; the sweete sympathie of affections which was in the members of this body one towards another; theire chearfullness in serueing and suffering together; how liberall they were without repineing, harbourers without grudgeing, and helpfull without reproaching; and all from hence, because they had feruent loue amongst them; which onely makes the practise of mercy constant and easie.

[. . . .]

From the former Considerations arise these Conclusions.—1. First, This loue among Christians is a reall thing, not imaginarie. 2ly. This loue is as absolutely necessary to the being of the body of Christ, as the sinews and other ligaments of a naturall body are to the being of that body. 3ly. This loue is a divine, spirituall, nature; free, active, strong, couragious, permanent; undervaluing all things beneathe its propper object and of all the graces, this makes us nearer to resemble the virtues of our heavenly father. 4thly It rests in the loue and wellfare of its beloued. For the full certain knowledge of those truthes concerning the nature, use, and excellency of this grace, that which the holy ghost hath left recorded, 1 Cor. 13, may give full satisfaction, which is needful for every true member of this louely body of the Lord Jesus, to worke upon theire heartes by prayer, meditation continuall exercise at least of the speciall [influence] of this grace, till Christ be formed in them and they in him, all in eache other, knitt together by this bond of loue.

[. . . .]

Now the onely way to avoyde this shipwracke, and to provide for our posterity, is to followe the counsell of Micah, *to doe justly, to love mercy, to walk humbly with our God.* For this end, wee must be knitt together, in this worke, as one man. Wee must entertaine each other in brotherly affection. Wee must be willing to abridge ourselves of our superfluities, for the supply of other's necessities. Wee must uphold a familiar commerce together in all meekeness, gentlenes, patience and liberality. Wee must delight in eache other; make other's conditions our oune; rejoice together, mourne together, labour and suffer together, allwayes haueuing before our eyes our commission and community in the worke, as members of the same body. Soe shall wee *keepe the unitie of the spirit in the bond of peace.* The Lord will be our God, and delight to dwell among us, as his oune people, and will command a blessing upon us in all our wayes. Soe that wee shall see much more of his wisdome, power, goodness and truthe, than formerly wee haue been acquainted with. Wee shall finde that the God of Israell is among us, when ten of us shall be able to resist a thousand of our enemies; when hee shall make us a prayse and glory that men shall say of succeeding plantations, "the Lord make it likely that of *New England.*" For wee must consider that wee shall be as a citty upon a hill. The eies of all people are uppon us. Soe that if wee shall deale falsely with our God in this worke wee haue undertaken, and soe cause him to withdrawe his present help from us, wee shall be made a story and a by-word through the world. Wee shall open the mouthes of enemies to speake evil of the wayes of God, and all professors for God's sake. Wee shall shame the faces of many of God's worthy servants, and cause theire prayers to be turned into curses upon us till wee be consumed out of the good land whither wee are a goeing.

85

René Descartes

from *Meditations on First Philosophy*

René Descartes (1596–1650) was a French intellectual of the highest order who made significant contributions to the disciplines of mathematics, geometry, physics, natural science, and philosophy. He is often heralded as the father of early modern philosophy, in part due to his influence on many of the key debates that would take place for centuries to come. The following is an excerpt from Descartes' best-known philosophical work, *Meditations on First Philosophy*, in which he attempts to combat epistemological skepticism, lay the groundwork for knowledge, and demonstrate (among other things) the existence of the soul and God by means of reasoning alone.

Meditation I: Of the Things on Which We May Doubt.

Several years have now elapsed since I first became aware that I had accepted, even from my youth, many false opinions for true, and that consequently what I afterward based on such principles was highly doubtful; and from that time I was convinced of the necessity of undertaking once in my life to rid myself of all the opinions I had adopted, and of commencing anew the work of building from the foundation, if I desired to establish a firm and abiding superstructure in the sciences. But as this enterprise appeared to me to be one of great magnitude, I waited until I had attained an age so mature as to leave me no hope that at any stage of life more advanced I should be better able to execute my design. On this account, I have delayed so long that I should henceforth consider I was doing wrong were I still to consume in deliberation any of the time that now remains for action. To-day, then, since I have opportunely

SOURCE: René Descartes, *The Method, Meditations, and Philosophy of Descartes*, trans. John Veitch (Washington: M. Walter Dunne, 1901), 219–29.

freed my mind from all cares [and am happily disturbed by no passions], and since I am in the secure possession of leisure in a peaceable retirement, I will at length apply myself earnestly and freely to the general overthrow of all my former opinions. But, to this end, it will not be necessary for me to show that the whole of these are false—a point, perhaps, which I shall never reach; but as even now my reason convinces me that I ought not the less carefully to withhold belief from what is not entirely certain and indubitable, than from what is manifestly false, it will be sufficient to justify the rejection of the whole if I shall find in each some ground for doubt. Nor for this purpose will it be necessary even to deal with each belief individually, which would be truly an endless labor; but, as the removal from below of the foundation necessarily involves the downfall of the whole edifice, I will at once approach the criticism of the principles on which all my former beliefs rested.

All that I have, up to this moment, accepted as possessed of the highest truth and certainty, I received either from or through the senses. I observed, however, that these sometimes misled us; and it is the part of prudence not to place absolute confidence in that by which we have even once been deceived.

But it may be said, perhaps, that, although the senses occasionally mislead us respecting minute objects, and such as are so far removed from us as to be beyond the reach of close observation, there are yet many other of their informations (presentations), of the truth of which it is manifestly impossible to doubt; as for example, that I am in this place, seated by the fire, clothed in a winter dressing gown, that I hold in my hands this piece of paper, with other intimations of the same nature. But how could I deny that I possess these hands and this body, and withal escape being classed with persons in a state of insanity, whose brains are so disordered and clouded by dark bilious vapors as to cause them pertinaciously to assert that they are monarchs when they are in the greatest poverty; or clothed [in gold] and purple when destitute of any covering; or that their head is made of clay, their body of glass, or that they are gourds? I should certainly be not less insane than they, were I to regulate my procedure according to examples so extravagant.

Though this be true, I must nevertheless here consider that I am a man, and that, consequently, I am in the habit of sleeping, and representing to myself in dreams those same things, or even sometimes others less probable, which the insane think are presented to them in their waking moments. How often have I dreamt that I was in these familiar circumstances, that I was dressed, and occupied this place by the fire, when I was lying undressed in bed? At the present moment, however, I certainly look upon this paper with eyes wide awake; the head which I now move is not asleep; I extend this hand consciously and with express purpose, and I perceive it; the occurrences in sleep are not so distinct as all this. But I cannot forget that, at other times I have been deceived in sleep by similar illusions; and, attentively considering those cases, I perceive so clearly that there exist no certain marks by which the state of waking can ever be distinguished from sleep, that I feel greatly astonished; and in amazement I almost persuade myself that I am now dreaming.

Let us suppose, then, that we are dreaming, and that all these particulars—namely, the opening of the eyes, the motion of the head, the forth-putting of the hands—are merely illusions; and even that we really possess neither an entire body nor hands such as we see. Nevertheless it must be admitted at least that the objects which appear to us in sleep are, as it were, painted representations which could not have been formed unless in the likeness of realities; and, therefore, that those general objects, at all events, namely, eyes, a head, hands, and an entire body, are not simply imaginary, but really existent. For, in truth, painters themselves, even when they study to represent sirens and satyrs by forms the most fantastic and extraordinary, cannot bestow upon them natures absolutely new, but can only make a certain medley of the members of different animals; or if they chance to imagine something so novel that nothing at all similar has ever been seen before, and such as is, therefore, purely fictitious and absolutely false, it is at least certain that the colors of which this is composed are real.

And on the same principle, although these general objects, viz, [a body], eyes, a head, hands, and the like, be imaginary, we are nevertheless absolutely necessitated to admit the reality at least of some other objects still more simple and universal than these, of which, just as of certain real colors, all those images of things, whether true and real, or false and fantastic, that are found in our consciousness . . . , are formed.

To this class of objects seem to belong corporeal nature in general and its extension; the figure of extended things, their quantity or magnitude, and their number, as also the place in, and the time during, which they exist, and other things of the same sort. We will not, therefore, perhaps reason illegitimately if we conclude from this that Physics, Astronomy, Medicine, and all the other sciences that have for their end the consideration of composite objects, are indeed of a doubtful character; but that Arithmetic, Geometry, and the other sciences of the same class, which regard merely the simplest and most general objects, and scarcely inquire whether or not these are really existent, contain somewhat that is certain and indubitable: for whether I am awake or dreaming, it remains true that two and three make five, and that a square has but four sides; nor does it seem possible that truths so apparent can ever fall under a suspicion of falsity [or incertitude].

Nevertheless, the belief that there is a God who is all powerful, and who created me, such as I am, has, for a long time, obtained steady possession of my mind. How, then, do I know that he has not arranged that there should be neither earth, nor sky, nor any extended thing, nor figure, nor magnitude, nor place, providing at the same time, however, for [the rise in me of the perceptions of all these objects, and] the persuasion that these do not exist otherwise than as I perceive them? And further, as I sometimes think that others are in error respecting matters of which they believe themselves to possess a perfect knowledge, how do I know that I am not also deceived each time I add together two and three, or number the sides of a square, or form some judgment still more simple, if more simple indeed can be imagined? But perhaps Deity has not been willing that I should be thus deceived, for he is said to be supremely good. If, however, it were repugnant to the goodness of Deity to have created me subject to constant deception, it would seem likewise to be contrary to his goodness to allow me to be occasionally deceived; and yet it is clear that this is permitted. Some, indeed, might perhaps be found who would be disposed rather to deny the existence of a Being so powerful than to believe that there is nothing certain. But let us for the present refrain from opposing this opinion, and grant that all which is here said of a Deity is fabulous: nevertheless, in whatever way it be supposed that I reach the state in which I exist, whether by fate, or chance, or by an endless series of antecedents and consequents, or by any other means, it is clear (since to be deceived and to err is a certain defect) that the probability of my being so imperfect as to be the constant victim of deception, will be increased exactly in proportion as the power possessed by the cause, to which they assign my origin, is lessened. To these reasonings I have assuredly nothing to reply, but am constrained at last to avow that there is nothing of all that I formerly believed to be true of which it is impossible to doubt, and that not through thoughtlessness or levity, but from cogent and maturely considered reasons; so that henceforward, if I desire to discover anything certain, I ought not the less carefully to refrain from assenting to those same opinions than to what might be shown to be manifestly false.

But it is not sufficient to have made these observations; care must be taken likewise to keep them in remembrance. For those old and customary opinions perpetually recur—long and familiar usage giving them the right of occupying my mind, even almost against my will, and subduing my belief; nor will I lose the habit of deferring to them and confiding in them so long as I shall consider them to be what in truth they are, viz, opinions to some extent doubtful, as I have already shown, but still highly probable, and such as it is much more reasonable to believe than deny. It is for this reason I am persuaded that I shall not be doing wrong, if, taking an opposite judgment of deliberate design, I become my own deceiver, by supposing, for a time, that all those opinions are entirely false and imaginary, until at length, having thus balanced my old by my new prejudices, my judgment shall no longer be turned aside by perverted usage from the path that may conduct to the perception of truth. For I am assured that, meanwhile, there will arise neither peril nor error from this course, and that I cannot for the present yield too much to distrust, since the end I now seek is not action but knowledge.

I will suppose, then, not that Deity, who is sovereignly good and the fountain of truth, but that some malignant demon, who is at once exceedingly potent and deceitful, has employed all his artifice to deceive me; I will suppose that the sky, the air, the earth, colors, figures, sounds, and all external things, are nothing better than the illusions of dreams, by means of which this being has laid snares for my credulity; I will consider myself as without hands, eyes, flesh, blood, or any of the senses, and as falsely believing that I am possessed of these; I will continue resolutely fixed in this belief, and if indeed by this means it be not in my power to arrive at the knowledge of truth, I shall at least do what is in my power, [viz., suspend my judgment], and guard with settled purpose against giving my assent to what is false, and being imposed upon by this deceiver, whatever be his power and artifice.

But this undertaking is arduous, and a certain indolence insensibly leads me back to my ordinary course of life; and just as the captive, who, perchance, was enjoying in his dreams an imaginary liberty, when he begins to suspect that it is but a vision, dreads awakening, and conspires with the agreeable illusions that the deception may be prolonged; so I, of my own accord, fall back into the train of my former beliefs, and fear to arouse myself from my slumber, lest the time of laborious wakefulness that would succeed this quiet rest, in place of bringing any light of day, should prove inadequate to dispel the darkness that will arise from the difficulties that have now been raised.

Meditation II: Of the Nature of the Human Mind; and That It Is More Easily Known than the Body.

The Meditation of yesterday has filled my mind with so many doubts, that it is no longer in my power to forget them. Nor do I see, meanwhile, any principle on which they can be resolved; and, just as if I had fallen all of a sudden into very deep water, I am so greatly disconcerted as to be unable either to plant my feet firmly on the bottom or sustain myself by swimming on the surface. I will, nevertheless, make an effort, and try anew the same path on which I had entered yesterday, that is, proceed by casting aside all that admits of the slightest doubt, not less than if I had discovered it to be absolutely false; and I will continue always in this track until I shall find something that is certain, or at least, if I can do nothing more, until I shall know with certainty that there is nothing certain. Archimedes, that he might transport the entire globe from the place it occupied to another, demanded only a point that was firm and immovable; so, also, I shall be entitled to entertain the highest expectations, if I am fortunate enough to discover only one thing that is certain and indubitable.

I suppose, accordingly, that all the things which I see are false (fictitious); I believe that none of those objects which my fallacious memory represents ever existed; I suppose that I possess no senses; I believe that body, figure, extension, motion, and place are merely fictions of my mind. What is there, then, that can be esteemed true? Perhaps this only, that there is absolutely nothing certain.

But how do I know that there is not something different altogether from the objects I have now enumerated, of which it is impossible to entertain the slightest doubt? Is there not a God, or some being, by whatever name I may designate him, who causes these thoughts to arise in my mind? But why suppose such a being, for it may be I myself am capable of producing them? Am I, then, at least not something? But I before denied that I possessed senses or a body; I hesitate, however, for what follows from that? Am I so dependent on the body and the senses that without these I cannot exist? But I had the persuasion that there was absolutely nothing in the world, that there was no sky and no earth, neither minds nor bodies; was I not, therefore, at the same time, persuaded that I did not exist? Far from it; I assuredly existed, since I was persuaded. But there is I know not what being, who is possessed at once of the highest power and the deepest cunning, who is constantly employing all his ingenuity in deceiving me. Doubtless, then, I exist, since I am deceived; and, let him deceive me as he may, he can never bring it about that I am nothing, so long as I shall be conscious that I am something. So that it must, in fine, be maintained, all things being maturely and carefully considered, that this proposition . . . I am, I exist, is necessarily true each time it is expressed by me, or conceived in my mind.

But I do not yet know with sufficient clearness what I am, though assured that I am; and hence, in the next place, I must take care, lest perchance I inconsiderately substitute some other object in room of what is properly myself, and thus wander from truth, even in that knowledge (cognition) which I hold to be of all others the most certain and evident. For this reason, I will now consider anew what I formerly believed myself to be, before I entered on the present train of thought; and of my previous opinion I will retrench all that can in the least be invalidated by the grounds of doubt I have adduced, in order that there may at length remain nothing but what is certain and indubitable. What then did I formerly think I was? Undoubtedly I judged that I was a man. But what is a man? Shall I say a rational animal? Assuredly not; for it would be necessary forthwith to inquire into what is meant by animal, and what by rational, and thus, from a single question, I should insensibly glide into others, and these more difficult than the first; nor do I now possess enough of leisure to warrant me in wasting my time amid subtleties of this sort. I prefer here to attend to the thoughts that sprung up of themselves in my mind, and were inspired by my own nature alone, when I applied myself to the consideration of what I was. In the first place, then, I thought that I possessed a countenance, hands, arms, and all the fabric of members that appears in a corpse, and which I called by the name of body. It further occurred to me that I was nourished, that I walked, perceived, and thought, and all those actions I referred to the soul; but what the soul itself was I either did not stay to consider, or, if I did, I imagined that it was something extremely rare and subtile, like wind, or flame, or ether, spread through my grosser parts. As regarded the body, I did not even doubt of its nature, but thought I distinctly knew it, and if I had wished to describe it according to the notions I then entertained, I should have explained myself in this manner: By body I understand all that can be terminated by a certain figure; that can be comprised in a certain place, and so fill a certain space as therefrom to exclude every other body; that can be perceived either by touch, sight, hearing, taste, or smell; that can be moved in different ways, not indeed of itself, but by something foreign to it by which it is touched [and from which it receives the impression]; for the power of self-motion, as likewise that of perceiving and thinking, I held as by no means pertaining to the nature of body; on the contrary, I was somewhat astonished to find such faculties existing in some bodies.

But [as to myself, what can I now say that I am], since I suppose there exists an extremely powerful, and, if I may so speak, malignant being, whose whole endeavors are directed toward deceiving me? Can I affirm that I possess any one of all those attributes of which I have lately spoken as belonging to the nature of body? After attentively considering them in my own mind, I find none of them that can properly be said to belong to myself. To recount them were idle and tedious. Let us pass, then, to the attributes of the soul. The first mentioned were the powers of nutrition and walking; but, if it be true that I have no body, it is true likewise that I am capable neither of walking nor of being nourished. Perception is another attribute of the soul; but perception too is impossible without the body; besides, I have frequently, during sleep, believed that I perceived objects which I afterward observed I did not in reality perceive. Thinking is another attribute of the soul; and here I discover what properly belongs to myself. This alone is inseparable from me. I am—I exist: this is certain; but how often? As often as I think; for perhaps it would even happen, if I should wholly cease to think, that I should at the same time altogether cease to be. I now admit nothing that is not necessarily true. I am therefore, precisely speaking, only a thinking thing, that is, a mind . . . , understanding, or reason, terms whose signification was before unknown to me. I am, however, a real thing, and really existent; but what thing? The answer was, a thinking thing. The question now arises, am I aught besides? I will stimulate my imagination with a view to discover whether I am not still something more than a thinking being. Now it is plain I am not the assemblage of members called the human body; I am not a thin and penetrating air diffused through all these members, or wind, or flame, or vapor, or breath, or any of all the things I can imagine; *for* I supposed that all these were not, and, without changing the supposition, I find that I still feel assured of my existence.

But it is true, perhaps, that those very things which I suppose to be nonexistent, because they are unknown to me, are not in troth different from myself whom I know. This is a point I cannot determine, and do not now enter into any dispute regarding it. I can only judge of things that are known to me: I am conscious that I exist, and I who know that I exist inquire into what I am. It is, however, perfectly certain that the knowledge of my existence, thus precisely taken, is not dependent on things, the existence of which is as yet unknown to me: and consequently it is not dependent on any of the things I can feign in imagination. Moreover, the phrase itself, I frame an image . . . , reminds me of my error; for I should in truth frame one if I were to imagine myself to be anything, since to imagine is nothing more than to contemplate the figure or image of a corporeal thing; but I already know that I exist, and that it is possible at the same time that all those images, and in general all that relates to the nature of body, are merely dreams [or chimeras]. From this I discover that it is not more reasonable to say, I will excite my imagination that I may know more distinctly what I am, than to express myself as follows: I am now awake, and perceive something real; but because my perception is not sufficiently clear, I will of express purpose go to sleep that my dreams may represent to me the object of my perception with more truth and clearness. And, therefore, I know that nothing of all that I can embrace in imagination belongs to the knowledge which I have of myself, and that there is need to recall with the utmost care the mind from this mode of thinking, that it may be able to know its own nature with perfect distinctness.

But what, then, am I? A thinking thing, it has been said. But what is a thinking thing? It is a thing that doubts, understands, [conceives], affirms, denies, wills, refuses; that imagines also, and perceives.

86

Thomas Hobbes

from *Leviathan*

Thomas Hobbes (1588–1679) was an English philosopher who is best known for his work in political thought, particularly in his presentation of the natural law and social contract theory in his most famous work, *Leviathan*. But Hobbes also made serious intellectual contributions in other areas of philosophy, as well as in physics, history, mathematics, and as a translator of Homer's epic poems. The following is perhaps the best-known excerpt from his *Leviathan* wherein he reflects on human life in state of nature, which he famously takes to be rather grim.

Chapter XIII: Of the Naturall Condition of Mankind, as concerning Their Felicity, and Misery.

Nature hath made men so equall, in the faculties of body, and mind; as that though there bee found one man sometimes manifestly stronger in body, or of quicker mind then another; yet when all is reckoned together, the difference between man, and man, is not so considerable, as that one man can thereupon claim to himselfe any benefit, to which another may not pretend, as well as he. For as to the strength of body, the weakest has strength enough to kill the strongest, either by secret machination, or by confederacy with others, that are in the same danger with himselfe.

And as to the faculties of the mind, (setting aside the arts grounded upon words, and especially that skill of proceeding upon generall, and infallible rules, called Science; which very few have, and but in few things; as being not a native faculty, born with us; nor attained, (as Prudence,) while we look

SOURCE: Thomas Hobbes, *Hobbes's Leviathan, Reprinted from the Edition of 1651, with an Essay by the Late W. G. Pogson Smith* (Oxford: Clarendon Press, 1909), 94–102, 110–11, 128–32.

after somewhat els,) I find yet a greater equality amongst men, than that of strength.

[. . . .]

From this equality of ability, ariseth equality of hope in the attaining of our Ends. And therefore if any two men desire the same thing, which neverthelesse they cannot both enjoy, they become enemies; and in the way to their End, (which is principally their owne conservation, and sometimes their delectation only,) endeavour to destroy, or subdue one an other. And from hence it comes to passe, that where an Invader hath no more to feare, than an other mans single power; if one plant, sow, build, or possesse a convenient Seat, others may probably be expected to come prepared with forces united, to dispossesse, and deprive him, not only of the fruit of his labour, but also of his life, or liberty. And the Invader again is in the like danger of another.

And from this diffidence of one another, there is no way for any man to secure himselfe, so reasonable, as Anticipation; that is, by force, or wiles, to master the persons of all men he can, so long, till he see no other power great enough to endanger him: And this is no more than his own conservation requireth, and is generally allowed. Also because there be some, that taking pleasure in contemplating their own power in the acts of conquest, which they pursue farther than their security requires; if others, that otherwise would be glad to be at ease within modest bounds, should not by invasion increase their power, they would not be able, long time, by standing only on their defence, to subsist. And by consequence, such augmentation of dominion over men, being necessary to a mans conservation, it ought to be allowed him.

Againe, men have no pleasure, (but on the contrary a great deale of griefe) in keeping company, where there is no power able to over-awe them all. For every man looketh that his companion should value him, at the same rate he sets upon himselfe: And upon all signes of contempt, or undervaluing, naturally endeavours, as far as he dares (which amongst them that have no common power to keep them in quiet, is far enough to make them destroy each other,) to extort a greater value from his contemners, by dommage; and from others, by the example.

So that in the nature of man, we find three principall causes of quarrell. First, Competition; Secondly, Diffidence; Thirdly, Glory.

The first, maketh men invade for Gain; the second, for Safety; and the third, for Reputation. The first use Violence, to make themselves Masters of other mens persons, wives, children, and cattell; the second, to defend them; the third, for trifles, as a word, a smile, a different opinion, and any other signe of undervalue, either direct in their Persons, or by reflexion in their Kindred, their Friends, their Nation, their Profession, or their Name.

Hereby it is manifest, that during the time men live without a common Power to keep them all in awe, they are in that condition which is called Warre; and such a warre, as is of every man, against every man. For Warre, consisteth not in Battell onely, or the act of fighting; but in a tract of time, wherein the Will to contend by Battell is sufficiently known: and therefore the notion of *Time*, is to be considered in the nature of Warre; as it is in the nature of Weather. For as the nature of Foule weather, lyeth not in a showre or two of rain; but in an inclination thereto of many dayes together; So the nature of War, consisteth not in actuall fighting; but in the known disposition thereto, during all the time there is no assurance to the contrary. All other time is Peace.

Whatsoever therefore is consequent to a time of Warre, where every man is Enemy to every man; the same is consequent to the time, wherein men live without other security, than what their own strength, and their own invention shall furnish them withall. In such condition, there is no place for Industry; because the fruit thereof is uncertain: and consequently no Culture of the Earth; no Navigation, nor use of the commodities that may be imported by Sea; no commodious Building; no Instruments of moving, and removing such things as require much force; no Knowledge of the face of the Earth; no account of Time; no Arts; no Letters; no Society; and which is worst of all, continuall feare, and danger of violent death; And the life of man, solitary, poore, nasty, brutish, and short.

It may seem strange to some man, that has not well weighed these things; that Nature should thus dissociate, and render men apt to invade, and destroy one another: and he may therefore, not trusting to this Inference, made from the Passions, desire perhaps to have the same confirmed by Experience. Let him therefore consider with himselfe, when taking a journey, he armes himselfe, and seeks to go well accompanied; when going to sleep, he locks his dores; when even in his house he locks his chests; and this when he knowes there bee Lawes, and publike Officers, armed, to revenge all injuries shall bee done him; what opinion he has of his fellow subjects, when he rides armed; of his fellow Citizens, when he locks his dores; and of his children, and servants, when he locks his chests. Does he not there as much accuse mankind by his actions, as I do by my words? But neither of us accuse mans nature in it. The Desires, and other Passions of man, are in themselves no Sin. No more are the Actions, that proceed from those Passions, till they know a Law that forbids them: which till Lawes be made they cannot know: nor can any Law be made, till they have agreed upon the Person that shall make it.

It may peradventure be thought, there was never such a time, nor condition of warre as this; and I believe it was never generally so, over all the world: but there are many places, where they live so now. For the savage people in many places of *America*, except the government of small Families, the concord whereof dependeth on naturall lust, have no government at all; and live at this day in that brutish manner, as I said before. Howsoever, it may be perceived what manner of life there would be, where there were no common Power to feare; by the manner of life, which men that have formerly lived under a peacefull government, use to degenerate into, in a civill Warre.

But though there had never been any time, wherein particular men were in a condition of warre one against another; yet in all times, Kings, and Persons of Soveraigne authority, because of their Independency, are in continuall jealousies, and in the state and posture of Gladiators; having their weapons pointing, and their eyes fixed on one another; that is, their Forts, Garrisons, and Guns upon the Frontiers of their Kingdomes; and continuall Spyes upon their neighbours; which is a posture of War. But because they uphold thereby, the Industry of their Subjects; there does not follow from it, that misery, which accompanies the Liberty of particular men.

To this warre of every man against every man, this also is consequent; that nothing can be Unjust. The notions of Right and Wrong, Justice and Injustice have there no place. Where there is no common Power, there is no Law: where no Law, no Injustice. Force, and Fraud, are in warre the two Cardinall vertues. Justice, and Injustice are none of the Faculties neither of the Body, nor Mind. If they were, they might be in a man that were alone in the world, as well as his Senses, and Passions. They are Qualities, that relate to men in Society, not in Solitude. It is consequent also to the same condition, that there be no Propriety, no Dominion, no *Mine* and *Thine* distinct; but onely that to be every mans, that he can get; and for so long, as he can keep it. And thus much for the ill condition, which man by meer Nature is actually placed in; though with a possibility to come out of it, consisting partly in the Passions, partly in his Reason.

The Passions that encline men to Peace, are Feare of Death; Desire of such things as are necessary to commodious living; and a Hope by their Industry to obtain them. And Reason suggesteth convenient Articles of Peace, upon which men may be drawn to agreement. These Articles, are they, which otherwise are called the Lawes of Nature: whereof I shall speak more particularly, in the two following Chapters.

Chapter XIV: Of the First and Second Naturall Lawes, and of Contracts.

The Right Of Nature, which Writers commonly call *Jus Naturale,* is the Liberty each man hath, to use his own power, as he will himselfe, for the preservation of his own Nature; that is to say, of his own Life; and consequently, of doing any thing, which in his own Judgement, and Reason, hee shall conceive to be the aptest means thereunto.

By Liberty, is understood, according to the proper signification of the word, the absence of externall Impediments: which Impediments, may oft take away part of a mans power to do what hee would; but cannot hinder him from using the power left him, according as his judgement, and reason shall dictate to him.

A Law Of Nature, (*Lex Naturalis,*) is a Precept, or generall Rule, found out by Reason, by which a man is forbidden to do, that, which is destructive of his life, or taketh away the means of preserving the same; and to omit, that, by which he thinketh it may be best preserved. For though they that speak of this subject, use to confound *Jus,* and *Lex, Right* and *Law*; yet they ought to be distinguished; because Right, consisteth in liberty to do, or to forbeare; Whereas Law, determineth, and bindeth to one of them: so that Law, and Right, differ as much, as Obligation, and Liberty; which in one and the same matter are inconsistent.

And because the condition of Man, (as hath been declared in the precedent Chapter) is a condition of Warre of every one against every one; in which case every one is governed by his own Reason; and there is nothing he can make use of, that may not be a help unto him, in preserving his life against his enemyes; It followeth, that in such a condition, every man has a Right to every thing; even to one anothers body. And therefore, as long as this naturall Right of every man to every thing endureth, there can be no security to any man, (how strong or wise soever he be,) of living out the time, which Nature ordinarily alloweth men to live. And consequently it is a precept, or generall rule of Reason, *That every man, ought to endeavour Peace, as farre as he has hope of obtaining it; and when he cannot obtain it, that he may seek, and use, all helps, and advantages of Warre.* The first branch of which Rule, containeth the first, and Fundamentall Law of Nature; which is, *to seek Peace, and follow it.* The Second, the summe of the Right of Nature; which is, *By all means we can, to defend our selves.*

From this Fundamentall Law of Nature, by which men are commanded to endeavour Peace, is derived this second Law; *That a man be willing, when others are so too, as farre-forth, as for Peace, and defence of himselfe he shall think it necessary, to lay down this right to all things; and be contented with so much liberty against other men, as he would allow other men against himselfe.* For as long as every man holdeth this Right, of doing any thing he liketh; so long are all men in the condition of Warre. But if other men will not lay down their Right, as well as he; then there is no Reason for any one, to devest himselfe of his: For that were to expose himselfe to Prey, (which no man is bound to) rather than to dispose himselfe to Peace. This is that Law of the Gospell; *Whatsoever you require that others should do to you, that do ye to them.* And that Law of all men, *Quod tibi fieri non vis, alteri ne feceris.*

To *lay downe* a mans *Right* to any thing, is to *devest* himselfe of the *Liberty*, of hindring another of the benefit of his own Right to the same. For he that renounceth, or passeth away his Right, giveth not to any other man a Right which he had not before; because there is nothing to which every man had not Right by Nature: but onely standeth out of his way, that he may enjoy his own originall Right, without hindrance from him; not without hindrance from another. So that the effect which redoundeth to one man, by another mans defect of Right, is but so much diminution of impediments to the use of his own Right originall.

Right is layd aside, either by simply Renouncing it; or by Transferring it to another. By *Simply* Renouncing; when he cares not to whom the benefit thereof redoundeth. By Transferring; when he intendeth the benefit thereof to some certain person, or persons. And when a man hath in either manner abandoned, or granted away his Right; then is he said to be Obliged, or Bound, not to hinder those, to whom such Right is granted, or abandoned, from the benefit of it: and that he *ought*, and it is his Duty, not to make voyd that voluntary act of his own: and that such hindrance is Injustice, and Injury, as being *Sine Jure*; the Right being before renounced, or transferred. So that *Injury*, or *Injustice*, in the controversies of the world, is somewhat like to that, which in the disputations of Scholers is called *Absurdity*. For as it is there called an Absurdity, to contradict what one maintained in the Beginning: so in the world, it is called Injustice, and injury voluntarily to undo that, which from the beginning he had voluntarily done. The way by which a man either simply Renounceth, or Transferreth his Right, is a Declaration, or Signification, by some voluntary and sufficient signe, or signes, that he doth so Renounce, or Transferre; or hath so Renounced, or Transferred the same, to him that accepteth it. And these Signes are either Words onely, or Actions onely; or (as it happeneth most often) both Words, and Actions. And the same are the Bonds, by which men are bound, and obliged: Bonds, that have their strength, not from their own Nature, (for nothing is more easily broken then a mans word,) but from Feare of some evill consequence upon the rupture.

Whensoever a man Transferreth his Right, or Renounceth it; it is either in consideration of some Right reciprocally transferred to himselfe; or for some other good he hopeth for thereby. For it is a voluntary act: and of the voluntary acts of every man, the object is some *Good to himselfe*. And therefore there be some Rights, which no man can be understood by any words, or other signes, to have abandoned, or transferred. As first a man cannot lay down the right of resisting them, that assault him by force, to take away his life; because he cannot be understood to ayme thereby, at any Good to himselfe. The same may be sayd of Wounds, and Chayns, and Imprisonment; both because there is no benefit consequent to such patience; as there is to the patience of suffering another to be wounded, or imprisoned: as also because a man cannot tell, when he seeth men proceed against him by violence, whether they intend his death or not. And lastly the motive, and end for which this renouncing, and transferring of Right is introduced, is nothing else but the security of a mans person, in his life, and in the means of so preserving life, as not to be weary of it. And therefore if a man by words, or other signes, seem to despoyle himselfe of the End, for which those signes were intended; he is not to be understood as if he meant it, or that it was his will; but that he was ignorant of how such words and actions were to be interpreted.

The mutuall transferring of Right, is that which men call Contract.

There is difference, between transferring of Right to the Thing; and transferring, or tradition, that is, delivery of the Thing it selfe. For the Thing may be delivered together with the Translation of the Right; as in buying and selling with ready mony; or exchange of goods, or lands: and it may be delivered some time after.

Again, one of the Contractors, may deliver the Thing contracted for on his part, and leave the other to perform his part at some determinate time after, and in the mean time be trusted; and then the Contract on his part, is called Pact, or Covenant: Or both parts may contract now, to performe hereafter: in which cases, he that is to performe in time to come, being trusted, his performance is called *Keeping of Promise*, or Faith; and the fayling of performance (if it be voluntary) *Violation of Faith*.

[. . . .]

Chapter XV: Of other Lawes of Nature.

From that law of Nature, by which we are obliged to transferre to another, such Rights, as being retained, hinder the peace of Mankind, there followeth a Third; which is this, *That men performe their Covenants made*: without which,

Covenants are in vain, and but Empty words; and the Right of all men to all things remaining, wee are still in the condition of Warre.

And in this law of Nature, consisteth the Fountain and Originall of Justice. For where no Covenant hath preceded, there hath no Right been transferred, and every man has right to every thing; and consequently, no action can be Unjust. But when a Covenant is made, then to break it is *Unjust*: And the definition of Iniustice, is no other than *the not Performance of Covenant*. And whatsoever is not Unjust, is *Just*.

But because Covenants of mutuall trust, where there is a feare of not performance on either part, (as hath been said in the former Chapter,) are invalid; though the Originall of Justice be the making of Covenants; yet Injustice actually there can be none, till the cause of such feare be taken away; which while men are in the naturall condition of Warre, cannot be done. Therefore before the names of Just, and Unjust can have place, there must be some coërcive Power, to compell men equally to the performance of their Covenants, by the terrour of some punishment, greater than the benefit they expect by the breach of their Covenant; and to make good that Propriety, which by mutuall Contract men acquire, in recompence of the universall Right they abandon: and such power there is none before the erection of a Common-wealth. And this is also to be gathered out of the ordinary definition of Justice in the Schooles: For they say, that *Justice is the constant Will of giving to every man his own*. And therefore where there is no *Own*, that is, no Propriety, there is no Injustice; and where there is no coërceive Power erected, that is, where there is no Common-wealth, there is no Propriety; all men having Right to all things: Therefore where there is no Common-wealth, there nothing is Unjust. So that the nature of Justice, consisteth in keeping of valid Covenants: but the Validity of Covenants begins not but with the Constitution of a Civill Power, sufficient to compell men to keep them: And then it is also that Propriety begins.

[. . . .]

Chapter XVII: Of the Causes, Generation, and Definition of a Common-Wealth.

The finall Cause, End, or Designe of men, (who naturally love Liberty, and Dominion over others,) in the introduction of that restraint upon themselves, (in which wee see them live in Common-wealths,) is the foresight of their own preservation, and of a more contented life thereby; that is to say, of getting themselves out from that miserable condition of Warre, which is necessarily consequent (as hath been shewn) to the naturall Passions of men, when there is no visible Power to keep them in awe, and tye them by feare of punishment to the performance of their Covenants, and observation of those Lawes of Nature set down in the fourteenth and fifteenth Chapters.

For the Lawes of Nature (as *Justice, Equity, Modesty, Mercy,* and (in summe) *doing to others, as wee would be done to*,) of themselves, without the terrour of some Power, to cause them to be observed, are contrary to our naturall Passions, that carry us to Partiality, Pride, Revenge, and the like. And Covenants, without the Sword, are but Words, and of no strength to secure a man at all. Therefore notwithstanding the Lawes of Nature, (which every one hath then kept, when he has the will to keep them, when he can do it safely,) if there be no Power erected, or not great enough for our security; every man will, and may lawfully rely on his own strength and art, for caution against all other men. And in all places, where men have lived by small Families, to robbe and spoyle one another, has been a Trade, and so farre from being reputed against the Law of Nature, that the greater spoyles they gained, the greater was their honour; and men observed no other Lawes therein, but the Lawes of Honour; that is, to abstain from cruelty, leaving to men their lives, and instruments of husbandry. And as small Familyes did then; so now do Cities and Kingdomes which are but greater Families (for their own security) enlarge their Dominions, upon all pretences of danger, and fear of Invasion, or assistance that may be given to Invaders, endeavour as much as they can, to subdue, or weaken their neighbours, by open force, and secret arts, for want of other Caution, justly; and are remembred for it in after ages with honour.

Nor is it the joyning together of a small number of men, that gives them this security; because in small numbers, small additions on the one side or the other, make the advantage of strength so great, as is sufficient to carry the Victory; and therefore gives encouragement to an Invasion. The Multitude sufficient to confide in for our Security, is not determined by any certain number, but by comparison with the Enemy we feare; and is then sufficient, when the odds of the Enemy is not of so visible and conspicuous moment, to determine the event of warre, as to move him to attempt.

And be there never so great a Multitude; yet if their actions be directed according to their particular judgements, and particular appetites, they can expect thereby no defence, nor protection, neither against a Common enemy, nor against the injuries of one another. For being distracted in opinions concerning the best use and application of their strength, they do not help, but hinder one another; and reduce their strength by mutuall opposition to nothing: whereby they are easily, not onely subdued by a very few that agree together; but also when there is no common enemy, they make warre upon each other, for their particular interests. For if we could suppose a great Multitude of men to consent in the observation of Justice, and other Lawes of Nature, without a common Power to keep them all in awe; we might as well suppose all Man-kind to do the same; and then there neither would be, nor need to be any Civill Government, or Common-wealth at all; because there would be Peace without subjection.

Nor is it enough for the security, which men desire should last all the time of their life, that they be governed, and directed by one judgement, for a limited time; as in one Battell, or one Warre. For though they obtain a Victory by their unanimous endeavour against a forraign enemy; yet afterwards, when either they have no common enemy, or he that by one part is held for an enemy, is by another part held for a friend, they must needs by the difference of their interests dissolve, and fall again into a Warre amongst themselves.

It is true, that certain living creatures, as Bees, and Ants, live sociably one with another, (which are therefore by *Aristotle* numbred amongst Politicall creatures;) and yet have no other direction, than their particular judgements and appetites; nor speech, whereby one of them can signifie to another, what he thinks expedient for the common benefit: and therefore some man may perhaps desire to know, why Man-kind cannot do the same. To which I answer,

First, that men are continually in competition for Honour and Dignity, which these creatures are not; and consequently amongst men there ariseth on that ground, Envy and Hatred, and finally Warre; but amongst these not so.

Secondly, that amongst these creatures, the Common good differeth not from the Private; and being by nature enclined to their private, they procure thereby the common benefit. But man, whose Joy consisteth in comparing himselfe with other men, can relish nothing but what is eminent.

Thirdly, that these creatures, having not (as man) the use of reason, do not see, nor think they see any fault, in the administration of their common businesse: whereas amongst men, there are very many, that thinke themselves wiser, and abler to govern the Publique, better than the rest; and these strive to reforme and innovate, one this way, another that way; and thereby bring it into Distraction and Civill warre.

Fourthly, that these creatures, though they have some use of voice, in making knowne to one another their desires, and other affections; yet they want that art of words, by which some men can represent to others, that which is Good, in the likenesse of Evill; and Evill, in the likenesse of Good; and augment, or diminish the apparent greatnesse of Good and Evill; discontenting men, and troubling their Peace at their pleasure.

Fiftly, irrationall creatures cannot distinguish betweene *Injury*, and *Dammage*; and therefore as long as they be at ease, they are not offended with their fellowes: whereas Man is then most troublesome, when he is most at ease: for then it is that he loves to shew his Wisdome, and controule the Actions of them that governe the Common-wealth.

Lastly, the agreement of these creatures is Naturall; that of men, is by Covenant only, which is Artificiall: and therefore it is no wonder if there be somwhat else required (besides Covenant) to make their Agreement constant and lasting; which is a Common Power, to keep them in awe, and to direct their actions to the Common Benefit.

The only way to erect such a Common Power, as may be able to defend them from the invasion of Forraigners, and the injuries of one another, and thereby to secure them in such sort, as that by their owne industrie, and by the fruites of the Earth, they may nourish themselves and live contentedly; is, to conferre all their power and strength upon one Man, or upon one Assembly of men, that may reduce all their Wills, by plurality of voices, unto one Will: which is as much as to say, to appoint one Man, or Assembly of men, to beare their Person; and every one to owne, and acknowledge himselfe to be Author of whatsoever he that so beareth their Person, shall Act, or cause to be Acted, in those things which concerne the Common Peace and Safetie; and therein to submit their Wills, every one to his Will, and their Judgements, to his Judgment. This is more than Consent, or Concord; it is a reall Unitie of them all, in one and the same Person, made by Covenant of every man with every man, in such manner, as if every man should say to every man, *I Authorise and give up my Right of Governing my selfe, to this Man, or to this Assembly of men, on this condition, that thou give up thy Right to him, and Authorise all his Actions in like manner.* This done, the Multitude so united in one Person, is called a Common-wealth, in latine Civitas. This is the Generation of that great Leviathan, or rather (to speake more reverently) of that *Mortall God*, to which wee owe under the *Immortall God*, our peace and defence. For by this Authoritie, given him by every particular man in the Common-Wealth, he hath the use of so much Power and Strength conferred on him, that by terror thereof, he is inabled to forme the wills of them all, to Peace at home, and mutuall ayd against their enemies abroad. And in him consisteth the Essence of the Common-wealth; which (to define it,) is *One Person, of whose Acts a great Multitude, by mutuall Covenants one with another, have made themselves every one the Author, to the end he may use the strength and means of them all, as he shall think expedient, for their Peace and Common Defence.*

87

John Locke

from *An Essay concerning Human Understanding*

John Locke (1632–1704) was a British Enlightenment philosopher and physician whose influence on the development of the modern world can be difficult to overstate. He made significant contributions in the areas of epistemology, political theory, Christian theology, and biblical studies. He is especially well known for his blank slate theory of mind and is commonly regarded as the father of modern empiricism, according to which the contents of our minds are derived exclusively of experience. The following are excerpts from his epistemological masterpiece work, *An Essay concerning Human Understanding*, wherein he develops his polemic against the view that we are innately endowed with certain ideas.

Book I: Chap. II: No Innate Principles in the Mind.

1. It is an established opinion amongst some men, that there are in the understanding certain innate principles; some primary notions . . ., characters, as it were, stamped upon the mind of man, which the soul receives in its very first being; and brings into the world with it. It would be sufficient to convince unprejudiced readers of the falseness of this supposition, if I should only shew (as I hope I shall in the following parts of this discourse) how men, barely by the use of their natural faculties, may attain to all the knowledge they have, without the help of any innate impressions; and may arrive at certainty, without any such original notions or principles. For I imagine any one will easily grant, that it would be impertinent to suppose, the ideas of colours innate in a creature, to whom God hath given sight, and a power to receive them by the

SOURCE: John Locke, *The Works of John Locke in Nine Volumes*, 12th ed., vol. 1 (London: C. and J. Rivington, et al., 1824), 13–17, 77–79.

eyes, from external objects: and no less unreasonable would it be to attribute several truths to the impressions of nature, and innate characters, when we may observe in ourselves faculties, fit to attain as easy and certain knowledge of them, as if they were originally imprinted on the mind.

But because a man is not permitted without censure to follow his own thoughts in the search of truth, when they lead him ever so little out of the common road; I shall set down the reasons that made me doubt of the truth of that opinion, as an excuse for my mistake, if I be in one; which I leave to be considered by those, who, with me, dispose themselves to embrace truth, wherever they find it.

2. There is nothing more commonly taken for granted, than that there are certain principles, both speculative and practical (for they speak of both) universally agreed upon by all mankind: which therefore, they argue, must needs be constant impressions, which the souls of men receive in their first beings, and which they bring into the world with them, as necessarily and really as they do any of their inherent faculties.

3. This argument, drawn from universal consent, has this misfortune in it, that if it were true in matter of fact, that there were certain truths, wherein all mankind agreed, it would not prove them innate, if there can be any other way shewn, how men may come to that universal agreement, in the things they do consent in; which I presume may be done.

4. But, which is worse, this argument of universal consent, which is made use of to prove innate principles, seems to me a demonstration that there are none such; because there are none to which all mankind give an universal assent. I shall begin with the speculative, and instance in those magnified principles of demonstration; "whatsoever is, is;" and, "it is impossible for the same thing to be, and not to be;" which, of all others, I think have the most allowed title to innate. These have so settled a reputation of maxims universally received, that it will, no doubt, be thought strange, if any one should seem to question it. But yet I take liberty to say, that these propositions are so far from having an universal assent, that there are a great part of mankind to whom they are not so much as known.

5. For, first, it is evident, that all children and idiots have not the least apprehension or thought of them; and the want of that is enough to destroy that universal assent, which must needs be the necessary concomitant of all innate truths: it seeming to me near a contradiction, to say, that there are truths imprinted on the soul, which it perceives or understands not; imprinting, if it signify any thing, being nothing else, but the making certain truths to be perceived. For to imprint any thing on the mind, without the mind's perceiving it, seems to me hardly intelligible. If therefore children and idiots have souls, have minds,

with those impressions upon them, they must unavoidably perceive them, and necessarily know and assent to these truths: which since they do not, it is evident that there are no such impressions. For if they are not notions naturally imprinted, how can they be innate? and if they are notions imprinted, how can they be unknown? To say a notion is imprinted on the mind, and yet at the same time to say, that the mind is ignorant of it, and never yet took notice of it, is to make this impression nothing. No proposition can be said to be in the mind, which it never yet knew, which it was never yet conscious of. For if any one may, then, by the same reason, all propositions that are true, and the mind is capable of ever assenting to, may be said to be in the mind, and to be imprinted: since, if any one can be said to be in the mind, which it never yet knew, it must be only, because it is capable of knowing it, and so the mind is of all truths it ever shall know. Nay, thus truths may be imprinted on the mind, which it never did, nor ever shall know: for a man may live long, and die at last in ignorance of many truths, which his mind was capable of knowing, and that with certainty. So that if the capacity of knowing, be the natural impression contended for, all the truths a man ever comes to know, will, by this account, be every one of them innate; and this great point will amount to no more, but only to a very improper way of speaking; which, whilst it pretends to assert the contrary, says nothing different from those, who deny innate principles. For nobody, I think, ever denied that the mind was capable of knowing several truths. The capacity, they say, is innate, the knowledge acquired. But then to what end such contest for certain innate maxims? If truths can be imprinted on the understanding without being perceived, I can see no difference there can be, between any truths the mind is capable of knowing, in respect of their original: they must all be innate, or all adventitious: in vain shall a man go about to distinguish them. He therefore, that talks of innate notions in the understanding, cannot (if he intend thereby any distinct sort of truths) mean such truths to be in the understanding, as it never perceived, and is yet wholly ignorant of. For if these words (to be in the understanding) have any propriety, they signify to be understood: so that, to be in the understanding, and not to be understood; to be in the mind, and never to be perceived; is all one, as to say, any thing is, and is not, in the mind or understanding. If therefore these two propositions, "whatsoever is, is;" and "it is impossible for the same thing to be, and not to be," are by nature imprinted, children cannot be ignorant of them; infants, and all that have souls, must necessarily have them in their understandings, know the truth of them, and assent to it.

6. To avoid this, it is usually answered, That all men know and assent to them, when they come to the use of reason, and this is enough to prove them innate. I answer,

7. Doubtful expressions that have scarce any signification, go for clear reasons, to those, who being prepossessed, take not the pains to examine, even what they themselves say. For to apply this answer with any tolerable sense to our present purpose, it must signify one of these two things; either, that, as soon as men come to the use of reason, these supposed native inscriptions come to be known, and observed by them: or else, that the use and exercise of men's reason assists them in the discovery of these principles, and certainly makes them known to them.

8. If they mean, that by the use of reason men may discover these principles; and that this is sufficient to prove them innate: their way of arguing will stand thus, (viz.) that, whatever truths reason can certainly discover to us, and make us firmly assent to, those are all naturally imprinted on the mind; since that universal assent, which is made the mark of them, amounts to no more but this; that by the use of reason, we are capable to come to a certain knowledge of, and assent to them; and, by this means, there will be no difference between the maxims of the mathematicians, and theorems they deduce from them; all must be equally allowed innate; they being all discoveries made by the use of reason, and truths that a rational creature may certainly come to know, if he apply his thoughts rightly that way.

9. But how can these men think the use of reason necessary, to discover principles that are supposed innate, when reason (if we may believe them) is nothing else but the faculty of deducing unknown truths from principles, or propositions, that are already known? That certainly can never be thought innate, which we have need of reason to discover; unless, as I have said, we will have all the certain truths, that reason ever teaches us, to be innate. We may as well think the use of reason necessary to make our eyes discover visible objects, as that there should be need of reason, or the exercise thereof, to make the understanding see what is originally engraven on it, and cannot be in the understanding before it be perceived by it. So that to make reason discover those truths, thus imprinted, is to say, that the use of reason discovers to a man what he knew before: and if men have those innate impressed truths originally, and before the use of reason, and yet are always ignorant of them, till they come to the use of reason, it is in effect to say, that men know, and know them not, at the same time.

[. . . .]

Book II: Chap. I: Of Ideas in general, and their Original.

1. Every man being conscious to himself that he thinks, and that which his mind is applied about, whilst thinking, being the ideas that are there, it is past doubt, that men have in their minds several ideas, such as are those

expressed by the words, Whiteness, Hardness, Sweetness, Thinking, Motion, Man, Elephant, Army, Drunkenness, and others. It is in the first place then to be inquired, how he comes by them. I know it is a received doctrine, that men have native ideas, and original characters, stamped upon their minds, in their very first being. This opinion I have, at large, examined already; and, I suppose, what I have said, in the foregoing book, will be much more easily admitted, when I have shewn, whence the understanding may get all the ideas it has, and by what ways and degrees they may come into the mind; for which I shall appeal to every one's own observation and experience.

2. Let us then suppose the mind to be, as we say, white paper, void of all characters, without any ideas; how comes it to be furnished? Whence comes it by that vast store which the busy and boundless fancy of man has painted on it, with an almost endless variety? Whence has it all the materials of reason and knowledge? To this I answer, in one word, from experience; in all that our knowledge is founded, and from that it ultimately derives itself. Our observation employed either about external sensible objects, or about the internal operations of our minds, perceived and reflected on by ourselves, is that which supplies our understandings with all the materials of thinking. These two are the fountains of knowledge, from whence all the ideas we have, or can naturally have, do spring.

3. First, Our senses, conversant about particular sensible objects, do convey into the mind several distinct perceptions of things, according to those various ways wherein those objects do affect them: and thus we come by those ideas we have, of Yellow, White, Heat, Cold, Soft, Hard, Bitter, Sweet, and all those which we call sensible qualities; which when I say the senses convey into the mind, I mean, they from external objects convey into the mind what produces there those perceptions. This great source of most of the ideas we have, depending wholly upon our senses, and derived by them to the understanding, I call sensation.

4. Secondly, The other fountain, from which experience furnisheth the understanding with ideas, is the perception of the operations of our own mind within us, as it is employed about the ideas it has got; which operations, when the soul comes to reflect on and consider, do furnish the understanding with another set of ideas, which could not be had from things without; and such are Perception, Thinking, Doubting, Believing, Reasoning, Knowing, Willing, and all the different actings of our own minds; which we being conscious of and observing in ourselves, do from these receive into our understandings as distinct ideas, as we do from bodies affecting our senses. This source of ideas every man has wholly in himself; and though

it be not sense, as having nothing to do with external objects, yet it is very like it, and might properly enough be called internal sense. But as I call the other sensation, so I call this reflection, the ideas it affords being such only as the mind gets by reflecting on its own operations within itself. By reflection then, in the following part of this discourse, I would be understood to mean that notice which the mind takes of its own operations, and the manner of them; by reason whereof there come to be ideas of these operations in the understanding. These two, I say, viz. external material things, as the objects of sensation; and the operations of our own minds within, as the objects of reflection; are to me the only originals from whence all our ideas take their beginnings.

88

John Locke

from *Second Treatise on Civil Government*

Locke's political philosophy was profoundly influential among the founders of the United States, which easily places Locke among the pantheon of history's most important political thinkers, especially within the classical liberal democratic and social contract traditions. The following are three significant excerpts from his most famous political work, *Second Treatise on Civil Government*. In these passages, Locke develops his influential labor-desert theory of property, he explains the chief ends for which governments should exist, and he gives an account of the conditions under which it is ultimately appropriate for governments to be dissolved—an account that can seem prescient when read with the U.S. Declaration of Independence in mind.

Chap. V: Of Property.

25. Whether we consider natural *reason*, which tells us, that men, being once born, have a right to their preservation, and consequently to meat and drink, and such other things as nature affords for their subsistence: or *revelation*, which gives us an account of those grants God made of the world to *Adam*, and to *Noah*, and his sons, it is very clear, that God, as king *David* says, *Psal.* CXV.16. *has given the earth to the children of men*; given it to mankind in common. But this being supposed, it seems to some a very great difficulty, how any one should ever come to have a *property* in any thing: I will not content myself to answer, that if it be difficult to make out *property*, upon a supposition that God gave the world to *Adam*, and his posterity in common, it is impossible that any man, but one universal monarch, should have any *property* upon a

SOURCE: John Locke, *Two Treatises of Government* (London: A Millar, et al., 1764), 215–19, 305–10, 384–416.

supposition, that God gave the world to *Adam*, and his heirs in succession, exclusive of all the rest of his posterity. But I shall endeavour to shew, how men might come to have a *property* in several parts of that which God gave to mankind in common, and that without any express compact of all the commoners.

26. God, who hath given the world to men in common, hath also given them reason to make use of it to the best advantage of life, and convenience. The earth, and all that is therein, is given to men for the support and comfort of their being. And tho' all the fruits it naturally produces, and beasts it feeds, belong to mankind in common, as they are produced by the spontaneous hand of nature; and no body has originally a private dominion, exclusive of the rest of mankind, in any of them, as they are thus in their natural state: yet being given for the use of men, there must of necessity be *a means to appropriate* them some way or other, before they can be of any use, or at all beneficial to any particular man. The fruit, or venison, which nourishes the wild *Indian*, who knows no inclosure, and is still a tenant in common, must be his, and so his, *i.e.* a part of him, that another can no longer have any right to it, before it can do him any good for the support of his life.

27. Though the earth, and all inferior creatures, be common to all men, yet every man has a *property* in his own *person*: this no body has any right to but himself. The *labour* of his body, and the *work* of his hands, we may say, are properly his. Whatsoever then he removes out of the state that nature hath provided, and left it in, he hath mixed his *labour* with, and joined to it something that is his own, and thereby makes it his *property*. It being by him removed from the common state nature hath placed it in, it hath by this *labour* something annexed to it, that excludes the common right of other men: for this *labour* being the unquestionable property of the labourer, no man but he can have a right to what that is once joined to, at least where there is enough, and as good, left in common for others.

28. He that is nourished by the acorns he picked up under an oak, or the apples he gathered from the trees in the wood, has certainly appropriated them to himself. No body can deny but the nourishment is his. I ask then, when did they begin to be his? when he digested? or when he eat? or when he boiled? or when he brought them home? or when he picked them up? and it is plain, if the first gathering made them not his, nothing else could. That *labour* put a distinction between them and common: that added something to them more than nature, the common mother of all, had done; and so they became his private right. And will any one say, he had no right to those acorns or apples, he thus appropriated, because he had not the consent of all mankind to make them his? Was it a robbery thus to assume to himself what belonged to all in

common? If such a consent as that was necessary, man had starved, notwith-standing the plenty God had given him. We see in *commons*, which remain so by compact, that it is the taking any part of what is common, and removing it out of the state nature leaves it in, which *begins the property*; without which the common is of no use. And the taking of this or that part, does not depend on the express consent of all the commoners. Thus the grass my horse has bit; the turfs my servant has cut; and the ore I have digged in any place, where I have a right to them in common with others, become my *property*, without the assignation or consent of any body. The *labour* that was mine, removing them out of that common state they were in, hath *fixed* my *property* in them.

29. By making an explicit consent of every commoner, necessary to any one's appropriating to himself any part of what is given in common, children or servants could not cut the meat, which their father or master had provided for them in common, without assigning to every one his peculiar part. Though the water running in the fountain be every one's, yet who can doubt, but that in the pitcher is his only who drew it out? His *labour* hath taken it out of the hands of nature, where it was common, and belonged equally to all her children, and *hath* thereby *appropriated* it to himself.

30. Thus this law of reason makes the deer that *Indian*'s who hath killed it; it is allowed to be his goods, who hath bestowed his labour upon it, though before it was the common right of every one. And amongst those who are counted the civilized part of mankind, who have made and multiplied positive laws to determine *property*, this original law of nature, for the *beginning of property*, in what was before common, still takes place; and by virtue thereof, what fish any one catches in the ocean, that great and still remaining common of mankind; or what ambergrise any one takes up here, is by the *labour* that removes it out of that common state nature left it in, *made* his *property*, who takes that pains about it. And even amongst us, the hare that any one is hunting, is thought his who pursues her during the chase: for being a beast that is still looked upon as common, and no man's private possession; whoever has employed so much labour about any of that kind, as to find and pursue her, has thereby removed her from the state of nature, wherein she was common, and hath *begun a property*.

[. . . .]

Chap. IX: Of the Ends of Political Society and Government.

123. If man in the state of nature be so free, as has been said; if he be absolute lord of his own person and possessions, equal to the greatest, and subject to no body, why will he part with his freedom? why will he give up this

empire, and subject himself to the dominion and controul of any other power? To which it is obvious to answer, that though in the state of nature he hath such a right, yet the enjoyment of it is very uncertain, and constantly exposed to the invasion of others: for all being kings as much as he, every man his equal, and the greater part no strict observers of equity and justice, the enjoyment of the property he has in this state is very unsafe, very unsecure. This makes him willing to quit a condition, which, however free, is full of fears and continual dangers: and it is not without reason, that he seeks out, and is willing to join in society with others, who are already united, or have a mind to unite, for the mutual preservation of their lives, liberties and estates, which I call by the general name, *property*.

124. The great and *chief end*, therefore, of men's uniting into commonwealths, and putting themselves under government, *is the preservation of their property*. To which in the state of nature there are many things wanting.

First, There wants an *established*, settled, known *law*, received and allowed by common consent to be the standard of right and wrong, and the common measure to decide all controversies between them: for though the law of nature be plain and intelligible to all rational creatures; yet men being biassed by their interest, as well as ignorant for want of study of it, are not apt to allow of it as a law binding to them in the application of it to their particular cases.

125. *Secondly*, In the state of nature there wants *a known and indifferent judge*, with authority to determine all differences according to the established law: for every one in that state being both judge and executioner of the law of nature, men being partial to themselves, passion and revenge is very apt to carry them too far, and with too much heat, in their own cases; as well as negligence, and unconcernedness, to make them too remiss in other men's.

126. *Thirdly*, In the state of nature there often wants *power* to back and support the sentence when right, and to *give* it due *execution*. They who by any injustice offended, will seldom fail, where they are able, by force to make good their injustice; such resistance many times makes the punishment dangerous, and frequently destructive, to those who attempt it.

127. Thus mankind, notwithstanding all the privileges of the state of nature, being but in an ill condition, while they remain in it, are quickly driven into society. Hence it comes to pass, that we seldom find any number of men live any time together in this state. The inconveniencies that they are therein exposed to, by the irregular and uncertain exercise of the power every man has of punishing the transgressions of others, make them take sanctuary under the established laws of government, and therein seek *the preservation of their property*. It is this makes them so willingly give up every one his single power of

punishing, to be exercised by such alone, as shall be appointed to it amongst them; and by such rules as the community, or those authorized by them to that purpose, shall agree on. And in this we have the original *right and rise of both the legislative and executive power*, as well as of the governments and societies themselves.

128. For in the state of nature, to omit the liberty he has of innocent delights, a man has two powers.

The first is to do whatsoever he thinks fit for the preservation of himself, and others within the permission of the *law of nature*: by which law, common to them all, he and all the rest of *mankind are one community*, make up one society, distinct from all other creatures. And were it not for the corruption and vitiousness of degenerate men, there would be no need of any other; no necessity that men should separate from this great and natural community, and by positive agreements combine into smaller and divided associations.

The other power a man has in the state of nature, is the *power to punish the crimes* committed against that law. Both these he gives up, when he joins in a private, if I may so call it, or particular politic society, and incorporates into any common-wealth, separate from the rest of mankind.

129. The first *power*, viz. *of doing whatsoever he thought for the preservation of himself*, and the rest of mankind, *he gives up* to be regulated by laws made by the society, so far forth as the preservation of himself, and the rest of that society shall require; which laws of the society in many things confine the liberty he had by the law of nature.

130. *Secondly*, The *power of punishing he wholly gives up*, and engages his natural force, (which he might before employ in the execution of the law of nature, by his own single authority, as he thought fit) to assist the executive power of the society, as the law thereof shall require: for being now in a new state, wherein he is to enjoy many conveniencies, from the labour, assistance, and society of others in the same community, as well as protection from its whole strength; he is to part also with as much of his natural liberty, in providing for himself, as the good, prosperity, and safety of the society shall require; which is not only necessary, but just, since the other members of the society do the like.

131. But though men, when they enter into society, give up the equality, liberty, and executive power they had in the state of nature, into the hands of the society, to be so far disposed of by the legislative, as the good of the society shall require; yet it being only with an intention in every one the better to preserve himself, his liberty and property; (for no rational creature can be supposed to change his condition with an intention to be worse) the power of the society, or *legislative* constituted by them, can *never be supposed to extend*

farther, than the common good; but is obliged to secure every one's property, by providing against those three defects above mentioned, that made the state of nature so unsafe and uneasy. And so whoever has the legislative or supreme power of any common-wealth, is bound to govern by established *standing laws*, promulgated and known to the people, and not by extemporary decrees; by *indifferent* and upright *judges*, who are to decide controversies by those laws; and to employ the force of the community at home, *only in the execution of such laws*, or abroad to prevent or redress foreign injuries, and secure the community from inroads and invasion. And all this to be directed to no other *end*, but the *peace, safety*, and *public good* of the people.

[. . . .]

Chap. XIX: Of the Dissolution of Government.

211. He that will with any clearness speak of the *dissolution of government*, ought in the first place to distinguish between the *dissolution of the society* and the *dissolution of the government*. That which makes the community, and brings men out of the loose state of nature, into *one politic society*, is the agreement which every one has with the rest to incorporate, and act as one body, and so be one distinct common-wealth. The usual, and almost only way whereby *this union is dissolved*, is the inroad of foreign force making a conquest upon them: for in that case, (not being able to maintain and support themselves, as *one intire* and *independent body)* the union belonging to that body which consisted therein, must necessarily cease, and so every one return to the state he was in before, with a liberty to shift for himself, and provide for his own safety, as he thinks fit, in some other society. Whenever the *society is dissolved*, it is certain the government of that society cannot remain. Thus conquerors swords often cut up governments by the roots, and mangle societies to pieces, separating the subdued or scattered multitude from the protection of, and dependence on, that society which ought to have preserved them from violence. The world is too well instructed in, and too forward to allow of, this way of dissolving of governments, to need any more to be said of it; and there wants not much argument to prove, that where the *society is dissolved*, the government cannot remain; that being as impossible, as for the frame of an house to subsist when the materials of it are scattered and dissipated by a whirl-wind, or jumbled into a confused heap by an earthquake.

212. Besides this over-turning from without, *governments are dissolved from within,*

First, When the *legislative* is *altered*. Civil society being a state of peace, amongst those who are of it, from whom the state of war is excluded by the umpirage, which they have provided in their legislative, for the ending all differences that may arise amongst any of them, it is in their *legislative*, that the members of a common-wealth are united, and combined together into one coherent living body. This *is the soul that gives form, life, and unity*, to the common-wealth: from hence the several members have their mutual influence, sympathy, and connexion: and therefore, when the *legislative* is broken, or *dissolved*, dissolution and death follows: for the *essence and union of the society* consisting in having one will, the legislative, when once established by the majority, has the declaring, and as it were keeping of that will. The *constitution of the legislative* is the first and fundamental act of society, whereby provision is made for the *continuation of their union*, under the direction of persons, and bonds of laws, made by persons authorized thereunto, by the consent and appointment of the people, without which no one man, or number of men, amongst them, can have authority of making laws that shall be binding to the rest. When any one, or more, shall take upon them to make laws, whom the people have not appointed so to do, they make laws without authority, which the people are not therefore bound to obey; by which means they come again to be out of subjection, and may constitute to themselves a *new legislative*, as they think best, being in full liberty to resist the force of those, who without authority would impose any thing upon them. Every one is at the disposure of his own will, when those who had, by the delegation of the society, the declaring of the public will, are excluded from it, and others usurp the place, who have no such authority or delegation.

[....]

221. There is therefore, secondly, another way whereby *governments are dissolved*, and that is, when the legislative, or the prince, either of them, act contrary to their trust.

First, The *legislative acts against the trust* reposed in them, when they endeavour to invade the property of the subject, and to make themselves, or any part of the community, masters, or arbitrary disposers of the lives, liberties, or fortunes of the people.

222. The reason why men enter into society, is the preservation of their property; and the end why they chuse and authorize a legislative, is, that there may be laws made, and rules set, as guards and fences to the properties of all the members of the society, to limit the power, and moderate the dominion, of every part and member of the society: for since it can never be supposed to be the will of the society, that the legislative should have a power to destroy that which every one designs to secure, by entering into society, and for which the people submitted themselves to legislators of their own making; whenever

the *legislators endeavour to take away, and destroy the property of the people,* or to reduce them to slavery under arbitrary power, they put themselves into a state of war with the people, who are thereupon absolved from any farther obedience, and are left to the common refuge, which God hath provided for all men, against force and violence. Whensoever therefore the *legislative* shall transgress this fundamental rule of society; and either by ambition, fear, folly or corruption, *endeavour to grasp* themselves, *or put into the hands of any other, an absolute power* over the lives, liberties, and estates of the people; by this breach of trust they forfeit *the power* the people had put into their hands for quite contrary ends, and it devolves to the people, who have a right to resume their original liberty, and, by the establishment of a new legislative, (such as they shall think fit) provide for their own safety and security, which is the end for which they are in society. What I have said here, concerning the legislative in general, holds true also concerning the supreme executor, who having a double trust put in him, both to have a part in the legislative, and the supreme execution of the law, acts against both, when he goes about to set up his own arbitrary will as the law of the society. He *acts* also *contrary to his trust,* when he either employs the force, treasure, and offices of the society, to corrupt the *representatives,* and gain them to his purposes; or openly pre-engages the *electors,* and prescribes to their choice, such, whom he has, by sollicitations, threats, promises, or otherwise, won to his designs; and employs them to bring in such, who have promised before-hand what to vote, and what to enact. Thus to regulate candidates and electors, and new-model the ways of election, what is it but to cut up the government by the roots, and poison the very fountain of public security? for the people having reserved to themselves the choice of their *representatives,* as the fence to their properties, could do it for no other end, but that they might always be freely chosen, and so chosen, freely act, and advise, as the necessity of the common-wealth, and the public good should, upon examination, and mature debate, be judged to require. This, those who give their votes before they hear the debate, and have weighed the reasons on all sides, are not capable of doing. To prepare such an assembly as this, and endeavour to set up the declared abettors of his own will, for the true *representatives* of the people, and the law-makers of the society, is certainly as great a *breach of trust,* and as perfect a declaration of a design to subvert the government, as is possible to be met with. To which, if one shall add rewards and punishments visibly employed to the same end, and all the arts of perverted law made use of, to take off and destroy all that stand in the way of such a design, and will not comply and consent to betray the liberties of their country, it will be past doubt what is doing. What power they ought to have in the society, who thus employ it contrary to the trust went along with it in its first institution, is easy to determine; and one cannot but see, that he, who has once attempted any such thing as this, cannot any longer be trusted.

223. To this perhaps it will be said, that the people being ignorant, and always discontented, to lay the foundation of government in the unsteady opinion and uncertain humour of the people, is to expose it to certain ruin; and *no government will be able long to subsist*, if the people may set up a new legislative, whenever they take offence at the old one. To this I answer, Quite the contrary. People are not so easily got out of their old forms, as some are apt to suggest. They are hardly to be prevailed with to amend the acknowledged faults in the frame they have been accustomed to. And if there be any original defects, or adventitious ones introduced by time, or corruption; it is not an easy thing to get them changed, even when all the world sees there is an opportunity for it. This slowness and aversion in the people to quit their old constitutions, has, in the many revolutions which have been seen in this kingdom, in this and former ages, still kept us to, or, after some interval of fruitless attempts, still brought us back again to our old legislative of king, lords and commons: and whatever provocations have made the crown be taken from some of our princes heads, they never carried the people so far as to place it in another line.

224. But it will be said, this *hypothesis* lays a *ferment for* frequent *rebellion*. To which I answer,

First, No more than any other *hypothesis*: for when the people are made miserable, and find themselves *exposed to the ill usage of arbitrary power*, cry up their governors, as much as you will, for sons of *Jupiter*; let them be sacred and divine, descended, or authorized from heaven; give them out for whom or what you please, the same will happen. *The people generally ill treated*, and contrary to right, will be ready upon any occasion to ease themselves of a burden that sits heavy upon them. They will wish, and seek for the opportunity, which in the change, weakness and accidents of human affairs, seldom delays long to offer itself. He must have lived but a little while in the world, who has not seen examples of this in his time; and he must have read very little, who cannot produce examples of it in all sorts of governments in the world.

225. *Secondly*, I answer, such *revolutions happen* not upon every little mismanagement in public affairs. *Great mistakes* in the ruling part, many wrong and inconvenient laws, and all the *slips* of human frailty, will be *born by the people* without mutiny or murmur. But if a long train of abuses, prevarications and artifices, all tending the same way, make the design visible to the people, and they cannot but feel what they lie under, and see whither they are going; it is not to be wondered, that they should then rouze themselves, and endeavour to

put the rule into such hands which may secure to them the ends for which government was at first erected; and without which, ancient names, and specious forms, are so far from being better, that they are much worse, than the state of nature, or pure anarchy; the inconveniencies being all as great and as near, but the remedy farther off and more difficult.

226. *Thirdly*, I answer, that *this doctrine* of a power in the people of providing for their safety a-new, by a new legislative, when their legislators have acted contrary to their trust, by invading their property, is *the best fence against rebellion*, and the probablest means to hinder it: for *rebellion* being an opposition, not to persons, but authority, which is founded only in the constitutions and laws of the government; those, whoever they be, who by force break through, and by force justify their violation of them, are truly and properly *rebels*: for when men, by entering into society and civil-government, have excluded force, and introduced laws for the preservation of property, peace, and unity amongst themselves, those who set up force again in opposition to the laws, do *rebellare*, that is, bring back again the state of war, and are properly rebels: which they who are in power, (by the pretence they have to authority, the temptation of force they have in their hands, and the flattery of those about them) being likeliest to do; the properest way to prevent the evil, is to shew them the danger and injustice of it, who are under the greatest temptation to run into it.

[. . . .]

228. But if they, who say *it lays a foundation for rebellion*, mean that it may occasion civil wars, or intestine broils, to tell the people they are absolved from obedience when illegal attempts are made upon their liberties or properties, and may oppose the unlawful violence of those who were their magistrates, when they invade their properties contrary to the trust put in them; and that therefore this doctrine is not to be allowed, being so destructive to the peace of the world: they may as well say, upon the same ground, that honest men may not oppose robbers or pirates, because this may occasion disorder or bloodshed. If any *mischief* come in such cases, it is not to be charged upon him who defends his own right, but *on him that invades* his neighbours. If the innocent honest man must quietly quit all he has, for peace sake, to him who will lay violent hands upon it, I desire it may be considered, what a kind of peace there will be in the world, which consists only in violence and rapine; and which is to be maintained only for the benefit of robbers and oppressors. Who would not think it an admirable peace betwixt the mighty and the mean, when the lamb, without resistance, yielded his throat to be torn by the imperious wolf? *Polyphemus's* den gives us a perfect pattern of such a peace, and such

a government, wherein *Ulysses* and his companions had nothing to do, but quietly to suffer themselves to be devoured. And no doubt *Ulysses*, who was a prudent man, preached up *passive obedience*, and exhorted them to a quiet submission, by representing to them of what concernment peace was to mankind; and by shewing the inconveniences might happen, if they should offer to resist *Polyphemus*, who had now the power over them.

229. The end of government is the good of mankind; and which is *best for mankind*, that the people should be always exposed to the boundless will of tyranny, or that the rulers should be sometimes liable to be opposed, when they grow exorbitant in the use of their power, and employ it for the destruction, and not the preservation of the properties of their people?

230. Nor let any one say, that mischief can arise from hence, as often as it shall please a busy head, or turbulent spirit, to desire the alteration of the government. It is true, such men may stir, whenever they please; but it will be only to their own just ruin and perdition: for till the mischief be grown general, and the ill designs of the rulers become visible, or their attempts sensible to the greater part, the people, who are more disposed to suffer than right themselves by resistance, are not apt to stir. The examples of particular injustice, or oppression of here and there an unfortunate man, moves them not. But if they universally have a persuasion, grounded upon manifest evidence, that designs are carrying on against their liberties, and the general course and tendency of things cannot but give them strong suspicions of the evil intention of their governors, who is to be blamed for it? Who can help it, if they, who might avoid it, bring themselves into this suspicion? Are the people to be blamed, if they have the sense of rational creatures, and can think of things no otherwise than as they find and feel them? And is it not rather *their fault*, who put things into such a posture, that they would not have them thought to be as they are? I grant, that the pride, ambition, and turbulency of private men have sometimes caused great disorders in common-wealths, and factions have been fatal to states and kingdoms. But whether *the mischief* hath *oftener* begun *in the peoples wantonness*, and a desire to cast off the lawful authority of their rulers, or *in the rulers insolence*, and endeavours to get and exercise an arbitrary power over their people; whether oppression, or disobedience, gave the first rise to the disorder, I leave it to impartial history to determine. This I am sure, whoever, either ruler or subject, by force goes about to invade the rights of either prince or people, and lays the foundation for *overturning* the constitution and frame of *any just government*, is highly guilty of the greatest crime, I think, a man is capable of, being to answer for all those mischiefs of blood, rapine, and desolation, which the breaking to pieces of governments bring on a country.

And he who does it, is justly to be esteemed the common enemy and pest of mankind, and is to be treated accordingly.

231. That *subjects* or *foreigners*, attempting by force on the properties of any people, may be *resisted* with force, is agreed on all hands. But that *magistrates*, doing the same thing, may be *resisted*, hath of late been denied: as if those who had the greatest privileges and advantages by the law, had thereby a power to break those laws, by which alone they were set in a better place than their brethren: whereas their offence is thereby the greater, both as being ungrateful for the greater share they have by the law, and breaking also that trust, which is put into their hands by their brethren.

232. Whosoever uses *force without right*, as every one does in society, who does it without law, puts himself into a *state of war* with those against whom he so uses it; and in that state all former ties are cancelled, all other rights cease, and every one has a right to defend himself, and *to resist the aggressor*. This is so evident, that *Barclay* himself, that great assertor of the power and sacredness of kings, is forced to confess, That it is lawful for the people, in some cases, to *resist* their king; and that too in a chapter, wherein he pretends to shew, that the divine law shuts up the people from all manner of rebellion. Whereby it is evident, even by his own doctrine, that, since they may in some cases *resist*, all resisting of *princes* is not rebellion. His words are these . . .

233. *But if any one should ask, Must the people then always lay themselves open to the cruelty and rage of tyranny? Must they see their cities pillaged, and laid in ashes, their wives and children exposed to the tyrant's lust and fury, and themselves and families reduced by their king to ruin, and all the miseries of want and oppression, and yet sit still? Must men alone be debarred the common privilege of opposing force with force, which nature allows so freely to all other creatures for their preservation from injury? I answer: Self-defence is a part of the law of nature; nor can it be denied the community, even against the king himself: but to revenge themselves upon him, must by no means be allowed them: it being not agreeable to that law. Wherefore if the king shall shew an hatred, not only to some particular persons, but sets himself against the body of the common-wealth, whereof he is the head, and shall, with intolerable ill usage, cruelly tyrannize over the whole, or a considerable part of the people, in this case the people have a right to resist and defend themselves from injury: but it must be with this caution, that they only defend themselves, but do not attack their prince: they may repair the damages received, but must not for any provocation exceed the bounds of due reverence and respect. They may repulse the present attempt, but must not revenge past violences: for it is natural for us to defend life and limb, but that an inferior should punish a superior, is against nature.*

The mischief which is designed them, the people may prevent before it be done; but when it is done, they must not revenge it on the king, though author of the villany. This therefore is the privilege of the people in general, above what any private person hath; that particular men are allowed by our adversaries themselves (Buchanan *only excepted) to have no other remedy but patience; but the body of the people may with respect resist intolerable tyranny; for when it is but moderate, they ought to endure it.*

[. . . .]

240. Here, it is like, the common question will be made, *Who shall be judge,* whether the prince or legislative act contrary to their trust? This, perhaps, ill-affected and factious men may spread amongst the people, when the prince only makes use of his due prerogative. To this I reply, *The people shall be judge;* for who shall be *judge* whether his trustee or deputy acts well, and according to the trust reposed in him, but he who deputes him, and must, by having deputed him, have still a power to discard him, when he fails in his trust? If this be reasonable in particular cases of private men, why should it be otherwise in that of the greatest moment, where the welfare of millions is concerned, and also where the evil, if not prevented, is greater, and the redress very difficult, dear, and dangerous?

[241.] But farther, this question, *(Who shall be judge?)* cannot mean, that there is no judge at all: for where there is no judicature on earth, to decide controversies amongst men, *God* in heaven is *judge.* He alone, it is true, is judge of the right. But *every man* is *judge* for himself, as in all other cases, so in this, whether another hath put himself into a state of war with him, and whether he should appeal to the Supreme Judge, as *Jeptha* did.

242. If a controversy arise betwixt a prince and some of the people, in a matter where the law is silent, or doubtful, and the thing be of great consequence, I should think the proper *umpire,* in such a case, should be the body of the *people:* for in cases where the prince hath a trust reposed in him, and is dispensed from the common ordinary rules of the law; there, if any men find themselves aggrieved, and think the prince acts contrary to, or beyond that trust, who so proper to *judge* as the body of the *people,* (who, at first, lodged that trust in him) how far they meant it should extend? But if the prince, or whoever they be in the administration, decline that way of determination, the appeal then lies no where but to heaven; force between either persons, who have no known superior on earth, or which permits no appeal to a judge on earth, being properly a state of war, wherein the appeal lies only to heaven; and in that state the *injured party must judge* for himself, when he will think fit to make use of that appeal, and put himself upon it.

243. To conclude, The *power that every individual gave the society*, when he entered into it, can never revert to the individuals again, as long as the society lasts, but will always remain in the community; because without this there can be no community, no common-wealth, which is contrary to the original agreement: so also when the society hath placed the legislative in any assembly of men, to continue in them and their successors, with direction and authority for providing such successors, *the legislative can never revert to the people* whilst that government lasts; because having provided a legislative with power to continue for ever, they have given up their political power to the legislative, and cannot resume it. But if they have set limits to the duration of their legislative, and made this supreme power in any person, or assembly, only temporary; or else, when by the miscarriages of those in authority, it is forfeited; upon the forfeiture, or at the determination of the time set, *it reverts to the society*, and the people have a right to act as supreme, and continue the legislative in themselves; or erect a new form, or under the old form place it in new hands, as they think good.

89

Sir Isaac Newton

from *Mathematical Principles of Natural Philosophy*

Few scientists could ever hope to rival the accomplishments or name recognition of the English intellectual Sir Isaac Newton (1643–1727). A central figure of the Scientific Revolution, Newton made groundbreaking contributions to optics, physics (particularly with his laws of motion and theory of gravity), and mathematics (in developing calculus), and he also made contributions to chemistry, alchemy, and theology. The following are excerpts from his most famous work, *Principia Mathematica*, or *The Mathematical Principles of Natural Philosophy*, in which he lays out his basic methodological strategy of induction and, later, speaks to his beliefs about God.

––––––––––––––––

Rules of Reasoning in Philosophy.

Rule I.

We are to admit no more causes of natural things than such as are both true and sufficient to explain their appearances.

To this purpose the philosophers say that Nature does nothing in vain, and more is in vain when less will serve; for Nature is pleased with simplicity, and affects not the pomp of superfluous causes.

Rule II.

Therefore to the same natural effects we must, as far as possible, assign the same causes.

As to respiration in a man and in a beast; the descent of stones in *Europe* and in *America*; the light of our culinary fire and of the sun; the reflection of light in the earth, and in the planets.

SOURCE: Sir Isaac Newton, *Newton's "Principia": The Mathematical Principles of Natural Philosophy*, trans. Andrew Motte (New York: Daniel Adee, 1846), 384–85, 503–7.

Rule III.

The qualities of bodies, which admit neither intension nor remission of degrees, and which are found to belong to all bodies within the reach of our experiments, are to be esteemed the universal qualities of all bodies whatsoever.

For since the qualities of bodies are only known to us by experiments, we are to hold for universal all such as universally agree with experiments; and such as are not liable to diminution can never be quite taken away. We are certainly not to relinquish the evidence of experiments for the sake of dreams and vain fictions of our own devising; nor are we to recede from the analogy of Nature, which uses to be simple, and always consonant to itself. We no other way know the extension of bodies than by our senses, nor do these reach it in all bodies; but because we perceive extension in all that are sensible, therefore we ascribe it universally to all others also. That abundance of bodies are hard, we learn by experience; and because the hardness of the whole arises from the hardness of the parts, we therefore justly infer the hardness of the undivided particles not only of the bodies we feel but of all others. That all bodies are impenetrable, we gather not from reason, but from sensation. The bodies which we handle we find impenetrable, and thence conclude impenetrability to be an universal property of all bodies whatsoever. That all bodies are moveable, and endowed with certain powers (which we call the *vires inertiæ*) of persevering in their motion, or in their rest, we only infer from the like properties observed in the bodies which we have seen. The extension, hardness, impenetrability, mobility, and *vis inertiæ* of the whole, result from the extension, hardness, impenetrability, mobility, and *vires inertiæ* of the parts; and thence we conclude the least particles of all bodies to be also all extended, and hard and impenetrable, and moveable, and endowed with their proper *vires inerti[æ]*. And this is the foundation of all philosophy. Moreover, that the divided but contiguous particles of bodies may be separated from one another, is matter of observation; and, in the particles that remain undivided, our minds are able to distinguish yet lesser parts, as is mathematically demonstrated. But whether the parts so distinguished, and not yet divided, may, by the powers of Nature, be actually divided and separated from one another, we cannot certainly determine. Yet, had we the proof of but one experiment that any undivided particle, in breaking a hard and solid body, suffered a division, we might by virtue of this rule conclude that the undivided as well as the divided particles may be divided and actually separated to infinity.

Lastly, if it universally appears, by experiments and astronomical observations, that all bodies about the earth gravitate towards the earth, and that in proportion to the quantity of matter which they severally contain; that the moon likewise, according to the quantity of its matter, gravitates towards the earth; that, on the other hand, our sea gravitates towards the moon; and all the planets mutually one towards another; and the comets in like manner towards the sun; we must, in consequence of this rule, universally allow that all bodies whatsoever are endowed with a principle of mutual gravitation. For the argument from the appearances concludes with more force for the universal gravitation of all bodies than for their impenetrability; of which, among those in the celestial regions, we have no experiments, nor any manner of observation. Not that I affirm gravity to be essential to bodies: by their *vis insita* I mean nothing but their *vis inertiæ*. This is immutable. Their gravity is diminished as they recede from the earth.

Rule IV.

> *In experimental philosophy we are to look upon propositions collected by general induction from phænomena as accurately or very nearly true, notwithstanding any contrary hypotheses that may be imagined, till such time as other phænomena occur, by which they may either be made more accurate, or liable to exceptions.*

This rule we must follow, that the argument of induction may not be evaded by hypotheses.

[. . . .]

General Scholium.

The hypothesis of vortices is pressed with many difficulties. That every planet by a radius drawn to the sun may describe areas proportional to the times of description, the periodic times of the several parts of the vortices should observe the duplicate proportion of their distances from the sun; but that the periodic times of the planets may obtain the sesquiplicate proportion of their distances from the sun, the periodic times of the parts of the vortex ought to be in the sesquiplicate proportion of their distances. That the smaller vortices may maintain their lesser revolutions about *Saturn, Jupiter*, and other planets, and swim quietly and undisturbed in the greater vortex of the sun, the periodic times of the parts of the sun's vortex should be equal; but the rotation of the sun and planets about their axes, which ought to correspond with the motions of their vortices, recede far from all these proportions. The motions of the comets are exceedingly regular, are governed by the same laws with the motions of the planets, and can by no means be accounted for by the hypothesis of vortices; for comets are carried with very eccentric motions through all parts of the heavens indifferently, with a freedom that is incompatible with the notion of a vortex.

Bodies projected in our air suffer no resistance but from the air. Withdraw the air, as is done in Mr. *Boyle's* vacuum, and the resistance ceases; for in this void a bit of fine down and a piece of solid gold descend with equal velocity. And the parity of reason must take place in the celestial spaces above the earth's atmosphere; in which spaces, where there is no air to resist their motions, all bodies will move with the greatest freedom; and the planets and comets will constantly pursue their revolutions in orbits given in kind and position, according to the laws above explained; but though these bodies may, indeed, persevere in their orbits by the mere laws of gravity, yet they could by no means have at first derived the regular position of the orbits themselves from those laws.

The six primary planets are revolved about the sun in circles concentric with the sun, and with motions directed towards the same parts, and almost in the same plane. Ten moons are revolved about the earth, Jupiter and Saturn, in circles concentric with them, with the same direction of motion, and nearly in the planes of the orbits of those planets; but it is not to be conceived that mere mechanical causes could give birth to so many regular motions, since the comets range over all parts of the heavens in very eccentric orbits; for by that kind of motion they pass easily through the orbs of the planets, and with great rapidity; and in their aphelions, where they move the slowest, and are detained the longest, they recede to the greatest distances from each other, and thence suffer the least disturbance from their mutual attractions. This most beautiful system of the sun, planets, and comets, could only proceed from the counsel and dominion of an intelligent and powerful Being. And if the fixed stars are the centres of other like systems, these, being formed by the like wise counsel, must be all subject to the dominion of One; especially since the light of the fixed stars is of the same nature with the light of the sun, and from every system light passes into all the other systems: and lest the systems of the fixed stars should, by their gravity, fall on each other mutually, he hath placed those systems at immense distances one from another.

This Being governs all things, not as the soul of the world, but as Lord over all; and on account of his dominion he is wont to be called *Lord God. . .* , or *Universal Ruler*; for *God* is a relative word, and has a respect to servants; and *Deity* is the dominion of God not over his own body, as those imagine who fancy God to be the soul of the world, but over servants. The Supreme God is a Being eternal, infinite, absolutely perfect; but a being, however perfect, without dominion, cannot be said to be Lord God; for we say, my God, your God, the God of *Israel*, the God of Gods, and Lord of Lords; but we do not say, my Eternal, your Eternal, the Eternal of *Israel*, the Eternal of Gods; we do not say, my Infinite, or my Perfect: these are titles which have no respect to servants. The word *God* usually signifies *Lord*; but every lord is not a God. It is the dominion of a spiritual being which constitutes a God: a true, supreme, or imaginary dominion makes a true, supreme, or imaginary God. And from his true dominion it follows that the true God is a living, intelligent, and powerful Being; and, from his other perfections, that he is supreme, or most perfect. He is eternal and infinite, omnipotent and omniscient; that is, his duration reaches from eternity to eternity; his presence from infinity to infinity; he governs all things, and knows all things that are or can be done. He is not eternity or infinity, but eternal and infinite; he is not duration or space, but he endures and is present. He endures for ever, and is every where present; and by existing always and every where, he constitutes duration and space. Since every particle of space is *always*, and every indivisible moment of duration is *every where*, certainly the Maker and Lord of all things cannot be *never* and *no where*. Every soul that has perception is, though in different times and in different organs of sense and motion, still the same indivisible person. There are given successive parts in duration, co-existent parts in space, but neither the one nor the other in the person of a man, or his thinking principle; and much less can they be found in the thinking substance of God. Every man, so far as he is a thing that has perception, is one and the same man during his whole life, in all and each of his organs of sense. God is the same God, always and every where. He is omnipresent not *virtually* only, but also *substantially*; for virtue cannot subsist without substance. In him are all things contained and moved; yet neither affects the other: God suffers nothing from the motion of bodies; bodies find no resistance from the omnipresence of God. It is allowed by all that the Supreme God exists necessarily; and by the same necessity he exists *always* and *every where*. Whence also he is all similar, all eye, all ear, all brain, all arm, all power to perceive, to understand, and to act; but in a manner not at all human, in a manner not at all corporeal, in a manner utterly unknown to us. As a blind man has no idea of colours, so have we no idea of the manner by which the all-wise God perceives and understands all things. He is utterly void of all body and bodily figure, and can therefore neither be seen, nor heard, nor touched; nor ought he to be worshipped under the representation of any corporeal thing. We have ideas of his attributes, but what the real substance of any thing is we know not. In bodies, we see only their figures and colours, we hear only the sounds, we touch only their outward surfaces, we smell only the smells, and taste the savours; but their inward substances are not to be known either by our senses, or by any reflex act of our minds: much less, then, have we any idea of the substance of God.

We know him only by his most wise and excellent contrivances of things, and final causes: we admire him for his perfections; but we reverence and adore him on account of his dominion: for we adore him as his servants; and a god without dominion, providence, and final causes, is nothing else but Fate and Nature. Blind metaphysical necessity, which is certainly the same always and every where, could produce no variety of things. All that diversity of natural things which we find suited to different times and places could arise from nothing but the ideas and will of a Being necessarily existing. But, by way of allegory, God is said to see, to speak, to laugh, to love, to hate, to desire, to give, to receive, to rejoice, to be angry, to fight, to frame, to work, to build; for all our notions of God are taken from the ways of mankind by a certain similitude, which, though not perfect, has some likeness, however. And thus much concerning God; to discourse of whom from the appearances of things, does certainly belong to Natural Philosophy.

Hitherto we have explained the phenomena of the heavens and of our sea by the power of gravity, but have not yet assigned the cause of this power. This is certain, that it must proceed from a cause that penetrates to the very centres of the sun and planets, without suffering the least diminution of its force; that operates not according to the quantity of the surfaces of the particles upon which it acts (as mechanical causes use to do), but according to the quantity of the solid matter which they contain, and propagates its virtue on all sides to immense distances, decreasing always in the duplicate proportion of the distances. Gravitation towards the sun is made up out of the gravitations towards the several particles of which the body of the sun is composed; and in receding from the sun decreases accurately in the duplicate proportion of the distances as far as the orb of Saturn, as evidently appears from the quiescence of the aphelions of the planets; nay, and even to the remotest aphelions of the comets, if those aphelions are also quiescent. But hitherto I have not been able to discover the cause of those properties of gravity from phænomena, and I frame no hypotheses; for whatever is not deduced from the phænomena is to be called an hypothesis; and hypotheses, whether metaphysical or physical, whether of occult qualities or mechanical, have no place in experimental philosophy. In this philosophy particular propositions are inferred from the phænomena, and afterwards rendered general by induction. Thus it was that the impenetrability, the mobility, and the impulsive force of bodies, and the laws of motion and of gravitation, were discovered. And to us it is enough that gravity does really exist, and act according to the laws which we have explained, and abundantly serves to account for all the motions of the celestial bodies, and of our sea.

And now we might add something concerning a certain most subtle Spirit which pervades and lies hid in all gross bodies; by the force and action of which Spirit the particles of bodies mutually attract one another at near distances, and cohere, if contiguous; and electric bodies operate to greater distances, as well repelling as attracting the neighbouring corpuscles; and light is emitted, reflected, refracted, inflected, and heats bodies; and all sensation is excited, and the members of animal bodies move at the command of the will, namely, by the vibrations of this Spirit, mutually propagated along the solid filaments of the nerves, from the outward organs of sense to the brain, and from the brain into the muscles. But these are things that cannot be explained in few words, nor are we furnished with that sufficiency of experiments which is required to an accurate determination and demonstration of the laws by which this electric and elastic Spirit operates.

from *English Bill of Rights, 1689*

England's seventeenth century proved particularly volatile. Contests between the authority of the Stuart monarchy (1603–1688), the rights of the
people, and the role of Parliament, were often at the center of the turmoil.
After the Glorious Revolution (1688–1689) and the elevation to the throne
of the Hanoverians, i.e., William and Mary of Orange, the English Bill of
Rights (1689) restated the foundation on which the English government operated. As seen in the following excerpt, the inviolable rights of the people
included limits on the power of the monarchy; a greater voice—through
Parliament—in the exercise of government; clearer participation in the
administration of justice; religious tolerance; and freedom of speech.
Precedent-setting for England's history, the English Bill of Rights served as
a model for many peoples and nations thereafter.

Extracts from the Bill of Rights

Whereas the said late King James II having abdicated the government, and
the throne being thereby vacant, his Highness the prince of Orange (whom
it hath pleased Almighty God to make the glorious instrument of delivering
this kingdom from popery and arbitrary power) did (by the advice of the lords
spiritual and temporal, and diverse principal persons of the Commons) caused
letters to be written to the lords spiritual and temporal, being Protestants, and
other letters to the several counties, cities, universities, boroughs, and Cinque
Ports, for the choosing of such persons to represent them, as were of right
to be sent to parliament, to meet and sit at Westminster upon the two-and-
twentieth day of January, in this year 1689, in order to such an establishment

SOURCE: Extracts from the English Bill of Rights, in *Readings in English History Drawn
from the Original Sources, Intended to Illustrate a Short History of England*, ed. Edward P.
Cheyney (Boston: Ginn, 1908), 545–47.

as that their religion, laws, and liberties might not again be in danger of being subverted; upon which letters elections have been accordingly made.

And thereupon the said lords spiritual and temporal and Commons, pursuant to their respective letters and elections, being now assembled in a full and free representation of this nation, taking into their most serious consideration the best means for attaining the ends aforesaid, do in the first place (as their ancestors in like case have usually done), for the vindicating and asserting of their ancient rights and liberties, declare:

1. That the pretended power of suspending laws, or the execution of laws, by regal authority, without consent of parliament, is illegal.

2. That the pretended power of dispensing with the laws, or the execution of law by regal authority, as it hath been assumed and exercised of late, is illegal.

3. That the commission for erecting the late court of commissioners for ecclesiastical causes, and all other commissions and courts of like nature, are illegal and pernicious.

4. That levying money for or to the use of the crown by pretense of prerogative, without grant of parliament, for longer time or in other manner than the same is or shall be granted, is illegal.

5. That it is the right of the subjects to petition the king, and all commitments and prosecutions for such petitioning are illegal.

6. That the raising or keeping a standing army within the kingdom in time of peace, unless it be with consent of parliament, is against law.

7. That the subjects which are Protestants may have arms for their defense suitable to their conditions, and as allowed by law.

8. That election of members of parliament ought to be free.

9. That the freedom of speech, and debates or proceedings in parliament, ought not to be impeached or questioned in any court or place out of parliament.

10. That excessive bail ought not to be required, nor excessive fines imposed, nor cruel and unusual punishments inflicted.

11. That jurors ought to be duly impaneled and returned, and jurors which pass upon men in trials for high treason ought to be freeholders.

12. That all grants and promises of fines and forfeitures of particular persons before conviction are illegal and void.

13. And that for redress of all grievance and for the amending, strengthening, and preserving of the laws, parliament ought to be held frequently.

And they do claim, demand, and insist upon all and singular the premises, as their undoubted rights and liberties; and that no declarations, judgments, doings, or proceedings, to the prejudice of the people in any of the said premises, ought in any wise to be drawn hereafter into consequence or example.

To which demand of their rights they are particularly encouraged by the declaration of his Highness the prince of Orange, as being the only means for obtaining a full redress and remedy therein.

Having therefore an entire confidence that his said Highness the prince of Orange will perfect the deliverance so far advanced by him, and will still preserve them from the violation of their rights which they have here asserted, and from all other attempts upon their religion, rights and liberties:

The said lords spiritual and temporal, and commons, assembled at Westminster, do resolve that William and Mary, prince and princess of Orange, be, and be declared king and queen of England, France, and Ireland, and the dominions thereunto belonging, to hold the crown and royal dignity of the said kingdoms and dominions to them the said prince and princess during their lives and the life of the survivor to them; and that the sole and full exercise of the regal power be only in, and executed by, the said prince of Orange, in the names of the said prince and princess, during their joint lives; and after their deceases, the said crown and royal dignity of the same kingdoms and dominions to be to the heirs of the body of the said princess, and for default of such issue to the Princess Anne of Denmark, and the heirs of her body; and for default of such issue to the heirs of the body of the said prince of Orange. And the lords spiritual and temporal and commons do pray the said prince and princess to accept the same accordingly. . . .

Upon which their said Majesties did accept the crown and royal dignity of the kingdoms of England, France, and Ireland, and the dominions thereunto belonging, according to the resolution and desire of the said lords and commons contained in the said declaration.

91

Adam Smith

from *Wealth of Nations*

Adam Smith (1723–1790) was a Scottish social philosopher who is often regarded as progenitor of the discipline of political economics and something
of an iconic figure in the history of capitalism. A leading figure in the Scottish
Enlightenment, his most influential work is commonly known as *Wealth of
Nations*. The following excerpts from that particular text include his famous
line of reasoning about the "invisible hand" that putatively guides free markets.

Book I: Chapter II: Of the Principle Which Gives Occasion to the Division of Labor

This division of labour, from which so many advantages are derived, is not
originally the effect of any human wisdom, which foresees and intends that
general opulence to which it gives occasion. It is the necessary, though very
slow and gradual, consequence of a certain propensity in human nature which
has in view no such extensive utility; the propensity to truck, barter, and exchange one thing for another.

Whether this propensity be one of those original principles in human nature, of which no further account can be given; or whether, as seems more
probable, it be the necessary consequence of the faculties of reason and speech,
it belongs not to our present subject to enquire. It is common to all men, and
to be found in no other race of animals, which seem to know neither this nor
any other species of contracts. Two greyhounds, in running down the same
hare, have sometimes the appearance of acting in some sort of concert. Each
turns her towards his companion, or endeavours to intercept her when his

SOURCE: Adam Smith, *An Inquiry into the Nature and Causes of the Wealth of Nations*, ed.
Edwin Cannan, vol. 1 (London: Methuen, 1904), 15–18, 421, 457–59.

companion turns her towards himself. This, however, is not the effect of any contract, but of the accidental concurrence of their passions in the same object at that particular time. Nobody ever saw a dog make a fair and deliberate exchange of one bone for another with another dog. Nobody ever saw one animal by its gestures and natural cries signify to another, this is mine, that yours; I am willing to give this for that. When an animal wants to obtain something either of a man or of another animal, it has no other means of persuasion but to gain the favour of those whose service it requires. A puppy fawns upon its dam, and a spaniel endeavours by a thousand attractions to engage the attention of its master who is at dinner, when it wants to be fed by him. Man sometimes uses the same arts with his brethren, and when he has no other means of engaging them to act according to his inclinations, endeavours by every servile and fawning attention to obtain their good will. He has not time, however, to do this upon every occasion. In civilized society he stands at all times in need of the co-operation and assistance of great multitudes, while his whole life is scarce sufficient to gain the friendship of a few persons. In almost every other race of animals each individual, when it is grown up to maturity, is entirely independent, and in its natural state has occasion for the assistance of no other living creature. But man has almost constant occasion for the help of his brethren, and it is in vain for him to expect it from their benevolence only. He will be more likely to prevail if he can interest their self-love in his favour, and shew them that it is for their own advantage to do for him what he requires of them. Whoever offers to another a bargain of any kind, proposes to do this: Give me that which I want, and you shall have this which you want, is the meaning of every such offer; and it is in this manner that we obtain from one another the far greater part of those good offices which we stand in need of. It is not from the benevolence of the butcher, the brewer, or the baker, that we expect our dinner, but from their regard to their own interest. We address ourselves, not to their humanity but to their self-love, and never talk to them of our own necessities but of their advantages. Nobody but a beggar chuses to depend chiefly upon the benevolence of his fellow-citizens. Even a beggar does not depend upon it entirely. The charity of well-disposed people, indeed, supplies him with the whole fund of his subsistence. But though this principle ultimately provides him with all the necessaries of life which he has occasion for, it neither does nor can provide him with them as he has occasion for them. The greater part of his occasional wants are supplied in the same manner as those of other people, by treaty, by barter, and by purchase. With the money which one man gives him he purchases food. The old cloaths which another bestows upon him he exchanges for other old cloaths which suit him better, or for lodging, or for food, or for money, with which he can buy either food, cloaths, or lodging, as he has occasion.

As it is by treaty, by barter, and by purchase, that we obtain from one another the greater part of those mutual good offices which we stand in need of, so it is this same trucking disposition which originally gives occasion to the division of labour. In a tribe of hunters or shepherds a particular person makes bows and arrows, for example, with more readiness and dexterity than any other. He frequently exchanges them for cattle or for venison with his companions; and he finds at last that he can in this manner get more cattle and venison, than if he himself went to the field to catch them. From a regard to his own interest, therefore, the making of bows and arrows grows to be his chief business, and he becomes a sort of armourer. Another excels in making the frames and covers of their little huts or moveable houses. He is accustomed to be of use in this way to his neighbours, who reward him in the same manner with cattle and with venison, till at last he finds it his interest to dedicate himself entirely to this employment, and to become a sort of house-carpenter. In the same manner a third becomes a smith or a brazier; a fourth a tanner or dresser of hides or skins, the principal part of the clothing of savages. And thus the certainty of being able to exchange all that surplus part of the produce of his own labour, which is over and above his own consumption, for such parts of the produce of other men's labour as he may have occasion for, encourages every man to apply himself to a particular occupation, and to cultivate and bring to perfection whatever talent or genius he may possess for that particular species of business.

The difference of natural talents in different men is, in reality, much less than we are aware of; and the very different genius which appears to distinguish men of different professions, when grown up to maturity, is not upon many occasions so much the cause, as the effect of the division of labour. The difference between the most dissimilar characters, between a philosopher and a common street porter, for example, seems to arise not so much from nature, as from habit, custom, and education. When they came into the world, and for the first six or eight years of their existence, they were, perhaps, very much alike, and neither their parents nor playfellows could perceive any remarkable difference. About that age, or soon after, they come to be employed in very different occupations. The difference of talents comes then to be taken notice of, and widens by degrees, till at last the vanity of the philosopher is willing to acknowledge scarce any resemblance. But without the disposition to truck, barter, and exchange, every man must have procured to himself every necessary and conveniency of life which he wanted. All must have had the same duties to perform, and the same work to do, and there could have been no such difference of employment as could alone give occasion to any great difference of talents.

As it is this disposition which forms that difference of talents, so remarkable among men of different professions, so it is this same disposition which renders that difference useful. Many tribes of animals acknowledged to be all of the same species, derive from nature a much more remarkable distinction of genius, than what, antecedent to custom and education, appears to take place among men. By nature a philosopher is not in genius and disposition half so different from a street porter, as a mastiff is from a greyhound, or a greyhound from a spaniel, or this last from a shepherd's dog. Those different tribes of animals, however, though all of the same species, are of scarce any use to one another. The strength of the mastiff is not in the least supported either by the swiftness of the greyhound, or by the sagacity of the spaniel, or by the docility of the shepherd's dog. The effects of those different geniuses and talents, for want of the power or disposition to barter and exchange, cannot be brought into a common stock, and do not in the least contribute to the better accommodation and conveniency of the species. Each animal is still obliged to support and defend itself, separately and independently, and derives no sort of advantage from that variety of talents with which nature has distinguished its fellows. Among men, on the contrary, the most dissimilar geniuses are of use to one another; the different produces of their respective talents, by the general disposition to truck, barter, and exchange, being brought, as it were, into a common stock, where every man may purchase whatever part of the produce of other men's talents he has occasion for.

[. . . .]

Book IV: Chapter II: Of Restraints upon the Importation from Foreign Countries of Such Goods as Can Be Produced at Home

... The produce of industry is what it adds to the subject or materials upon which it is employed. In proportion as the value of this produce is great or small, so will likewise be the profits of the employer. But it is only for the sake of profit that any man employs a capital in the support of industry; and he will always, therefore, endeavour to employ it in the support of that industry of which the produce is likely to be of the greatest value, or to exchange for the greatest quantity either of money or of other goods.

But the annual revenue of every society is always precisely equal to the exchangeable value of the whole annual produce of its industry, or rather is precisely the same thing with that exchangeable value. As every individual, therefore, endeavours as much as he can both to employ his capital in the support of domestic industry, and so to direct that industry that its produce may be of the greatest value; every individual necessarily labours to render the annual revenue of the society as great as he can. He generally, indeed, neither intends to promote the public interest, nor knows how much he is promoting it. By preferring the support of domestic to that of foreign industry, he intends only his own security; and by directing that industry in such a manner as its produce may be of the greatest value, he intends only his own gain, and he is in this, as in many other cases, led by an invisible hand to promote an end which was no part of his intention. Nor is it always the worse for the society that it was no part of it. By pursuing his own interest he frequently promotes that of the society more effectually than when he really intends to promote it. I have never known much good done by those who affected to trade for the public good. It is an affectation, indeed, not very common among merchants, and very few words need be employed in dissuading them from it.

What is the species of domestic industry which his capital can employ, and of which the produce is likely to be of the greatest value, every individual, it is evident, can, in his local situation, judge much better than any statesman or lawgiver can do for him. The statesman, who should attempt to direct private people in what manner they ought to employ their capitals, would not only load himself with a most unnecessary attention, but assume an authority which could safely be trusted, not only to no single person, but to no council or senate whatever, and which would no-where be so dangerous as in the hands of a man who had folly and presumption enough to fancy himself fit to exercise it.

[. . . .]

Book IV: Chapter III: Of the Extraordinary Restraints upon the Importation of Goods of Almost All Kinds, from Those Countries with Which the Balance Is Supposed to Be Disadvantageous

. . . Each nation has been made to look with an invidious eye upon the prosperity of all the nations with which it trades, and to consider their gain as its own loss. Commerce, which ought naturally to be, among nations, as among individuals, a bond of union and friendship, has become the most fertile source of discord and animosity. The capricious ambition of kings and ministers has not, during the present and the preceding century, been more fatal to the repose of Europe, than the impertinent jealousy of merchants and manufacturers. The violence and injustice of the rulers of mankind is an ancient evil, for which, I am afraid, the nature of human affairs can scarce admit of a remedy. But the mean rapacity, the monopolizing spirit of merchants and manufacturers, who neither are, nor ought to be, the rulers of mankind, though it cannot perhaps be corrected, may very easily be prevented from disturbing the tranquillity of any body but themselves.

That it was the spirit of monopoly which originally both invented and propagated this doctrine, cannot be doubted; and they who first taught it were by no means such fools as they who believed it. In every country it always is and must be the interest of the great body of the people to buy whatever they want of those who sell it cheapest. The proposition is so very manifest, that it seems ridiculous to take any pains to prove it; nor could it ever have been called in question, had not the interested sophistry of merchants and manufacturers confounded the common sense of mankind. Their interest is, in this respect, directly opposite to that of the great body of the people. As it is the interest of the freemen of a corporation to hinder the rest of the inhabitants from employing any workmen but themselves, so it is the interest of the merchants and manufacturers of every country to secure to themselves the monopoly of the home market. Hence in Great Britain, and in most other European countries, the extraordinary duties upon almost all goods imported by alien merchants. Hence the high duties and prohibitions upon all those foreign manufactures which can come into competition with our own. Hence too the extraordinary restraints upon the importation of almost all sorts of goods from those countries with which the balance of trade is supposed to be disadvantageous; that is, from those against whom national animosity happens to be most violently inflamed.

The wealth of a neighbouring nation, however, though dangerous in war and politics, is certainly advantageous in trade. In a state of hostility it may enable our enemies to maintain fleets and armies superior to our own; but in a state of peace and commerce it must likewise enable them to exchange with us to a greater value, and to afford a better market, either for the immediate produce of our own industry, or for whatever is purchased with that produce. As a rich man is likely to be a better customer to the industrious people in his neighbourhood, than a poor, so is likewise a rich nation. A rich man, indeed, who is himself a manufacturer, is a very dangerous neighbour to all those who deal in the same way. All the rest of the neighbourhood, however, by far the greatest number, profit by the good market which his expence affords them. They even profit by his underselling the poorer workmen who deal in the same way with him. The manufacturers of a rich nation, in the same manner, may no doubt be very dangerous rivals to those of their neighbours. This very competition, however, is advantageous to the great body of the people, who profit greatly besides by the good market which the great expence of such a nation affords them in every other way. Private people who want to make a fortune, never think of retiring to the remote and poor provinces of the country, but resort either to the capital, or to some of the great commercial towns. They know, that, where little wealth circulates, there is little to be got, but that where a great deal is in motion, some share of it may fall to them. The same maxims which would in this manner direct the common sense of one, or ten, or twenty individuals, should regulate the judgment of one, or ten, or twenty millions, and should make a whole nation regard the riches of its neighbours, as a probable cause and occasion for itself to acquire riches. A nation that would enrich itself by foreign trade, is certainly most likely to do so when its neighbours are all rich, industrious, and commercial nations. A great nation surrounded on all sides by wandering savages and poor barbarians might, no doubt, acquire riches by the cultivation of its own lands, and by its own interior commerce, but not by foreign trade. It seems to have been in this manner that the ancient Egyptians and the modern Chinese acquired their great wealth. The ancient Egyptians, it is said, neglected foreign commerce, and the modern Chinese, it is known, hold it in the utmost contempt, and scarce deign to afford it the decent protection of the laws. The modern maxims of foreign commerce, by aiming at the impoverishment of all our neighbours, so far as they are capable of producing their intended effect, tend to render that very commerce insignificant and contemptible.

92

Immanuel Kant

from Fundamental Principles of the Metaphysic of Ethics

Immanuel Kant (1724–1804) was a Prussian philosopher who played a vital role in the Enlightenment and in the development of late modern philosophy, in part by offering a middle path of sorts between rationalism and empiricism with his transcendental idealism. Kant easily stands out as one of the most influential philosophers of all time, particularly with respect to moral philosophy. In his view, reason is the root source of the moral law and it issues a singular fundamental imperative—the categorical imperative. The following are excerpts from his *Fundamental Principles of the Metaphysic of Ethics* in which he discusses what it takes to have a good will, as well as his first and second formulations of the categorical imperative of practical reason.

Nothing can possibly be conceived in the world, or even out of it, which can be called good without qualification, except a Good Will. Intelligence, wit, judgment, and the other *talents* of the mind, however they may be named, or courage, resolution, perseverance, as qualities of temperament, are undoubtedly good and desirable in many respects; but these gifts of nature may also become extremely bad and mischievous if the will which is to make use of them, and which, therefore, constitutes what is called *character*, is not good. It is the same with the *gifts of fortune*. Power, riches, honour, even health, and the general well-being and contentment with one's condition which is called *happiness*, inspire pride, and often presumption, if there is not a good will to correct the influence of these on the mind, and with this also to rectify the whole principle of acting, and adapt it to its end. The sight of a being who is not adorned with a single

SOURCE: Immanuel Kant, *Fundamental Principles of the Metaphysic of Ethics*, trans. Thomas Kingsmill Abbott, 5th ed. (London: Longmans, Green, and Co., 1916), 10–24, 45–50, 55–56.

feature of a pure and good will, enjoying unbroken prosperity, can never give pleasure to an impartial rational spectator. Thus a good will appears to constitute the indispensable condition even of being worthy of happiness.

[. . . .]

We have then to develop the notion of a will which deserves to be highly esteemed for itself, and is good without a view to anything further, a notion which exists already in the sound natural understanding, requiring rather to be cleared up than to be taught, and which in estimating the value of our actions always takes the first place, and constitutes the condition of all the rest. In order to do this we will take the notion of duty, which includes that of a good will, although implying certain subjective restrictions and hindrances. These, however, far from concealing it, or rendering it unrecognisable, rather bring it out by contrast, and make it shine forth so much the brighter.

I omit here all actions which are already recognised as inconsistent with duty, although they may be useful for this or that purpose, for with these the question whether they are done *from duty* cannot arise at all, since they even conflict with it. I also set aside those actions which really conform to duty, but to which men have *no* direct *inclination*, performing them because they are impelled thereto by some other inclination. For in this case we can readily distinguish whether the action which agrees with duty is done *from duty*, or from a selfish view. It is much harder to make this distinction when the action accords with duty, and the subject has besides a *direct* inclination to it. For example, it is always a matter of duty that a dealer should not overcharge an inexperienced purchaser, and wherever there is much commerce the prudent tradesman does not overcharge, but keeps a fixed price for everyone, so that a child buys of him as well as any other. Men are thus *honestly* served; but this is not enough to make us believe that the tradesman has so acted from duty and from principles of honesty: his own advantage required it; it is out of the question in this case to suppose that he might besides have a direct inclination in favour of the buyers, so that, as it were, from love he should give no advantage to one over another. Accordingly the action was done neither from duty nor from direct inclination, but merely with a selfish view.

On the other hand, it is a duty to maintain one's life; and, in addition, everyone has also a direct inclination to do so. But on this account the often anxious care which most men take for it has no intrinsic worth, and their maxim has no moral import. They preserve their life *as duty requires*, no doubt, but not *because duty requires*. On the other hand, if adversity and hopeless sorrow have completely taken away the relish for life; if the unfortunate one, strong in mind, indignant at his fate rather than desponding or dejected, wishes for death, and yet preserves his life without loving it—not from inclination or fear, but from duty—then his maxim has a moral worth.

To be beneficent when we can is a duty; and besides this, there are many minds so sympathetically constituted that, without any other motive of vanity or self-interest, they find a pleasure in spreading joy around them, and can take delight in the satisfaction of others so far as it is their own work. But I maintain that in such a case an action of this kind, however proper, however amiable it may be, has nevertheless no true moral worth, but is on a level with other inclinations, *e.g.*, the inclination to honour, which, if it is happily directed to that which is in fact of public utility and accordant with duty and consequently honourable, deserves praise and encouragement, but not esteem. For the maxim lacks the moral import, namely, that such actions be done *from duty*, not from inclination. Put the case that the mind of that philanthropist were clouded by sorrow of his own extinguishing all sympathy with the lot of others, and that while he still has the power to benefit others in distress, he is not touched by their trouble because he is absorbed with his own; and now suppose that he tears himself out of this dead insensibility, and performs the action without any inclination to it, but simply from duty, then first has his action its genuine moral worth. Further still; if nature has put little sympathy in the heart of this or that man; if he, supposed to be an upright man, is by temperament cold and indifferent to the sufferings of others, perhaps because in respect of his own he is provided with the special gift of patience and fortitude, and supposes, or even requires, that others should have the same—and such a man would certainly not be the meanest product of nature—but if nature had not specially framed him for a philanthropist, would he not still find in himself a source from whence to give himself a far higher worth than that of a good-natured temperament could be? Unquestionably. It is just in this that the moral worth of the character is brought out which is incomparably the highest of all, namely, that he is beneficent, not from inclination, but from duty.

To secure one's own happiness is a duty, at least indirectly; for discontent with one's condition, under a pressure of many anxieties and amidst unsatisfied wants, might easily become a great *temptation to transgression of duty*. But here again, without looking to duty, all men have already the strongest and most intimate inclination to happiness, because it is just in this idea that all inclinations are combined in one total. But the precept of happiness is often of such a sort that it greatly interferes with some inclinations, and yet a man cannot form any definite and certain conception of the sum of satisfaction of all of them which is called happiness. It is not then to be wondered at that a single inclination, definite both as to what it promises and as to the time within which it can be gratified, is often able to overcome such a fluctuating idea, and that a gouty patient, for instance, can choose to enjoy what he likes, and to suffer what he may, since, according to his calculation, on this occasion at least, he has [only] not sacrificed the enjoyment of the present moment to a possibly mistaken expectation of a happiness which is supposed to be found in health. But even in this case, if the general desire for happiness did not influence his will, and supposing that in his particular case health was not a necessary element in this calculation, there yet remains in this, as in all other cases, this law, namely, that he should promote his happiness not from inclination but from duty, and by this would his conduct first acquire true moral worth.

It is in this manner, undoubtedly, that we are to understand those passages of Scripture also in which we are commanded to love our neighbour, even our enemy. For love, as an affection, cannot be commanded, but beneficence for duty's sake may; even though we are not impelled to it by any inclination—nay, are even repelled by a natural and unconquerable aversion. This is *practical* love, and not *pathological*—a love which is seated in the will, and not in the propensions of sense—in principles of action and not of tender sympathy; and it is this love alone which can be commanded.

The second proposition is: That an action done from duty derives its moral worth, *not from the purpose* which is to be attained by it, but from the maxim by which it is determined, and therefore does not depend on the realization of the object of the action, but merely on the *principle of volition* by which the action has taken place, without regard to any object of desire. It is clear from what precedes that the purposes which we may have in view in our actions, or their effects regarded as ends and springs of the will, cannot give to actions any unconditional or moral worth. In what, then, can their worth lie, if it is not to consist in the will and in reference to its expected effect? It cannot lie anywhere but in the *principle of the will* without regard to the ends which can be attained by the action. For the will stands between its *á priori* principle, which is formal, and its *á posteriori* spring, which is material, as between two roads, and as it must be determined by something, it follows that it must be determined by the formal principle of volition when an action is done from duty, in which case every material principle has been withdrawn from it.

The third proposition, which is a consequence of the two preceding, I would express thus: *Duty is the necessity of acting from respect for the law.* I may have *inclination* for an object as the effect of my proposed action, but I cannot have *respect* for it, just for this reason, that it is an effect and not an energy of will. Similarly, I cannot have respect for inclination, whether my own or another's; I can at most, if my own, approve it; if another's, sometimes even love it; *i.e.*, look on it as favourable to my own interest. It is only what is connected with my will as a principle, by no means as an effect—what does not subserve my inclination, but overpowers it, or at least in case of choice excludes it from its calculation—in other words, simply the law of itself, which can be an object of respect, and hence a command. Now an action done from duty must wholly exclude the influence of inclination and with it every object of the will, so that nothing remains which can determine the will except objectively the *law*, and subjectively *pure respect* for this practical law, and consequently the maxim that I should follow this law even to the thwarting of all my inclinations.

Thus the moral worth of an action does not lie in the effect expected from it, nor in any principle of action which requires to borrow its motive from this expected effect. For all these effects—agreeableness of one's condition, and even the promotion of the happiness of others—could have been also brought about by other causes, so that for this there would have been no need of the will of a rational being; whereas it is in this alone that the supreme and unconditional good can be found. The pre-eminent good which we call moral can therefore consist in nothing else than *the conception of law* in itself, *which certainly is only possible in a rational being*, in so far as this conception, and not the expected effect, determines the will. This is a good which is already present in the person who acts accordingly, and we have not to wait for it to appear first in the result.

But what sort of law can that be, the conception of which must determine the will, even without paying any regard to the effect expected from it, in order that this will may be called good absolutely and without qualification? As I have deprived the will of every impulse which could arise to it from obedience to any law, there remains nothing but the universal conformity of its actions to law in general, which alone is to serve the will as a principle, *i.e.*, I am never to act otherwise than so *that I could also will that my maxim should become a universal law*. Here now, it is the simple conformity to law in general, without assuming any particular law applicable to certain actions, that serves the will as its principle, and must so serve it, if duty is not to be a vain delusion and a chimerical notion. The common reason of men in its practical judgments perfectly coincides with this and always has in view the principle here suggested. Let the question be, for example: May I when in distress make a promise with the intention not to keep it? I readily distinguish here between the two significations which the question may have: Whether it is prudent, or whether it is right, to make a false promise. The former may undoubtedly often be the case. I see clearly indeed that it is not enough to extricate myself from a present difficulty by means of this subterfuge, but it must be well considered whether there may not hereafter spring from this lie much greater inconvenience than that from which I now free myself, and as, with all my supposed *cunning*, the consequences cannot be so easily foreseen but that credit once lost may be much more injurious to me than any mischief which I seek to avoid at present, it should be considered whether it would not be more *prudent* to act herein according to a universal maxim and to make it a habit to promise nothing except with the intention of keeping it. But it is soon clear to me that such a maxim will still only be based on the fear of consequences. Now it is a wholly different thing to be truthful from duty, and to be so from apprehension of injurious consequences. In the first case, the very notion of the action already implies a law for me; in the second case, I must first look about elsewhere to see what results may be combined with it which would affect myself. For to deviate from the principle of duty is beyond all doubt wicked; but to be unfaithful to my maxim of prudence may often be very advantageous to me, although to abide by it is certainly safer. The shortest way, however, and an unerring one, to discover the answer to this question whether a lying promise is consistent with duty, is to ask myself, Should I be content that my maxim (to extricate myself from difficulty by a false promise) should hold good as a universal law, for myself as well as for others? and should I be able to say to myself, Every one may make a deceitful promise when he finds himself in a difficulty from which he cannot otherwise extricate himself? Then I presently become aware that while I can will the lie, I can by no means will that lying should be a universal law. For with such a law there would be no promises at all, since it would be in vain to allege my intention in regard to my future actions to those who would not believe this allegation, or if they over-hastily did so would pay me back in my own coin. Hence my maxim, as soon as it should be made a universal law, would necessarily destroy itself.

I do not, therefore, need any far-reaching penetration to discern what I have to do in order that my will may be morally good. Inexperienced in the course of the world, incapable of being prepared for all its contingencies, I only ask myself: Canst thou also will that thy maxim should be a universal law? If not, then it must be rejected, and that not because of a disadvantage accruing from it to myself or even to others, but because it cannot enter as a principle into a possible universal legislation, and reason extorts from me immediate respect for such legislation. I do not indeed as yet *discern* on what this respect is based (this the philosopher may inquire), but at least I understand this, that it is an estimation of the worth which far outweighs all worth of what is recommended by inclination, and that the necessity of acting from *pure* respect for the practical law is what constitutes duty, to which every other motive must give place, because it is the condition of a will being good *in itself*, and the worth of such a will is above everything.

Thus, then, without quitting the moral knowledge of common human reason, we have arrived at its principle. And although, no doubt, common men do not conceive it in such an abstract and universal form, yet they always have it really before their eyes and use it as the standard of their decision. Here it would be easy to show how, with this compass in hand, men are well able to distinguish, in every case that occurs, what is good, what bad, conformably to duty or inconsistent with it, if, without in the least teaching them anything new, we only, like Socrates, direct their attention to the principle they themselves employ; and that, therefore, we do not need science and philosophy to know what we should do to be honest and good, yea, even wise and virtuous. Indeed we might well have conjectured beforehand that the knowledge of what every man is bound to do, and therefore also to know, would be within the reach of every man, even the commonest.

[. . . .]

When I conceive a hypothetical imperative in general I do not know beforehand what it will contain until I am given the condition. But when I conceive a categorical imperative I know at once what it contains. For as the imperative contains besides the law only the necessity that the maxims shall conform to this law, while the law contains no conditions restricting it, there remains nothing but the general statement that the maxim of the action should conform to a universal law, and it is this conformity alone that the imperative properly represents as necessary.

There is therefore but one categorical imperative, namely this: *Act only on that maxim whereby thou canst at the same time will that it should become a universal law.*

Now if all imperatives of duty can be deduced from this one imperative as from their principle, then, although it should remain undecided whether what is called duty is not merely a vain notion, yet at least we shall be able to show what we understand by it and what this notion means.

Since the universality of the law according to which effects are produced constitutes what is properly called *nature* in the most general sense (as to form), that is, the existence of things so far as it is determined by general laws, the imperative of duty may be expressed thus: *Act as if the maxim of thy action were to become by thy will a Universal Law of Nature.*

We will now enumerate a few duties, adopting the usual division of them into duties to ourselves and ourselves and to others, and into perfect and imperfect duties.

1. A man reduced to despair by a series of misfortunes feels wearied of life, but is still so far in possession of his reason that he can ask himself whether it would not be contrary to his duty to himself to take his own life. Now he inquires whether the maxim of his action could become a universal law of nature. His maxim is: From self-love I adopt it as a principle to shorten my life when its longer duration is likely to bring more evil than satisfaction. It is asked then simply whether this principle founded on self-love can become a universal law of nature. Now we see at once that a system of nature of which it should be a law to destroy life by means of the very feeling whose special nature it is to impel to the improvement of life would contradict itself, and therefore, could not exist as a system of nature; hence that maxim cannot possibly exist as a universal law of nature, and consequently would be wholly inconsistent with the supreme principle of all duty.

2. Another finds himself forced by necessity to borrow money. He knows that he will not be able to repay it, but sees also that nothing will be lent to him, unless he promises stoutly to repay it in a definite time. He desires to make this promise, but he has still so much conscience as to ask himself: Is it not unlawful and inconsistent with duty to get out of a difficulty in this way? Suppose however that he resolves to do so, then the maxim of his action would be expressed thus: When I think myself in want of money, I will borrow money and promise to repay it, although I know that I never can do so. Now this principle of self-love or of one's own advantage may perhaps be consistent with my whole future welfare; but the question now is, Is it right? I change then the suggestion of self-love into a universal law, and state the question thus: How would it be if my maxim were a universal law? Then I see at once that it could never hold as a universal law of nature but would necessarily contradict itself. For supposing it to be a universal law that everyone when he thinks himself in a difficulty should be able to promise whatever he pleases, with the purpose of not keeping his promise, the promise itself would become impossible, as well as the end that one might have in view in it, since no one would consider that anything was promised to him, but would ridicule all such statements as vain pretences.

3. A third finds in himself a talent which with the help of some culture might make him a useful man in many respects. But he finds himself in comfortable circumstances and prefers to indulge in pleasure rather than to take pains in enlarging and improving his happy natural capacities. He asks, however, whether his maxim of neglect of his natural gifts, besides agreeing with his inclination to indulgence, agrees also with what is called duty. He sees then that a system of nature could indeed subsist with such a universal law

although men (like the South Sea islanders) should let their talents rust and resolve to devote their lives merely to idleness, amusement, and propagation of their species—in a word, to enjoyment; but he cannot possibly *will* that this should be a universal law of nature, or be implanted in us as such by a natural instinct. For, as a rational being, he necessarily wills that his faculties be developed, since they serve him and have been given him, for all sorts of possible purposes.

4. A fourth, who is in prosperity, while he sees that others have to contend with great wretchedness and that he could help them, thinks: What concern is it of mine? Let everyone be as happy as Heaven pleases, or as he can make himself; I will take nothing from him nor even envy him, only I do not wish to contribute anything to his welfare or to his assistance in distress! Now no doubt if such a mode of thinking were a universal law, the human race might very well subsist and doubtless even better than in a state in which everyone talks of sympathy and good-will, or even takes care occasionally to put it into practice, but on the other side, also cheats when he can, betrays the rights of men, or otherwise violates them. But although it is possible that a universal law of nature might exist in accordance with that maxim, it is impossible to *will* that such a principle should have the universal validity of a law of nature. For a will which resolved this would contradict itself, inasmuch as many cases might occur in which one would have need of the love and sympathy of others, and in which, by such a law of nature, sprung from his own will, he would deprive himself of all hope of the aid he desires.

These are a few of the many actual duties, or at least what we regard as such, which obviously fall into two classes on the one principle that we have laid down. We must be *able to will* that a maxim of our action should be a universal law. This is the canon of the moral appreciation of the action generally. Some actions are of such a character that their maxim cannot without contradiction be even *conceived* as a universal law of nature, far from it being possible that we should *will* that it *should* be so. In others this intrinsic impossibility is not found, but still it is impossible to *will* that their maxim should be raised to the universality of a law of nature, since such a will would contradict itself. It is easily seen that the former violate strict or rigorous (inflexible) duty; the latter only laxer (meritorious) duty. Thus it has been completely shown how all duties depend as regards the nature of the obligation (not the object of the action) on the same principle.

[. . . .]

Supposing, however, that there were something whose *existence* has *in itself* an absolute worth, something which, being *an end in itself,* could be a source of definite laws, then in this and this alone would lie the source of a possible categorical imperative, *i.e.*, a practical law.

Now I say: man and generally any rational being *exists* as an end in himself, *not merely as a means* to be arbitrarily used by this or that will, but in all his actions, whether they concern himself or other rational beings, must be always regarded at the same time as an end. All objects of the inclinations have only a conditional worth, for if the inclinations and the wants founded on them did not exist, then their object would be without value. But the inclinations, themselves being sources of want, are so far from having an absolute worth for which they should be desired, that on the contrary it must be the universal wish of every rational being to be wholly free from them. Thus the worth of any object which is *to be acquired* by our action is always conditional. Beings whose existence depends not on our will but on nature's, have nevertheless, if they are irrational beings, only a relative value as means, and are therefore called *things*; rational beings, on the contrary, are called *persons*, because their very nature points them out as ends in themselves, that is as something which must not be used merely as means, and so far therefore restricts freedom of action (and is an object of respect). These, therefore, are not merely subjective ends whose existence has a worth *for us* as an effect of our action, but *objective ends*, that is things whose existence is an end in itself: an end moreover for which no other can be substituted, which they should subserve *merely* as means, for otherwise nothing whatever would possess *absolute worth*; but if all worth were conditioned and therefore contingent, then there would be no supreme practical principle of reason whatever.

If then there is a supreme practical principle or, in respect of the human will, a categorical imperative, it must be one which, being drawn from the conception of that which is necessarily an end for everyone because it is *an end in itself*, constitutes an *objective* principle of will, and can therefore serve as a universal practical law. The foundation of this principle is: *rational nature exists as an end in itself*. Man necessarily conceives his own existence as being so: so far then this is a *subjective* principle of human actions. But every other rational being regards its existence similarly, just on the same rational principle that holds for me: so that it is at the same time an objective principle, from which as a supreme practical law all laws of the will must be capable of being deduced. Accordingly the practical imperative will be as follows: *So act as to treat humanity, whether in thine own person or in that of any other, in every case as an end withal, never as means only.*

93

J. Hector St. Jean de Crevecoeur

from *What Is an American?*

Born to an impoverished family in Normandy (France), J. Hector St. Jean Crevecoeur (1735–1813) traveled in 1755 to New France as a soldier under the command of Gen. Louis-Joseph de Montcalm to fight the British in North America during the Seven Years War. Under terms of the Treaty of Paris 1763, the defeated French vacated their claims in North America. Crevecoeur remained, however. Composing his *Letters from an American Farmer* before the American Revolution, he sought to explain distinctive American characteristics for European readers. The letters would only find publication in 1782, near the conclusion of the Revolutionary War for U.S. independence. For more than two hundred years, these letters have served as an important early portrait of the American identity. The following selection poses Crevecoeur's famous question, "What is an American?"

Letter III: What Is an American.

I wish I could be acquainted with the feelings and thoughts which must agitate the heart and present themselves to the mind of an enlightened Englishman, when he first lands on this continent. He must greatly rejoice that he lived at a time to see this fair country discovered and settled; he must necessarily feel a share of national pride, when he views the chain of settlements which embellishes these extended shores. When he says to himself, this is the work of my countrymen, who, when convulsed by factions, afflicted by a variety of miseries and wants, restless and impatient, took refuge here. They brought along with them their national genius, to which they principally owe what

SOURCE: J. Hector St. John [Jean] Crevecoeur, *Letters from an American Farmer* (New York: Fox, Duffield, 1904), 48–56.

liberty they enjoy, and what substance they possess. Here he sees the industry of his native country displayed in a new manner, and traces in their works the embrios of all the arts, sciences, and ingenuity which flourish in Europe. Here he beholds fair cities, substantial villages, extensive fields, an immense country filled with decent houses, good roads, orchards, meadows, and bridges, where an hundred years ago all was wild, woody and uncultivated! What a train of pleasing ideas this fair spectacle must suggest; it is a prospect which must inspire a good citizen with the most heartfelt pleasure. The difficulty consists in the manner of viewing so extensive a scene. He is arrived on a new continent; a modern society offers itself to his contemplation, different from what he had hitherto seen. It is not composed, as in Europe, of great lords who possess everything, and of a herd of people who have nothing. Here are no aristocratical families, no courts, no kings, no bishops, no ecclesiastical dominion, no invisible power giving to a few a very visible one; no great manufacturers employing thousands, no great refinements of luxury. The rich and the poor are not so far removed from each other as they are in Europe. Some few towns excepted, we are all tillers of the earth, from Nova Scotia to West Florida. We are a people of cultivators, scattered over an immense territory, communicating with each other by means of good roads and navigable rivers, united by the silken bands of mild government, all respecting the laws, without dreading their power, because they are equitable. We are all animated with the spirit of an industry which is unfettered and unrestrained, because each person works for himself. If he travels through our rural districts he views not the hostile castle, and the haughty mansion, contrasted with the clay-built hut and miserable cabbin, where cattle and men help to keep each other warm, and dwell in meanness, smoke, and indigence. A pleasing uniformity of decent competence appears throughout our habitations. The meanest of our log-houses is a dry and comfortable habitation. Lawyer or merchant are the fairest titles our towns afford; that of a farmer is the only appellation of the rural inhabitants of our country. It must take some time ere he can reconcile himself to our dictionary, which is but short in words of dignity, and names of honour. There, on a Sunday, he sees a congregation of respectable farmers and their wives, all clad in neat homespun, well mounted, or riding in their own humble waggons. There is not among them an esquire, saving the unlettered magistrate. There he sees a parson as simple as his flock, a farmer who does not riot on the labour of others. We have no princes, for whom we toil, starve, and bleed: we are the most perfect society now existing in the world. Here man is free as he ought to be; nor is this pleasing equality so transitory as many others are. Many ages will not see the shores of our great lakes replenished with inland nations, nor the unknown bounds of North America entirely peopled. Who can tell how far it extends? Who can tell the millions of men whom it will feed and contain? for no European foot has as yet travelled half the extent of this mighty continent!

The next wish of this traveller will be to know whence came all these people? they are a mixture of English, Scotch, Irish, French, Dutch, Germans, and Swedes. From this promiscuous breed, that race now called Americans have arisen. The eastern provinces must indeed be excepted, as being the unmixed descendents of Englishmen. I have heard many wish that they had been more intermixed also: for my part, I am no wisher, and think it much better as it has happened. They exhibit a most conspicuous figure in this great and variegated picture; they too enter for a great share in the pleasing perspective displayed in these thirteen provinces. I know it is fashionable to reflect on them, but I respect them for what they have done; for the accuracy and wisdom with which they have settled their territory; for the decency of their manners; for their early love of letters; their ancient college, the first in this hemisphere; for their industry; which to me who am but a farmer, is the criterion of everything. There never was a people, situated as they are, who with so ungrateful a soil have done more in so short a time. Do you think that the monarchical ingredients which are more prevalent in other governments, have purged them from all foul stains? Their histories assert the contrary.

In this great American asylum, the poor of Europe have by some means met together, and in consequence of various causes; to what purpose should they ask one another what countrymen they are? Alas, two thirds of them had no country. Can a wretch who wanders about, who works and starves, whose life is a continual scene of sore affliction or pinching penury; can that man call England or any other kingdom his country? A country that had no bread for him, whose fields procured him no harvest, who met with nothing but the frowns of the rich, the severity of the laws, with jails and punishments; who owned not a single foot of the extensive surface of this planet? No! urged by a variety of motives, here they came. Everything has tended to regenerate them; new laws, a new mode of living, a new social system; here they are become men: in Europe they were as so many useless plants, wanting vegitative mould, and refreshing showers; they withered, and were mowed down by want, hunger, and war; but now by the power of transplantation, like all other plants they have taken root and flourished! Formerly they were not numbered in any civil lists of their country, except in those of the poor; here they rank as citizens. By what invisible power has this surprising metamorphosis been performed? By that of the laws and that of their industry. The laws, the indulgent laws, protect them as they arrive, stamping on them the symbol of adoption; they receive ample rewards for their labours; these accumulated rewards procure them lands; those lands confer on them the title of freemen, and to that title every benefit is affixed which men can possibly require. This is the great operation daily performed by our laws. From whence proceed these laws? From our government. Whence the government? It is derived from the original genius and strong desire of the people ratified and confirmed by the crown. This is the great chain which links us all, this is the picture which every province exhibits, Nova Scotia excepted. There the crown has done all; either there were no people who had genius, or it was not much attended to: the consequence is, that the province is very thinly inhabited indeed; the power of the crown in conjunction with the musketos has prevented men from settling there. Yet some parts of it flourished once, and it contained a mild harmless set of people. But for the fault of a few leaders, the whole were banished. The greatest political error the crown ever committed in America, was to cut off men from a country which wanted nothing but men!

What attachment can a poor European emigrant have for a country where he had nothing? The knowledge of the language, the love of a few kindred as poor as himself, were the only cords that tied him: his country is now that which gives him land, bread, protection, and consequence: *Ubi panis ibi patria*, is the motto of all emigrants. What then is the American, this new man? He is either an European, or the descendant of an European, hence that strange mixture of blood, which you will find in no other country. I could point out to you a family whose grandfather was an Englishman, whose wife was Dutch, whose son married a French woman, and whose present four sons have now four wives of different nations. *He* is an American, who leaving behind him all his ancient prejudices and manners, receives new ones from the new mode of life he has embraced, the new government he obeys, and the new rank he holds. He becomes an American by being received in the broad lap of our great *Alma Mater*. Here individuals of all nations are melted into a new race of men, whose labours and posterity will one day cause great changes in the world. Americans are the western pilgrims, who are carrying along with them that great mass of arts, sciences, vigour, and industry which began long since in the east; they will finish the great circle. The Americans were once scattered all over Europe; here they are incorporated into one of the finest systems of population which has ever appeared, and which will hereafter become distinct by the power of the different climates they inhabit. The American ought therefore to love this country much better than that wherein either he or his forefathers were born. Here the rewards of his industry follow with equal steps the progress of his labour; his labour is founded on the basis of nature, *self-interest*; can it want a stronger allurement? Wives and children, who before in vain demanded of him a morsel of bread, now, fat and frolicsome, gladly help their father to clear those fields whence exuberant crops are to arise to feed and to clothe them all; without any part being claimed, either by a despotic prince, a rich abbot, or a mighty lord. Here religion demands but little of him; a small voluntary salary to the minister, and gratitude to God; can he refuse these? The American is a new man, who acts upon new principles; he must therefore entertain new ideas, and form new opinions. From involuntary idleness, servile dependence, penury, and useless labour, he has passed to toils of a very different nature, rewarded by ample subsistence.—This is an American.

94

Thomas Paine

from *Common Sense*

Thomas Paine (1737–1809) was an English-born American thinker, revolutionary, and essayist, whose most famous published work, *Common Sense*, helped to
shape public opinion in 1776 in the direction of breaking with the British crown
toward American independence. He later used his influential pen to defend the
French Revolution during the 1790s and, years later, to bring a controversial
deistic critique against institutionalized forms of religion and the Christian faith.
The following is an excerpt from the opening pages of his *Common Sense*.

Introduction

Perhaps the sentiments contained in the following pages, are not *yet* sufficiently fashionable to procure them general favor; a long habit of not thinking
a thing *wrong*, gives it a superficial appearance of being *right*, and raises at first a
formidable outcry in defense of custom. But the tumult soon subsides. Time
makes more converts than reason.

As a long and violent abuse of power, is generally the Means of calling
the right of it in question (and in Matters too which might never have been
thought of, had not the Sufferers been aggravated into the inquiry) and as the
King of England hath undertaken in his *own Right*, to support the Parliament
in what he calls *Theirs*, and as the good people of this country are grievously
oppressed by the combination, they have an undoubted privilege to inquire
into the pretensions of both, and equally to reject the usurpation of either.

In the following sheets, the author hath studiously avoided every thing
which is personal among ourselves. Compliments as well as censure to

SOURCE: Thomas Paine, *Common Sense; Addressed to the Inhabitants of America, on the
Following Interesting Subjects* (Philadelphia: W. and T. Bradford, 1776), 3–17.

individuals make no part thereof. The wise, and the worthy, need not the triumph of a pamphlet; and those whose sentiments are injudicious, or unfriendly, will cease of themselves unless too much pains are bestowed upon their conversion.

The cause of America is in a great measure the cause of all mankind. Many circumstances hath, and will arise, which are not local, but universal, and through which the principles of all Lovers of Mankind are affected, and in the Event of which, their Affections are interested. The laying a Country desolate with Fire and Sword, declaring War against the natural rights of all Mankind, and extirpating the Defenders thereof from the Face of the Earth, is the Concern of every Man to whom Nature hath given the Power of feeling; of which Class, regardless of Party Censure, is the

AUTHOR

P.S. The Publication of this new Edition hath been delayed, with a View of taking notice (had it been necessary) of any Attempt to refute the Doctrine of Independance: As no Answer hath yet appeared, it is now presumed that none will, the Time needful for getting such a Performance ready for the Public being considerably past.

Who the Author of this Production is, is wholly unnecessary to the Public, as the Object for Attention is the *Doctrine itself*, not the *Man*. Yet it may not be unnecessary to say, That he is unconnected with any Party, and under no sort of Influence public or private, but the influence of reason and principle.

PHILADELPHIA, FEBRUARY 14, 1776

Of the Origin and Design of Government in General, with Concise Remarks on the English Constitution.

Some writers have so confounded society with government, as to leave little or no distinction between them; whereas they are not only different, but have different origins. Society is produced by our wants, and government by our wickedness; the former promotes our happiness *positively* by uniting our affections, the latter *negatively* by restraining our vices. The one encourages intercourse, the other creates distinctions. The first a patron, the last a punisher.

Society in every state is a blessing, but government even in its best state is but a necessary evil; in its worst state an intolerable one; for when we suffer, or are exposed to the same miseries *by a government*, which we might expect in a country *without government*, our calamity is heightened by reflecting that we furnish the means by which we suffer. Government, like dress, is the badge of lost innocence; the palaces of kings are built on the ruins of the bowers of paradise. For were the impulses of conscience clear, uniform, and irresistibly obeyed, man would need no other lawgiver; but that not being the case, he finds it necessary to surrender up a part of his property to furnish means for the protection of the rest; and this he is induced to do by the same prudence which in every other case advises him out of two evils to choose the least. *Wherefore*, security being the true design and end of government, it unanswerably follows that whatever *form* thereof appears most likely to ensure it to us, with the least expence and greatest benefit, is preferable to all others.

In order to gain a clear and just idea of the design and end of government, let us suppose a small number of persons settled in some sequestered part of the earth, unconnected with the rest, they will then represent the first peopling of any country, or of the world. In this state of natural liberty, society will be their first thought. A thousand motives will excite them thereto, the strength of one man is so unequal to his wants, and his mind so unfitted for perpetual solitude, that he is soon obliged to seek assistance and relief of another, who in his turn requires the same. Four or five united would be able to raise a tolerable dwelling in the midst of a wilderness, but *one* man might labour out of the common period of life without accomplishing any thing; when he had felled his timber he could not remove it, nor erect it after it was removed; hunger in the mean time would urge him from his work, and every different want call him a different way. Disease, nay even misfortune would be death, for though neither might be mortal, yet either would disable him from living, and reduce him to a state in which he might rather be said to perish than to die.

Thus necessity, like a gravitating power, would soon form our newly arrived emigrants into society, the reciprocal blessings of which, would supersede, and render the obligations of law and government unnecessary while they remained perfectly just to each other; but as nothing but heaven is impregnable to vice, it will unavoidably happen, that in proportion as they surmount the first difficulties of emigration, which bound them together in a common cause, they will begin to relax in their duty and attachment to each other; and this remissness, will point out the necessity, of establishing some form of government to supply the defect of moral virtue.

Some convenient tree will afford them a State-House, under the branches of which, the whole colony may assemble to deliberate on public matters. It is more than probable that their first laws will have the title only of Regulations, and be enforced by no other penalty than public disesteem. In this first parliament every man, by natural right, will have a seat.

But as the colony increases, the public concerns will increase likewise, and the distance at which the members may be separated, will render it too inconvenient for all of them to meet on every occasion as at first, when their number was small, their habitations near, and the public concerns few and trifling. This will point out the convenience of their consenting to leave the legislative part to be managed by a select number chosen from the whole body, who are supposed to have the same concerns at stake which those who appointed them, and who will act in the same manner as the whole body would act were they present. If the colony continue increasing, it will become necessary to augment the number of the representatives, and that the interest of every part of the colony may be attended to, it will be found best to divide the whole into convenient parts, each part sending its proper number; and that the *elected* might never form to themselves an interest separate from the *electors*, prudence will point out the propriety of having elections often; because as the *elected* might by that means return and mix again with the general body of the *electors* in a few months, their fidelity to the public will be secured by the prudent reflexion of not making a rod for themselves. And as this frequent interchange will establish a common interest with every part of the community, they will mutually and naturally support each other, and on this (not on the unmeaning name of king) depends the *strength of government, and the happiness of the governed.*

Here then is the origin and rise of government; namely, a mode rendered necessary by the inability of moral virtue to govern the world; here too is the design and end of government, viz. freedom and security. And however our eyes may be dazzled with show, or our ears deceived by sound; however prejudice may warp our wills, or interest darken our understanding, the simple voice of nature and of reason will say, it is right.

I draw my idea of the form of government from a principle in nature, which no art can overturn, viz. that the more simple any thing is, the less liable it is to be disordered; and the easier repaired when disordered; and with this maxim in view, I offer a few remarks on the so much boasted constitution of England. That it was noble for the dark and slavish times in which it was erected, is granted. When the world was over run with tyranny the least remove therefrom was a glorious rescue. But that it is imperfect, subject to convulsions, and incapable of producing what it seems to promise, is easily demonstrated.

Absolute governments (tho' the disgrace of human nature) have this advantage with them, that they are simple; if the people suffer, they know the head from which their suffering springs, know likewise the remedy, and are not bewildered by a variety of causes and cures. But the constitution of England is so exceedingly complex, that the nation may suffer for years together without being able to discover in which part the fault lies, some will say in one and some in another, and every political physician will advise a different medicine.

I know it is difficult to get over local or long standing prejudices, yet if we will suffer ourselves to examine the component parts of the English constitution, we shall find them to be the base remains of two ancient tyrannies, compounded with some new republican materials.

First.—The remains of monarchical tyranny in the person of the king.

Secondly.—The remains of aristocratical tyranny in the persons of the peers.

Thirdly.—The new republican materials, in the persons of the commons, on whose virtue depends the freedom of England.

The two first, by being hereditary, are independent of the people; wherefore in a *constitutional sense* they contribute nothing towards the freedom of the state.

To say that the constitution of England is a *union* of three powers reciprocally *checking* each other, is farcical, either the words have no meaning, or they are flat contradictions.

To say that the commons is a check upon the king, presupposes two things.

First.—That the king is not to be trusted without being looked after, or in other words, that a thirst for absolute power is the natural disease of monarchy.

Secondly.—That the commons, by being appointed for that purpose, are either wiser or more worthy of confidence than the crown.

But as the same constitution which gives the commons a power to check the king by withholding the supplies, gives afterwards the king a power to check the commons, by empowering him to reject their other bills; it again supposes that the king is wiser than those whom it has already supposed to be wiser than him. A mere absurdity!

There is something exceedingly ridiculous in the composition of monarchy; it first excludes a man from the means of information, yet empowers him to act in cases where the highest judgment is required. The state of a king shuts him from the world, yet the business of a king requires him to know it thoroughly; wherefore the different parts, by unnaturally opposing and destroying each other, prove the whole character to be absurd and useless.

Some writers have explained the English constitution thus; the king, say they, is one, the people another; the peers are an house in behalf of the king; the commons in behalf of the people; but this hath all the distinctions of a house divided against itself; and though the expressions be pleasantly arranged, yet when examined they appear idle and ambiguous; and it will always happen, that the nicest construction that words are capable of, when applied to the description of some thing which either cannot exist, or is too incomprehensible to be within the compass of description, will be words of sound only, and though they may amuse the ear, they cannot inform the mind, for this explanation includes a previous question, viz. *How came the king by a power which the people are afraid to trust, and always obliged to check?* Such a power could not be the gift of a wise people, neither can any power, *which needs checking*, be from God; yet the provision, which the constitution makes, supposes such a power to exist.

But the provision is unequal to the task; the means either cannot or will not accomplish the end, and the whole affair is a *felo de se*; for as the greater weight will always carry up the less, and as all the wheels of a machine are put in motion by one, it only remains to know which power in the constitution has the most weight, for that will govern; and though the others, or a part of them, may clog, or, as the phrase is, check the rapidity of its motion, yet so long as they cannot stop it, their endeavors will be ineffectual; the first moving power will at last have its way, and what it wants in speed is supplied by time.

That the crown is this overbearing part in the English constitution needs not be mentioned, and that it derives its whole consequence merely from being the giver of places and pensions is self-evident, wherefore, though we have been wise enough to shut and lock a door against absolute monarchy, we at the same time have been foolish enough to put the crown in possession of the key.

The prejudice of Englishmen, in favour of their own government by king, lords and commons, arises as much or more from national pride than reason. Individuals are undoubtedly safer in England than in some other countries, but the *will* of the king is as much the *law* of the land in Britain as in France, with this difference, that instead of proceeding directly from his mouth, it is handed to the people under the more formidable shape of an act of parliament. For the fate of Charles the First, hath only made kings more subtle—not more just.

Wherefore, laying aside all national pride and prejudice in favour of modes and forms, the plain truth is, that *it is wholly owing to the constitution of the people, and not to the constitution of the government* that the crown is not as oppressive in England as in Turkey.

An inquiry into the *constitutional errors* in the English form of government is at this time highly necessary, for as we are never in a proper condition of doing justice to others, while we continue under the influence of some leading partiality, so neither are we capable of doing it to ourselves while we remain fettered by any obstinate prejudice. And as a man, who is attached to a prostitute, is unfitted to choose or judge of a wife, so any prepossession in favour of a rotten constitution of government will disable us from discerning a good one.

95

David Hume

from *An Enquiry concerning Human Understanding*

David Hume (1711–1776) was a Scottish philosopher whose lasting influence makes him one of the most important thinkers of the Enlightenment period. He is perhaps best known today for his empiricism, his skepticism, and his critical posture toward religion. The following are excerpts from section four of his work *An Enquiry concerning Human Understanding*, in which he gives an empiricist analysis of causality and, in turn, argues that our indispensable reliance on inductive reasoning lacks a rational basis but, rather, has a psychological basis.

_____

Section IV: Sceptical Doubts concerning the Operations of the Understanding.

Part I.

All the objects of human reason or enquiry may naturally be divided into two kinds, to wit, *Relations of Ideas*, and *Matters of Fact*. Of the first kind are the sciences of Geometry, Algebra, and Arithmetic; and in short, every affirmation which is either intuitively or demonstratively certain. *That the square of the hypothenuse is equal to the square of the two sides*, is a proposition which expresses a relation between these figures. *That three times five is equal to the half of thirty*, expresses a relation between these numbers. Propositions of this kind are discoverable by the mere operation of thought, without dependence on what is anywhere existent in the universe. Though there never were a circle or triangle in nature, the truths demonstrated by Euclid would for ever retain their certainty and evidence.

SOURCE: David Hume, *Enquiries concerning the Human Understanding and concerning the Principles of Morals*, ed. L. A. Selby-Bigge, 2nd ed. (Oxford: Clarendon Press, 1902), 25–39.

Matters of fact, which are the second objects of human reason, are not ascertained in the same manner; nor is our evidence of their truth, however great, of a like nature with the foregoing. The contrary of every matter of fact is still possible; because it can never imply a contradiction, and is conceived by the mind with the same facility and distinctness, as if ever so conformable to reality. *That the sun will not rise to-morrow* is no less intelligible a proposition, and implies no more contradiction than the affirmation, *that it will rise.* We should in vain, therefore, attempt to demonstrate its falsehood. Were it demonstratively false, it would imply a contradiction, and could never be distinctly conceived by the mind.

It may, therefore, be a subject worthy of curiosity, to enquire what is the nature of that evidence which assures us of any real existence and matter of fact, beyond the present testimony of our senses, or the records of our memory. This part of philosophy, it is observable, has been little cultivated, either by the ancients or moderns; and therefore our doubts and errors, in the prosecution of so important an enquiry, may be the more excusable; while we march through such difficult paths without any guide or direction. They may even prove useful, by exciting curiosity, and destroying that implicit faith and security, which is the bane of all reasoning and free enquiry. The discovery of defects in the common philosophy, if any such there be, will not, I presume, be a discouragement, but rather an incitement, as is usual, to attempt something more full and satisfactory than has yet been proposed to the public.

All reasonings concerning matter of fact seem to be founded on the relation of *Cause and Effect.* By means of that relation alone we can go beyond the evidence of our memory and senses. If you were to ask a man, why he believes any matter of fact, which is absent; for instance, that his friend is in the country, or in France; he would give you a reason; and this reason would be some other fact; as a letter received from him, or the knowledge of his former resolutions and promises. A man finding a watch or any other machine in a desert island, would conclude that there had once been men in that island. All our reasonings concerning fact are of the same nature. And here it is constantly supposed that there is a connexion between the present fact and that which is inferred from it. Were there nothing to bind them together, the inference would be entirely precarious. The hearing of an articulate voice and rational discourse in the dark assures us of the presence of some person: Why? because these are the effects of the human make and fabric, and closely connected with it. If we anatomize all the other reasonings of this nature, we shall find that they are founded on the relation of cause and effect, and that this relation is either near or remote, direct or collateral. Heat and light are collateral effects of fire, and the one effect may justly be inferred from the other.

If we would satisfy ourselves, therefore, concerning the nature of that evidence, which assures us of matters of fact, we must enquire how we arrive at the knowledge of cause and effect.

I shall venture to affirm, as a general proposition, which admits of no exception, that the knowledge of this relation is not, in any instance, attained by reasonings *a priori*; but arises entirely from experience, when we find that any particular objects are constantly conjoined with each other. Let an object be presented to a man of ever so strong natural reason and abilities; if that object be entirely new to him, he will not be able, by the most accurate examination of its sensible qualities, to discover any of its causes or effects. Adam, though his rational faculties be supposed, at the very first, entirely perfect, could not have inferred from the fluidity and transparency of water that it would suffocate him, or from the light and warmth of fire that it would consume him. No object ever discovers, by the qualities which appear to the senses, either the causes which produced it, or the effects which will arise from it; nor can our reason, unassisted by experience, ever draw any inference concerning real existence and matter of fact.

This proposition, *that causes and effects are discoverable, not by reason but by experience*, will readily be admitted with regard to such objects, as we remember to have once been altogether unknown to us; since we must be conscious of the utter inability, which we then lay under, of foretelling what would arise from them. Present two smooth pieces of marble to a man who has no tincture of natural philosophy; he will never discover that they will adhere together in such a manner as to require great force to separate them in a direct line, while they make so small a resistance to a lateral pressure. Such events, as bear little analogy to the common course of nature, are also readily confessed to be known only by experience; nor does any man imagine that the explosion of gunpowder, or the attraction of a loadstone, could ever be discovered by arguments *a priori*. In like manner, when an effect is supposed to depend upon an intricate machinery or secret structure of parts, we make no difficulty in attributing all our knowledge of it to experience. Who will assert that he can give the ultimate reason, why milk or bread is proper nourishment for a man, not for a lion or a tiger?

But the same truth may not appear, at first sight, to have the same evidence with regard to events, which have become familiar to us from our first appearance in the world, which bear a close analogy to the whole course of nature, and which are supposed to depend on the simple qualities of objects, without any secret structure of parts. We are apt to imagine that we could discover these effects by the mere operation of our reason, without experience. We fancy, that were we brought on a sudden into this world, we could at first have inferred that one Billiard-ball would communicate motion to another upon impulse; and that we needed not to have waited for the event, in order to pronounce with certainty concerning it. Such is the influence of custom, that, where it is strongest, it not only covers our natural ignorance, but even conceals itself, and seems not to take place, merely because it is found in the highest degree.

But to convince us that all the laws of nature, and all the operations of bodies without exception, are known only by experience, the following reflections may, perhaps, suffice. Were any object presented to us, and were we required to pronounce concerning the effect, which will result from it, without consulting past observation; after what manner, I beseech you, must the mind proceed in this operation? It must invent or imagine some event, which it ascribes to the object as its effect; and it is plain that this invention must be entirely arbitrary. The mind can never possibly find the effect in the supposed cause, by the most accurate scrutiny and examination. For the effect is totally different from the cause, and consequently can never be discovered in it. Motion in the second Billiard-ball is a quite distinct event from motion in the first; nor is there anything in the one to suggest the smallest hint of the other. A stone or piece of metal raised into the air, and left without any support, immediately falls: but to consider the matter *a priori*, is there anything we discover in this situation which can beget the idea of a downward, rather than an upward, or any other motion, in the stone or metal?

And as the first imagination or invention of a particular effect, in all natural operations, is arbitrary, where we consult not experience; so must we also esteem the supposed tie or connexion between the cause and effect, which binds them together, and renders it impossible that any other effect could result from the operation of that cause. When I see, for instance, a Billiard-ball moving in a straight line towards another; even suppose motion in the second ball should by accident be suggested to me, as the result of their contact or impulse; may I not conceive, that a hundred different events might as well follow from that cause? May not both these balls remain at absolute rest? May not the first ball return in a straight line, or leap off from the second in any line or direction? All these suppositions are consistent and conceivable. Why then should we give the preference to one, which is no more consistent or conceivable than the rest? All our reasonings *a priori* will never be able to show us any foundation for this preference.

[. . . .]

Part II.

But we have not yet attained any tolerable satisfaction with regard to the question first proposed. Each solution still gives rise to a new question as difficult as the foregoing, and leads us on to farther enquiries. When it is asked, *What is the nature of all our reasonings concerning matter of fact?* the proper answer seems to be, that they are founded on the relation of cause and effect. When again it is asked, *What is the foundation of all our reasonings and conclusions concerning that relation?* it may be replied in one word, Experience. But if we still carry on our sifting humour, and ask, *What is the foundation of all conclusions from experience?* this implies a new question, which may be of more difficult solution and explication. Philosophers, that give themselves airs of superior wisdom and sufficiency, have a hard task when they encounter persons of inquisitive dispositions, who push them from every corner to which they retreat, and who are sure at last to bring them to some dangerous dilemma. The best expedient to prevent this confusion, is to be modest in our pretensions; and even to discover the difficulty ourselves before it is objected to us. By this means, we may make a kind of merit of our very ignorance.

I shall content myself, in this section, with an easy task, and shall pretend only to give a negative answer to the question here proposed. I say then, that, even after we have experience of the operations of cause and effect, our conclusions from that experience are *not* founded on reasoning, or any process of the understanding. This answer we must endeavour both to explain and to defend.

It must certainly be allowed, that nature has kept us at a great distance from all her secrets, and has afforded us only the knowledge of a few superficial qualities of objects; while she conceals from us those powers and principles on which the influence of those objects entirely depends. Our senses inform us of the colour, weight, and consistence of bread; but neither sense nor reason can ever inform us of those qualities which fit it for the nourishment and support of a human body. Sight or feeling conveys an idea of the actual motion of bodies; but as to that wonderful force or power, which would carry on a moving body for ever in a continued change of place, and which bodies never lose but by communicating it to others; of this we cannot form the most distant conception. But notwithstanding this ignorance of natural powers and principles, we always presume, when we see like sensible qualities, that they have like secret powers, and expect that effects, similar to those which we have experienced, will follow from them. If a body of like colour and consistence with that bread, which we have formerly eat, be presented to us, we make no scruple of repeating the experiment, and foresee, with certainty, like nourishment and support. Now this is a process of the mind or thought, of which I would willingly know the foundation. It is allowed on all hands that there is no known connexion between the sensible qualities and the secret powers; and consequently, that the mind is not led to form such a conclusion concerning their constant and regular conjunction, by anything which it knows of their nature. As to past *Experience*, it can be allowed to give *direct* and *certain* information of those precise objects only, and that precise period of time, which fell under its cognizance: but why this experience should be extended to future times, and to other objects, which for aught we know, may be only in appearance similar; this is the main question on which I would insist. The bread, which I formerly eat, nourished me; that is, a body of such sensible qualities was, at that time, endued with such secret powers: but does it follow, that other bread must also nourish me at another time, and that like sensible qualities must always be attended with like secret powers? The consequence seems nowise necessary. At least, it must be acknowledged that there is here a consequence drawn by the mind; that there is a certain step taken; a process of thought, and an inference, which wants to be explained. These two propositions are far from being the same, *I have found that such an object has always been attended with such an effect*, and *I foresee, that other objects, which are, in appearance, similar, will be attended with similar effects*. I shall allow, if you please, that the one proposition may justly be inferred from the other: I know, in fact, that it always is inferred. But if you insist that the inference is made by a chain of reasoning, I desire you to produce that reasoning. The connexion between these propositions is not intuitive. There is required a medium, which may enable the mind to draw such an inference, if indeed it be drawn by reasoning and argument. What that medium is, I must confess, passes my comprehension; and it is incumbent on those to produce it, who assert that it really exists, and is the origin of all our conclusions concerning matter of fact.

This negative argument must certainly, in process of time, become altogether convincing, if many penetrating and able philosophers shall turn their enquiries this way and no one be ever able to discover any connecting proposition or intermediate step, which supports the understanding in this conclusion. But as the question is yet new, every reader may not trust so far to his own penetration, as to conclude, because an argument escapes his enquiry, that therefore it does not really exist. For this reason it may be requisite to venture upon a more difficult task; and enumerating all the branches of human knowledge, endeavour to show that none of them can afford such an argument.

All reasonings may be divided into two kinds, namely, demonstrative reasoning, or that concerning relations of ideas, and moral reasoning, or that concerning matter of fact and existence. That there are no demonstrative arguments in the case seems evident; since it implies no contradiction that the course of nature may change, and that an object, seemingly like those which we have experienced, may be attended with different or contrary effects. May I not clearly and distinctly conceive that a body, falling from the clouds, and which, in all other respects, resembles snow, has yet the taste of salt or feeling of fire? Is there any more intelligible proposition than to affirm, that all the trees will flourish in December and January, and decay in May and June? Now whatever is intelligible, and can be distinctly conceived, implies no contradiction, and can never be proved false by any demonstrative argument or abstract reasoning *a priori*.

If we be, therefore, engaged by arguments to put trust in past experience, and make it the standard of our future judgement, these arguments must be probable only, or such as regard matter of fact and real existence, according to the division above mentioned. But that there is no argument of this kind, must appear, if our explication of that species of reasoning be admitted as solid and satisfactory. We have said that all arguments concerning existence are founded on the relation of cause and effect; that our knowledge of that relation is derived entirely from experience; and that all our experimental conclusions proceed upon the supposition that the future will be conformable to the past. To endeavour, therefore, the proof of this last supposition by probable arguments, or arguments regarding existence, must be evidently going in a circle, and taking that for granted, which is the very point in question.

In reality, all arguments from experience are founded on the similarity which we discover among natural objects, and by which we are induced to expect effects similar to those which we have found to follow from such objects. And though none but a fool or madman will ever pretend to dispute the authority of experience, or to reject that great guide of human life, it may surely be allowed a philosopher to have so much curiosity at least as to examine the principle of human nature, which gives this mighty authority to experience, and makes us draw advantage from that similarity which nature has placed among different objects. From causes which appear *similar* we expect similar effects. This is the sum of all our experimental conclusions. Now it seems evident that, if this conclusion were formed by reason, it would be as perfect at first, and upon one instance, as after ever so long a course of experience. But the case is far otherwise. Nothing so like as eggs; yet no one, on account of this appearing similarity, expects the same taste and relish in all of them. It is only after a long course of uniform experiments in any kind, that we attain a firm reliance and security with regard to a particular event. Now where is that process of reasoning which, from one instance, draws a conclusion, so different from that which it infers from a hundred instances that are nowise different from that single one? This question I propose as much for the sake of information, as with an intention of raising difficulties. I cannot find, I cannot imagine any such reasoning. But I keep my mind still open to instruction, if any one will vouchsafe to bestow it on me.

Should it be said that, from a number of uniform experiments, we *infer* a connexion between the sensible qualities and the secret powers; this, I must confess, seems the same difficulty, couched in different terms. The question still recurs, on what process of argument this *inference* is founded? Where is the medium, the interposing ideas, which join propositions so very wide of each other? It is confessed that the colour, consistence, and other sensible qualities of bread appear not, of themselves, to have any connexion with the secret powers of nourishment and support. For otherwise we could infer these secret powers from the first appearance of these sensible qualities, without the aid of experience; contrary to the sentiment of all philosophers, and contrary to plain matter of fact. Here, then, is our natural state of ignorance with regard to the powers and influence of all objects. How is this remedied by experience? It only shows us a number of uniform effects, resulting from certain objects, and teaches us that those particular objects, at that particular time, were endowed with such powers and forces. When a new object, endowed with similar sensible qualities, is produced, we expect similar powers and forces, and look for a like effect. From a body of like colour and consistence with bread we expect like nourishment and support. But this surely is a step or progress of the mind, which wants to be explained. When a man says, *I have found, in all past instances, such sensible qualities conjoined with such secret powers*: And when he says, *Similar sensible qualities will always be conjoined with similar secret powers*, he is not guilty of a tautology, nor are these propositions in any respect the same. You say that the one proposition is an inference from the other. But you must confess that the inference is not intuitive; neither is it demonstrative: Of what nature is it, then? To say it is experimental, is begging the question. For all inferences from experience suppose, as their foundation, that the future will resemble the past, and that similar powers will be conjoined with similar sensible qualities. If there be any suspicion that the course of nature may change, and that the past may be no rule for the future, all experience becomes useless, and can give rise to no inference or conclusion. It is impossible, therefore, that any arguments from experience can prove this resemblance of the past to the future; since all these arguments are founded on the supposition of that resemblance. Let the course of things be allowed hitherto ever so regular; that alone, without some new argument or inference, proves not that, for the future, it will continue so. In vain do you pretend to have learned the nature of bodies from your past experience. Their secret nature, and consequently all their effects and influence, may change, without any change in their sensible qualities. This happens sometimes, and with regard to some objects: Why may it not happen always, and with regard to all objects? What logic, what process of argument secures you against this supposition? My practice, you say, refutes my doubts. But you mistake the purport of my question. As an agent, I am quite satisfied in the point; but as a philosopher, who has some share of curiosity, I will not say scepticism, I want to learn the foundation of this inference. No reading, no enquiry has yet been able to remove my difficulty, or give me satisfaction in a matter of such importance. Can I do better than propose the difficulty to the public, even though, perhaps, I have small hopes of obtaining a solution? We shall at least, by this means, be sensible of our ignorance, if we do not augment our knowledge.

I must confess that a man is guilty of unpardonable arrogance who concludes, because an argument has escaped his own investigation, that therefore it does not really exist. I must also confess that, though all the learned, for several ages, should have employed themselves in fruitless search upon any subject, it may still, perhaps, be rash to conclude positively that the subject must, therefore, pass all human comprehension. Even though we examine all the sources of our knowledge, and conclude them unfit for such a subject, there may still remain a suspicion, that the enumeration is not complete, or the examination not accurate. But with regard to the present subject, there are some considerations which seem to remove all this accusation of arrogance or suspicion of mistake.

It is certain that the most ignorant and stupid peasants—nay infants, nay even brute beasts—improve by experience, and learn the qualities of natural objects, by observing the effects which result from them. When a child has felt the sensation of pain from touching the flame of a candle, he will be careful not to put his hand near any candle; but will expect a similar effect from a cause which is similar in its sensible qualities and appearance. If you assert, therefore, that the understanding of the child is led into this conclusion by any process of argument or ratiocination, I may justly require you to produce that argument; nor have you any pretence to refuse so equitable a demand. You cannot say that the argument is abstruse, and may possibly escape your enquiry; since you confess that it is obvious to the capacity of a mere infant. If you hesitate, therefore, a moment, or if, after reflection, you produce any intricate or profound argument, you, in a manner, give up the question, and confess that it is not reasoning which engages us to suppose the past resembling the future, and to expect similar effects from causes which are, to appearance, similar. This is the proposition which I intended to enforce in the present section. If I be right, I pretend not to have made any mighty discovery. And if I be wrong, I must acknowledge myself to be indeed a very backward scholar; since I cannot now discover an argument which, it seems, was perfectly familiar to me long before I was out of my cradle.

96

David Hume

from *Dialogues concerning Natural Religion* (on the Design Argument)

The following is an excerpt from David Hume's *Dialogues concerning Natural Religion*, which is widely regarded as one of the most important works of philosophy of religion ever written in the English language. This passage is largely a conversation between the characters Demea, Cleanthes (who defends a design argument for religious belief), and the religious skeptic Philo (who brings several objections against that design argument).

Part II

... Not to lose any time in circumlocutions, said Cleanthes, addressing himself to Demea, much less in replying to the pious declamations of Philo; I shall briefly explain how I conceive this matter. Look round the world: contemplate the whole and every part of it: You will find it to be nothing but one great machine, subdivided into an infinite number of lesser machines, which again admit of subdivisions to a degree beyond what human senses and faculties can trace and explain. All these various machines, and even their most minute parts, are adjusted to each other with an accuracy which ravishes into admiration all men who have ever contemplated them. The curious adapting of means to ends, throughout all nature, resembles exactly, though it much exceeds, the productions of human contrivance; of human designs, thought, wisdom, and intelligence. Since, therefore, the effects resemble each other, we are led to infer, by all the rules of analogy, that the causes also resemble; and that the Author of Nature is somewhat similar to the mind of man, though

SOURCE: David Hume, *Dialogues concerning Natural Religion*, in *The Philosophical Works of David Hume Including All the Essays, and Exhibiting the More Important Alterations and Corrections in the Successive Editions Published by the Author*, 4 vols., vol. 2 (Edinburgh: Adam Black and William Tait, 1826), 440–42, 445–49, 467–73.

possessed of much larger faculties, proportioned to the grandeur of the work which he has executed. By this argument *a posteriori*, and by this argument alone, do we prove at once the existence of a Deity, and his similarity to human mind and intelligence.

[. . . .]

What I chiefly scruple in this subject, said Philo, is not so much that all religious arguments are by Cleanthes reduced to experience, as that they appear not to be even the most certain and irrefragable of that inferior kind. That a stone will fall, that fire will burn, that the earth has solidity, we have observed a thousand and a thousand times; and when any new instance of this nature is presented, we draw without hesitation the accustomed inference. The exact similarity of the cases gives us a perfect assurance of a similar event; and a stronger evidence is never desired nor sought after. But wherever you depart, in the least, from the similarity of the cases, you diminish proportionably the evidence; and may at last bring it to a very weak *analogy*, which is confessedly liable to error and uncertainty. . . .

If we see a house, Cleanthes, we conclude, with the greatest certainty, that it had an architect or builder; because this is precisely that species of effect which we have experienced to proceed from that species of cause. But surely you will not affirm, that the universe bears such a resemblance to a house, that we can with the same certainty infer a similar cause, or that the analogy is here entire and perfect. The dissimilitude is so striking, that the utmost you can here pretend to is a guess, a conjecture, a presumption concerning a similar cause; and how that pretension will be received in the world, I leave you to consider.

It would surely be very ill received, replied Cleanthes; and I should be deservedly blamed and detested, did I allow, that the proofs of a Deity amounted to no more than a guess or conjecture. But is the whole adjustment of means to ends in a house and in the universe so slight a resemblance? The economy of final causes? The order, proportion, and arrangement of every part? Steps of a stair are plainly contrived, that human legs may use them in mounting; and this inference is certain and infallible. Human legs are also contrived for walking and mounting; and this inference, I allow, is not altogether so certain, because of the dissimilarity which you remark; but does it, therefore, deserve the name only of presumption or conjecture?

[. . . .]

When Cleanthes had assented, Philo, after a short pause, proceeded in the following manner.

That all inferences, Cleanthes, concerning fact, are founded on experience; and that all experimental reasonings are founded on the supposition that similar causes prove similar effects, and similar effects similar causes; I shall not at present much dispute with you. But observe, I entreat you, with what extreme caution all just reasoners proceed in the transferring of experiments to similar cases. Unless the cases be exactly similar, they repose no perfect confidence in applying their past observation to any particular phenomenon. Every alteration of circumstances occasions a doubt concerning the event; and it requires new experiments to prove certainly, that the new circumstances are of no moment or importance. A change in bulk, situation, arrangement, age, disposition of the air, or surrounding bodies; any of these particulars may be attended with the most unexpected consequences: And unless the objects be quite familiar to us, it is the highest temerity to expect with assurance, after any of these changes, an event similar to that which before fell under our observation. The slow and deliberate steps of philosophers here, if any where, are distinguished from the precipitate march of the vulgar, who, hurried on by the smallest similitude, are incapable of all discernment or consideration.

But can you think, Cleanthes, that your usual phlegm and philosophy have been preserved in so wide a step as you have taken, when you compared to the universe houses, ships, furniture, machines, and, from their similarity in some circumstances, inferred a similarity in their causes? Thought, design, intelligence, such as we discover in men and other animals, is no more than one of the springs and principles of the universe, as well as heat or cold, attraction or repulsion, and a hundred others, which fall under daily observation. It is an active cause, by which some particular parts of nature, we find, produce alterations on other parts. But can a conclusion, with any propriety, be transferred from parts to the whole? Does not the great disproportion bar all comparison and inference? From observing the growth of a hair, can we learn any thing concerning the generation of a man? Would the manner of a leaf's blowing, even though perfectly known, afford us any instruction concerning the vegetation of a tree?

But, allowing that we were to take the *operations* of one part of nature upon another, for the foundation of our judgment concerning the *origin* of the whole, (which never can be admitted,) yet why select so minute, so weak, so bounded a principle, as the reason and design of animals is found to be upon this planet? What peculiar privilege has this little agitation of the brain which we call *thought*, that we must thus make it the model of the whole universe? Our partiality in our own favour does indeed present it on all occasions; but sound philosophy ought carefully to guard against so natural an illusion.

So far from admitting, continued Philo, that the operations of a part can afford us any just conclusion concerning the origin of the whole, I will not allow any one part to form a rule for another part, if the latter be very remote from the former. Is there any reasonable ground to conclude, that the inhabitants of other planets possess thought, intelligence, reason, or any thing similar to these faculties in men? When nature has so extremely diversified her manner of operation in this small globe, can we imagine that she incessantly copies herself throughout so immense a universe? And if thought, as we may well suppose, be confined merely to this narrow corner, and has even there so limited a sphere of action, with what propriety can we assign it for the original cause of all things? The narrow views of a peasant, who makes his domestic economy the rule for the government of kingdoms, is in comparison a pardonable sophism.

But were we ever so much assured, that a thought and reason, resembling the human, were to be found throughout the whole universe, and were its activity elsewhere vastly greater and more commanding than it appears in this globe; yet I cannot see, why the operations of a world constituted, arranged, adjusted, can with any propriety be extended to a world which is in its embryo state, and is advancing towards that constitution and arrangement. By observation, we know somewhat of the economy, action, and nourishment of a finished animal; but we must transfer with great caution that observation to the growth of a fœtus in the womb, and still more to the formation of an animalcule in the loins of its male parent. Nature, we find, even from our limited experience, possesses an infinite number of springs and principles, which incessantly discover themselves on every change of her position and situation. And what new and unknown principles would actuate her in so new and unknown a situation as that of the formation of a universe, we cannot, without the utmost temerity, pretend to determine.

[. . . .]

Part V

But to show you still more inconveniences, continued Philo, in your Anthropomorphism, please to take a new survey of your principles. *Like effects prove like causes.* This is the experimental argument; and this, you say too, is the sole theological argument. Now, it is certain, that the liker the effects are which are seen, and the liker the causes which are inferred, the stronger is the argument. Every departure on either side diminishes the probability, and renders the experiment less conclusive. You cannot doubt of the principle; neither ought you to reject its consequences.

All the new discoveries in astronomy, which prove the immense grandeur and magnificence of the works of Nature, are so many additional arguments for a Deity, according to the true system of Theism; but, according to your hypothesis of experimental Theism, they become so many objections, by removing the effect still further from all resemblance to the effects of human art and contrivance. . . . If this argument, I say, had any force in former ages, how much greater must it have at present, when the bounds of Nature are so infinitely enlarged, and such a magnificent scene is opened to us? It is still more unreasonable to form our idea of so unlimited a cause from our experience of the narrow productions of human design and invention.

The discoveries by microscopes, as they open a new universe in miniature, are still objections, according to you, arguments, according to me. The further we push our researches of this kind, we are still led to infer the universal cause of all to be vastly different from mankind, or from any object of human experience and observation.

And what say you to the discoveries in anatomy, chemistry, botany? . . . These surely are no objections, replied Cleanthes; they only discover new instances of art and contrivance. It is still the image of mind reflected on us from innumerable objects. Add, a mind *like the human*, said Philo. I know of no other, replied Cleanthes. And the liker the better, insisted Philo. To be sure, said Cleanthes.

Now, Cleanthes, said Philo, with an air of alacrity and triumph, mark the consequences. *First*, By this method of reasoning, you renounce all claim to infinity in any of the attributes of the Deity. For, as the cause ought only to be proportioned to the effect, and the effect, so far as it falls under our cognizance, is not infinite; what pretensions have we, upon your suppositions, to ascribe that attribute to the Divine Being? You will still insist, that, by removing him so much from all similarity to human creatures, we give in to the most arbitrary hypothesis, and at the same time weaken all proofs of his existence.

Secondly, You have no reason, on your theory, for ascribing perfection to the Deity, even in his finite capacity, or for supposing him free from every error, mistake, or incoherence, in his undertakings. There are many inexplicable difficulties in the works of Nature, which, if we allow a perfect author to be proved *a priori*, are easily solved, and become only seeming difficulties, from the narrow capacity of man, who cannot trace infinite relations. But according to your method of reasoning, these difficulties become all real; and perhaps will be insisted on, as new instances of likeness to human art and contrivance. At least, you must acknowledge, that it is impossible for us to tell, from our limited views, whether this system contains any great faults, or deserves any considerable praise, if compared to other possible, and even real systems. Could a peasant, if the Æneid were read to him, pronounce that poem to be absolutely faultless, or even assign to it its proper rank among the productions of human wit, he, who had never seen any other production?

But were this world ever so perfect a production, it must still remain uncertain, whether all the excellences of the work can justly be ascribed to the workman. If we survey a ship, what an exalted idea must we form of the ingenuity of the carpenter who framed so complicated, useful, and beautiful a machine? And what surprise must we feel, when we find him a stupid mechanic, who imitated others, and copied an art, which, through a long succession of ages, after multiplied trials, mistakes, corrections, deliberations, and controversies, had been gradually improving? Many worlds might have been botched and bungled, throughout an eternity, ere this system was struck out; much labour lost, many fruitless trials made; and a slow, but continued improvement carried on during infinite ages in the art of world-making. In such subjects, who can determine, where the truth; nay, who can conjecture where the probability lies, amidst a great number of hypotheses which may be proposed, and a still greater which may be imagined?

And what shadow of an argument, continued Philo, can you produce, from your hypothesis, to prove the unity of the Deity? A great number of men join in building a house or ship, in rearing a city, in framing a commonwealth; why may not several deities combine in contriving and framing a world? This is only so much greater similarity to human affairs. By sharing the work among several, we may so much further limit the attributes of each, and get rid of that extensive power and knowledge, which must be supposed in one deity, and which, according to you, can only serve to weaken the proof of his existence. And if such foolish, such vicious creatures as man, can yet often unite in framing and executing one plan, how much more those deities or demons, whom we may suppose several degrees more perfect!

To multiply causes without necessity, is indeed contrary to true philosophy: but this principle applies not to the present case. Were one deity antecedently proved by your theory, who were possessed of every attribute requisite to the production of the universe; it would be needless, I own, (though not absurd), to suppose any other deity existent. But while it is still a question, Whether all these attributes are united in one subject, or dispersed among several independent beings, by what phenomena in nature can we pretend to decide the controversy? Where we see a body raised in a scale, we are sure that there is in the opposite scale, however concealed from sight, some counterpoising weight equal to it; but it is still allowed to doubt, whether that weight be an aggregate of several distinct bodies, or one uniform united mass. And if the weight requisite very much exceeds any thing which we have ever seen conjoined in any single body, the former supposition becomes still more probable and natural. An intelligent being of such vast power and capacity as is necessary to produce the universe, or, to speak in the language of ancient philosophy, so prodigious an animal exceeds all analogy, and even comprehension.

But farther, Cleanthes: Men are mortal, and renew their species by generation; and this is common to all living creatures. The two great sexes of male and female, says Milton, animate the world. Why must this circumstance, so universal, so essential, be excluded from those numerous and limited deities? Behold, then, the theogeny of ancient times brought back upon us.

And why not become a perfect Anthropomorphite? Why not assert the deity or deities to be corporeal, and to have eyes, a nose, mouth, ears, &c.? Epicurus maintained, that no man had ever seen reason but in a human figure; therefore the gods must have a human figure. And this argument, which is deservedly so much ridiculed by Cicero, becomes, according to you, solid and philosophical.

In a word, Cleanthes, a man who follows your hypothesis is able perhaps to assert, or conjecture, that the universe, sometime, arose from something like design: but beyond that position he cannot ascertain one single circumstance; and is left afterwards to fix every point of his theology by the utmost license of fancy and hypothesis. This world, for aught he knows, is very faulty and imperfect, compared to a superior standard; and was only the first rude essay of some infant deity, who afterwards abandoned it, ashamed of his lame performance: it is the work only of some dependent, inferior deity; and is the object of derision to his superiors: it is the production of old age and dotage in some superannuated deity; and ever since his death, has run on at adventures, from the first impulse and active force which it received from him. You justly give signs of horror, Demea, at these strange suppositions; but these, and a thousand more of the same kind, are Cleanthes's suppositions, not mine. From the moment the attributes of the Deity are supposed finite, all these have place. And I cannot, for my part, think that so wild and unsettled a system of theology is, in any respect, preferable to none at all.

These suppositions I absolutely disown, cried Cleanthes: they strike me, however, with no horror, especially when proposed in that rambling way in which they drop from you. On the contrary, they give me pleasure, when I see, that, by the utmost indulgence of your imagination, you never get rid of the hypothesis of design in the universe, but are obliged at every turn to have recourse to it. To this concession I adhere steadily; and this I regard as a sufficient foundation for religion.

97

David Hume

from *Dialogues concerning Natural Religion* (on the Problem of Evil)

The following is an excerpt from David Hume's *Dialogues concerning Natural Religion*, which is a conversation between the characters Demea, Cleanthes, and the skeptic Philo. In this passage, Philo raises one of the notorious problems facing religious belief, namely, the problem of evil: if God is all-knowing, all-powerful, and perfectly good, then why is there so much evil in the world?

[I]s it possible, Cleanthes, said Philo, that after all these reflections, and infinitely more, which might be suggested, you can still persevere in your Anthropomorphism, and assert the moral attributes of the Deity, his justice, benevolence, mercy, and rectitude, to be of the same nature with these virtues in human creatures? His power we allow is infinite: whatever he wills is executed: but neither man nor any other animal is happy: therefore he does not will their happiness. His wisdom is infinite: he is never mistaken in choosing the means to any end: but the course of Nature tends not to human or animal felicity: therefore it is not established for that purpose. Through the whole compass of human knowledge, there are no inferences more certain and infallible than these. In what respect, then, do his benevolence and mercy resemble the benevolence and mercy of men?

Epicurus's old questions are yet unanswered.

Is he willing to prevent evil, but not able? then is he impotent. Is he able, but not willing? then is he malevolent. Is he both able and willing? whence then is evil?

SOURCE: David Hume, *Dialogues concerning Natural Religion*, in *The Philosophical Works of David Hume Including All the Essays, and Exhibiting the More Important Alterations and Corrections in the Successive Editions Published by the Author*, 4 vols., vol. 2 (Edinburgh: Adam Black and William Tait, 1826), 509–18.

You ascribe, Cleanthes (and I believe justly), a purpose and intention to Nature. But what, I beseech you, is the object of that curious artifice and machinery, which she has displayed in all animals? The preservation alone of individuals, and propagation of the species. It seems enough for her purpose, if such a rank be barely upheld in the universe, without any care or concern for the happiness of the members that compose it. No resource for this purpose: no machinery, in order merely to give pleasure or ease: no fund of pure joy and contentment: no indulgence, without some want or necessity accompanying it. At least, the few phenomena of this nature are overbalanced by opposite phenomena of still greater importance.

Our sense of music, harmony, and indeed beauty of all kinds, gives satisfaction, without being absolutely necessary to the preservation and propagation of the species. But what racking pains, on the other hand, arise from gouts, gravels, megrims, toothachs, rheumatisms, where the injury to the animal machinery is either small or incurable? Mirth, laughter, play, frolic, seem gratuitous satisfactions, which have no further tendency: spleen, melancholy, discontent, superstition, are pains of the same nature. How then does the Divine benevolence display itself, in the sense of you Anthropomorphites? None but we Mystics, as you were pleased to call us, can account for this strange mixture of phenomena, by deriving it from attributes, infinitely perfect, but incomprehensible.

And have you at last, said Cleanthes smiling, betrayed your intentions, Philo? Your long agreement with Demea did indeed a little surprise me; but I find you were all the while erecting a concealed battery against me. And I must confess, that you have now fallen upon a subject worthy of your noble spirit of opposition and controversy. If you can make out the present point, and prove mankind to be unhappy or corrupted, there is an end at once of all religion. For to what purpose establish the natural attributes of the Deity, while the moral are still doubtful and uncertain?

You take umbrage very easily, replied Demea, at opinions the most innocent, and the most generally received, even amongst the religious and devout themselves: and nothing can be more surprising than to find a topic like this, concerning the wickedness and misery of man, charged with no less than Atheism and profaneness. Have not all pious divines and preachers, who have indulged their rhetoric on so fertile a subject; have they not easily, I say, given a solution of any difficulties which may attend it? This world is but a point in comparison of the universe; this life but a moment in comparison of eternity. The present evil phenomena, therefore, are rectified in other regions, and in some future period of existence. And the eyes of men, being then opened to larger views of things, see the whole connection of general laws; and trace with adoration, the benevolence and rectitude of the Deity, through all the mazes and intricacies of his providence.

No! replied Cleanthes, No! These arbitrary suppositions can never be admitted, contrary to matter of fact, visible and uncontroverted. Whence can any cause be known but from its known effects? Whence can any hypothesis be proved but from the apparent phenomena? To establish one hypothesis upon another, is building entirely in the air; and the utmost we ever attain, by these conjectures and fictions, is to ascertain the bare possibility of our opinion; but never can we, upon such terms, establish its reality.

The only method of supporting Divine benevolence, and it is what I willingly embrace, is to deny absolutely the misery and wickedness of man. Your representations are exaggerated; your melancholy views mostly fictitious; your inferences contrary to fact and experience. Health is more common than sickness; pleasure than pain; happiness than misery. And for one vexation which we meet with, we attain, upon computation, a hundred enjoyments.

Admitting your position, replied Philo, which yet is extremely doubtful, you must at the same time allow, that if pain be less frequent than pleasure, it is infinitely more violent and durable. One hour of it is often able to outweigh a day, a week, a month of our common insipid enjoyments; and how many days, weeks, and months, are passed by several in the most acute torments? Pleasure, scarcely in one instance, is ever able to reach ecstasy and rapture; and in no one instance can it continue for any time at its highest pitch and altitude. The spirits evaporate, the nerves relax, the fabric is disordered, and the enjoyment quickly degenerates into fatigue and uneasiness. But pain often, good God, how often! rises to torture and agony; and the longer it continues, it becomes still more genuine agony and torture. Patience is exhausted, courage languishes, melancholy seizes us, and nothing terminates our misery but the removal of its cause, or another event, which is the sole cure of all evil, but which, from our natural folly, we regard with still greater horror and consternation.

But not to insist upon these topics, continued Philo, though most obvious, certain, and important; I must use the freedom to admonish you, Cleanthes, that you have put the controversy upon a most dangerous issue, and are unawares introducing a total scepticism into the most essential articles of natural and revealed theology. What! no method of fixing a just foundation for religion, unless we allow the happiness of human life, and maintain a continued existence even in this world, with all our present pains, infirmities, vexations, and follies, to be eligible and desirable! But this is contrary to every one's feeling and experience: It is contrary to an authority so established as nothing can subvert. No decisive proofs can ever be produced against this authority; nor is it possible for you to compute, estimate, and compare, all the pains and all the pleasures in the lives of all men and of all animals: And thus, by your resting the whole system of religion on a point, which, from its very nature, must for ever be uncertain, you tacitly confess, that that system is equally uncertain.

But allowing you what never will be believed, at least what you never possibly can prove, that animal, or at least human happiness, in this life, exceeds its misery, you have yet done nothing: For this is not, by any means, what we expect from infinite power, infinite wisdom, and infinite goodness. Why is there any misery at all in the world? Not by chance surely. From some cause then. Is it from the intention of the Deity? But he is perfectly benevolent. Is it contrary to his intention? But he is almighty. Nothing can shake the solidity of this reasoning, so short, so clear, so decisive; except we assert, that these subjects exceed all human capacity, and that our common measures of truth and falsehood are not applicable to them; a topic which I have all along insisted on, but which you have, from the beginning, rejected with scorn and indignation.

But I will be contented to retire still from this entrenchment, for I deny that you can ever force me in it. I will allow, that pain or misery in man is *compatible* with infinite power and goodness in the Deity, even in your sense of these attributes: What are you advanced by all these concessions? A mere possible compatibility is not sufficient. You must *prove* these pure, unmixt, and uncontrollable attributes from the present mixt and confused phenomena, and from these alone. A hopeful undertaking! Were the phenomena ever so pure and unmixt, yet being finite, they would be insufficient for that purpose. How much more, where they are also so jarring and discordant!

[. . . .]

I scruple not to allow, said Cleanthes, that I have been apt to suspect the frequent repetition of the word *infinite*, which we meet with in all theological writers, to savour more of panegyric than of philosophy; and that any purposes of reasoning, and even of religion, would be better served, were we to rest contented with more accurate and more moderate expressions. The terms, *admirable, excellent, superlatively great, wise,* and *holy*; these sufficiently fill the imaginations of men; and any thing beyond, besides that it leads into absurdities, has no influence on the affections or sentiments. Thus, in the present subject, if we abandon all human analogy, as seems your intention, Demea, I am afraid we abandon all religion, and retain no conception of the great object of our adoration. If we preserve human analogy, we must for ever find it impossible to reconcile any mixture of evil in the universe with infinite attributes; much less can we ever prove the latter from the former. But supposing the

Author of Nature to be finitely perfect, though far exceeding mankind, a satisfactory account may then be given of natural and moral evil, and every untoward phenomenon be explained and adjusted. A less evil may then be chosen, in order to avoid a greater; inconveniences be submitted to, in order to reach a desirable end; and in a word, benevolence, regulated by wisdom, and limited by necessity, may produce just such a world as the present. You, Philo, who are so prompt at starting views, and reflections, and analogies, I would gladly hear, at length, without interruption, your opinion of this new theory; and if it deserve our attention, we may afterwards, at more leisure, reduce it into form.

My sentiments, replied Philo, are not worth being made a mystery of; and therefore, without any ceremony, I shall deliver what occurs to me with regard to the present subject. It must, I think, be allowed, that if a very limited intelligence, whom we shall suppose utterly unacquainted with the universe, were assured, that it were the production of a very good, wise, and powerful Being, however finite, he would, from his conjectures, form *beforehand* a different notion of it from what we find it to be by experience; nor would he ever imagine, merely from these attributes of the cause, of which he is informed, that the effect could be so full of vice and misery and disorder, as it appears in this life. Supposing now, that this person were brought into the world, still assured that it was the workmanship of such a sublime and benevolent Being; he might, perhaps, be surprised at the disappointment; but would never retract his former belief, if founded on any very solid argument; since such a limited intelligence must be sensible of his own blindness and ignorance, and must allow, that there may be many solutions of those phenomena, which will for ever escape his comprehension. But supposing, which is the real case with regard to man, that this creature is not antecedently convinced of a supreme intelligence, benevolent, and powerful, but is left to gather such a belief from the appearances of things; this entirely alters the case, nor will he ever find any reason for such a conclusion. He may be fully convinced of the narrow limits of his understanding; but this will not help him in forming an inference concerning the goodness of superior powers, since he must form that inference from what he knows, not from what he is ignorant of. The more you exaggerate his weakness and ignorance, the more diffident you render him, and give him the greater suspicion that such subjects are beyond the reach of his faculties. You are obliged, therefore, to reason with him merely from the known phenomena, and to drop every arbitrary supposition or conjecture.

Did I show you a house or palace, where there was not one apartment convenient or agreeable; where the windows, doors, fires, passages, stairs, and the whole economy of the building, were the source of noise, confusion, fatigue, darkness, and the extremes of heat and cold; you would certainly blame the contrivance, without any further examination. The architect would in vain display his subtilty, and prove to you, that if this door or that window were altered, greater ills would ensue. What he says may be strictly true: The alteration of one particular, while the other parts of the building remain, may only augment the inconveniences. But still you would assert in general, that, if the architect had had skill and good intentions, he might have formed such a plan of the whole, and might have adjusted the parts in such a manner, as would have remedied all or most of these inconveniences. His ignorance, or even your own ignorance of such a plan, will never convince you of the impossibility of it. If you find any inconveniences and deformities in the building, you will always, without entering into any detail, condemn the architect.

In short, I repeat the question: Is the world, considered in general, and as it appears to us in this life, different from what a man, or such a limited being, would, *beforehand*, expect from a very powerful, wise, and benevolent Deity? It must be strange prejudice to assert the contrary. And from thence I conclude, that however consistent the world may be, allowing certain suppositions and conjectures, with the idea of such a Deity, it can never afford us an inference concerning his existence. The consistence is not absolutely denied, only the inference. Conjectures, especially where infinity is excluded from the Divine attributes, may perhaps be sufficient to prove a consistence, but can never be foundations for any inference.

98

John Adams

from *Thoughts on Government*

A creative visionary in the founding of the United States of America, John Adams (1735–1826) served in numerous roles. His important contributions included: representative to the Continental Congress before the American Revolution; authoring the Massachusetts state constitution during the Revolution; signing the Treaty of Paris (1783) that confirmed U.S. independence; U.S. ambassador to the United Kingdom; first Vice President; and the second President of the United States. Adams was also a keen student of political theory, collecting and comparing historic documents and constitutions. In this letter, Adams responds to George Wythe of Virginia, who in January of 1776 asked Adams what he might envision—should the colonies rebel—as a replacement to England's colonial government. Inspired by this moment of responsibility and opportunity, Adams draws upon the best of great traditions to empower the populace with agency in their own just governing.

———————————

MY DEAR SIR,—If I was equal to the task of forming a plan for the government of a colony, I should be flattered with your request, and very happy to comply with it; because, as the divine science of politics is the science of social happiness, and the blessings of society depend entirely on the constitutions of government, which are generally institutions that last for many generations, there can be no employment more agreeable to a benevolent mind than a research after the best.

Pope flattered tyrants too much when he said, "For forms of government let fools contest, That which is best administered is best."

SOURCE: John Adams, "Thoughts on Government," in *The Works of John Adams, Second President of the United States: With a Life of the Author, Notes and Illustrations, by his Grandson Charles Francis Adams*, vol. 4 (Boston: Charles C. Little and James Brown, 1851), 193–200.

Nothing can be more fallacious than this. But poets read history to collect flowers, not fruits; they attend to fanciful images, not the effects of social institutions. Nothing is more certain, from the history of nations and nature of man, than that some forms of government are better fitted for being well administered than others.

We ought to consider what is the end of government, before we determine which is the best form. Upon this point all speculative politicians will agree, that the happiness of society is the end of government, as all divines and moral philosophers will agree that the happiness of the individual is the end of man. From this principle it will follow, that the form of government which communicates ease, comfort, security, or, in one word, happiness, to the greatest number of persons, and in the greatest degree, is the best.

All sober inquirers after truth, ancient and modern, pagan and Christian, have declared that the happiness of man, as well as his dignity, consists in virtue. Confucius, Zoroaster, Socrates, Mahomet, not to mention authorities really sacred, have agreed in this.

If there is a form of government, then, whose principle and foundation is virtue, will not every sober man acknowledge it better calculated to promote the general happiness than any other form?

Fear is the foundation of most governments; but it is so sordid and brutal a passion, and renders men in whose breasts it predominates so stupid and miserable, that Americans will not be likely to approve of any political institution which is founded on it.

Honor is truly sacred, but holds a lower rank in the scale of moral excellence than virtue. Indeed, the former is but a part of the latter, and consequently has not equal pretensions to support a frame of government productive of human happiness.

The foundation of every government is some principle or passion in the minds of the people. The noblest principles and most generous affections in our nature, then, have the fairest chance to support the noblest and most generous models of government.

A man must be indifferent to the sneers of modern Englishmen, to mention in their company the names of Sidney, Harrington, Locke, Milton, Nedham, Neville, Burnet, and Hoadly. No small fortitude is necessary to confess that one has read them. The wretched condition of this country, however, for ten or fifteen years past, has frequently reminded me of their principles and reasonings. They will convince any candid mind, that there is no good government but what is republican. That the only valuable part of the British constitution is so; because the very definition of a republic is "an empire of laws, and not of men." That, as a republic is the best of governments, so that particular arrangement of the powers of society, or, in other words, that form of government which is best contrived to secure an impartial and exact execution of the laws, is the best of republics.

Of republics there is an inexhaustible variety, because the possible combinations of the powers of society are capable of innumerable variations.

As good government is an empire of laws, how shall your laws be made? In a large society, inhabiting an extensive country, it is impossible that the whole should assemble to make laws. The first necessary step, then, is to depute power from the many to a few of the most wise and good. But by what rules shall you choose your representatives? Agree upon the number and qualifications of persons who shall have the benefit of choosing, or annex this privilege to the inhabitants of a certain extent of ground.

The principal difficulty lies, and the greatest care should be employed, in constituting this representative assembly. It should be in miniature an exact portrait of the people at large. It should think, feel, reason, and act like them. That it may be the interest of this assembly to do strict justice at all times, it should be an equal representation, or, in other words, equal interests among the people should have equal interests in it. Great care should be taken to effect this, and to prevent unfair, partial, and corrupt elections. Such regulations, however, may be better made in times of greater tranquillity than the present; and they will spring up themselves naturally, when all the powers of government come to be in the hands of the people's friends. At present, it will be safest to proceed in all established modes, to which the people have been familiarized by habit.

A representation of the people in one assembly being obtained, a question arises, whether all the powers of government, legislative, executive, and judicial, shall be left in this body? I think a people cannot be long free, nor ever happy, whose government is in one assembly. My reasons for this opinion are as follow:—

1. A single assembly is liable to all the vices, follies, and frailties of an individual; subject to fits of humor, starts of passion, flights of enthusiasm, partialities, or prejudice, and consequently productive of hasty results and absurd judgments. And all these errors ought to be corrected and defects supplied by some controlling power.

2. A single assembly is apt to be avaricious, and in time will not scruple to exempt itself from burdens, which it will lay, without compunction, on its constituents.

3. A single assembly is apt to grow ambitious, and after a time will not hesitate to vote itself perpetual. This was one fault of the Long Parliament;

but more remarkably of Holland, whose assembly first voted themselves from annual to septennial, then for life, and after a course of years, that all vacancies happening by death or otherwise, should be filled by themselves, without any application to constituents at all.

4. A representative assembly, although extremely well qualified, and absolutely necessary, as a branch of the legislative, is unfit to exercise the executive power, for want of two essential properties, secrecy and despatch.

5. A representative assembly is still less qualified for the judicial power, because it is too numerous, too slow, and too little skilled in the laws.

6. Because a single assembly, possessed of all the powers of government, would make arbitrary laws for their own interest, execute all laws arbitrarily for their own interest, and adjudge all controversies in their own favor.

But shall the whole power of legislation rest in one assembly? Most of the foregoing reasons apply equally to prove that the legislative power ought to be more complex; to which we may add, that if the legislative power is wholly in one assembly, and the executive in another, or in a single person, these two powers will oppose and encroach upon each other, until the contest shall end in war, and the whole power, legislative and executive, be usurped by the strongest.

The judicial power, in such case, could not mediate, or hold the balance between the two contending powers, because the legislative would undermine it. And this shows the necessity, too, of giving the executive power a negative upon the legislative, otherwise this will be continually encroaching upon that.

To avoid these dangers, let a distinct assembly be constituted, as a mediator between the two extreme branches of the legislature, that which represents the people, and that which is vested with the executive power.

Let the representative assembly then elect by ballot, from among themselves or their constituents, or both, a distinct assembly, which, for the sake of perspicuity, we will call a council. It may consist of any number you please, say twenty or thirty, and should have a free and independent exercise of its judgment, and consequently a negative voice in the legislature.

These two bodies, thus constituted, and made integral parts of the legislature, let them unite, and by joint ballot choose a governor, who, after being stripped of most of those badges of domination, called prerogatives, should have a free and independent exercise of his judgment, and be made also an integral part of the legislature. This, I know, is liable to objections; and, if you please, you may make him only president of the council, as in Connecticut. But as the governor is to be invested with the executive power, with consent of council, I think he ought to have a negative upon the legislative. If he is annually elective, as he ought to be, he will always have so much reverence and affection for the people, their representatives and counsellors, that, although you give him an independent exercise of his judgment, he will seldom use it in opposition to the two houses, except in cases the public utility of which would be conspicuous; and some such cases would happen.

In the present exigency of American affairs, when, by an act of Parliament, we are put out of the royal protection, and consequently discharged from our allegiance, and it has become necessary to assume government for our immediate security, the governor, lieutenant-governor, secretary, treasurer, commissary, attorney-general, should be chosen by joint ballot of both houses. And these and all other elections, especially of representatives and counsellors, should be annual, there not being in the whole circle of the sciences a maxim more infallible than this, "where annual elections end, there slavery begins."

These great men, in this respect, should be, once a year,

> "Like bubbles on the sea of matter borne,
> They rise, they break, and to that sea return."

This will teach them the great political virtues of humility, patience, and moderation, without which every man in power becomes a ravenous beast of prey.

This mode of constituting the great offices of state will answer very well for the present; but if by experiment it should be found inconvenient, the legislature may, at its leisure, devise other methods of creating them, by elections of the people at large, as in Connecticut, or it may enlarge the term for which they shall be chosen to seven years, or three years, or for life, or make any other alterations which the society shall find productive of its ease, its safety, its freedom, or, in one word, its happiness.

A rotation of all offices, as well as of representatives and counsellors, has many advocates, and is contended for with many plausible arguments. It would be attended, no doubt, with many advantages; and if the society has a sufficient number of suitable characters to supply the great number of vacancies which would be made by such a rotation, I can see no objection to it. These persons may be allowed to serve for three years, and then be excluded three years, or for any longer or shorter term.

Any seven or nine of the legislative council may be made a quorum, for doing business as a privy council, to advise the governor in the exercise of the executive branch of power, and in all acts of state.

The governor should have the command of the militia and of all your armies. The power of pardons should be with the governor and council.

Judges, justices, and all other officers, civil and military, should be nominated and appointed by the governor, with the advice and consent of council, unless you choose to have a government more popular; if you do, all officers, civil and military, may be chosen by joint ballot of both houses; or, in order to preserve the independence and importance of each house, by ballot of one house, concurred in by the other. Sheriffs should be chosen by the freeholders of counties; so should registers of deeds and clerks of counties.

All officers should have commissions, under the hand of the governor and seal of the colony.

The dignity and stability of government in all its branches, the morals of the people, and every blessing of society depend so much upon an upright and skilful administration of justice, that the judicial power ought to be distinct from both the legislative and executive, and independent upon both, that so it may be a check upon both, as both should be checks upon that. The judges, therefore, should be always men of learning and experience in the laws, of exemplary morals, great patience, calmness, coolness, and attention. Their minds should not be distracted with jarring interests; they should not be dependent upon any man, or body of men. To these ends, they should hold estates for life in their offices; or, in other words, their commissions should be during good behavior, and their salaries ascertained and established by law. For misbehavior, the grand inquest of the colony, the house of representatives, should impeach them before the governor and council, where they should have time and opportunity to make their defence; but, if convicted, should be removed from their offices, and subjected to such other punishment as shall be thought proper.

A militia law, requiring all men, or with very few exceptions besides cases of conscience, to be provided with arms and ammunition, to be trained at certain seasons; and requiring counties, towns, or other small districts, to be provided with public stocks of ammunition and intrenching utensils, and with some settled plans for transporting provisions after the militia, when marched to defend their country against sudden invasions; and requiring certain districts to be provided with field-pieces, companies of matrosses, and perhaps some regiments of light-horse, is always a wise institution, and, in the present circumstances of our country, indispensable.

Laws for the liberal education of youth, especially of the lower class of people, are so extremely wise and useful, that, to a humane and generous mind, no expense for this purpose would be thought extravagant.

The very mention of sumptuary laws will excite a smile. Whether our countrymen have wisdom and virtue enough to submit to them, I know not; but the happiness of the people might be greatly promoted by them, and a revenue saved sufficient to carry on this war forever. Frugality is a great revenue, besides curing us of vanities, levities, and fopperies, which are real antidotes to all great, manly, and warlike virtues.

But must not all commissions run in the name of a king? No. Why may they not as well run thus, "The colony of [ ] to A. B. greeting," and be tested by the governor?

Why may not writs, instead of running in the name of the king, run thus, "The colony of [] to the sheriff," &c., and be tested by the chief justice?

Why may not indictments conclude, "against the peace of the colony of [ ] and the dignity of the same?"

A constitution founded on these principles introduces knowledge among the people, and inspires them with a conscious dignity becoming freemen; a general emulation takes place, which causes good humor, sociability, good manners, and good morals to be general. That elevation of sentiment inspired by such a government, makes the common people brave and enterprising. That ambition which is inspired by it makes them sober, industrious, and frugal. You will find among them some elegance, perhaps, but more solidity; a little pleasure, but a great deal of business; some politeness, but more civility. If you compare such a country with the regions of domination, whether monarchical or aristocratical, you will fancy yourself in Arcadia or Elysium.

If the colonies should assume governments separately, they should be left entirely to their own choice of the forms; and if a continental constitution should be formed, it should be a congress, containing a fair and adequate representation of the colonies, and its authority should sacredly be confined to these cases, namely, war, trade, disputes between colony and colony, the postoffice, and the unappropriated lands of the crown, as they used to be called.

These colonies, under such forms of government, and in such a union, would be unconquerable by all the monarchies of Europe.

You and I, my dear friend, have been sent into life at a time when the greatest lawgivers of antiquity would have wished to live. How few of the human race have ever enjoyed an opportunity of making an election of government, more than of air, soil, or climate, for themselves or their children! When, before the present epocha, had three millions of people full power and a fair opportunity to form and establish the wisest and happiest government that human wisdom can contrive? I hope you will avail yourself and your country of that extensive learning and indefatigable industry which you possess, to assist her in the formation of the happiest governments and the best character of a great people. For myself, I must beg you to keep my name out of sight; for this feeble attempt, if it should be known to be mine, would oblige me to apply to myself those lines of the immortal John Milton, in one of his sonnets:—

> "I did but prompt the age to quit their clogs
> By the known rules of ancient liberty,
> When straight a barbarous noise environs me
> Of owls and cuckoos, asses, apes, and dogs."

99

Abigail Adams

Letter from Abigail Adams to John Adams, 31 March–5 April 1776

Abigail Adams (1744–1818) was the wife and confidante of the second U.S. President, John Adams (1735–1826), as well as the mother of the sixth U.S. President, John Quincy Adams (1767–1848). Evidence suggests that she advised her husband throughout his political career, often through written correspondence, on a number of important issues of the day. Among other things, she advocated for the abolition of slavery and for women's rights and education. The following is her most famous letter to her husband, in which she encourages him to "Remember the Ladies" in the laws of the new nation he was helping to forge.

———————————

Braintree March 31 1776

I wish you would ever write me a Letter half as long as I write you; and tell me if you may where your Fleet are gone? What sort of Defence Virginia can make against our common Enemy? Whether it is so situated as to make an able Defence? Are not the Gentery Lords and the common people vassals, are they not like the uncivilized Natives Brittain represents us to be? I hope their Riffel Men who have shewen themselves very savage and even Blood thirsty; are not a specimen of the Generality of the people.

I am willing to allow the Colony great merrit for having produced a Washington but they have been shamefully duped by a Dunmore.

I have sometimes been ready to think that the passion for Liberty cannot be Eaquelly Strong in the Breasts of those who have been accustomed to deprive their fellow Creatures of theirs. Of this I am certain that it is not founded

SOURCE: "Abigail Adams to John Adams, 31 March 1776," Founders Online, National Archives, https://founders.archives.gov/documents/Adams/04-01-02-0241.

upon that generous and christian principal of doing to others as we would that others should do unto us.

Do not you want to see Boston; I am fearfull of the small pox, or I should have been in before this time. I got Mr. Crane to go to our House and see what state it was in. I find it has been occupied by one of the Doctors of a Regiment, very dirty, but no other damage has been done to it. The few things which were left in it are all gone. Cranch has the key which he never deliverd up. I have wrote to him for it and am determined to get it cleand as soon as possible and shut it up. I look upon it a new acquisition of property, a property which one month ago I did not value at a single Shilling, and could with pleasure have seen it in flames.

The Town in General is left in a better state than we expected, more oweing to a percipitate flight than any Regard to the inhabitants, tho some individuals discoverd a sense of honour and justice and have left the rent of the Houses in which they were, for the owners and the furniture unhurt, or if damaged sufficent to make it good.

Others have committed abominable Ravages. The Mansion House of your President is safe and the furniture unhurt whilst both the House and Furniture of the Solisiter General have fallen a prey to their own merciless party. Surely the very Fiends feel a Reverential awe for Virtue and patriotism, whilst they Detest the paricide and traitor.

I feel very differently at the approach of spring to what I did a month ago. We knew not then whether we could plant or sow with safety, whether when we had toild we could reap the fruits of our own industery, whether we could rest in our own Cottages, or whether we should not be driven from the sea coasts to seek shelter in the wilderness, but now we feel as if we might sit under our own vine and eat the good of the land.

I feel a gaieti de Coar to which before I was a stranger. I think the Sun looks brighter, the Birds sing more melodiously, and Nature puts on a more chearfull countanance. We feel a temporary peace, and the poor fugitives are returning to their deserted habitations.

Tho we felicitate ourselves, we sympathize with those who are trembling least the Lot of Boston should be theirs. But they cannot be in similar circumstances unless pusilanimity and cowardise should take possession of them. They have time and warning given them to see the Evil and shun it.—I long to hear that you have declared an independancy—and by the way in the new Code of Laws which I suppose it will be necessary for you to make I desire you would Remember the Ladies, and be more generous and favourable to them than your ancestors. Do not put such unlimited power into the hands of the

Husbands. Remember all Men would be tyrants if they could. If perticuliar care and attention is not paid to the Laidies we are determined to foment a Rebelion, and will not hold ourselves bound by any Laws in which we have no voice, or Representation.

That your Sex are Naturally Tyrannical is a Truth so thoroughly established as to admit of no dispute, but such of you as wish to be happy willingly give up the harsh title of Master for the more tender and endearing one of Friend. Why then, not put it out of the power of the vicious and the Lawless to use us with cruelty and indignity with impunity. Men of Sense in all Ages abhor those customs which treat us only as the vassals of your Sex. Regard us then as Beings placed by providence under your protection and in immitation of the Supreem Being make use of that power only for our happiness.

April 5

Not having an opportunity of sending this I shall add a few lines more; tho not with a heart so gay. I have been attending the sick chamber of our Neighbour Trot whose affliction I most sensibly feel but cannot discribe, striped of two lovely children in one week. Gorge the Eldest died on wedensday and Billy the youngest on fryday, with the Canker fever, a terible disorder so much like the thr[o]at distemper, that it differs but little from it. Betsy Cranch has been very bad, but upon the recovery. Becky Peck they do not expect will live out the day. Many grown person[s] are now sick with it, in this [street?] 5. It rages much in other Towns. The Mumps too are very frequent. Isaac is now confined with it. Our own little flock are yet well. My Heart trembles with anxiety for them. God preserve them.

I want to hear much oftener from you than I do. March 8 was the last date of any that I have yet had.—You inquire of whether I am making Salt peter. I have not yet attempted it, but after Soap making believe I shall make the experiment. I find as much as I can do to manufacture cloathing for my family which would else be Naked. I know of but one person in this part of the Town who has made any, that is Mr. Tertias Bass as he is calld who has got very near an hundred weight which has been found to be very good. I have heard of some others in the other parishes. Mr. Reed of Weymouth has been applied to, to go to Andover to the mills which are now at work, and has gone. I have lately seen a small Manuscrip de[s]cribing the proportions for the various sorts of powder, fit for cannon, small arms and pistols. If it would be of any Service your way I will get it transcribed and send it to you.—Every one of your Friend[s] send their Regards, and all the little ones. Your Brothers youngest child lies bad with convulsion fitts. Adieu. I need not say how much I am Your ever faithfull Friend.

100

U.S. Declaration of Independence

The U.S. Declaration of Independence represents a new nation's formal proclamation of its own self-identity, as well as an articulation of the justification for separating with its former ruler. Drafted largely by Thomas Jefferson (with input from the so-called Committee of Five, which included John Adams and Benjamin Franklin, along with Robert Livingston and Roger Sherman) the declaration was adopted by the Second Continental Congress convened at the Pennsylvania State House in Philadelphia on July 4, 1776.

In Congress, July 4, 1776.

The unanimous Declaration of the thirteen united States of America, When in the Course of human events, it becomes necessary for one people to dissolve the political bands which have connected them with another, and to assume among the powers of the earth, the separate and equal station to which the Laws of Nature and of Nature's God entitle them, a decent respect to the opinions of mankind requires that they should declare the causes which impel them to the separation.

We hold these truths to be self-evident, that all men are created equal, that they are endowed by their Creator with certain unalienable Rights, that among these are Life, Liberty and the pursuit of Happiness.—That to secure these rights, Governments are instituted among Men, deriving their just powers from the consent of the governed,—That whenever any Form of Government becomes destructive of these ends, it is the Right of the People to alter or to abolish it, and to institute new Government, laying its foundation on such principles and organizing its powers in such form, as to them shall seem most likely to effect their Safety and Happiness. Prudence, indeed, will dictate that

SOURCE: U.S. Declaration of Independence, Philadelphia, July 4, 1776, "Declaration of Independence: A Transcription," National Archives, https://www.archives.gov/founding-docs/declaration-transcript.

Governments long established should not be changed for light and transient causes; and accordingly all experience hath shewn, that mankind are more disposed to suffer, while evils are sufferable, than to right themselves by abolishing the forms to which they are accustomed. But when a long train of abuses and usurpations, pursuing invariably the same Object evinces a design to reduce them under absolute Despotism, it is their right, it is their duty, to throw off such Government, and to provide new Guards for their future security.—Such has been the patient sufferance of these Colonies; and such is now the necessity which constrains them to alter their former Systems of Government. The history of the present King of Great Britain is a history of repeated injuries and usurpations, all having in direct object the establishment of an absolute Tyranny over these States. To prove this, let Facts be submitted to a candid world.

He has refused his Assent to Laws, the most wholesome and necessary for the public good.

He has forbidden his Governors to pass Laws of immediate and pressing importance, unless suspended in their operation till his Assent should be obtained; and when so suspended, he has utterly neglected to attend to them.

He has refused to pass other Laws for the accommodation of large districts of people, unless those people would relinquish the right of Representation in the Legislature, a right inestimable to them and formidable to tyrants only.

He has called together legislative bodies at places unusual, uncomfortable, and distant from the depository of their public Records, for the sole purpose of fatiguing them into compliance with his measures.

He has dissolved Representative Houses repeatedly, for opposing with manly firmness his invasions on the rights of the people.

He has refused for a long time, after such dissolutions, to cause others to be elected; whereby the Legislative powers, incapable of Annihilation, have returned to the People at large for their exercise; the State remaining in the mean time exposed to all the dangers of invasion from without, and convulsions within.

He has endeavoured to prevent the population of these States; for that purpose obstructing the Laws for Naturalization of Foreigners; refusing to pass others to encourage their migrations hither, and raising the conditions of new Appropriations of Lands.

He has obstructed the Administration of Justice, by refusing his Assent to Laws for establishing Judiciary powers.

He has made Judges dependent on his Will alone, for the tenure of their offices, and the amount and payment of their salaries.

He has erected a multitude of New Offices, and sent hither swarms of Officers to harrass our people, and eat out their substance.

He has kept among us, in times of peace, Standing Armies without the Consent of our legislatures.

He has affected to render the Military independent of and superior to the Civil power.

He has combined with others to subject us to a jurisdiction foreign to our constitution, and unacknowledged by our laws; giving his Assent to their Acts of pretended Legislation:

For Quartering large bodies of armed troops among us:

For protecting them, by a mock Trial, from punishment for any Murders which they should commit on the Inhabitants of these States:

For cutting off our Trade with all parts of the world:

For imposing Taxes on us without our Consent:

For depriving us in many cases, of the benefits of Trial by Jury:

For transporting us beyond Seas to be tried for pretended offences

For abolishing the free System of English Laws in a neighbouring Province, establishing therein an Arbitrary government, and enlarging its Boundaries so as to render it at once an example and fit instrument for introducing the same absolute rule into these Colonies:

For taking away our Charters, abolishing our most valuable Laws, and altering fundamentally the Forms of our Governments:

For suspending our own Legislatures, and declaring themselves invested with power to legislate for us in all cases whatsoever.

He has abdicated Government here, by declaring us out of his Protection and waging War against us.

He has plundered our seas, ravaged our Coasts, burnt our towns, and destroyed the lives of our people.

He is at this time transporting large Armies of foreign Mercenaries to compleat the works of death, desolation and tyranny, already begun with circumstances of Cruelty & perfidy scarcely paralleled in the most barbarous ages, and totally unworthy the Head of a civilized nation.

He has constrained our fellow Citizens taken Captive on the high Seas to bear Arms against their Country, to become the executioners of their friends and Brethren, or to fall themselves by their Hands.

He has excited domestic insurrections amongst us, and has endeavoured to bring on the inhabitants of our frontiers, the merciless Indian Savages, whose known rule of warfare, is an undistinguished destruction of all ages, sexes and conditions.

In every stage of these Oppressions We have Petitioned for Redress in the most humble terms: Our repeated Petitions have been answered only by repeated injury. A Prince whose character is thus marked by every act which may define a Tyrant, is unfit to be the ruler of a free people.

Nor have We been wanting in attentions to our Brittish brethren. We have warned them from time to time of attempts by their legislature to extend an unwarrantable jurisdiction over us. We have reminded them of the circumstances of our emigration and settlement here. We have appealed to their native justice and magnanimity, and we have conjured them by the ties of our common kindred to disavow these usurpations, which, would inevitably interrupt our connections and correspondence. They too have been deaf to the voice of justice and of consanguinity. We must, therefore, acquiesce in the necessity, which denounces our Separation, and hold them, as we hold the rest of mankind, Enemies in War, in Peace Friends.

We, therefore, the Representatives of the united States of America, in General Congress, Assembled, appealing to the Supreme Judge of the world for the rectitude of our intentions, do, in the Name, and by Authority of the good People of these Colonies, solemnly publish and declare, That these United Colonies are, and of Right ought to be Free and Independent States; that they are Absolved from all Allegiance to the British Crown, and that all political connection between them and the State of Great Britain, is and ought to be totally dissolved; and that as Free and Independent States, they have full Power to levy War, conclude Peace, contract Alliances, establish Commerce, and to do all other Acts and Things which Independent States may of right do. And for the support of this Declaration, with a firm reliance on the protection of divine Providence, we mutually pledge to each other our Lives, our Fortunes and our sacred Honor.

[Signed by: Button Gwinnett, Lyman Hall, George Walton, William Hooper, Joseph Hewes, John Penn, Edward Rutledge, Thomas Heyward, Jr., Thomas Lynch, Jr., Arthur Middleton, John Hancock, Samuel Chase, William Paca, Thomas Stone, Charles Carroll of Carrollton, George Wythe, Richard Henry Lee, Thomas Jefferson, Benjamin Harrison, Thomas Nelson, Jr., Francis Lightfoot Lee, Carter Braxton, Robert Morris, Benjamin Rush, Benjamin Franklin, John Morton, George Clymer, James Smith, George Taylor, James Wilson, George Ross, Caesar Rodney, George Read, Thomas McKean, William Floyd, Philip Livingston, Francis Lewis, Lewis Morris, Richard Stockton, John Witherspoon, Francis Hopkinson, John Hart, Abraham Clark, Josiah Bartlett, William Whipple, Samuel Adams, John Adams, Robert Treat Paine, Elbridge Gerry, Stephen Hopkins, William Ellery, Roger Sherman, Samuel Huntington, William Williams, Oliver Wolcott, Matthew Thornton.]

101

U.S. Constitution

During their fight for independence (1776–1783), the thirteen American states ratified the Articles of Confederation and Perpetual Union (1781) as the law for their fledgling nation. Time, however, revealed weaknesses in the document. Thus, in 1787, twelve of the thirteen states (Rhode Island abstaining) sent delegates to a constitutional convention in Philadelphia. The new constitution created a stronger centralized federal government, adding an executive branch, a federal judiciary (e.g., the Supreme Court), and the Senate to the legislative branch. Concerned that the document did not enumerate and protect key civil rights, the authors of the Constitution added a Bill of Rights as the Constitution's first ten amendments. The Constitution was ratified and became the law of the United States in 1789.

We the People of the United States, in Order to form a more perfect Union, establish Justice, insure domestic Tranquility, provide for the common defence, promote the general Welfare, and secure the Blessings of Liberty to ourselves and our Posterity, do ordain and establish this Constitution for the United States of America.

Article. I.

Section. 1.

All legislative Powers herein granted shall be vested in a Congress of the United States, which shall consist of a Senate and House of Representatives.

SOURCE: U.S. Constitution, Philadelphia, 1789, "The Constitution of the United States: A Transcription," National Archives, https://www.archives.gov/founding-docs/constitution -transcript.

Section. 2.

The House of Representatives shall be composed of Members chosen every second Year by the People of the several States, and the Electors in each State shall have the Qualifications requisite for Electors of the most numerous Branch of the State Legislature.

No Person shall be a Representative who shall not have attained to the Age of twenty five Years, and been seven Years a Citizen of the United States, and who shall not, when elected, be an Inhabitant of that State in which he shall be chosen.

Representatives and direct Taxes shall be apportioned among the several States which may be included within this Union, according to their respective Numbers, which shall be determined by adding to the whole Number of free Persons, including those bound to Service for a Term of Years, and excluding Indians not taxed, three fifths of all other Persons. The actual Enumeration shall be made within three Years after the first Meeting of the Congress of the United States, and within every subsequent Term of ten Years, in such Manner as they shall by Law direct. The Number of Representatives shall not exceed one for every thirty Thousand, but each State shall have at Least one Representative; and until such enumeration shall be made, the State of New Hampshire shall be entitled to chuse three, Massachusetts eight, Rhode-Island and Providence Plantations one, Connecticut five, New-York six, New Jersey four, Pennsylvania eight, Delaware one, Maryland six, Virginia ten, North Carolina five, South Carolina five, and Georgia three.

When vacancies happen in the Representation from any State, the Executive Authority thereof shall issue Writs of Election to fill such Vacancies.

The House of Representatives shall chuse their Speaker and other Officers; and shall have the sole Power of Impeachment.

Section. 3.

The Senate of the United States shall be composed of two Senators from each State, chosen by the Legislature thereof, for six Years; and each Senator shall have one Vote.

Immediately after they shall be assembled in Consequence of the first Election, they shall be divided as equally as may be into three Classes. The Seats of the Senators of the first Class shall be vacated at the Expiration of the second Year, of the second Class at the Expiration of the fourth Year, and of the third Class at the Expiration of the sixth Year, so that one third may be chosen every second Year; and if Vacancies happen by Resignation, or otherwise, during the Recess of the Legislature of any State, the Executive thereof may make temporary Appointments until the next Meeting of the Legislature, which shall then fill such Vacancies.

No Person shall be a Senator who shall not have attained to the Age of thirty Years, and been nine Years a Citizen of the United States, and who shall not, when elected, be an Inhabitant of that State for which he shall be chosen.

The Vice President of the United States shall be President of the Senate, but shall have no Vote, unless they be equally divided.

The Senate shall chuse their other Officers, and also a President pro tempore, in the Absence of the Vice President, or when he shall exercise the Office of President of the United States.

The Senate shall have the sole Power to try all Impeachments. When sitting for that Purpose, they shall be on Oath or Affirmation. When the President of the United States is tried, the Chief Justice shall preside: And no Person shall be convicted without the Concurrence of two thirds of the Members present.

Judgment in Cases of Impeachment shall not extend further than to removal from Office, and disqualification to hold and enjoy any Office of honor, Trust or Profit under the United States: but the Party convicted shall nevertheless be liable and subject to Indictment, Trial, Judgment and Punishment, according to Law.

Section. 4.

The Times, Places and Manner of holding Elections for Senators and Representatives, shall be prescribed in each State by the Legislature thereof; but the Congress may at any time by Law make or alter such Regulations, except as to the Places of chusing Senators.

The Congress shall assemble at least once in every Year, and such Meeting shall be on the first Monday in December, unless they shall by Law appoint a different Day.

Section. 5.

Each House shall be the Judge of the Elections, Returns and Qualifications of its own Members, and a Majority of each shall constitute a Quorum to do Business; but a smaller Number may adjourn from day to day, and may be authorized to compel the Attendance of absent Members, in such Manner, and under such Penalties as each House may provide.

Each House may determine the Rules of its Proceedings, punish its Members for disorderly Behaviour, and, with the Concurrence of two thirds, expel a Member.

Each House shall keep a Journal of its Proceedings, and from time to time publish the same, excepting such Parts as may in their Judgment require Secrecy; and the Yeas and Nays of the Members of either House on any question shall, at the Desire of one fifth of those Present, be entered on the Journal.

Neither House, during the Session of Congress, shall, without the Consent of the other, adjourn for more than three days, nor to any other Place than that in which the two Houses shall be sitting.

Section. 6.

The Senators and Representatives shall receive a Compensation for their Services, to be ascertained by Law, and paid out of the Treasury of the United States. They shall in all Cases, except Treason, Felony and Breach of the Peace, be privileged from Arrest during their Attendance at the Session of their respective Houses, and in going to and returning from the same; and for any Speech or Debate in either House, they shall not be questioned in any other Place.

No Senator or Representative shall, during the Time for which he was elected, be appointed to any civil Office under the Authority of the United States, which shall have been created, or the Emoluments whereof shall have been encreased during such time; and no Person holding any Office under the United States, shall be a Member of either House during his Continuance in Office.

Section. 7.

All Bills for raising Revenue shall originate in the House of Representatives; but the Senate may propose or concur with Amendments as on other Bills.

Every Bill which shall have passed the House of Representatives and the Senate, shall, before it become a Law, be presented to the President of the United States; If he approve he shall sign it, but if not he shall return it, with his Objections to that House in which it shall have originated, who shall enter the Objections at large on their Journal, and proceed to reconsider it. If after such Reconsideration two thirds of that House shall agree to pass the Bill, it shall be sent, together with the Objections, to the other House, by which it shall likewise be reconsidered, and if approved by two thirds of that House, it shall become a Law. But in all such Cases the Votes of both Houses shall be determined by yeas and Nays, and the Names of the Persons voting for and against the Bill shall be entered on the Journal of each House respectively. If any Bill shall not be returned by the President within ten Days (Sundays excepted) after it shall have been presented to him, the Same shall be a Law, in like Manner as if he had signed it, unless the Congress by their Adjournment prevent its Return, in which Case it shall not be a Law.

Every Order, Resolution, or Vote to which the Concurrence of the Senate and House of Representatives may be necessary (except on a question of Adjournment) shall be presented to the President of the United States; and before the Same shall take Effect, shall be approved by him, or being disapproved by him, shall be repassed by two thirds of the Senate and House of Representatives, according to the Rules and Limitations prescribed in the Case of a Bill.

Section. 8.

The Congress shall have Power To lay and collect Taxes, Duties, Imposts and Excises, to pay the Debts and provide for the common Defence and general Welfare of the United States; but all Duties, Imposts and Excises shall be uniform throughout the United States;

To borrow Money on the credit of the United States;

To regulate Commerce with foreign Nations, and among the several States, and with the Indian Tribes;

To establish an uniform Rule of Naturalization, and uniform Laws on the subject of Bankruptcies throughout the United States;

To coin Money, regulate the Value thereof, and of foreign Coin, and fix the Standard of Weights and Measures;

To provide for the Punishment of counterfeiting the Securities and current Coin of the United States;

To establish Post Offices and post Roads;

To promote the Progress of Science and useful Arts, by securing for limited Times to Authors and Inventors the exclusive Right to their respective Writings and Discoveries;

To constitute Tribunals inferior to the supreme Court;

To define and punish Piracies and Felonies committed on the high Seas, and Offences against the Law of Nations;

To declare War, grant Letters of Marque and Reprisal, and make Rules concerning Captures on Land and Water;

To raise and support Armies, but no Appropriation of Money to that Use shall be for a longer Term than two Years;

To provide and maintain a Navy;

To make Rules for the Government and Regulation of the land and naval Forces;

To provide for calling forth the Militia to execute the Laws of the Union, suppress Insurrections and repel Invasions;

To provide for organizing, arming, and disciplining, the Militia, and for governing such Part of them as may be employed in the Service of the United States, reserving to the States respectively, the Appointment of the Officers, and the Authority of training the Militia according to the discipline prescribed by Congress;

To exercise exclusive Legislation in all Cases whatsoever, over such District (not exceeding ten Miles square) as may, by Cession of particular States, and the Acceptance of Congress, become the Seat of the Government of the United States, and to exercise like Authority over all Places purchased by the Consent of the Legislature of the State in which the Same shall be, for the Erection of Forts, Magazines, Arsenals, dock-Yards, and other needful Buildings;—And

To make all Laws which shall be necessary and proper for carrying into Execution the foregoing Powers, and all other Powers vested by this Constitution in the Government of the United States, or in any Department or Officer thereof.

Section. 9.

The Migration or Importation of such Persons as any of the States now existing shall think proper to admit, shall not be prohibited by the Congress prior to the Year one thousand eight hundred and eight, but a Tax or duty may be imposed on such Importation, not exceeding ten dollars for each Person.

The Privilege of the Writ of Habeas Corpus shall not be suspended, unless when in Cases of Rebellion or Invasion the public Safety may require it.

No Bill of Attainder or ex post facto Law shall be passed.

No Capitation, or other direct, Tax shall be laid, unless in Proportion to the Census or enumeration herein before directed to be taken.

No Tax or Duty shall be laid on Articles exported from any State.

No Preference shall be given by any Regulation of Commerce or Revenue to the Ports of one State over those of another: nor shall Vessels bound to, or from, one State, be obliged to enter, clear, or pay Duties in another.

No Money shall be drawn from the Treasury, but in Consequence of Appropriations made by Law; and a regular Statement and Account of the Receipts and Expenditures of all public Money shall be published from time to time.

No Title of Nobility shall be granted by the United States: And no Person holding any Office of Profit or Trust under them, shall, without the Consent of the Congress, accept of any present, Emolument, Office, or Title, of any kind whatever, from any King, Prince, or foreign State.

Section. 10.

No State shall enter into any Treaty, Alliance, or Confederation; grant Letters of Marque and Reprisal; coin Money; emit Bills of Credit; make any Thing but gold and silver Coin a Tender in Payment of Debts; pass any Bill of Attainder, ex post facto Law, or Law impairing the Obligation of Contracts, or grant any Title of Nobility.

No State shall, without the Consent of the Congress, lay any Imposts or Duties on Imports or Exports, except what may be absolutely necessary for executing its inspection Laws: and the net Produce of all Duties and Imposts, laid by any State on Imports or Exports, shall be for the Use of the Treasury of the United States; and all such Laws shall be subject to the Revision and Controul of the Congress.

No State shall, without the Consent of Congress, lay any Duty of Tonnage, keep Troops, or Ships of War in time of Peace, enter into any Agreement or Compact with another State, or with a foreign Power, or engage in War, unless actually invaded, or in such imminent Danger as will not admit of delay.

Article. II.

Section. 1.

The executive Power shall be vested in a President of the United States of America. He shall hold his Office during the Term of four Years, and, together with the Vice President, chosen for the same Term, be elected, as follows

Each State shall appoint, in such Manner as the Legislature thereof may direct, a Number of Electors, equal to the whole Number of Senators and Representatives to which the State may be entitled in the Congress: but no Senator or Representative, or Person holding an Office of Trust or Profit under the United States, shall be appointed an Elector.

The Electors shall meet in their respective States, and vote by Ballot for two Persons, of whom one at least shall not be an Inhabitant of the same State with themselves. And they shall make a List of all the Persons voted for, and of the Number of Votes for each; which List they shall sign and certify, and transmit sealed to the Seat of the Government of the United States, directed to the President of the Senate. The President of the Senate shall, in the Presence of the Senate and House of Representatives, open all the Certificates, and the Votes shall then be counted. The Person having the greatest Number of Votes shall be the President, if such Number be a Majority of the whole Number of Electors appointed; and if there be more than one who have such Majority, and have an equal Number of Votes, then the House of Representatives shall immediately chuse by Ballot one of them for President; and if no Person have a Majority, then from the five highest on the List the said House shall in like Manner chuse the President. But in chusing the President, the Votes shall be taken by States, the Representation from each State having one Vote; A quorum for this Purpose shall consist of a Member or Members from two thirds of the States, and a Majority of all the States shall be necessary to a Choice. In every Case, after the Choice of the President, the Person having the greatest Number of Votes of the Electors shall be the Vice President. But if there should remain two or more who have equal Votes, the Senate shall chuse from them by Ballot the Vice President.

The Congress may determine the Time of chusing the Electors, and the Day on which they shall give their Votes; which Day shall be the same throughout the United States.

No Person except a natural born Citizen, or a Citizen of the United States, at the time of the Adoption of this Constitution, shall be eligible to the Office of President; neither shall any Person be eligible to that Office who shall not have attained to the Age of thirty five Years, and been fourteen Years a Resident within the United States.

In Case of the Removal of the President from Office, or of his Death, Resignation, or Inability to discharge the Powers and Duties of the said Office, the Same shall devolve on the Vice President, and the Congress may by Law provide for the Case of Removal, Death, Resignation or Inability, both of the President and Vice President, declaring what Officer shall then act as President, and such Officer shall act accordingly, until the Disability be removed, or a President shall be elected.

The President shall, at stated Times, receive for his Services, a Compensation, which shall neither be encreased nor diminished during the Period for which he shall have been elected, and he shall not receive within that Period any other Emolument from the United States, or any of them.

Before he enter on the Execution of his Office, he shall take the following Oath or Affirmation:—"I do solemnly swear (or affirm) that I will faithfully execute the Office of President of the United States, and will to the best of my Ability, preserve, protect and defend the Constitution of the United States."

Section. 2.

The President shall be Commander in Chief of the Army and Navy of the United States, and of the Militia of the several States, when called into the actual Service of the United States; he may require the Opinion, in writing, of the principal Officer in each of the executive Departments, upon any Subject relating to the Duties of their respective Offices, and he shall have Power to grant Reprieves and Pardons for Offences against the United States, except in Cases of Impeachment.

He shall have Power, by and with the Advice and Consent of the Senate, to make Treaties, provided two thirds of the Senators present concur; and he shall nominate, and by and with the Advice and Consent of the Senate, shall appoint Ambassadors, other public Ministers and Consuls, Judges of the supreme Court, and all other Officers of the United States, whose Appointments are not herein otherwise provided for, and which shall be established by Law: but the Congress may by Law vest the Appointment of such inferior Officers, as they think proper, in the President alone, in the Courts of Law, or in the Heads of Departments.

The President shall have Power to fill up all Vacancies that may happen during the Recess of the Senate, by granting Commissions which shall expire at the End of their next Session.

Section. 3.

He shall from time to time give to the Congress Information of the State of the Union, and recommend to their Consideration such Measures as he shall judge necessary and expedient; he may, on extraordinary Occasions, convene both Houses, or either of them, and in Case of Disagreement between them, with Respect to the Time of Adjournment, he may adjourn them to such Time as he shall think proper; he shall receive Ambassadors and other public Ministers; he shall take Care that the Laws be faithfully executed, and shall Commission all the Officers of the United States.

Section. 4.

The President, Vice President and all civil Officers of the United States, shall be removed from Office on Impeachment for, and Conviction of, Treason, Bribery, or other high Crimes and Misdemeanors.

Article III.

Section. 1.

The judicial Power of the United States, shall be vested in one supreme Court, and in such inferior Courts as the Congress may from time to time ordain and establish. The Judges, both of the supreme and inferior Courts, shall hold their Offices during good Behaviour, and shall, at stated Times, receive for their Services, a Compensation, which shall not be diminished during their Continuance in Office.

Section. 2.

The judicial Power shall extend to all Cases, in Law and Equity, arising under this Constitution, the Laws of the United States, and Treaties made, or which shall be made, under their Authority;—to all Cases affecting Ambassadors, other public Ministers and Consuls;—to all Cases of admiralty and maritime Jurisdiction;—to Controversies to which the United States shall be a Party;—to Controversies between two or more States;—between a State and Citizens of another State,—between Citizens of different States,—between Citizens of the same State claiming Lands under Grants of different States, and between a State, or the Citizens thereof, and foreign States, Citizens or Subjects.

In all Cases affecting Ambassadors, other public Ministers and Consuls, and those in which a State shall be Party, the supreme Court shall have original Jurisdiction. In all the other Cases before mentioned, the supreme Court shall have appellate Jurisdiction, both as to Law and Fact, with such Exceptions, and under such Regulations as the Congress shall make.

The Trial of all Crimes, except in Cases of Impeachment, shall be by Jury; and such Trial shall be held in the State where the said Crimes shall have been committed; but when not committed within any State, the Trial shall be at such Place or Places as the Congress may by Law have directed.

Section. 3.

Treason against the United States, shall consist only in levying War against them, or in adhering to their Enemies, giving them Aid and Comfort. No Person shall be convicted of Treason unless on the Testimony of two Witnesses to the same overt Act, or on Confession in open Court.

The Congress shall have Power to declare the Punishment of Treason, but no Attainder of Treason shall work Corruption of Blood, or Forfeiture except during the Life of the Person attainted.

Article. IV.

Section. 1.

Full Faith and Credit shall be given in each State to the public Acts, Records, and judicial Proceedings of every other State. And the Congress may by general Laws prescribe the Manner in which such Acts, Records and Proceedings shall be proved, and the Effect thereof.

Section. 2.

The Citizens of each State shall be entitled to all Privileges and Immunities of Citizens in the several States.

A Person charged in any State with Treason, Felony, or other Crime, who shall flee from Justice, and be found in another State, shall on Demand of the executive Authority of the State from which he fled, be delivered up, to be removed to the State having Jurisdiction of the Crime.

No Person held to Service or Labour in one State, under the Laws thereof, escaping into another, shall, in Consequence of any Law or Regulation therein, be discharged from such Service or Labour, but shall be delivered up on Claim of the Party to whom such Service or Labour may be due.

Section. 3.

New States may be admitted by the Congress into this Union; but no new State shall be formed or erected within the Jurisdiction of any other State; nor any State be formed by the Junction of two or more States, or Parts of States, without the Consent of the Legislatures of the States concerned as well as of the Congress.

The Congress shall have Power to dispose of and make all needful Rules and Regulations respecting the Territory or other Property belonging to the United States; and nothing in this Constitution shall be so construed as to Prejudice any Claims of the United States, or of any particular State.

Section. 4.

The United States shall guarantee to every State in this Union a Republican Form of Government, and shall protect each of them against Invasion; and on Application of the Legislature, or of the Executive (when the Legislature cannot be convened) against domestic Violence.

Article. V.

The Congress, whenever two thirds of both Houses shall deem it necessary, shall propose Amendments to this Constitution, or, on the Application of the Legislatures of two thirds of the several States, shall call a Convention for proposing Amendments, which, in either Case, shall be valid to all Intents and Purposes, as Part of this Constitution, when ratified by the Legislatures of three fourths of the several States, or by Conventions in three fourths thereof, as the one or the other Mode of Ratification may be proposed by the Congress; Provided that no Amendment which may be made prior to the Year One thousand eight hundred and eight shall in any Manner affect the first and fourth Clauses in the Ninth Section of the first Article; and that no State, without its Consent, shall be deprived of its equal Suffrage in the Senate.

Article. VI.

All Debts contracted and Engagements entered into, before the Adoption of this Constitution, shall be as valid against the United States under this Constitution, as under the Confederation.

This Constitution, and the Laws of the United States which shall be made in Pursuance thereof; and all Treaties made, or which shall be made, under the Authority of the United States, shall be the supreme Law of the Land; and the Judges in every State shall be bound thereby, any Thing in the Constitution or Laws of any State to the Contrary notwithstanding.

The Senators and Representatives before mentioned, and the Members of the several State Legislatures, and all executive and judicial Officers, both of the United States and of the several States, shall be bound by Oath or Affirmation, to support this Constitution; but no religious Test shall ever be required as a Qualification to any Office or public Trust under the United States.

Article. VII.

The Ratification of the Conventions of nine States, shall be sufficient for the Establishment of this Constitution between the States so ratifying the Same.

The Word, "the," being interlined between the seventh and eighth Lines of the first Page, The Word "Thirty" being partly written on an Erazure in the fifteenth Line of the first Page, The Words "is tried" being interlined between the thirty second and thirty third Lines of the first Page and the Word "the" being interlined between the forty third and forty fourth Lines of the second Page.

ATTEST WILLIAM JACKSON SECRETARY

done in Convention by the Unanimous Consent of the States present the Seventeenth Day of September in the Year of our Lord one thousand seven hundred and Eighty seven and of the Independance of the United States of America the Twelfth In witness whereof We have hereunto subscribed our Names,

G°. WASHINGTON
Presidt and deputy from Virginia

[Signed also by: Geo: Read, Gunning Bedford jun, John Dickinson, Richard Bassett, Jaco: Broom, James McHenry, Dan of St Thos. Jenifer, Danl. Carroll, John Blair, James Madison Jr., Wm. Blount, Richd. Dobbs Spaight, Hu Williamson, J. Rutledge, Charles Cotesworth Pinckney, Charles Pinckney, Pierce Butler, William Few, Abr Baldwin, John Langdon, Nicholas Gilman, Nathaniel Gorham, Rufus King, Wm. Saml. Johnson, Roger Sherman, Alexander Hamilton, Wil: Livingston, David Brearley, Wm. Paterson, Jona: Dayton, B Franklin, Thomas Mifflin, Robt. Morris, Geo. Clymer, Thos. FitzSimons, Jared Ingersoll, James Wilson, Gouv Morris.]

102

U.S. Bill of Rights

The Bill of Rights—the first ten amendments to the U.S. Constitution—enumerates important individual liberties and places explicit limitations on the powers of the government. It is thought to have been inspired by, among other things, the Magna Carta of 1215, the English Bill of Rights of 1689, and the Virginia Declaration of Rights of 1776. Drafted largely by James Madison, the amendments comprising the Bill of Rights were initially proposed in part to shore up support for ratification of the Constitution by all of the states. They were formally ratified on December 15, 1791.

Amendment I

Congress shall make no law respecting an establishment of religion, or prohibiting the free exercise thereof; or abridging the freedom of speech, or of the press; or the right of the people peaceably to assemble, and to petition the Government for a redress of grievances.

Amendment II

A well regulated Militia, being necessary to the security of a free State, the right of the people to keep and bear Arms, shall not be infringed.

Amendment III

No Soldier shall, in time of peace be quartered in any house, without the consent of the Owner, nor in time of war, but in a manner to be prescribed by law.

SOURCE: U.S. Bill of Rights, 1791, "The Bill of Rights: A Transcription," National Archives, https://www.archives.gov/founding-docs/bill-of-rights-transcript.

Amendment IV

The right of the people to be secure in their persons, houses, papers, and effects, against unreasonable searches and seizures, shall not be violated, and no Warrants shall issue, but upon probable cause, supported by Oath or affirmation, and particularly describing the place to be searched, and the persons or things to be seized.

Amendment V

No person shall be held to answer for a capital, or otherwise infamous crime, unless on a presentment or indictment of a Grand Jury, except in cases arising in the land or naval forces, or in the Militia, when in actual service in time of War or public danger; nor shall any person be subject for the same offence to be twice put in jeopardy of life or limb; nor shall be compelled in any criminal case to be a witness against himself, nor be deprived of life, liberty, or property, without due process of law; nor shall private property be taken for public use, without just compensation.

Amendment VI

In all criminal prosecutions, the accused shall enjoy the right to a speedy and public trial, by an impartial jury of the State and district wherein the crime shall have been committed, which district shall have been previously ascertained by law, and to be informed of the nature and cause of the accusation; to be confronted with the witnesses against him; to have compulsory process for obtaining witnesses in his favor, and to have the Assistance of Counsel for his defence.

Amendment VII

In Suits at common law, where the value in controversy shall exceed twenty dollars, the right of trial by jury shall be preserved, and no fact tried by a jury, shall be otherwise re-examined in any Court of the United States, than according to the rules of the common law.

Amendment VIII

Excessive bail shall not be required, nor excessive fines imposed, nor cruel and unusual punishments inflicted.

Amendment IX

The enumeration in the Constitution, of certain rights, shall not be construed to deny or disparage others retained by the people.

Amendment X

The powers not delegated to the United States by the Constitution, nor prohibited by it to the States, are reserved to the States respectively, or to the people.

103

Federalist No. 10

The Federalist Papers is a historically important collection of eighty-five articles severally written by Alexander Hamilton, James Madison, and John Jay that were anonymously published under the pen name "Publius" in several New York newspapers during the late 1780s in a sustained effort to convince New Yorkers to support ratification of the U.S. Constitution. These articles offer valuable insight into at least some the original intentions of the framers of the Constitution, if for no other reason than because both Hamilton and Madison were members of the Constitutional Convention. Federalist No. 10 was authored by James Madison and was originally published in the *New York Packet* on November 23, 1787. It addresses how a representative republican form of government can help mitigate the dangers associated with partisan factions in a pluralistic society in service to the public good.

The Same Subject Continued: The Union as a Safeguard Against Domestic Faction and Insurrection

To the People of the State of New York:

AMONG the numerous advantages promised by a well-constructed Union, none deserves to be more accurately developed than its tendency to break and control the violence of faction. The friend of popular governments never finds himself so much alarmed for their character and fate, as when he contemplates their propensity to this dangerous vice. He will not fail, therefore, to set a due value on any plan which, without violating the principles to which he is attached, provides a proper cure for it. The instability, injustice, and confusion introduced into the public councils, have, in truth, been the

SOURCE: James Madison, "Federalist No. 10: The Same Subject Continued: The Union as a Safeguard against Domestic Faction and Insurrection," *New York Packet*, November 23, 1787, *Federalist Papers: Primary Documents in American History*, Library of Congress website, https://guides.loc.gov/federalist-papers/text-1-10#s-lg-box-wrapper-25493273.

mortal diseases under which popular governments have everywhere perished; as they continue to be the favorite and fruitful topics from which the
adversaries to liberty derive their most specious declamations. The valuable
improvements made by the American constitutions on the popular models, both ancient and modern, cannot certainly be too much admired; but it
would be an unwarrantable partiality, to contend that they have as effectually
obviated the danger on this side, as was wished and expected. Complaints are
everywhere heard from our most considerate and virtuous citizens, equally
the friends of public and private faith, and of public and personal liberty, that
our governments are too unstable, that the public good is disregarded in the
conflicts of rival parties, and that measures are too often decided, not according to the rules of justice and the rights of the minor party, but by the superior
force of an interested and overbearing majority. However anxiously we may
wish that these complaints had no foundation, the evidence, of known facts
will not permit us to deny that they are in some degree true. It will be found,
indeed, on a candid review of our situation, that some of the distresses under which we labor have been erroneously charged on the operation of our
governments; but it will be found, at the same time, that other causes will not
alone account for many of our heaviest misfortunes; and, particularly, for that
prevailing and increasing distrust of public engagements, and alarm for
private rights, which are echoed from one end of the continent to the other.
These must be chiefly, if not wholly, effects of the unsteadiness and injustice
with which a factious spirit has tainted our public administrations.

By a faction, I understand a number of citizens, whether amounting to a
majority or a minority of the whole, who are united and actuated by some
common impulse of passion, or of interest, adversed to the rights of other citizens, or to the permanent and aggregate interests of the community.

There are two methods of curing the mischiefs of faction: the one, by removing its causes; the other, by controlling its effects.

There are again two methods of removing the causes of faction: the one, by
destroying the liberty which is essential to its existence; the other, by giving
to every citizen the same opinions, the same passions, and the same interests.

It could never be more truly said than of the first remedy, that it was worse
than the disease. Liberty is to faction what air is to fire, an aliment without
which it instantly expires. But it could not be less folly to abolish liberty, which
is essential to political life, because it nourishes faction, than it would be to
wish the annihilation of air, which is essential to animal life, because it imparts
to fire its destructive agency.

The second expedient is as impracticable as the first would be unwise. As long as the reason of man continues fallible, and he is at liberty to exercise it, different opinions will be formed. As long as the connection subsists between his reason and his self-love, his opinions and his passions will have a reciprocal influence on each other; and the former will be objects to which the latter will attach themselves. The diversity in the faculties of men, from which the rights of property originate, is not less an insuperable obstacle to a uniformity of interests. The protection of these faculties is the first object of government. From the protection of different and unequal faculties of acquiring property, the possession of different degrees and kinds of property immediately results; and from the influence of these on the sentiments and views of the respective proprietors, ensues a division of the society into different interests and parties.

The latent causes of faction are thus sown in the nature of man; and we see them everywhere brought into different degrees of activity, according to the different circumstances of civil society. A zeal for different opinions concerning religion, concerning government, and many other points, as well of speculation as of practice; an attachment to different leaders ambitiously contending for pre-eminence and power; or to persons of other descriptions whose fortunes have been interesting to the human passions, have, in turn, divided mankind into parties, inflamed them with mutual animosity, and rendered them much more disposed to vex and oppress each other than to co-operate for their common good. So strong is this propensity of mankind to fall into mutual animosities, that where no substantial occasion presents itself, the most frivolous and fanciful distinctions have been sufficient to kindle their unfriendly passions and excite their most violent conflicts. But the most common and durable source of factions has been the various and unequal distribution of property. Those who hold and those who are without property have ever formed distinct interests in society. Those who are creditors, and those who are debtors, fall under a like discrimination. A landed interest, a manufacturing interest, a mercantile interest, a moneyed interest, with many lesser interests, grow up of necessity in civilized nations, and divide them into different classes, actuated by different sentiments and views. The regulation of these various and interfering interests forms the principal task of modern legislation, and involves the spirit of party and faction in the necessary and ordinary operations of the government.

No man is allowed to be a judge in his own cause, because his interest would certainly bias his judgment, and, not improbably, corrupt his integrity. With equal, nay with greater reason, a body of men are unfit to be both judges and parties at the same time; yet what are many of the most important acts of legislation, but so many judicial determinations, not indeed concerning the rights of single persons, but concerning the rights of large bodies of citizens? And what are the different classes of legislators but advocates and parties to the causes which they determine? Is a law proposed concerning private debts? It is a question to which the creditors are parties on one side and the debtors on the other. Justice ought to hold the balance between them. Yet the parties are, and must be, themselves the judges; and the most numerous party, or, in other words, the most powerful faction must be expected to prevail. Shall domestic manufactures be encouraged, and in what degree, by restrictions on foreign manufactures? are questions which would be differently decided by the landed and the manufacturing classes, and probably by neither with a sole regard to justice and the public good. The apportionment of taxes on the various descriptions of property is an act which seems to require the most exact impartiality; yet there is, perhaps, no legislative act in which greater opportunity and temptation are given to a predominant party to trample on the rules of justice. Every shilling with which they overburden the inferior number, is a shilling saved to their own pockets.

It is in vain to say that enlightened statesmen will be able to adjust these clashing interests, and render them all subservient to the public good. Enlightened statesmen will not always be at the helm. Nor, in many cases, can such an adjustment be made at all without taking into view indirect and remote considerations, which will rarely prevail over the immediate interest which one party may find in disregarding the rights of another or the good of the whole.

The inference to which we are brought is, that the CAUSES of faction cannot be removed, and that relief is only to be sought in the means of controlling its EFFECTS.

If a faction consists of less than a majority, relief is supplied by the republican principle, which enables the majority to defeat its sinister views by regular vote. It may clog the administration, it may convulse the society; but it will be unable to execute and mask its violence under the forms of the Constitution. When a majority is included in a faction, the form of popular government, on the other hand, enables it to sacrifice to its ruling passion or interest both the public good and the rights of other citizens. To secure the public good and private rights against the danger of such a faction, and at the same time to preserve the spirit and the form of popular government, is then the great object to which our inquiries are directed. Let me add that it is the great desideratum by which this form of government can be rescued from the opprobrium under which it has so long labored, and be recommended to the esteem and adoption of mankind.

By what means is this object attainable? Evidently by one of two only. Either the existence of the same passion or interest in a majority at the same time must be prevented, or the majority, having such coexistent passion or interest, must be rendered, by their number and local situation, unable to concert and carry into effect schemes of oppression. If the impulse and the opportunity be suffered to coincide, we well know that neither moral nor religious motives can be relied on as an adequate control. They are not found to be such on the injustice and violence of individuals, and lose their efficacy in proportion to the number combined together, that is, in proportion as their efficacy becomes needful.

From this view of the subject it may be concluded that a pure democracy, by which I mean a society consisting of a small number of citizens, who assemble and administer the government in person, can admit of no cure for the mischiefs of faction. A common passion or interest will, in almost every case, be felt by a majority of the whole; a communication and concert result from the form of government itself; and there is nothing to check the inducements to sacrifice the weaker party or an obnoxious individual. Hence it is that such democracies have ever been spectacles of turbulence and contention; have ever been found incompatible with personal security or the rights of property; and have in general been as short in their lives as they have been violent in their deaths. Theoretic politicians, who have patronized this species of government, have erroneously supposed that by reducing mankind to a perfect equality in their political rights, they would, at the same time, be perfectly equalized and assimilated in their possessions, their opinions, and their passions.

A republic, by which I mean a government in which the scheme of representation takes place, opens a different prospect, and promises the cure for which we are seeking. Let us examine the points in which it varies from pure democracy, and we shall comprehend both the nature of the cure and the efficacy which it must derive from the Union.

The two great points of difference between a democracy and a republic are: first, the delegation of the government, in the latter, to a small number of citizens elected by the rest; secondly, the greater number of citizens, and greater sphere of country, over which the latter may be extended.

The effect of the first difference is, on the one hand, to refine and enlarge the public views, by passing them through the medium of a chosen body of citizens, whose wisdom may best discern the true interest of their country, and whose patriotism and love of justice will be least likely to sacrifice it to temporary or partial considerations. Under such a regulation, it may well happen that the public voice, pronounced by the representatives of the people, will be more consonant to the public good than if pronounced by the people themselves, convened for the purpose. On the other hand, the effect may be inverted. Men of factious tempers, of local prejudices, or of sinister designs, may, by intrigue, by corruption, or by other means, first obtain the suffrages, and then betray the interests, of the people. The question resulting is, whether small or extensive republics are more favorable to the election of proper guardians of the public weal; and it is clearly decided in favor of the latter by two obvious considerations:

In the first place, it is to be remarked that, however small the republic may be, the representatives must be raised to a certain number, in order to guard against the cabals of a few; and that, however large it may be, they must be limited to a certain number, in order to guard against the confusion of a multitude. Hence, the number of representatives in the two cases not being in proportion to that of the two constituents, and being proportionally greater in the small republic, it follows that, if the proportion of fit characters be not less in the large than in the small republic, the former will present a greater option, and consequently a greater probability of a fit choice.

In the next place, as each representative will be chosen by a greater number of citizens in the large than in the small republic, it will be more difficult for unworthy candidates to practice with success the vicious arts by which elections are too often carried; and the suffrages of the people being more free, will be more likely to centre in men who possess the most attractive merit and the most diffusive and established characters.

It must be confessed that in this, as in most other cases, there is a mean, on both sides of which inconveniences will be found to lie. By enlarging too much the number of electors, you render the representatives too little acquainted with all their local circumstances and lesser interests; as by reducing it too much, you render him unduly attached to these, and too little fit to comprehend and pursue great and national objects. The federal Constitution forms a happy combination in this respect; the great and aggregate interests being referred to the national, the local and particular to the State legislatures.

The other point of difference is, the greater number of citizens and extent of territory which may be brought within the compass of republican than of democratic government; and it is this circumstance principally which renders factious combinations less to be dreaded in the former than in the latter. The smaller the society, the fewer probably will be the distinct parties and interests composing it; the fewer the distinct parties and interests, the more frequently will a majority be found of the same party; and the smaller the number of individuals composing a majority, and the smaller the compass within which they are placed, the more easily will they concert and execute their plans of oppression. Extend the sphere, and you take in a greater variety of parties and interests; you make it less probable that a majority of the whole will have a common motive to invade the rights of other citizens; or if such a common motive exists, it will be more difficult for all who feel it to discover their own strength, and to act in unison with each other. Besides other impediments, it may be remarked that, where there is a consciousness of unjust or dishonorable purposes, communication is always checked by distrust in proportion to the number whose concurrence is necessary.

Hence, it clearly appears, that the same advantage which a republic has over a democracy, in controlling the effects of faction, is enjoyed by a large over a small republic,—is enjoyed by the Union over the States composing it. Does the advantage consist in the substitution of representatives whose enlightened views and virtuous sentiments render them superior to local prejudices and schemes of injustice? It will not be denied that the representation of the Union will be most likely to possess these requisite endowments. Does it consist in the greater security afforded by a greater variety of parties, against the event of any one party being able to outnumber and oppress the rest? In an equal degree does the increased variety of parties comprised within the Union, increase this security. Does it, in fine, consist in the greater obstacles opposed to the concert and accomplishment of the secret wishes of an unjust and interested majority? Here, again, the extent of the Union gives it the most palpable advantage.

The influence of factious leaders may kindle a flame within their particular States, but will be unable to spread a general conflagration through the other States. A religious sect may degenerate into a political faction in a part of the Confederacy; but the variety of sects dispersed over the entire face of it must secure the national councils against any danger from that source. A rage for paper money, for an abolition of debts, for an equal division of property, or for any other improper or wicked project, will be less apt to pervade the whole body of the Union than a particular member of it; in the same proportion as such a malady is more likely to taint a particular county or district, than an entire State.

In the extent and proper structure of the Union, therefore, we behold a republican remedy for the diseases most incident to republican government. And according to the degree of pleasure and pride we feel in being republicans, ought to be our zeal in cherishing the spirit and supporting the character of Federalists.

104

Federalist No. 51

Federalist No. 51 was originally published under the pen name "Publius" in *New York Packet* on February 8, 1788. It was authored by either Alexander Hamilton or James Madison and defends the system of checks and balances provided for by the U.S. Constitution. Together with Federalist No. 10, it is widely considered to be one of the most important political writings in American history.

The Structure of the Government Must Furnish the Proper Checks and Balances Between the Different Departments

To the People of the State of New York:

TO WHAT expedient, then, shall we finally resort, for maintaining in practice the necessary partition of power among the several departments, as laid down in the Constitution? The only answer that can be given is, that as all these exterior provisions are found to be inadequate, the defect must be supplied, by so contriving the interior structure of the government as that its several constituent parts may, by their mutual relations, be the means of keeping each other in their proper places. Without presuming to undertake a full development of this important idea, I will hazard a few general observations, which may perhaps place it in a clearer light, and enable us to form a more correct judgment of the principles and structure of the government planned by the convention. In order to lay a due foundation for that separate and distinct exercise of the different powers of government, which to a certain extent is admitted on all hands to be essential to the preservation of liberty, it

source: Alexander Hamilton or James Madison, "Federalist No. 51: The Structure of the Government Must Furnish the Proper Checks and Balances between the Different Departments," *New York Packet*, February 8, 1788, *Federalist Papers: Primary Documents in American History*, Library of Congress website, https://guides.loc.gov/federalist-papers/text-51-60#s-lg-box-wrapper-25493427.

is evident that each department should have a will of its own; and consequently should be so constituted that the members of each should have as little agency as possible in the appointment of the members of the others. Were this principle rigorously adhered to, it would require that all the appointments for the supreme executive, legislative, and judiciary magistracies should be drawn from the same fountain of authority, the people, through channels having no communication whatever with one another. Perhaps such a plan of constructing the several departments would be less difficult in practice than it may in contemplation appear. Some difficulties, however, and some additional expense would attend the execution of it. Some deviations, therefore, from the principle must be admitted. In the constitution of the judiciary department in particular, it might be inexpedient to insist rigorously on the principle: first, because peculiar qualifications being essential in the members, the primary consideration ought to be to select that mode of choice which best secures these qualifications; secondly, because the permanent tenure by which the appointments are held in that department, must soon destroy all sense of dependence on the authority conferring them. It is equally evident, that the members of each department should be as little dependent as possible on those of the others, for the emoluments annexed to their offices. Were the executive magistrate, or the judges, not independent of the legislature in this particular, their independence in every other would be merely nominal. But the great security against a gradual concentration of the several powers in the same department, consists in giving to those who administer each department the necessary constitutional means and personal motives to resist encroachments of the others. The provision for defense must in this, as in all other cases, be made commensurate to the danger of attack. Ambition must be made to counteract ambition. The interest of the man must be connected with the constitutional rights of the place. It may be a reflection on human nature, that such devices should be necessary to control the abuses of government. But what is government itself, but the greatest of all reflections on human nature? If men were angels, no government would be necessary. If angels were to govern men, neither external nor internal controls on government would be necessary. In framing a government which is to be administered by men over men, the great difficulty lies in this: you must first enable the government to control the governed; and in the next place oblige it to control itself. A dependence on the people is, no doubt, the primary control on the government; but experience has taught mankind the necessity of auxiliary precautions. This policy of supplying, by opposite and rival interests, the defect of better motives, might be traced through the whole system of human affairs, private as well as public. We see it particularly displayed in all the subordinate distributions of power, where the constant aim is to divide and arrange the several offices in such a manner as that each may be a check on the other that the private interest of every individual may be a sentinel over the public rights. These inventions of prudence cannot be less requisite in the distribution of the supreme powers of the State. But it is not possible to give to each department an equal power of self-defense. In republican government, the legislative authority necessarily predominates. The remedy for this inconveniency is to divide the legislature into different branches; and to render them, by different modes of election and different principles of action, as little connected with each other as the nature of their common functions and their common dependence on the society will admit. It may even be necessary to guard against dangerous encroachments by still further precautions. As the weight of the legislative authority requires that it should be thus divided, the weakness of the executive may require, on the other hand, that it should be fortified. An absolute negative on the legislature appears, at first view, to be the natural defense with which the executive magistrate should be armed. But perhaps it would be neither altogether safe nor alone sufficient. On ordinary occasions it might not be exerted with the requisite firmness, and on extraordinary occasions it might be perfidiously abused. May not this defect of an absolute negative be supplied by some qualified connection between this weaker department and the weaker branch of the stronger department, by which the latter may be led to support the constitutional rights of the former, without being too much detached from the rights of its own department? If the principles on which these observations are founded be just, as I persuade myself they are, and they be applied as a criterion to the several State constitutions, and to the federal Constitution it will be found that if the latter does not perfectly correspond with them, the former are infinitely less able to bear such a test. There are, moreover, two considerations particularly applicable to the federal system of America, which place that system in a very interesting point of view. First. In a single republic, all the power surrendered by the people is submitted to the administration of a single government; and the usurpations are guarded against by a division of the government into distinct and separate departments. In the compound republic of America, the power surrendered by the people is first divided between two distinct governments, and then the portion allotted to each subdivided among distinct and separate departments. Hence a double security arises to the rights of the people. The different governments will control each other, at the same time that each will be controlled by itself. Second. It is of great importance in a republic not only to guard the society against the oppression of its rulers, but to guard one part of the society against the injustice of the other part. Different interests necessarily exist in different classes of citizens. If a majority be united by a common interest, the rights of the minority will be insecure. There are but two methods of providing against this evil: the one by creating a will in the community independent of the majority that is, of the society itself; the other, by comprehending in the society so many separate descriptions of citizens as will render an unjust combination of a majority of the whole very improbable, if not impracticable. The first method prevails in all governments possessing an hereditary or self-appointed authority. This, at best, is but a precarious security; because a power independent of the society may as well espouse the unjust views of the major, as the rightful interests of the minor party, and may possibly be turned against both parties. The second method will be exemplified in the federal republic of the United States. Whilst all authority in it will be derived from and dependent on the society, the society itself will be broken into so many parts, interests, and classes of citizens, that the rights of individuals, or of the minority, will be in little danger from interested combinations of the majority. In a free government the security for civil rights must be the same as that for religious rights. It consists in the one case in the multiplicity of interests, and in the other in the multiplicity of sects. The degree of security in both cases will depend on the number of interests and sects; and this may be presumed to depend on the extent of country and number of people comprehended under the same government. This view of the subject must particularly recommend a proper federal system to all the sincere and considerate friends of republican government, since it shows that in exact proportion as the territory of the Union may be formed into more circumscribed Confederacies, or States[,] oppressive combinations of a majority will be facilitated: the best security, under the republican forms, for the rights of every class of citizens, will be diminished: and consequently the stability and independence of some member of the government, the only other security, must be proportionately increased. Justice is the end of government. It is the end of civil society. It ever has been and ever will be pursued until it be obtained, or until liberty be lost in the pursuit. In a society under the forms of which the stronger faction can readily unite and oppress the weaker, anarchy may as truly be said to reign as in a state of nature, where the weaker individual is not secured against the violence of the stronger; and as, in the latter state, even the stronger individuals are prompted, by the uncertainty of their condition, to submit to a government which may protect the weak as well as themselves; so, in the former state, will the more powerful factions or parties be gradually induced, by a like motive, to wish for a government which will protect all parties, the weaker as well as the more powerful. It can be little doubted that if the State of Rhode Island was separated from the Confederacy and left to itself, the insecurity of rights under the popular form of government within such narrow limits would be displayed by such reiterated oppressions of factious majorities that some power altogether independent of the people would soon be called for by the voice of the very factions whose misrule had proved the necessity of it. In the extended republic of the United States, and among the great variety of interests, parties, and sects which it embraces, a coalition of a majority of the whole society could seldom take place on any other principles than those of justice and the general good; whilst there being thus less danger to a minor from the will of a major party, there must be less pretext, also, to provide for the security of the former, by introducing into the government a will not dependent on the latter, or, in other words, a will independent of the society itself. It is no less certain than it is important, notwithstanding the contrary opinions which have been entertained, that the larger the society, provided it lie within a practical sphere, the more duly capable it will be of self-government. And happily for the REPUBLICAN CAUSE, the practicable sphere may be carried to a very great extent, by a judicious modification and mixture of the FEDERAL PRINCIPLE.

PUBLIUS.

105

Mary Wollstonecraft

from *A Vindication of the Rights of Woman*

English author and early pioneer of women's rights Mary Wollstonecraft (1759–1797) confronted the chauvinism of the eighteenth century with strategy and tact. Her work *A Vindication of the Rights of Woman* (1792) has both inspired and challenged societies wherever it has been read. The following excerpt is the dedication to that volume, in which she addresses Charles-Maurice de Talleyrand-Périgord, the French politician, diplomat, and clergyman, whose "Report on Public Instruction" for the French National Assembly in 1791 contended that an education in the domestic arts was sufficient for women. Wollstonecraft explains the logic of educating males and females equally, and in a common curriculum.

TO M. TALLEYRAND-PERIGORD,
Late Bishop of Autun.

SIR,—Having read with great pleasure a pamphlet which you have lately published, I dedicate this volume to you; to induce you to reconsider the subject, and maturely weigh what I have advanced respecting the rights of woman and national education: and I call with the firm tone of humanity; for my arguments, sir, are dictated by a disinterested spirit—I plead for my sex—not for myself. Independence I have long considered as the grand blessing of life, the basis of every virtue—and independence I will ever secure by contracting my wants, though I were to live on a barren heath.

It is then an affection for the whole human race that makes my pen dart rapidly along to support what I believe to be the cause of virtue; and the same motive leads me earnestly to wish to see woman placed in a station in which

SOURCE: Mary Wollstonecraft, *A Vindication of the Rights of Woman with Strictures on Political and Moral Subjects* (London: T. Fisher Unwin, 1891), vii–xii.

she would advance, instead of retarding, the progress of those glorious principles that give a substance to morality. My opinion, indeed, respecting the rights and duties of woman, seems to flow so naturally from these simple principles, that I think it scarcely possible, but that some of the enlarged minds who formed your admirable constitution will coincide with me.

In France there is undoubtedly a more general diffusion of knowledge than in any part of the European world, and I attribute it, in a great measure, to the social intercourse which has long subsisted between the sexes. It is true, I utter my sentiments with freedom, that in France the very essence of sensuality has been extracted to regale the voluptuary, and a kind of sentimental lust has prevailed, which, together with the system of duplicity that the whole tenor of their political and civil government taught, have given a sinister sort of sagacity to the French character, properly termed finesse; from which naturally flow a polish of manners that injures the substance, by hunting sincerity out of society. And, modesty, the fairest garb of virtue! has been more grossly insulted in France than even in England, till their women have treated as *prudish* that attention to decency which brutes instinctively observe.

Manners and morals are so nearly allied that they have often been confounded; but, though the former should only be the natural reflection of the latter, yet, when various causes have produced factitious and corrupt manners, which are very early caught, morality becomes an empty name. The personal reserve, and sacred respect for cleanliness and delicacy in domestic life, which French women almost despise, are the graceful pillars of modesty; but, far from despising them, if the pure flame of patriotism have reached their bosoms, they should labour to improve the morals of their fellow-citizens, by teaching men, not only to respect modesty in women, but to acquire it themselves, as the only way to merit their esteem.

Contending for the rights of woman, my main argument is built on this simple principle, that if she be not prepared by education to become the companion of man, she will stop the progress of knowledge and virtue; for truth must be common to all, or it will be inefficacious with respect to its influence on general practice. And how can woman be expected to co-operate unless she know why she ought to be virtuous? unless freedom strengthen her reason till she comprehend her duty, and see in what manner it is connected with her real good? If children are to be educated to understand the true principle of patriotism, their mother must be a patriot; and the love of mankind, from which an orderly train of virtues spring, can only be produced by considering the moral and civil interest of mankind; but the education and situation of woman, at present, shuts her out from such investigations.

In this work I have produced many arguments, which to me were conclusive, to prove that the prevailing notion respecting a sexual character was subversive of morality, and I have contended, that to render the human body and mind more perfect, chastity must more universally prevail, and that chastity will never be respected in the male world till the person of a woman is not, as it were, idolized, when little virtue or sense embellish it with the grand traces of mental beauty, or the interesting simplicity of affection.

Consider, sir, dispassionately, these observations—for a glimpse of this truth seemed to open before you when you observed, "that to see one half of the human race excluded by the other from all participation of government, was a political phenomenon that, according to abstract principles, it was impossible to explain." If so, on what does your constitution rest? If the abstract rights of man will bear discussion and explanation, those of woman, by a parity of reasoning, will not shrink from the same test; though a different opinion prevails in this country, built on the very arguments which you use to justify the oppression of woman—prescription.

Consider—I address you as a legislator—whether, when men contend for their freedom, and to be allowed to judge for themselves respecting their own happiness, it be not inconsistent and unjust to subjugate women, even though you firmly believe that you are acting in the manner best calculated to promote their happiness? Who made man the exclusive judge, if woman partake with him the gift of reason.

In this style, argue tyrants of every denomination, from the weak king to the weak father of a family; they are all eager to crush reason; yet always assert that they usurp its throne only to be useful. Do you not act a similar part, when you *force* all women, by denying them civil and political rights, to remain immured in their families groping in the dark? for surely, sir, you will not assert that a duty can be binding which is not founded on reason? If, indeed, this be their destination, arguments may be drawn from reason: and thus augustly supported, the more understanding women acquire, the more they will be attached to their duty—comprehending it—for unless they comprehend it, unless their morals be fixed on the same immutable principle as those of man, no authority can make them discharge it in a virtuous manner. They may be convenient slaves, but slavery will have its constant effect, degrading the master and the abject dependent.

But, if women are to be excluded, without having a voice, from a participation of the natural rights of mankind, prove first, to ward off the charge of injustice and inconsistency, that they want reason—else this flaw in your NEW CONSTITUTION will ever show that man must, in some shape, act like a tyrant; and tyranny, in whatever part of society it rears its brazen front, will ever undermine morality.

I have repeatedly asserted, and produced what appeared to me irrefragable arguments drawn from matters of fact, to prove my assertion, that women cannot, by force, be confined to domestic concerns; for they will, however ignorant, intermeddle with more weighty affairs, neglecting private duties only to disturb, by cunning tricks, the orderly plans of reason which rise above their comprehension.

Besides, whilst they are only made to acquire personal accomplishments, men will seek for pleasure in variety, and faithless husbands will make faithless wives: such ignorant beings, indeed, will be very excusable when, not taught to respect public good, nor allowed any civil rights, they attempt to do themselves justice by retaliation.

The box of mischief thus opened in society, what is to preserve private virtue, the only security of public freedom and universal happiness?

Let there be then no coercion *established* in society, and the common law of gravity prevailing, the sexes will fall into their proper places. And, now that more equitable laws are forming your citizens, marriage may become more sacred: your young men may choose wives from motives of affection, and your maidens allow love to root out vanity.

The father of a family will not then weaken his constitution and debase his sentiments by visiting the harlot, nor forget, in obeying the call of appetite, the purpose for which it was implanted. And, the mother will not neglect her children to practise the arts of coquetry, when sense and modesty secure her the friendship of her husband.

But, till men become attentive to the duty of a father, it is vain to expect women to spend that time in their nursery which they, "wise in their generation," choose to spend at their glass; for this exertion of cunning is only an instinct of nature to enable them to obtain indirectly a little of that power of which they are unjustly denied a share: for, if women are not permitted to enjoy legitimate rights, they will render both men and themselves vicious, to obtain illicit privileges.

I wish, sir, to set some investigations of this kind afloat in France; and should they lead to a confirmation of my principles when your constitution is revised the Rights of Woman may be respected, if it be fully proved that reason calls for this respect, and loudly demands JUSTICE for one half of the human race.—I am, sir, yours respectfully,

M.W.

106

George Washington

from *Farewell Address to the People of the United States*
of America

The imprint of George Washington (1732–1799) on the early history of the United States is incalculable; hence, the attribution "Father of his country." In 1775 the Continental Congress called him to serve as commander in chief of the colonial armies, a role he held until the end of the Revolution (1783). In 1787 he served as president of the Constitutional Convention. Then in 1788 he was elected as the first President of the United States. Completing two four-year terms as the nation's executive, he drafted a valediction to counsel the nation he had worked diligently to form. In this Farewell Address (1796) he thanks the citizenry for their fidelity and support, but also provides "parental" advice, warning of tendencies and challenges that could stifle the promise and potential of the new nation.

To the People of the United States.

FRIENDS AND FELLOW CITIZENS:—The period for a new election of a citizen to administer the executive government of the United States being not far distant, and the time actually arrived when your thoughts must be employed in designating the person who is to be clothed with that important trust, it appears to me proper, especially as it may conduce to a more distinct expression of the public voice, that I should now apprize you of the resolution I have formed, to decline being considered among the number of those, out of whom a choice is to be made.

[. . . .]

SOURCE: George Washington, *Farewell Address to the People of the United States of America: Published in September, 1796* (Harrisburg: Isaac G. M'Kinley, state printer, 1844), 3–13.

Here, perhaps, I ought to stop. But a solicitude for your welfare, which cannot end but with my life, and the apprehension of danger, natural to that solicitude, urge me, on an occasion like the present, to offer to your solemn contemplation, and to recommend to your frequent review, some sentiments which are the result of much reflection, of no inconsiderable observation, and which appear to me all important to the permanency of your felicity as a people. These will be offered to you with the more freedom, as you can only see in them the disinterested warnings of a parting friend, who can possibly have no personal motive to bias his counsel. Nor can I forget, as an encouragement to it, your indulgent reception of my sentiments on a former and not dissimilar occasion.

Interwoven as is the love of liberty with every ligament of your hearts, no recommendation of mine is necessary to fortify or confirm the attachment.

The unity of government which constitutes you one people, is also now dear to you. It is justly so; for it is a main pillar in the edifice of your real independence; the support of your tranquility at home; your peace abroad; of your safety; of your prosperity; of that very liberty which you so highly prize. But as it is easy to foresee that, from different causes and from different quarters, much pains will be taken, many artifices employed, to weaken in your minds the conviction of this truth; as this is the point in your political fortress against which the batteries of internal and external enemies will be most constantly and actively, (though often covertly and insidiously,) directed; it is of infinite moment, that you should properly estimate the immense value of your national union to your collective and individual happiness . . . .

[. . . .]

While then every part of our country thus feels an immediate and particular interest in union, all the parts combined cannot fail to find in the united mass of means and efforts, greater strength, greater resource, proportionably greater security from external danger, a less frequent interruption of their peace by foreign nations; and, what is of inestimable value, they must derive from union, an exemption from those broils and wars between themselves, which so frequently afflict neighboring countries, not tied together by the same government; which their own rivalship alone would be sufficient to produce, but which opposite foreign alliances, attachments and intrigues, would stimulate and embitter. Hence, likewise, they will avoid the necessity of those overgrown military establishments, which under any form of government, are inauspicious to liberty, and which are to be regarded as particularly hostile to republican liberty. In this sense it is, that your union ought to be considered as a main prop of your liberty, and that the love of the one ought to endear to you the preservation of the other.

[. . . .]

In contemplating the causes which may disturb our union, it occurs as matter of serious concern, that any ground should have been furnished for characterizing parties by *geographical* discriminations—*northern* and *southern*—*Atlantic* and *western*; whence designing men may endeavor to excite a belief that there is a real difference of local interests and views. One of the expedients of party to acquire influence within particular districts, is to misrepresent the opinions and aims of other districts. You cannot shield yourselves too much against the jealousies and heart-burnings which spring from these misrepresentations: they tend to render alien to each other those who ought to be bound together by fraternal affection. . . .

[. . . .]

I have already intimated to you the danger of parties in the State, with particular references to the founding them on geographical discrimination. Let me now take a more comprehensive view, and warn you in the most solemn manner against the baneful effects of the spirit of party generally.

This spirit, unfortunately, is inseparable from our nature, having its root in the strongest passions of the human mind. It exists under different shapes in all governments, more or less stifled, controlled, or repressed; but in those of the popular form, it is seen in its greatest rankness, and is truly their worst enemy.

The alternate domination of one faction over another, sharpened by the spirit of revenge natural to party dissension, which, in different ages and countries, has perpetrated the most horrid enormities, is itself a frightful despotism. But this leads at length to a more formal and permanent despotism. The disorders and miseries which result, gradually incline the minds of men to seek security and repose in the absolute power of an individual and, sooner or later, the chief of some prevailing faction, more able or more fortunate than his competitors, turns this disposition to the purpose of his own elevation, on the ruins of public liberty.

Without looking forward to an extremity of this kind, (which, nevertheless, ought not to be entirely out of sight,) the common and continual mischiefs of the spirit of party are sufficient to make it the interest and duty of a wise people to discourage and restrain it.

It serves always to distract the public councils, and enfeeble the public administration. It agitates the community with ill-founded jealousies and false alarms; kindles the animosity of one part against another; foments occasional riot and insurrection. It opens the door to foreign influence and corruption, which finds a facilitated access to the government itself, through the channels of party passions. Thus, the policy and the will of one country are subjected to the policy and will of another.

[. . . .]

It is important, likewise, that the habits of thinking in a free country should inspire caution in those intrusted with its administration, to confine themselves within their respective constitutional spheres, avoiding, in the exercise of the powers of one department, to encroach upon another. The spirit of encroachment tends to consolidate the powers of all the departments in one, and thus to create, whatever the form of government, a real despotism. A just estimate of that love of power and proneness to abuse it which predominate in the human heart, is sufficient to satisfy us of the truth of this position. The necessity of reciprocal checks, in the exercise of political power, by dividing and distributing it into different depositories, and constituting each the guardian of the public weal against invasions of the others, has been evinced by experiments, ancient and modern; some of them in our country and under our own eyes. To preserve them must be as necessary as to institute them. If, in the opinion of the people, the distribution or modification of the constitutional powers be in any particular wrong, let it be corrected by an amendment in the way which the constitution designates. But let there be no change by usurpation; for though this, in one instance, may be the instrument of good, it is the customary weapon by which free governments are destroyed. The precedent must always greatly overbalance, in permanent evil, any partial or transient benefit which the use can at any time yield.

Of all the dispositions and habits which lead to political prosperity, Religion and Morality are indispensable supports. In vain would that man claim the tribute of patriotism, who should labor to subvert these great pillars of human happiness, these firmest props of the duties of men and citizens. The mere politician, equally with the pious man, ought to respect and to cherish them. A volume could not trace all their connexions with private and public felicity. Let it simply be asked, where is the security for property, for reputation, for life, if the sense of religious obligation *desert* the oaths which are the instruments of investigation in courts of justice? And let us, with caution, indulge the supposition that morality can be maintained without religion. Whatever may be conceded to the influence of refined education on minds of peculiar structure, reason and experience both forbid us to expect, that national morality can [p]revail in exclusion of religious principle.

It is substantially true, that virtue or morality is a necessary spring of popular government. The rule indeed extends, with more or less force, to every species of free government. Who, that is a sincere friend to it, can look with indifference upon attempts to shake the foundation of the fabric?

Promote then, as an object of primary importance, institutions for the general diffusion of knowledge. In proportion as the structure of a government gives force to public opinion, it should be enlightened.

As a very important source of strength and security, cherish public credit. One method of preserving it, is to use it as sparingly as possible, avoiding occasions of expense by cultivating peace, but remembering also, that timely disbursements, to prepare for danger, frequently prevent much greater disbursements to repel it; avoiding, likewise, the accumulation of debt, not only by shunning occasions of expense, but by vigorous exertions, in time of peace, to discharge the debts which unavoidable wars may have occasioned, not ungenerously throwing upon posterity the burden which we ourselves ought to bear. The execution of those maxims belongs to your representatives, but it is necessary that public opinion should co-operate. To facilitate to them the performance of their duty, it is essential that you should practically bear in mind, that towards the payment of debts there must be revenue, that to have revenue there must be taxes; that no taxes can be devised, which are not more or less inconvenient and unpleasant; that the intrinsic embarrassment, inseparable from the selection of the proper object, (which is always a choice of difficulties,) ought to be a decisive motive for a candid construction of the conduct of the government in making it, and for a spirit of acquiescence in the measures for obtaining revenue, which the public exigencies may at any time dictate.

Observe good faith and justice towards all nations; cultivate peace and harmony with all. Religion and morality enjoin this conduct, and can it be that good policy does not equally enjoin it? It will be worthy of a free, enlightened, and, at no distant period, a great nation, to give to mankind the magnanimous and too novel example of a people always guided by an exalted justice and benevolence. Who can doubt but, in the course of time and things, the fruits of such a plan would richly repay any temporary advantages which might be lost by a steady adherence to it; can it be that Providence has not connected the permanent felicity of a nation with its virtue? The experiment, at least, is recommended by every sentiment which ennobles human nature. Alas! it is rendered impossible by its vices.

[. . . .]

The great rule of conduct for us, in regard to foreign nations, is, in extending our commercial relations, to have with them as little *political* connexion as possible. So far as we have already formed engagements, let them be fulfilled with perfect good faith: Here let us stop.

Europe has a set of primary interests, which to us have none, or a very remote relation. Hence, she must be engaged in frequent controversies, the causes of which are essentially foreign to our concerns. Hence, therefore, it must be unwise in us to implicate ourselves, by artificial ties, in the ordinary vicissitudes of her politics, or the ordinary combinations and collisions of her friendships or enmities.

[. . . .]

Relying on its kindness in this as in other things, and actuated by that fervent love towards it, which is so natural to a man who views in it the native soil of himself and his progenitors for several generations; I anticipate with pleasing expectations that retreat in which I promise myself to realize, without alloy, the sweet enjoyment of partaking, in the midst of my fellow citizens, the benign influence of good laws under a free government—the ever favorite object of my heart, and the happy reward, as I trust, of our mutual cares, labors and dangers.

GEO. WASHINGTON.

UNITED STATES, *17th September,* 1796.

107

Declaration of the Rights of Man and Citizen

Adopted by the French National Assembly in 1789, the Declaration of the Rights of Man and Citizen sets forth the central affirmations concerning universal human rights that helped animate the French Revolution. It would ultimately be enshrined as the preamble to the French Constitution of 1791. Along with the Magna Carta and the U.S. Bill of Rights, it stands out as a prominent document in the history of civil rights.

The representatives of the French people, organized in National Assembly, considering that ignorance, forgetfulness or contempt of the rights of man, are the sole causes of the public miseries and of the corruption of governments, have resolved to set forth in a solemn declaration the natural, inalienable, and sacred rights of man, in order that this declaration, being ever present to all the members of the social body, may unceasingly remind them of their rights and their duties in order that the acts of the legislative power and those of the executive power may be each moment compared with the aim of every political institution and thereby may be more respected; and in order that the demands of the citizens, grounded henceforth upon simple and incontestable principles, may always take the direction of maintaining the constitution and the welfare of all.

In consequence, the National Assembly recognizes and declares, in the presence and under the auspices of the Supreme Being, the following rights of man and citizen.

1. Men are born and remain free and equal in rights. Social distinctions can be based only upon public utility.

SOURCE: "Declaration of the Rights of Man and Citizen," in Frank Maloy Anderson, *The Constitutions and Other Select Documents Illustrative of the History of France, 1789–1901* (Minneapolis: H. W. Wilson, 1904), 58–60.

2. The aim of every political association is the preservation of the natural and imprescriptible rights of man. These rights are liberty, property, security, and resistance to oppression.

3. The source of all sovereignty is essentially in the nation; no body, no individual can exercise authority that does not proceed from it in plain terms.

4. Liberty consists in the power to do anything that does not injure others; accordingly, the exercise of the natural rights of each man has for its only limits those that secure to the other members of society the enjoyment of these same rights. These limits can be determined only by law.

5. The law has the right to forbid only such actions as are injurious to society. Nothing can be forbidden that is not interdicted by the law, and no one can be constrained to do that which it does not order.

6. Law is the expression of the general will. All citizens have the right to take part personally or by their representatives in its formation. It must be the same for all, whether it protects or punishes. All citizens being equal in its eyes, are equally eligible to all public dignities, places, and employments, according to their capacities, and without other distinction than that of their virtues and their talents.

7. No man can be accused, arrested, or detained except in the cases determined by the law and according to the forms that it has prescribed. Those who procure, expedite, execute, or cause to be executed arbitrary orders ought to be punished: but every citizen summoned or seized in virtue of the law ought to render instant obedience; he makes himself guilty by resistance.

8. The law ought to establish only penalties that are strictly and obviously necessary, and no one can be punished except in virtue of a law established and promulgated prior to the offence and legally applied.

9. Every man being presumed innocent until he has been pronounced guilty, if it is thought indispensable to arrest him, all severity that may not be necessary to secure his person ought to be strictly suppressed by law.

10. No one ought to be disturbed on account of his opinions, even religious, provided their manifestation does not derange the public order established by law.

11. The free communication of ideas and opinions is one of the most precious of the rights of man; every citizen then can freely speak, write, and print, subject to responsibility for the abuse of this freedom in the cases determined by law.

12. The guarantee of the rights of man and citizen requires a public force; this force then is instituted for the advantage of all and not for the personal benefit of those to whom it is entrusted.

13. For the maintenance of the public force and for the expenses of administration a general tax is indispensable; it ought to be equally apportioned among all the citizens according to their means.

14. All the citizens have the right to ascertain, by themselves or by their representatives, the necessity of the public tax, to consent to it freely, to follow the employment of it, and to determine the quota, the assessment, the collection, and the duration of it.

15. Society has the right to call for an account of his administration from every public agent.

16. Any society in which the guarantee of the rights is not secured or the separation of powers not determined has no constitution at all.

17. Property being a sacred and inviolable right, no one can be deprived of it unless a legally established public necessity evidently demands it, under the condition of a just and prior indemnity.

108

Edmund Burke

from *Reflections on the Revolution in France*

Edmund Burke (1729–1797) was an Irish-British political thinker, traditionalist, and politician who is often regarded as a father of modern conservatism. He was supportive of the colonies during the American Revolution, but he is perhaps most famous for his scathing critique of the French Revolution. The following is an excerpt from his best-known work, *Reflections on the Revolution in France*, in which he expresses his apprehension over what he took to be the hopelessly abstract and metaphysical underpinnings of the French Revolution.

Government is not made in virtue of natural rights, which may and do exist in total independence of it,—and exist in much greater clearness, and in a much greater degree of abstract perfection: but their abstract perfection is their practical defect. By having a right to everything they want everything. Government is a contrivance of human wisdom to provide for human *wants*. Men have a right that these wants should be provided for by this wisdom. Among these wants is to be reckoned the want, out of civil society, of a sufficient restraint upon their passions. Society requires not only that the passions of individuals should be subjected, but that even in the mass and body, as well as in the individuals, the inclinations of men should frequently be thwarted, their will controlled, and their passions brought into subjection. This can only be done *by a power out of themselves*, and not, in the exercise of its function, subject to that will and to those passions which it is its office to bridle and subdue. In this sense the restraints on men, as well as their liberties, are to be reckoned among their rights. But as the liberties and the

SOURCE: Edmund Burke, *Reflections on the Revolution in France*, in *The Writings & Speeches of Edmund Burke, in Twelve Volumes*, vol. 3, *On the Nabob of Arcot's Debts; Speech on the Army Estimates; Reflections on the Revolution in France* (Boston: Little, Brown, and Co., 1901), 310–16.

restrictions vary with times and circumstances, and admit of infinite modifications, they cannot be settled upon any abstract rule; and nothing is so foolish as to discuss them upon that principle.

The moment you abate anything from the full rights of men each to govern himself, and suffer any artificial, positive limitation upon those rights, from that moment the whole organization of government becomes a consideration of convenience. This it is which makes the constitution of a state, and the due distribution of its powers, a matter of the most delicate and complicated skill. It requires a deep knowledge of human nature and human necessities, and of the things which facilitate or obstruct the various ends which are to be pursued by the mechanism of civil institutions. The state is to have recruits to its strength and remedies to its distempers. What is the use of discussing a man's abstract right to food or medicine? The question is upon the method of procuring and administering them. In that deliberation I shall always advise to call in the aid of the farmer and the physician, rather than the professor of metaphysics.

The science of constructing a commonwealth, or renovating it, or reforming it, is, like every other experimental science, not to be taught *a priori*. Nor is it a short experience that can instruct us in that practical science; because the real effects of moral causes are not always immediate, but that which in the first instance is prejudicial may be excellent in its remoter operation, and its excellence may arise even from the ill effects it produces in the beginning. The reverse also happens; and very plausible schemes, with very pleasing commencements, have often shameful and lamentable conclusions. In states there are often some obscure and almost latent causes, things which appear at first view of little moment, on which a very great part of its prosperity or adversity may most essentially depend. The science of government being, therefore, so practical in itself, and intended for such practical purposes, a matter which requires experience, and even more experience than any person can gain in his whole life, however sagacious and observing he may be, it is with infinite caution that any man ought to venture upon pulling down an edifice which has answered in any tolerable degree for ages the common purposes of society, or on building it up again without having models and patterns of approved utility before his eyes.

These metaphysic rights entering into common life, like rays of light which pierce into a dense medium, are, by the laws of Nature, refracted from their straight line. Indeed, in the gross and complicated mass of human passions and concerns, the primitive rights of men undergo such a variety of refractions and reflections that it becomes absurd to talk of them as if they continued in the simplicity of their original direction. The nature of man is intricate;

the objects of society are of the greatest possible complexity: and therefore no simple disposition or direction of power can be suitable either to man's nature or to the quality of his affairs. When I hear the simplicity of contrivance aimed at and boasted of in any new political constitutions, I am at no loss to decide that the artificers are grossly ignorant of their trade or totally negligent of their duty. The simple governments are fundamentally defective, to say no worse of them. If you were to contemplate society in but one point of view, all these simple modes of polity are infinitely captivating. In effect each would answer its single end much more perfectly than the more complex is able to attain all its complex purposes. But it is better that the whole should be imperfectly and anomalously answered than that while some parts are provided for with great exactness, others might be totally neglected, or perhaps materially injured, by the over-care of a favorite member.

The pretended rights of these theorists are all extremes; and in proportion as they are metaphysically true, they are morally and politically false. The rights of men are in a sort of *middle*, incapable of definition, but not impossible to be discerned. The rights of men in governments are their advantages; and these are often in balances between differences of good,—in compromises sometimes between good and evil, and sometimes between evil and evil. Political reason is a computing principle: adding, subtracting, multiplying, and dividing, morally, and not metaphysically or mathematically, true moral denominations.

By these theorists the right of the people is almost always sophistically confounded with their power. The body of the community, whenever it can come to act, can meet with no effectual resistance; but till power and right are the same, the whole body of them has no right inconsistent with virtue, and the first of all virtues, prudence. Men have no right to what is not reasonable, and to what is not for their benefit; for though a pleasant writer said, "*Liceat perire poetis,*" when one of them, in cold blood, is said to have leaped into the flames of a volcanic revolution, "*ardentem frigidus Ætnam insiluit,*" I consider such a frolic rather as an unjustifiable poetic license than as one of the franchises of Parnassus; and whether he were poet, or divine, or politician, that chose to exercise this kind of right, I think that more wise, because more charitable, thoughts would urge me rather to save the man than to preserve his brazen slippers as the monuments of his folly.

The kind of anniversary sermons to which a great part of what I write refers, if men are not shamed out of their present course, in commemorating the fact, will cheat many out of the principles and deprive them of the benefits of the Revolution they commemorate. I confess to you, Sir, I never liked this continual talk of resistance and revolution, or the practice of making the extreme medicine of the Constitution its daily bread. It renders the habit of society dangerously valetudinary; it is taking periodical doses of mercury sublimate, and swallowing down repeated provocatives of cantharides to our love of liberty.

This distemper of remedy, grown habitual, relaxes and wears out, by a vulgar and prostituted use, the spring of that spirit which is to be exerted on great occasions. It was in the most patient period of Roman servitude that themes of tyrannicide made the ordinary exercise of boys at school,—*cum perimit sævos classis numerosa tyrannos*. In the ordinary state of things, it produces in a country like ours the worst effects, even on the cause of that liberty which it abuses with the dissoluteness of an extravagant speculation. Almost all the high-bred republicans of my time have, after a short space, become the most decided, thorough-paced courtiers; they soon left the business of a tedious, moderate, but practical resistance, to those of us whom, in the pride and intoxication of their theories, they have slighted as not much better than Tories. Hypocrisy, of course, delights in the most sublime speculations; for, never intending to go beyond speculation, it costs nothing to have it magnificent. But even in cases where rather levity than fraud was to be suspected in these ranting speculations, the issue has been much the same. These professors, finding their extreme principles not applicable to cases which call only for a qualified, or, as I may say, civil and legal resistance, in such cases employ no resistance at all. It is with them a war or a revolution, or it is nothing. Finding their schemes of politics not adapted to the state of the world in which they live, they often come to think lightly of all public principle, and are ready, on their part, to abandon for a very trivial interest what they find of very trivial value. Some, indeed, are of more steady and persevering natures; but these are eager politicians out of Parliament, who have little to tempt them to abandon their favorite projects. They have some change in the Church or State, or both, constantly in their view. When that is the case, they are always bad citizens, and perfectly unsure connections. For, considering their speculative designs as of infinite value, and the actual arrangement of the state as of no estimation, they are, at best, indifferent about it. They see no merit in the good, and no fault in the vicious management of public affairs; they rather rejoice in the latter, as more propitious to revolution. They see no merit or demerit in any man, or any action, or any political principle, any further than as they may forward or retard their design of change; they therefore take up, one day, the most violent and stretched prerogative, and another time the wildest democratic ideas of freedom, and pass from the one to the other without any sort of regard to cause, to person, or to party.

109

David Rice

from *Slavery Inconsistent with Justice and Good Policy*

Born and reared in Virginia, David Rice (1733–1816) studied at the College of New Jersey (Princeton). Upon his ordination as a Presbyterian minister, he served among the enslaved of his home state before migrating westward to Kentucky. As that territory prepared for statehood, Rice was elected to the Constitutional Convention. In preparation for the 1792 convention, Rice published *Slavery Inconsistent with Justice and Good Policy* under the pseudonym "Philanthropos." When it became clear that the convention would endorse Kentucky's entrance into the Union as a slave state, Rice resigned his seat and refused to endorse Kentucky's constitution. He remained a lifelong abolitionist.

MR. CHAIRMAN,

[. . . .]

As creatures of God we are, with respect to liberty, all equal. If one has a right to live among his fellow creatures, and enjoy his freedom, so has another: if one has a right to enjoy that property he acquires by an honest industry, so has another. If I by force take that from another, which he has a just right to according to the law of nature, (which is a divine law) which he has never forfeited, and to which he has never relinquished his claim, I am certainly guilty of injustice and robbery; and when the thing taken is the man's liberty, when it is himself, it is the greatest injustice. I injure him much more, than if I robbed him of his property on the high-way. In this case, it does not belong to him to prove a negative, but to me to prove that such forfeiture has been made; because, if it has not, he is certainly still the proprietor. All he has to do is to show the insufficiency of my proofs.

SOURCE: David Rice, *Slavery Inconsistent with Justice and Good Policy: Proved by a Speech Delivered in the Convention, Held at Danville, Kentucky* (London: M. Gurney, 1793), 4–6, 24.

A slave claims his freedom; he pleads that he is a man, that he was by nature free, that he has not forfeited his freedom, nor relinquished it. Now, unless his master can prove that he is not a man, that he was not born free, or that he has forfeited or relinquished his freedom, he must be judged free; the justice of his claim must be acknowledged. His being long deprived of this right, by force or fraud, does not annihilate it, it remains; it is still his right. When I rob a man of his property, I leave him his liberty, and a capacity of acquiring and possessing more property; but when I deprive him of his liberty, I also deprive him of this capacity; therefore I do him greater injury, when I deprive him of his liberty, than when I rob him of his property. It is in vain for me to plead, that I have the sanction of law; for this makes the injury the greater: it arms the community against him, and makes his case desperate.

If my definition of a slave is true, he is a rational creature reduced by the power of legislation to the state of a brute, and thereby deprived of every privilege of humanity, except as above, that he may minister to the ease, luxury, lust, or avarice of another, no better than himself.

We only want a law enacted that no owner of a brute, nor other person, should kill or dismember it, and then in law the case of a slave and of a brute is in most respects parallel; and where they differ, the state of the brute is to be preferred. The brute may steal or rob, to supply his hunger; the law does not condemn him to die for his offence, it only permits his death; but the slave, though in the most starving condition, dares not do either, on penalty of death or some severe punishment.

Is there any need of arguments to prove, that it is in a high degree unjust and cruel, to reduce one human creature to such an abject wretched state as this, that he may minister to the ease, luxury, or avarice of another? Has not that other the same right to have him reduced to this state, that he may minister to his interest or pleasure? On what is this right founded? Whence was it derived? Did it come from heaven, from earth, or from hell? Has the great King of heaven, the absolute sovereign disposer of all men, given this extraordinary right to white men over black men? Where is the charter? In whose hands is it lodged? Let it be produced, and read, that we may know our privilege.

Thus reducing men is an indignity, a degradation to our own nature. Had we not lost a true sense of its worth and dignity, we should blush to see it converted into brutes. We should blush to see our houses filled, or surrounded with cattle, in our own shapes. We should look upon it to be a fouler, a blacker stain, than that with which the vertical suns have tinged the blood of Africa. When we plead for slavery, we plead for the disgrace and ruin of our nature.

If we are capable of it, we may ever after claim kindred with the brutes, and renounce our own superior dignity.

From our definition it will appear, that a slave is a creature made after the image of God, and accountable to him for the maintenance of innocence and purity; but by law reduced to a liableness to be debauched by men, without any prospect or hope of redress.

That a slave is made after the image of God, no Christian will deny: that a slave is absolutely subjected to be debauched by men, is so apparent from the nature of slavery, that it needs no proof. This is evidently the unhappy case of female slaves; a number of whom have been remarkable for their chastity and modesty. If their master attempts their chastity, they dare neither resist nor complain. If another man should make the attempt, though resistance may not be so dangerous, complaints are equally vain. They cannot be heard in their own defense; their testimony cannot be admitted. The injurious person has a right to be heard, may accuse the innocent sufferer of malicious slander, and have her severely chastised.

A virtuous woman, and virtuous Africans no doubt there are, esteems her chastity above every other thing: some have preferred it even to their lives. Then, forcibly to deprive her of this, is treating her with the greatest injustice. Therefore, since law leaves the chastity of a female slave entirely in the power of her master, and greatly in the power of others, it permits this injustice; it provides no remedy; it refuses to redress this insufferable grievance, it denies even the small privilege of complaining.

From our definition it will follow, that a slave is a free moral agent, legally deprived of free agency, and obliged to act according to the will of another free agent of the same species: and yet he is accountable to his Creator for the use he makes of his own free agency.

When a man, though he can exist independent of another, cannot act independent of him, his agency must depend upon the will of that other; and therefore he is deprived of his own free agency: and yet, as a free agent, he is accountable to his Maker for all the deeds done in the body. This comes to pass through a great omission and inconsistency in the legislature. They ought farther to have enacted, in order to have been consistent, that the slave should not have been accountable for any of his actions; but that his master should have answered for him in all things, here and hereafter.

That a slave has the capacities of a free moral agent, will be allowed by all. That he is, in many instances, deprived by law of the exercise of these powers, evidently appears from his situation. That he is accountable to his Maker for his conduct, will be allowed by those who do not believe that human legislatures are omnipotent, and can free men from this allegiance and subjection to the King of heaven.

The principles of conjugal love and fidelity in the breast of a virtuous pair, of natural affection in parents, and a sense of duty in children, are inscribed there by the finger of God; they are the laws of heaven: but an inslaving law directly opposes them, and virtually forbids obedience. The relations of husband and wife, of parent and child, are formed by divine authority, and founded on the laws of nature. But it is in the power of a cruel master, and often of a needy creditor, to break these tender connections, and for ever to separate these dearest relatives. This is ever done, in fact, at the call of interest, or of humour. The poor sufferers may expostulate; they may plead; may plead with tears; their hearts may break; but all in vain. The laws of nature are violated, the tender ties are dissolved, a final separation takes place, and the duties of these relations can no longer be performed, nor their comforts enjoyed. Would these slaves perform the duties of husbands and wives, parents and children; the law disables them, it puts it altogether out of their power.

In these cases, it is evident that the laws of nature, or the laws of man, are wrong; and which, none will be at a loss to judge. The divine law says, Whom God hath joined together, let no man put asunder: the law of man says, to the master of the slave, Though the divine law has joined them together, you may put them asunder when you please. The divine law says, Train up your child in the way he should go: the law of man says, You shall not train up your child, but as your master thinks proper. The divine law says, Honor your father and your mother, and obey them in all things: but the law of man says, Honor and obey your master in all things, and your parents just as far as he shall direct you.

[. . . .]

The slavery of the Negroes began in iniquity; a curse has attended it, and a curse will follow it. National vices will be punished with national calamities. Let us avoid these vices, that we may avoid the punishment which they deserve; and endeavour so to act, as to secure the approbation and smiles of Heaven.

Holding men in slavery is the national vice of Virginia; and, while a part of that state, we were partakers of the guilt. As a separate state, we are just now come to the birth; and it depends upon our free choice, whether we shall be born in this sin, or innocent of it. We now have it in our power to adopt it as our national crime; or to bear a national testimony against it. I hope the latter will be our choice; that we shall wash our hands of this guilt, and not leave it in the power of a future legislature, ever more to stain our reputation or our conscience with it.

THE END.

110

Alexis de Tocqueville

from *Democracy in America*

Based on his travels throughout the United States in 1831 and 1832, Alexis de Tocqueville (1805–1859) published his four-volume *Democracy in America* (1835–1840). The collection quickly found its place among the most important political works of the nineteenth century. In this expansive work, Tocqueville provides insight into key elements of American life and thought, e.g., philosophy, religion, and politics, the proper role of the press, and the power of the majority in this Jacksonian moment. His research centered on the questions of whether a democratic society, properly knit together, could sustain liberty, and what presented the greatest threat to its survival.

Second Part, First Book: Influence of Democracy on the Progress of Opinion in the United States. Chapter I: *Philosophical Method Among the Americans*

I think that in no country in the civilized world is less attention paid to philosophy than in the United States. The Americans have no philosophical school of their own; and they care but little for all the schools into which Europe is divided, the very names of which are scarcely known to them. Nevertheless it is easy to perceive that almost all the inhabitants of the United States conduct their understanding in the same manner, and govern it by the same rules; that is to say, that without ever having taken the trouble to define the rules of a philosophical method, they are in possession of one, common to the whole people. To evade the bondage of system and habit, of family maxims, class opinions, and, in some degree, of national prejudices; to accept tradition only as a means

SOURCE: Alexis de Tocqueville, *Democracy in America*, trans. Henry Reeve, rev. ed., vol. 2 (New York: Colonial Press, 1899), 3–8, 99–103.

of information, and existing facts only as a lesson used in doing otherwise, and doing better; to seek the reason of things for one's self, and in one's self alone; to tend to results without being bound to means, and to aim at the substance through the form;—such are the principal characteristics of what I shall call the philosophical method of the Americans. But if I go further, and if I seek amongst these characteristics that which predominates over and includes almost all the rest, I discover that in most of the operations of the mind, each American appeals to the individual exercise of his own understanding alone. America is therefore one of the countries in the world where philosophy is least studied, and where the precepts of Descartes are best applied. Nor is this surprising. The Americans do not read the works of Descartes, because their social condition deters them from speculative studies; but they follow his maxims because this very social condition naturally disposes their understanding to adopt them. In the midst of the continual movement which agitates a democratic community, the tie which unites one generation to another is relaxed or broken; every man readily loses the trace of the ideas of his forefathers or takes no care about them. Nor can men living in this state of society derive their belief from the opinions of the class to which they belong, for, so to speak, there are no longer any classes, or those which still exist are composed of such mobile elements, that their body can never exercise a real control over its members. As to the influence which the intelligence of one man has on that of another, it must necessarily be very limited in a country where the citizens, placed on the footing of a general similitude, are all closely seen by each other; and where, as no signs of incontestable greatness or superiority are perceived in any one of them, they are constantly brought back to their own reason as the most obvious and proximate source of truth. It is not only confidence in this or that man which is then destroyed, but the taste for trusting the *ipse dixit* of any man whatsoever. Everyone shuts himself up in his own breast, and affects from that point to judge the world.

The practice which obtains amongst the Americans of fixing the standard of their judgment in themselves alone, leads them to other habits of mind. As they perceive that they succeed in resolving without assistance all the little difficulties which their practical life presents, they readily conclude that everything in the world may be explained, and that nothing in it transcends the limits of the understanding. Thus they fall to denying what they cannot comprehend; which leaves them but little faith for whatever is extraordinary, and an almost insurmountable distaste for whatever is supernatural. As it is on their own testimony that they are accustomed to rely, they like to discern the object which engages their attention with extreme clearness; they therefore strip off as much as possible all that covers it, they rid themselves of whatever separates them from it, they remove whatever conceals it from sight, in order to view it more closely and in the broad light of day. This disposition of the mind soon leads them to contemn forms, which they regard as useless and inconvenient veils placed between them and the truth.

The Americans then have not required to extract their philosophical method from books; they have found it in themselves. The same thing may be remarked in what has taken place in Europe. This same method has only been established and made popular in Europe in proportion as the condition of society has become more equal, and men have grown more like each other. Let us consider for a moment the connection of the periods in which this change may be traced. In the sixteenth century the Reformers subjected some of the dogmas of the ancient faith to the scrutiny of private judgment; but they still withheld from it the discussion of all the rest. In the seventeenth century, Bacon in the natural sciences, and Descartes in the study of philosophy in the strict sense of the term, abolished recognized formulas, destroyed the empire of tradition, and overthrew the authority of the schools. The philosophers of the eighteenth century, generalizing at length the same principle, undertook to submit to the private judgment of each man all the objects of his belief.

Who does not perceive that Luther, Descartes, and Voltaire employed the same method, and that they differed only in the greater or less use which they professed should be made of it? Why did the Reformers confine themselves so closely within the circle of religious ideas? Why did Descartes, choosing only to apply his method to certain matters, though he had made it fit to be applied to all, declare that men might judge for themselves in matters philosophical but not in matters political? How happened it that in the eighteenth century those general applications were all at once drawn from this same method, which Descartes and his predecessors had either not perceived or had rejected? To what, lastly, is the fact to be attributed, that at this period the method we are speaking of suddenly emerged from the schools, to penetrate into society and become the common standard of intelligence; and that, after it had become popular among the French, it has been ostensibly adopted or secretly followed by all the nations of Europe?

[. . . .]

It must never be forgotten that religion gave birth to Anglo-American society. In the United States religion is therefore commingled with all the habits of the nation and all the feelings of patriotism; whence it derives a peculiar force. To this powerful reason another of no less intensity may be added: in America religion has, as it were, laid down its own limits. Religious institutions have remained wholly distinct from political institutions, so that former laws have been easily changed whilst former belief has remained unshaken. Christianity has therefore retained a strong hold on the public mind in America; and, I would more particularly remark, that its sway is not only that of a philosophical doctrine which has been adopted upon inquiry, but of a religion which is believed without discussion. In the United States Christian sects are infinitely diversified and perpetually modified; but Christianity itself is a fact so irresistibly established, that no one undertakes either to attack or to defend it. The Americans, having admitted the principal doctrines of the Christian religion without inquiry, are obliged to accept in like manner a great number of moral truths originating in it and connected with it. Hence the activity of individual analysis is restrained within narrow limits, and many of the most important of human opinions are removed from the range of its influence. . . .

There are no revolutions which do not shake existing belief, enervate authority, and throw doubts over commonly received ideas. The effect of all revolutions is therefore, more or less, to surrender men to their own guidance, and to open to the mind of every man a void and almost unlimited range of speculation. When equality of conditions succeeds a protracted conflict between the different classes of which the elder society was composed, envy, hatred, and uncharitableness, pride, and exaggerated self-confidence are apt to seize upon the human heart, and plant their sway there for a time. This, independently of equality itself, tends powerfully to divide men—to lead them to mistrust the judgment of others, and to seek the light of truth nowhere but in their own understandings. Everyone then attempts to be his own sufficient guide, and makes it his boast to form his own opinions on all subjects. Men are no longer bound together by ideas, but by interests; and it would seem as if human opinions were reduced to a sort of intellectual dust, scattered on every side, unable to collect, unable to cohere.

Thus, that independence of mind which equality supposes to exist, is never so great, nor ever appears so excessive, as at the time when equality is beginning to establish itself, and in the course of that painful labor by which it is established. That sort of intellectual freedom which equality may give ought, therefore, to be very carefully distinguished from the anarchy which revolution brings. Each of these two things must be severally considered, in order not to conceive exaggerated hopes or fears of the future.

I believe that the men who will live under the new forms of society will make frequent use of their private judgment; but I am far from thinking that they will often abuse it. This is attributable to a cause of more general application to all democratic countries, and which, in the long run, must needs restrain in them the independence of individual speculation within fixed, and sometimes narrow, limits. . . .

[. . . .]

Second Part, Second Book: Influence of Democracy on the Feelings of the Americans. Chapter I: *Why Democratic Nations Show a More Ardent and Enduring Love of Equality than of Liberty*

The first and most intense passion which is engendered by the equality of conditions is, I need hardly say, the love of that same equality. My readers will therefore not be surprised that I speak of it before all others. Everybody has remarked that in our time, and especially in France, this passion for equality is every day gaining ground in the human heart. It has been said a hundred times that our contemporaries are far more ardently and tenaciously attached to equality than to freedom; but as I do not find that the causes of the fact have been sufficiently analyzed, I shall endeavor to point them out.

It is possible to imagine an extreme point at which freedom and equality would meet and be confounded together. Let us suppose that all the members of the community take a part in the government, and that each one of them has an equal right to take a part in it. As none is different from his fellows, none can exercise a tyrannical power: men will be perfectly free, because they will all be entirely equal; and they will all be perfectly equal, because they will be entirely free. To this ideal state democratic nations tend. Such is the completest form that equality can assume upon earth; but there are a thousand others which, without being equally perfect, are not less cherished by those nations.

The principle of equality may be established in civil society, without prevailing in the political world. Equal rights may exist of indulging in the same pleasures, of entering the same professions, of frequenting the same places—in a word, of living in the same manner and seeking wealth by the same means, although all men do not take an equal share in the government. A kind of equality may even be established in the political world, though there should be no political freedom there. A man may be the equal of all his countrymen save one, who is the master of all without distinction, and who selects equally from among them all the agents of his power. Several other combinations might be easily imagined, by which very great equality would be united to institutions more or less free, or even to institutions wholly without freedom. Although men cannot become absolutely equal unless they be entirely free, and consequently equality, pushed to its furthest extent, may be confounded with freedom, yet there is good reason for distinguishing the one from the other. The taste which men have for liberty, and that which they feel for equality, are, in fact, two different things; and I am not afraid to add that, amongst democratic nations, they are two unequal things.

Upon close inspection, it will be seen that there is in every age some peculiar and preponderating fact with which all others are connected; this fact almost always gives birth to some pregnant idea or some ruling passion, which attracts to itself, and bears away in its course, all the feelings and opinions of the time: it is like a great stream, towards which each of the surrounding rivulets seems to flow. Freedom has appeared in the world at different times and under various forms; it has not been exclusively bound to any social condition, and it is not confined to democracies. Freedom cannot, therefore, form the distinguishing characteristic of democratic ages. The peculiar and preponderating fact which marks those ages as its own is the equality of conditions; the ruling passion of men in those periods is the love of this equality. Ask not what singular charm the men of democratic ages find in being equal, or what special reasons they may have for clinging so tenaciously to equality rather than to the other advantages which society holds out to them: equality is the distinguishing characteristic of the age they live in; that, of itself, is enough to explain that they prefer it to all the rest.

But independently of this reason there are several others, which will at all times habitually lead men to prefer equality to freedom. If a people could ever succeed in destroying or even in diminishing, the equality which prevails in its own body, this could only be accomplished by long and laborious efforts. Its social condition must be modified, its laws abolished, its opinions superseded, its habits changed, its manners corrupted. But political liberty is more easily lost; to neglect to hold it fast is to allow it to escape. Men therefore not only cling to equality because it is dear to them; they also adhere to it because they think it will last forever.

That political freedom may compromise in its excesses the tranquillity, the property, the lives of individuals, is obvious to the narrowest and most unthinking minds. But, on the contrary, none but attentive and clear-sighted men perceive the perils with which equality threatens us, and they commonly avoid pointing them out. They know that the calamities they apprehend are remote, and flatter themselves that they will only fall upon future generations, for which the present generation takes but little thought. The evils which freedom sometimes brings with it are immediate; they are apparent to all, and all are more or less affected by them. The evils which extreme equality may produce are slowly disclosed; they creep gradually into the social frame; they are only seen at intervals, and at the moment at which they become most violent habit already causes them to be no longer felt. The advantages which freedom brings are only shown by length of time; and it is always easy to mistake the cause in which they originate. The advantages of equality are instantaneous, and they may constantly be traced from their source. Political liberty bestows exalted pleasures, from time to time, upon a certain number of citizens. Equality every day confers a number of small enjoyments on every man. The charms of equality are every instant felt, and are within the reach of all; the noblest hearts are not insensible to them, and the most vulgar souls exult in them. The passion which equality engenders must therefore be at once strong and general. Men cannot enjoy political liberty unpurchased by some sacrifices, and they never obtain it without great exertions. But the pleasures of equality are self-proffered: each of the petty incidents of life seems to occasion them, and in order to taste them nothing is required but to live.

Democratic nations are at all times fond of equality, but there are certain epochs at which the passion they entertain for it swells to the height of fury. This occurs at the moment when the old social system, long menaced, completes its own destruction after a last intestine struggle, and when the barriers of rank are at length thrown down. At such times men pounce upon equality as their booty, and they cling to it as to some precious treasure which they fear to lose. The passion for equality penetrates on every side into men's hearts, expands there, and fills them entirely. Tell them not that by this blind surrender of themselves to an exclusive passion they risk their dearest interests: they are deaf. Show them not freedom escaping from their grasp, whilst they are looking another way: they are blind—or rather, they can discern but one sole object to be desired in the universe.

What I have said is applicable to all democratic nations: what I am about to say concerns the French alone. Amongst most modern nations, and especially amongst all those of the Continent of Europe, the taste and the idea of freedom only began to exist and to extend themselves at the time when social conditions were tending to equality, and as a consequence of that very equality. Absolute kings were the most efficient levellers of ranks amongst their subjects. Amongst these nations equality preceded freedom: equality was therefore a fact of some standing when freedom was still a novelty: the one had already created customs, opinions, and laws belonging to it, when the other, alone and for the first time, came into actual existence. Thus the latter was still only an affair of opinion and of taste, whilst the former had already crept into the habits of the people, possessed itself of their manners, and given a particular turn to the smallest actions of their lives. Can it be wondered that the men of our own time prefer the one to the other?

I think that democratic communities have a natural taste for freedom: left to themselves, they will seek it, cherish it, and view any privation of it with regret. But for equality, their passion is ardent, insatiable, incessant, invincible: they call for equality in freedom; and if they cannot obtain that, they still call for equality in slavery. They will endure poverty, servitude, barbarism—but they will not endure aristocracy. This is true at all times, and especially true in our own. All men and all powers seeking to cope with this irresistible passion, will be overthrown and destroyed by it. In our age, freedom cannot be established without it, and despotism itself cannot reign without its support.

111

Søren Kierkegaard

from *Fear and Trembling*

Søren Kierkegaard (1813–1855) was a Danish Christian philosopher who is sometimes regarded as one of the early forerunners to what would become known as existentialism and, more generally, as continental philosophy. The following is an excerpt from one of the opening parts of his best-known work, *Fear and Trembling*, in which Kierkegaard wrestles with the Abraham and Isaac story and the concept of faith.

A Panegyric on Abraham

If a consciousness of the eternal were not implanted in man; if the basis of all that exists were but a confusedly fermenting element which, convulsed by obscure passions, produced all, both the great and the insignificant; if under everything there lay a bottomless void never to be filled—what else were life but despair? If it were thus, and if there were no sacred bonds between man and man; if one generation arose after another, as in the forest the leaves of one season succeed the leaves of another, or like the songs of birds which are taken up one after another; if the generations of man passed through the world like a ship passing through the sea and the wind over the desert—a fruitless and a vain thing; if eternal oblivion were ever greedily watching for its prey and there existed no power strong enough to wrest it from its clutches—how empty were life then, and how dismal! And therefore it is not thus; but, just as God created man and woman, he likewise called into being the hero and the poet or orator. The latter cannot perform the deeds of the hero—he can only admire and love him and rejoice in him. And yet he also is happy and not less so; for the hero

SOURCE: Søren Kierkegaard, *Fear and Trembling*, in *Selections from the Writings of Kierkegaard*, trans. L. M. Hollander, *University of Texas Bulletin* no. 2326: July 8, 1923 (Austin: The University of Texas, 1923), 125–34.

is, as it were, his better self with which he has fallen in love, and he is glad he is not himself the hero, so that his love can express itself in admiration.

The poet is the genius of memory, and does nothing but recall what has been done, can do nothing but admire what has been done. He adds nothing of his own, but he is jealous of what has been entrusted to him. He obeys the choice of his own heart; but once he has found what he has been seeking, he visits every man's door with his song and with his speech, so that all may admire the hero as he does, and be proud of the hero as he is. This is his achievement, his humble work, this is his faithful service in the house of the hero. If thus, faithful to his love, he battles day and night against the guile of oblivion which wishes to lure the hero from him, then has he accomplished his task, then is he gathered to his hero who loves him as faithfully; for the poet is [as] it were the hero's better self, unsubstantial, to be sure, like a mere memory, but also transfigured as is a memory. Therefore shall no one be forgotten who has done great deeds; and even if there be delay, even if the cloud of misunderstanding obscure the hero from our vision, still his lover will come some time; and the more time has passed, the more faithfully will he cleave to him.

No, no one shall be forgotten who was great in this world. But each hero was great in his own way, and each one was eminent in proportion to the great things he loved. For he who loved himself became great through himself, and he who loved others became great through his devotion, but he who loved God became greater than all of these. Everyone of them shall be remembered, but each one became great in proportion to his trust. One became great by hoping for the possible; another, by hoping for the eternal; but he who hoped for the impossible, he became greater than all of these. Every one shall be remembered; but each one was great in proportion to the power with which he strove. For he who strove with the world became great by overcoming himself; but he who strove with God, he became the greatest of them all. Thus there have been struggles in the world, man against man, one against a thousand; but he who struggled with God, he became greatest of them all. Thus there was fighting on this earth, and there was he who conquered everything by his strength, and there was he who conquered God by his weakness. There was he who, trusting in himself, gained all; and there was he who, trusting in his strength sacrificed everything; but he who believed in God was greater than all of these. There was he who was great through his strength, and he who was great through his wisdom, and he who was great through his hopes, and he who was great through his love; but Abraham was greater than all of these—great through the strength whose power is weakness, great through the wisdom whose secret is folly, great through the hope whose expression is madness, great through the love which is hatred of one's self.

Through the urging of his faith Abraham left the land of his forefathers and became a stranger in the land of promise. He left one thing behind and took one thing along: he left his worldly wisdom behind and took with him faith. For else he would not have left the land of his fathers, but would have thought it an unreasonable demand. Through his faith he came to be a stranger in the land of promise, where there was nothing to remind him of all that had been dear to him, but where everything by its newness tempted his soul to longing. And yet was he God's chosen, he in whom the Lord was well pleased! Indeed, had he been one cast off, one thrust out of God's mercy, then might he have comprehended it; but now it seemed like a mockery of him and of his faith. There have been others who lived in exile from the fatherland which they loved. They are not forgotten, nor is the song of lament forgotten in which they mournfully sought and found what they had lost. Of Abraham there exists no song of lamentation. It is human to complain, it is human to weep with the weeping; but it is greater to believe, and more blessed to consider him who has faith.

Through his faith Abraham received the promise that in his seed were to be blessed all races of mankind. Time passed, there was still the possibility of it, and Abraham had faith. Another man there was who also lived in hopes. Time passed, the evening of his life was approaching; neither was he paltry enough to have forgotten his hopes: neither shall he be forgotten by us! Then he sorrowed, and his sorrow did not deceive him, as life had done, but gave him all it could; for in the sweetness of sorrow he became possessed of his disappointed hopes. It is human to sorrow, it is human to sorrow with the sorrowing; but it is greater to have faith, and more blessed to consider him who has faith.

No song of lamentation has come down to us from Abraham. He did not sadly count the days as time passed; he did not look at Sarah with suspicious eyes, whether she was becoming old; he did not stop the sun's course lest Sarah should grow old and his hope with her; he did not lull her with his songs of lamentation. Abraham grew old, and Sarah became a laughing-stock to the people; and yet was he God's chosen, and heir to the promise that in his seed were to be blessed all races of mankind. Were it, then, not better if he had not been God's chosen? For what is it to be God's chosen? Is it to have denied to one in one's youth all the wishes of youth in order to have them fulfilled after great labor in old age?

But Abraham had faith and steadfastly lived in hope. Had Abraham been less firm in his trust, then would he have given up that hope. He would have said to God: "So it is, perchance, not Thy will, after all, that this shall come to pass. I shall surrender my hope. It was my only one, it was my bliss. I am sincere, I conceal no secret grudge for that Thou didst deny it to me." He would not have remained forgotten, his example would have saved many a one; but he would not have become the Father of Faith. For it is great to surrender one's hope, but greater still to abide by it steadfastly after having surrendered it; for it is great to seize hold of the eternal hope, but greater still to abide steadfastly by one's worldly hopes after having surrendered them.

Then came the fulness of time. If Abraham had not had faith, then Sarah would probably have died of sorrow, and Abraham, dulled by his grief, would not have understood the fulfillment, but would have smiled about it as a dream of his youth. But Abraham had faith, and therefore he remained young; for he who always hopes for the best, him life will deceive, and he will grow old; and he who is always prepared for the worst, he will soon age; but he who has faith, he will preserve eternal youth. Praise, therefore, be to this story! For Sarah, though advanced in age, was young enough to wish for the pleasures of a mother, and Abraham, though grey of hair, was young enough to wish to become a father. In a superficial sense it may be considered miraculous that what they wished for came to pass, but in a deeper sense the miracle of faith is to be seen in Abraham's and Sarah's being young enough to wish, and their faith having preserved their wish and therewith their youth. The promise he had received was fulfilled, and he accepted it in faith, and it came to pass according to the promise and his faith; whereas Moses smote the rock with his staff but believed not.

There was joy in Abraham's house when Sarah celebrated the day of her Golden Wedding.

But it was not to remain thus; for once more was Abraham to be tempted. He had struggled with that cunning power to which nothing is impossible, with that ever watchful enemy who never sleeps, with that old man who out-lives all—he had struggled with Time and had preserved his faith. And now all the terror of that fight was concentrated in one moment. "And God tempted Abraham, saying to him: take now thine only son Isaac, whom thou lovest, and get thee into the land of Moriah; and offer him there for a burnt offering upon one of the mountains which I will tell thee of."

All was lost, then, and more terribly than if a son had never been given him! The Lord had only mocked Abraham, then! Miraculously he had realized the unreasonable hopes of Abraham; and now he wished to take away what he had given. A foolish hope it had been, but Abraham had not laughed when the promise had been made him. Now all was lost—the trusting hope of seventy years, the brief joy at the fulfilment of his hopes. Who, then, is he that snatches away the old man's staff, who that demands that he himself shall break it in two? Who is he that renders disconsolate the grey hair of old age, who is he that demands that he himself shall do it? Is there no pity for the venerable old man, and none for the innocent child? And yet was Abraham God's chosen one, and yet was it the Lord that tempted him. And now all was to be lost! The glorious remembrance of him by a whole race, the promise of Abraham's seed—all that was but a whim, a passing fancy of the Lord, which Abraham was now to destroy forever! That glorious treasure, as old as the faith in Abraham's heart, and many, many years older than Isaac, the fruit of Abraham's life, sanctified by prayers, matured in struggles—the blessing on the lips of Abraham: this fruit was now to be plucked before the appointed time, and to remain without significance; for of what significance were it if Isaac was to be sacrificed? That sad and yet blessed hour when Abraham was to take leave from all that was dear to him, the hour when he would once more lift up his venerable head, when his face would shine like the countenance of the Lord, the hour when he would collect his whole soul for a blessing strong enough to render Isaac blessed all the days of his life—that hour was not to come! He was to say farewell to Isaac, to be sure, but in such wise that he himself was to remain behind; death was to part them, but in such wise that Isaac was to die. The old man was not in happiness to lay his hand on Isaac's head when the hour of death came, but, tired of life, to lay violent hands on Isaac. And it was God who tempted him. Woe, woe to the messenger who would have come before Abraham with such a command! Who would have dared to be the messenger of such dread tidings? But it was God that tempted Abraham.

But Abraham had faith, and had faith for this life. Indeed, had his faith been but concerning the life to come, then might he more easily have cast away all, in order to hasten out of this world which was not his. . . .

But Abraham had faith and doubted not, but trusted that the improbable would come to pass. If Abraham had doubted, then would he have undertaken something else, something great and noble; for what could Abraham have undertaken but was great and noble! He would have proceeded to Mount Moriah, he would have cloven the wood, and fired it, and unsheathed his knife—he would have cried out to God: "Despise not this sacrifice; it is not, indeed, the best I have; for what is an old man against a child foretold of God; but it is the best I can give thee. Let Isaac never know that he must find consolation in his youth." He would have plunged the steel in his own breast. And he would have been admired throughout the world, and his name would not have been forgotten; but it is one thing to be admired and another, to be a lode-star which guides one troubled in mind.

But Abraham had faith. He prayed not for mercy and that he might prevail upon the Lord: it was only when just retribution was to be visited upon Sodom and Gomorrha that Abraham ventured to beseech Him for mercy.

We read in Scripture: "And God did tempt Abraham, and said unto him, Abraham: and he said, Behold here I am." You, whom I am now addressing[,] did you do likewise? When you saw the dire dispensations of Providence approach threateningly, did you not then say to the mountains, Fall on me; and to the hills, Cover me? Or, if you were stronger in faith, did not your step linger along the way, longing for the old accustomed paths, as it were? And when the voice called you, did you answer, then, or not at all, and if you did, perchance in a low voice, or whispering? Not thus Abraham, but gladly and cheerfully and trustingly, and with a resonant voice he made answer: "Here am I." And we read further: "And Abraham rose up early in the morning." He made haste as though for some joyous occasion, and early in the morning he was in the appointed place, on Mount Moriah. He said nothing to Sarah, nothing to Eliezer, his steward; for who would have understood him? Did not his temptation by its very nature demand of him the vow of silence? "He laid the wood in order, and bound Isaac his son, and laid him on the altar upon the wood. And Abraham stretched forth his hand, and took the knife to slay his son." My listener! Many a father there has been who thought that with his child he lost the dearest of all there was in the world for him; yet assuredly no child ever was in that sense a pledge of God as was Isaac to Abraham. Many a father there has been who lost his child; but then it was God, the unchangeable and inscrutable will of the Almighty and His hand which took it. Not thus with Abraham. For him was reserved a more severe trial, and Isaac's fate was put into Abraham's hand together with the knife. And there he stood, the old man, with his only hope! Yet did he not doubt, nor look anxiously to the left or right, nor challenge Heaven with his prayers. He knew it was God the Almighty who now put him to the test; he knew it was the greatest sacrifice which could be demanded of him; but he knew also that no sacrifice was too great which God demanded—and he drew forth his knife.

Who strengthened Abraham's arm, who supported his right arm that it drooped not powerless? For he who contemplates this scene is unnerved. Who strengthened Abraham's soul so that his eyes grew not too dim to see either Isaac or the ram? For he who contemplates this scene will be struck with blindness. And yet, it is rare enough that one is unnerved or is struck with blindness, and still more rare that one narrates worthily what there did take place between father and son. To be sure, we know well enough—it was but a trial!

If Abraham had doubted, when standing on Mount Moriah; if he had looked about him in perplexity; if he had accidentally discovered the ram before drawing his knife; if God had permitted him to sacrifice it instead of

Isaac—then would he have returned home, and all would have been as before, he would have had Sarah and would have kept Isaac; and yet how different all would have been! For then had his return been a flight, his salvation an accident, his reward disgrace; his future, perchance, perdition. Then would he have borne witness neither to his faith nor to God's mercy, but would have witnessed only to the terror of going to Mount Moriah. Then Abraham would not have been forgotten, nor either Mount Moriah. It would be mentioned, then, not as is Mount Ararat on which the Ark landed, but as a sign of terror, because it was there Abraham doubted.

Venerable patriarch Abraham! When you returned home from Mount Moriah you required no encomiums to console you for what you had lost; for, indeed, you did win all and still kept Isaac, as we all know. And the Lord did no more take him from your side, but you sate gladly at table with him in your tent as in the life to come you will, for all times. Venerable patriarch Abraham! Thousands of years have passed since those times, but still you need no late-born lover to snatch your memory from the power of oblivion, for every language remembers you—and yet do you reward your lover more gloriously than any one, rendering him blessed in your bosom, and taking heart and eyes captive by the marvel of your deed. Venerable patriarch Abraham! Second father of the race! You who first perceived and bore witness to that unbounded passion which has but scorn for the terrible fight with the raging elements and the strength of brute creation, in order to struggle with God; you who first felt that sublimest of all passions, you who found the holy, pure, humble expression for the divine madness which was a marvel to the heathen—forgive him who would speak in your praise, in case he did it not fittingly. He spoke humbly, as if it concerned the desire of his heart; he spoke briefly, as is seemly; but he will never forget that you required a hundred years to obtain a son of your old age, against all expections; that you had to draw the knife before being permitted to keep Isaac; he will never forget that in a hundred and thirty years you never got farther than to faith.

112

Henry David Thoreau

from *Civil Disobedience*

Poet, naturalist, philosopher, and political activist, Henry David Thoreau (1817–1882) was well-read in ancient and contemporary thought. Fearing that he might arrive at the end of his life only to realize that he had failed to live, his quest was "to live deliberately." Instead of conforming, he inquired. And if the answer was not compelling, he would resist. *Civil Disobedience*, for instance, was sparked by a tax bill. After following where the tax revenues went, he concluded that the funds, and much of government's machinery, ultimately supported slavery, which he opposed. Consequently, he refused to pay the tax, a protest for which he was arrested and jailed for a couple days. The reasoning Thoreau offered would ultimately influence the likes of Leo Tolstoy, Mohandas Gandhi, and Martin Luther King Jr.

I heartily accept the motto—"That government is best which governs least"; and I should like to see it acted up to more rapidly and systematically. Carried out, it finally amounts to this, which also I believe—"That government is best which governs not at all"; and when men are prepared for it, that will be the kind of government which they will have. Government is at best but an expedient; but most governments are usually, and all governments are sometimes, inexpedient.

[. . . .]

But, to speak practically and as a citizen, unlike those who call themselves no-government men, I ask for, not at once no government, but *at once* a better government. Let every man make known what kind of government would command his respect, and that will be one step toward obtaining it.

SOURCE: Henry David Thoreau, *On the Duty of Civil Disobedience* (London: Simple Life Press, 1903), 7–11, 14–15, 19, 22–23, 33–34.

After all, the practical reason why, when the power is once in the hands of the people, a majority are permitted, and for a long period continue, to rule, is not because they are most likely to be in the right, nor because this seems fairest to the minority, but because they are physically the strongest. But a government in which the majority rule in all cases cannot be based on justice, even as far as men understand it.

Can there not be a government in which majorities do not virtually decide right and wrong, but conscience?—in which majorities decide only those questions to which the rule of expediency is applicable? Must the citizen ever for a moment, or in the least degree, resign his conscience to the legislator? Why has every man a conscience, then? I think that we should be men first, and subjects afterward. It is not desirable to cultivate a respect for the law, so much as for the right. The only obligation which I have a right to assume is to do at any time what I think right. It is truly enough said, that a corporation has no conscience; but a corporation of conscientious men is a corporation *with* a conscience.

Law never made men a whit more just; and, by means of their respect for it, even the well-disposed are daily made the agents of injustice. A common and natural result of an undue respect for law is that you may see a file of soldiers, colonel, captain, corporal, privates, powder-monkeys, and all, marching in admirable order over hill and dale to the wars, against their wills, ay, against their common sense and consciences, which makes it very steep marching indeed, and produces a palpitation of the heart. They have no doubt that it is a damnable business in which they are concerned; they are all peaceably inclined. Now, what are they? Men at all? or small movable forts and magazines, at the service of some unscrupulous man in power?

[. . . .]

The mass of men serve the State thus, not as men mainly, but as machines, with their bodies. They are the standing army, and the militia, gaolers [jailers], constables, posse comitatus, etc. In most cases there is no free exercise whatever of the judgment or of the moral sense; but they put themselves on a level with wood and earth and stones; and wooden men can perhaps be manufactured that will serve the purpose as well. Such command no more respect than men of straw or a lump of dirt. They have the same sort of worth only as horses and dogs. Yet such as these even are commonly esteemed good citizens.

Others—as most legislators, politicians, lawyers, ministers, and office-holders—serve the State chiefly with their heads; and, as they rarely make any moral distinctions, they are as likely to serve the Devil, without *intending* it, as God.

A very few, as heroes, patriots, martyrs, reformers in the great sense, and *men*, serve the State with their consciences also, and so necessarily resist it for the most part; and they are commonly treated as enemies by it.

[. . . .]

All voting is a sort of gaming, like checkers or backgammon with a slight moral tinge to it, a playing with right and wrong, with moral questions; and betting naturally accompanies it. The character of the voters is not staked. I cast my vote, perchance, as I think right; but I am not vitally concerned that that right should prevail. I am willing to leave it to the majority. Its obligation, therefore, never exceeds that of expediency.

Even voting *for the right* is *doing* nothing for it. It is only expressing to men feebly your desire that it should prevail. A wise man will not leave the right to the mercy of chance, nor wish it to prevail through the power of the majority. There is but little virtue in the action of masses of men. When the majority shall at length vote for the abolition of slavery, it will be because they are indifferent to slavery, or because there is but little slavery left to be abolished by their vote. *They* will then be the only slaves. Only *his* vote can hasten the abolition of slavery who asserts his own freedom by his vote.

[. . . .]

If the injustice is part of the necessary friction of the machine of government, let it go, let it go: perchance it will wear smooth—certainly the machine will wear out. If the injustice has a spring, or a pulley, or a rope, or a crank, exclusively for itself, then perhaps you may consider whether the remedy will not be worse than the evil; but if it is of such a nature that it requires you to be the agent of injustice to another, then, I say, break the law. Let your life be a counter friction to stop the machine. What I have to do is to see, at any rate, that I do not lend myself to the wrong which I condemn.

[. . . .]

Under a government which imprisons any unjustly, the true place for a just man is also a prison. The proper place to-day, the only place which Massachusetts has provided for her freer and less desponding spirits, is in her prisons, to be put out and locked out of the State by her own act, as they have already put themselves out by their principles. It is there that the fugitive slave, and the Mexican prisoner on parole, and the Indian come to plead the wrongs of his race, should find them; on that separate, but more free and honourable ground, where the State places those who are not *with* her but *against* her, the only house in a slave State in which a free man can abide with honour.

[. . . .]

Cast your whole vote, not a strip of paper merely, but your whole influence. A minority is powerless while it conforms to the majority; it is not even a minority then; but it is irresistible when it clogs by its whole weight.

If the alternative is to keep all just men in prison, or give up war and slavery, the State will not hesitate which to choose. If a thousand men were not to pay their tax-bills this year, that would not be a violent and bloody measure, as it would be to pay them, and enable the State to commit violence and shed innocent blood.

This is, in fact, the definition of a peaceful revolution, if any such is possible. If the tax-gatherer or any other public officer asks me, as one has done, "But what shall I do?" my answer is, "If you really wish to do anything, resign your office." When the subject has refused allegiance, and the officer has resigned his office, then the revolution is accomplished.

But even suppose blood should flow. Is there not a sort of blood shed when the conscience is wounded? Through this wound a man's real manhood and immortality flow out, and he bleeds to an everlasting death. I see this blood flowing now.

[. . . .]

There will never be a really free and enlightened State until the State comes to recognize the individual as a higher and independent power, from which all its own power and authority are derived, and treats him accordingly. I please myself with imagining a State at last which can afford to be just to all men, and to treat the individual with respect as a neighbour; which even would not think it inconsistent with its own repose if a few were to live aloof from it, not meddling with it, nor embraced by it, who fulfilled all the duties of neighbours and fellow-men. A State which bore this kind of fruit, and suffered it to drop off as fast as it ripened, would prepare the way for a still more perfect and glorious State, which also I have imagined, but not yet anywhere seen.

113

John Stuart Mill

from *Utilitarianism*

John Stuart Mill (1806–1873) was a British child prodigy, philosopher, and public official of immense significance during the nineteenth century. Among his other contributions to philosophy and politics, he is perhaps best known today as the chief architect (along with Jeremy Bentham) of classical utilitarianism, which is one of the most influential theories of ethics in the history of moral reflection. The following is a brief excerpt from his famous book, *Utilitarianism*, wherein Mill gives an initial articulation and defense of the principle of utility, or the greatest happiness principle.

The creed which accepts as the foundation of morals, Utility, or the Greatest Happiness Principle, holds that actions are right in proportion as they tend to promote happiness, wrong as they tend to produce the reverse of happiness. By happiness is intended pleasure, and the absence of pain; by unhappiness, pain, and the privation of pleasure. To give a clear view of the moral standard set up by the theory, much more requires to be said; in particular, what things it includes in the ideas of pain and pleasure; and to what extent this is left an open question. But these supplementary explanations do not affect the theory of life on which this theory of morality is grounded—namely, that pleasure, and freedom from pain, are the only things desirable as ends; and that all desirable things (which are as numerous in the utilitarian as in any other scheme) are desirable either for the pleasure inherent in themselves, or as means to the promotion of pleasure and the prevention of pain.

Now, such a theory of life excites in many minds, and among them in some of the most estimable in feeling and purpose, inveterate dislike. To suppose

SOURCE: John Stuart Mill, *Utilitarianism*, reprinted from "Fraser's Magazine," 7th ed. (London: Longmans, Green, and Co., 1879), 8–17.

that life has (as they express it) no higher end than pleasure—no better and nobler object of desire and pursuit—they designate as utterly mean and grovelling; as a doctrine worthy only of swine, to whom the followers of Epicurus were, at a very early period, contemptuously likened; and modern holders of the doctrine are occasionally made the subject of equally polite comparisons by its German, French, and English assailants.

When thus attacked, the Epicureans have always answered, that it is not they, but their accusers, who represent human nature in a degrading light; since the accusation supposes human beings to be capable of no pleasures except those of which swine are capable. If this supposition were true, the charge could not be gainsaid, but would then be no longer an imputation; for if the sources of pleasure were precisely the same to human beings and to swine, the rule of life which is good enough for the one would be good enough for the other. The comparison of the Epicurean life to that of beasts is felt as degrading, precisely because a beast's pleasures do not satisfy a human being's conceptions of happiness. Human beings have faculties more elevated than the animal appetites, and when once made conscious of them, do not regard anything as happiness which does not include their gratification. I do not, indeed, consider the Epicureans to have been by any means faultless in drawing out their scheme of consequences from the utilitarian principle. To do this in any sufficient manner, many Stoic, as well as Christian elements require to be included. But there is no known Epicurean theory of life which does not assign to the pleasures of the intellect, of the feelings and imagination, and of the moral sentiments, a much higher value as pleasures than to those of mere sensation. It must be admitted, however, that utilitarian writers in general have placed the superiority of mental over bodily pleasures chiefly in the greater permanency, safety, uncostliness, &c., of the former—that is, in their circumstantial advantages rather than in their intrinsic nature. And on all these points utilitarians have fully proved their case; but they might have taken the other, and, as it may be called, higher ground, with entire consistency. It is quite compatible with the principle of utility to recognise the fact, that some *kinds* of pleasure are more desirable and more valuable than others. It would be absurd that while, in estimating all other things, quality is considered as well as quantity, the estimation of pleasures should be supposed to depend on quantity alone.

If I am asked, what I mean by difference of quality in pleasures, or what makes one pleasure more valuable than another, merely as a pleasure, except its being greater in amount, there is but one possible answer. Of two pleasures, if there be one to which all or almost all who have experience of both give a decided preference, irrespective of any feeling of moral obligation to prefer it, that is the more desirable pleasure. If one of the two is, by those who are competently acquainted with both, placed so far above the other that they prefer it, even though knowing it to be attended with a greater amount of discontent, and would not resign it for any quantity of the other pleasure which their nature is capable of, we are justified in ascribing to the preferred enjoyment a superiority in quality, so far outweighing quantity as to render it, in comparison, of small account.

Now it is an unquestionable fact that those who are equally acquainted with, and equally capable of appreciating and enjoying, both, do give a most marked preference to the manner of existence which employs their higher faculties. Few human creatures would consent to be changed into any of the lower animals, for a promise of the fullest allowance of a beast's pleasures; no intelligent human being would consent to be a fool, no instructed person would be an ignoramus, no person of feeling and conscience would be selfish and base, even though they should be persuaded that the fool, the dunce, or the rascal is better satisfied with his lot than they are with theirs. They would not resign what they possess more than he, for the most complete satisfaction of all the desires which they have in common with him. If they ever fancy they would, it is only in cases of unhappiness so extreme, that to escape from it they would exchange their lot for almost any other, however undesirable in their own eyes. A being of higher faculties requires more to make him happy, is capable probably of more acute suffering, and is certainly accessible to it at more points, than one of an inferior type; but in spite of these liabilities, he can never really wish to sink into what he feels to be a lower grade of existence. We may give what explanation we please of this unwillingness; we may attribute it to pride, a name which is given indiscriminately to some of the most and to some of the least estimable feelings of which mankind are capable; we may refer it to the love of liberty and personal independence, an appeal to which was with the Stoics one of the most effective means for the inculcation of it; to the love of power, or to the love of excitement, both of which do really enter into and contribute to it: but its most appropriate appellation is a sense of dignity, which all human beings possess in one form or other, and in some, though by no means in exact, proportion to their higher faculties, and which is so essential a part of the happiness of those in whom it is strong, that nothing which conflicts with it could be, otherwise than momentarily, an object of desire to them. Whoever supposes that this preference takes place at a sacrifice of happiness—that the superior being, in anything like equal circumstances, is not happier than the inferior—confounds the two very different ideas, of happiness, and content. It is indisputable that the being whose capacities of enjoyment are low, has the greatest chance of having them fully satisfied; and a highly-endowed being will always feel that any happiness which he can look for, as the world is constituted, is imperfect. But he can learn to bear its imperfections, if they are at all bearable; and they will not make him envy the being who is indeed unconscious of the imperfections, but only because he feels not at all the good which those imperfections qualify. It is better to be a human being dissatisfied than a pig satisfied; better to be Socrates dissatisfied than a fool satisfied. And if the fool, or the pig, is of a different opinion, it is because they only know their own side of the question. The other party to the comparison knows both sides.

It may be objected, that many who are capable of the higher pleasures, occasionally, under the influence of temptation, postpone them to the lower. But this is quite compatible with a full appreciation of the intrinsic superiority of the higher. Men often, from infirmity of character, make their election for the nearer good, though they know it to be the less valuable; and this no less when the choice is between two bodily pleasures, than when it is between bodily and mental. They pursue sensual indulgences to the injury of health, though perfectly aware that health is the greater good. It may be further objected, that many who begin with youthful enthusiasm for everything noble, as they advance in years sink into indolence and selfishness. But I do not believe that those who undergo this very common change, voluntarily choose the lower description of pleasures in preference to the higher. I believe that before they devote themselves exclusively to the one, they have already become incapable of the other. Capacity for the nobler feelings is in most natures a very tender plant, easily killed, not only by hostile influences, but by mere want of sustenance; and in the majority of young persons it speedily dies away if the occupations to which their position in life has devoted them, and the society into which it has thrown them, are not favourable to keeping that higher capacity in exercise. Men lose their high aspirations as they lose their intellectual tastes, because they have not time or opportunity for indulging them; and they addict themselves to inferior pleasures, not because they deliberately prefer them, but because they are either the only ones to which they have access, or the only ones which they are any longer capable of enjoying. It may be questioned whether any one who has remained equally susceptible to both classes of pleasures, ever knowingly and calmly preferred the lower; though many, in all ages, have broken down in an ineffectual attempt to combine both.

From this verdict of the only competent judges, I apprehend there can be no appeal. On a question which is the best worth having of two pleasures, or which of two modes of existence is the most grateful to the feelings, apart from its moral attributes and from its consequences, the judgment of those who are qualified by knowledge of both, or, if they differ, that of the majority among them, must be admitted as final. And there needs be the less hesitation to accept this judgment respecting the quality of pleasures, since there is no other tribunal to be referred to even on the question of quantity. What means are there of determining which is the acutest of two pains, or the intensest of two pleasurable sensations, except the general suffrage of those who are familiar with both? Neither pains nor pleasures are homogeneous, and pain is always heterogeneous with pleasure. What is there to decide whether a particular pleasure is worth purchasing at the cost of a particular pain, except the feelings and judgment of the experienced? When, therefore, those feelings and judgment declare the pleasures derived from the higher faculties to be preferable *in kind*, apart from the question of intensity, to those of which the animal nature, disjoined from the higher faculties, is susceptible, they are entitled on this subject to the same regard.

I have dwelt on this point, as being a necessary part of a perfectly just conception of Utility or Happiness, considered as the directive rule of human conduct. But it is by no means an indispensable condition to the acceptance of the utilitarian standard; for that standard is not the agent's own greatest happiness, but the greatest amount of happiness altogether; and if it may possibly be doubted whether a noble character is always the happier for its nobleness, there can be no doubt that it makes other people happier, and that the world in general is immensely a gainer by it. Utilitarianism, therefore, could only attain its end by the general cultivation of nobleness of character, even if each individual were only benefited by the nobleness of others, and his own, so far as happiness is concerned, were a sheer deduction from the benefit. But the bare enunciation of such an absurdity as this last, renders refutation superfluous.

According to the Greatest Happiness Principle, as above explained, the ultimate end, with reference to and for the sake of which all other things are desirable (whether we are considering our own good or that of other people), is an existence exempt as far as possible from pain, and as rich as possible in enjoyments, both in point of quantity and quality; the test of quality, and the rule for measuring it against quantity, being the preference felt by those who, in their opportunities of experience, to which must be added their habits of self-consciousness and self-observation, are best furnished with the means of comparison. This, being, according to the utilitarian opinion, the end of human action, is necessarily also the standard of morality; which may accordingly be defined, the rules and precepts for human conduct, by the observance of which an existence such as has been described might be, to the greatest extent possible, secured to all mankind; and not to them only, but, so far as the nature of things admits, to the whole sentient creation.

114

John Stuart Mill

from *On Liberty*

In addition to his contributions to moral philosophy, John Stuart Mill also made important contributions to political thought, and he is commonly regarded as one of the towering figures in the history of classical liberalism and libertarianism. The following are excerpts from his most important political work, *On Liberty*. Here, Mill discusses the inherent tension between state authority and individual liberty in making a case for liberal democracy and legal rights that are justified by their utility in maximizing happiness. This passage also includes his discussion of what is often referred to as the "harm principle," which is an influential view about the conditions under which laws restricting individual liberty are justified.

The subject of this Essay is not the so-called Liberty of the Will, so unfortunately opposed to the misnamed doctrine of Philosophical Necessity; but Civil, or Social Liberty: the nature and limits of the power which can be legitimately exercised by society over the individual. A question seldom stated, and hardly ever discussed, in general terms, but which profoundly influences the practical controversies of the age by its latent presence, and is likely soon to make itself recognised as the vital question of the future. It is so far from being new, that, in a certain sense, it has divided mankind, almost from the remotest ages; but in the stage of progress into which the more civilized portions of the species have now entered, it presents itself under new conditions, and requires a different and more fundamental treatment.

The struggle between Liberty and Authority is the most conspicuous feature in the portions of history with which we are earliest familiar, particularly

SOURCE: John Stuart Mill, *On Liberty*, 4th ed. (London: Longmans, Green, Reader and Dyer, 1869), 7–15, 21–27.

in that of Greece, Rome, and England. But in old times this contest was between subjects, or some classes of subjects, and the Government. By liberty, was meant protection against the tyranny of the political rulers. The rulers were conceived (except in some of the popular governments of Greece) as in a necessarily antagonistic position to the people whom they ruled. They consisted of a governing One, or a governing tribe or caste, who derived their authority from inheritance or conquest, who, at all events, did not hold it at the pleasure of the governed, and whose supremacy men did not venture, perhaps did not desire, to contest, whatever precautions might be taken against its oppressive exercise. Their power was regarded as necessary, but also as highly dangerous; as a weapon which they would attempt to use against their subjects, no less than against external enemies. To prevent the weaker members of the community from being preyed upon by innumerable vultures, it was needful that there should be an animal of prey stronger than the rest, commissioned to keep them down. But as the king of the vultures would be no less bent upon preying on the flock than any of the minor harpies, it was indispensable to be in a perpetual attitude of defence against his beak and claws. The aim, therefore, of patriots was to set limits to the power which the ruler should be suffered to exercise over the community; and this limitation was what they meant by liberty. It was attempted in two ways. First, by obtaining a recognition of certain immunities, called political liberties or rights, which it was to be regarded as a breach of duty in the ruler to infringe, and which, if he did infringe, specific resistance, or general rebellion, was held to be justifiable. A second, and generally a later expedient, was the establishment of constitutional checks, by which the consent of the community, or of a body of some sort, supposed to represent its interests, was made a necessary condition to some of the more important acts of the governing power. To the first of these modes of limitation, the ruling power, in most European countries, was compelled, more or less, to submit. It was not so with the second; and, to attain this, or when already in some degree possessed, to attain it more completely, became everywhere the principal object of the lovers of liberty. And so long as mankind were content to combat one enemy by another, and to be ruled by a master, on condition of being guaranteed more or less efficaciously against his tyranny, they did not carry their aspirations beyond this point.

A time, however, came, in the progress of human affairs, when men ceased to think it a necessity of nature that their governors should be an independent power, opposed in interest to themselves. It appeared to them much better that the various magistrates of the State should be their tenants or delegates, revocable at their pleasure. In that way alone, it seemed, could they have complete security that the powers of government would never be abused to their disadvantage. By degrees this new demand for elective and temporary rulers became the prominent object of the exertions of the popular party, wherever any such party existed; and superseded, to a considerable extent, the previous efforts to limit the power of rulers. As the struggle proceeded for making the ruling power emanate from the periodical choice of the ruled, some persons began to think that too much importance had been attached to the limitation of the power itself. *That* (it might seem) was a resource against rulers whose interests were habitually opposed to those of the people. What was now wanted was, that the rulers should be identified with the people; that their interest and will should be the interest and will of the nation. The nation did not need to be protected against its own will. There was no fear of its tyrannizing over itself. Let the rulers be effectually responsible to it, promptly removable by it, and it could afford to trust them with power of which it could itself dictate the use to be made. Their power was but the nation's own power, concentrated, and in a form convenient for exercise. This mode of thought, or rather perhaps of feeling, was common among the last generation of European liberalism, in the Continental section of which it still apparently predominates. Those who admit any limit to what a government may do, except in the case of such governments as they think ought not to exist, stand out as brilliant exceptions among the political thinkers of the Continent. A similar tone of sentiment might by this time have been prevalent in our own country, if the circumstances which for a time encouraged it, had continued unaltered.

But, in political and philosophical theories, as well as in persons, success discloses faults and infirmities which failure might have concealed from observation. The notion, that the people have no need to limit their power over themselves, might seem axiomatic, when popular government was a thing only dreamed about, or read of as having existed at some distant period of the past. Neither was that notion necessarily disturbed by such temporary aberrations as those of the French Revolution, the worst of which were the work of an usurping few, and which, in any case, belonged, not to the permanent working of popular institutions, but to a sudden and convulsive outbreak against monarchical and aristocratic despotism. In time, however, a democratic republic came to occupy a large portion of the earth's surface, and made itself felt as one of the most powerful members of the community of nations; and elective and responsible government became subject to the observations and criticisms which wait upon a great existing fact. It was now perceived that such phrases as 'self-government,' and 'the power of the people over themselves,' do not express the true state of the case. The 'people' who exercise the power are not always the same people with those over whom it is exercised; and the 'self-government' spoken of is not the government of each by himself, but of each by all the rest. The will of the people, moreover, practically means the will of the most numerous or the most active *part* of the people; the majority, or those who succeed in making themselves accepted as the majority; the people, consequently, *may* desire to oppress a part of their number; and precautions are as much needed against this as against any other abuse of power. The limitation, therefore, of the power of government over individuals loses none of its importance when the holders of power are regularly accountable to the community, that is, to the strongest party therein. This view of things, recommending itself equally to the intelligence of thinkers and to the inclination of those important classes in European society to whose real or supposed interests democracy is adverse, has had no difficulty in establishing itself; and in political speculations "the tyranny of the majority" is now generally included among the evils against which society requires to be on its guard.

Like other tyrannies, the tyranny of the majority was at first, and is still vulgarly, held in dread, chiefly as operating through the acts of the public authorities. But reflecting persons perceived that when society is itself the tyrant—society collectively, over the separate individuals who compose it—its means of tyrannizing are not restricted to the acts which it may do by the hands of its political functionaries. Society can and does execute its own mandates: and if it issues wrong mandates instead of right, or any mandates at all in things with which it ought not to meddle, it practises a social tyranny more formidable than many kinds of political oppression, since, though not usually upheld by such extreme penalties, it leaves fewer means of escape, penetrating much more deeply into the details of life, and enslaving the soul itself. Protection, therefore, against the tyranny of the magistrate is not enough: there needs protection also against the tyranny of the prevailing opinion and feeling; against the tendency of society to impose, by other means than civil penalties, its own ideas and practices as rules of conduct on those who dissent from them; to fetter the development, and, if possible, prevent the formation, of any individuality not in harmony with its ways, and compel all characters to fashion themselves upon the model of its own. There is a limit to the legitimate interference of collective opinion with individual independence: and to find that limit, and maintain it against encroachment, is as indispensable to a good condition of human affairs, as protection against political despotism.

But though this proposition is not likely to be contested in general terms, the practical question, where to place the limit—how to make the fitting adjustment between individual independence and social control—is a subject on which nearly everything remains to be done. All that makes existence valuable to any one, depends on the enforcement of restraints upon the actions of other people. Some rules of conduct, therefore, must be imposed, by law in the first place, and by opinion on many things which are not fit subjects for the operation of law. What these rules should be, is the principal question in human affairs; but if we except a few of the most obvious cases, it is one of those which least progress has been made in resolving. No two ages, and scarcely any two countries, have decided it alike; and the decision of one age or country is a wonder to another. Yet the people of any given age and country no more suspect any difficulty in it, than if it were a subject on which mankind had always been agreed. The rules which obtain among themselves appear to them self-evident and self-justifying. This all but universal illusion is one of the examples of the magical influence of custom, which is not only, as the proverb says, a second nature, but is continually mistaken for the first. The effect of custom, in preventing any misgiving respecting the rules of conduct which mankind impose on one another, is all the more complete because the subject is one on which it is not generally considered necessary that reasons should be given, either by one person to others, or by each to himself.

[. . . .]

The object of this Essay is to assert one very simple principle, as entitled to govern absolutely the dealings of society with the individual in the way of compulsion and control, whether the means used be physical force in the form of legal penalties, or the moral coercion of public opinion. That principle is, that the sole end for which mankind are warranted, individually or collectively, in interfering with the liberty of action of any of their number, is self-protection. That the only purpose for which power can be rightfully exercised over any member of a civilized community, against his will, is to prevent harm to others. His own good, either physical or moral, is not a sufficient warrant. He cannot rightfully be compelled to do or forbear because it will be better for him to do so, because it will make him happier, because, in the opinions of others, to do so would be wise, or even right. These are good reasons for remonstrating with him, or reasoning with him, or persuading him, or entreating him, but not for compelling him, or visiting him with any evil in case he do otherwise. To justify that, the conduct from which it is desired to deter him, must be calculated to produce evil to some one else. The only part of the conduct of any one, for which he is amenable to society, is that which concerns others. In the part which merely concerns himself, his independence is, of right, absolute. Over himself, over his own body and mind, the individual is sovereign.

It is, perhaps, hardly necessary to say that this doctrine is meant to apply only to human beings in the maturity of their faculties. We are not speaking of children, or of young persons below the age which the law may fix as that of manhood or womanhood. Those who are still in a state to require being taken care of by others, must be protected against their own actions as well as against external injury. For the same reason, we may leave out of consideration those backward states of society in which the race itself may be considered as in its nonage. The early difficulties in the way of spontaneous progress are so great, that there is seldom any choice of means for overcoming them; and a ruler full of the spirit of improvement is warranted in the use of any expedients that will attain an end, perhaps otherwise unattainable. Despotism is a legitimate mode of government in dealing with barbarians, provided the end be their improvement, and the means justified by actually effecting that end. Liberty, as a principle, has no application to any state of things anterior to the time when mankind have become capable of being improved by free and equal discussion. Until then, there is nothing for them but implicit obedience to an Akbar or a Charlemagne, if they are so fortunate as to find one. But as soon as mankind have attained the capacity of being guided to their own improvement by conviction or persuasion (a period long since reached in all nations with whom we need here concern ourselves), compulsion, either in the direct form or in that of pains and penalties for non-compliance, is no longer admissible as a means to their own good, and justifiable only for the security of others.

It is proper to state that I forego any advantage which could be derived to my argument from the idea of abstract right, as a thing independent of utility. I regard utility as the ultimate appeal on all ethical questions; but it must be utility in the largest sense, grounded on the permanent interests of man as a progressive being. Those interests, I contend, authorize the subjection of individual spontaneity to external control, only in respect to those actions of each, which concern the interest of other people. If any one does an act hurtful to others, there is a *primâ facie* case for punishing him, by law, or, where legal penalties are not safely applicable, by general disapprobation. There are also many positive acts for the benefit of others, which he may rightfully be compelled to perform; such as, to give evidence in a court of justice; to bear his fair share in the common defence, or in any other joint work necessary to the interest of the society of which he enjoys the protection; and to perform certain acts of individual beneficence, such as saving a fellow-creature's life, or interposing to protect the defenceless against ill-usage, things which whenever it is obviously a man's duty to do, he may rightfully be made responsible to society for not doing. A person may cause evil to others not only by his actions but by his inaction, and in either case he is justly accountable to them for the injury. The latter case, it is true, requires a much more cautious exercise of compulsion than the former. To make any one answerable for doing evil to others, is the rule; to make him answerable for not preventing evil, is, comparatively speaking, the exception. Yet there are many cases clear enough and grave enough to justify that exception. In all things which regard the external relations of the individual, he is *de jure* amenable to those whose interests are concerned, and if need be, to society as their protector. There are often good reasons for not holding him to the responsibility; but these reasons must arise from the special expediencies of the case: either because it is a kind of case in which he is on the whole likely to act better, when left to his own discretion, than when controlled in any way in which society have it in their power to control him; or because the attempt to exercise control would produce other evils, greater than those which it would prevent. When such reasons as these preclude the enforcement of responsibility, the conscience of the agent himself should step into the vacant judgment seat, and protect those interests of others which have no external protection; judging himself all the more rigidly, because the case does not admit of his being made accountable to the judgment of his fellow-creatures.

But there is a sphere of action in which society, as distinguished from the individual, has, if any, only an indirect interest; comprehending all that portion of a person's life and conduct which affects only himself, or if it also affects others, only with their free, voluntary, and undeceived consent and participation. When I say only himself, I mean directly, and in the first instance: for whatever affects himself, may affect others through himself; and the objection which may be grounded on this contingency, will receive consideration in the sequel. This, then, is the appropriate region of human liberty. It comprises, first, the inward domain of consciousness; demanding liberty of conscience, in the most comprehensive sense; liberty of thought and feeling; absolute freedom of opinion and sentiment on all subjects, practical or speculative, scientific, moral, or theological. The liberty of expressing and publishing opinions may seem to fall under a different principle, since it belongs to that part of the conduct of an individual which concerns other people; but, being almost of as much importance as the liberty of thought itself, and resting in great part on the same reasons, is practically inseparable from it. Secondly, the principle requires liberty of tastes and pursuits; of framing the plan of our life to suit our own character; of doing as we like, subject to such consequences as may follow: without impediment from our fellow-creatures, so long as what we do does not harm them, even though they should think our conduct foolish, perverse, or wrong. Thirdly, from this liberty of each individual, follows the liberty, within the same limits, of combination among individuals; freedom to unite, for any purpose not involving harm to others: the persons combining being supposed to be of full age, and not forced or deceived.

No society in which these liberties are not, on the whole, respected, is free, whatever may be its form of government; and none is completely free in which they do not exist absolute and unqualified. The only freedom which deserves the name, is that of pursuing our own good in our own way, so long as we do not attempt to deprive others of theirs, or impede their efforts to obtain it. Each is the proper guardian of his own health, whether bodily, or mental and spiritual. Mankind are greater gainers by suffering each other to live as seems good to themselves, than by compelling each to live as seems good to the rest.

115

Seneca Falls Women's Rights Convention Declaration of Sentiments

Despite the rhetoric of equality and empowerment in the U.S. Declaration of Independence (1776), the nation that emerged out of the American Revolution changed the status of women only very little. Impatient with pledges of rights long delayed, Lucretia Mott, Elizabeth Cady Stanton, and others held a women's rights convention at Seneca Falls, New York, in July 1848. The convention ratified its Declaration of Sentiments, which closely mimics the language and logic of the more famous 1776 text. It enumerated grievances, explaining the unbearable nature of the injustices, and calling on women and their male allies to organize and effect the necessary remedies.

Declaration of Sentiments.

When, in the course of human events, it becomes necessary for one portion of the family of man to assume among the people of the earth a position different from that which they have hitherto occupied, but one to which the laws of nature and of nature's God entitle them, a decent respect to the opinions of mankind requires that they should declare the causes that impel them to such a course.

We hold these truths to be self-evident: that all men and women are created equal; that they are endowed by their Creator with certain inalienable rights; that among these are life, liberty, and the pursuit of happiness; that to secure these rights governments are instituted, deriving their just powers from

SOURCE: *History of Woman Suffrage*, ed. Elizabeth Cady Stanton, Susan B. Anthony, and Matilda Joslyn Gage, 2nd ed., 3 vols., *Volume 1: 1848–1861* (Rochester, N.Y.: Charles Mann, 1889), 70–71.

the consent of the governed. Whenever any form of Government becomes destructive of these ends, it is the right of those who suffer from it to refuse allegiance to it, and to insist upon the institution of a new government, laying its foundation on such principles, and organizing its powers in such form as to them shall seem most likely to effect their safety and happiness. Prudence, indeed, will dictate that governments long established should not be changed for light and transient causes; and accordingly, all experience hath shown that mankind are more disposed to suffer, while evils are sufferable, than to right themselves by abolishing the forms to which they are accustomed. But when a long train of abuses and usurpations, pursuing invariably the same object, evinces a design to reduce them under absolute despotism, it is their duty to throw off such government, and to provide new guards for their future security. Such has been the patient sufferance of the women under this government, and such is now the necessity which constrains them to demand the equal station to which they are entitled.

The history of mankind is a history of repeated injuries and usurpations on the part of man toward woman, having in direct object the establishment of an absolute tyranny over her. To prove this, let facts be submitted to a candid world.

He has never permitted her to exercise her inalienable right to the elective franchise.

He has compelled her to submit to laws, in the formation of which she had no voice.

He has withheld from her rights which are given to the most ignorant and degraded men—both natives and foreigners.

Having deprived her of this first right of a citizen, the elective franchise, thereby leaving her without representation in the halls of legislation, he has oppressed her on all sides.

He has made her, if married, in the eye of the law, civilly dead.

He has taken from her all right in property, even to the wages she earns.

He has made her, morally, an irresponsible being, as she can commit many crimes with impunity, provided they be done in the presence of her husband. In the covenant of marriage, she is compelled to promise obedience to her husband, he becoming, to all intents and purposes, her master—the law giving him power to deprive her of her liberty, and to administer chastisement.

He has so framed the laws of divorce, as to what shall be the proper causes, and in case of separation, to whom the guardianship of the children shall be given, as to be wholly regardless of the happiness of women—the law, in all cases, going upon the false supposition of the supremacy of man, and giving all power into his hands.

After depriving her of all rights as a married woman, if single, and the owner of property, he has taxed her to support a government which recognizes her only when her property can be made profitable to it.

He has monopolized nearly all the profitable employments, and from those she is permitted to follow, she receives but a scanty remuneration. He closes against her all the avenues to wealth and distinction, which he considers most honorable to himself. As a teacher of theology, medicine, or law, she is not known.

He has denied her the facilities for obtaining a thorough education, all colleges being closed against her.

He allows her in Church, as well as State, but a subordinate position, claiming Apostolic authority for her exclusion from the ministry, and with some exceptions, from any public participation in the affairs of the Church.

He has created a false public sentiment, by giving to the world a different code of morals for men and women, by which moral delinquencies which exclude women from society, are not only tolerated, but deemed of little account in man.

He has usurped the prerogative of Jehovah himself, claiming it as his right to assign for her a sphere of action, when that belongs to her conscience and her God.

He has endeavored, in every way that he could, to destroy her confidence in her own powers, to lessen her self-respect, and to make her willing to lead a dependent and abject life.

Now, in view of this entire disfranchisement of one-half the people of this country, their social and religious degradation—in view of the unjust laws above mentioned, and because women do feel themselves aggrieved, oppressed, and fraudulently deprived of their most sacred rights, we insist that they have immediate admission to all the rights and privileges which belong to them as citizens of the United States.

In entering upon the great work before us, we anticipate no small amount of misconception, misrepresentation, and ridicule; but we shall use every instrumentality within our power to effect our object. We shall employ agents, circulate tracts, petition the State and National legislatures, and endeavor to enlist the pulpit and the press in our behalf. We hope this Convention will be followed by a series of Conventions embracing every part of the country.

116

Karl Marx and Frederick Engels

from *Communist Manifesto*

In 1848, German philosophers Karl Marx (1818–1883) and Frederick Engels (1820–1895) penned the *Communist Manifesto*, which has proven to be one of the most influential, if controversial, political pamphlets in human history. This brief work summarized their theories about the history of class warfare, as well as their anticipation that the arc of human history will ultimately bend toward the abolition of private property and the rise of communism. The following is an excerpt from their manifesto, in which they offer a variety of distinct predictions along those lines.

II. Proletarians and Communists.

In what relation do the Communists stand to the proletarians as a whole?

The Communists do not form a separate party opposed to other working-class parties.

They have no interests separate and apart from those of the proletariat as a whole.

They do not set up any sectarian principles of their own, by which to shape and mould the proletarian movement.

The Communists are distinguished from the other working class parties by this only: 1. In the national struggles of the proletarians of the different countries, they point out and bring to the front the common interests of the entire proletariat, independently of all nationality. 2. In the various stages of development which the struggle of the working class against the bourgeoisie

SOURCE: Karl Marx and Frederick Engels, *Manifesto of the Communist Party, Authorized English Translation: Edited and Annotated by Frederick Engels*, trans. Samuel Moore (Chicago: Charles H. Kerr, 1906), 32–47.

has to pass through, they always and everywhere represent the interests of the movement as a whole.

The Communists, therefore, are on the one hand, practically, the most advanced and resolute section of the working class parties of every country, that section which pushes forward all others; on the other hand, theoretically, they have over the great mass of the proletariat the advantage of clearly understanding the line of march, the conditions, and the ultimate general results of the proletarian movement.

The immediate aim of the Communists is the same as that of all the other proletarian parties; formation of the proletariat into a class, overthrow of the bourgeois supremacy, conquest of political power by the proletariat.

The theoretical conclusions of the Communists are in no way based on ideas or principles that have been invented, or discovered, by this or that would-be universal reformer.

They merely express, in general terms, actual relations springing from an existing class struggle, from a historical movement going on under our very eyes. The abolition of existing property relations is not at all a distinctive feature of Communism.

All property relations in the past have continually been subject to historical change consequent upon the change in historical conditions.

The French Revolution, for example, abolished feudal property in favour of bourgeois property.

The distinguishing feature of Communism is not the abolition of property generally, but the abolition of bourgeois property. But modern bourgeois private property is the final and most complete expression of the system of producing and appropriating products, that is based on class antagonism, on the exploitation of the many by the few.

In this sense, the theory of the Communists may be summed up in the single sentence: Abolition of private property.

We Communists have been reproached with the desire of abolishing the right of personally acquiring property as the fruit of a man's own labour, which property is alleged to be the ground work of all personal freedom, activity and independence.

Hard-won, self-acquired, self-earned property! Do you mean the property of the petty artizan and of the small peasant, a form of property that preceded the bourgeois form? There is no need to abolish that; the development of industry has to a great extent already destroyed it, and is still destroying it daily.

Or do you mean modern bourgeois private property?

But does wage-labour create any property for the labourer? Not a bit. It creates capital, i.e., that kind of property which exploits wage-labour, and which cannot increase except upon condition of getting a new supply of wage-labour for fresh exploitation. Property, in its present form, is based on the antagonism of capital and wage-labour. Let us examine both sides of this antagonism.

To be a capitalist, is to have not only a purely personal, but a social status in production. Capital is a collective product, and only by the united action of many members, nay, in the last resort, only by the united action of all members of society, can it be set in motion.

Capital is therefore not a personal, it is a social power.

When, therefore, capital is converted into common property, into the property of all members of society, personal property is not thereby transformed into social property. It is only the social character of the property that is changed. It loses its class-character.

Let us now take wage-labour.

The average price of wage-labour is the minimum wage, i.e., that quantum of the means of subsistence, which is absolutely requisite to keep the labourer in bare existence as a labourer. What, therefore, the wage-labourer appropriates by means of his labour, merely suffices to prolong and reproduce a bare existence. We by no means intend to abolish this personal appropriation of the products of labour, an appropriation that is made for the maintenance and reproduction of human life, and that leaves no surplus wherewith to command the labour of others. All that we want to do away with is the miserable character of this appropriation, under which the labourer lives merely to increase capital, and is allowed to live only in so far as the interest of the ruling class requires it.

In bourgeois society, living labour is but a mean to increase accumulated labour. In Communist society, accumulated labour is but a means to widen, to enrich, to promote the existence of the labourer.

In bourgeois society, therefore, the past dominates the present; in communist society, the present dominates the past. In bourgeois society capital is independent and has individuality, while the living person is dependent and has no individuality.

And the abolition of this state of things is called by the bourgeois, abolition of individuality and freedom! And rightly so. The abolition of bourgeois individuality, bourgeois independence, and bourgeois freedom is undoubtedly aimed at.

By freedom is meant, under the present bourgeois conditions of production, free trade, free selling and buying.

But if selling and buying disappears, free selling and buying disappears also. This talk about free selling and buying, and all the other "brave words" of our bourgeoisie about freedom in general, have a meaning, if any, only in contrast with restricted selling and buying, with the fettered traders of the Middle Ages, but have no meaning when opposed to the Communistic abolition of buying and selling, of the bourgeois conditions of production, and of the bourgeoisie itself.

You are horrified at our intending to do away with private property. But in your existing society, private property is already done away with for nine-tenths of the population; its existence for the few is solely due to its non-existence in the hands of those nine-tenths. You reproach us, therefore, with intending to do away with a form of property, the necessary condition for whose existence is, the non-existence of any property for the immense majority of society.

In one word, you reproach us with intending to do away with your property. Precisely so: that is just what we intend.

From the moment when labour can no longer be converted into capital, money, or rent, into a social power capable of being monopolised, i.e., from the moment when individual property can no longer be transformed into bourgeois property, into capital, from that moment, you say, individuality vanishes.

You must, therefore, confess that by "individual" you mean no other person than the bourgeois, than the middle-class owner of property. This person must, indeed, be swept out of the way, and made impossible.

Communism deprives no man of the power to appropriate the products of society: all that it does is to deprive him of the power to subjugate the labour of others by means of such appropriation.

It has been objected, that upon the abolition of private property all work will cease, and universal laziness will overtake us.

According to this, bourgeois society ought long ago to have gone to the dogs through sheer idleness; for those of its members who work, acquire nothing, and those who acquire anything, do not work. The whole of this objection is but another expression of the tautology: that there can no longer be any wage-labour when there is no longer any capital.

All objections urged against the Communistic mode of producing and appropriating material products, have, in the same way, been urged against the Communistic modes of producing and appropriating intellectual products. Just as, to the bourgeois, the disappearance of class property is the disappearance of production itself, so the disappearance of class culture is to him identical with the disappearance of all culture.

That culture, the loss of which he laments, is, for the enormous majority, a mere training to act as a machine.

But don't wrangle with us so long as you apply, to our intended abolition of bourgeois property, the standard of your bourgeois notions of freedom, culture, law, etc. Your very ideas are but the outgrowth of the conditions of your bourgeois production and bourgeois property, just as your jurisprudence is but the will of your class made into a law for all, a will, whose essential character and direction are determined by the economic conditions of existence of your class.

The selfish misconception that induces you to transform into eternal laws of nature and of reason, the social forms springing from your present mode of production and form of property—historical relations that rise and disappear in the progress of production—this misconception you share with every ruling class that has preceded you. What you see clearly in the case of ancient property, what you admit in the case of feudal property, you are of course forbidden to admit in the case of your own bourgeois form of property.

Abolition of the family! Even the most radical flare up at this infamous proposal of the Communists.

On what foundation is the present family, the bourgeois family, based? On capital, on private gain. In its completely developed form this family exists only among the bourgeoisie. But this state of things finds its complement in the practical absence of the family among the proletarians, and in public prostitution.

The bourgeois family will vanish as a matter of course when its complement vanishes, and both will vanish with the vanishing of capital.

Do you charge us with wanting to stop the exploitation of children by their parents? To this crime we plead guilty.

But, you will say, we destroy the most hallowed of relations, when we replace home education by social.

And your education! Is not that also social, and determined by the social conditions under which you educate, by the intervention, direct or indirect, of society by means of schools, &c.? The Communists have not invented the intervention of society in education; they do but seek to alter the character of that intervention, and to rescue education from the influence of the ruling class.

The bourgeois clap-trap about the family and education, about the hallowed co-relation of parent and child, becomes all the more disgusting, the more, by the action of Modern Industry, all family ties among the proletarians are torn asunder, and their children transformed into simple articles of commerce and instruments of labor.

But you Communists would introduce community of women, screams the whole bourgeoisie in chorus.

The bourgeois sees in his wife a mere instrument of production. He hears that the instruments of production are to be exploited in common, and, naturally, can come to no other conclusion, than that the lot of being common to all will likewise fall to the women.

He has not even a suspicion that the real point aimed at is to do away with the status of women as mere instruments of production.

For the rest, nothing is more ridiculous than the virtuous indignation of our bourgeois at the community of women which, they pretend, is to be openly and officially established by the Communists. The Communists have no need to introduce community of women; it has existed almost from time immemorial.

Our bourgeois, not content with having the wives and daughters of their proletarians at their disposal, not to speak of common prostitutes, take the greatest pleasure in seducing each others' wives.

Bourgeois marriage is in reality a system of wives in common and thus, at the most, what the Communists might possibly be reproached with, is that they desire to introduce, in substitution for a hypocritically concealed, an openly legalised community of women. For the rest, it is self-evident, that the abolition of the present system of production must bring with it the abolition of the community of women springing from that system, i.e., of prostitution both public and private.

The Communists are further reproached with desiring to abolish countries and nationalities.

The working men have no country. We cannot take from them what they have not got. Since the proletariat must first of all acquire political supremacy, must rise to be the leading class of the nation, must constitute itself the nation, it is, so far, itself national, though not in the bourgeois sense of the word.

National differences, and antagonisms between peoples, are daily more and more vanishing, owing to the development of the bourgeoisie, to freedom of commerce, to the world-market, to uniformity in the mode of production and in the conditions of life corresponding thereto.

The supremacy of the proletariat will cause them to vanish still faster. United action, of the leading civilised countries at least, is one of the first conditions for the emancipation of the proletariat.

In proportion as the exploitation of one individual by another is put an end to, the exploitation of one nation by another will also be put an end to. In proportion as the antagonism between classes within the nation vanishes, the hostility of one nation to another will come to an end.

The charges against Communism made from a religious, a philosophical, and generally, from an ideological standpoint, are not deserving of serious examination.

Does it require deep intuition to comprehend that man's ideas, views, and conceptions, in one word, man's consciousness, changes with every change in the conditions of his material existence, in his social relations and in his social life?

What else does the history of ideas prove, than that intellectual production changes in character in proportion as material production is changed? The ruling ideas of each age have ever been the ideas of its ruling class.

When people speak of ideas that revolutionize society, they do but express the fact, that within the old society, the elements of a new one have been created, and that the dissolution of the old ideas keeps even pace with the dissolution of the old conditions of existence.

When the ancient world was in its last throes, the ancient religions were overcome by Christianity. When Christian ideas succumbed in the 18th century to rationalist ideas, feudal society fought its death-battle with the then revolutionary bourgeoisie. The ideas of religious liberty and freedom of conscience, merely gave expression to the sway of free competition within the domain of knowledge.

"Undoubtedly," it will be said, "religious, moral, philosophical and juridical ideas have been modified in the course of historical development. But religion, morality, philosophy, political science, and law, constantly survived this change."

"There are, besides, eternal truths, such as Freedom, Justice, etc., that are common to all states of society. But Communism abolishes eternal truths, it abolishes all religion, and all morality, instead of constituting them on a new basis; it therefore acts in contradiction to all past historical experience."

What does this accusation reduce itself to? The history of all past society has consisted in the development of class antagonisms, antagonisms that assumed different forms at different epochs.

But whatever form they may have taken, one fact is common to all past ages, viz., the exploitation of one part of society by the other. No wonder, then, that the social consciousness of past ages, despite all the multiplicity and variety it displays, moves within certain common forms, or general ideas, which cannot completely vanish except with the total disappearance of class antagonisms.

The Communist revolution is the most radical rupture with traditional property-relations; no wonder that its development involves the most radical rupture with traditional ideas.

But let us have done with the bourgeois objections to Communism.

We have seen above, that the first step in the revolution by the working class, is to raise the proletariat to the position of ruling class, to win the battle of democracy.

The proletariat will use its political supremacy, to wrest, by degrees, all capital from the bourgeoisie, to centralise all instruments of production in the hands of the State, i.e., of the proletariat organised as the ruling class; and to increase the total of productive forces as rapidly as possible.

Of course, in the beginning, this cannot be effected except by means of despotic inroads on the rights of property, and on the conditions of bourgeois production; by means of measures, therefore, which appear economically insufficient and untenable, but which, in the course of the movement, outstrip themselves, necessitate further inroads upon the old social order, and are unavoidable as a means of entirely revolutionising the mode of production.

These measures will of course be different in different countries.

Nevertheless in the most advanced countries the following will be pretty generally applicable:

1. Abolition of property in land and application of all rents of land to public purposes.
2. A heavy progressive or graduated income tax.
3. Abolition of all right of inheritance.
4. Confiscation of the property of all emigrants and rebels.
5. Centralisation of credit in the hands of the state, by means of a national bank with State capital and an exclusive monopoly.
6. Centralisation of the means of communication and transport in the hands of the State.
7. Extension of factories and instruments of production owned by the State; the bringing into cultivation of waste lands, and the improvement of the soil generally in accordance with a common plan.
8. Equal liability of all to labour. Establishment of industrial armies, especially for agriculture.
9. Combination of agriculture with manufacturing industries; gradual abolition of the distinction between town and country, by a more equable distribution of population over the country.
10. Free education for all children in public schools. Abolition of children's factory labour in its present form. Combination of education with industrial production, etc., etc.

When, in the course of development, class distinctions have disappeared, and all production has been concentrated in the hands of a vast association of the whole nation, the public power will lose its political character. Political power, properly so called, is merely the organised power of one class for oppressing another. If the proletariat during its contest with the bourgeoisie is compelled, by the force of circumstances, to organise itself as a class, if, by means of a revolution, it makes itself the ruling class, and, as such, sweeps away by force the old conditions of production, then it will, along with these conditions, have swept away the conditions for the existence of class antagonisms, and of classes generally, and will thereby have abolished its own supremacy as a class.

In place of the old bourgeois society, with its classes and class antagonisms, we shall have an association, in which the free development of each is the condition for the free development of all.

117

Charles Darwin

from *On the Origin of Species*

As one of the seminal texts of the last two centuries, Charles Darwin's *On the Origin of Species* sparked what amounted to a revolution in thought. Until the mid-nineteenth century, prevailing scientific models had generally provided for supernatural creation, intervention, control, and/or oversight. Darwin (1809–1882), along with others, such as his cousin Herbert Spencer, deleted this provision, thereby proposing that biological diversity is fully explainable by natural processes and selection. The implications of this view for theology, science, and social theory were profound, and have reverberated ever since the book's publication in 1859. Although it was the American sociologist William Graham Sumner who first coined the phrase "survival of the fittest," the concept is patently Darwinian.

Introduction.

. . . No one ought to feel surprise at much remaining as yet unexplained in regard to the origin of species and varieties, if he makes due allowance for our profound ignorance in regard to the mutual relations of all the beings which live around us. Who can explain why one species ranges widely and is very numerous, and why another allied species has a narrow range and is rare? Yet these relations are of the highest importance, for they determine the present welfare, and, as I believe, the future success and modification of every inhabitant of this world. Still less do we know of the mutual relations of the innumerable inhabitants of the world during the many past geological epochs in its history. Although much remains obscure, and will long remain obscure,

SOURCE: Charles Darwin, *On the Origin of Species by Means of Natural Selection, or the Preservation of Favoured Races in the Struggle for Life* (New York: Appleton, 1864), 13, 47, 52–53, 60–61, 80–81, 150, 152–53, 417–19.

I can entertain no doubt, after the most deliberate study and dispassionate judgment of which I am capable, that the view which most naturalists entertain, and which I formerly entertained—namely, that each species has been independently created—is erroneous. I am fully convinced that species are not immutable; but that those belonging to what are called the same genera are lineal descendants of some other and generally extinct species, in the same manner as the acknowledged varieties of any one species are the descendants of that species. Furthermore, I am convinced that Natural Selection has been the main but not exclusive means of modification.

[. . . .]

Chapter II: VARIATION UNDER NATURE.

Again, we have many slight differences which may be called individual differences, such as are known frequently to appear in the offspring from the same parents, or which may be presumed to have thus arisen, from being frequently observed in the individuals of the same species inhabiting the same confined locality. No one supposes that all the individuals of the same species are cast in the very same mould. These individual differences are highly important for us, as they afford materials for natural selection to accumulate, in the same manner as man can accumulate in any given direction individual differences in his domesticated productions. These individual differences generally affect what naturalists consider unimportant parts; but I could show by a long catalogue of facts, that parts which must be called important, whether viewed under a physiological or classificatory point of view, sometimes vary in the individuals of the same species. I am convinced that the most experienced naturalist would be surprised at the number of the cases of variability, even in important parts of structure, which he could collect on good authority, as I have collected, during a course of years.

[. . . .]

Hence I look at individual differences, though of small interest to the systematist, as of high importance for us, as being the first step towards such slight varieties as are barely thought worth recording in works on natural history. And I look at varieties which are in any degree more distinct and permanent, as steps leading to more strongly marked and more permanent varieties; and at these latter, as leading to sub-species, and to species. The passage from one stage of difference to another and higher stage may be, in some cases, due merely to the long-continued action of different physical conditions in two different regions; but I have not much faith in this view; and I attribute the passage of a variety, from a state in which it differs very slightly from its parent to one in which it differs more, to the action of natural selection in accumulating (as will hereafter be more fully explained) differences of structure in certain definite directions. Hence I believe a well-marked variety may be called an incipient species; but whether this belief be justifiable must be judged of by the general weight of the several facts and views given throughout this work.

It need not be supposed that all varieties or incipient species necessarily attain the rank of species. They may whilst in this incipient state become extinct, or they may endure as varieties for very long periods.

[. . . .]

Chapter III: STRUGGLE FOR EXISTENCE.

. . . How have all those exquisite adaptations of one part of the organisation to another part, and to the conditions of life, and of one distinct organic being to another being, been perfected? We see these beautiful co-adaptations most plainly in the woodpecker and mistletoe; and only a little less plainly in the humblest parasite which clings to the hairs of a quadruped or feathers of a bird; in the structure of the beetle which dives through the water; in the plumed seed which is wafted by the gentlest breeze; in short, we see beautiful adaptations everywhere and in every part of the organic world.

Again, it may be asked, how is it that varieties, which I have called incipient species, become ultimately converted into good and distinct species, which in most cases obviously differ from each other far more than do the varieties of the same species? How do those groups of species, which constitute what are called distinct genera, and which differ from each other more than do the species of the same genus, arise? All these results, as we shall more fully see in the next chapter, follow from the struggle for life. Owing to this struggle for life, any variation, however slight, and from whatever cause proceeding, if it be in any degree profitable to an individual of any species, in its infinitely complex relations to other organic beings and to external nature, will tend to the preservation of that individual, and will generally be inherited by its offspring. The offspring, also, will thus have a better chance of surviving, for, of the many individuals of any species which are periodically born, but a small number can survive. I have called this principle, by which each slight variation, if useful, is preserved, by the term of Natural Selection, in order to mark its relation to man's power of selection. We have seen that man by selection can certainly produce great results, and can adapt organic beings to his own uses, through the accumulation of slight but useful variations, given to him by the hand of Nature. But Natural Selection, as we shall hereafter see, is a power incessantly ready for action, and is as immeasurably superior to man's feeble efforts, as the works of Nature are to those of Art.

[. . . .]

Chapter IV: NATURAL SELECTION

. . . It may be said that natural selection is daily and hourly scrutinising, throughout the world, every variation, even the slightest; rejecting that which is bad, preserving and adding up all that is good; silently and insensibly working, whenever and wherever opportunity offers, at the improvement of each organic consequently how being in relation to its organic and inorganic conditions of life. We see nothing of these slow changes in progress, until the hand of time has marked the long lapse of ages, and then so imperfect is our view into long past geological ages, that we only see that the forms of life are now different from what they formerly were.

Although natural selection can act only through and for the good of each being, yet characters and structures, which we are apt to consider as of very trifling importance, may thus be acted on. When we see leaf-eating insects green, and bark-feeders mottled-grey; the alpine ptarmigan white in winter, the red-grouse the colour of heather, and the black-grouse that of peaty earth, we must believe that these tints are of service to these birds and insects in preserving them from danger. . . . Hence I can see no reason to doubt that natural selection might be most effective in giving the proper column to each kind of grouse, and in keeping that colour, when once acquired, true and constant.

[. . . .]

Chapter V: LAWS OF VARIATION.

. . . He who believes that each equine species was independently created, will, I presume, assert that each species has been created with a tendency to vary, both under nature and under domestication, in this particular manner, so as often to become striped like other species of the genus; and that each has been created with a strong tendency, when crossed with species inhabiting distant quarters of the world, to produce hybrids resembling in their stripes, not their own parents, but other species of the genus. To admit this view is, as it seems to me, to reject a real for an unreal, or at least for an unknown, cause. It makes the works of God a mere mockery and deception; I would almost as soon believe with the old and ignorant cosmogonists, that fossil shells had never lived, but had been created in stone so as to mock the shells now living on the sea-shore.

[. . . .]

Whatever the cause may be of each slight difference in the offspring from their parents—and a cause for each must exist—it is the steady accumulation, through natural selection, of such differences, when beneficial to the individual, that gives rise to all the more important modifications of structure, by which the innumerable beings on the face of this earth are enabled to struggle with each other, and the best adapted to survive.

[. . . .]

Chapter XIV: RECAPITULATION AND CONCLUSION.

. . . Why, it may be asked, have all the most eminent living naturalists and geologists rejected this view of the mutability of species? It cannot be asserted that organic beings in a state of nature are subject to no variation; it cannot be proved that the amount of variation in the course of long ages is a limited quantity; no clear distinction has been, or can be, drawn between species and well-marked varieties. It cannot be maintained that species when intercrossed are invariably sterile, and varieties invariably fertile; or that sterility is a special endowment and sign of creation. The belief that species were immutable productions was almost unavoidable as long as the history of the world was thought to be of short duration; and now that we have acquired some idea of the lapse of time, we are too apt to assume, without proof, that the geological record is so perfect that it would have afforded us plain evidence of the mutation of species, if they had undergone mutation.

But the chief cause of our natural unwillingness to admit that one species has given birth to other and distinct species, is that we are always slow in admitting any great change of which we do not see the intermediate steps. The difficulty is the same as that felt by so many geologists, when Lyell first insisted that long lines of inland cliffs had been formed, and great valleys excavated, by the slow action of the coast-waves. The mind cannot possibly grasp the full meaning of the term of a hundred million years; it cannot add up and perceive the full effects of many slight variations, accumulated during an almost infinite number of generations.

Although I am fully convinced of the truth of the views given in this volume under the form of an abstract, I by no means expect to convince experienced naturalists whose minds are stocked with a multitude of facts all viewed, during a long course of years, from a point of view directly opposite to mine. It is so easy to hide our ignorance under such expressions as the "plan of creation," "unity of design," &c., and to think that we give an explanation when we only restate a fact. Any one whose disposition leads him to attach more weight to unexplained difficulties than to the explanation of a certain number of facts will certainly reject my theory. A few naturalists, endowed with much flexibility of mind, and who have already begun to doubt on the immutability of species, may be influenced by this volume; but I look with confidence to the future, to young and rising naturalists, who will be able to view both sides of the question with impartiality. Whoever is led to believe that species are mutable will do good service by conscientiously expressing his conviction; for only thus can the load of prejudice by which this subject is overwhelmed be removed.

118

Frederick Douglass

from What to the Slave Is the Fourth of July?

Frederick Douglass (1817–1895) escaped slavery in Maryland as a young man to become one of the most prominent intellectuals, lecturers, suffragists, and spokespersons for equality and the abolitionist movement in nineteenth century America. He was the first African American to be nominated for Vice President of the United States. The following is an excerpt from his famous July Fourth oration, originally delivered to the Rochester (New York) Ladies' Anti-Slavery Society on July 5, 1852. In it, Douglass offers a scathing critique of America's long and hypocritical endorsement of slavery.

———————

Fellow-citizens—Pardon me and allow me to ask, why am I called upon to speak here to-day? What have I, or those I represent, to do with your national independence? Are the great principles of political freedom and of natural justice, embodied in that Declaration of Independence, extended to us? and am I, therefore, called upon to bring our humble offering to the national altar, and to confess the benefits and express devout gratitude for the blessings, resulting from your independence to us?

Would to God, both for your sakes and ours, that an affirmative answer could be truthfully returned to these questions! Then would my task be light, and my burden easy and delightful. For who is there so cold, that a nation's sympathy could not warm him? Who so obdurate and dead to the claims of gratitude, that would not thankfully acknowledge such priceless benefits? Who so stolid and selfish, that would not give his voice to swell the hallelujahs of a nation's jubilee, when the chains of servitude had been torn from his limbs? I

SOURCE: Frederick Douglass, *My Bondage and My Freedom* (New York: Miller, Orton & Mulligan, 1855), 441–45.

am not that man. In a case like that, the dumb might eloquently speak, and the "lame man leap as an hart."

But, such is not the state of the case. I say it with a sad sense of the disparity between us. I am not included within the pale of this glorious anniversary! Your high independence only reveals the immeasurable distance between us. The blessings in which you this day rejoice, are not enjoyed in common. The rich inheritance of justice, liberty, prosperity, and independence, bequeathed by your fathers, is shared by you, not by me. The sunlight that brought life and healing to you, has brought stripes and death to me. This Fourth of July is *yours*, not *mine. You* may rejoice, *I* must mourn. To drag a man in fetters into the grand illuminated temple of liberty, and call upon him to join you in joyous anthems, were inhuman mockery and sacrilegious irony. Do you mean, citizens, to mock me, by asking me to speak to-day? If so, there is a parallel to your conduct. And let me warn you that it is dangerous to copy the example of a nation whose crimes, towering up to heaven, were thrown down by the breath of the Almighty, burying that nation in irrecoverable ruin! I can to-day take up the plaintive lament of a peeled and woe-smitten people!

"By the rivers of Babylon, there we sat down. Yea! we wept when we remembered Zion. We hanged our harps upon the willows in the midst thereof. For there, they that carried us away captive, required of us a song; and they who wasted us required of us mirth, saying, Sing us one of the songs of Zion. How can we sing the Lord's song in a strange land? If I forget thee, O Jerusalem, let my right hand forget her cunning. If I do not remember thee, let my tongue cleave to the roof of my mouth."

Fellow-citizens, above your national, tumultuous joy, I hear the mournful wail of millions, whose chains, heavy and grievous yesterday, are to-day, rendered more intolerable by the jubilant shouts that reach them. If I do forget, if I do not faithfully remember those bleeding children of sorrow this day, "may my right hand forget her cunning, and may my tongue cleave to the roof of my mouth!" To forget them, to pass lightly over their wrongs, and to chime in with the popular theme, would be treason most scandalous and shocking, and would make me a reproach before God and the world. My subject, then, fellow-citizens, is AMERICAN SLAVERY. I shall see this day and its popular characteristics, from the slave's point of view. Standing, there, identified with the American bondman, making his wrongs mine, I do not hesitate to declare, with all my soul, that the character and conduct of this nation never looked blacker to me than on this Fourth of July. Whether we turn to the declarations of the past, or to the professions of the present, the conduct of the nation seems equally hideous and revolting. America is false to the past, false to the present, and solemnly binds herself to be false to the future. Standing with God and the crushed and bleeding slave on this occasion, I will, in the name of humanity which is outraged, in the name of liberty which is fettered, in the name of the constitution and the bible, which are disregarded and trampled upon, dare to call in question and to denounce, with all the emphasis I can command, everything that serves to perpetuate slavery—the great sin and shame of America! "I will not equivocate; I will not excuse;" I will use the severest language I can command; and yet not one word shall escape me that any man, whose judgment is not blinded by prejudice, or who is not at heart a slaveholder, shall not confess to be right and just.

But I fancy I hear some one of my audience say, it is just in this circumstance that you and your brother abolitionists fail to make a favorable impression on the public mind. Would you argue more, and denounce less, would you persuade more and rebuke less, your cause would be much more likely to succeed. But, I submit, where all is plain there is nothing to be argued. What point in the anti-slavery creed would you have me argue? On what branch of the subject do the people of this country need light? Must I undertake to prove that the slave is a man? That point is conceded already. Nobody doubts it. The slaveholders themselves acknowledge it in the enactment of laws for their government. They acknowledge it when they punish disobedience on the part of the slave. There are seventy-two crimes in the state of Virginia, which, if committed by a black man, (no matter how ignorant he be), subject him to the punishment of death; while only two of the same crimes will subject a white man to the like punishment. What is this but the acknowledgement that the slave is a moral, intellectual, and responsible being[?] The manhood of the slave is conceded. It is admitted in the fact that southern statute books are covered with enactments forbidding, under severe fines and penalties, the teaching of the slave to read or to write. When you can point to any such laws, in reference to the beasts of the field, then I may consent to argue the manhood of the slave. When the dogs in your streets, when the fowls of the air, when the cattle on your hills, when the fish of the sea, and the reptiles that crawl, shall be unable to distinguish the slave from a brute, *then* will I argue with you that the slave is a man!

For the present, it is enough to affirm the equal manhood of the negro race. Is it not astonishing that, while we are ploughing, planting, and reaping, using all kinds of mechanical tools, erecting houses, constructing bridges, building ships, working in metals of brass, iron, copper, silver, and gold; that, while we are reading, writing, and cyphering, acting as clerks, merchants, and secretaries, having among us lawyers, doctors, ministers, poets, authors, editors, orators, and teachers; that, while we are engaged in all manner of enterprises common to other men—digging gold in California, capturing the whale in the Pacific, feeding sheep and cattle on the hill-side, living, moving, acting, thinking, planning, living in families as husbands, wives, and children, and, above all, confessing and worshiping the christian's God, and looking hopefully for life and immortality beyond the grave,—we are called upon to prove that we are men!

Would you have me argue that man is entitled to liberty? that he is the rightful owner of his own body? You have already declared it. Must I argue the wrongfulness of slavery? Is that a question for republicans? Is it to be settled by the rules of logic and argumentation, as a matter beset with great difficulty, involving a doubtful application of the principle of justice, hard to be understood? How should I look to-day, in the presence of Americans, dividing and subdividing a discourse, to show that men have a natural right to freedom? speaking of it relatively and positively, negatively and affirmatively. To do so, would be to make myself ridiculous, and to offer an insult to your understanding. There is not a man beneath the canopy of heaven, that does not know that slavery is wrong *for him*.

What! am I to argue that it is wrong to make men brutes, to rob them of their liberty, to work them without wages, to keep them ignorant of their relations to their fellow men, to beat them with sticks, to flay their flesh with the lash, to load their limbs with irons, to hunt them with dogs, to sell them at auction, to sunder their families, to knock out their teeth, to burn their flesh, to starve them into obedience and submission to their masters? Must I argue that a system, thus marked with blood, and stained with pollution, is wrong? No; I will not. I have better employments for my time and strength than such arguments would imply.

What, then, remains to be argued? Is it that slavery is not divine; that God did not establish it; that our doctors of divinity are mistaken? There is blasphemy in the thought. That which is inhuman cannot be divine. Who can reason on such a proposition? They that can, may; I cannot. The time for such argument is passed.

At a time like this, scorching irony, not convincing argument, is needed. Oh! had I the ability, and could I reach the nation's ear, I would, to-day, pour out a fiery stream of biting ridicule, blasting reproach, withering sarcasm, and stern rebuke. For it is not light that is needed, but fire; it is not the gentle shower, but thunder. We need the storm, the whirlwind, and the earthquake. The feeling of the nation must be quickened; the conscience of the nation must be roused; the propriety of the nation must be startled; the hypocrisy of the nation must be exposed; and its crimes against God and man must be proclaimed and denounced.

What to the American slave is your Fourth of July? I answer, a day that reveals to him, more than all other days in the year, the gross injustice and cruelty to which he is the constant victim. To him, your celebration is a sham; your boasted liberty, an unholy license; your national greatness, swelling vanity; your sounds of rejoicing are empty and heartless; your denunciations of tyrants, brass-fronted impudence; your shouts of liberty and equality, hollow mockery; your prayers and hymns, your sermons and thanksgivings, with all your religious parade and solemnity, are to him mere bombast, fraud, deception, impiety, and hypocrisy—a thin veil to cover up crimes which would disgrace a nation of savages. There is not a nation on the earth guilty of practices more shocking and bloody than are the people of these United States, at this very hour.

Go where you may, search where you will, roam through all the monarchies and despotisms of the old world, travel through South America, search out every abuse, and when you have found the last, lay your facts by the side of the every-day practices of this nation, and you will say with me, that, for revolting barbarity and shameless hypocrisy, America reigns without a rival.

119

Abraham Lincoln

Gettysburg Address

In July 1863, President Abraham Lincoln's Union army had gained a strategic military victory in the American Civil War at Gettysburg, Pennsylvania. The victory, however, cost some fifty-one thousand casualties. As the crowds gathered four months later, on November 19, 1863, to dedicate the battle-field cemetery at Gettysburg, Lincoln was not the chosen keynote speaker. That honor went to Edward Everett, who delivered a speech of some thirteen thousand words, with celebratory references to numerous historic battles. By contrast, Lincoln, shouldering the weight of such carnage, gave a poignant address in fewer than three hundred words, which is often recognized as one of the greatest speeches in human history.

Four score and seven years ago our fathers brought forth on this continent, a new nation, conceived in Liberty, and dedicated to the proposition that all men are created equal.

Now we are engaged in a great civil war, testing whether that nation, or any nation so conceived and so dedicated, can long endure. We are met on a great battle field of that war. We have come to dedicate a portion of that field, as a final resting place for those who here gave their lives that that nation might live. It is altogether fitting and proper that we should do this.

But, in a larger sense, we can not dedicate—we can not consecrate—we can not hallow—this ground. The brave men, living and dead, who struggled here, have consecrated it, far above our poor power to add or detract. The world will little note, nor long remember what we say here, but it can never forget what they did here. It is for us the living, rather, to be dedicated here

SOURCE: Abraham Lincoln, "The Gettysburg Address," 1863, Library of Congress website, https://tile.loc.gov/storage-services/service/rbc/lprbscsm/scsm0717/scsm0717.pdf.

to the unfinished work which they who fought here have thus far so nobly advanced. It is rather for us to be here dedicated to the great task remaining before us—that from these honored dead we take increased devotion to that cause for which they gave the last full measure of devotion—that we here highly resolve that these dead shall not have died in vain—that this nation, under God, shall have a new birth of freedom—and that government of the people, by the people, for the people, shall not perish from the earth.

ABRAHAM LINCOLN
November 19, 1863

120

Abraham Lincoln

Second Inaugural Address

The sixteenth President of the United States, Abraham Lincoln (1809–1865) was re-elected in November 1864, amidst the American Civil War. By Inauguration Day, the outcome of the war was all but a foregone conclusion: the Union would prevail. Thus, as Lincoln took the Oath of Office and delivered his Second Inaugural Address, he struck a conciliatory tone, looking to "bind up the nation's wounds." Unknown on that afternoon of March 4, 1865, however, was that an assassin would soon silence Lincoln's voice, and deny his leadership in restoring the nation. Heard in terms of those events, the speech engenders an eerily prophetic feel.

FELLOW-COUNTRYMEN,—At this second appearing to take the oath of the Presidential office, there is less occasion for an extended address than there was at the first. Then, a statement, somewhat in detail, of a course to be pursued seemed very fitting and proper. Now, at the expiration of four years, during which public declarations have been constantly called forth on every point and phase of the great contest which still absorbs the attention and engrosses the energies of the nation, little that is new could be presented. The progress of our arms, upon which all else chiefly depends, is as well known to the public as to myself, and it is, I trust, reasonably satisfactory and encouraging to all. With high hope for the future, no prediction in regard to it is ventured.

On the occasion corresponding to this, four years ago, all thoughts were anxiously directed to an impending civil war. All dreaded it, all sought to avert it. While the inaugural address was being delivered from this place, devoted

SOURCE: Abraham Lincoln, "Lincoln's Second Inaugural Address," in *The International Library of Famous Literature: Selections from the World's Great Writers, Ancient, Mediæval, and Modern, with Biographical and Explanatory Notes and Critical Essays by Many Eminent Writers*, ed. Richard Garnett, vol. 15 (London: The Standard, 1899), 7288–90.

altogether to saving the Union without war, insurgent agents were in the city, seeking to destroy it without war,—seeking to dissolve the Union, and divide effects by negotiation. Both parties deprecated war; but one of them would make war rather than let the nation survive, and the other would accept war rather than let it perish; and the war came.

One eighth of the whole population were colored slaves, not distributed generally over the Union, but localized in the southern part of it. These slaves constituted a peculiar and powerful interest. All knew that this interest was somehow the cause of the war. To strengthen, perpetuate, and extend this interest was the object for which the insurgents would rend the Union by war, while the government claimed no right to do more than to restrict the territorial enlargement of it.

Neither party expected for the war the magnitude or the duration which it has already attained. Neither anticipated that the cause of the conflict might cease with, or even before the conflict itself should cease. Each looked for an easier triumph, and a result less fundamental and astounding. Both read the same Bible, and pray to the same God, and each invokes His aid against the other. It may seem strange that any men should dare to ask a just God's assistance in wringing their bread from the sweat of other men's faces. But let us judge not, that we be not judged. The prayers of both could not be answered. That of neither has been answered fully. The Almighty has His own purposes. "Woe unto the world because of offenses, for it must needs be that offenses come; but woe to that man by whom the offense cometh."

If we shall suppose that American slavery is one of those offenses, which, in the providence of God, must needs come, but which, having continued through His appointed time, He now wills to remove, and that He gives to both North and South this terrible war as the woe due to those by whom the offense came, shall we discern therein any departure from those divine attributes which the believers in a living God always ascribe to Him?

Fondly do we hope, fervently do we pray, that this mighty scourge of war may speedily pass away. Yet, if God wills that it continue until all the wealth piled by the bondsman's two hundred and fifty years of unrequited toil shall be sunk, and until every drop of blood drawn by the lash shall be paid by another drawn with the sword, as was said three thousand years ago, so still it must be said that "the judgments of the Lord are true and righteous altogether."

With malice towards none, with charity for all, with firmness in the right, as God gives us to see the right, let us strive on to finish the work we are in, to bind up the nation's wounds, to care for him who shall have borne the battle, and for his widow and orphans, to do all which may achieve and cherish a just and lasting peace among ourselves and with all nations.

121

Susan B. Anthony

from *Address Prior to Her Trial, June 1873*

Nearly fifty years before the Nineteenth Amendment granted women the right to vote in the United States, Susan B. Anthony (1820–1906) committed an act of civil disobedience when she cast a ballot in the presidential election of 1872. Three elections officials counted her vote. Within only a matter of days, a warrant was issued for her arrest, as well as the arrest of the three polling officials. Charged with violating the Enforcement Act of 1870, while out on bail and before her trial in 1873, Anthony delivered the following speech. This is one of the clearest summations of the suffragist petition. Anthony was ultimately convicted and fined $100, which she refused to pay. Nearly 150 years later, on the one-hundredth anniversary of the ratification of the Nineteenth Amendment (August 18, 2020), Anthony was formally pardoned by President Donald J. Trump.

Friends and Fellow-citizens: I stand before you to-night, under indictment for the alleged crime of having voted at the last Presidential election, without having a lawful right to vote. It shall be my work this evening to prove to you that in thus voting, I not only committed no crime, but, instead, simply exercised my *citizen's right*, guaranteed to me and all United States citizens by the National Constitution, beyond the power of any State to deny.

Our democratic-republican government is based on the idea of the natural right of every individual member thereof to a voice and a vote in making and executing the laws. We assert the province of government to be to secure the

SOURCE: *An Account of the Proceedings of the Trial of Susan B. Anthony, on the Charge of Illegal Voting, at the Presidential Election in Nov. 1872, and on the Trial of Beverly W. Jones, Edwin T. Marsh and William B. Hall, the Inspectors of Election by Whom Her Vote Was Received* (Rochester, N.Y.: Daily Democrat and Chronicle Book Print, 1874), 151–54, 157, 164–65, 178.

people in the enjoyment of their unalienable rights. We throw to the winds the old dogma that governments can give rights. Before governments were organized, no one denies that each individual possessed the right to protect his own life, liberty and property. And when 100 or 1,000,000 people enter into a free government, they do not barter away their natural rights; they simply pledge themselves to protect each other in the enjoyment of them, through prescribed judicial and legislative tribunals. They agree to abandon the methods of brute force in the adjustment of their differences, and adopt those of civilization.

Nor can you find a word in any of the grand documents left us by the fathers that assumes for government the power to create or to confer rights. The Declaration of Independence, the United States Constitution, the constitutions of the several states and the organic laws of the territories, all alike propose to protect the people in the exercise of their God-given rights. Not one of them pretends to bestow rights.

"All men are created equal, and endowed by their Creator with certain unalienable rights. Among these are life, liberty and the pursuit of happiness. That to secure these, governments are instituted among men, deriving their just powers from the consent of the governed."

Here is no shadow of government authority over rights, nor exclusion of any from their full and equal enjoyment. Here is pronounced the right of all men, and "consequently," as the Quaker preacher said, "of all women," to a voice in the government. And here, in this very first paragraph of the declaration, is the assertion of the natural right of all to the ballot; for, how can "the consent of the governed" be given, if the right to vote be denied. Again:

"That whenever any form of government becomes destructive of these ends, it is the right of the people to alter or abolish it, and to institute a new government, laying its foundations on such principles, and organizing its powers in such forms as to them shall seem most likely to effect their safety and happiness."

Surely, the right of the whole people to vote is here clearly implied. For however destructive in their happiness this government might become, a disfranchised class could neither alter nor abolish it, nor institute a new one, except by the old brute force method of insurrection and rebellion. One-half of the people of this nation to-day are utterly powerless to blot from the statute books an unjust law, or to write there a new and a just one. The women, dissatisfied as they are with this form of government, that enforces taxation without representation,—that compels them to obey laws to which they have never given their consent,—that imprisons and hangs them without a trial by a jury of their peers, that robs them, in marriage, of the custody of their own persons, wages and children,—are this half of the people left wholly at the mercy of the other half, in direct violation of the spirit and letter of the declarations of the framers of this government, every one of which was based on the immutable principle of equal rights to all. By those declarations, kings, priests, popes, aristocrats, were all alike dethroned, and placed on a common level, politically, with the lowliest born subject or serf. By them, too, men, as such, were deprived of their divine right to rule, and placed on a political level with women. By the practice of those declarations all class and caste distinction will be abolished; and slave, serf, plebeian, wife, woman, all alike, bound from their subject position to the proud platform of equality.

The preamble of the federal constitution says: "We, the people of the United States, in order to form a more perfect union, establish justice, insure *domestic* tranquility, provide for the common defence, promote the general welfare and secure the blessings of liberty to ourselves and our posterity, do ordain and established this constitution for the United States of America."

It was we, the people, not we, the white male citizens, nor yet we, the male citizens; but we, the whole people, who formed this Union. And we formed it, not to give the blessings or liberty, but to secure them; not to the half of ourselves and the half of our posterity, but to the whole people—women as well as men. And it is downright mockery to talk to women of their enjoyment of the blessings of liberty while they are denied the use of the only means of securing them provided by this democratic-republican government—the ballot.

The early journals of Congress show that when the committee reported to that body the original articles of confederation, the very first article which became the subject of discussion was that respecting equality of suffrage. Article 4th said: "The better to secure and perpetuate mutual friendship and intercourse between the people of the different States of this Union, the free inhabitants of each of the States, (paupers, vagabonds and fugitives from justice excepted,) shall be entitled to all the privileges and immunities of the free citizens of the several States."

Thus, at the very beginning, did the fathers see the necessity of the universal application of the great principle of equal rights to all—in order to produce the desired result—a harmonious union and a homogeneous people.

Luther Martin, attorney-general of Maryland, in his report to the Legislature of that State of the convention that framed the United States Constitution, said: "Those who advocated the equality of suffrage took the matter up on the original principles of government: that the reason why each individual man in forming a State government should have an equal vote, is because each individual, before he enters into government, is equally free and equally independent."

James Madison said; "Under every view of the subject, it seems indispensable that the mass of the citizens should not be without a voice in making the laws which they are to obey, and in choosing the magistrates who are to administer them." Also, "Let it be remembered, finally, that it has ever been the pride and the boast of America that the rights for which she contended were the rights of human nature."

And these assertions of the framers of the United States Constitution of the equal and natural rights of all the people to a voice in the government, have been affirmed and reaffirmed by the leading statesmen of the nation, throughout the entire history of our government.

[. . . .]

But I submit that in view of the explicit assertions of the equal right of the whole people, both in the preamble and previous article of the constitution, this omission of the adjective "female" in the second, should not be construed into a denial; but, instead, counted as of no effect. Mark the direct prohibition: "No member of this State shall be disfranchised, unless by the 'law of the land,' or the judgment of his peers." "The law of the land," is the United States Constitution: and there is no provision in that document that can be fairly construed into a permission to the States to deprive any class of their citizens of their right to vote. Hence New York can get no power from that source to disfranchise one entire half of her members. Nor has "the judgment of their peers" been pronounced against women exercising their right to vote; no disfranchised person is allowed to be judge or juror—and none but disfranchised persons can be women's peers; nor has the legislature passed laws excluding them on account of idiocy or lunacy; nor yet the courts convicted them of bribery, larceny, or any infamous crime. Clearly, then, there is no constitutional ground for the exclusion of women from the ballot-box in the State of New York, No barriers whatever stand to-day between women and the exercise of their right to vote save those of precedent and prejudice.

[. . . .]

The only question left to be settled, now, is: Are women persons? And I hardly believe any of our opponents will have the hardihood to say they are not. Being persons, then, women are citizens, and no state has a right to make any new law, or to enforce any old law, that shall abridge their privileges or immunities. Hence, every discrimination against women in the constitutions and laws of the several states, is to-day null and void, precisely as is every one against negroes.

Is the right to vote one of the privileges or immunities of citizens? I think the disfranchised ex-rebels, and the ex-state prisoners will all agree with me, that it is not only one of them, but the one without which all the others are nothing. Seek the first kingdom of the ballot, and all things else shall be given thee, is the political injunction.

Webster, Worcester and Bouvier all define citizen to be a person, in the United States, entitled to vote and hold office.

[. . . .]

We no longer petition Legislature or Congress to give us the right to vote. We appeal to the women everywhere to exercise their too long neglected "citizen's right to vote." We appeal to the inspectors of election everywhere to receive the votes of all United States citizens as it is their duty to do. We appeal to United States commissioners and marshals to arrest the inspectors who reject the names and votes of United States citizens, as it is their duty to do, and leave those alone who, like our eighth ward inspectors, perform their duties faithfully and well.

We ask the juries to fail to return verdicts of "guilty" against honest, law-abiding, tax-paying United States citizens for offering their votes at our elections. Or against intelligent, worthy young men, inspectors of elections, for receiving and counting such citizens' votes.

We ask the judges to render true and unprejudiced opinions of the law, and wherever there is room for a doubt to give its benefit on the side of liberty and equal rights to women, remembering that "the true rule of interpretation under our national constitution, especially since its amendments, is that anything for human rights is constitutional, everything against human rights unconstitutional."

And it is on this line that we propose to fight our battle for the ballot—all peaceably, but nevertheless persistently through to complete triumph, when all United States citizens shall be recognized as equals before the law.

Appendix: A Thematic Guide to the Selections

Asceticism

- from *The Passion of Perpetua and Felicitas*
- Athanasius of Alexandria, from *Life of Antony*
- Basil of Caesarea, from *Homily VI on Luke 12*
- Benedict of Nursia, from *The Rule of St. Benedict*
- Julian of Norwich, from *Revelations of Divine Love*
- Catherine of Siena, from *Dialogue of the Seraphic Virgin*
- Teresa of Avila, from *Interior Castle*

Authority—see Government and Power

Baptism

- *Nicene Creed*, Three Versions
- from *Schleitheim Confession of Faith, 1527*
- from *Canons and Decrees of the Sacred and Ecumenical Council of Trent*

Body

- from *Bhagavad-Gita*
- Ibn Sina (Avicenna), from *Avicenna's Offering to the Prince: A Compendium on the Soul*
- Ibn Tufail, from *Hayy ibn Yaqdhan*
- Moses Maimonides, from *Guide for the Perplexed*
- René Descartes, from *Meditations on First Philosophy*
- Sir Isaac Newton, from *Mathematical Principles of Natural Philosophy*

Buddhism

- *Doctrines of Gautama Buddha: The Four Noble Truths and Eightfold Path*

Christianity

- Ignatius of Antioch, *Epistle to the Magnesians*
- from *Didache*, chapters 1–5
- Justin Martyr, from *Second Apology*
- Irenaeus, from *Against Heresies*
- Clement of Alexandria, from *Stromata*
- Tertullian, from *Prescription against Heretics*
- Origen, from *Against Celsus*
- *Apostles' Creed*, Two Versions
- from *The Passion of Perpetua and Felicitas*
- Eusebius of Caesarea, from *Life of Constantine*
- *Edict of Milan*
- *Nicene Creed*, Three Versions
- Athanasius of Alexandria, from *Life of Antony*
- Basil of Caesarea, from *Homily VI on Luke 12*
- Sulpicius Severus, from *Life of St. Martin*
- Benedict of Nursia, from *The Rule of St. Benedict*
- John of Damascus, from *Exposition of the Orthodox Faith*
- The Venerable Bede, from *Ecclesiastical History of England* (Caedmon's Story)
- Eginhard, from *Life of Charlemagne*
- Pope Urban II, from Fulcher of Chartres' *Speech of Urban II at the Council of Clermont*
- Pope Boniface VIII, *Unam Sanctam* (November 18, 1302)
- Julian of Norwich, from *Revelations of Divine Love*
- Catherine of Siena, from *Dialogue of the Seraphic Virgin*
- Thomas à Kempis, from *Imitation of Christ*
- Bartolomé de Las Casas, from *Tears of the Indians*
- Ignatius of Loyola, from *Spiritual Exercises*
- Martin Luther, *Ninety-Five Theses*
- from *Schleitheim Confession of Faith, 1527*
- from *Canons and Decrees of the Sacred and Ecumenical Council of Trent*
- Teresa of Avila, from *Interior Castle*
- David Rice, from *Slavery Inconsistent with Justice and Good Policy*

Confucianism

- Confucius, from *Analects*
- Mencius, from *Kung-Sun Ch'ow*

Constitutions

- Aristotle, from *Politics*
- *Edict of Milan*
- Benedict of Nursia, from *The Rule of St. Benedict*
- *Magna Carta, 1215*
- from *Canons and Decrees of the Sacred and Ecumenical Council of Trent*
- *Mayflower Compact*
- John Winthrop, from *A Model of Christian Charity*
- from *English Bill of Rights, 1689*
- John Locke, from *Second Treatise on Civil Government*
- Thomas Paine, from *Common Sense*
- John Adams, from *Thoughts on Government*
- *U.S. Declaration of Independence*
- *U.S. Constitution*
- *U.S. Bill of Rights*
- *Federalist No. 10*
- *Federalist No. 51*
- *Declaration of the Rights of Man and Citizen*
- *Seneca Falls Women's Rights Convention Declaration of Sentiments*
- Frederick Douglass, from *What to the Slave Is the Fourth of July?*
- Susan B. Anthony, from *Address Prior to Her Trial, June 1873*

Creation

- Hesiod, from *Theogony*
- *Apostles' Creed*, Two Versions
- *Nicene Creed*, Three Versions
- The Venerable Bede, from *Ecclesiastical History of England* (Caedmon's Story)
- Moses Maimonides, *Thirteen Principles of the Faith*

Creeds/Confessions/Statements of Faith

- from *Didache*, chapters 1–5
- *Apostles' Creed*, Two Versions
- *Nicene Creed*, Three Versions
- Moses Maimonides, *Thirteen Principles of the Faith*
- from *Schleitheim Confession of Faith, 1527*

Crusades

- Pope Urban II, from Fulcher of Chartres' *Speech of Urban II at the Council of Clermont*
- Ibn al-Athir, from *Account of the Outbreak of the Tartars into the Lands of Islam*

Daoism/Taoism

- Lao-Tze, from *Tao Teh King*
- Sun Tzŭ, from *On the Art of War*
- Chuang Tzŭ (Zhuangzi), Nourishment of the Soul, from *Chuang Tzŭ*

Death

- Thucydides, from *History of the Peloponnesian War*
- Plato, from *Apology*
- Epicurus, *Letter to Menoeceus*
- Epictetus, from *Enchiridion*
- Marcus Aurelius, from *Meditations*
- from *The Passion of Perpetua and Felicitas*
- Li Po, *The Sun*
- Ibn Sina (Avicenna), from *Avicenna's Offering to the Prince: A Compendium on the Soul*
- Ibn Tufail, from *Hayy ibn Yaqdhan*
- Dante Alighieri, from *Divine Comedy (Inferno)*
- Abraham Lincoln, *Gettysburg Address*

Democracy

- Herodotus, from *The History*
- Aristotle, from *Politics*
- Thomas Paine, from *Common Sense*
- *U.S. Declaration of Independence*
- *U.S. Constitution*
- George Washington, from *Farewell Address to the People of the United States of America*
- Karl Marx and Frederick Engels, from *Communist Manifesto*
- *Seneca Falls Women's Rights Convention Declaration of Sentiments*
- Susan B. Anthony, from *Address Prior to Her Trial, June 1873*

Eastern Orthodoxy

- Basil of Caesarea, from *Homily VI on Luke 12*
- John of Damascus, from *Exposition of the Orthodox Faith*

Education

- Plato, from *Meno*
- Plato, from *Republic*
- Karl Marx and Frederick Engels, from *Communist Manifesto*

England

- The Venerable Bede, from *Ecclesiastical History of England* (Caedmon's Story)
- *Magna Carta, 1215*
- Joan of Arc, *Letter to the King of England, March 22, 1429*
- from *Thirty-Nine Articles of Religion* (Church of England)
- Thomas Paine, from *Common Sense*
- *U.S. Declaration of Independence*

Ethics

- Confucius, from *Analects*
- Lao-Tze, from *Tao Teh King*
- Plato, from *Euthyphro*
- Plato, from *Republic*
- Aristotle, from *Nicomachean Ethics*
- Mencius, from *Kung-Sun Ch'ow*
- Epicurus, *Letter to Menoeceus*
- from *Bhagavad-Gita*
- Marcus Tullius Cicero, from *Treatise on the Laws*
- Marcus Tullius Cicero, from *De Officiis*
- Epictetus, from *Enchiridion*
- Livy, from *History of Rome* (Stories of Lucretia and Cincinnatus)
- Plutarch, from *Lives*
- from *Didache*, chapters 1–5
- Marcus Aurelius, from *Meditations*
- Basil of Caesarea, from *Homily VI on Luke 12*
- Augustine of Hippo, from *Confessions*
- Thomas Aquinas, from *Summa Theologica* (from the Treatise on the Law)
- Bartolomé de Las Casas, from *Tears of the Indians*
- Francisco de Vitoria, from *De Indis et de Ivre Belli Reflectiones*
- John Winthrop, from *A Model of Christian Charity*
- Immanuel Kant, from *Fundamental Principles of the Metaphysic of Ethics*
- Søren Kierkegaard, from *Fear and Trembling*
- John Stuart Mill, from *Utilitarianism*

Faith and Reason

- Plato, from *Euthyphro*
- Justin Martyr, from *Second Apology*
- Clement of Alexandria, from *Stromata*
- Tertullian, from *Prescription against Heretics*
- Anselm of Canterbury and Gaunilon, from *Proslogium* (on the Ontological Argument)
- Al Ghazzali, from *Confessions of Al Ghazzali*
- Ibn Tufail, from *Hayy ibn Yaqdhan*
- Thomas Aquinas, from *Summa Theologica* ("The Five Ways")
- Petrarch, *The Ascent of Mount Ventoux*
- John Calvin, from *Institutes of the Christian Religion*
- Sir Isaac Newton, from *Mathematical Principles of Natural Philosophy*
- David Hume, from *Dialogues concerning Natural Religion* (on the Design Argument)
- David Hume, from *Dialogues concerning Natural Religion* (on the Problem of Evil)
- Søren Kierkegaard, from *Fear and Trembling*
- Charles Darwin, from *On the Origin of Species*

Freedom

- William Bradford, from *History of Plymouth Plantation*
- Thomas Hobbes, from *Leviathan*
- John Locke, from *Second Treatise on Civil Government*
- from *English Bill of Rights, 1689*
- J. Hector St. Jean de Crevecoeur, from *What Is an American?*
- Abigail Adams, *Letter from Abigail Adams to John Adams, 31 March–5 April 1776*
- *U.S. Declaration of Independence*
- *U.S. Constitution*
- *U.S. Bill of Rights*
- George Washington, from *Farewell Address to the People of the United States of America*
- *Declaration of the Rights of Man and Citizen*
- Edmund Burke, from *Reflections on the Revolution in France*
- David Rice, from *Slavery Inconsistent with Justice and Good Policy*
- Henry David Thoreau, from *Civil Disobedience*
- John Stuart Mill, from *On Liberty*
- *Seneca Falls Women's Rights Convention Declaration of Sentiments*

- Frederick Douglass, from *What to the Slave Is the Fourth of July?*
- Abraham Lincoln, *Gettysburg Address*
- Abraham Lincoln, *Second Inaugural Address*
- Susan B. Anthony, from *Address Prior to Her Trial, June 1873*

God/gods

- Homer, from *Iliad*
- Hesiod, from *Theogony*
- Plato, from *Apology*
- Plato, from *Euthyphro*
- Epicurus, *Letter to Menoeceus*
- from *Bhagavad-Gita*
- *Apostles' Creed*, Two Versions
- *Nicene Creed*, Three Versions
- Augustine of Hippo, from *Confessions*
- Li Po, *The Sun*
- Ibn Sina (Avicenna), from *Avicenna's Offering to the Prince: A Compendium on the Soul*
- Anselm of Canterbury and Gaunilon, from *Proslogium* (on the Ontological Argument)
- Al Ghazzali, from *Confessions of Al Ghazzali*
- Ibn Tufail, from *Hayy ibn Yaqdhan*
- Moses Maimonides, from *Guide for the Perplexed*
- Moses Maimonides, *Thirteen Principles of the Faith*
- Thomas Aquinas, from *Summa Theologica* ("The Five Ways")
- Julian of Norwich, from *Revelations of Divine Love*
- Catherine of Siena, from *Dialogue of the Seraphic Virgin*
- Thomas à Kempis, from *Imitation of Christ*
- Ignatius of Loyola, from *Spiritual Exercises*
- Martin Luther, *Ninety-Five Theses*
- John Calvin, from *Institutes of the Christian Religion*
- from *Schleitheim Confession of Faith, 1527*
- Teresa of Avila, from *Interior Castle*
- John Winthrop, from *A Model of Christian Charity*
- Sir Isaac Newton, from *Mathematical Principles of Natural Philosophy*
- David Hume, from *Dialogues concerning Natural Religion* (on the Design Argument)
- David Hume, from *Dialogues concerning Natural Religion* (on the Problem of Evil)

Government

- Aristotle, from *Politics*
- *Edict of Milan*
- Eginhard, from *Life of Charlemagne*
- *Magna Carta, 1215*
- Pope Boniface VIII, *Unam Sanctam* (November 18, 1302)
- Joan of Arc, *Letter to the King of England, March 22, 1429*
- Niccolò Machiavelli, from *The Prince*
- Niccolò Machiavelli, from *Discourses on the First Decade of Titus Livius*
- from *Edict of Nantes*
- *Mayflower Compact*
- John Locke, from *Second Treatise on Civil Government*
- from *English Bill of Rights, 1689*
- Adam Smith, from *Wealth of Nations*
- Thomas Paine, from *Common Sense*
- John Adams, from *Thoughts on Government*
- Abigail Adams, *Letter from Abigail Adams to John Adams, 31 March–5 April 1776*
- *U.S. Declaration of Independence*
- *U.S. Constitution*
- George Washington, from *Farewell Address to the People of the United States of America*
- *Declaration of the Rights of Man and Citizen*
- Edmund Burke, from *Reflections on the Revolution in France*
- Alexis de Tocqueville, from *Democracy in America*
- Henry David Thoreau, from *Civil Disobedience*
- John Stuart Mill, from *On Liberty*
- *Seneca Falls Women's Rights Convention Declaration of Sentiments*
- Karl Marx and Frederick Engels, from *Communist Manifesto*
- Frederick Douglass, from *What to the Slave Is the Fourth of July?*
- Abraham Lincoln, *Second Inaugural Address*
- Susan B. Anthony, from *Address Prior to Her Trial, June 1873*

Happiness

- Aristotle, from *Nicomachean Ethics*
- Epicurus, *Letter to Menoeceus*
- Epictetus, from *Enchiridion*
- Marcus Aurelius, from *Meditations*
- Boethius, from *Consolation of Philosophy*

- Immanuel Kant, from *Fundamental Principles of the Metaphysic of Ethics*
- John Stuart Mill, from *Utilitarianism*

Hell

- Dante Alighieri, from *Divine Comedy (Inferno)*

History, Study of

- Herodotus, from *The History*
- The Venerable Bede, from *Ecclesiastical History of England* (Caedmon's Story)
- Eginhard, from *Life of Charlemagne*
- Ibn Khaldun, from *Muqaddimah*

Iconography

- John of Damascus, from *Exposition of the Orthodox Faith*

Innate Ideas

- John Calvin, from *Institutes of the Christian Religion*
- René Descartes, from *Meditations on First Philosophy*
- John Locke, from *An Essay concerning Human Understanding*

Islam

- Ibn Sina (Avicenna), from *Avicenna's Offering to the Prince: A Compendium on the Soul*
- Al Ghazzali, from *Confessions of Al Ghazzali*
- Ibn al-Athir, from *Account of the Outbreak of the Tartars into the Lands of Islam*
- Ibn Tufail, from *Hayy ibn Yaqdhan*
- Ibn Batuta, from *Travels* (in Africa)
- Ibn Khaldun, from *Muqaddimah*

Judaism

- Josephus, from *The Jewish War*
- Moses Maimonides, from *Guide for the Perplexed*
- Moses Maimonides, *Thirteen Principles of the Faith*

Justice

- Marcus Tullius Cicero, from *Treatise on the Laws*
- *Magna Carta, 1215*
- Bartolomé de Las Casas, from *Tears of the Indians*

- Francisco de Vitoria, from *De Indis et de Ivre Belli Reflectiones*
- Thomas Hobbes, from *Leviathan*
- John Locke, from *Second Treatise on Civil Government*
- from *English Bill of Rights, 1689*
- *U.S. Declaration of Independence*
- *U.S. Constitution*
- *U.S. Bill of Rights*
- *Declaration of the Rights of Man and Citizen*
- David Rice, from *Slavery Inconsistent with Justice and Good Policy*
- Henry David Thoreau, from *Civil Disobedience*
- *Seneca Falls Women's Rights Convention Declaration of Sentiments*
- Frederick Douglass, from *What to the Slave Is the Fourth of July?*
- Abraham Lincoln, *Second Inaugural Address*
- Susan B. Anthony, from *Address Prior to Her Trial, June 1873*

Knowledge

- Plato, from *Meno*
- Plato, from *Republic*
- Petrarch, *The Ascent of Mount Ventoux*
- John Calvin, from *Institutes of the Christian Religion*
- René Descartes, from *Meditations on First Philosophy*
- John Locke, from *An Essay concerning Human Understanding*
- David Hume, from *An Enquiry concerning Human Understanding*
- Alexis de Tocqueville, from *Democracy in America*

Law

- Marcus Tullius Cicero, from *Treatise on the Laws*
- *Edict of Milan*
- *Magna Carta, 1215*
- Niccolò Machiavelli, from *Discourses on the First Decade of Titus Livius*
- Francisco de Vitoria, from *De Indis et de Ivre Belli Reflectiones*
- from *Canons and Decrees of the Sacred and Ecumenical Council of Trent*
- from *Edict of Nantes*
- *Mayflower Compact*
- William Bradford, from *History of Plymouth Plantation*
- John Winthrop, from *A Model of Christian Charity*
- Thomas Hobbes, from *Leviathan*
- John Locke, from *Second Treatise on Civil Government*
- from *English Bill of Rights, 1689*

- John Adams, from *Thoughts on Government*
- Abigail Adams, *Letter from Abigail Adams to John Adams, 31 March–5 April 1776*
- *U.S. Declaration of Independence*
- *U.S. Constitution*
- *U.S. Bill of Rights*
- *Declaration of the Rights of Man and Citizen*
- David Rice, from *Slavery Inconsistent with Justice and Good Policy*
- Henry David Thoreau, from *Civil Disobedience*
- John Stuart Mill, from *On Liberty*
- Frederick Douglass, from *What to the Slave Is the Fourth of July?*
- Susan B. Anthony, from *Address Prior to Her Trial, June 1873*

Liberty—see Freedom

Lives of the Saints (hagiography)

- from *The Passion of Perpetua and Felicitas*
- Eusebius of Caesarea, from *Life of Constantine*
- Athanasius of Alexandria, from *Life of Antony*
- Sulpicius Severus, from *Life of St. Martin*

Love

- Andreas Capellanus, from *The Art of Courtly Love* ("The Rules of Love")
- John Winthrop, from *A Model of Christian Charity*

Martyrdom

- Ignatius of Antioch, *Epistle to the Magnesians*
- Tertullian, from *Prescription against Heretics*
- from *The Passion of Perpetua and Felicitas*

Monasticism

- Athanasius of Alexandria, from *Life of Antony*
- Benedict of Nursia, from *The Rule of St. Benedict*
- Julian of Norwich, from *Revelations of Divine Love*
- Catherine of Siena, from *Dialogue of the Seraphic Virgin*
- Teresa of Avila, from *Interior Castle*

Mysticism

- Chuang Tzŭ (Zhuangzi), Nourishment of the Soul, from *Chuang Tzŭ*
- Al Ghazzali, from *Confessions of Al Ghazzali*

- Julian of Norwich, from *Revelations of Divine Love*
- Catherine of Siena, from *Dialogue of the Seraphic Virgin*
- Teresa of Avila, from *Interior Castle*

Natural Law

- Mencius, from *Kung-Sun Ch'ow*
- Marcus Tullius Cicero, from *Treatise on the Laws*
- Marcus Tullius Cicero, from *De Officiis*
- Thomas Aquinas, from *Summa Theologica* (from the Treatise on the Law)
- Francisco de Vitoria, from *De Indis et de Ivre Belli Reflectiones*
- Thomas Hobbes, from *Leviathan*
- *U.S. Declaration of Independence*

Nonviolence

- Origen, from *Against Celsus*
- Sulpicius Severus, from *Life of St. Martin*
- from *Schleitheim Confession of Faith, 1527*

Political Theology

- Ignatius of Antioch, *Epistle to the Magnesians*
- Tertullian, from *Prescription against Heretics*
- from *The Passion of Perpetua and Felicitas*
- Origen, from *Against Celsus*
- Eusebius of Caesarea, from *Life of Constantine*
- *Edict of Milan*
- Athanasius of Alexandria, from *Life of Antony*
- Basil of Caesarea, from *Homily VI on Luke 12*
- Sulpicius Severus, from *Life of St. Martin*
- Pope Urban II, from Fulcher of Chartres' *Speech of Urban II at the Council of Clermont*
- Thomas Aquinas, from *Summa Theologica* (from the Treatise on the Law)
- Pope Boniface VIII, *Unam Sanctam* (November 18, 1302)
- Joan of Arc, *Letter to the King of England, March 22, 1429*
- Bartolomé de Las Casas, from *Tears of the Indians*
- from *Schleitheim Confession of Faith, 1527*
- from *Canons and Decrees of the Sacred and Ecumenical Council of Trent*
- John Winthrop, from *A Model of Christian Charity*
- David Rice, from *Slavery Inconsistent with Justice and Good Policy*

Power

- Origen, from *Against Celsus*
- Sulpicius Severus, from *Life of St. Martin*
- Pope Boniface VIII, *Unam Sanctam* (November 18, 1302)
- Joan of Arc, *Letter to the King of England, March 22, 1429*
- from *Schleitheim Confession of Faith, 1527*
- Thomas Hobbes, from *Leviathan*
- John Locke, from *Second Treatise on Civil Government*
- Henry David Thoreau, from *Civil Disobedience*
- John Stuart Mill, from *On Liberty*
- *Seneca Falls Women's Rights Convention Declaration of Sentiments*
- Susan B. Anthony, from *Address Prior to Her Trial, June 1873*

Problem of Evil

- David Hume, from *Dialogues concerning Natural Religion* (on the Problem of Evil)

Property

- Basil of Caesarea, from *Homily VI on Luke 12*
- *Magna Carta, 1215*
- William Bradford, from *History of Plymouth Plantation*
- Thomas Hobbes, from *Leviathan*
- John Locke, from *Second Treatise on Civil Government*
- Adam Smith, from *Wealth of Nations*
- *U.S. Bill of Rights*
- *Declaration of the Rights of Man and Citizen*
- Karl Marx and Frederick Engels, from *Communist Manifesto*

Protestantism

- Martin Luther, *Ninety-Five Theses*
- John Calvin, from *Institutes of the Christian Religion*
- from *Schleitheim Confession of Faith, 1527*
- from *Thirty-Nine Articles of Religion* (Church of England)

Reason

- Marcus Tullius Cicero, from *Treatise on the Laws*
- Justin Martyr, from *Second Apology*
- Clement of Alexandria, from *Stromata*
- René Descartes, from *Meditations on First Philosophy*

- John Locke, from *An Essay concerning Human Understanding*
- Sir Isaac Newton, from *Mathematical Principles of Natural Philosophy*
- Immanuel Kant, from *Fundamental Principles of the Metaphysic of Ethics*
- David Hume, from *An Enquiry concerning Human Understanding*

Religious Conversion

- Eusebius of Caesarea, from *Life of Constantine*
- Athanasius of Alexandria, from *Life of Antony*
- Sulpicius Severus, from *Life of St. Martin*

Resistance/Reform (Dissent)

- Tertullian, from *Prescription against Heretics*
- from *The Passion of Perpetua and Felicitas*
- Athanasius of Alexandria, from *Life of Antony*
- Sulpicius Severus, from *Life of St. Martin*
- Joan of Arc, *Letter to the King of England, March 22, 1429*
- Martin Luther, *Ninety-Five Theses*
- from *Schleitheim Confession of Faith, 1527*
- from *Canons and Decrees of the Sacred and Ecumenical Council of Trent*
- William Bradford, from *History of Plymouth Plantation*
- John Winthrop, from *A Model of Christian Charity*
- *U.S. Declaration of Independence*
- Mary Wollstonecraft, from *A Vindication of the Rights of Woman*
- Henry David Thoreau, from *Civil Disobedience*
- *Seneca Falls Women's Rights Convention Declaration of Sentiments*
- Karl Marx and Frederick Engels, from *Communist Manifesto*
- Frederick Douglass, from *What to the Slave Is the Fourth of July?*
- Susan B. Anthony, from *Address Prior to Her Trial, June 1873*

Roman Catholicism

- Desiderius Erasmus, from *In Praise of Folly*
- Ignatius of Loyola, from *Spiritual Exercises*
- from *Canons and Decrees of the Sacred and Ecumenical Council of Trent*

Science

- John Locke, from *An Essay concerning Human Understanding*
- Sir Isaac Newton, from *Mathematical Principles of Natural Philosophy*
- David Hume, from *An Enquiry concerning Human Understanding*
- Charles Darwin, from *On the Origin of Species*

Sin

- Augustine of Hippo, from *Confessions*
- John Calvin, from *Institutes of the Christian Religion*

Slavery

- Ibn Batuta, from *Travels* (in Africa)
- Bartolomé de Las Casas, from *Tears of the Indians*
- Francisco de Vitoria, from *De Indis et de Ivre Belli Reflectiones*
- David Rice, from *Slavery Inconsistent with Justice and Good Policy*
- Frederick Douglass, from *What to the Slave Is the Fourth of July?*
- Abraham Lincoln, *Second Inaugural Address*

Soul

- from *Bhagavad-Gita*
- Ibn Sina (Avicenna), from *Avicenna's Offering to the Prince: A Compendium on the Soul*
- Ibn Tufail, from *Hayy ibn Yaqdhan*
- René Descartes, from *Meditations on First Philosophy*

Stoicism

- Epictetus, from *Enchiridion*
- Marcus Aurelius, from *Meditations*

Valedictory Counsel

- Thucydides, from *History of the Peloponnesian War*
- Ignatius of Antioch, *Epistle to the Magnesians*
- from *The Passion of Perpetua and Felicitas*
- George Washington, from *Farewell Address to the People of the United States of America*
- Abraham Lincoln, *Gettysburg Address*
- Abraham Lincoln, *Second Inaugural Address*

Virtue

- Confucius, from *Analects*
- Lao-Tze, from *Tao Teh King*
- Thucydides, from *History of the Peloponnesian War*
- Plato, from *Meno*
- Aristotle, from *Nicomachean Ethics*
- Mencius, from *Kung-Sun Ch'ow*

- Marcus Tullius Cicero, from *Treatise on the Laws*
- Marcus Tullius Cicero, from *De Officiis*
- Livy, from *History of Rome* (Stories of Lucretia and Cincinnatus)
- Plutarch, from *Lives*
- Niccolò Machiavelli, from *Discourses on the First Decade of Titus Livius*

War

- Homer, from *Iliad*
- Sun Tzŭ, from *On the Art of War*
- Thucydides, from *History of the Peloponnesian War*
- from *Bhagavad-Gita*
- Josephus, from *The Jewish War*
- Origen, from *Against Celsus*
- Sulpicius Severus, from *Life of St. Martin*
- Pope Urban II, from Fulcher of Chartres' *Speech of Urban II at the Council of Clermont*
- Joan of Arc, *Letter to the King of England, March 22, 1429*
- Niccolò Machiavelli, from *The Prince*
- Bartolomé de Las Casas, from *Tears of the Indians*
- Francisco de Vitoria, from *De Indis et de Ivre Belli Reflectiones*
- from *Schleitheim Confession of Faith, 1527*
- Abigail Adams, *Letter from Abigail Adams to John Adams, 31 March–5 April 1776*
- *U.S. Declaration of Independence*
- Abraham Lincoln, *Gettysburg Address*
- Abraham Lincoln, *Second Inaugural Address*

Wealth

- Aristotle, from *Politics*
- Basil of Caesarea, from *Homily VI on Luke 12*
- John Winthrop, from *A Model of Christian Charity*
- John Locke, from *Second Treatise on Civil Government*
- Adam Smith, from *Wealth of Nations*
- Karl Marx and Frederick Engels, from *Communist Manifesto*

Women's Rights

- Abigail Adams, *Letter from Abigail Adams to John Adams, 31 March–5 April 1776*

- Mary Wollstonecraft, from *A Vindication of the Rights of Woman*
- *Seneca Falls Women's Rights Convention Declaration of Sentiments*
- Karl Marx and Frederick Engels, from *Communist Manifesto*
- Susan B. Anthony, from *Address Prior to Her Trial, June 1873*